# THE HARMONY
## ILLUSTRATED ENCYCLOPEDIA OF
# ROCK

# THE HARMONY
# ILLUSTRATED ENCYCLOPEDIA OF
# ROCK

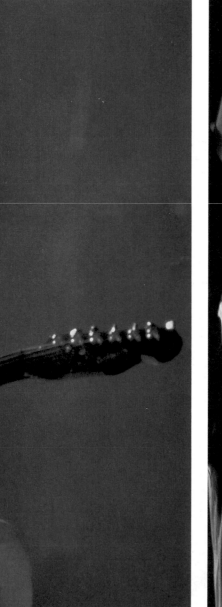

Consultant: **Mike Clifford**

Authors: Pete Frame, John Tobler, Ed Hanel, Roger St. Pierre, Chris Trengove, John Beecher, Clive Richardson, Gary Cooper, Marsha Hanlon, Linda Sandahl.

**SIXTH EDITION**

HARMONY BOOKS
NEW YORK

a Salamander book

Copyright © 1988 by Salamander Books Ltd.

Published by Harmony Books, a division of Crown Publishers, Inc., 225 Park Avenue South, New York, New York 10003 and represented in Canada by the Canadian Manda Group.

Originally published in Great Britain as The New Illustrated Rock Handbook by Salamander Books Ltd.

HARMONY and Colophon are trademarks of Crown Publishers, Inc.

Manufactured in Belgium

Library of Congress Cataloging-in-Publication Data

Clifford, Mike.
    The Harmony Illustrated encyclopedia of rock
    by Mike Clifford—6th ed.

    p. cm.
    ISBN 0-517-57164-1: $30.00
    1. Rock Music—Dictionaries. I. Title.
ML 102.R6C6 1988
784.5'4'00321—dc19        88-21473 CIP MN

© 1988 Salamander Books Ltd.

## Acknowledgements

*The publishers would like to thank Johnny Waller, Chris Welch, and Chris Whyte for writing new entries, and Virgin Records for supplying us with album covers and CD sleeves.*

*We also wish to thank all the record companies and publicity/management agencies who supplied and gave their permission to use promotional photos and record sleeves. All other photos by Pictorial Press, Terry Lott, Phil Gorton, Keith Bernstein, Tom Sheehan, Trinifold, Chris Morphet, Adrian Boot, Michael Putland, Robert Ellis, John Timbers, Victor Skrebneski, MTV, Jill Furmanovsky, Barry Plummer, Paul Slattery, Fin Costello, Martin Godard, Duane Michaels, Peter Anderson, Scope Features, Brian Aris, Simon Fowler, Eric Watson, Rex Features, and DeMonde Advertising.*

*US chart positions © 1955 through 1988 by Billboard Publications, Inc. Compiled by the Billboard Research Department and reprinted with permission. UK chart positions from 1956 through 1988 by kind permission of Music And Video Week/BBC/Gallup.*

*We would also like to recognize the contributions and assistance of the Schwann Music Catalog, the Music Master Catalogue, and Joel Whitburn.*

## Credits

*Managing Editor: Terence Monaighan*
*Editorial Assistant: Roseanne Eckart*
*Designers: Mike Jolley, Richard Hawke*
*Family Trees: Pete Frame*
*Chart and Discography Research: Heather Robinson*
*Picture Research: Helen Donlon*
*Filmset by H&P Graphics Ltd.*
*Colour Reproduction by Rodney Howe Ltd.*
*Printed in Belgium by Proost International Book Production, Turnhout.*

# Contents

# Authors

### The Consultant

MIKE CLIFFORD played bass with '60s soul outfit the Errol Dixon Band. He has worked with Bad Company and Led Zeppelin and handled public relations for Aretha Franklin, James Brown, the Drifters, Richie Havens, and many other performers. Mike has written extensively on rock 'n' roll and was chief author and consultant of Salamander's 'Black Music' and consultant co-author of their 'Illustrated Encyclopedia of Rock' (third edition).

### Contributors

PETE FRAME is probably best known for his intricate Rock Family Trees, but he has also been a freelance rock journalist since 1969 when he founded Zig Zag magazine, which he edited for several years. Following work for Charisma and Stiff Records in the '70s, he specialized in group genealogies. Three volumes of his Rock Family Trees have been published to date.

JOHN TOBLER has written for all the major music weeklies in the UK at one time or another, but concentrates on rock books, such as '25 Years Of Rock' (co-written with Pete Frame), 'The Record Producers', and 'Guitar Greats', all of which have also been successful BBC Radio One series. He has also written books on the Beach Boys, Buddy Holly, Cliff Richard, and Elvis Presley, plus rock trivia books such as 'The Rock Lists Album'.

ED HANEL plunged into rock journalism when he founded the Who fanzine 'Who's News'. Still a fan himself and an avid record collector, Ed specializes in discographies. He has contributed to various US and UK rock publications, including 'Trouser Press', 'Zig Zag', and the 'History of Rock' series. He is the author of 'The Omnibus Rock Bibliography' and 'The Who: The Illustrated Discography'.

ROGER ST. PIERRE has worked for nearly 20 years in the music industry, mostly as a publicist for such acts as the Drifters, Johnnie Ray, Frankie Laine, Marvin Gaye, the Temptations, Diana Ross, and the Jacksons. He is also the author of several books, has contributed to 'Record Mirror', 'Blues And Soul', and 'New Musical Express', written several hundred sleeve notes, and was a co-author of Salamander's 'Black Music'.

CHRIS TRENGOVE played tenor sax with soul band Lester Square and the GTs and the John Dummer Blues in the '60s. In the '70s he worked as a publicist for Status Quo, Thin Lizzy, and Bill Withers, among others. He has co-authored two novels and a biography of Keith Moon, and has contributed to 'Beat Instrumental', 'Album Tracking', 'Black Echoes', and Salamander's 'Black Music' and 'Illustrated Encyclopedia of Rock'.

JOHN BEECHER is a rock historian, rock music publisher, and owner of an oldies record shop. He compiled the comprehensive boxed set of Buddy Holly LPs.

CLIVE RICHARDSON was editor of 'Shout' soul magazine from 1967 until its demise in 1976. He then became a regular contributor to 'Black Echoes' and 'Blues Unlimited' and has written sleeve notes for numerous soul and R&B albums. He was a contributor to Salamander's 'Black Music' and 'Illustrated Encyclopedia of Rock' publications.

GARY COOPER became editor of 'Beat Instrumental' in the '70s and since then has been writing for musical instrument/musicians magazines throughout the world, including 'Spotlight' (West Germany), 'Music Maker' (Holland), and 'Sonix' (Australia), and UK publications 'Sounds', 'Music World', and 'Sound International'. In 1981 co-founded and became editor of 'Music UK'.

MARSHA HANLON has been a rock 'n' roll fan since she danced in the aisles of New York's Paramount in the '50s. In the '60s she co-founded a weekly entertainment newspaper in Boston. She has worked as a freelance publicist/journalist since.

LINDA SANDAHL gained her early writing experience as assistant to James Robert Parish. Since then she has worked on Steven H. Scheuer's 'Movies On TV', of which she is now an associate editor. Linda recently began researching and writing for the collector's magazine 'Goldmine'.

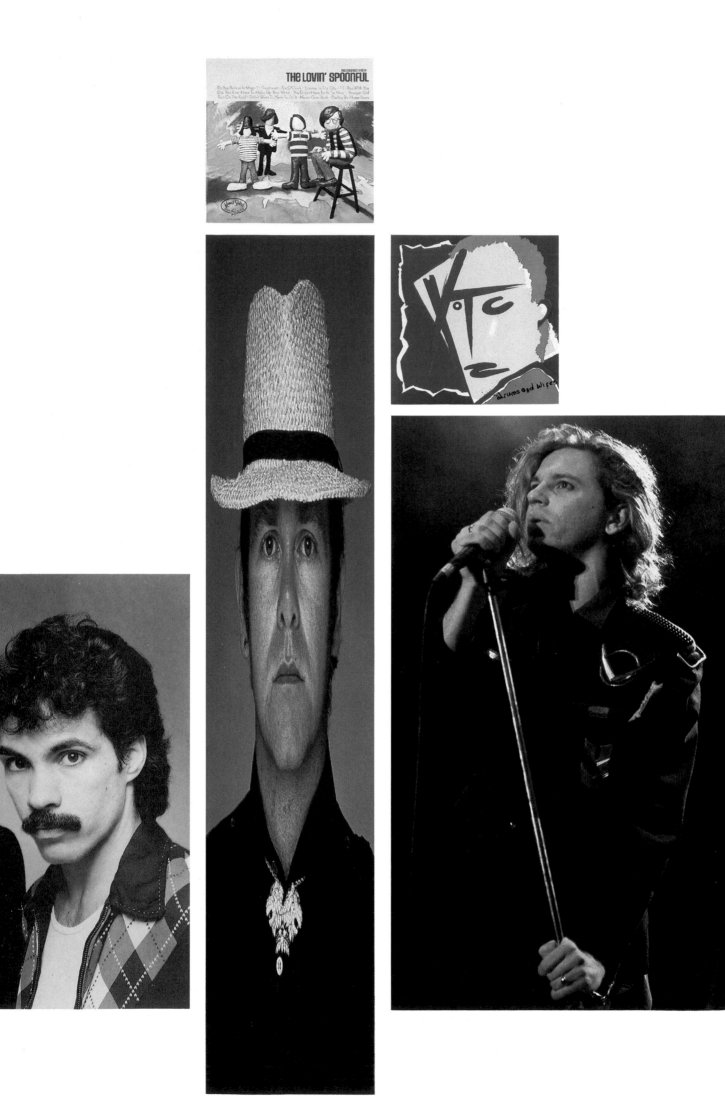

# Introduction

**W**elcome to **The Harmony Illustrated Encyclopedia of Rock**. So much has happened in the rock world since the last edition of 1986 it has been necessary to extensively update hundreds of the existing entries and highlight for the first time the careers of the new superstars — Terence Trent D'Arby, Simply Red, Alexander O'Neal, INXS, Pet Shop Boys, Suzanne Vega, Communards and many more. We now also have a clearer idea of the megastars who are likely to last the distance through the 1990s — U2, Whitney Houston, Madonna, Michael Jackson, George Michael, among them.

The last few years have all seen rock stars giving back to the community in a way that has never happened before. Vast concerts led by die-hards such as Phil Collins, Peter Gabriel, Stevie Wonder and Dire Straits have brought people together for Live Aid, Amnesty and Nelson Mandela, a trend that seems sure to continue well into the next decade.

As ever, we are bound to cause disputes and upset people when trying to narrow down the field from potentially thousands to only 700! This makes the selection fairly subjective, with more than a few 'borderline' cases included because of their originality, influence on other artists, or contribution to rock, rather than popularity or chart success. This time round, to give recognition to some of the lesser-known performers, bands who just might become massive overnight, 'One Hit Wonders' and faded glories, we have put together an Appendix with brief notes on over 500 additional personalities.

How To Read this Book:
1. Within the main text, individual artists are listed under their surnames, groups under group name. The name of an individual performer is followed by his/her country of origin and a description of talents (US vocalist, producer, composer) in order of renown. His/her date and place of birth and real name (if known by a pseudonym) comes next. Group headings are followed by place of origin, year founded, and the original line-up listing members and instruments played. In cases where a musician is particularly well known, his preference of instrument is listed, i.e. Guitar: Fender Stratocaster. (Where an artist has his/her own entry separate to group, this instrument would be listed in their own entry.)
2. The biography beneath the heading outlines the career of the artist(s). Within the entry, the symbol(▶) is likely to appear; this indicates that the reader may refer to a related entry in the main text of the book or in the Appendix.

The industry terms AOR, MOR, Gold Record, and Platinum Record also appear frequently.

AOR stands for 'Adult Oriented Rock', meaning that which is easily digested by the record buying public (the Eagles, Billy Joel, rather than Motorhead, Kiss, or the Ramones). MOR stands for 'Middle of the Road', meaning easy-listening music which isn't heavy metal, rock, blues, or any other distinct sound.

Gold and Platinum albums are awarded by the RIAA (Recording Industry Association of America) in the US and the BPI (British Phonographic Industries Association) in the UK, and the criteria required by each country differs slightly. In the US, a million singles sold earns a Gold record; two million singles earns Platinum. An LP which goes gold in the US has sold half a million copies. If it goes on to sell a million copies, it becomes Platinum (12" singles are awarded in the same way).

In the UK, the singles version is based on sales figures, or 'pounds sterling', thus: £250,000 = Silver, £500,000 = Gold, and one million pounds = Platinum. For LPs however, awards are based on units (as in the US) rather than sales, 60,000 copies sold = Silver, 100,000 = Gold, and 300,000 = Platinum. But then, things have changed over the years as values change.
3. A discography follows the biography, beginning with Hit Singles. To be listed in this category, a single must have made the Top 20 in either the US or UK charts. If so, the position it reached in the corresponding chart, up to and including No. 60 (but not 61-100) would also be listed. Single positions were taken from the most respected chart compilers/publications in the trade, Billboard (US) and Music And Video Week/BBC/Gallup (UK). Billboard began a regular Hot 100 chart in November 1955, while Music And Video Week commenced their charts in January 1956 (figures were compiled by Record Mirror, now owned by Music And Video Week, at that time).

We are aware that some artists included in this book had million-selling records prior to the publication of charts; in such cases we have mentioned their biggest hits with their biographies. Our official cut-off date for charts was May 1, 1988 though we have followed through the positions of any singles in the charts at that time.
4. Albums and CDs listed are currently available according to the trade catalogues, Schwann (US) and Music Master (UK) through May 1, 1988. We have added on new LP releases through to press date whenever possible. In certain cases, (selected) appears after the 'Albums' heading; such instances usually involve a 'fringe' artist from country, R&B, soul, etc, and therefore we have listed only the pertinent albums. Albums not available but which are essential to the understanding and appreciation of a performer and therefore merit looking in second hand record shops for, appear under the heading 'Worth Searching Out'. Following the title of an album is the label it is currently available on. (Atlantic) would mean the album is available on Atlantic in both the US and the UK; (MCA, Polydor) means the album is available on MCA in the US and on Polydor in the UK.
5. Group geneology expert Pete Frame has updated his 12 Family Trees where appropriate for this edition. These trees serve as a visual aid in relationships of several groups, and allow us to introduce some of the more obscure performers in rock.

Enough of the technicalities, read on...

Mike Clifford
Terence Monaighan
September 1988

# ABC

UK group formed 1980.

**Original line-up:** Martin Fry, vocals; Mark Lickley, bass; David Robinson, drums; Stephen Singleton, saxophone; Mark White, guitar.

**Career:** Martin Fry formed ABC out of demise of synth band Vice Versa. From experience gained as editor of fanzine ('Modern Drugs') began creating an image of glamour and style for group. A year after signing with Phonogram, Fry had led ABC into UK pop charts with three hit singles and a gold album.

**The Lexicon Of Love, ABC. Courtesy Mercury Records.**

Band won widespread acceptance with American audience via MTV through strong, well-made videos. ABC's sound combines clever lyrics and good melody but relies heavily on Fry's excellent vocals, as well as good production, and tends to be a mite too polished.

Latterly outfit has regrouped as duo scoring heavily with superb single **When Smokey Sings**. Acute sense of style and intelligent interpretation of current mood likely to ensure longevity.

**Current line-up:** Fry; David Clayton, keyboard; Graham Broad, drums; Brad Land. bass; Danny Thompson, double bass; Pandit Dinesh and Louis Jardim, percussion; Howie Casey, saxophone; Judd Lander, harp

| Hit Singles: | US | UK |
|---|---|---|
| Tears Are Not Enough 1981[1] | | 19 |
| Poison Arrow, 1982 | | 6 |
| The Look Of Love, 1982 | 19 | 4 |
| All Of My Heart, 1982 | | 5 |
| That Was Then But This is Now 1983 | - | 18 |
| Be Near Me, 1985 | 9 | |
| Night You Murdered Love, 1987 | | 31 |
| When Smokey Sings. 1987 | 5 | 11 |

**Albums:**
The Lexicon Of Love (Mercury/ Neutron), 1982 **CD**
Beauty Stab (Phonogram/Neutron), 1983 **CD**
How To Be A Zillionaire (Phonogram/ Neutron), 1985 **CD**
Alphabet City (Neutron), 1987 **CD**

# AC/DC

Australian group formed 1974.

**Original line-up:** Malcolm Young, guitar; Angus Young, Gibson SG guitar; Phil Rudd, drums; Mark Evans, bass; Bon Scott, vocals.

**Career:** Malcolm and Angus Young formed band in Sydney, Australia, but moved to Melbourne where original line-up evolved. Malcolm and Angus are younger brothers of George Young of '60s pop outfit Easybeats This connection has proved invaluable to AC/DC in terms of experience and production

However, there is no trace of the Easybeats' pop melodies in the sonic, frontal assaults of AC/DC.

Now superstars on heavy-metal circuit, AC/DC were instrumental in breaking down prejudices against Australian rock. Strong home following was gained via release of two 1975 albums: **High Voltage** and **TNT**. Then came low-budget, hard-working tour of UK which earned enough favourable response for UK album release. (Entitled **High Voltage**, UK LP is actually **TNT** minus two tracks, with two added from the Australian release **High Voltage**.)

Making every performance an athletic endurance contest for both band and audience, AD/DC gained notoriety in US. Clearly everyone else was back-up to Scott's rivet-driving vocals and Angus' head-bobbing gyrotechnics. (Change in bass players in 1977 from Mark Evans to Cliff Williams almost went unnoticed.) Bon Scott's death from alcohol abuse in April 1980 occurred when AC/DC was on fringe of super-group status. In a fortunate twist of fate, AC/DC hired Scott-soundalike Brian Johnson (from band Geordie).

**Back In Black** set proved band could overcome loss of one of its main attractions, and led to less hectic touring and recording schedule. AC/DC are real heavy-metal heavies, with deserved success and should be a force for many years to come.

**Current line-up:** Malcolm Young; Angus Young; Rudd; Cliff Williams, bass; Brian Johnson, vocals.

| Hit Singles: | US | UK |
|---|---|---|
| Rock'n'Roll Ain't Noise Pollution, 1981 | — | 15 |
| Let's Get It Up, 1982 | 44 | 13 |
| For Those About To Rock, 1982 | — | 15 |
| Who Made Who, 1986 | — | 16 |
| Shake Your Foundations, 1986 | — | 24 |
| Heatseeker, 1988 | — | 12 |

**Albums:**
High Voltage (ATCO/Atlantic), 1976 **CD**
Dirty Deeds Done Dirty Cheap (Atlantic), 1976 **CD**
Let There Be Rock (Atlantic), 1977
Powerage (Atlantic), 1978
If You Want Blood (Atlantic), 1978
Highway To Hell (Atlantic), 1979 **CD**
Back In Black (Atlantic), 1980 **CD**
For Those About To Rock (Atlantic), 1981 **CD**
Flick Of The Switch (Atlantic), 1983
Fly On The Wall (Atlantic), 1985 **CD**
Who Made Who (Atlantic), 1986 **CD**

# Abba

Swedish group formed 1971.

**Original/Final line-up:** Agnetha Fältskog, vocals; Anni-Frid Lyngstad-Fredriksson, vocals; Bjorn Ulvaeus, guitar, vocals; Benny Andersson, keyboards, synthesiser, vocals.

**Career:** Reputed to earn more for the Swedish economy each year than the vast Volvo car and truck company, Abba leapt to international prominence when they won the 1974 Eurovision Song Contest. Before that, they had already put in long service as leading figures of Swedish pop scene.

Anni-Frid (born Norway, November 15, 1945; raised in Toshala, Sweden) moved to Stockholm in 1967 to start singing career. Agnetha (born Jonkopping, April 5, 1950) started recording at 17 and had several local hits. Bjorn (born Gothenburg, April 25, 1945) was the star of successful Hootenanny Singers in late '60s. Benny (born Stockholm, December 16, 1946) was leader of popular rock band the Hep Cats.

Pop industry entrepreneur Stikkan Andersson persuaded Bjorn, whom he already had under contract to his Polar Music company, and Benny to leave their groups and pool resources. Benny and Anni-Frid had been living together in Stockholm since 1970; Bjorn and Agnetha married in July 1971, a major event on Sweden's pop scene as both were already national figures. After Benny and Bjorn cut **Lycka** album as duo, Abba gradually came into being. The girls had been doing vocal back-ups on Benny and Bjorn recordings and as foursome had made some stage appearances.

Anni-Frid was unsuccessful solo entrant in 1971 Eurovision song contest; for next two years foursome worked hard on their act with view to using that event as springboard to stardom. Name Abba was chosen in 1973 and the group represented Sweden in that year's Eurovision with **Ring Ring** but failed to win. Next year, despite strongest ever competition, they came out on top with **Waterloo**. The event was televised from Brighton, England, to an audience of some 500 million. Eurovision triumph does not automatically spell big record sales but in Abba's case it did. **Waterloo** not only went to No. 1 in most

**Below: Angus Young of AC/DC adds to the group's visual image with his schoolboy shorts and head banging.**

European countries, but made No. 6 in the US where Eurovision is unknown.

However, Eurovision's market is not normally the same as the pop market, its appeal being largely to mums and dads rather than young rock fans. It was 18 months before Abba could crack the true pop market. They did it with **S.O.S.**, which made charts all over Europe, precipitating them to superstardom.

**Mama Mia, Fernando, Dancing Queen** and **Knowing Me, Knowing You** were all UK No. 1s, while **Money, Money, Money** went to No. 2. In 1977 **Dancing Queen** gave them their first American chart-topper. Every record was a perfectly crafted piece of pop commercialism, employing perfect harmonies, irresistible hooks, and impeccable production. Their accompanying promotional videos utilised equally flawless formula.

When they finally embarked on a world tour in 1977 it was done in the grandest manner with 14 musicians, elaborate sets and full-blown productions. Hits continued to flow, both albums and singles racking amazing sales. Personal problems, however, began to overshadow their artistic and commercial success (besides musical activities they invested heavily in property and other business spheres).

Bjorn and Agnetha divorced in 1979. Agnetha reverted to maiden name Fältskog. Anni-Frid and Benny divorced in 1981. For some time they did not allow this to interfere with their career as a group, but eventually they drifted apart, embarking solo ventures, notably Ulvaeus' and Andersson's involvement with 'Chess' musical.

| Hit Singles: | US | UK |
|---|---|---|
| Waterloo, 1974 | 6 | 1 |
| S.O.S., 1975 | 15 | 6 |
| Mamma Mia, 1975 | 32 | 1 |
| Fernando, 1976 | 13 | 1 |
| I Do I Do I Do I Do, 1976 | 15 | 38 |
| Dancing Queen, 1976 | 1 | 1 |
| Money Money Money, 1976 | 56 | 3 |
| Knowing Me Knowing You, 1977 | 14 | 1 |
| The Name Of The Game, 1977 | 12 | 1 |
| Take A Chance On Me, 1978 | 3 | 1 |
| Summer Night City, 1978 | — | 15 |
| Chiquitita, 1979 | 29 | 2 |
| Does Your Mother Know, 1979 | 19 | 4 |
| Angeleyes/Voulez-Vous, 1979 | — | 3 |
| Gimme Gimme Gimme (A Man After Midnight), 1979 | — | 3 |
| I Have A Dream, 1979 | — | 2 |
| The Winner Takes It All, 1980 | 8 | 1 |
| Super Trouper, 1980 | 45 | 1 |
| Lay All Your Love On Me, 1981 | — | 7 |
| One Of Us, 1981 | | 3 |

**Albums:**
Waterloo (Atlantic/Epic), 1974
Abba (Atlantic/Epic), 1975
Arrival (Atlantic/Epic), 1976
Greatest Hits (Atlantic/Epic), 1976 **CD**
The Album (Atlantic/Epic), 1978
Greatest Hits Volume II (Atlantic/Epic), 1979
Voulez-Vous (Atlantic/Epic), 1979
Super Trouper (Atlantic/Epic), 1980 **CD**
The Visitors (Atlantic/Epic), 1981 **CD**
Gracias Pour La Musica (—/Epic), 1981
The Singles (Atlantic/Epic), 1982 **CD**
Thank You For The Music (—/Epic), 1983
The Singles (Atlantic/Epic), 1982

*Frida Solo:*
Something's Going On (Atlantic/Epic), 1982
Shine (Epic), 1984

*Agnetha Fältskog Solo:*
Wrap Your Arms Around Me (Atlantic/Epic), 1983
Eyes Of A Woman (Epic), 1985

*Benny & Bjorn (with Tim Rice):*
Chess (RCA), 1984

# Bryan Adams

Canadian singer/songwriter.
Born Kingston, Ontario, November 1959.

**Career:** Adams' 1985 European concert tour with Tina Turner(▶) finally focused the big-time limelight on an artist who had been building a steadily growing reputation over the decade since he started in club groups around Vancouver, British Columbia, at 16. Within a year of starting out, Adams was writing with Jim Vallance, their songs giving hits to Prism, Bachman-Turner Overdrive(▶), Ian Lloyd,

Into The Fire, Bryan Adams.
Courtesy A&M Records.

Bob Welch, Kiss(▶) and others. Late 1979 recording deal with A&M led to four solid months touring USA.

Touring as opening act for Kinks, Loverboy and Foreigner in 1982 led to breakthrough album **Cuts Like A Knife** which went platinum and contained US hit single **Straight From The Heart**, covered successfully by Ian Lloyd and Bonnie Tyler.

Since then Adams has successfully pursued policy of touring almost continually throughout US and world, establishing reputation as consistent if hardly original performer. Policy has also paid off in terms of record sales, with platinum album **Into The Fire** latest example of Adams' across-the-board appeal.

All-round journeyman rocker who takes craftsmanlike approach to his profession, Adams may well outlast some of the flashier and more gimmicky artists currently on offer.

**Hit Singles:**

| | US | UK |
|---|---|---|
| Straight From The Heart, 1983 | 10 | — |
| Cuts Like A Knife, 1983 | 15 | — |
| Run To Him, 1985 | 6 | 11 |
| Somebody, 1985 | 11 | — |
| Heaven, 1985 | 1 | — |
| Summer Of '69, 1985 | 5 | — |
| One Night Love Affair, 1985 | 13 | — |
| It's Only Love, 1985 | 19 | 29 |
| Heats On Fire, 1987 | 26 | — |
| Heat Of The Night, 1987 | 6 | — |
| Victim Of Love, 1987 | 32 | — |

**Albums:**
You Want It You Got It (A&M), 1982 **CD**
Cuts Like A Knife (A&M), 1983
Reckless (A&M), 1985
Into The Fire (A&M), 1987 **CD**
One Good Reason (A&M), 1985 **CD**

# Aerosmith

US group formed 1970.

**Original/current line-up:** Steve Tyler vocals; Joe Perry, guitar; Tom Hamilton, bass; Joey Kramer, drums; Brad Whitford, guitar.

**Career:** Legend has band forming in Sunapee, New Hampshire, during summer 1970. Lots of local gigging in Boston led to dates at

Max's Kansas City where they were seen and signed by Clive Davis for CBS in late 1972. Despite emphasis on group participation, focal point was Jagger look-alike Tyler and guitarist Perry. Duo were main writers of original material and also took brunt of universal criticism as Rolling Stones(▶)/Yardbirds(▶) rip-offs.

Long-term liaison with producer Jack Douglas began with widely criticised second album **Get Your Wings**. By 1975 extensive touring

Aerosmith's Draw The Line.
Courtesy CBS Records.

finally paid off with success in American singles and album charts. **Toys In The Attic** went platinum within months of release and stayed in charts for two years. This sparked interest in first two albums which went platinum by the release of **Rocks**. 1976 saw re-issue of **Dream On**, which earned gold record three years after first appearance. Aerosmith

**Above: Without flash and without gimmick, Bryan Adams has across-the-board rock appeal that looks to continue.**

seemed destined for long run as high-class Grand Funk Railroad(▶), a people's band, working diligently for fans.

A well-deserved rest from touring may have caused **Draw The Line** to miss the fire of earlier albums. Original LP sleeve, which featured only a cartoon of band, also seemed ego trip which did not mesh with spirit of '77 punk revolution. Instead of being allowed to enjoy hard-won success, Aerosmith found themselves part of establishment about to be assaulted by new wave.

1979 saw Perry quit, having devoted more time to solo projects than the band. His replacement was New Yorker Jimmy Crespo, former member of Flame.

Brad Whitford became the second original member to depart when he joined forces with former Ted Nugent guitarist Derek St. Holmes in Whitford/St. Holmes. Rick Dufay took his place and this new aggregate cut just one album **Rock In A Hard Place**, release of which was delayed by Tyler's motorcycle injury.

Unhappy with new line-up, Tyler approached Perry, who had cut three LPs as Joe Perry Project and, later, Whitford, to rejoin Aerosmith. They agreed and reformed band quickly put a tour together and returned to the studios, hopefully to recreate the old excitement.

In 1986 Steven Tyler and Joe Perry forged an alliance between heavy metal and hip hop when they joined forces with Run DMC in remake of the Aerosmith hit **Walk This Way**.

Featured on **Raising Hell** which went double platinum and the single was a big hit, boosted by a witty video.

In Spring 1987 Aerosmith recorded new album **Permanent Vacation** in Vancouver, Canada, produced by Bruce Fairburn and released in October. Earlier in June that year, the band played for 82,000 fans at the Texas Jam. The album sold out its first pressing and yielded a major hit single **Dude (Looks Like A Lady)** completing a triumphant comeback.

**Hit Singles:**

| | US | UK |
|---|---|---|
| Dream On, 1976 | 6 | — |
| Walk This Way, 1977 | 10 | — |
| Dude (Looks Like A Lady), 1987 | 14 | — |

**Albums:**
Aerosmith (Columbia/CBS), 1973
Get Your Wings (Columbia/CBS), 1974
Toys In The Attic (Columbia/CBS), 1975 **CD**
Rocks (Columbia/CBS), 1976 **CD**
Draw The Line (Columbia/CBS), 1977
Live! Bootleg (Columbia/CBS), 1978
Greatest Hits (Columbia/CBS), 1980 **CD**
Night In The Ruts (Columbia/CBS), 1979
Rock In A Hard Place (Columbia/CBS), 1982
Done With Mirrors (Geffen), 1985 **CD**
Classics Live (CBS), 1986
Classics Live 2 (Columbia), 1987
Permanent Vacation (Geffen), 1987 **CD**

# Allman Brothers Band

US group formed 1969.

**Original line-up:** Duane Allman, Gibson Les Paul, Fender Stratocaster guitar; Gregg Allman, guitar, vocals, keyboards; Dickie Betts, Gibson Les Paul guitar; Berry Oakley, bass; Jai Johnny Johanson, drums; Butch Trucks, drums.

**Career:** Duane Allman (born Nashville, November 20, 1946) was raised in Daytona Beach, Florida; moved to Los Angeles in '60s. Formed Hour Glass with brother Gregg (born December 8, 1947) on keyboards, guitar, vocals; Paul Hornsby, keyboards, guitar, vocals; Jesse Willard Carr, bass, vocals; John Sandlin, drums, guitar. Debut Liberty album was cut at label's own LA studio. Band recorded follow-up at Rick Hall's Muscle Shoals Studio. Duane Allman had previously worked there as session guitarist (on Clarence Carter's 1967 **Road Of Love** sessions). Tapes for second album were rejected by Liberty and band broke up.

Allman stayed at Fame to work on sessions with Percy Sledge, Aretha Franklin(▶), Boz Scaggs(▶), Wilson Pickett and others. Also cut material for projected but unreleased Atlantic solo album before signing to Phil Walden's Capricorn label (based in nearby Macon, Georgia, and distributed by Atlantic).

Walden had previously managed the late Otis Redding(▶) and helped Allman put together what became Allman Brothers Band. The Brothers had been working informally with Butch Truck's band 31st February; when outfit jammed with Betts and Oakley's band Second Coming, in Jacksonville, foundations of Allman Brothers band were laid.

New band gigged around Southern States building big following. Debut album **The Allman Brothers Band**, 1969 (cut in New York), was potent mixture of progressive rock and R&B/blues roots. Interplay between Duane Allman's potent slide work and forceful technique of Dickie Betts was focal point of band's attractive new sound. From **Idlewild South** album (1970) single **Midnight Rider** was smash, pushing LP to gold status.

While band's reputation grew ever bigger, Duane Allman continued session work, both at Muscle Shoals and elsewhere. Among artists who benefited from his creative playing were Johnny Jenkins, Delaney and Bonnie and Friends(▶), King Curtis(▶), Lulu(▶), Herbie Mann(▶), Ronnie Hawkins(▶), Sam Samudio, The Duck and The Bear (a pseudonym for Canned Heat's Bob Hite), blues legend Otis Rush and, most especially, Eric Clapton(▶). Allman's trading-off of licks with Clapton on the Derek and the Dominoes' **Layla** album was among his finest work.

Tragedy hit band when Duane Allman died in motorcycle crash on October 29, 1971; he was just 24 years old. Last testament was superlative **The Allman Brothers Band At Fillmore East** album, recorded shortly before. Contained superb versions of blues standards **Statesboro' Blues** and **Stormy Monday** plus a 22-minute 40-second workout on **Whipping Post** which filled whole of one side of double LP set.

Three tracks for **Eat A Peach** had been laid down before Duane's death; it was decided to finish album without recruiting replacement guitarist. LP proved another massive seller.

Unbelievably, lightning struck twice: on November 11, 1972, Berry Oakley died in another motorcycle accident, also in Macon.

Band susbequently added Chuck Leavill, keyboards, and Lamar Williams, bass. Sound softened out into more melodic country-rock idiom for **Brothers And Sisters** album. From this, **Jessica** instrumental hit proved to be Betts' tour-de-force; revealed depth of talent which had previously been, to some degree, overshadowed by Duane Allman.

Following **Win, Lose Or Draw,** Betts and Gregg Allman embarked on solo projects. Gregg toured States under own name with new band. Allman Brothers' Band LP **The Road Goes On Forever** was compilation rather than new material.

End seemed to have arrived when Allman testified against his personal road manager Scooter Herring who received a 75-year sentence on narcotics' charges. 'There is no way we can ever work with Gregg again', aggrieved Betts told 'Rolling Stone' magazine. Betts promptly departed to form own band, Great Southern, with debut album on Arista (1977). Jazz-rock group Sea Level was formed by Johnson, Williams and Leavill, plus guitarist Jimmy Nalls.

By now married to Cher Bono, Gregg Allman issued **Playin' Up A Storm** under own name in 1977. Rift was healed, however, when at a Great Southern concert in Central Park, Betts

**Below: Duane Allman, who died in a motorcycle crash at 24.**

was joined on stage for finale by Gregg and Butch Trucks. Soon after, at Capricorn Records' annual barbecue, core of Allman Brothers Band, plus David Goldflies, bass, and Dan Toler, drums, played 90-minute set; band was back in business with a vengeance.

Following 1980 move to Arista and **Reach For The Sky** album, band's internal problems resurfaced. Greg Allman eventually broke away to form Greg Allman Band which enjoyed US album success, most recently with **I'm No Angel** on Epic.

**Final line-up:** Gregg Allman; Betts.

**Hit Singles:**

| | US | UK |
|---|---|---|
| Ramblin' Man, 1973 | 2 | — |

**Albums:**
The Allman Brothers Band (Capricorn), 1969
Idlewild South (Capricorn), 1970
At Fillmore East (Capricorn), 1971
Eat A Peach (Capricorn), 1972
Beginnings (Capricorn), 1973
Brothers & Sisters (Capricorn), 1973 **CD**
Win, Loose Or Draw (Capricorn), 1975
The Road Goes On Forever (Capricorn), 1975
Wipe The Windows, Check The Oil, Dollar Gas (Capricorn), 1976
Enlightened Rogues (Capricorn) 1979
Best Of (Capricorn), 1980
Reach For The Sky (Arista), 1980
Brothers Of The Road (Arista), 1981

*Duane Allman Solo:*
Anthology (Polydor/Capricorn), 1972
Anthology Volume 2 (Polydor/Capricorn), 1974
Best Of (Polydor/Capricorn), 1979

*Gregg Allman:*
Laid Back (Polydor/Capricorn), 1973
Playing Up A Storm (Polydor/Capricorn), 1977
Dickie Betts And The Great Southern (Arista), 1977

*Worth Searching Out:*
The Hour Glass (Liberty), 1968
Duane And Gregg Allman (Bold/Polydor), 1972

# Marc Almond
UK vocalist, composer.
Born Southport, near Liverpool, 1957

**Career:** Studied design and fine art at college where he discovered performance art. Met multi-instrumentalist Dave Ball in 1978 and formed highly successful duo Soft Cell.

Also formed Marc And The Mambas as occasional off-shoot project to indulge in love of melodramatic ballads, covering songs by Scott Walker, Lou Reed and Jacques Brel, and released **Untitled** in 1982.

Almond left Soft Cell in mid-83 to go solo and released second Mambas LP, flamenco-influenced **Torment And Toreros** before immediately announcing he was quitting the recording business. Changed his mind the next day, and later formed Marc Almond And The Willing Sinners to release **Vermine In Ermine** LP and played series of one-man shows in London theatres. Recorded **I Feel Love** hit single with label-mates Bronski Beat, fuelling (unfounded) rumours that he would replace Jimmy Somerville as BB vocalist.

Left Phonogram and joined Virgin for **Stories Of Johnny** LP — his most commercial record since Soft Cell days, despite excellent title track failing to chart when released as single.

Follow-up album **Mother Fist And Her Five Daughters** explored darker side of

Almond's songwriting, but once more proved his stunning interpretive talent on **A Woman's Story** single, which again failed to chart. In late 1987 he signed new deal with EMI, while EMI released compilation LP **Singles**.

Having established unique style star embraces hopeless romanticism and sordid realism (his fan club is called Gutter Hearts) he is an unrepentant modern recreation of tragic chanteuses like Judy Garland and Edith Piaf. Brilliant, disastrous, trashy, glamorous, over-emotional. Marc Almond is all of these and regrets nothing.

**Hit Singles:**

| | US | UK |
|---|---|---|
| *With Bronski Beat:* | | |
| I Feel Love, 1985 | — | 3 |

**Albums:**
Vermine in Ermine (Some Bizarre), 1984
Mother Fist And Her Five Daughters (Some Bizarre), 1985
Stories of Johnny (Some Bizarre), 1985
Singles (EMI), 1987

*Marc and the Mambas:*
Untitled (Some Bizarre), 1982
Torment & Toreros (Sire/Some Bizarre), 1983

**Above: Hopeless romantic and tragic chanteur Marc Almond. His work with Mari Wilson and Genesis P. Orridge show his eclectic taste.**

**Left: Singles, Courtesy EMI Records.**

# The Animals
UK group formed 1960.

**Original line-up:** Eric Burdon, vocals; Alan Price, keyboards; Hilton Valentine, guitar; Chas Chandler, bass; John Steel, drums.

**Career:** One of several important groups to emerge from vibrant British R&B scene of early '60s, the band started out with Saturday residency at Newcastle's Downbeat Club around 1960 before moving to city centre Club A Go-Go, changing name from Alan Price (▶) Combo to the Animals when Eric Burdon joined in 1962.

Cutting a demo disc they sold 500 copies to local fans while their manager took a copy to London where it impressed producer Mickie Most enough to persuade him to travel North to see group. Most brought them to London to record cover of **Baby Let Me Take You Home** (from the first Bob Dylan(▶) album), and it charted in April 1964, winning the group

a slot on that month's Chuck Berry(▶) tour. (As the Alan Price Combo they had backed Jerry Lee Lewis(▶) on tour.)

A semi-residency at London's Scene Club cemented their following and for their second release they lifted another song from same Dylan LP, the traditional New Orleans number **House Of The Rising Sun**. This plaintive blues ballad shot straight to No. 1 both sides of Atlantic, leading to debut US tour that summer. (Both re-issues have charted.)

1965 produced succession of hits kicking off with brilliant reading of Nina Simone(▶) masterpiece **Don't Let Me Be Misunderstood**, but despite the success he had brought them, band—and Burdon in particular—were unhappy with Most's choice of material and when their Columbia contract expired they refused to renew it, switching to Decca.

Never keen on air travel, Alan Price quit group to form the Alan Price Set, touring solely

**Below: The Animals in 1966, minus Alan Price, with Burdon in centre.**

in UK, going on to work prodigiously with Georgie Fame(▶), while Dave Rowberry was drafted in from the Mike Cotton Sound to replace him. In February 1966 John Steel was replaced by Barry Jenkins.

After two more hits, **Inside—Looking Out** and **Don't Bring Me Down**, the Animals split in July, largely due to rows over Burdon's hard drinking and heavy flirtation with LSD.

Burdon moved to Los Angeles, then to San Francisco where he formed the New Animals with Jenkins and newcomers Mick Briggs (ex-Steampacket), guitar, and Danny McCullough, bass.

The New Animals made UK charts with **Help Me Girl** (1966), **Good Times** (1967) and **San Francisco Nights** (1967) before Burdon disbanded them to gig around LA rock scene with Jimi Hendrix(▶) (Andy Summers of Police(▶) was a member briefly in 1968). He met up with producers Jerry Goldstein and Steve Gold who teamed him with the rhythm section of black LA band Nite Shift to form new unit known as War(▶) featuring the brilliant Danish harmonica player Lee Oskar and Burdon's hoarse vocals. (Hilton Valentine worked as unit's roadie.)

War went on to become one of the most successful of new wave of black funk bands. The wild-natured Burdon once more went into limbo, drifting round the rock scene, recording with blues veteran Jimmy Witherspoon, touring UK in 1973 and 1976, retiring to France for a time, then returning to California.

Back in Britain, Alan Price had become TV regular while Chas Chandler had sold his bass guitars to launch Jimi Hendrix's solo career, then masterminded the campaign which took Slade to stardom.

During his 1976 UK visit, Burdon and the other original Animals got together to cut **Before We Were So Rudely Interrupted** album, released in 1977 on Jet in US.

Original Animals line-up reformed in 1983 and undertook six-week tour of America in summer '83.

**Current line-up:** Original line-up plus sessioneers.

**Hit Singles:**

| | US | UK |
|---|---|---|
| House Of The Rising Sun, 1964 | 1 | 1 |
| I'm Crying, 1964 | 19 | 8 |
| Don't Let Me Be Misunderstood, 1965 | 15 | 5 |
| Bring It On Home To Me, 1965 | 32 | 7 |
| We Gotta Get Out Of This Place, 1965 | 13 | 2 |
| It's My Life, 1965 | 23 | 7 |
| Inside—Looking Out, 1966 | 34 | 12 |
| Don't Bring Me Down, 1966 | 12 | 6 |
| See See Rider, 1966 | 10 | — |
| When I Was Young, 1967 | 15 | — |
| San Francisco Nights, 1967 | 9 | — |
| Monterey, 1968 | 15 | — |
| Sky Pilot, 1968 | 14 | — |

**Albums (selected):**
The Animals (—/Starline), 1969
Most Of The Animals (—/MFP), 1971
Best Of (Abcko/—), 1975
Newcastle December 1963 (with Sonny Boy Williamson) (—/Charly), 1977
Greatest Hits (Live) (—/IRS), 1984
Singles Plus (EMI), 1987 **CD**

# Joan Armatrading

West Indian vocalist, guitarist, composer.
Born St Kitts, December 9, 1950.

**Career:** One of five children, Joan emigrated to Birmingham, UK, with her family in 1958. She starred in local production of rock musical

**Above: West Indian vocalist, guitarist, composer, Joan Armatrading.**

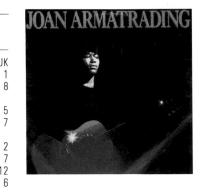

**Joan Armatrading's 1976 album. Courtesy A&M Records.**

'Hair' and formed songwriting partnership with fellow West Indian immigrant Pam Nester.

Moving to London in 1971, duo signed production and management deal with Cube Records but, when Gus Dudgeon-produced **Whatever's For Us** album appeared, Nester received no label credit and resultant friction led to break-up of both partnership and Cube deal.

After two years in limbo, Joan was signed by A&M and, adding own lyrics to previous melody-writing, came up with praised **Back To The Night** album (1975). Lack of sales success led A&M to team her with legendary producer Glyn Johns (Rolling Stones(▶), the Who(▶), Eagles(▶), Steve Miller(▶), etc) whose work proved totally sympathetic to her mood-laden introverted style. **Joan Armatrading** (1976) yielded **Love And Affection** hit single; and her third album **Show Some Emotion** spent four months on US charts, breaking her into American market.

A third Glyn Johns-produced LP, **To The Limit** (1978), introduced harder cutting edge while in 1980 **Me, Myself I** was successful single and album (produced by Richard Gottehrer of Blondie(▶), Link Wray, and Robert Johnson fame).

1983 album **The Key** spawned major hit in **Drop The Pilot**, and Armatrading has continued to maintain low-key but distinctive presence throughout 80s. A perennial concert draw, Armatrading has the talent to buck pop trends and establish permanent niche for herself.

**Hit Singles:**

| | US | UK |
|---|---|---|
| Love And Affection, 1976 | — | 10 |
| Drop The Pilot, 1983 | — | 11 |

**Albums:**
Whatever's For Us (Hifly/Cube), 1974
Back To The Night (A&M), 1975
Joan Armatrading (A&M), 1976
Show Some Emotion (A&M), 1977
To The Limit (A&M), 1978
Steppin' Out (A&M), 1979
My Myself I (A&M), 1980
Walk Under Ladders (A&M), 1981
The Key (A&M), 1983 **CD**
Track Record (A&M), 1983 **CD**
Back To The Night (A&M), 1984
Secret Secrets (A&M), 1985 **CD**
Sleight Of Hand (A&M), 1986 **CD**

# Asia

UK group formed 1981.
**Original line-up:** John Wetton, bass, vocals; Steve Howe, guitar; Geoffrey Downes, keyboards; Carl Palmer, drums.

**Career:** Wetton was England's premier utility man, playing in Family(▶), King Crimson(▶), Roxy Music(▶), Uriah Heep(▶) and UK. In late 1980 he teamed up with Steve Howe who was free following the break-up of Yes(▶). Last line-up of Yes had merged with UK band, Buggles (who had No.1 UK single **Video Killed The Radio Star**). Geoff Downes was re-forming Buggles when Howe asked him to join Wetton's group.

Carl Palmer's past included original King Crimson and megastardom with Emerson, Lake and Palmer(▶). After 1979 demise of ELP, Palmer tried solo career. Grand style of playing seemed anachronistic and 1981 UK tour/album flopped. Asia beckoned.

Self-named album appeared in early 1982 to universal condemnation *before* release. Critics judged public would not support 'supergroup' of dinosaur rockers from '70s. Through word of mouth, US sales rocketed, LP zooming to platinum despite recession and critics. After nine weeks at No.1, criticism shifted to complaints of selling out to undiscriminating youth of America.

Asia continued to defy critics and please public. Carl Palmer's old cohort from ELP days, Greg Lake temporarily replaced Wetton

in October 1983 but five months later Wetton returned with new material and Lake left. In late 1984, Steve Howe was replaced by Swiss guitarist 'Mandy' Meyer, formerly of heavy metal outfit Krokus(▶).

Howe went on to form GTR with ex-Genesis guitarist Steve Hackett, and hit album **GTR** ensued in 1986.

**Current line-up:** John Wetton, bass, vocals; Armand 'Mandy' Meyer, guitar; Geoffrey Downes, keyboards; Carl Palmer, drums.

**Hit Singles:**

| | US | UK |
|---|---|---|
| Heat Of The Moment, 1982 | 4 | 46 |
| Only Time Will Tell, 1982 | 17 | 54 |

**Albums:**
Asia (Geffen), 1982 **CD**
Alpha (Geffen), 1983
Astra (Geffen), 1985 **CD**

# Bad Company

UK group formed 1973

**Original line up:** Paul Rodgers, guitar, vocals; Mick Ralphs, guitar; Boz Burrell, bass; Simon Kirke, drums.

**Career:** Formed from the remnants of Free(▶) (Kirke and Rodgers), Bad Company—named after the Robert Benton western—carved no new ground in their lifetime but made one hell of a dent on the British and American markets during '70s.

The sparse, tight rhythm section of Burrell (ex King Crimson(▶)), Kirke and Ralphs (ex-Mott the Hoople(▶)) was the perfect foil for Rodgers' explosive vocal talents, and on the right night they were among the best of live bands.

After brief breaking-in period, Bad Company hit the road in March 1974, debuting at Rodgers' home gig, Newcastle Town Hall (which remained group's favourite venue).

First album **Bad Company** went platinum in States, with debut single **Can't Get Enough** making US Top 10 and UK Top 20. All material released on manager Peter Grant(▶)'s and Led Zeppelin(▶)'s Swan Song label, breaking Company in States, and furthering Grant's managerial reputation.

Grant's policy of a world tour every two years kept audiences hungry, and explained group's life-span of nearly ten years. Their later material was certainly not worthy of the adulation it received.

Apart from sax player Mel Collins' contribution to first album, Bad Company was a com-

**Below: Astute management earned Bad Company near decade of album chart action.**

pletely self-contained unit, working both studio and live with minimum of frills.

Although Rodgers was an aggressive power-house front man (not unlike his personality) and centre of attention, Ralphs, Burrell and Kirke always turned in some memorable riffs and melodies.

1979 release **Desolation Angels** was surrounded by rumour of split, although this was not confirmed until summer 1982 (after successful **Rough Diamond** set), when Kirke and Burrell began putting together new bands. Paul Rodgers re-surfaced with former Swan Song label sidekick Jimmy Page(▶) in The Firm (bassist Tony Franklin, drummer Chris Slade), who enjoyed considerable US success.

Latterly Bad Company reformed featuring ex-Ted Nugent vocalist Brian Howe, and, perhaps surprisingly in view of loss of Paul Rodgers' distinctive vocals, achieved retread success with **Fame And Fortune** set in US.

**Final line-up:** Ralphs, guitar; Burrell, bass; Kirke, drums; Brian Howe, vocals.

| Hit Singles: | US | UK |
|---|---|---|
| Can't Get Enough, 1974 | 5 | 15 |
| Movin' On, 1975 | 19 | — |
| Feel Like Making Love, 1975 | 10 | 20 |
| Young Blood, 1976 | 20 | — |
| Rock'n'Roll Fantasy, 1979 | 13 | — |

**Albums:**
Bad Company (Swan Song/Island), 1974
Straight Shooter (Swan Song/Island), 1975
Run With The Pack (Swan Song/Island), 1976
Burning Sky (Swan Song/Island), 1977
Desolation Angels (Swan Song/Island), 1979
Rough Diamonds (Swan Song), 1982
10 From 6 (Atlantic), 1986 **CD**
Fame And Fortune (Atlantic), 1986 **CD**

# Bad Manners

UK group formed 1980.
**Line-up:** Fatty 'Buster' Bloodvessel (Doug Trendle), vocals; Gus 'Hot Lips' Herman, trumpet; Andrew 'Marcus Absent' Marson, saxophone; Chris Kane, saxophone; Louis Alphonso (L. Cook), guitar; David Farren, bass; Martin Stewart, keyboards; Brian Chew-It (Brian Tuitt), drums; Winston Bazoomies (Alan Sayag), harmonica.

**Career:** Formed in North London, Bad Manners quickly gained success as part of ska revival movement along with Madness(▶) and the Specials(▶). Despite controversy at one time surrounding 'skinhead' following, band relies on showmanship, raucous enthusiasm and easily assimilable music to make impact. Stage act was based around antics of bald, 17-stone Buster Bloodvessel, one of Britain's most unlikely pop stars. Extrovert to outrageous degree, Bloodvessel was given to wearing dresses and other outlandish cos-

**Gosh It's, Bad Manners. Courtesy Magnet Records.**

tumes along with Doctor Marten 'bovver' boots.

'Good time' image sometimes obscures fact that band are solid musicians capable of exciting music. Act has very British nature but direct signing to US Portrait label in 1983 showed intent to win international audience.

| Hit Singles: | US | UK |
|---|---|---|
| Lip Up Fatty, 1980 | — | 15 |
| Special Brew, 1980 | — | 3 |
| Just A Feeling, 1981 | — | 13 |
| Can Can, 1981 | — | 3 |
| Walkin' In The Sunshine, 1981 | — | 10 |
| My Girl Lollipop (My Boy Lollipop), 1982 | — | 9 |

**Albums:**
Ska'n'B (—/Magnet), 1980
Loonee Tunes (—/Magnet), 1981
Gosh It's . . . (—/Magnet), 1981
Forging Ahead (—/Magnet), 1982

# The Band

Canadian group formed late '50s.
**Original/final line-up:** Jamie 'Robbie' Robertson, guitar: Garth Hudson, organ, saxophone; Richard Manuel, piano, vocals; Rick Danko, bass, vocals; Levon Helm, drums, vocals, mandolin.

**Career:** Levon Helm came from Arkansas, rest are Canadians. Group started as backing band for Toronto-based rock 'n' roller Ronnie Hawkins(▶), with whom they recorded covers of urban blues hits featuring Helm's vocals and Robertson's incisive guitar (classic example, Hawkins' **Who Do You Love**). Billed first as Canadian Squires then as Levon and the Hawks, they left Hawkins and toured Canada and US. Recorded classic single **The Stones I Throw** while in New York, where they met white blues singer John Hammond Jr, whose father was A&R boss of Columbia.

Through the Hammond connection, the Band met Bob Dylan(▶), who was then moving more heavily into electric music and saw their musical versatility (all play several instruments) as ideal backing. First collaboration was single **Can You Please Crawl Out Your Window** some members played on **Blonde On Blonde** album. With Mickey Jones playing drums instead of Helm, the Band accompanied Dylan on 1965-66 US/European tour. A motorcycle accident in July 1966 put Dylan out of action and the Band settled in Woodstock, New York. Rehearsed and recorded with him while he recovered, the results being heard on **The Basement Tapes,** a bootleg so successful that much of its material was officialy released on LP of same name by Columbia in 1975.

The crossflow influence between Dylan and the Band can be heard on Dylan's **John Wesley Harding** album and the Band's own **Music From Big Pink** (Capitol, 1968), from which **The Weight** remains true classic.

Robertson's songs for second LP, **The Band,** included **Up On Cripple Creek** and **The Night They Drove Old Dixie Down,** both subtle yet powerfully evocative traditional-style, truly American songs. Became first North American band to make the cover of 'Time' magazine.

Undertaking lengthy tours on their own led to **Stage Fright** LP; titletrack told of perils of being on road. **Cahoots** (1971) reflected their weariness at then current American values, but seemed a trifle pretentious; it included track cut in collaboration with Van Morrison(▶).

There followed four-year hiatus before Robertson came up with new material; after

**The Band. Courtesy Capitol Records.**

December 1971 concert at New York Academy Of Music (recorded live as **Rock Of Ages),** Band made no appearances until Watkins Glen Festival of July 1973. Their studio efforts, a planned thematic work by Robertson, was shelved and next record release was **Moondog Matinee,** a tribute to their rock 'n' roll roots.

**Before The Flood** encapsulated live work with Dylan on 1974 tour; they provided all back-up work on his **Planet Waves** album. In late 1975, own long-awaited album of new material hit stores, but **Northern Lights Southern Cross** did not quite have stunning effect expected, though musicianship remained superb.

In late 1976 came shock announcement— their current tour was to be the Band's last and stage career was to climax with a special Thanksgiving Day concert at San Francisco's Winterland, to be dubbed 'The Last Waltz'. It was a triumphant occasion with such friends and collaborators as Bob Dylan, Ronnie Hawkins, Neil Young, Bobby Charles, Van Morrison, Joni Mitchell, Eric Clapton, Dr John, Neil Diamond and Muddy Waters turning out. (Robertson had produced two Neil Diamond(▶) albums, **Beautiful Noise** (1976) and **Love At The Greek** (1977), while Helm had produced **Muddy Waters in Woodstock,** 1976.)

**Islands** (1977), a very laid-back effort, completed group's contractual obligations to Capitol and they embarked on solo projects leaving the album and movie of 'The Last Waltz' as their testament.

Robbie Robertson co-wrote, produced and starred in 'Carny' with Garey Busey (Buddy Holly in 'The Buddy Holly Story' and Jodie Foster in 1980, and re-surfaced with critically acclaimed **Robbie Robertson** LP in 1987. Levon Helm received plaudits for role in 'Coal Miners Daughter' (1980), and also starred in Tom Wolfe's 'The Right Stuff', and 'The Dollmaker' with Jane Fonda; toured with Rick Danko as country duo in early 80s. Both recorded solo albums, released in 1978. Richard Manuel committed suicide in March 1986. Levon Helm continues working away, having made no less than 4 solo albums, and the Band's history is kept alive by enthusiastic Appreciation Society based in UK.

| Hit Singles: | US | UK |
|---|---|---|
| Rag Mama Rag, 1970 | 57 | 16 |

**Albums:**
Music From Big Pink (Capitol), 1968 **CD**
The Band (Capitol), 1969 **CD**
Stage Fright (Capitol), 1970
Cahoots (Capitol), 1971
Rock Of Ages (Capitol), 1972 **CD**
Rock Of Ages Volume II (-/Capitol), 1972
Moondog Matinee (Capitol), 1973
Northern Lights, Southern Cross (Capitol), 1975
Best Of (Capitol/Fame), 1976 **CD**
Islands (Capitol), 1977
The Last Waltz (Warner Bros), 1978
Anthology Volume I (Capitol), 1978

Anthology Volume II (Capitol), 1980
*(With Bob Dylan)* Before The Flood (Island), 1974

*Levon Helm Solo:*
American Son (MCA), 1978
The Legend of Jesse James (A&M), 1980*
*With various artists

*Rick Danko Solo:*
Rick Danko (Arista), 1978

# The Beach Boys

US group formed 1950s.
**Original line-up:** Brian Wilson, vocals; Dennis Wilson, vocals, drums; Carl Wilson, vocals, guitar; Mike Love, vocals; Al Jardine, vocals, guitar.

**Career:** Sons of California's 1960s surfing boom, the Beach Boys were based around the Wilson brothers. Songwriting genius Brian Wilson (born June 20, 1942), Dennis Wilson (born December 4, 1944), Carl Wilson (born December 21, 1946), cousin Mike Love (born March 15, 1941) and friend Al Jardine (born September 3, 1942) grew up in middle-class Los Angeles district of Hawthorne. Started out singing barber-shop/Four Freshmen-styled harmonies at homes of friends and relatives. Then launched themselves as Carl and the Passions; name soon changed to Kenny and the Cadets (Brian being Kenny).

Dennis, already a surfing addict, suggested to Brian and Mike that they write a song about the cult sport. Result was **Surfin'.** The Wilson brothers' father Murray, himself an established songwriter, took them along to his music publisher. A cheapo production found Carl on guitar, Al on acoustic bass and Brian providing percussion courtesy of a garbage can. Record was issued on tiny local X label then switched to slightly bigger Candix label. It hung around low limits of US Hot 100 for six weeks.

**Below: These are Boys? (Left to Right) Wilson, Johnston, Jardine, Wilson, Love during the late '70s.**

Group worked for while as the Pendletones, a name taken from a make of heavy plaid shirt which was standard surfer wear and which they adopted as stage garb. Candix promotion man suggested the Beach Boys as better tag. First appearance under new name was at Ritchie Valens'(▶) Memorial Concert, Long Beach Municipal Auditorium, December 31, 1961 (Mexicano rock singer Valens had perished in recent air-crash along with Buddy Holly(▶) and the Big Bopper).

Al Jardine left group to take up dental studies at college and he was temporarily replaced by neighbour David L. Marks (featured on sleeve pics of debut album).

Candix folded early 1962. Murray persuaded Capitol Records' producer Nik Venet to pick up group. With smooth harmonies, his own falsetto and a twangy guitar, Brian Wilson had created a whole new sound. What's more, his songs went beyond Tin Pan Alley-style romance and dealt with real teenage concerns — and fantasies — like surfing, hot rod cars and motorcycles.

First Capitol release, **Surfin' Safari**, went US Top 20. **Ten Little Indians** bombed, then **Surfin' USA** (a clever parody of Chuck Berry's(▶) **Sweet Little Sixteen**) went all the way to No. 3. **Surfin' USA** album (1963) brought the group first gold record. In same year Brian Wilson had further success when his composition **Surf City** gave his friends Jan and Dean(▶) a million-seller.

Al Jardine rejoined the fold, Marks passing into rock history. Meanwhile, ballad **Surfer Girl, Fun Fun Fun, Little Honda** and chart-topping **I Get Around** continued run of hits. The Beach Boys' flawless harmonies impressed and influenced many artists, and group's success opened flood-gates for profusion of imitators. When Wilson switched from songs about the wild surf to songs about drag strips, imitators followed suit.

**When I Grow Up To Be A Man, Dance Dance Dance, Help Me Rhonda** (another chart-topper) kept things going but Brian, always something of an introvert, was feeling the strain. Suffering from working pressures, he had nervous breakdown in early 1965; also suffered loss of hearing in one ear. He decided to stop touring with band, though he

**Above: Brian Wilson when it all began — in the early 1960s.**

continued to mastermind their records. Glen Campbell(▶) joined group as temporary replacement but left following argument over uneven split of income. He was replaced by Bruce Johnston who, as Bruce and Terry (with Terry Melcher), had been among Beach Boys imitators.

Increasingly influenced by Phil Spector's 'Wall Of Sound' technique (Beach Boys eventually cut version of Spector song **Then I Kissed Her**), Brian Wilson's productions became ever more inventive (with occasional relapses, like the beach party sing-along **Barbara Ann**). This sophistication helped band compete successfully with British invasion of US charts.

However, when Brian came up with his tour-de-force **Pet Sounds**, (a monumental concept album on which he worked with lyricist Tony Asher) it was totally upstaged by the Beatles'(▶) **Sergeant Pepper**, which came right on its heels. Brian was by now hanging out with Van Dyke Parks, who later wrote Beach Boys lyrics. Brian got into the drug scene, dropping acid, and drifted away from his brothers. (They had been on tour overseas at time of **Pet Sounds** release, of which they did not totally approve.)

**Good Vibrations** proved to be *the* classic Beach Boys' single but it took nine months to piece together. Complex though record was, this time-lag was due more to Brian's untogetherness than anything else.

Follow-up album project **Smile**, which eventually appeared as **Smiley Smile**, found Van Dyke Parks heavily involved with Brian, to disapproval of rest of group. Rather than being Brian's dreamed-of masterwork LP was eclipsed by emergent West Coast psychedelia movement; it seemed old hat.

With Brian more and more out of things the Beach Boys continued to churn out pleasant if time-warped singles — including **Wild Honey, Do It Again** and **I Can Hear Music.** Their albums also maintained totally distinctive sound. In 1967 formed own Brother Records label but ran into immediate legal problems. Their dispute with Capitol did not end until 1970 when label's distribution was switched to Warner Bros/Reprise. Brother was one of first artist-owned labels (preceding Beatles' Apple set-up but meeting similar problems).

New management by Jack Rieley, who also wrote lyrics for them, helped put group back on course. Rieley dug up some old, incomplete tapes for a song called **Surf's Up**, which had been intended as part of **Smile.** He got group

to finish it off and make it titletrack of new album. Rieley also encouraged group to drop stage uniforms and come up with less structured stage show. Sets now ran for as much as two hours and included newer, more obscure material alongside hits.

Bruce Johnston quit group after **Surf's Up.** In 1972 Rieley took band off to the Netherlands to cut critically applauded but commercially unspectacular **Holland** album. This led to his split from group. (Band had moved Brother studios to Holland — then Brian decided to return to California.)

At this time, a new rhythm section was formed, including black South Africans Blondie Chaplin, guitar, and Ricky Fataar, drums (both of SA Group Fire), making group more potent in concert, but the hits stopped.

Chaplin and Fataar quit in 1974. James Guercio, who had been associated with both Blood Sweat and Tears(▶) and Chicago(▶), came in as manager also played bass on-stage in line-up which reverted to original format.

Dennis and Carl Wilson were proving to be songwriters of some talent but magic spark of Brian Wilson was missing. Numerous attempts were made to tempt him out of his hermit-like existence at Bel-Air mansion. After nearly a decade of virtual inactivity, and following course of therapeutic songwriting prescribed by an analyst, 1976 album **15 Big Ones** (title referring both to number of tracks and the group's age) found Brian back with Beach Boys as singer, songwriter and 'director'. LP won plenty of publicity but did not really stand up. 1977's **The Beach Boys Love You** was more promising. Brian was now firmly back in command of his faculties, composing and producing all material; performed on US tour in summer 1977.

1978's **M.I.U.** album sold poorly and members of band seemed to be going off in own directions. Bruce Johnston came back to help with first Caribou/CBS album **The Beach Boys L.A. Light Album**; and also helped on **Keepin' The Summer Alive** project. Explained Carl: 'He was exactly what we needed. He helped us sort the good from the bad and get back to the basics — the vocals and harmonies — which have been our

**The Beach Boys.
Courtesy Caribou Records.**

strength from the beginning.'

It was truly a joint effort: Carl Wilson and Randy Bachman of Guess Who and Bachman Turnover Overdrive fame wrote title cut; Brian Wilson/Al Jardine co-wrote five songs and did a new arrangement of Chuck Berry's **School Day;** and Bruce Johnston contributed **Endless Harmony** — an apt Beach Boys theme.

**Keepin' The Summer Alive** (1979) and **Ten Years Of Harmony** kept show rolling and concert appearances, usually before huge crowds, continued into mid-'80s but group had long since lost creative edge. Death by drowning of Dennis Wilson at 39 at Marina Del Rey, California in December 1983 seemed

symbolic of the fun having finally deserted surf music.

However, band gained just accolade of induction into Rock'n'Roll Hall Of Fame in January 1988 (although ceremony was somewhat marred by bizarre behaviour of Mike Love.)

**Current line-up:** Brian Wilson; Carl Wilson; Love; Jardine; plus sessioneers.

**Hit Singles:**

| | US | UK |
|---|---|---|
| Surfin' Safari, 1962 | 14 | — |
| Surfin' USA, 1963 | 3 | 34 |
| Surfer Girl, 1963 | 7 | — |
| Little Deuce Coupe, 1963 | 15 | — |
| Be True To Your School, 1963 | 6 | — |
| Fun Fun Fun, 1964 | 5 | — |
| I Get Around, 1964 | 1 | 7 |
| When I Grow Up (To Be A Man), 1964 | 9 | 27 |
| Dance Dance Dance, 1964 | 8 | 24 |
| Do You Wanna Dance, 1965 | 12 | — |
| Help Me Rhonda, 1965 | 1 | 27 |
| California Girls, 1965 | 3 | 26 |
| The Little Girl I Once Knew, 1965 | 20 | — |
| Barbara Ann, 1966 | 2 | 3 |
| Sloop John B., 1966 | 3 | 2 |
| Wouldn't It Be Nice, 1966 | 8 | — |
| God Only Knows, 1966 | 39 | 2 |
| Good Vibrations, 1966 | 1 | 1 |
| Then I Kissed Her, 1967 | — | 4 |
| Heroes And Villains, 1967 | 12 | 8 |
| Darlin', 1968 | 19 | 11 |
| Do It Again, 1968 | 20 | 1 |
| I Can Hear Music, 1969 | 24 | 10 |
| Break Away, 1969 | — | 6 |
| Cottonfields, 1970 | — | 5 |
| Good Vibrations, 1976 | — | 8 |
| Rock And Roll Music, 1976 | 5 | 36 |
| Lady Lynda, 1979 | — | 6 |
| Beach Boys Medley, 1981 | 12 | 47 |
| Come Go With Me, 1981 | 18 | — |
| (With the Fat Boys) Wipeout | 12 | — |

**Albums:**

Surfin' Safari (Capitol/Greenlight), 1962
Surfin' USA (Capitol), 1963
Surfer Girl (Capitol/Pickwick), 1963
Little Deuce Coupe (Capitol/Greenlight), 1963
All Summer Long (Capitol/MFP), 1964
Concert (Capitol/—), 1964*
Party (Capitol), 1965
Pet Sounds (Capitol/Greenlight), 1966
Best Of (Capitol), 1966
Smiley Smile (Capitol), 1967
Best Of Volume 2 (Capitol), 1967
Wild Honey (Capitol), 1967
Friends (Capitol), 1968
20/20 (Capitol), 1969
Sunflower (Reprise/Caribou), 1970
Surf's Up (Reprise/Caribou), 1971
Live In London (Capitol/MFP), 1972
Endless Summer (Capitol/MFP), 1974 **CD**
Spirit Of America (Capitol), 1975 **CD**
The Beach Boys Love You (Reprise), 1977
Fun Fun Fun (Capitol), 1978
California Girls (Capitol/—), 1978
Keepin' The Summer Alive (Caribou), 1979
L.A. (Light Album) (Caribou), 1979
Ten Years Of Harmony (Caribou), 1981
Sunshine Dream (Capitol/—), 1982
The Very Best Of (Capitol), 1983
Beach Boys Rarities (Capitol), 1985
Beach Boys (Caribou), 1981 **CD**
Made In The USA (Capitol), 1986 **CD**

*Live

*Worth Searching Out*
Surf's Up (Reprise/Stateside), 1971
Holland (Reprise) 1972

*Dennis Wilson Solo*
Pacific Ocean Blue (Caribou), 1977
One Of Those People (Elektra) 1979

*Carl Wilson Solo.*
Carl Wilson (Caribou), 1981

# Beastie Boys

US group formed 1983.

**Original/Current line-up:** Adam Horovitz; Adam Yauch; Michael Diamond.

**Career:** Much-hyped US band whose 1987 activities owed not a little to those of The Sex Pistols' a decade before. A god-send for the downmarket daily tabloids, their Montreux Rock Festival antics stole the headlines from every other act appearing. First single **Cookie Puss/Beastie Revolution** surfaced in August 1983 and had the accolade of being nominated by Billy Idol alongside records by Little Richard, Presley and The Beatles.

**Licensed to III, Beastie Boys. Courtesy Columbia Records.**

Signed by Rick Rubin to Def Jam theirs was the second Def Jam release **Rock Hard, DJ 002** after LL Cool J's **I Need A Beat**. The band's 1985 summer tour with Madonna was likened to "Jimi Hendrix and The Monkees appearing together in 1967" and ended at Madison Square Garden with Mike D soaking Madonna with a water-pistol and chasing her into the wings.

Band visited UK in February 1986, returning later in the year for the Raisin' Hell Tour. Their double A-sided single **She's Crafty/Girls** released in September 1987. Whether they have the true musical ability to have a sustained chart career remains to be seen.

**Hit Singles:**

|  | US | UK |
|---|---|---|
| She's On It, 1986 | — | 10 |
| Fight for Your Right To Party, 1987 | 12 | 11 |
| No Sleep Till Brooklyn, 1987 | — | 14 |

**Albums:**
Licenced to III (Def Jam USA—Columbia), 1987 **CD**

# The Beatles

UK group formed 1959.

**Original line-up:** John Lennon, vocals, guitar; Paul McCartney, guitar, vocals; George Harrison, guitar, vocals; Stuart Sutcliffe, bass; Pete Best, drums.

**Career:** Formed in Liverpool area: influenced strongly by American rock 'n' roll and R&B records brought to port by sailors. After becoming local success, began to work in Hamburg, West Germany, where bookings involved playing 8-10 hours per night for little money. However, this experience perfected crowd-pleasing ability (recordings from era are high on energy, short on polish). First studio records were in Germany 1961 as backing group for Tony Sheridan, legendary UK rocker. Sessions also provided first genuine Beatles tracks, notably **Ain't She Sweet,** although tracks not released until much later.

Discovered by Liverpool record shop manager Brian Epstein in late 1961, by which time Sutcliffe had left group, preferring to remain in Germany. McCartney(▶) then moved to bass, and group became quartet (Sutcliffe died of brain haemorrhage, 1962). Epstein tried to acquire recording contract for Beatles, but without success. Group cut demo tracks for Decca Records, but were rejected in favour of Brian Poole & Tremeloes. Finally, Epstein convinced then minor Parlophone label to provide audition. George Martin, head of label, signed group in late 1962, but suggested replacement of Pete Best—rest of band not unhappy, and recruited Ringo Starr(▶) from Rory Storme and the Hurricanes, fellow Merseyside group.

Prior to this, group had gone through several name changes—initially known as the Quarrymen (after school which Lennon(▶) attended), they became Silver Beatles, then simply the Beatles (name inspired by the Crickets, Buddy Holly's(▶) group). Sessions for Parlophone proved promising—first single, **Love Me Do,** released October 1962, reached No. 17 in UK while follow-up, **Please Please Me,** released early 1962, became huge hit. Similarly titled debut LP topped UK charts. Three further chart-toppers, **From Me To You**, **She Loves You**, and **I Want To Hold Your Hand**, followed in 1963.

US success delayed until 1964 when **I Want To Hold Your Hand** (fifth UK hit) topped US singles chart, beginning deluge of releases in US, almost all becoming major hits. At one point in first half of 1964, the Beatles held positions 1, 2, 3, 4 and 5 in US chart, with seven *other* singles in Top 100, and LPs at No. 1 and No. 2. While this success was never equalled, group enjoyed enormous worldwide success through mid-'60s, with strings of chart-toppers in both US and UK. Almost all Beatles B-sides charted on their own in US.

Beatles' success opened floodgates for the 'British Invasion', when numerous British acts broke through in US charts, including Rolling Stones(▶), Gerry & the Pacemakers, Dave Clark Five(▶) and many more. Beatles also starred in pair of ground-breaking rock films, 'A Hard Day's Night' and 'Help!', which were enormously successful both artistically and commercially. Lennon and McCartney were recognised as most potent songwriting partnership of rock'n'roll era; besides providing all Beatle hits, they also wrote chart-toppers for Billy J. Kramer and Peter & Gordon.

**Below: Vastly underrated as a 'live' band, the Beatles paid dues with gruelling schedule of German clubs in early days.**

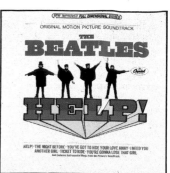

**Help! from the fab four film. Courtesy Capitol Records.**

**The American issue, Beatles '65. Courtesy Capitol Records.**

**US release, Meet The Beatles. Courtesy Capitol Records.**

Early beat group style, influenced by Chuck Berry(▶), Everly Brothers(▶), Carl Perkins(▶) and Tamla-Motown, evolved by 1966 LP **Rubber Soul** into much more original sound and approach, without affecting commercial success; by late 1966, as psychedelic album **Revolver** released, group gave up touring, mostly because hysterical fans made it too risky. This led to lengthy studio experimentation (and often, in retrospect, self-indulgence) culminating in arguably finest LP ever made.

**Sergeant Pepper's Lonely Hearts Club Band**, released in June 1967. Group also got involved with Indian guru Maharishi Mahesh Yogi; during their attendance at transcendental meditation course in August, Brian Epstein, who had directed group's career throughout hugely successful period, died (of alcohol/drug overdose).

Beatles plunged back into work, creating **Magical Mystery Tour** LP and TV film, an extension of **Sergeant Pepper**, and equally influenced by hallucinogenic drugs. It received critical roasting but latterly has been regarded as legendary. Although group by this time beginning to argue internally, they created remarkable double LP in 1968, known as **The White Album** because of completely white sleeve; it was preceded by **Lady Madonna** single, which heralded return to more basic rock 'n' roll, and by anthemic **Hey Jude,** single lasting seven minutes plus. Year also saw formation of Beatles' company, Apple Corps, with record label, shop, film company etc. 'Yellow Submarine' cartoon movie was created around fictional characters suggested by Beatle songs.

1969 was final year of Beatles activities, including fated film project 'Let It Be' which produced two chart-topping singles in title song and **Get Back.** Apple Records achieved great success with Mary Hopkin (recommended to Paul McCartney by Twiggy), but 'Let It Be' film was virtually abandoned, as each Beatle wanted to work without the others. Having left producer and svengali George Martin for **Let It Be,** group returned to him for final classic LP, **Abbey Road,** but opposing business interests, particularly of Lennon and McCartney, were becoming impossible.

Lennon and new wife, Japanese avant-garde artist Yoko Ono, formed splinter group, Plastic Ono Band, who scored with first single, **Give Peace A Chance.** Eventually, in 1970, new manager Allen Klein and famed record producer Phil Spector pulled together **Let It Be** project, but this further annoyed McCartney, who announced that he was leaving group. Subsequently, each Beatle enjoyed solo success to a greater or lesser extent. Compilations, re-issues and a few new recordings have kept group in charts ever since, although solo careers (see under individual entries) have in some cases tarnished reputation of undoubtedly most popular group of rock 'n' roll era, whose success and influence are unlikely ever to be equalled.

Rumours of unreleased material being made available arose during refitting of Abbey Road Studios (July 1983) and subsequent opening to public.

1987 saw 25th anniversary of release of **Love Me Do**, and 20th birthday of **Sergeant Pepper**. Memorial celebrations included release of plethora of tracks on compact disc, introducing music to new generation of high-tech buyers. Warts-and-all effect of CD technology was nevertheless welcomed by producer George Martin, who commented that medium captured raw vitality of original sessions.

**Final line-up:** Lennon; McCartney, bass; Harrison; Ringo Starr, drums.

**Above: Near the end. One of the last publicity shots.**

**Right: Sergeant Pepper's Lonely Hearts Club Band. Courtesy Parlophone Records.**

**Hit Singles:**

| | US | UK |
|---|---|---|
| Love Me Do, 1962 | 1 | 17 |
| Please Please Me, 1963 | 3 | 2 |
| From Me To You, 1963 | 41 | 1 |
| She Loves You, 1963 | 1 | 1 |
| I Want To Hold Your Hand, 1963 | 1 | 1 |
| Can't Buy Me Love, 1964 | 1 | 1 |
| I Saw Her Standing There, 1964 | 14 | — |
| Twist & Shout, 1964 | 2 | — |
| Do You Want To Know A Secret, 1964, | 2 | — |
| P.S. I Love You, 1964 | 10 | — |
| A Hard Day's Night, 1964 | 1 | 1 |
| Ain't She Sweet, 1964 | 19 | 29 |
| And I Love Her, 1964 | 12 | — |
| Matchbox, 1964 | 17 | — |
| I Feel Fine, 1964 | 1 | 1 |
| She's A Woman, 1964 | 4 | — |
| Eight Days A Week, 1965 | 1 | — |
| Ticket To Ride, 1965 | 1 | 1 |
| Help, 1965 | 1 | 1 |
| Yesterday, 1965 | 1 | — |
| Day Tripper/We Can Work It Out, 1965 | — | 1 |
| Day Tripper, 1966 | 5 | — |
| We Can Work It Out, 1966 | 1 | — |
| Nowhere Man, 1966 | 3 | — |
| Paperback Writer, 1966 | 1 | 1 |
| Yellow Submarine/Eleanor Rigby, 1966 | — | 1 |
| Yellow Submarine, 1966 | 2 | — |
| Eleanor Rigby, 1966 | 11 | — |
| Penny Lane/Strawberry Fields Forever, 1967 | — | 2 |
| Penny Lane, 1967 | 1 | — |
| Strawberry Fields Forever, 1967 | 8 | — |
| All You Need Is Love, 1967 | 1 | 1 |
| Hello Goodbye, 1967 | 1 | 1 |
| Magical Mystery Tour (EP), 1967 | — | 2 |
| Lady Madonna, 1968 | 1 | 1 |
| Hey Jude, 1968 | 1 | 1 |
| Revolution, 1968 | 12 | — |
| Get Back, 1969 | 1 | 1 |
| Ballad Of John And Yoko, 1969 | 8 | 1 |
| Something/Come Together, 1969 | — | 4 |
| Come Together/Something, 1969 | 1 | — |
| Let It Be, 1970 | 1 | 2 |
| Long And Winding Road, 1970 | 1 | — |
| Yesterday, 1976 | — | 8 |
| Got To Get You Into My Life, 1976 | 7 | — |
| Back In The U.S.S.R., 1976 | — | 19 |
| Beatles Movie Medley, 1982 | 12 | 9 |
| Love Me Do, 1982 | — | 4 |

**Albums:**

*UK:*
Please Please Me (Parlophone), 1963 **CD**
With The Beatles (Parlophone), 1963 **CD**
A Hard Day's Night (Parlophone), 1964 **CD**
Beatles For Sale (Parlophone), 1964 **CD**
Help (Parlophone), 1965 **CD**
Rubber Soul (Parlophone), 1965 **CD**
Revolver (Parlophone), 1966 **CD**
A Collection of Beatles' Oldies (But Goldies) (Parlophone), 1966
Sergeant Pepper's Lonely Hearts Club Band (Parlophone), 1967 **CD**
The Beatles (White Album) (Parlophone), 1968 **CD**
Yellow Submarine (Parlophone), 1969 **CD**
Abbey Road (Parlophone), 1969 **CD**
Let It Be (Parlophone), 1970 **CD**
The Beatles 1962-1966 (Parlophone), 1973
The Beatles 1967-1970 (Parlophone), 1973
Rock 'n' Roll Music (Parlophone, 1976
Magical Mystery Tour (Parlophone), 1976 **CD**
The Beatles At The Hollywood Bowl, (Parlophone), 1977
Love Songs (Parlophone), 1977
Hey Jude (Parlophone), 1979
Rarities, 1979
The Beatles Ballads (Parlophone), 1980
Reel Music (Parlophone), 1982
20 Greatest Hits (Parlophone), 1982
Decca Sessions (Topline) **CD**

*US:*
(excluding Boxed Sets and superfluous compilations)
Introducing The Beatles (Capitol), 1963
Meet The Beatles (Capitol), 1964
The Beatles' Second Album (Capitol), 1964
A Hard Day's Night (Capitol), 1964
Something New (Capitol), 1964
The Beatles Story (Capitol), 1964
Beatles '65 (Capitol), 1965
The Early Beatles (Capitol), 1965
Beatles VI (Capitol), 1965
Help (Capitol), 1965
Rubber Soul (Capitol), 1965
Yesterday And Today (Capitol), 1966
Revolver (Capitol), 1966
Sergeant Pepper's Lonely Hearts Club Band (Capitol), 1967
Magical Mystery Tour (Capitol), 1967
The Beatles (White Album) (Capitol), 1968
Yellow Submarine (Capitol), 1969

Abbey Road (Capitol), 1969
Hey Jude (Capitol), 1970
Let It Be (Capitol), 1970
The Beatles 1962-1966 (Capitol), 1973
The Beatles 1967-1970 (Capitol), 1973
Rock 'n' Roll Music (Capitol), 1976
The Beatles At The Hollywood Bowl, (Capitol), 1977
Love Songs (Capitol), 1977
The Beatles Rarities (Capitol), 1980
Reel Music (Capitol), 1982
20 Greatest Hits (Capitol), 1982

**Below: The fab four at the time they held the top five positions in US chart.**

# Jeff Beck

UK guitarist, composer, vocalist.
Born Surrey, June 24, 1944.

**Career:** Studied at Wimbledon Art College. Played lead guitar for Tridents before being recommended to Yardbirds(▶) by Jimmy Page as replacement for Eric Clapton(▶). Spent two years with group, contributing to new, more experimental, sound on singles like **Shapes Of Things To Come** and **Over Under Sideways Down**.

Left Yardbirds in December 1966 to sign solo deal on EMI's Columbia label. Scored with out-of-character sing-along **Hi Ho Silver Lining** (again hit on re-release via Rak in 1972 and still a UK disco/pub/juke-box/party standard). Also cut version of **Love Is Blue** and played guitar solo on Donovan's(▶) hit **Goo Goo Barabajagel** before forming Jeff Beck Group featuring Rod Stewart(▶), vocals; Ron Wood, bass; Ray Cook, drums. (Cook was replaced by Mickey Waller after group was thrown off Roy Orbison/Small Faces(▶) package tour in March 1967.)

Nicky Hopkins (keyboards) joined later, and group won big reputation in US with **Truth** and **Beck-Ola** LPs. Playing biting, R&B-edged heavy rock, group had exciting but tempestuous career, developing reputation for potent music and bawdy life-style. Wood and Stewart split to join Faces(▶) in 1969.

Beck planned new group with ex-Vanilla Fudge(▶) players Tim Bogert (bass) and Carmine Appice (drums) — friends met on early Yardbirds visit to New York — but when car accident kept Beck out of action for 18 months the other two formed Cactus.

**Beck-Ola, Jeff Beck. Courtesy Columbia Records.**

Beck re-appeared in late 1971 to form new Jeff Beck Group with Robert Tench, vocals; Max Middleton, piano; Clive Chapman, bass, and Cozy Powell, drums. After two albums he declared band wasn't what he wanted and, on break-up of Cactus, formed trio with Bogert and Appice. This broke up after one album, **Beck Bogert Appice** (1973), and tour.

Beck retired again until, in 1975, George Martin produced **Blow By Blow** set, which found Beck experimenting heavily with jazz/rock fusion. Joining Jan Hammer Group for co-billing tour (which produced joint album **Live** in 1977), Beck featured Hammer's synthesiser work on 1976 album **Wired**.

Yet another inactive period ended in 1980 with appearance of **There And Back** album, again featuring Hammer, plus Tony Hymas, keyboards; Mo Foster, bass, and Simon Phillips, drums (Beck's first all-British band since Yardbirds).

In 1984, Beck joined up with old mate Rod Stewart, but relationship lasted just a few stormy days. Together with Plant and Page (ex-Led Zep(▶)) and Nile Rodgers(▶) had Top 5 hit at beginning of 1985 as Honeydrippers but as one of rock's greatest rock guitarists

**Above: Jeff Beck laces into his favourite Strat.**

ever, deserves more than his so far sadly fragmented career.

**Hit Singles:**

| | US | UK |
|---|---|---|
| Hi Ho Silver Lining, 1967 | — | 14 |
| Hi Ho Silver Lining, 1972 | — | 17 |

*(as member of)* The Honeydrippers:

| | | |
|---|---|---|
| Sea Of Love, 1985 | 3 | — |

**Albums:**
Truth (Epic/Columbia), 1968*
Beck-Ola (Epic/Columbia), 1969*
Rough And Ready (Epic), 1971
Jeff Beck Group (Epic), 1972
Beck, Bogert, Appice (Epic), 1973
Wired (Epic), 1976
Live (with the Jan Hammer Group), (Epic), 1977
There And Back (Epic), 1980
Early Anthology (Accord/—), 1981
The Best Of (1967-69) (Fame), 1985
Flash (Epic), 1985 **CD**
*Released as double LP (Epic/—), 1975

# The Bee Gees

UK group formed 1950s.

**Original line-up:** Barry Gibb, vocals, guitar; Robin Gibb, vocals; Maurice Gibb, vocals, guitar; Vince Melouney, guitar; Colin Petersen, drums.

**Career:** Formed in Manchester, England (Barry born September, 1946; non-identical twins Robin and Maurice born December 1949), Bee Gees performed on-stage in home city as pre-teens (father, Hugh, was bandleader). Emigrated to Australia with parents in 1958.

After winning radio talent contest, trio graduated to hosting own TV show. First single **Three Kisses Of Love** (1963) was mildly successful. Group's name was taken from Barry Gibbs' initials. By 1966 they were top

Antipodean group but market had limitations. Australian pomoter/manager/entrepreneur Robert Stigwood decided to take band to UK in 1967 as challenge to Beatles. Former child actor Colin Petersen was recruited to go with them as drummer. On arrival in London, another Australian, Vince Melouney, was added on guitar. Their **Spicks and Specks** reached top of Australian charts after they arrived in UK.

This group scored almost immediately with **New York Mining Disaster 1941** in both Britain and America. Follow-ups **To Love Somebody** and **Holiday** were hits, while **Massachusetts** topped UK charts. **I've Got To Get A Message To You** confirmed brothers' songwriting talent. On one early Royal Albert Hall concert they had support from 60-piece orchestra, huge choir and Royal Air Force Brass Band.

Melouney left to form own short-lived band in 1969. Robin Gibb fell out with others and went solo; scored with **Robin's Reign** album and hit single **Saved By The Bell** but career soon floundered. His brothers remained relatively inactive (Maurice married Scottish singer Lulu; they subsequently divorced); Colin Petersen had departed amid much acrimony. Brothers reunited as trio in late 1970.

Bee Gees had two million-selling American singles in 1971, with **Lonely Days** and **How Can You Mend A Broken Heart** but then languished. It was mid-'70s disco explosion which not only revived their career but made them superstars.

Switching from somewhat self-pitying storyline-songs to an emasculated brand of soul/disco did trick. Robin's high-pitched lead matched to nasal falsetto harmonies gave unique sound. 1975 Arif Mardin-produced album **Main Course** went platinum. **Jive Talkin'** was the disco smash of 1975.

Follow-up set **Children Of The Night** was self-produced; contained **You Should Be Dancing** and **Love So Right** monster singles.

Their music for RSO movies 'Saturday Night awards in 1979; **Saturday Night Fever** soundtrack included three No. 1's for group. Two further chart-toppers from studio album **Spirits Having Flown** made it a remarkable six No. 1's in a row. Bee Gees-penned title song from 'Grease' gave Frankie Valli No. 1 in 1978.

Their 1979 'Music For Unicef' charity project found them headlining worldwide televised New York spectacular. Also on bill were Abba(▶), John Denver(▶), Rod Stewart (▶), Earth, Wind And Fire(▶), Elton John(▶) and other major artists. Youngest Gibb brother Andy had four hit singles and became teeny-bopper hearthrob in late '70s. In 1980 Barry Gibb co-wrote, co-produced and contributed vocals to Barbra Streisand's(▶) smash album **Guilty**; he went on to revive Dionne Warwick's (▶) career as her new producer. Robin Gibb produced an LP on soul star Jimmy Ruffin and wrote, performed and produced **Help Me** for movie 'Times Square'. Group appeared in Stigwood's 'Sgt. Pepper' film with Peter Frampton(▶).

Now based in Miami, where they have their own recording studio, the brothers emerged from hitless period late in 1987 with international chart-topper **You Win Again**.

In a twenty-plus year career the Bee Gees have wielded enormous influence — the disco boom was practically their invention — and suffered less than most from fads and fashions of pop industry. Authorized biography 'The Illustrated Bee Gees' was published in 1979.

**Current line-up:** Barry Gibb; Maurice Gibb; Robin Gibb.

**Hit Singles:**

| | US | UK |
|---|---|---|
| New York Mining Disaster 1941, 1967 | 12 | 12 |
| To Love Somebody, 1967 | 15 | 41 |
| (The Lights Went Out In) Massachusetts, 1967 | 11 | 1 |
| World, 1967 | — | 9 |
| Holiday, 1967 | 16 | — |
| Words, 1968 | 15 | 8 |
| I've Gotta Get A Message To You, 1968 | 8 | 1 |
| I Started A Joke, 1969 | 6 | — |
| First Of May, 1969 | 37 | 6 |
| Don't Forget To Remember, 1969 | — | 2 |
| Lonely Days, 1971 | 3 | 33 |
| How Can You Mend A Broken Heart, 1971 | 1 | — |
| My World, 1972 | 16 | 16 |
| Run To Me, 1972 | 16 | 9 |
| Jive Talkin', 1975 | 1 | 5 |

**Spirits Having Flown, the Bee Gees. Courtesy RSO Records.**

| | US | UK |
|---|---|---|
| Fanny (Be Tender With My Love), 1976 | 12 | — |
| You Should Be Dancing, 1976 | 1 | 5 |
| Love So Right, 1976 | 3 | 41 |

| | | |
|---|---|---|
| Boogie Child, 1977 | 12 | — |
| How Deep Is Your Love, 1977 | 1 | 3 |
| Stayin' Alive, 1978 | 1 | 4 |
| Night Fever, 1978 | 1 | 1 |
| Too Much Heaven, 1978 | 1 | 3 |
| Tragedy, 1979 | 1 | 1 |
| Love You Inside Out, 1979 | 1 | 13 |
| Spirits Having Flown, 1980 | — | 16 |
| You Win Again, 1987 | — | 1 |

*Robin Gibb Solo:*

| | | |
|---|---|---|
| Saved By The Bell, 1969 | — | 2 |
| Oh! Darling, 1978* | 15 | — |

*From Sgt. Pepper soundtrack featuring all Bee Gees.

**Albums:**
Odessa (RSO/Polydor), 1969 **CD**
Best Of (—/RSO), 1969 **CD**
Best Of Volume 2 (RSO), 1973
Main Course (RSO), 1975
Children Of The World (RSO), 1976
Gold (RSO/—), 1976
Massachusetts (—/Contour), 1976
Here At Last—Live (RSO), 1977
I've Gotta Get A Message To You (—/Contour), 1977
Bonanza—Early Days (—/Pickwick), 1978
Greatest Hits (RSO), 1979
Spirits Having Flown (RSO), 1979
The Bee Gees (—/Impact), 1979
Early Days Volume 1 (—/Pickwick), 1979
Early Days Volume 2 (—/Pickwick), 1979
Early Days Volume 3 (—/Pickwick), 1979
Living Eyes (RSO), 1981 **CD**
ESP (Warner Bros) 1987 **CD**
Staying Alive (RSO, USA), 1983 **CD**

*Worth Searching Out:*
Bee Gees First (Polydor), 1967

**Below: Pat Benatar quickly dispensed with operatic background to make macho metal music.**

# Pat Benatar

US vocalist.
Born Pat Andrejewski, Brooklyn, New York, 1953.

**Career:** Possessed of undeniably unusual vocal ability, Pat Benatar trained in opera, but never actually attempted professional classical career. After short early marriage, she supported herself by singing in nightclubs, and quickly found her voice as the ultimate female hard-rocker.

**Seven The Hard Way, Pat Benatar. Courtesy Chrysalis Records.**

Her musical and performing stance is original only in that she *is* female, however. Whether the power-chord clichés and humorless posturing of heavy metal are rendered any more interesting when performed by a tiny, spandex-clad redhead (even with natural talent) rather than by the usual macho howlers is questionable.

Still, Benatar's appearance on the rock scene in 1979 certainly filled a niche. **In The Heat Of The Night** was surprisingly successful, and was followed by two hit singles in 1980 and 1981, **Heartbreaker** and **Hit Me**

**With Your Best Shot.** Her second album, **Crimes of Passion,** went straight to the top in 1981; quick follow-up LP **Precious Time** did just as well. She made acting debut in 'Union City Blues' same year.

Handicapped by not being a proficient songwriter, Benatar's own attempts have been naive, and guitarist-producer (and her husband) Neil Geraldo's writing seldom rises above clichés of the genre. Nevertheless, she has shown taste and daring in her selection of covers, which include John Cougar's(▶) **I Need A Lover,** Lennon and McCartney's **Helter Skelter** and Kate Bush's(▶) **Wuthering Heights**.

**Hit Singles:**

| | US | UK |
|---|---|---|
| Hit Me With Your Best Shot, 1981 | 9 | — |
| Treat Me Right, 1981 | 13 | — |
| Fire And Ice, 1981 | 5 | — |
| Shadows In The Night, 1982 | 13 | — |
| Little Too Late, 1983 | 20 | — |
| We Belong, 1984 | 5 | — |
| *Love Is A Battlefield, 1985 | 5 | 17 |
| Invincible, 1985 | 10 | — |

*1983 in US

**Albums:**
In The Heat Of The Night (Mobile/Chrysalis), 1979
Crimes Of Passion (Chrysalis), 1980
Precious Time (Chrysalis), 1981
Get Nervous (Chrysalis), 1982
Live From Earth (Chrysalis), 1983
Tropico (Chrysalis), 1984
Seven The Hard Way (Chrysalis), 1985
Best Shots (Chrysalis), 1987

# George Benson

US guitarist, vocalist.
Born Pittsburgh, Pennsylvania, March 22, 1943.

**Career:** Began learning guitar at eight, and played and sang with several Pittsburgh R&B outfits during teens. However, models for guitar style were jazz men like Charlie Christian and Wes Montgomery rather than R&B practitioners.

Benson moved to New York in 1963 and joined band of organist Brother Jack McDuff; two years on road with McDuff's funky tenor- and organ-led outfit honed Benson's guitar style. In mid-60s recorded for Columbia with own group, before forming working relationship with Creed Taylor's CTI label in 1970, becoming 'house guitarist' and releasing albums under own name.

CTI period resulted in recognition of Benson's skills, and moderate success, including Grammy nomination for album **White Rabbit**. His vocal talents, however, were largely ignored.

Real success came when Benson joined Warner Bros in mid-'70s, and was teamed with producer Tommy LiPuma. Result was **Breezin'**, a lightweight jazz-funk effort that struck lucrative chord with record-buying public. Eventually going double platinum, it yielded two hit singles in title track (an instrumental) and **This Masqerade**, on which Benson exhibited his attractive Stevie Wonder(▶)-influenced voice. Next album, **In Flight**, followed similar formula and also achieved double platinum sales.

Further hit singles and albums ensued, and Benson established himself as major concert draw throughout world. Always accompanied by the very best musicians, Benson vocalises to good effect, plays inventive guitar in effortless style, and occasionally combines both in unison scat-singing/guitar improvisations.

In 1980, partnership with renowned music-

ian and producer Quincy Jones brought about renewed success with **Give Me The Night** LP and further hit singles through early '80s.

One of handful of jazz-orientated musicians to have achieved wide crossover success, Benson continues to sell out concerts world wide. He has opened up large market for well-crafted, easy-listening funk, bringing a touch of jazz sophistication to popular music.

Guitars: Ibanez G310, Gibson Super 400 CES.

**Hit Singles:**

| | US | UK |
|---|---|---|
| This Masquerade, 1976 | 10 | — |
| On Broadway, 1978 | 7 | — |
| Love Ballad, 1979 | 18 | 29 |
| Give Me The Night, 1980 | 4 | 7 |
| Love X Love, 1980 | — | 10 |
| Turn Your Love Around, 1981 | 5 | 29 |
| Never Give Up, 1982 | 52 | 14 |
| Lady Love, 1983 | 30 | 11 |
| In Your Eyes, 1983 | — | 7 |

**Albums:**
George Benson & Jack McDuff (Prestige/—), 1960s
It's Uptown (Columbia/—), 1965
Cookbook (Columbia/—), 1966
Shape Of Things To Come (A&M), 1968
White Rabbit (CTI), 1973
Breezin' (Warner Bros), 1977 **CD**
Summertime: In Concert (CTI), 1977
In Flight (Warner Bros), 1977
Best Of (A&M/—), 1978
Stormy Weather (—/Embassy), 1978
Weekend In L.A. (Warner Bros), 1978
Livin' Inside Your Love (Warner Bros), 1979
Cast Your Fate To The Wind (CTI/—), 1979
Blue Benson (Polydor/—), 1980
New Boss Guitar (Prestige/—), 1980
Give Me The Night (Warner Bros), 1980 **CD**
The George Benson Collection (Warner Bros), 1981
In Your Eyes (Warner Bros), 1983
20/20 (Warner Bros), 1985 **CD**
The Love Songs (K-Tel), 1985
Collaboration (Warner Bros), 1987 (with Earl Klugh)
Best Of George Benson (CTI), 1984 **CD**
Body Talk (Musidisc, France), 1984 **CD**
Early Years (CTI), 1983 **CD**
The Electrifying George Benson (Charly), 1985 **CD**
The Silver Collection (Polydor), 1985 **CD**
While The City Sleeps (Warner Bros), 1986 **CD**

# Chuck Berry

US vocalist, guitarist, composer.
Born Charles Edward Berry, San Jose, California, October 18, 1926.

**Career:** Arguably the most influential guitarist and songwriter of the entire rock genre; a musically adequate vocalist, his highly articulate diction ensured maximum impact from inventive lyrics. Many of his songs became anthems of teenage life.

Family moved to St Louis, Missouri, in 1930s; young Berry gained musical experience in school glee-clubs and church choirs. Trained as hairdresser, then worked in car factory; performed with small group evenings and weekends.

In 1955 recorded some songs for audition tape and travelled North to Chicago to look for successful bluesman Muddy Waters(▶). Muddy suggested Berry take tape to Chess Records. Leonard Chess was interested in embryonic version of **Maybellene** and had the young hopeful record polished version for Chess debut; disc topped R&B chart and began prolific succession of hits like **Brown Eyed Handsome Man, Roll Over Beethoven, Sweet Little Sixteen, School Day,**

**Johnny B. Goode, Rock 'n' Roll Music, Reelin' & Rockin'** and **Memphis Tennessee.**

Berry's records are notable for their lyrical content and distinctive guitar style; most discs had guitar introductions and incisive solos midway. On stage, Berry played solo while hopping around in squatting posture; this came to be described as a 'duckwalk'.

Consistency of hit singles resulted in several movie parts; Chuck was committed to celluloid in 'Go Johnny Go' and 'Rock Rock Rock'; also featured in film of 1958 Newport Jazz Festival 'Jazz On A Summers Day' singing **Sweet Little Sixteen.** His performance considered quite revolutionary in such context! Convicted for immorality offence (for taking underage girl across state lines) in 1959; Chess still issued Berry singles but with minimal sales.

Recorded fresh material upon release in 1964; scored hits with **Nadine, No Particular Place To Go** and **You Never Can Tell.** Made first overseas tour and played in England with Carl Perkins(▶). Left Chess after financial temptation from Mercury but only decent Mercury disc was **Club Nitty Gritty**— others were mainly re-hashes of old hits; returned to Chess in 1969. During 1972 toured England and recorded 'live' and studio material; from live set, **My Ding A Ling** was issued as single. This version of old blues song with suggestive lyric topped US and UK charts (sadly Berry's only No. 1).

As Chess label faded, Chuck cut final **Bio** LP. Began to concentrate more on tours than recording; gained reputation for being hard to deal with financially. Has become regular attraction at cosmopolitan music festivals. Brief contract with Atlantic yielded solitary 1979 LP **Rock It,** patchy in quality, a commercial failure.

1988 saw interest in rock legend flare yet again with publication of **Chuck Berry: The Autobiography**, and movie **Hail! Hail! Rock And Roll**.

| Hit Singles: | US | UK |
|---|---|---|
| Maybellene, 1955 | 5 | — |
| School Day, 1957 | 3 | 24 |

**Above: Chuck Berry glides into the 'duckwalk'.**

| Rock 'n' Roll Music, 1957 | 8 | — |
|---|---|---|
| Sweet Little Sixteen, 1958 | 2 | 16 |
| Johnny B. Goode, 1958 | 8 | — |
| Carol | 18 | — |
| Let It Rock/Memphis Tennessee, 1963 | — | 16 |
| No Particular Place To Go, 1964 | 10 | 3 |
| You Never Can Tell, 1964 | 14 | 23 |
| My Ding-A-Ling, 1972 | 1 | 1 |
| Reelin' And Rockin', 1972 | 27 | 18 |

**Albums:**
Golden Hits (Mercury/—), 1967
Greatest Hits (Archive Of Folk And Jazz Music/—), 1967
Chuck Berry Volume 1 (—/Impact), 1979
Chuck Berry Volume 2 (—/Impact), 1979
Chess Masters (Chess/PRT), 1983
21 Greatest Hits (Bescol), 1987 **CD**
Best Of Chuck Berry (Vogue, France), 1983 **CD**
Greatest Hits (Charly), 1986 **CD**
Reelin And A Rockin (The Collection), 1985 **CD**
Rock 'N' Roll Rareities (Vogue, France), 1987 **CD**
Two Dozen Berrys (Vogue), 1986 **CD**
*Worth Searching Out:*
After School Sessions (Chess/—), 1958
One Dozen Berry's (Chess/—), 1958
Golden Decade Volumes 1-3 (—/Chess), 1973

# Big Country
UK group formed 1983.

**Original/current line-up:** Stuart Adamson, guitar, vocals; Bruce Watson, guitar; Tony Butler, bass; Mark Brzezicki, drums.

**Career:** Rhythm For Hire session team Butler and Brzezicki decided to throw in lot with Scots Adamson and Watson after working for them on demo session of **Harvest Home** at Phonogram Studios, London, at end of 1983.

Catchy chorus and exciting guitar crescendos of debut record became group's hallmark but single **Chance** was a Springsteen-esque ballad

revealing another side to group's talent.

Debut album **The Crossing** produced, like singles, by Steve Lillywhite, established band.

Big Country's strident brand of rock is imbued with strong Celtic influence, reflecting Adamson's upbringing on diet of Scottish and Irish folk songs in his native Dunferline.

Adamson had earlier career with Skids for four years up to 1981 before going back home to write songs and germinate Big Country.

Big Country's songs have a strong element of social comment, as in **Steeltown,** but album failed to live up to promise of debut set. Matters were not helped by long recording hiatus which followed, although band maintained busy touring schedule. Third album **The Seer** did not break new ground and there are fears that group's repetitive formula may have limited potential.

| Hit Singles: | US | UK |
|---|---|---|
| Fields Of Fire (400 Miles), 1983 | — | 10 |
| In A Big Country, 1983 | 17 | 17 |
| Chance, 1983 | — | 9 |
| Wonderland, 1984 | — | 8 |
| East Of Eden, 1984 | — | 17 |
| Where The Rose Is Sown, 1984 | — | 29 |
| Just A Shadow, 1985 | — | 26 |
| Look Away, 1986 | — | 7 |
| The Teacher, 1986 | — | 28 |
| One Great Thing, 1986 | — | 19 |

**Albums:**
The Crossing (Mercury/Phonogram), 1983
Steeltown (Mercury/Phonogram), 1984
The Seer (Mercury), 1986

# Black Sabbath
UK group formed 1969.

**Original line-up:** Ozzy Osbourne, vocals; Tony Iommi, Jay-dee guitar; Terry 'Geezer' Butler, bass; Bill Ward, drums.

**Career:** Started in Birmingham as blues band Earth; in late 1969 they changed name to Black Sabbath and recorded first album of same name, developing quasi occult, 'evil' image. Although album was largely ignored by radio and media, word of mouth eventually hoisted it into UK charts where it remained for 13 weeks.

International success followed quickly with release of 1970 album **Paranoid**; LP and single of same name hit on both sides of Atlantic. Band played first successful American tour in autumn 1970.

**Below: They sold their souls for rock 'n' roll — Black Sabbath.**

**Technical Ecstasy, Black Sabbath. Courtesy Warner Bros Records.**

From that time until 1973, band toured regularly and recorded prolifically, establishing themselves as one of world's foremost heavy metal bands, though critical acclaim continued to elude them.

In 1973 managerial problems forced cessation of activities until 1975 release of album **Sabotage** re-established band as major force in heavy metal, a position they have maintained ever since.

Since 1978 band has undergone several personnel changes. Ozzy Osbourne(▶) left, to return a few months later, but in 1979 he departed for good to form own band, Ozzy Osbourne's Blizzard of Oz, which has achieved considerable success. He was replaced by Ronnie James Dio, formerly singer with Ritchie Blackmore's Rainbow(▶). At end of 1980 Bill Ward left for personal reasons, and Vinnie Appice, brother of the more famous Carmine, was recruited.

Fluctuating line-up saw Ian Gillan as new vocalist, until he left to rejoin Deep Purple(▶), replaced by Dave Donato. Dio and Appice also split and Ward returned.

In July 1985 the original Sabbath with Ozzy reunited for an appearance at Live Aid in Philadelphia. Subsequently Sabbath suffered a series of personnel changes which led to dwindling audiences. Singer Dave Donato did not record with Sabbath but his successor Glenn Hughes cut the **Seventh Star** album with them in 1986 and the band under the leadership of Tony Iommi, toured the UK with Eric Singer (drums), Dave Spitz (bass), Geoff Nichols (keyboards) and Ray Gillen (vocals).

In November 1987 the Sabs released critically acclaimed **The Eternal Idol** with vocalist Tony Martin. However band criticised for visiting South Africa's Sun City to play. Then they cancelled a concert at London's Odeon Hammersmith at the last minute during Christmas,

which upset even their most loyal fans.

Sabbath still have a strong reputation and are hailed as the founders of Heavy Metal. The dogged spirit of Tony Iommi may yet see a revival of their fortunes.

**Current line-up:** Iommi; Tony Martin, vocals; Geoff Nicholls, keyboard; Bev Bevan, percussion; Eric Singer, drums; Dave Spitz and Bob Daisley, bass.

| Hit Singles: | US | UK |
|---|---|---|
| Paranoid, 1970 | — | 4 |
| Paranoid, 1980 | — | 14 |

**Albums:**
Black Sabbath (Nems/Warner Bros), 1970 **CD**
Paranoid (Nems/Warner Bros), 1970 **CD**
Master Of Reality (Nems/Warner Bros), 1971 **CD**
Black Sabbath 4 (Nems/Warner Bros), 1972 **CD**
Sabbath Bloody Sabbath (Nems/Warner Bros), 1973 **CD**
Sabotage (Nems/Warner Bros), 1975 **CD)**
We Sold Our Souls For Rock 'N' Roll (Nems/Warner Bros), 1975
Technical Ecstasy (Nems/Warner Bros), 1976
Greatest Hits (Nems/Warner Bros), 1977 **CD**
Never Say Die (Vertigo/Warner Bros), 1978
Heaven & Hell (Vertigo/Warner Bros), 1980
Mob Rules (Vertigo/Warner Bros), 1981
Live Evil (Vertigo/Warner Bros), 1983
Born Again (Vertigo), 1983
Seventh Star (Vertigo), 1986 **CD**
The Eternal Idol (Vertigo), 1987
*Ronnie James Dio:*
Holy Diver (Vertigo), 1983
The Last In Line (Vertigo), 1984
*(with ELF)* Trying to Burn The Sun (Safari), 1984
Sacred Heart (Vertigo), 1985

# Blondie

US group formed 1975.
**Original line-up:** Debbie Harry, vocals; Chris Stein, guitar; Jimmy Destri, keyboards; Gary Valentine, bass; Clem Burke, drums.

**Career:** Band born out of mid-'70s New York new wave, a splinter group of punk/sleaze outfit the Stilettoes. Lead singer was Debbie Harry, one-time front person of folk-rock band the Wind In The Willows, and well-known figure around New York music/art/night-life scene. Briefly calling themselves Angel and the Snake, band consisted of Harry, Chris Stein (guitar), Billy O'Connor (drums), Fred Smith (bass), and two back-up singers, Tish and Snooky. By 1975 had reached line-up (above) known as Blondie.

In 1976 band signed with producer Richard Gottehrer and released first single, **X Offender/In The Sun**. In October same year they contracted to Private Stock, and released first album, **Blondie**. Promotion concentrated on Monroesque good looks of Debbie Harry, as has much of publicity throughout life of band.

Lack of success with Private Stock prompted move to Chrysalis, who re-released first album and followed it with **Plastic Letters** in 1978. Gary Valentine had left, and was replaced by guitarist Frank Infante, who played bass on **Letters**. Album spawned international hits **Denis** and **(I'm Always Touched By Your) Presence Dear** and set band on road to success. Next album, **Parallel Lines**, with addition of bassist Nigel Harrison, established band as top international attraction and went on to eventually sell 20 million copies.

From 1978 to 1981 band was among most successful in world. Winning formula combined commercial material, clear, pop-style vocals,

**Above: Blondie, in better days. Harry's solo career has not yet matched former success with group.**

and rock backing with hint of punk aggression. Audiences were drawn from both pop and rock aficionados. Harry became much-photographed sex symbol of rock.

In 1982, however, it became apparent that runaway pace of success was slowing down. Album **The Hunter** was relatively unsuccessful (although it still made UK Top 10 and US Top 40), and British tour was cancelled because it failed to attract interest anticipated. Critics cited lack of regular live work.

In meantime, Debbie Harry had some success with solo album **Koo Koo** (produced by Chic(▶) supremos Nile Rodgers and Bernard Edwards) and acting debut in 'Union City Blues' and 'Roadie' (1980). (Her career on Broadway lasted precisely one evening in 1983 New York play.) Other members of Blondie also branched out into production and projects with other musicians. In February 1983 band announced break-up. Burke went on to play with Eurythmics(▶).

**Plastic Letters, Blondie. Courtesy Chrysalis Records.**

With refreshing honesty, Debbie Harry eventually admitted that solo career was relative failure, and early in 1988 announced formation of **Tiger Bomb**, featuring Blondie guitarist and former beau Chris Stein. Although now in her early forties, the well-preserved Ms. Harry may still possess sufficient aura to do it all over again.

**Final line-up:** Harry; Stein; Destri; Frank Infante, guitar; Nigel Harrison, bass; Burke.

| Hit Singles: | US | UK |
|---|---|---|
| Denis, 1978 | — | 2 |
| (I'm Always Touched By Your) Presence Dear, 1978 | — | 10 |
| Picture This, 1978 | — | 12 |
| Hanging On The Telephone, 1978 | — | 5 |
| Heart Of Glass, 1979 | 1 | 1 |
| Sunday Girl, 1979 | — | 1 |
| Dreaming, 1979 | 27 | 2 |
| Union City Blues, 1979 | — | 13 |
| Atomic, 1980 | 39 | 1 |
| Call Me, 1980 | 1 | 1 |
| The Tide Is High, 1980 | 1 | 1 |
| Rapture, 1981 | 1 | 5 |
| Island Of Lost Souls, 1982 | 37 | 11 |

**Albums:**
Blondie (Private Stock), 1977
Plastic Letters (Chrysalis), 1978
Parallel Lines (Chrysalis), 1978 **CD**
Eat To The Beat (Chrysalis), 1979 **CD**
Autoamerican (Chrysalis), 1980
The Best Of (Chrysalis), 1981 **CD**
The Hunter (Chrysalis), 1982
Heart Of Glass (Old Gold), 1987 **CD**

*Debbie Harry solo:*

| | US | UK |
|---|---|---|
| Koo Koo (Chrysalis), 1981 | — | — |
| French Kissin' In The USA, 1987 | — | 8 |

# Blue Oyster Cult

US group formed 1970.
**Original line-up:** Eric Bloom, vocals, guitar; Allen Lanier, keyboards, synthesiser; Donald 'Buck Dharma' Roeser, guitar, vocals; Joe Bouchard, bass, vocals; Albert Bouchard, drums, vocals.

**Career:** America's prime exponents of heavy-metal idiom started in New York as Stalk Forrest Group and Soft White Underbelly. Recorded two unreleased albums for Elektra before name change and Columbia contract, earned via mentor Sandy Pearlman, 'Crawdaddy' magazine critic, in 1971. Released eponymous debut album.

Breakthrough came with third album **Secret Treaties** in 1974, which included Patti Smith(▶)-penned **Career Of Evil;** 1975 live double set **On Your Feet Or On Your Knees** captured their explosive stage presence — screaming vocals and savage guitar riffs overlaying a pounding rhythm section.

Patti Smith wrote two songs and guested on 1976 album **Agents Of Fortune** from which **(Don't Fear) The Reaper** was US hit. Since then, somewhat sinister mysticism of lyrics, album cover designs and image, and increasingly heavy playing has marked work. With Rick Downey replacing Albert Bouchard on drums, band have maintained reputation as premier cult HM band.

In 1985 band returned to Europe for concerts and released their 13th album **Club Ninja** produced by Sandy Pearlman, his first with the band since **Spectres** in 1977. Allen Lanier (keyboards), quit the band in protest at material on album which he didn't like and was replaced by Tony Zvancheck. New drummer Jimmy Wilcox was recruited at the same time. Asked how long the band could keep going,

Eric Bloom mused: 'Probably into our seventies!'

**Current line-up:** Bloom; Roeser; Joe Bouchard; Jimmy Wilcox, drums; Tony Zvancheck, vocals.

| Hit Singles: | US | UK |
|---|---|---|
| (Don't Fear) The Reaper, 1976 | 12 | — |
| (Don't Fear) The Reaper, 1978 | — | 16 |

**Albums:**
Blue Oyster Cult (Columbia/CBS), 1972
Tyranny And Mutation (Columbia/CBS), 1974
Secret Treaties (Columbia/CBS), 1974
On Your Feet Or On Your Knees (Columbia/CBS), 1975
Agents Of Fortune (Columbia/CBS), 1976
Spectres (Columbia/CBS), 1977
Some Enchanted Evening (Columbia/CBS), 1978
Mirrors (Columbia/CBS), 1979
Cultasaurus Erectus (Columbia/CBS), 1980
Fire Of Unknown Origin (Columbia/CBS), 1981
Extraterrestrial/Live (Columbia/CBS), 1982
Revolution By Night (Columbia/CBS), 1983
Club Ninja (CBS), 1985

*Buck Dharma Solo:*
Flat Out (Columbia), 1982

**Secret Treaties, Blue Oyster Cult. Courtesy CBS Records.**

# Marc Bolan

UK vocalist, guitarist, composer.
Born Mark Feld, London, July 30, 1947; died September 16, 1977.

**Career:** Always adept at self-promotion, in early '60s then 15-year-old Feld managed to win wide exposure in media as archetypal mod, which led to brief career as male model. Later dropped sharp besuited image for loose-fitting flowery clothes, beads and espousal of 'flower power'. Changed name to Bolan for debut single **The Wizard** on Decca (1966). Briefly joined pioneer glam-rock band John's Children, scoring with **Desdemona**. Their **Go Go Girl** backing track was used for Bolan's later **Mustang Ford.** On leaving group, Bolan cut sides for Track which did not surface until 1974, as **Beginning Of Doves** LP.

Joined by Steve Peregrine Took, Bolan attempted to form five-piece electronic band but hire-purchase company snatched back equipment. Bolan and Took consequently started working in 1968 as acoustic folksy-rock duo Tyrannosaurus Rex. Full of elves, fairies and flower-power mythology, Tyrannosaurus Rex albums **My People Were Fair And Had Sky In Their Hair But Now They're Content To Wear Stars On Their Brows** (1968), **Prophets, Seers And Sages** (1969), **The Angels Of The Ages** (1969) and **Unicorn** (1969) may have been somewhat pretentious, but captured essence of the

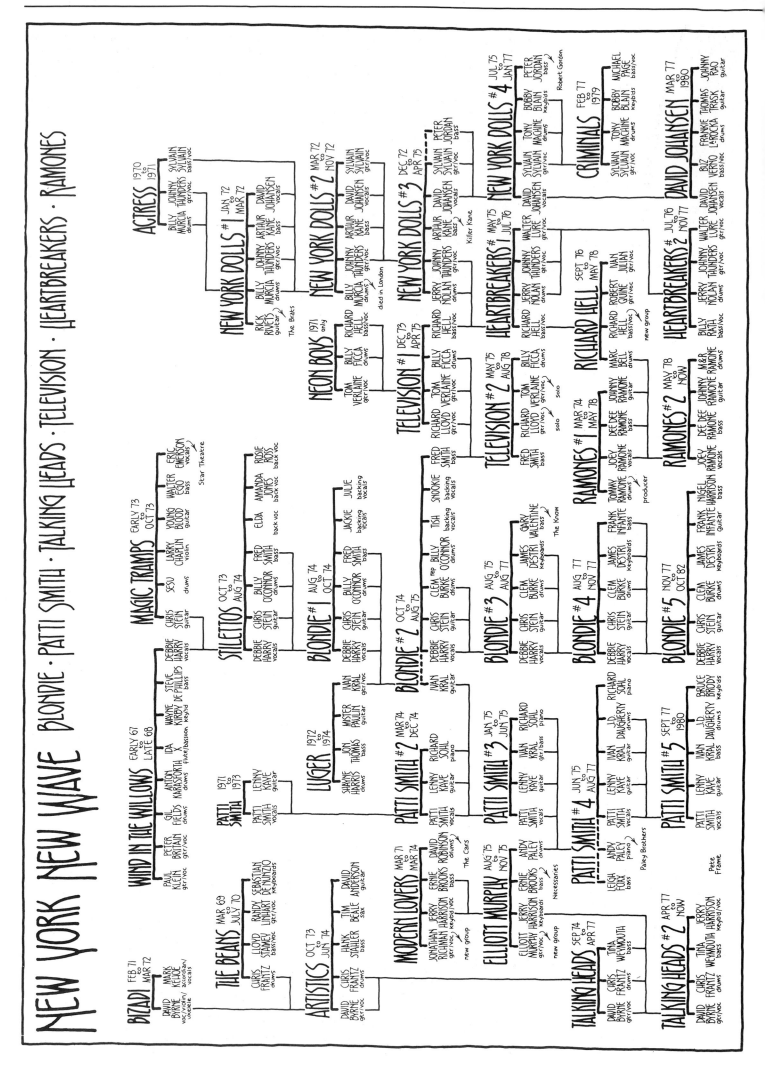

**You Scare Me To Death, Marc Bolan. Courtesy Decca Records.**

love-and-peace philosophy. Duo also benefited from support of influential BBC radio DJ John Peel (as did Bolan's book of poetry).

Overshadowed in duo by Bolan, Took quit in 1970, replaced by Mickey Finn (who met Bolan in a health food restaurant). On their **Beard Of Stars** album Bolan switched to electric guitar. Later that year, with name shortened to T.Rex, they notched surprise UK No. 2 with soft-rock but uptempo **Ride A White Swan**. Added drummer Bill Legend and bass player Steve Currie in time for next single **Hot Love**. Aimed direct at teenybop pop audience, it topped chart for six weeks in early 1971. **Get It On** was second No. 1 later same year; re-titled **Bang A Gong**, became group's biggest US success.

T. Rex had now fully undergone transition from esoteric folk-rock outfit to rocking pop band. Bolan had become pre-teen idol to rival earlier Beatles(▶) and Monkees(▶).

Though **Jeepster** made UK No. 2, Fly

Records had pulled it from **Electric Warrior** album without consulting Bolan. Angered, he split to start own T.Rex label, via EMI.

String of UK hits made 1972 big year. In 1973 ex-Beatle Ringo Starr(▶) directed movie, 'Born To Boogie', about T.Rex phenomenon but it flopped. By end of year Bolan's fickle young audiences were deserting him in droves for younger artists like the Osmonds(▶) and David Cassidy, and more exciting bands like Slade(▶).

The glamour and glitter became tarnished. Bolan left wife June Child to live with black American soul singer Gloria Jones (who bore him a child). He put on weight alarmingly, churned out ever less satisfying material, split with Finn (in March 1975) and broke up T.Rex before slinking off to tax exile in Los Angeles.

Bolan undertook comeback tour with Jones early in 1976 and formed new T.Rex with veteran studio musicians Herbie Flowers, Miller Anderson and Tony Newman, and keyboard player Dino Dines.

Seeking rising star to hitch on to, Marc tried to become self-proclaimed guru of British new-wave movement and used the Damned(▶) as support on his spring 1977 tour. Hosted a rather unsatisfactory weekly TV music show and fought hard to rebuild career. Early one September morning in 1977, the mini car driven by Gloria Jones careered off road on dangerous bend and passenger Bolan was killed, aged 30. Totally shattered, Jones—who blamed tragedy on herself—had hard time until, with help of songwriter brother, she

**Below: Marc Bolan—a master of the changing pop genre, in at the start of punk. Photo from inside of T. Rex album.**

rebuilt career, wrote hit records for several artists, notably British soul act Gonzalez (worldwide disco smash **Haven't Stopped Dancing Yet**). Her composition **Tainted Love**, written back in '60s, became big 1981 hit for Soft Cell.

| Hit Singles: | US | UK |
|---|---|---|
| *As Tyrannosaurus Rex:* | | |
| Deborah/One Inch Rock, 1972 | — | 7 |
| *As T.Rex:* | | |
| Ride A White Swan, 1970 | — | 2 |
| Hot Love, 1971 | — | 1 |
| Get It On, 1971 | 10 | 1 |
| Jeepster, 1971 | — | 2 |
| Telegram Sam, 1972 | — | 1 |
| Metal Guru, 1972 | — | 1 |
| Children Of The Revolution, 1972 | — | 2 |
| Solid Gold Easy Action, 1972 | — | 2 |
| 20th Century Boy, 1973 | — | 3 |
| The Groover, 1973 | — | 4 |
| Truck On (Tyke), 1973 | — | 12 |
| Teenage Dream, 1974 | — | 13 |
| New York City, 1975 | — | 15 |
| I Love To Boogie, 1976 | — | 13 |

**Albums:**
*As Tyrannosaurus Rex:*
Prophet/My People (—/Cube), 1972*
Beard Of Stars/Unicorn (—/Cube), 1972*
*As T.Rex:*
T.Rex (—/Cube), 1970
Electric Warrior (Reprise/Cube), 1971
Bolan Boogie (—/Cube), 1972
The Slider (Reprise/EMI), 1972
Greatest Hits Volume I (—/Hallmark), 1978
Collection (—/Hallmark), 1978
Solid Gold (—/Fame), 1979
Unobtainable (—/Nut), 1980
In Concert (—/Marc), 1981
Patinum Collection (—/Cube), 1981
Best Of 20th Century Boy (K-Tel), 1985
Zinc Alloy & The Hidden Riders Of Tomorrow (Marc On Wax), 1985 **CD**
Bolans Zip Gun (Marc On Wax), 1985 **CD**
Dandy In The Underworld (Marc On Wax), 1985 **CD**
Love & Death (Cherry Red), 1985 **CD**
Marc Bolan & T. Rex (The Collection), 1987 **CD**

*Released as double albums two years after original release as singles.

# Gary 'US' Bonds

US vocalist.
Born Gary Anderson, Jacksonville, Florida, June 6, 1939.

**Career:** Former street-corner singer who found success after ingenious 'con' by producer Frank Guida. Guida sent promotional copies of Anderson's first single **New Orleans** to record stations in a sleeve marked 'Buy US Bonds'. Gary had no idea his new name was being taken in vain, although quickly accepted this promotional device as record charted.

**Greatest Hits, Gary 'US' Bonds. Courtesy Ensign Records.**

Bonds followed **New Orleans** with similar series of raucous R&B belters, amateurishly but effectively produced by enthusiastic Guida.

When hits dried up, Bonds moved to lounge circuit, where he was 're-discovered' by Bruce Springsteen(▶) in 1980. With producer Miami Steve Van Zandt and Springsteen at the helm, Bonds went back into the studio to cut **Dedication** LP, which understandably paid homage to Bonds' earlier recordings, provided minor chart action, and led to further Springsteen/Van Zandt assistance on 1982 album, **On The Line**.

| Hit Singles: | US | UK |
|---|---|---|
| New Orleans, 1960 | 6 | 16 |
| Quarter To Three, 1961 | 1 | 7 |
| School Is Out, 1961 | 5 | — |
| Dear Lady Twist, 1962 | 9 | — |
| Twist Twist Senora, 1962 | 9 | — |
| This Little Girl, 1981 | 11 | — |

**Albums:**
Certified Soul (Rhino/—), 1980s
Dedication (EMI), 1981
Greatest Hits (—/Ensign), 1981
On The Line (Capitol), 1982
Standing In The Line Of Fire (Making Waves), 1985

# Boston

US group formed 1975.

**Original:** Tom Scholz, guitar, keyboards; Brad Delp, guitar, vocals; Barry Goudreau, guitar; Fran Sheehan, bass; Sib Hashian, drums.

**Boston. Courtesy Epic Records.**

**Career:** Band formed around Tom Scholz who utilised own 12-track studio to prepare meticulous demo tapes. After series of record company rejections Scholz signed to Epic, and duly formed Boston. A recording phenomenon (though members only played in part on first LP), band earned double platinum album within first year for debut set **Boston** which included worldwide hit **More Than A Feeling**.

In 1984 Goudreau left to form Orion while continued low-key presence of Scholz made group's resurrection in 1986 real surprise, but Boston's third album **Third Stage** duly savaged the US charts, and the band took to the road in 1987, for the first time in eight years.

**Current line-up:** Tom Scholz, guitar, keyboards, bass; Brad Delp, vocals; Gary Pihl, guitar; Jim Masdea, drums.

| Hit Singles: | US | UK |
|---|---|---|
| More Than A Feeling, 1976 | 5 | 22 |
| Don't Look Back, 1978 | 4 | 43 |
| Amanda, 1987 | 1 | — |
| We're Ready, 1987 | 7 | — |

**Albums:**
Boston (Epic), 1976
Don't Look Back (Epic), 1978
Third Stage (MCA), 1986

# David Bowie

UK vocalist, composer, producer, actor.
Born David Robert Jones, London, January 8, 1947.

**Career:** Began musical career playing tenor sax in school group. Suffered eye injury following a fight; subsequent surgery left him with paralysed pupil. Leaving Bromley High School, secured job as commercial artist before forming succession of progressive R&B groups: Davie Jones and the King Bees, the Manish Boys, and the Lower Third. All recorded without success. Upsurge of Monkees(▶) forced name change from Jones to Bowie.

Subsequent contract with Pye and Decca as soloist produced series of pop/love songs, strongly influenced by Anthony Newley. Originally issued as **The World Of David Bowie,** these were re-released in 1973 as **Images 1966/67.** Included in set was embarrassing **The Laughing Gnome,** which actually reached Top 10 on re-release in 1973.

For brief period Bowie dropped out of music and flirted with Buddhism. Also joined Lindsay Kemp's mime company, a move that would greatly influence his later theatrical work. Re-emerged in 1969 and started an arts lab in Beckenham, recording **Space Oddity** for Mercury during same period. Song became surprise hit, followed by average album of same title. Toured as support act, but returned, disillusioned, to one-man show in Beckenham. Failure to follow up novelty **Space Oddity** strongly indicated that he was little more than a one-hit-wonder.

By 1970, Bowie had consolidated resources, combining interest in mime, Buddhism, novelty and whatever else to produce epic **The Man Who Sold The World.**

Album was complete contrast to predecessor; acoustic strumming was replaced by heavy guitar work of Mick Ronson. Thematically, work was chilling: an Orwellian vision of a future riddled with sexual perversion, dominance by machines, loneliness and helplessness. Many of these themes would be extended to produce later albums, not least the Nietzschean vision of **The Supermen.**

Although initially a relatively poor seller, **The Man Who Sold The World** gave Bowie cult following and was hailed as excellent work by more perceptive buyers/critics of the period. An important and much-publicised US tour followed, with Bowie decked out as 1970s Garbo, complete with flowing dress. Switch to RCA proved timely, and with further publicity critics were well-primed for release of **Hunky Dory.** Work was more mellow than its predecessor but still haunting, original and commercially appealing in range of themes.

1972 was year of the breakthrough with most commerical work to date, **The Rise And Fall Of Ziggy Stardust And The Spiders From Mars.** Where he had used a number of different ideas/personae on previous LPs, Bowie now created a single figure, Ziggy, the ultimate rock superstar destroyed by the fanaticism he creates. Negotiating ground between the heaviness of **The Man Who Sold The World** and the diverse quirkiness of **Hunky Dory,** an image of Ziggy was created that almost subsumed Bowie in later years. Artist and art, actor and part were inextricably linked. From this point on Bowie became the most important rock figure of '70s.

Activities broadened following hit single **Starman** and Bowie took on role as producer, literally saving the faltering career of Lou Reed(▶) (**Transformer**) and resurrecting the already dead Mott the Hoople(▶) (**All The Young Dudes**). 1972 US tour provided ideas for next conceptual work, **Aladdin Sane.** Album was not classic, though Ronson's work was exceptional and two hit singles were forthcoming via **Jean Genie** and **Drive In Saturday. Pin Ups** was a surprise *volte face* that brought suspicion from some critical quarters; a re-working of selected oldies from 1964-67 pop scene, it seemed rather too lightweight as concept. Period of uncertainty was punctuated by 'retirement' following Hammersmith Odeon concert in July 1973.

Later in year, recorded an NBC Midnight Special at London's Marquee Club titled 'The 1980 Floor Show'. Production inspired next album **Diamond Dogs** (1974), a return to Orwellian gloom of **Man Who Sold The World,** but minus fine guitar work of Ronson. Show was taken on road in US and performance at Philadelphia's Tower Theatre was used for double **David Live.** During tour, a new course was charted as Bowie picked up on soul/R&B style. Results were evident enough on Philly-influenced **Young Americans,** which included another couple of hit singles in titletrack and **Fame.** Latter, co-written by John Lennon(▶), provided first US No. 1

single. Incredibly, 1975 UK re-release of first hit **Space Oddity** went to top in same year, the slowest No. 1 of all time (6 years 63 days!).

For remainder of 1975 Bowie involved himself in filming 'The Man Who Fell To Earth' (directed by Nicholas Roeg), released the following year. Long-awaited return to England in spring '76 provided memorable gigs at Wembley Empire Pool. Having re-established himself commercially, Bowie felt free to record more adventurous material. **Station To Station,** consisting of six lengthy cuts, was return to top form, paving way for three albums recorded under supervision of Brian Eno(▶). **Low,** originally titled **New Music: Night And Day,** was essentially a mood piece, consisting largely of instrumental music. (Nick Lowe(▶) 'retaliated' by calling his 1977 EP **Bowi.**) The experiment was continued on **Heroes,** but with enough conventional rock to attract larger listening audience. Trilogy was interrupted by **Stage,** an uninspired double LP documenting 1978 tour. Final Bowie/Eno collaboration **Lodger** proved only partially successful in spite of strong tracks (**Boys Keep Swingin', Repetition**).

With **Scary Monsters (And Super Creeps),** commitment and commerciality were neatly fused in old tradition. Album spawned several hit singles, including excellent **Ashes To Ashes,** which hit No. 1 in UK in August '80. Since then there have been a series of re-issues, re-packages and film soundtracks, though for his next album, Bowie promised some positive dance-orientated music as reaction against apocalyptic themes of yore.

This was forthcoming in 1983 Nile Rodgers produced album **Let's Dance,** a worldwide chart topper with its titletrack single. Soon after release, Bowie toured Europe and UK for first time in seven years.

Rightly acknowledged as '70s rock's most important figure, Bowie continues to wield

Above: Young Americans, David Bowie. Courtesy RCA Records.

Above: Bowie models a dress— androgynous?

Below: Ziggy with Stratocaster on stage in 1974.

Above: David Live, David Bowie. Courtesy RCA Records.

Above: Fresh-faced, while recording for a Xmas TV show with Bing Crosby.

Left: Bowie circa 1965. 'Ground Control to Major...Fred? Joe?

enormous influence on '80s rock scene. Acting commitments and extra-curricular work may appear distracting but his 1985 hit single duet with Mick Jagger reworking Martha and the Vandellas' **Dancing In The Street** indicates no sign of decline.

Acting credits include films 'The Man Who Fell To Earth' (1975), 'Just A Gigolo' (1979), and, more recently, 'The Hunger' (1983) and 'Merry Christmas Mr. Lawrence' (1983). Played main role of disfigured John Merrick in Broadway play 'The Elephant Man' (1980) and the lead in BBC TV's production of Berthold Brecht's 'Baal' (1981).

Bowie's movie career escalated still further with bravado performance as English detective in John Landis comedy thriller 'Into The Night' and featured role in ambitious British feature 'Absolute Beginners' (1986).

Like a chameleon, Bowie has moulded and adapted career to the whims and changes of a fickle and critical audience. They seem ever satisfied.

Bowie's movie career spluttered slightly after amusing cameo as English detective in John Landis 'Into The Night' (1985) when 'Absolute Beginners' (1986) found the wrath of reviewers and limited public interest.

Since his nervous debut in The Virgin Soldiers (1969), following the unfinished 'Love You Til Tuesday' (1968) and three-reeler 'The Image' (1967), Bowie has fought hard to establish his place as the premier rock/film performer. He has, however, failed to impress the movie moguls, who see him as little more than a novelty.

Bowie's selection of films has hardly helped, and whilst 'Labyrinth' (1987) earned a little money for producer George Lucas, it was hardly a career enhancer. This enigmatic Londoner may need to settle on rock 'n roll until the equivalent of 'From Here To Eternity' arrives.

**Hit Singles:**

| | US | UK |
|---|---|---|
| Space Oddity, 1969 | — | 5 |
| Starman, 1972 | — | 10 |
| John I'm Only Dancing, 1972 | — | 12 |
| The Jean Genie, 1972 | — | 2 |
| Space Oddity, 1973 | 15 | — |
| Drive In Saturday, 1973 | — | 3 |
| Life On Mars, 1973 | — | 3 |
| The Laughing Gnome, 1973 | — | 6 |
| Sorrow, 1973 | — | 3 |
| Rebel Rebel, 1974 | — | 5 |
| Knock On Wood, 1974 | — | 10 |
| Space Oddity, 1975 | — | 1 |
| Young Americans, 1975 | — | 18 |
| Fame, 1975 | 1 | 17 |
| Golden Years, 1975 | 10 | 8 |
| Sound And Vision, 1977 | — | 3 |
| Boys Keep Swinging, 1979 | — | 7 |

**Above: Scary Monsters, David Bowie. Courtesy RCA Records.**

| | US | UK |
|---|---|---|
| John I'm Only Dancing (Again), 1979 | — | 12 |
| Ashes To Ashes, 1980 | — | 1 |
| Fashion, 1980 | — | 5 |
| Scary Monsters, 1981 | — | 20 |
| Let's Dance, 1983 | 1 | 1 |
| China Girl, 1983 | 10 | 2 |
| Modern Love, 1983 | 14 | 2 |
| Blue Jean, 1984 | 8 | 6 |
| This Is Not America, 1985 | — | 14 |
| Loving The Alien, 1985 | — | 19 |
| Day In Day Out, 1987 | — | 17 |
| Never Let Me Down, 1987 | 27 | 34 |

*With Queen:*

| | | |
|---|---|---|
| Under Pressure, 1981 | 29 | 1 |

*With Bing Crosby:*

| | | |
|---|---|---|
| Peace On Earth, 1982 | — | 3 |

*With Mick Jagger:*

| | | |
|---|---|---|
| Dancing In The Street, 1985 | 7 | 1 |

**Albums:**

The World Of David Bowie (Decca), 1970
The Man Who Sold The World (Mercury/RSA), 1971 **CD**
Hunky Dory (RCA), 1971 **CD**
The Rise And Fall Of Ziggy Stardust And The Spiders From Mars (RCA), 1972 **CD**
Space Oddity (RCA), 1972 **CD**
Aladin Sane (RCA), 1973
Pin Ups (RCA), 1973 **CD**
Diamond Dogs (RCA), 1974 **CD**
David Live (RCA), 1974
Young Americans (RCA), 1975 **CD**
Images (Decca), 1975
Station To Station (RCA), 1976 **CD**
Changesonebowie (RCA), 1976 **CD**
Low (RCA), 1977 **CD**
Starting Point (London/—), 1977
Heroes (RCA), 1977 **CD**
Stage (RCA), 1978
Lodger (RCA), 1979 **CD**
Scary Monsters (And Super Creeps) (RCA), 1980 **CD**

**Above: Never Let Me Down, David Bowie. Courtesy EMI Records.**

**Left: The new look in 1976 — the return of the Thin White Duke.**

The Best Of (—/K-Tel), 1980
Another Face (Decca), 1981
Don't Be Fooled By The Name (PRT), 1981*
Changes (RCA), 1981†
Christianne F (Soundtrack) (RCA), 1981
Changestwobowie (RCA), 1981 **CD**
The Manish Boys, Davy Jones And The Lower Third (Charly), 1981
Rare Bowie (RCA), 1982
Lets Dance (EMI), 1983 **CD**
Tonight (EMI), 1984 **CD**
Labyrinth (EMI), 1986 **CD**
Never Let Me Down (EMI), 1987 **CD**
*Tracks From 1966
†Hunky Dory & Ziggy Stardust

# Billy Bragg

UK singer/songwriter, guitarist.
Born Barking, Essex, December 20, 1957.

**Career:** Total expenditure of just £175 paid for two-track 'live' recording of **Life's A Riot With Spy Vs Spy** album, subsequently rejected by virtually every record label before Go! Disc decided to give it a shot and was rewarded with more than 120,000 sales and a 12-week stint at number one on the independent chart, turning Billy Bragg into instant cult hero.

Having previously worked in punk/R&B band Riff Raff, with an instantly deleted EP **I Wanna Be A Cosmonaut** on Chiswick, Bragg decided in 1982 to go solo, singing self-penned songs with strong political content but with international appeal, witness his growing success in America and Europe.

In many ways a latter-day Dylan, Bragg's protest songs made him a perfect candidate for the 1985 Labour Party 'Red Wedge' rock tour, part of a 'Jobs For Youth' campaign.

Bragg continues to maintain his links with left-wing causes, and has established an audience sufficiently wide to support his quirky one-man shows.

**Hit Single:**

| | US | UK |
|---|---|---|
| Between The Wars (EP) | — | 18 |
| Levi Stubbs Tears, 1986 | — | 29 |

**Albums:**
Life's A Riot With Spy Vs Spy (—?Go! Disc), 1983
Brewing Up With Billy Bragg (—Go! Disc), 1984
Back To Basics (Go! Disc), 1987
Talking With The Taxman About Poetry (Go! Disc), 1986

# James Brown

US vocalist, composer, also arranger, multi-instrumentalist.
Born Macon, Georgia, May 3, 1933.

**Career:** Born into rural poverty, Brown first came to music via gospel. He formed first version of Famous Flames, which included long-time colleague Bobby Byrd, in 1954. Group quickly gained local reputation, Brown already showing impassioned style that was to become trademark. Gospel material gradually shelved in favour of secular songs; **Please Please Please** came to attention of King Records, who signed Brown and Flames and released it as single. Record became major R&B chart success.

Successful follow-up was elusive, and group spent next few years touring small-time club circuit. In September 1958 they went to New York to record; result was gospel-flavoured **Try Me**, group's second hit. Brown consolidated success with string of hit records between 1959 and 1961.

By 1962 Famous Flames had metamorphosised into entire revue, consisting of back-up singers, sizeable band and even own support acts. Brown had developed dynamic stage act and offered most exciting live performance of era. Exhilaration of Brown live in front of black audience is captured on seminal double album, **Live At The Apollo**. One of the first live recordings, it was also one of the most successful records by a black artist up to that point and marked beginning of acceptance by white American and international markets.

Hits continued throughout '60s, Brown achieving position as number one black superstar and figurehead for American black consciousness movement. He also acquired

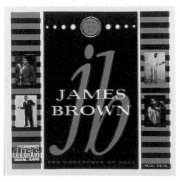

**The Compact Disc of James Brown. Courtesy Polydor Records.**

reputation as no-nonsense businessman and disciplinarian employer. He toured to capacity audiences all over world, and was especially successful in UK.

After disappearance of King Records in 1970, Brown signed to Polydor; hits continued unabated. During '70s his influence was discernible in work of many newer soul/rock/funk bands. Sly and the Family Stone(▶) adapted Brown rhythmic patterns and combined them with rock sensibility; others such as Kool and the Gang(▶), Ohio Players, Blackbyrds and Earth, Wind and Fire(▶) evolved directly out of Brown's musical approach, creating new funk/dance movement. Brown himself enjoyed massive success with **Body Heat** LP in 1976.

While late 70s were relatively fallow period for Brown, he came back in 1981 with **Rap Payback** his response to success of New York hip-hop cult.

By mid-eighties, Brown's rehabilitation was in full swing, with release of Dan Hartman-produced **Gravity** set on **Scotti Brothers** label, and live set featuring notables like Wilson Pickett and Robert Palmer. Whilst no **Live At The Apollo**, this album nevertheless made most live offerings pale by comparison.

Despite career hiccups, Brown's stature has never seriously waned, most particularly amongst dance-floor afficionados, and his tally of forty-plus US Top Forty hits has been surpassed only by Presley and Beatles.

**Below: Number one black superstar of the '60s, and figurehead for American black consciousness movement, James Brown.**

| Hit Singles: | US | UK |
|---|---|---|
| Prisoner Of Love, 1963 | 18 | — |
| Papa's Got A Brand New Bag, —Pt 1, 1965 | 8 | 25 |
| I Got You (I Feel Good), 1965 | 3 | 29 |
| It's A Man's Man's World, 1966 | 8 | 13 |
| Cold Sweat—Pt 1, 1967 | 7 | — |
| I Got The Feelin', 1968 | 6 | — |
| Licking Stick—Pt 1, 1968 | 14 | — |
| Say It Loud—I'm Black And I'm Proud, 1968 | 10 | — |
| Give It Up Or Turnit A Loose, 1969 | 15 | — |
| I Don't Want Nobody To Give Me Nothing (Open Up The Door, I'll Get It Myself), 1969 | 20 | — |
| Mother Popcorn—Pt 1, 1969 | 11 | — |
| Get Up I Feel Like Being A Sex Machine, 1970 | 15 | 32 |
| Super Bad (Pts I & II), 1970 | 13 | — |
| Hot Pants (She Got To Use What She Got To Get What She Wants)—Pt 1, 1971 | 15 | — |
| Get On The Good Foot—Pt. 1, 1972 | 18 | — |
| Living In America, 1985 | — | 5 |

**Albums (selected):**
Live At The Apollo (Polydor), 1962 **CD**
Best Of (Polydor), 1975
Body Heat (Polydor), 1977
Solid Gold (Polydor), 1977
Special (Polydor), 1981
Soul Syndrome (RCA), 1980
Bring It On (Sonet), 1983
Greatest Hits (Polydor), 1985
The Compact Disc Of James Brown (Polydor), 1985 **CD**
Gravity (Scotti Bros., USA), 1986 **CD**
In The Jungle Groove (Polydor), 1986 **CD**
Live In New York (SOPI Milan, France), 1981 **CD**
Sex Machine & Other Soul Classics (Polydor), 1987 **CD**
*Worth Searching Out:*
It's A Man's Man's World (Polydor), 1966
Say It Loud I'm Black And I'm Proud (King/Polydor), 1968
Get On The Good Foot (Polydor), 1973
Sex Machine Today (Polydor), 1975

# Jackson Browne

US composer, vocalist, guitarist.
Born Heidelberg, Germany, October 9, 1948.

**Career:** Raised in Los Angeles, Browne moved to New York in 1967 and began playing guitar for Nico. She liked his original songs and used three on **Chelsea Girl** album. Soon Browne was placing songs with folk-rock artists such as Johnny Rivers, Nitty Gritty Dirt Band(▶) and Tom Rush(▶). Although now largely forgotten or overlooked. Tom Rush was then important musician whose opinion carried great weight in folk community; if Rush was recording songs by somebody named Browne, then Browne must be good.

Browne's multi-talents could never be channelled into one area, so it's not surprising that he signed with Asylum in his own right. **Jackson Browne** LP (1971) contained mostly material already recorded by others.

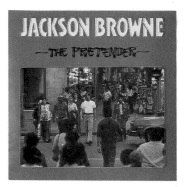

**The Pretender, Jackson Browne. Courtesy Asylum Records.**

Sales not impressive, but critical reviews were strongly favourable. Browne worked closely with newly formed Eagles(▶), co-writing first major hit, **Take It Easy**. His version is on his second LP, 1973's **For Everyman**. Again reviews bordered on ecstatic; again sales bordered on non-existent. Browne seemed doomed to cult status as excellent composer. His low-key stage performance also seemed antithetical to usual excess prevalent in rock.

But Browne's reputation for heartfelt emotion began spreading and with 1974 release **Late For The Sky** his back catalogue began selling well. Browne's careful approach is not conducive to dashing off albums. His next effort was delayed even further by March 1976 suicide of his wife. **The Pretender** seemed to strip Browne to essentials and suddenly he was a big star.

Refusing to cash in on success, he made extended tour of US and Europe, releasing **Running On Empty** in 1978. This album seemed radical departure from past work in that it had rough edges not normally associated with Browne. Critics did not know quite what to make of it, so emphasised risk Browne took in recording under adverse conditions while on tour. The public loved it and sales boomed.

**Hold Out** seemed to mark return of some peace in Jackson's personal life. Only time will tell if **The Pretender** and **Running On Empty** marked high point of Browne's career. But he has firmly established himself as intellectual lyricist with compassionate eye on concerns and problems of the person in the street.

| Hit Singles: | US | UK |
|---|---|---|
| Doctor My Eyes, 1972 | 8 | — |
| Running On Empty, 1978 | 11 | — |
| Stay, 1978 | 20 | 12 |
| Somebody's Baby, 1982 | 7 | — |
| Lawyers In Love, 1983 | 13 | — |

**Albums:**
Jackson Browne, Saturate Before Using (Asylum), 1971
For Everyman (Asylum), 1973
Late For The Sky (Asylum), 1974
The Pretender (Asylum), 1976
Running On Empty (Asylum), 1978
Hold Out (Asylum), 1980
Lawyers In Love (Asylum), 1983
Lives In The Balance (Elektra, USA)

# Eric Burdon

UK vocalist.
Born Newcastle, May 11, 1941.

**Career:** Raised in Newcastle, Burdon discovered black music via a merchant seaman living in flat below who brought records home from US. Finding friends had developed same interest in R&B Burdon joined with them to set up band, originally as Alan Price Combo, which became the Animals(▶). Burdon soon built reputation as hard-drinking, hard-talking Geordie with brash, husky blues-laced vocal delivery. His frenetic stage demeanour led to his being described as 'a black man in a white skin'.

On break-up of original Animals in 1966 following tempestuous US tour, Burdon moved from hard-edged R&B to then emergent acid-rock format with new band known as Eric Burdon and the Animals (Denny McCulloch, guitar; Vic Briggs, keyboards; John Weider, bass; Barry Jenkins, drums). Burdon espoused flower-power and, like John Lennon(▶) switched reputation as brawling boozer for that of gentle prophet of love image. Concentrated activities in America, and US hits **San Franciscan Nights** and **Sky Pilot** summed up his new philosophy.

After **Love Is** album (double set in US, single in Britain), Burdon dropped out from music scene and went into obscurity on West Coast amid rumours of drug problems. He suddenly re-emerged in 1970 as front-man for War(▶), an aggressive black progressive band with whom he enjoyed US chart-topper **Spill The Wine** from **Eric Burdon Declares War** album. After follow-up set, **Black Man's Burdon,** War went own way as heavy R&B group. Burdon, still closely associated

**Above: Eric Burdon making 1983 comeback with reformed Animals.**

with War's management/production team of Steve Gold and Jerry Goldstein, fulfilled personal ambition by working with their artist, blues veteran Jimmy Witherspoon, on joint album **Guilty.**

In 1973, Burdon returned to stage scene, playing three gigs in Britain and some dates in US with Aaron Butler (guitar), Randy Rice (bass) and Alvin Taylor (drums) in heavy-rock idiom.

Various abortive comebacks in '70s, together with contractual entanglements and personal problems, kept Burdon's name in press but out of charts. In 1983 the original Animals re-formed in London again, but whether past glories can be repeated remains to be seen.

**Hit Singles:**

| | US | UK |
|---|---|---|
| San Franciscan Nights, 1967 | — | 7 |

**Albums:**
Survivor (Polydor), 1978
Black And White Blues (MCA), 1979
Winds Of Change (Polydor), 1985 **CD**

# Kate Bush

UK vocalist, composer.
Born London, July 30, 1958.

**Career:** Born into a musical family, Kate studied violin and piano. Leaving school at 16, she signed to EMI having recorded demo

The Whole Story, Kate Bush.
Courtesy EMI Records.

tape under aegis of Pink Floyd's(▶) Dave Gilmour. She then spent several years writing, making demos, and studying dance and mime.

Recorded first album, **The Kick Inside**, in 1977. Single from album, **Wuthering Heights**, shot to top of UK charts on release in early 1978. Instant impact of record was due partly to originality of subject matter and musical treatment, partly to unearthly quality of Bush's voice. Critics were divided as to worth of artist, some decrying record as mere gimmickry.

However, **Heights** was first of string of hit singles for Bush, which established her as highly creative and innovative artist. Bush's writing style and vocal delivery are instantly recognisable, and her individuality is stamped on clutch of big-selling albums. She has also become renowned for her showmanship and idiosyncratic stage act, which involves elements of dance and mime.

Kate Bush is now regarded as all-round professional, and looks set to sustain career into '80s. Her most recent LP, **The Dreaming**, made No.3 in UK but had little impact in US, a territory which has so far largely resisted her undoubted talents. A three year hiatus ended with 1985 release **Hounds Of Love** followed a year later by a retrospective look back at her career with **Whole Story** LP.

**Hit Singles:**

| | US | UK |
|---|---|---|
| Wuthering Heights, 1978 | — | 1 |
| Man With The Child In His Eyes, 1978 | — | 6 |
| Wow, 1979 | — | 14 |
| Kate Bush On Stage (EP), 1979 | — | 10 |
| Breathing, 1980 | — | 16 |
| Babooshka, 1980 | — | 5 |
| Army Dreamers, 1980 | — | 16 |
| Sat In Your Lap, 1981 | — | 11 |
| Running Up That Hill, 1985 | 21 | 3 |
| Cloudbusting, 1985 | — | 20 |
| Hounds Of Love, 1986 | — | 18 |
| Experiment IV, 1986 | — | 23 |
| Don't Give Up, 1987 | — | 9 |

**Albums:**
The Kick Inside (EMI), 1978 **CD**
Lionheart (EMI), 1978 **CD**
Never For Ever (—/EMI), 1980 **CD**
The Dreaming (EMI), 1982 **CD**
Hounds Of Love (EMI), 1985 **CD**
Whole Story (EMI), 1986 **CD**

# The Byrds

US group formed 1964.

**Original line-up:** Roger McGuinn, lead guitar, vocals; David Crosby, rhythm guitar, vocals; Gene Clark, vocals, tambourine; Chris Hillman, bass; Michael Clarke, drums.

**Career:** Originally called the Jet Set before arrival of Hillman and Clarke; recorded series of demos for World Pacific, later released as **Preflyte.** As trio, cut one unsuccessful single for Elektra, **Please Let Me Love You**, then signed to Columbia as the Byrds. Acclaimed as America's answer to the Beatles(▶) they successfully combined the lyrical genius of Dylan(▶) with the Beatles' melodic expertise to produce a distinctive style exemplified by million-selling **Mr Tambourine Man,** which topped US and UK charts during summer 1965.

Generally acknowledged as pioneers of 'folk rock', Byrds produced a string of consistently excellent singles during 1965-67, including **Turn! Turn! Turn!, Eight Miles High, So You Want To Be A Rock 'n' Roll Star** and **My Back Pages.** First two albums consisted mainly of Dylan covers and love songs from the prolific Gene Clark.

By early 1966, folk-rock repertoire was extended to include a number of jazz and hard-rock items. The seminal **Eight Miles High** rivalled the output of such contempora-

**Above: Wow! Kate Bush—a very special vocal ability.**

ries as the Beatles and the Stones(▶) but Byrds suffered from radio bans; some numbers were unjustly labelled 'drug songs'.

In March, career development was further complicated by shock departure of Gene Clark. Continuing as quartet, they released **Fifth Dimension**—a neat amalgam of folk-rock orchestration, jazz and raga-tinged rock that fully demonstrated their ability to survive and thrive.

In late 1966, Byrds retired temporarily from live appearances amid speculation that they were breaking up.

1967 was most crucial year in their history, beginning with brilliant **Younger Than Yesterday** LP, which fully demonstrated David Crosby's growing importance as singer/songwriter. More surprisingly, album featured several country-flavoured songs from Chris Hillman, the fourth singer/songwriter to emerge from original line-up. Creative tensions in group led to several flare ups and a struggle for leadership between McGuinn and Crosby. Loss of management team, Jim Dickson and Eddie Tickner, only made matters worse.

Arguments over musical direction precipitated Crosby's sacking in October 1967. He was replaced by former Byrd Gene Clark, who lasted only three weeks before quitting due to ever-present fear of flying. Drummer Michael Clarke quit in disillusionment shortly afterwards, leaving McGuinn and Hillman to complete the excellent **Notorious Byrd Brothers**, generally hailed as a creative peak in their illustrious career.

Early in 1968, McGuinn and Hillman recruited Kevin Kelley (drums) and Gram Parsons (guitar/vocals) and plunged headlong into new musical direction. Although McGuinn was intent on recording an electronic-jazz album, it was Parsons and Hillman who proved strongest in determining group's subsequent musical policy. Country and western styled **Sweetheart Of The Rodeo** was a perfectly timed reaction against the excesses of psychedelia, predating Dylan's **Nashville Skyline** by a year. The Byrds' interest in country music continued, even after Parsons decided to quit on eve of an abortive South African tour.

Late 1968 was another period of flux, culminating in departure of Hillman following a dispute with McGuinn. By end of year, group was almost totally restructured with introduction of bluegrass virtuoso Clarence White (guitar), John York (bass) and Gene Parsons (drums).

From 1969 onwards, McGuinn assumed sole control of Byrds while ex-members went on to fame and fortune in offshoot groups, including Flying Burrito Brothers(▶), Dillard and Clark, Crosby Stills Nash & Young(▶), Manassas, the Souther-Hillman Furay Band and Firefall.

Recruitment of bassist Skip Battin (replacing York) produced settled line-up during early '70s, but quality of group's work declined significantly. There were, however, occasional highpoints, particularly the double album **(Untitled)** which included group's last hit single, **Chestnut Mare.**

By 1972, several members had drifted into various unproductive solo ventures and group shortly disbanded. Original quintet re-formed for one album, but results were not encouraging enough to inspire follow-up. During same disastrous year, former members Clarence White and Gram Parsons died in tragic

**Mr. Tambourine Man, the Byrds.
Courtesy Columbia Records.**

circumstances: White in hit and run accident, Parsons of drug overdose.

Following an erratic series of solo outings, McGuinn, Clark and Hillman reunited during late '70s but failed to establish themselves as supergroup. All five original Byrds have found difficulty in securing record contracts in recent years and their futures in the rock business seem very uncertain. Although Byrds were plagued by ego clashes and disputes, there is little doubt that at their peak in mid-'60s, they were the most important group in American rock music.

Having pioneered folk rock, raga rock and space rock, Byrds must also be credited for spearheading country rock boom of late '60s/early '70s. Influence on such units as Poco ( ) and the Eagles ( ) is incalculable.

**Final line-up:** McGuinn; Clarence White, guitar, vocals; Skip Battin, bass, vocals; John Guerin, drums.

| Hit Singles: | US | UK |
|---|---|---|
| Mr Tambourine Man, 1965 | 1 | 1 |
| All I Really Want To Do, 1965 | 40 | 4 |
| Turn! Turn! Turn!, 1965 | 1 | — |
| Eight Miles High, 1966 | 14 | — |
| Chestnut Mare, 1971 | — | 19 |

**Albums:**
Preflyte (Together) (Columbia/CBS), 1969
Mr Tambourine Man (Columbia/CBS), 1965*
Turn! Turn! Turn! (Columbia/CBS), 1965*
Fifth Dimension (Columbia/CBS), 1966
Younger Than Yesterday (Columbia/CBS), 1967 **CD**
Greatest Hits (Columbia/CBS), 1967
The Notorious Byrd Brothers (Columbia/CBS), 1968†
Sweetheart Of The Rodeo (Columbia/CBS), 1968† **CD**
Dr Byrd And Mr Hyde (Columbia/CBS), 1969
Ballad Of Easy Rider (Columbia/CBS), 1969
Greatest Hits Volume II (Columbia/CBS), 1971
(Columbia/CBS), 1971
History Of The Byrds (CBS), 1973
The Byrds Play Dylan (Columbia/CBS), 1979
The Original Singles Volume I (Columbia/CBS), 1980
The Original Singles Volume II (Columbia/CBS), 1982
*Available as double LP set (Columbia) US only.
†Available as double album, UK only, 1976.

*Worth Searching Out:*
(Untitled) (Columbia/CBS), 1970

**Safe As Milk, Captain Beefheart. Courtesy Kama Sutra Records.**

# Captain Beefheart

US composer, vocalist, multi-instrumentalist. Born Don Van Vliet, Glendale, California, January 15, 1941.

**Career:** As young man in California Van Vliet tried playing straight with group called Blackouts. Assuming name Captain Beefheart (a name not so unusual now, but rather outrageous in 1964) he formed loose confederation of forever-changing musicians called the Magic Band. In what some called his last touch with reality, he released 'commercial' single **Diddy Wah Diddy** on A&M. Then he began changing record labels almost as fast as he changed band members.
**Safe As Milk** in spring 1967 was very avant-garde, very original, and very much an inside joke. Critics like to consider themselves insiders and Beefheart quickly became known as someone to like, not because you listened to his records, but to be 'cool'.
Beefheart recorded **Mirror Man** next but no one would release it until Buddah took a chance in 1973. With third line-up in 12 months, Beefheart recorded **Strictly Personal** which he got Blue Thumb to release in December 1968. Beefheart's excuse for this one was that it was mixed without his supervision. Next record was definitely going to be *it*. He signed with old friend Frank Zappa(▶)'s label, Straight.
**Trout Mask Replica** was made with no restraints, and no effort to be commerical. This was art. Critics fell over themselves praising it as one of rock's truly innovative

**Below: Don Van Vliet, alias the notorious Captain Beefheart.**

moments; rock public fell over itself avoiding it. Zappa and Beefheart fell out over who was responsible. Straight released a second Beefheart album with one of rock's better titles, **Lick My Decals Off, Baby**.
Moving to Reprise, Captain released somewhat blues-based **The Spotlight Kid**, then **Clear Spot**. Both were departures in containing some identifiable tunes. Another record deal in 1974 (Mercury/Virgin) launched Captain yet again. **Unconditionally Guaranteed** was commercial sell-out of his career. To avoid falling into rut, he quickly followed up with demented **Blue Jeans And Moonbeams**.
In 1975 he dissolved Magic Band (who resented dismissal and went on to fail on own as Mallard). Beefheart collaborated with Zappa on **Bongo Fury** album and in 1976 recorded 'solo' effort. (Warner Bros eventually released **Shiney Beast Bat Chain Puller** in 1978.) With new Magic Band, Beefheart released 1980 **Doc At The Radar Station** and has continued to record since.
Some call this music with a personal vision; others call it eccentric nonsense. Beefheart would probably agree with both. In any case Captain has always been original, and remained somewhat immune to criticism. Rave on Captain.

**Albums:**
Safe As Milk (Kama Sutra/Pye), 1967
Strictly Personal (Blue Thumb/Liberty), 1968
Trout Mask Replica (Straight), 1970
Lick My Decals Off, Baby (Straight), 1970*
The Spotlight Kid (Reprise), 1972*
Clear Spot (Reprise), 1972
Mirror Man (Buddah/Pye), 1973
Unconditionally Guaranteed (Mercury/Fame), 1974 **CD**
The Captain Beefheart File (—/Pye), 1977
Shiney Beast Bat Chain Puller (Warner Bros/Virgin), 1978 **CD**
Two Originals Of... (—/Reprise), 1979 **CD**
Doc At The Radar Station (Virgin), 1980 **CD**
Ice Cream For Crow (Virgin), 1982
Blue Jeans And Moonbeams (Virgin), 1984 **CD**

*Released as double album set (—/Reprise), 1976

# Kim Carnes

US vocalist, pianist, composer. Born Los Angeles, July 20, 1945.

**Career:** Former member of New Christy Minstrel, Carnes' career was taking a distinctly MOR direction when **Bette Davis Eyes** cut loose in 1981.
One-time commercials writer/performer, Carnes first attracted attention with A&M albums **Kim Carnes** and **Sailin'**, produced by Mentor Williams and Jerry Wexler respectively. A prolific writer (with husband David Ellingson), her material has been recorded by Anne Murray, Frank Sinatra(▶) and Barbra Streisand(▶).
Cut **Don't Fall In Love With A Dreamer** with Kenny Rogers(▶), another ex-New Christy Minstrel, in '79. Rogers subsequently recorded album of Carnes/Ellingson material, **Gideon** (1980).
**Bette Davis Eyes** (written by Jackie De Shannon, whose husky vocals Carnes successfully emulated) pushed the LA native into the rock mainstream where she has continued to flourish.

| Hit Singles: | US | UK |
|---|---|---|
| More Love, 1980 | 10 | — |
| Bette Davis Eyes, 1981 | 1 | 10 |

*With Kenny Rogers:*

| | | |
|---|---|---|
| Don't Fall In Love With A Dreamer, 1980 | 4 | — |

**Albums:**
Kim Carnes (A&M), 1976
Sailin' (A&M), 1977
St Vincents Court (EMI), 1979
Romance Dance (EMI), 1980
Best Of (A&M), 1981
Mistaken Identity (EMI), 1981
Voyeur (EMI), 1982
Café Racers (EMI), 1983
Mistaken Identity (EMI), 1985
Lighthouse (EMI), 1986

# The Carpenters

US duo formed 1969.
Richard Carpenter, vocals, keyboards; born New Haven, Connecticut, October 15, 1945.
Karen Carpenter, vocals, drums; born New Haven, Connecticut, March 2, 1950; died December, 1982.

**Career:** Richard began playing piano at 12, while younger sister Karen developed interest in drums. When Carpenter family moved to Downey, California, in early '60s brother and

**A Song For You, The Carpenters. Courtesy A&M Records.**

sister recruited bass player to form jazz outfit. Trio won Hollywood Battle Of The Bands contest, but was soon disbanded as Richard and Karen developed interest in vocal harmonies. Next band, Spectrum, comprised Richard and Karen plus four others, and was equally short-lived.
Duo decided to experiment on their own with vocal harmony effects, using overdubbing techniques. Demo tapes were eventually heard by Herb Alpert(▶) of A&M Records, who signed pair as the Carpenters. Success was almost immediate; 1970 Bacharach-David million-seller **Close To You** set pattern for string of hit singles lasting into mid-'70s. At same time duo notched up massive album sales worldwide (1973 album **The Singles 1969-73** became one of the all-time biggest-selling albums). Concert appearances were equally popular.
Appeal of act was based on Karen Carpenter's limpid voice, excellent material from writers such as Bacharach-David and Paul Williams, and unique vocal harmony blend. Richard Carpenter was mainly responsible for arranging and musical direction. Although often critically berated for blandness and wholesome, clean-cut image, the Carpenters were praised by musicians and industry insiders for musicianship, excellent choice of sidemen (e.g. virtuoso guitarist Tony Peluso) and professionalism.
In late '70s duo kept relatively low profile, although 1981 album **Made In America** brought them back into limelight (especially in UK where it made No.12). Unfortunately,

**Above: The late Karen Carpenter with brother Richard.**

career ended in February, 1983 with death of Karen Carpenter (caused by heart trouble/anorexia).

| Hit Singles: | US | UK |
| --- | --- | --- |
| (They Long To Be) Close To You, 1970 | 1 | 6 |
| We've Only Just Begun, 1970 | 2 | 28 |
| For All We Know, 1971 | 3 | — |
| Rainy Days And Mondays, 1971 | 2 | — |
| Superstar/For All We Know, 1971 | — | 18 |
| Superstar, 1971 | 2 | — |
| Hurting Each Other, 1972 | 2 | — |
| It's Going To Take Some Time, 1972 | 12 | — |
| I Won't Last A Day Without You/ Goodbye To Love, 1972 | — | 9 |
| Goodbye To Love, 1972 | 7 | — |
| Sing, 1973 | 3 | — |
| Yesterday Once More, 1973 | 2 | 2 |
| Top Of The World, 1973 | 1 | 5 |
| Jambalaya/Mr Guder, 1974 | — | 12 |
| I Won't Last A Day Without You, 1974 | 11 | 32 |
| Please Mr Postman, 1975 | 1 | 2 |
| Only Yesterday, 1975 | 4 | 7 |
| Solitaire, 1975 | 17 | 32 |
| There's A Kind Of Hush, 1976 | 12 | 22 |

**Below: Front-line American unit the Cars, bumper to bumper.**

| | US | UK |
| --- | --- | --- |
| Calling Occupants Of Interplanetary Craft, 1977 | 32 | 9 |
| Touch Me When We're Dancing, 1981 | 16 | — |

**Albums:**
Close To You (A&M), 1971
The Carpenters (A&M), 1971
Ticket To Ride (A&M), 1972
A Song For You (A&M), 1972
Now And Then (A&M), 1973
The Singles 1969-73 (A&M), 1974 **CD**
Greatest Hits (—/Hallmark), 1974
Horizon (A&M), 1975
Live In Japan (A&M), 1975
A Kind Of Hush (A&M), 1976
The Carpenters Collection (—/A&M), 1976
Live At The Palladium (A&M), 1977
Passage (A&M), 1977
The Singles 1974-78 (A&M), 1978
Made In America (A&M), 1981
An Old Fashioned Christmas (A&M), 1984
Yesterday Once More (EMI), 1985
Voice Of The Heart (A&M), 1987 **CD**

# The Cars

US group formed 1976.

**Original/Current line-up:** Ric Ocasek, guitar, vocals; Ben Orr, bass, vocals; Greg Hawkes, keyboards, vocals, sax, percussion; Elliot Easton, guitar; David Robinson, drums.

**Career:** Richard Otcasek was born and raised near Cleveland, Ohio. He went East to Boston and became Ric Ocasek. In early '70s he met and began working with Ben Orr in various small local bands. Mid-'70s brought in Greg Hawkes. Ocasek was clearly focal point of this melting pot but he was also very much open to others' ideas and opinions. Trio did various demo tapes and kept in touch with each other while Ocasek came across Elliot Easton in another local band.

Meanwhile Bostonian David Robinson, who had been playing in Jonathan Richman's Modern Lovers, moved to Los Angeles. After short time with highly underrated the Pop, he returned to Boston. There he joined Ocasek's group, was impressed by team spirit and offered up name he had been saving: the Cars.

In February 1977 Cars began playing at Boston's 'The Rat' where ability to mix enthusiasm with professional musicianship marked them as special. In 1978 they signed to Elektra who teamed them with Roy Thomas Baker as producer, and first album followed. As strong as album became after several plays, several tracks were masterpieces in own right as singles. Even new-wave orientated UK proved susceptible to Cars' music and made **My Best Friend's Girl** No.3.

**Candy-O** (1979) could only prove anti-

**The Cars. Courtesy Elektra Records.**

climactic, especially as recorded quickly between tours. But Cars proved their commitment to rock by refusing to do US TV's 'Midnight Special' unless they got complete control of guests and presentation. They turned fall '79 show into masterpiece of what rock *could* be on television.

**Panorama** (1980) seemed a reaction to the critics who complained Cars were too slick and too mechanical. 1981 saw release of **Shake It Up** which almost recaptured first

album's balance. Despite public effort to present Cars in group image, Ocasek's personality is too strong not to emerge as head Car. 1982 proved this as no new Cars album appeared. US got **Beatitude**, Ocasek solo album sounding a lot like . . .a new Cars album.

March 1984 saw release of fifth album, **Heartbeat City**, produced by Robert John 'Mutt' Lange of AC/DC and Foreigner renown and major hit single **Drive** (latter entering UK charts in 1985 after its use during Live Aid concert.) Since that time Cars albums have continued to be major sellers, and provided Ocasek continues in driving seat, longevity seems assured.

Band has often won plaudits for innovative videos, including one directed by avant garde icon Andy Warhol.

| Hit Singles: | US | UK |
| --- | --- | --- |
| My Best Friend's Girl, 1978 | 35 | 3 |
| Just What I Needed, 1979 | 27 | 17 |
| Let's Go, 1979 | 14 | — |
| Shake It Up, 1982 | 4 | — |
| You Might Think, 1984 | 7 | — |
| Magic, 1984 | 12 | — |
| *Drive, 1984 | 3 | 4 |
| Hello Again, 1984 | 20 | — |
| Tonight She Comes, 1986 | 9 | — |
| You Are The Girl, 1987 | 17 | — |

*1985 in UK

**Albums:**
The Cars (Elektra), 1978
Candy-O (Elektra), 1979
Panorama (Elektra), 1980
Shake It Up (Elektra), 1981
Heartbeat City (Elektra), 1984
Greatest Hits (Elektra), 1985

*Ric Ocasek Solo:*
Beatitude, 1982

# Ray Charles

US vocalist, pianist, composer, arranger.
Born Ray Charles Robinson, Albany, Georgia, September 23, 1930.

**Career:** Brought up in Greenville, Florida, Charles was blinded by glaucoma at age six. He showed early signs of musical talent, and was sent to State School for Blind at seven. He remained until 15, concentrating on musical studies, and by early teens was already playing piano semi-professionally. On death of his mother in 1945 he became full-time musician.

Early experience on road included stint as part of blues singer Lowell Fulsom's band. First band Charles led was called McSon Trio. Recorded number of Nat Cole(▶)-influenced sides for small local labels.

Big career break was signing with nascent black music label Atlantic; **It Should Have Been Me**, a semi-humorous blues number, was R&B hit in 1954.

During this period Charles began to move away from Cole influence and developed idiosyncratic style based on mixture of secularised gospel and blues. At same time he put together band of top-echelon jazz musicians; result was commercial and critical success.

Charles broke pop market in 1959 with **What'd I Say**, a wildly exciting single that synthesised blues, gospel, and rock'n'roll in one dynamic package. Made Top 10 of pop charts and started Charles' career as performer of wide appeal.

Following big money offer, Charles left Atlantic for ABC-Paramount at end of 1959. He continued to make excellent recordings, particularly of blues-based material, and notch up major hits. **Georgia On My Mind**, a reading of Hoagy Carmichael standard which set

Charles' emotion-filled voice against strings backing, was Top-30 hit in UK and established Charles internationally.

Further landmark was created in 1962 when Charles recorded album of country songs, **Modern Sounds In Country And Western**. Idea of black R&B star covering country songs seemed outlandish at time, but concept was successful both artistically and commercially, and resulted in huge album sales and hit singles like **I Can't Stop Loving You**. That year Charles sold then phenomenal amount of eight million dollars worth of records (he has had nearly 70 US chart singles), and became major international star, in demand for TV and concert dates all over world.

During '60s Charles' career assumed fairly consistent pattern; albums contained mixture of R&B and more pop-orientated material, and live appearances became well-oiled and disciplined runthroughs of hits.

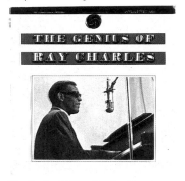

**The Genius Of Ray Charles. Courtesy Atlantic Records.**

Charles' power as vocalist continued unabated. The '70s saw changes in record company arrangements. In 1973, he severed connections with ABC to form own label, Crossover, and in 1977 Crossover became distributed and marketed by his old company, Atlantic.

In '80s Charles seems content to follow formula which has kept him at top for 20 years. A living legend, he is still capable of powerful music and remains an important influence on many contemporary rock singers —particularly Joe Cocker(▶). His Atlantic and early ABC material is a testimony to one of the most exhilarating talents in popular music.

**Hit Singles:**

| | US | UK |
|---|---|---|
| What'd I Say, 1959 | 6 | — |
| Georgia On My Mind, 1960 | 1 | 24 |
| One Mint Julep, 1961 | 8 | — |
| Hit The Road Jack, 1961 | 1 | 6 |
| Unchain My Heart, 1961 | 9 | — |
| Hide Nor Hair, 1962 | 20 | — |
| I Can't Stop Loving You, 1962 | 1 | 1 |
| You Don't Know Me, 1962 | 2 | 9 |
| You Are My Sunshine, 1962 | 7 | — |
| Your Cheating Heart, 1962 | 29 | 13 |
| Don't Set Me Free, 1963 | 20 | 37 |
| Take These Chains From My Heart, 1963 | 8 | 5 |
| Busted, 1963 | 4 | 21 |
| That Lucky Old Sun, 1964 | 20 | — |
| Crying Time, 1966 | 6 | 50 |
| Together Again, 1966 | 19 | 48 |
| Here We Go Again, 1967 | 15 | 38 |

**Albums:**
Ray Charles At Newport (Atlantic), 1958
The Great Ray Charles (Atlantic/London), 1958
Genius Of Ray Charles (Atlantic/Boulevard), 
Ray Charles Live (Atlantic/—), 1965
25th Anniversary In Showbusiness (ABC/Atlantic), 1971
Come Live With Me (Crossover/London), 1974
World Of (—/Decca), 1974
World Of Volume 2 (—/Decca), 1975
Focus On Ray Charles (London), 1975
My Kind Of Jazz Volume 3 (Crossover/—), 1975
Renaissance (Crossover/London), 1975
Porgy And Bess (with Cleo Laine) (RCA/London), 1976
What Have I Done To Their Songs (London), 1977
True To Life (Atlantic/London), 1977
Love And Peace (Atco/London), 1978
Ray Charles Blues (—/Ember), 1978
20 Golden Pieces Of (—/Bulldog), 1979
Ain't It So (—/London), 1979
A Ray Of Hope (—/Manhattan), 1980
Brother Ray (London), 1980
Everything (—/Manhattan), 1980
I Can't Stop Loving You (—/Pickwick), 1980

**Below: The legendary 'Brother' Ray Charles, R&B giant of four decades, a great influence on rock singers.**

Simply Ray (—/Manhattan), 1980
Great Hits (—/Phoenix), 1982
Standing On The Edge (Epic), 1985
The Right Time (Atlantic), 1987 **CD**
Ray Charles (Entertainers), 1987 **CD**

*With Milt Jackson:*
Soul Brothers (Atlantic/London), 1959
Soul Meeting (Atlantic), 1962

*Worth Searching Out:*
Yes Indeed (Atlantic/London), 1958
What'd I Say (Atlantic/London), 1959
Ray Charles And Betty Carter (HMV/ABC), 1960
Genius + Soul = Jazz (Atlantic/HMV), 1961
Modern Sounds In Country & Western (ABC/HMV), 1962
Do I Ever Cross Your Mind (CBS), 1984
Tell The Truth (Charly), 1984
The Fantastic Ray Charles (Musidisc), 1985

# Chicago

US group formed 1968.

**Original line-up:** Robert Lamm, keyboards, lead vocals; Terry Kath, guitar, lead vocals; Peter Cetera, bass, lead vocals; Lee Loughnana, trumpet, background vocals; James Pankow, trombone; Walter Parazaider, woodwinds, background vocals; Daniel Seraphine, drums.

**Career:** Formed as the Big Thin in 1968, name changed to Chicago Transit Authority. Made big reputation in Chicago (shortening name to simply 'Chicago' when sued by Mayor Daley) before moving to Los Angeles and linking with producer/manager James William Guercio. Debut album **Chicago Transit Authority** (1969) won immediate acclaim for its blend of black-influenced rhythm section and jazzy brass section—in similar mode to also emergent Blood Sweat And Tears(▶). Album was massive seller, staying in chart for amazing six years.

Subsequent albums, called Chicago I-VIII etc., appeared at regular annual intervals and run of singles like **I'm A Man** (a punchy 1970 version of Spencer Davis Group(▶) oldie) **Make Me Smile, 25 Or 6 To 4** and romantic chart-topping ballad **If You Leave Me Now**

**If You Leave Me Now, Chicago. Courtesy CBS Records.**

have made them one of the highest-earning groups in rock. They are reputed to have generated more than $160 million in sales, their 14 albums selling 20 million copies.

Following death of guitarist Terry Kath (playing Russian roulette), band went into limbo for short time. He was eventually replaced by Donnie Dacus. Comeback 1980 world tour included concert before 150,000 audience at Chicago Festival.

Unceremoniously dumped by Columbia, who felt that band had outlived their appeal, Chicago found welcome at Full Moor in 1982. Move revitalized stagnating recording career.

Loss of bass player and vocalist Peter Cetera, who himself enjoyed immediate single success with **Glory Of Love**, did not halt Chicago bandwagon. Move to Warner Brothers in late 80s resulted in band achieving further success. Outfit seems likely to become one of handful of pop acts to achieve double-decade longevity.

**Current line-up:** Lamm; Loughnana; Pankow; Parazaider; Seraphine; Chris Pinnick; Bill Champlin.

**Hit Singles:**

| | US | UK |
|---|---|---|
| I'm A Man, 1970 | — | 8 |
| Make Me Smile, 1970 | 9 | — |
| 25 Or 6 To 4, 1970 | 4 | 7 |
| Does Anybody Really Know What Time It Is? 1970 | 7 | — |
| Free, 1971 | 20 | — |
| Beginnings/Colour My World, 1971 | 7 | — |
| Saturday In The Park, 1972 | 3 | — |
| Feelin' Stronger Every Day, 1973 | 10 | — |
| Just You 'n' Me, 1973 | 4 | — |
| (I've Been) Searchin' So Long, 1974 | 9 | — |
| Call On Me, 1974 | 6 | — |
| Wishing You Were Here, 1974 | 11 | — |
| Harry Truman, 1975 | 13 | — |
| Old Days, 1975 | 5 | — |
| If You Leave Me Now, 1976 | 1 | 1 |
| Baby What A Big Surprise, 1977 | 4 | 41 |
| Live Again, 1978 | 14 | — |
| No Tell Lover, 1979 | 14 | — |
| Hard For Me To Say I'm Sorry, 1982 | 1 | 4 |
| Stay The Night, 1984 | 16 | — |
| Hard Habit To Break, 1984 | 3 | 8 |
| You're The Inspiration, 1985 | 3 | 14 |
| Long Comes A Woman, 1985 | 14 | — |
| If She Would Have Been Faithful, 1987 | 12 | — |
| Will You Still Love Me, 1987 | 2 | — |

**Albums:**
Chicago Transit Authority (Columbia/CBS), 1968
Chicago (Columbia/CBS), 1970
III (Columbia/CBS), 1971
IV Live At Carnegie Hall* (Columbia/CBS), 1971
V (Columbia/CBS), 1972
VI (Columbia/CBS), 1973
VII (Columbia/CBS), 1974
VIII (Columbia/CBS), 1975
IX Greatest Hits (Columbia/CBS), 1975
X (Columbia/CBS), 1976
XI (Columbia/CBS), 1977
Hot Streets (Columbia/CBS), 1978
XIII (Columbia/CBS), 1979
XIV (Columbia/CBS), 1980
Greatest Hits Volume 2 (Columbia/CBS), 1982
If You Leave Me Now (—/CBS), 1982
Love Songs (—/TV), 1982
Toronto Rock 'n' Roll Revival 1969, Volume 1 (Accord/—), 1982
Chicago 16 (Full Moon), 1982 **CD**
Chicago 17 (Full Moon), 1984 **CD**
Chicago 18 (Warner Bros), 1986 **CD**
*4 album live set

# China Crisis

UK group formed 1982

**Original line-up:** Eddie Lundon, vocals, guitar, keyboard, composer; Garry Daly, vocals, keyboards, guitar, composer.

**Career:** Initial single **African and White** on Lewis's Inevitable label, did well enough to be picked up by Virgin for minor chart success. Ponderously titled **Difficult Shapes And Passive Rhythms Some People Think It's**

**Fun To Entertain** debut album contained Top 20 hit **Christian**.

Adding bassist Gary Johnson and other musicians who came and went, China Crisis toured with Simple Minds, Kevin Wilkinson eventually becoming regular drummer.

Frequently accused of wimpering, China Crisis nevertheless show strength of working-class roots and subsequent albums showed growing stature as creative force as performers and writers.

1985 car crash involving Daly and Johnson did not impair band's progress, with their third album **Flaunt The Imperfection** (produced by former Steely Dan bassman Walter Becker) making UK top thirty. Singles **Black Man Ray** and **King In A Catholic Style** culled from LP both made UK top twenty. 1987 set **What Price Paradise?** received mixed reviews, with detractors still looking for more substance from band.

**Current line-up:** Lundon; Stuart Rushet, guitar; Martin Ditcham, percussion; Gary Barnacle, saxophone; Pete Thoms, trombone; Luke Tunney, trumpet and flugelhorn.

| Hit Singles: | US | UK |
|---|---|---|
| Christian, 1983 | — | 12 |
| Wishful Thinking, 1984 | — | 9 |
| Black Man Ray, 1985 | — | 14 |
| King In A Catholic Style, 1985 | — | 19 |
| Arizona Sky, 1986 | — | 47 |

**Albums:**
Difficult Shapes And Passive Rhythms (Virgin), 1982
Working With Fire And Steel (Virgin), 1983
Flaunt The Imperfection (Virgin), 1985
What Price Paradise? (Virgin), 1986

# Clannad

Eire group formed 1976.

**Original/Current line-up:** Maire Ni Bhraonain; Pol O Braonain; Ciaran O Braonain; Noel O Dugain; Padraig O Dugain.

**Career:** Formed originally with the intention of entering local folk festivals Clannad soon came to the forefront of Irish music. Early records were released in Ireland only but after writing the music for UK TV Series "Harry's Game", Clannad's title song single reached number 5 in UK and won them an Ivor Novello songwriting award.

Debut LP for RCA **Magical Ring** followed and went gold. After a lengthy European tour Clannad worked on songs for the UK TV series "Robin Of Sherwood". Apart from the resulting album **Legend**, the group also wrote and performed all the atmospheric pieces for the 26 episodes. February 1985 Clannad received British Academy Award for best soundtrack of the year — the first Irish group to receive the award.

Third album **Macalla** recorded in Dublin, London and Switzerland included single **In A Lifetime**. Featuring U2's Bono duetting with Maire; it charted as the group undertook a 23 date sell-out UK tour. Clannad's most recent album **Sirius** was recorded in Wales and London, and mixed in Los Angeles, with Gred Ladanyi and Russ Kunkel producing.

Clannad's musical appeal has managed to surmount parochial boundaries and their 1988 world tour including US dates is an indication of their international appeal.

| Hit Singles: | US | UK |
|---|---|---|
| Theme From Harry's Game, 1982 | — | 5 |
| In A Lifetime, 1986 | — | 20 |

**Albums:**
Clannad In Concert (Ogham), 1979
Clannad Vol 2 (Gael-Linn) (Ireland), 1979
Dulaman (Gael-Linn) (Ireland), 1979

**Above: Chicago earned the wrath of Mayor Daly before moving to L.A.**

**Sirius, Clannad.
Courtesy RCA Records.**

The Pretty Maid (Phillips), 1982
Crannull (Phillips), 1982
Fuain (Tara) (Ireland), 1982
The Legend (RCA), 1984 **CD**
Magical Ring (RCA), 1984 **CD**
Macalla (RCA), 1985 **CD**
Sirius (RCA), 1987 **CD**

**Below: Clannad, whose Macalla album featured U2's Bono in a duet with Maire Ni Bhraonain.**

# Eric Clapton

UK guitarist, vocalist, composer.
Born Ripley, Surrey, March 30, 1945.

**Career:** Brought up by foster-parents. At 15 he started to listen to blues recordings by Muddy Waters(▶), Chuck Berry(▶), Big Bill Broonzy et al, and bought first guitar at 17. Taught himself to play while studying at Kingston Art College.

Formed first band in 1963, an R&B outfit called Roosters which also included at various times Paul Jones and Tom McGuinness later of Manfred Mann(▶) and Brian Jones later of Rolling Stones(▶). Band was short-lived; and in late 1963 Clapton spent two weeks with Casey Jones and the Engineers before replacing Anthony 'Top' Topham as lead guitarist in recently formed Yardbirds(▶).

While with Yardbirds Clapton established reputation as blues stylist, and recorded **Five Live Yardbirds** and **Sonny Boy Williamson & The Yardbirds** albums. But when band took more commercial direction with 1965 single **For Your Love,** Clapton took off for more purist environment of John Mayall's(▶) Bluesbreakers.

Straight-down-the-line blues approach of Mayall's band provided perfect backdrop for Clapton, and the guitarist attracted even more fervent following. Shown to good effect on **Bluesbreakers** album, Clapton's playing began to influence other British players; he became widely regarded as *the* guitar hero.

Sitters-in with Bluesbreakers included Jack Bruce(▶) and Ginger Baker(▶), bass player and drummer respectively, with Graham Bond Organization. Empathy with both musicians led to break from Mayall (Clapton replaced by Peter Green(▶)) and formation of Cream(▶) in 1967.

With Cream Clapton enjoyed first major commercial success and fully blown rock star status. Although band was important link in development of heavy rock—the first power trio—it was relatively short-lived, and folded in November 1968.

Period which followed saw Clapton involved with variety of projects, including ill-fated Blind Faith(▶) supergroup, touring and recording with Delaney & Bonnie(▶), guesting on other artists' albums, and his first solo album in 1970. From this time onwards Clapton seemed to be trying to live down his axe hero past. He immersed himself in group as Derek of Derek and the Dominoes(▶) December 1970 Dominoes album featured Duane Allman(▶) and is regarded by many as Clapton's best recorded effort. Single **Layla**—dedicated to then wife of George Harrison(▶), Patti, whom Clapton was later to marry—has achieved classic status.

Nevertheless, Derek and the Dominoes were not huge commercial success, and this relative failure plus increasing drug problem

**Backless, Eric Clapton. Courtesy RSO Records.**

took Clapton off music scene for several years. Eventually, with help of friends like Pete Townshend(▶) and course of electro-acupuncture, Clapton regained health.

Since 1974 Clapton has pursued fairly low-profile career, making relaxed, down-home albums, occasionally coming up with hit singles, and working live sporadically. He has continued to play down guitar hero persona, and has developed pleasing J.J. Cale(▶)-like voice to go with his simple but appealing compositions. Nowadays as often influenced by country and other forms of blues (he is for example fan of super-relaxed country artist Don Williams(▶)), Clapton appeals both to AOR audiences and diehard rock fans.

This crossover appeal has ensured massive success of albums like 1987 blockbuster **August**, and continuing demand for live appearances.

One of the most important British musicians to have come out of rock, Clapton now seems to have come to terms with his legendary status, and looks set to garner commercial—if not ncessarily critical—success for years to come.

Guitars: Fender Stratocaster, Gibson Les Paul.

**Hit Singles:**

| | US | UK |
|---|---|---|
| After Midnight, 1970 | 18 | — |
| I Shot The Sherriff, 1974 | 1 | 9 |
| Swing Low Sweet Chariot, 1975 | — | 19 |
| Lay Down Sally, 1978 | 3 | 39 |
| Wonderful Tonight, 1978 | 16 | — |
| Promises, 1979 | 9 | 37 |
| I Can't Stand It, 1981 | 10 | — |
| I've Got A Rock'n'Roll Heart, 1983 | 18 | — |
| Behind The Mask, 1987 | — | 15 |

**Albums:**
Eric Clapton (Polydor), 1970
History of Eric Clapton (Polydor), 1972
Eric Clapton At His Best (Polydor), 1973
Eric Clapton's Rainbow Concert (RSO), 1973
461 Ocean Boulevard* (RSO), 1974 **CD**
There's One In Every Crowd (RSO), 1975 **CD**
E.C. Was Here (RSO), 1975
The Blues World Of (—/Decca), 1975
No Reason To Cry (RSO), 1976 **CD**
Slowhand* (RSO), 1977 **CD**
Backless* (RSO), 1978
Just One Night (RSO), 1980 **CD**
Another Ticket (RSO), 1981 **CD**
Steppin' Out (—/Decca), 1981
Time Pieces (Best Of) (RSO), 1982 **CD**
Money And Cigarettes (Warner Bros), 1983 **CD**
Time Pieces, Volume II (RSO), 1983 **CD**
Behind The Sun (Warner Bros), 1984 **CD**
August (Warner Bros), 1987 **CD**
Cream Of Eric Clapton (Polydor), 1987 **CD**
Backtrackin (RSO, USA), 1985 **CD**
Layla (RSO, Import), 1983 **CD**
Live 85 (Duck), 1985 **CD**
Too Much Monkey Business (Astan), 1984 **CD**

*Available as triple album set.

**August, Eric Clapton.
Courtesy Warner Bros. Records**

**Above: Eric Clapton, with Ron Wood and Freddie King at the Crystal Palace.**

*Eric Clapton & John Mayall:*
Bluebreaker (Decca) **CD**
Bluesbreakers (Decca) **CD**

# The Dave Clark Five

UK group formed 1963.
**Original/Final line-up:** Dave Clark, drums, vocals; Lenny Davidson, guitar; Rick Huxley, guitar, banjo; Dennis Payton, saxophone, guitar, clarinet, harmonica; Mike Smith, keyboards, vibraphone, vocals.

**Career:** This 'British invasion' group followed the Beatles(▶) to US and found great, if temporary, fame and fortune there. Nowadays often considered pale imitation of Beatles, but in fact the Five had distinctive sound (called 'Tottenham Sound') of their own, based on Clark's steadily thudding drums and chanting vocals. Smash hit single **Glad All Over** was amazingly considered rather risqué at the time. Group became involved in a ridiculous publicity war with the Beatles, the Five being touted as a neat, well-groomed London alternative. Then the Rolling Stones(▶) arrived. It was all a contrived tempest in a teapot, anyway, indicative of the innocent controversies that filled the pages of teen magazines at the time.

Band also starred in what turned out to be one of the best rock movies, 'Having A Wild Weekend', directed by then unknown John Boorman in 1965. Despite title, it is a bitter-sweet story that looks at the price of sudden fame and at the hysteria that briefly surrounds popular young musicians. There's no great acting here, of course, but it is one of the few rock exploitation films that holds up.

Group had several hit singles in the States, including **Do You Love Me**, a cover of the 1962 dance hit by the Contours, and raucous stomper **Bits And Pieces**. After that, popularity faded; although the Five had an original and identifiable sound, it never varied. They weren't capable of the changes that more lasting bands were beginning to explore. They stayed together, a constant live attraction until 1973 when they finally broke up. Clark became successful in the business end of music by buying rights to near legendary 'Ready Steady Go' TV series and also staging musical 'Time' starring Cliff Richard, Julian Lennon and Sir Laurence Olivier.

**The Best of the Dave Clark Five. Courtesy EMI Records.**

**Hit Singles:**

| | US | UK |
|---|---|---|
| Glad All Over, 1963 | 6 | 1 |
| Bits And Pieces, 1964 | 4 | 2 |
| Can't You See That She's Mine, 1964, | 4 | 10 |
| Do You Love Me, 1964 | 11 | 30 |
| Because, 1964 | 3 | — |
| Everybody Knows (I Still Love, You), 1964 | 15 | 37 |
| Any Way You Want It, 1964 | 14 | 25 |

**Below: London's answer to the 'Mersey' sound, the Dave Clark Five with Ed Sullivan, who introduced many UK acts.**

| | | |
|---|---|---|
| Come Home, 1965 | 14 | 16 |
| I Like It Like That, 1965 | 7 | — |
| Catch Us If You Can, 1965 | 4 | 5 |
| Over And Over, 1965 | 1 | 45 |
| At The Scene, 1966 | 18 | — |
| Try Too Hard, 1966 | 12 | — |
| You Got What It Takes, 1967 | 7 | 28 |
| Everybody Knows (I Still Love You) 1967 | 43 | 2 |
| Red Balloon, 1968 | — | 7 |
| Good Old Rock 'n' Roll, 1969 | — | 7 |
| Everybody Get Together, 1970 | — | 8 |

**Albums:**
Best Of (—/Starline), 1970
Plays Good Old Rock 'n' Roll (—/MFP), 1975
25 Thumping Great Hits (—/Polydor), 1978

*Worth Searching Out:*
Greatest Hits (Epic/Columbia), 1966

# The Clash

UK group formed 1976.
**Original line-up:** Joe Strummer, vocals, guitar; Paul Simonon, bass; Mick Jones, guitar; Keith Levine, guitar; Terry Chimes, drums.

**Career:** Group formed in squat in London's Shepherd's Bush area in May 1976. Simonon and Jones were previously part of prototype punk outfit London SS and approached Strummer, then with 101ers. Keith Levine became group's second guitarist but was soon replaced by Nicky 'Topper' Headon. After several auditions, Terry Chimes (drums) completed line-up.

Moving headquarters to disused warehouse in Camden Town, group rehearsed under direction and guidance of manager Bernie Rhodes. An unpublicised appearance with the Sex Pistols(▶) was followed by their official unveiling in August 1976. The publicity afforded the Pistols and punk led to lucrative contract with CBS. Move regarded as treason by some hard-core punk fans. Nevertheless, the Clash quickly established themselves as one of the most forceful and committed spokesmen of the new wave; their impact was immediately felt.

First single **'White Riot'** reached No. 38 and was hailed as mini-classic of punk genre.

Debut album **The Clash** entered LP chart at No. 12. During same period, drummer Terry Chimes left, disillusioned with trappings of punk; antipathy felt by other members reflected on LP sleeve where Chimes is renamed Tory Crimes. An endless series of auditions followed before Nicky 'Topper' Headon was brought in as replacement.

Third single **Complete Control,** a riposte to CBS, was produced by Lee Perry and reached Top 30. Tour with Richard Hell and the Voidoids was followed by publicity in the form of group arrests on charges of petty vandalism and shooting racing pigeons. Another tour, appropriately titled 'The Clash Out On Parole', and new single, **White Man In Hammersmith Palais/The Prisoner,** maintained momentum.

Second LP **Give 'Em Enough Rope** hit No. 2 on album charts and provided first Top 20 hit single, **Tommy Gun.** Production by Sandy Pearlman caused further controversy amongst punk elite, who feared that Clash were being transformed into heavy-metal unit. Following split with manager Rhodes, group embarked on first US visit, dubbed the 'Pearl Harbour Tour'. Positive response from US critics helped subsequent career prospects.

Returning to UK, began work on film 'Rude Boy' (1980). On the day of Britain's General Election (May 11, 1979) **The Cost Of Living** (EP) was issued. Included a version of Bobby Fuller's **I Fought The Law.** Group's political credibility was promoted further by appearances at Rock Against Racism gigs. Another US tour saw group augmented by Blockheads' keyboardist Micky Gallagher.

Third LP, produced by Guy Stevens, was scheduled as **The New Testament,** a pretentious title finally dropped in favour of **London Calling.** Released in Christmas 1979 as a two for the price of one, the work was a strong seller. Follow up **Sandinista,** a triple album, followed same pattern, though less successfully.

Headon's increasingly idiosyncratic (drug related) behaviour resulted in his removal from group on eve of crucial US tour in May 1982. At short notice, Terry Chimes agreed to return to drummer's seat—a position he filled ably until December, when close-knit trio were once again diverted to search for a compatible cohort. Former Cold Fish Peter Howard was named in 1983.

**Below: Survivors of the London punk movement, the Clash.**

Clash have continued to reach wider audience without greatly diverging from original punk stance. Purists, however, would contend this. Their appearance on the cover of **Rolling Stone** caused strong ripples of indignation among punk hard core, but most mainstream critics accepted their political integrity and credited them for commitment and lack of obvious compromise. US Top 10

**London Calling, The Clash.
Courtesy CBS Records.**

breakthrough came with Glyn Johns' produced Combat Rock album in 1982. Band then played support on Who's 1982 farewell tour of US. New drummer Peter Howard joined in May 1983, but internal strife continued. Jones left to form own successful band Big Audio Dynamite, and was replaced by two guitarists, Vince White and Nick Shepherd, at beginning of 1984.

Fallow period was broken by release of delightfully titled 1985 album **Cut The Crap,** but band disintegrated before going on road.

At end of day, basic concept of band and volatile nature of members were always likely to ensure state of ongoing implosion.

**Current line-up:** Strummer; Simonon; Jones; Peter Howard, drums.

| Hit Singles: | US | UK |
|---|---|---|
| Tommy Gun, 1978 | — | 19 |
| London Calling, 1979 | — | 11 |
| Bank Robber, 1980 | — | 12 |
| Rock The Casbah, 1982 | 8 | 30 |
| Should I Stay Or Should I Go Straight To Hell, 1982 | — | 17 |

**Albums:**
The Clash (Columbia/CBS), 1977

Give 'Em Enough Rope (Columbia/CBS), 1978
London Calling (Columbia/CBS), 1979
Sandinista (Columbia/CBS), 1980
Combat Rock (Columbia/CBS), 1982
Cut The Crap (CBS), 1985

# The Coasters
US vocal group formed 1955.
**Original line-up:** Carl Gardner; Bobby Nunn; Billy Guy; Leon Hughes.

**Career:** Legendary vocal quartet who added large dose of fun to classic age of rock 'n' roll. Group have such an involved history that it took whole book ('The Coasters' by Bill Millar) to explain. The legend began in 1949 with Los Angeles group the Robins; they had local R&B hits on Savoy and RCA. Moving to Spark Records, incepted in 1954, scored big with R&B **Smokey Joe's Cafe.** Jerry Leiber and Mike Stoller's material became major factor in Coasters' success.

When Atlantic negotiated for acquisition of Spark, Robins' management didn't approve; Leiber and Stoller persuaded lead voice Carl Gardner and bassman Bobby Nunn to leave group. Joined Billy Guy and Leon Hughes to form Coasters; name derived from their west-coast origins. Debut **Down In Mexico** hit R&B Top 10. String of smash hits followed over next five years, with varying personnel; Nunn and Hughes left, replaced by Cornel Gunter and Will 'Dub' Jones, first session yielding **Yakety Yak,** Coasters' first pop chart topper in summer 1958.

Magical ingredients were Gardner's earthy, good-humoured tenor lead contrasted by Jones' rumbling bass; inventive Leiber/Stoller lyrics were punctuated by King Curtis'(▶) raunchy tenor sax solos and embellished by Mickey Baker's catchy guitar phrases. Songs like **Searching, Charlie Brown, Poison Ivy** and **Little Egypt** are rock 'n' roll classics.

Hits dwindled by late 1961; Cornel Gunter left, replaced by Earl Carroll from Cadillacs. Standards declined until 1964 when **'Tain't Nothin' To Me,** cut 'live' at the Apollo Theatre, was hit.

Connections with Leiber and Stoller were severed. Final Atco release revived Louis Jordan's jumping **Saturday Night Fish Fry.** In 1967 group signed with Columbia soul

subsidiary Date; produced again by Leiber and Stoller in contemporary idiom. **Soul Pad** and **She Can** resulted, artistically excellent but commercial failures. Solitary single appeared on Lloyd's Price's Turntable label in 1969.

In 1971 King Records bought all Date material, did doctoring in studio with overdubs, and hit with group's revival of Clovers'

**The Coasters' Greatest Hits. Courtesy Atco Records.**

**Love Potion No. 9.** Coasters continue to tour with varying personnel; managed another disc outing in 1976 on Wilson Pickett's Wicked label. Various line-ups capitalised on name throughout '70s and '80s, but the spirit had gone.

**1974 line-up:** Gardner; Earl Carroll; Ronnie Bright; Jimmy Norman.

| Hit Singles: | US | UK |
|---|---|---|
| Searchin'/Young Blood, 1957 | 3 | 30 |
| Young Blood/Searchin', 1957 | 8 | — |
| Yakkety Yak, 1958 | 1 | 12 |
| Charlie Brown, 1959 | 2 | 6 |
| Along Came Jones, 1959 | 9 | — |
| Poison Ivy, 1959 | 7 | 15 |

**Albums (selected):**
Greatest Hits (Atco/London), 1962
Greatest Hits (Power/—), 1979
Greatest Recordings/The Early Years (Atco/Atlantic), 1978
20 Great Originals (—/Atlantic), 1978
Juke Box Giants (—/Audio Fidelity) 1982
Thumbing A Ride (—/Edsel) 1985

# Eddie Cochran
US vocalist, guitarist, composer.
Born Oklahoma City, October 3, 1938; died April 17, 1960.

**Career:** Teamed with Hank Cochran (unrelated) as Cochran Brothers in 1954; recorded first single for Ekko label in hillbilly style. Met songwriter (later manager) Jerry Capehart in 1956 and signed to Crest Records in Los Angeles as solo. When first Crest single failed, Capehart negotiated contract with Liberty Records on strength of Cochran's successful audition for appearance in movie 'The Girl Can't Help It'. First Liberty single **Sittin' In The Balcony** became hit, and album that followed revealed soft pop style. Returned, however, to rock 'n' roll with subsequent singles and biggest US hit **Summertime Blues.**

Two further cameo appearances in typical exploitive rock 'n' roll movies failed to capture dynamic stage performance, but nationwide tours soon established Cochran as teen idol. Made first British appearances early in 1960 with Gene Vincent(▶) and popularity in UK much increased by spots on 'Boy Meets Girl' television show and tour of major UK theatres.

During tour many British guitarists were influenced by Cochran's individual style and tuning of Gretsch semi-acoustic guitar with humbucker pickup.

Interrupted British tour in April 1960 intending to make brief visit to Los Angeles, died as result of injuries received in car crash when returning to London for flight. Biggest UK hit in May marked beginning of cult following and subsequent releases included material culled from demo sessions and studio jams. Cochran had recorded extensively as solo and as sideman and tapes of hitherto unheard of performances are still being discovered and released.

Cochran's involvement in studio production and arranging (he was first artist to make own demos, and innovated multi-tracking techniques) revealed talents which could hardly have failed to influence popular music had he lived. However, his death did not stop his influence through songs and style which found reflection in New Wave records of '70s, notably the Sex Pistols(▶) covers of **Somethin' Else** and **C'mon Everybody**. The latter was re-released in 1988 to advertise a well-known brand of jeans.

Guitar: Semi-acoustic Gretsch.

| Hit Singles: | US | UK |
|---|---|---|
| Sittin' In The Balcony, 1957 | 18 | — |
| Summertime Blues, 1958 | 8 | 18 |
| C'mon Everybody, 1959 | 35 | 6 |
| Three Steps To Heaven, 1960 | — | 1 |
| Weekend, 1961 | — | 15 |

**Albums:**
Memorial Album (Liberty), 1960
C'mon Everybody (—/Sunset), 1970
Legendary Masters (United Artists), 1971
Very Best Of (15th Anniversary), 1975 Anniversary), 1975
Many Sides Of (—/Rollercoaster), 1979
A Legend In Our Time (Union Pacific), 1979
Cherished Memories (Liberty/EMI), 1983
25th Anniversary Album (Liberty), 1985
The Eddie Cochran Singles Album (United Artists), 1979
20th Anniversary Album (—/United Artists), 1980
Gene Vincent & Eddie Cochran — Together Again (Capitol), 1980
Gene Vincent & Eddie Cochran — Rock 'n' Roll Heroes (Rockstar), 1981
Words and Music (Rockstar), (United Artists) 1982
Rock 'N' Roll Greats (EMI), 1986
Somethin' Else (Capehart), 1987
Best of Eddie Cochran (EMI America), 1987 **CD**
Rock 'N' Roll Legend (Rockstar), 1987 **CD**

# Joe Cocker

UK vocalist, composer.
Born Sheffield, May 20, 1944.

**Career:** 'Blue-eyed soul' exponent Cocker joined brother Victor's Cavaliers skiffle group at 12 as drummer/harmonica player. Became hooked on rock 'n' roll, blues and, especially, music of Ray Charles(▶), on whom he based subsequent vocal style. First pro band was Big Blues, which evolved into Vance Arnold and the Avengers. Cocker was given six months' leave of absence by employers (the gas board), while he worked with band as support act for Rolling Stones(▶), Manfred Mann(▶) and Hollies(▶). Group's debut single, Beatles'(▶) song **I'll Cry Instead,** on Decca (1964), flopped. Cocker went back to work as gas fitter then as packer for magazine distributor before co-writing **Marjorine** with fellow Sheffield musician Chris Stainton; they sent demo to Denny Cordell (producer of Move

**Joe Cocker! Courtesy A&M Records.**

and Procol Harum), who secured release via Deram.

Cocker and bass player Stainton headed semi-pro Grease Band with Henry McCullough, guitar, Tommy Eyre, keyboards, and Kenny Slade, drums, playing Northern clubs and residency at Sheffield's King Mojo Club. Recorded limited issue live single for Sheffield University Rag Week. With **Marjorine,** issued under his name, hitting UK Top-50, Cocker moved to London. Follow-up single, a Ray Charles-styled cover of Lennon/McCartney's **With A Little Help From My Friends,** was massive European hit and title cut from debut album. It featured Grease Band plus guest musicians, including Jimmy Page(▶), Stevie Winwood(▶), Albert Lee and Procol Harum's(▶) drummer B.J. Wilson (who later became member of Cocker's touring band).

Success of record, plus appearance at Windsor Jazz and Blues Festival, made international reputation. During 1969 US tour Cocker appeared at Woodstock Festival and met Leon Russell(▶) who co-produced (with Cordell) his second album and hit single **Delta Lady**.

When Grease Band (except Stainton), went own way a year later, Bruce Rowland and Alan Spenner having replaced Eyre and Slade, Russell put together ambitious 40-strong musical entourage under title **Mad Dogs And Englishmen.** Tour yielded double album and movie of same title for Cocker. Excellent single **High Time We Went** made it to No. 22 in US

Unfortunately, Cocker failed to follow-up on success; though it seemed he was used to handling cigarettes and booze, he couldn't cope with drugs. His hyper-energetic stage performances and emotion-laden recordings contributed to near mental and physical collapse. Became temporary recluse on West Coast at end of Mad Dogs tour, later slipping home to UK to live with parents. Made one fleeting live appearance when called up on-stage by Rita Coolidge in 1971.

With help of Stainton, Cocker formed new 12-piece band for 1972 comeback tour of US, Britain and Australia, where he was busted on drugs charge. When band split, Stainton helped his friend put together combination of concert tapes and studio material for **Something To Say** album.

Had 1974 US hit with Billy Preston's(▶) **You Are So Beautiful.** Regular album releases were counterbalanced by repeated on and off-stage traumas and a succession of abortive comeback attempts as major live act. Made guest vocal appearance on Crusaders' Top 100 single **I'm So Glad** (1981)

Cocker's 1982 Island album, **Sheffield Steel,** mixed soul, rock and ballads and following its success Cocker contributed to soundtrack of hit movie 'An Officer And A Gentleman', recording ballad **Up Where We Belong** with Jennifer Warnes for his first US chart-topper. Since then, he has contributed **You Can Keep Your Hat On** to '9½ Weeks' movie soundtrack and successfully toured Europe, spring 1986 and winter 1987.

**Below: "Who's nicked me guitar?" Joe Cocker belts it out.**

| Hit Singles: | US | UK |
|---|---|---|
| With A Little Help From My Friends, 1968 | — | 1 |
| Delta Lady, 1969 | — | 10 |
| The Letter, 1970 | 7 | 39 |
| Cry Me A River, 1970 | 11 | — |
| You Are So Beautiful, 1974 | 5 | — |

*With Jennifer Warnes:*
| | | |
|---|---|---|
| Up Where We Belong, 1983 | 1 | 4 |

**Albums:**
With A Little Help From My Friends (A&M), 1969
Joe Cocker! (A&M), 1970
Mad Dogs And Englishmen (A&M), 1971
I Can Stand A Little Rain (A&M), 1974
Stingray (A&M), 1976
Luxury You Can Afford (Asylum), 1978
Platinum Collection (—/Cube), 1981
Sheffield Steel (Island), 1982
Space Captain (—/Cube), 1982
Civilised Man (Capitol), 1984 **CD**
Cocker (Capital), 1986 **CD**
Unchain My Heart (Capitol), 1987
The Joe Cocker Collection (Castle Classics), 1986 **CD**

# Lloyd Cole and the Commotions

UK group formed 1983

**Original/Current line-up:** Lloyd Cole, vocals, guitar; Blair Cowan, vocals, keyboards; Neil Clark, guitar; Lawrence Donegan, bass; Steven Irvine, drums.

**Career:** One of Britain's brightest new bands for the '80s, Lloyd Cole and the Commotions were conceived above infamous Tennant's Bar

**Mainstream, Lloyd Cole and the Commotions. Courtesy Polydor Records.**

in Glasgow's West End by Cole, Cowan and Clark and signed to management deal by Derek MacKellop who introduced Donegan and Irvine to complete line-up. With producer Paul Hardiman, band released debut single **Perfect Skin** in 1984 and quickly built strong reputation, enhanced by first album **Rattlesnakes**. Follow-up **Easy Pieces** spawned top twenty singles and confirmed band's early promise. Latterly, group have steadily increased following in Europe and UK, with 1987 LP **Mainstream** further strengthening credibility. Although Commotions can now fill arena-style venues, breakthrough to the first division is proving puzzlingly elusive.

| Hit Singles: | US | UK |
|---|---|---|
| Brand New Friend, 1985 | — | 19 |
| Lost Weekend, 1985 | — | 17 |
| Jennifer She Said, 1987 | — | 31 |

**Albums:**
Rattlesnakes (Polydor), 1984
Easy Pieces (Polydor), 1985
Mainstream (Polydor), 1987

| Sussudio, 1985 | 1 | 12 |
| One More Night, 1985 | 1 | 4 |
| Don't Lose My Number, 1985 | 4 | — |
| Take Me Home, 1985 | — | 19 |
| Separate Lives (with Marilyn Martin), 1985 | 1 | 4 |

**Albums:**
Face Value (Atlantic/Virgin), 1981 **CD**
Hello I Must Be Going (Atlantic/Virgin), 1982 **CD**
No Jacket Required (Atlantic/Virgin), 1985 **CD**

# Commodores

US group formed 1960s

**Original line-up:** Lionel Richie, vocals, tenor saxophone; William King, trumpet; Thomas McClary, guitar; Milan Williams, keyboards.

**Career:** Original four were school-friends in Tuskegee, Alabama; formed Commodores after merger of two other school groups, Mystics and Jays. With two additional musicians played local gigs and gained strong reputation.

Eventually signed management deal with Benjamin Ashburn who secured band New York gigs. At one of these, Commodores were spotted by Suzanne DePasse, Motown vice-president; result was support spot on Jackson Five(▶) worldwide tour. In 1972, band signed contract with Motown; two latest recruits had by this time moved on and been replaced by drummer and vocalist Walter 'Clyde' Orange and bass player Ronald LaPread.

After three singles had made impact on

**Below: Phil Collins, the man who appeared on both sides of the Atlantic in one day (courtesy Concorde) for Live Aid gigs.**

soul market, simple but effective instrumental **Machine Gun** became hit on both sides of Atlantic. This and another single, **Do The Bump,** helped **Machine Gun** LP to eventual gold status. Following initial success band toured with Rolling Stones(▶) and Stevie Wonder(▶).

From that time Commodores diversified material; **Sweet Love,** from 1975 album **Movin' On,** was melodic ballad, and showed direction in which writer Lionel Richie(▶) would lead group.

By late '70s group were a headlining international act, shipping platinum with every album. Band had also made impact with appearance in disco film 'Thank God It's Friday' with Donna Summer(▶); but high spot was 1978 single **Three Times A Lady.** Beautiful Richie-composed song went double platinum in US and became biggest-ever Motown single in UK, also gained numerous songwriting awards.

Following massive international hit with Diana Ross(▶) on movie theme **Endless Love,** Lionel Richie(▶) split to pursue highly successful solo career.

Black British singer J.D. Nicholas, formerly

**Zoom, the Commodores. Courtesy Motown Records.**

# Phil Collins

UK drummer, vocalist, keyboard player, composer.
Born London, January 31, 1951

**Career:** Former child actor—he played the Artful Dodger in stage version of 'Oliver Twist'—Collins joined Genesis(▶) as drummer after stint with Flaming Youth. He was brought forward as vocalist for group's 1976 album **A Trick Of The Tail** which promptly revived their flagging career.

In tandem with work as member of Genesis, Collins has played drums on all but one of six albums released by jazz-rock outfit Brand X.

In February 1981, issued first solo album **Face Value;** shot to top of UK album charts. In totally different musical vein to Genesis, Collins' solo sound got him UK No. 2 hit with **In The Air Tonight.** Then worked reggae backbeat and heavy percussion for compulsive **I Missed Again** hit single; also scored with **If Leaving Me Is Easy.** Magic of Earth Wind And Fire's(▶) brass section, great melodic songs and Collins' soul-tinged vocals added up to potent package. Not so inventive, however, was second solo set. Single **You Can't Hurry Love** was straight re-make of Supremes(▶) soul oldie, but it was what public wanted, rocketing to No. 1. Its success was aided by clever promotional video in which Collins appeared as cross between the Supremes and the Blues Brothers(▶).

With Genesis activities slowing down, new-found freedom for solo work found Collins involved in production. Worked with Adam Ant(▶), former Abba vocalist Frida(▶), John Martyn(▶) and Eric Clapton(▶).

**Above: Lloyd Cole, tipped with the Commotions to be stars of the '80s, have yet to reach a mainstream audience.**

Appetite for live work undiminished, 1983 saw US tour with Robert Plant under title of 'Principle Of Moments' and further concerts with Genesis.

In 1984 produced album for Earth, Wind and Fire(▶) vocalist Phillip Bailey. Collins and Bailey duetted on hit single, **Easy Lover.**

Year also saw inclusion on **Do They Know It's Christmas** single, in aid of Ethiopian Famine Appeal. With help of Concorde, featured in both US and UK Live Aid concerts on the same day.

Third solo LP **No Jacket Required,** movie songs **Against All Odds** and **Separate Lives** (with Marilyn Martin) and subsequent Grammy awards established Collins as major force in own right.

Collins has subsequently made the inevitable return into acting, having appeared as rock star in 'Miami Vice.' and as great train robber Buster Edwards in movie 'Buster', with Julie Walters.

Reluctance to adopt 'poseur' stance may restrict Collins efforts at more serious work, but as backbone of benefit (▶) resident side musician (most recently for Eric Clapton's UK gigs) and all round good egg, he is second to none.

| Hit Singles: | US | UK |
| --- | --- | --- |
| In The Air Tonight, 1981 | 19 | 2 |
| I Missed Again, 1981 | 19 | 14 |
| If Leaving Me Is Easy, 1981 | — | 17 |
| You Can't Hurry Love, 1982 | 10 | 1 |
| Against All Odds, 1984 | 1 | 2 |
| Easy Lover (with Philip Bailey), 1985 | 2 | 1 |

lead singer with Heatwave was brought in during 1984 to share lead vocals with Walter 'Clyde' Orange.

By group's 14th album, **Nightshift**, their total sales top 40-million unit mark. Band quit Motown February 1986.

**Current line-up:** Walter 'Clyde' Orange, vocals, drums; J.D. Nicholas, vocals; Milan Williams, keyboards; Ronald LaPraed, bass, piano, trumpet, drums, horns; William King, trumped, arp synthesisers, percussion.

**Hit Singles:**

| | US | UK |
|---|---|---|
| Machine Gun, 1974 | 22 | 20 |
| Slippery When Wet, 1975 | 19 | — |
| Sweet Love, 1976 | 5 | — |
| Easy, 1977 | 4 | 9 |
| Brickhouse/Sweet Love, 1977 | 5 | 32 |
| Three Times A Lady, 1978 | 1 | 1 |
| Just To Be Close To You, 1978 | 7 | — |
| Sail On, 1979 | 4 | 8 |
| Still, 1979 | 1 | 4 |
| Old Fashioned Love, 1980 | 20 | — |
| Lady (You Bring Me Up), 1981 | 8 | 56 |
| Oh No, 1981 | 4 | 44 |
| Nightshift, 1985 | 3 | 3 |
| Goin To The Bank, 1986 | — | 43 |

**Albums:**
Machine Gun (Motown), 1974
Caught In The Act (Motown), 1975
Movin' On (Motown), 1975
Hot On The Tracks (Motown), 1976
Commodores* (Motown), 1977
Live (Motown), 1978
Natural High (Motown), 1978 **CD**
Greatest Hits (Motown), 1978
Midnight Magic (Motown), 1979
Heroes (Motown), 1980
In The Pocket (Motown), 1981
All The Greatest Hits (Motown), 1982
13 (Motown), 1983
14 Greatest Hits (Motown), 1984 **CD**
Nightshift (Motown), 1985 **CD**
Best Of (Telstar), 1985
Rise Up (Blue Moon), 1987 **CD**
United (Polydor) **CD**
All The Great Love Songs (Motown) **CD**
*Titled **Zoom** in UK.

# The Communards

UK vocal/instrumental duo formed 1985.

**Original line-up:** Jimmy Somerville, vocals; Richard Coles, keyboards.

**Career:** Formed when vocalist Somerville quit chart act Bronski Beat and teamed up with long-time friend (and occasional Bronski sidekick) Coles, originally as The Committee, then renamed the Communards after 19th Century French radicals.

First two singles, grandiose ballad **You Are My World** and electro-disco **Disenchanted**, both failed to chart. Concentrated instead on series of benefit concerts (especially Gay Switchboard and Red Wedge) featuring full backing band of eight females. This line-up recorded debut LP **The Communards** which contained soul standard **Don't Leave Me This Way**.

Embracing sexual and social politics, Communards' musical mix of disco rhythms and soaring melodies found perfect match in lyrical combination of facts and frivolity on second LP **Red**. **Victims** and **If I Could Tell You** dealt with AIDS crisis, while another 70s classic, **Never Can Say Goodbye** was sheer exuberant dancefloor fun. Both this and **Tomorrow** became UK hits, maintaining impressive record for a duo determined to indulge in both frothy pop and serious polemics.

With Coles' classical training and Somer-

ville's angelic voice, Communards have all the necessary talent to transcend pointless categorisation and will continue to create serious emotional music with an irresistible dancebeat for some time to come.

**Hit Singles:**

| | US | UK |
|---|---|---|
| Disenchanted, 1986 | — | 29 |
| Don't Leave Me This Way, 1986 | — | 1 |
| So Cold the Night, 1986 | — | 8 |
| Tomorrow, 1987 | — | 23 |
| Never Can Say Goodbye, 1987 | — | 4 |

**Albums:**
Communards (London) 1986
Red (London), 1987

**Red, The Communards. Courtesy London Records.**

# Ry Cooder

US guitarist, vocalist, producer, arranger. Born Los Angeles, March 15, 1947.

**Career:** Former session player (predominantly slide guitar, also mandolin); one-time member of Taj Mahal(▶) and Captain Beefheart(▶) bands. Now fronts formidable R&B group consisting of keyboard players Jim Dickenson and William D. Smith, bass guitarist Tim Drummond, drummer Jim Keltner, percussionist Baboo and vocalists Bobby King, Willie Greene and Herman Johnson.

Worked on film scores 'Candy' and 'Performance' (which starred Mick Jagger) and made notable contribution to Rolling Stones'(▶) **Let It Bleed** album. Other sessions include Marc Benno, Crazy Horse(▶), Randy

Newman(▶), John Sebastian(▶) and Maria Muldaur(▶).

First solo LP **Ry Cooder** released by Reprise in 1970. Established Cooder's mean bottle-neck guitar style and strangled, authentic R&B vocalising. Has run entire musical heritage of America with more than a smattering of cajun and country, '20s and '30s swing (**Jazz**), eclectic (**Chicken Skin Music**), down-home R&B (**Borderline**) and further soundtrack albums (**The Long Riders**, **Southern Comfort**, **The Border**, **Paris, Texas** and **Alamo Bay**).

Cooder's work has never fallen into rock mainstream, and this has prevented permanent niche in upper reaches of album charts. Concerts, however, are a different matter, with Cooder now established as major stage performer, particularly in Britain; on bi-annual pilgrimage plays to capacity audiences.

True spirit of R&B is deeply implanted in this multi-talented veteran, and never better expounded than on Jimmy Reed's(▶) **How Can A Poor Man Stand Such Times And Live** from live **Show Time** album.

Guitars: Various Fenders, primarily 1968 Stratocaster, Washburn solid-body electric, Martin and Ovation acoustics; also Gibson F-style mandolin.

**Albums:**
Ry Cooder (Reprise) 1970
Into The Purple Valley (Reprise), 1971
Boomer's Story (Reprise), 1972
Paradise And Lunch (Reprise), 1974 **CD**
Chicken Skin Music (Warner Bros), 1976
Show Time (Warner Bros), 1977*
Jazz (Warner Bros), 1978
Bop Till You Drop (Warner Bros), 1979 **CD**
Borderline (Warner Bros), 1980 **CD**
The Long Riders (Warner Bros), 1980**
Southern Comfort (Warner Bros), 1981**
The Border (Warner Bros), 1982**
The Slide Area (Warner Bros), 1982
Paris, Texas (Warner Bros), 1985**
Music From Alamo Bay (Slash), 1985**
Blue City (Warner Bros), 1986
Crossroads (Warner Bros), 1986
Who Don't You Try Me Tonight (Warner Bros), 1986 **CD**
Get Rhythm (Warner Bros), 1987

\* Live
\*\* Soundtracks

**Left: Richard Coles (standing) and Jimmy Somerville — The Communards.**

**Borderline, Ry Cooder. Courtesy Warner Bros Records. The versatile Ry Cooder has experimented with Cajun, country, R&B, swing, and even rock.**

# Sam Cooke

US vocalist, composer. Born Chicago, Illinois, January 22, 1931; died December 11, 1964.

**Career:** Influential black performer/writer whose songs and vocal style have remained in vogue over three decades. Originally member of Soul Stirrers gospel group, Cooke turned to secular music in late '50s.

First hit **You Send Me** (1957) was followed by classics **Only Sixteen, Wonderful World, Cupid, Bring It On Home To Me** and **A Change Is Gonna Come**. He started own label Sar in 1960, recording Sims Twins, Johnnie Taylor, and the Valentinos.

Under aegis of Hugo & Luigi (who later groomed the Stylistics(▶)), Cooke remained chart-bound until his untimely demise: he was shot by a woman in December 1964, after entering wrong motel room. The courts ruled the shooting 'justifiable homicide'.

Cooke is still considered the definitive soul vocalist some 20 years after his death. His phrasing and articulation may never be surpassed. His material has since been recorded by Aretha Franklin(▶), Otis Redding(▶), Dawn, Rod Stewart(▶) and countless others.

**Hit Singles:**

| | US | UK |
|---|---|---|
| You Send Me/Summertime, 1957 | 1 | 29 |
| (I Love You) For Sentimental Reasons, 1958 | 17 | — |
| I'll Come Running Back To You, 1958 | 18 | — |
| Only Sixteen, 1959 | 28 | 13 |
| Wonderful World, 1960 | 12 | 27 |
| Chain Gang, 1960 | 2 | 9 |
| Cupid, 1961 | 17 | 7 |
| Twistin' The Night Away, 1962 | 9 | 6 |
| Having A Party, 1962 | 17 | — |
| Bring It On Home To Me, 1963 | 10 | 23 |

| | US | UK |
|---|---|---|
| Nothing Can Change This Love, 1962 | 12 | — |
| Another Saturday Night, 1963 | 10 | 23 |
| Frankie And Johnny, 1963 | 14 | 30 |
| Send Me Some Lovin', 1963 | 13 | — |
| Little Red Rooster, 1963 | 11 | — |
| Good News, 1964 | 11 | — |
| Good Times, 1964 | 11 | — |
| Shake, 1965 | 7 | — |
| Wonderful World, 1986 | — | 3 |

**Albums:**
Best Of (RCA/—), 1961
Golden Age Of (RCA/—), 1969
Two Sides Of (Specialty/Sonet), 1971
This Is Sam Cooke (RCA), 1971
When I Fall In Love (—/EMI), 1979
Mr Soul (—/RCA), 1980
When I Fall In Love (Arena), 1987
20 Greatest Hits (the compact collection), 1987 **CD**
You Send Me (the collection), 1987 **CD**

# Alice Cooper

US vocalist, composer.
Born Vincent Furnier, Detroit, Michigan, February 4, 1948.

**Career:** Raised in Phoenix, Arizona. Formed first band at high school, which performed variously as Spiders, Earwigs, Nazz. Members included Glen Buxton (guitar), Michael Bruce (guitar, keyboards), Dennis Dunaway (bass), and Neal Smith (drums). Recorded locally with minor success.

After move to Los Angeles, group changed name to Alice Cooper. Signed to Frank Zappa's Straight label in 1969 by manager Shep Gordon. Debut LP **Pretties For You** released 1969.

After running up massive debts, outfit shifted to Detroit, working under aegis of Bob Ezrin. First album produced by Ezrin **Love It To Death** earned group instant credibility, and first chart single **I'm 18.**

As a live act, Alice Cooper's (his name alone attracted enough attention) bizarre antics disguised mediocrity of performance. Nevertheless, band was now on frontline of rock scene; scored further chart successes including million-selling **School's Out.**

1974 saw wholesale change of group personnel; Cooper recruited former Lou Reed(▶) sidemen Dick Wagner (guitar), Prakash John (bass), Steve Hunter (guitar), Whitney (Panti) Glan (drums), and Josef Chirowski (keyboards).

Last major tour undertaken in 1975 after release of **Welcome To My Nightmare.** Cooper's long-term drink problem caused period of inactivity. Had re-think in face of developing punk scene (which made band's formerly outrageous tactics seem about as revolutionary as a Pat Boone concert).

During '80s Cooper has made persistent attempts at comeback, particularly in '82 with new band and album **Special Forces.** At time of writing, rock iconoclast and golf fanatic Cooper was embarking upon European tour.

| **Hit Singles:** | US | UK |
|---|---|---|
| School's Out, 1972 | 7 | — |
| Only Women Bleed, 1975 | 12 | — |
| I Never Cry, 1976 | 12 | — |
| You And Me, 1977 | 9 | — |
| How You Gonna See Me Now, 1978 | 12 | — |

**Albums:**
Love It To Death (Warner Bros), 1971
Killer (Warner Bros), 1971
School's Out (Warner Bros), 1972
Billion Dollar Babies (Warner Bros), 1973
Greatest Hits (Warner Bros), 1974
Welcome To My Nightmare (ATCO/Anchor), 1974
Goes To Hell (Warner Bros), 1976

Lace And Whiskey (Warner Bros), 1977
Alice Cooper Show (Warner Bros), 1977
From The Inside (Warner Bros), 1978
Flush The Fashion (Warner Bros), 1980
Special Forces (Warner Bros), 1981
Zipper Catches Skin (Warner Bros), 1982
Da Da (Warner Bros), 1983
Constrictor (MCA), 1986
Freak Out Song (Showcase), 1986
Raise Your Fist And Yell (MCA), 1987 **CD**

# Elvis Costello

UK composer, vocalist, guitarist.
Born Declan McManus, London, August 25, 1954.

**Career:** After unsuccessful early career in pub/country-rock band Flip City, Costello (son of erstwhile Joe Loss Band singer Ross McManus) took demo tapes in 1976 to then fledgling Stiff label. Jake Riviera was impressed enough not only to sign Declan, but also to manage him. With name change to Elvis Costello, first three singles built strong cult following, and debut LP reached UK Top 20, backing provided by San Francisco band Clover, performing under name of the Shamrocks.

**Imperial Bedroom, Elvis Costello. Courtesy F-Beat Records.**

June 1977 saw formation of permanent backing group, the Attractions. Pete Thomas (drums, ex-Chilli Willi), Bruce Thomas (bass, ex-Quiver) and Steve Nieve (keyboards, ex-Royal Academy of Music). Elvis and band toured with first Stiff Records package along with Ian Dury(▶) Nick Lowe(▶) (who had produced all Costello records up to this point), Dave Edmunds(▶) and Wreckless Eric—concurrently scored first Top 20 hit with **Watching The Detectives.**

By early 1978 had made major US impact; moved with Riviera and Lowe to newly formed Radar label; three Top 30 hits followed in 1978, plus second acclaimed album; third LP released during first days of 1979. Biggest UK hit so far was **Oliver's Army;** 1979 also saw production of first LP by the Specials(▶) and collapse of Radar Records. Riviera subsequently set up new F-Beat label, launched with Top 5 Costello single, **I Can't Stand Up For Falling Down** (cover of ancient Sam & Dave song). Made further hit singles (although smaller successes) during 1980, plus classic LP **Get Happy.**

1981 chiefly notable for release of Billy Sherrill-produced country LP **Almost Blue,** which polarised fans. Played concert at Royal Albert Hall with Royal Philharmonic Orchestra at start of 1982. Rest of year saw return to original abrasive style—thoughtful, meaningful, but often bitter songs—with **Imperial Bedroom** LP.

1984 album **Goodbye Cruel World** was also well received, and in that year Costello also performed theme tune of and acted in UK TV series 'Scully'.

During 1984 and 1985 Costello toured extensively without regular backing band The Attractions, and also scored a personal success at the 1985 Live Aid concert. His acting career continued with a cameo role in the Liverpool-set black comedy movie 'No Surrender'.

1986 album **King Of America,** featuring US West Coast session men, created new wave of approval for mercurial artist, acclaim which continued next year with **Blood and Chocolates** set.

Universally acknowledged as great songwriter, Costello provides welcome dose of gritty intelligence amidst pap and pretentiousness which make up most of pop and rock scene. Greatest potential possibly still yet to be realized.

Guitar: Fender Jaguar.

**Below: Elvis Costello, a diverse talent, with the Attractions.**

| **Hit Singles:** | US | UK |
|---|---|---|
| Watching The Detectives, 1977 | — | 15 |
| (I Don't Want To Go To) Chelsea, 1977 | — | 16 |
| Oliver's Army, 1979 | — | 2 |
| I Can't Stand Up For Falling Down, 1980 | — | 4 |
| Good Year For The Roses, 1981 | — | 6 |

**Albums:**
My Aim Is True (Columbia/Stiff), 1977 **CD**
This Year's Model (Columbia/F-Beat), 1978 **CD**
Armed Forces (Columbia/Radar), 1979 **CD**
Get Happy (Columbia/F-Beat), 1980 **CD**
Trust (Columbia/F-Beat), 1981 **CD**
Almost Blue (Columbia/F-Beat), 1981 **CD**
Imperial Bedroom (Columbia/F-Beat), 1982 **CD**
Goodbye Cruel World (Columbia/F-Beat), 1984 **CD**
Punch The Clock (Columbia/F-Beat), 1984 **CD**
The Best Of (Telstar), 1985
King Of America (Columbia/F-Beat), 1986 **CD**
Out Of Our Idiot (Demon), 1986 **CD**
The Man (Demon), 1987 **CD**
Blood and Chocolate (IMP), 1986 **CD**
10 Bloody Marys (Demon), 1984 **CD**

# Randy Crawford

US vocalist, composer.
Born Macon, Georgia, 1952.

**Career:** Prime claimant to title 'Queen of '80s Soul', Randy Crawford manages to mix deep-soul stylings of South with urban disco-slant.

Raised in Cincinnati, Ohio, grounded in gospel, she became regular night club performer from 15. During school holidays she had two-week gig in St Tropez, France, which was extended to three months and brought record deal offers, but she returned to US to complete education and take six-night-a-week stint at Cincinnati's Buccaneer Club.

On graduation, moved to New York where she sang with George Benson(▶) before signing with Cannonball Adderley's manager John Levy and guesting on Adderley's final

album **Big Man**.

Shifting base to Los Angeles, Randy appeared before capacity 5,500 audience at Shrine Auditorium as part of World Jazz Association all-star package in tribute concert to Adderley who had just died. Show was taped and some of her set was used on her 1980s' Warner Bros album, **Everything Must Change**, acceptance of which led to formation of own five-piece band.

First writer credit came with **I Got Myself A Happy Song** on second album **Raw Silk** (1979).

Though uncredited on label, Randy was chosen to sing vocal on titletrack of Crusaders' (▶) **Street Life** album, a transatlantic hit which established her reputation. Subsequently she undertook two successful European tours with Crusaders, who became involved with producing **Now We May Begin** set, star cut of which was haunting Joe Sample ballad **One Day I'll Fly Away**, Crawford's first major hit single (winning her Most Outstanding Performance award at 1980 Tokyo Music Festival).

Veteran West Coast producer Tommy LiPuma came in for **Secret Combination** LP from which **You Might Need Somebody** was perfect sample of her wistful and soul-searching style.

Though lacking raw power of Etta James or Aretha Franklin(▶), or pure commericalism of Diana Ross(▶), Randy Crawford has displayed rare penchant for understated performances which nevertheless wring last drop of emotion from a song.

**Hit Singles:**

| | US | UK |
|---|---|---|
| Street Life (featured vocalist with Crusaders), 1979 | 36 | 5 |
| One Day I'll Fly Away, 1980 | — | 2 |
| You Might Need Somebody, 1981 | — | 11 |
| Rainy Night In Georgia, 1981 | — | 18 |
| Almaz, 1986 | — | 4 |

**Albums:**
Miss Randy Crawford (Warner Bros), 1977
Raw Silk (Warner Bros), 1979
Now We May Begin (Warner Bros), 1980
Everything Must Change (Warner Bros), 1980
Secret Combination (Warner Bros), 1981 **CD**
Windsong (Warner Bros), 1982
Nightline (Warner Bros), 1983 **CD**
The Greatest Hits (K-Tel), 1984
Abstract Emotions (Warner Bros), 1986 **CD**

**Below: Southern soulstress Randy Crawford**

# Cream

UK group formed 1966.

**Original/final line-up:** Eric Clapton, guitar; Jack Bruce, vocals, bass; Ginger Baker, drums.

**Career:** Clapton(▶), previously with John Mayall's Bluesbreakers(▶), joined forces with former Graham Bond Organization sidemen Bruce(▶) and Baker(▶) with object of forming blues supergroup. Immediate acclaim followed first gig at 1966 Windsor Festival.

First album, **Fresh Cream,** revealed winning format of blues-influenced songs plus extended improvised solos. Group also had ability to come up with hit singles, and during just over two years of existence scored with handful of unusual but effective cuts which, although showcasing Clapton's guitar work, were remarkably restrained and inventive by comparison with the products of later 'power trios'.

From 1967, however, band spent most of time in US where they had quickly gained huge reputation. Every Cream album exceeded sales of one million dollars, and gigs throughout country were standing room only.

In 1968, however, members decided that outfit had run its course, and in autumn played farewell concert at London's Royal Albert Hall. Shortly afterwards recorded last album, **Goodbye.**

Although somewhat given to overstatement, especially in live context—thunderous volume and seemingly endless solos being order of day—Cream were highly influential band; they set pattern for 'power trio' format, later endlessly copied by generally lesser talents. Group also acted as springboard to superstardom for Clapton, and to lesser extent for other members. Immediately following demise of band Clapton and Baker became involved in short-lived Blind Faith(▶), while Bruce took up solo career.

**Hit Singles:**

| | US | UK |
|---|---|---|
| I Feel Free, 1966 | — | 11 |
| Strange Brew, 1967 | — | 17 |
| Sunshine Of Your Love, 1968 | 5 | 25 |
| White Room, 1968 | 6 | 28 |
| Badge, 1969 | 60 | 18 |

**Albums:**
Fresh Cream (RSO/Polydor), 1966 **CD**
Disraeli Gears (RSO/Polydor), 1967 **CD**

**Fresh Cream, the first Cream album. Courtesy Atco Records.**

Wheels Of Fire (RSO/Polydor), 1968 **CD**
Goodbye (RSO/Polydor), 1969 **CD**
Cream Live (RSO/Polydor), 1970 **CD**
Cream Live 2 (RSO/Polydor), 1972 **CD**
Off The Top (RSO/—), 1972
Heavy Cream (RSO/Polydor), 1973
Cream (—/Polydor), 1975
Cream Volume 2 (—/RSO), 1978
The Very Best Of Vols I & II (Polydor), 1983

Original version of Fresh Cream on Atco has more tracks.

# Creedence Clearwater Revival

US group, formed 1967.

**Original line-up:** John Fogerty, vocals, guitar; Tom Fogerty, rhythm guitar; Stu Cook, bass; Doug 'Cosmo' Clifford, drums.

**Career:** While attending junior high school in San Francisco Bay area of El Cerritto, foursome got together as Tommy Fogerty and the Blue Velvets. Locally based Fantasy Records offered recording deal on proviso that band changed name to the Golliwogs (in attempt to cash-in on then current British beat boom). Band reluctantly agreed and debut single was released in 1965. Further singles followed but none made impact except local hit **Brown Eyed Girl**. Group evolved new 'swamp rock' style based on mixture of R&B and cajun rhythms. They persuaded label's new boss Saul Zaentz to agree to change of name to Creedence Clearwater Revival.

New sound and image coincided with San Francisco rock music explosion. Band's eponymous debut album, a mix of rock 'n' roll/R&B standards and John Fogerty originals, made immediate impression. Two singles were lifted simultaneously. A version of Dale Hawkins' oldie **Suzie Q** registered first in charts then classy reading of Screamin' Jay Hawkins' **I Put A Spell On You** also scored.

Group's albums were essentially collections of potential hits and CCR went against then current trend by remaining singles-orientated. John Fogerty-penned **Proud Mary** became instant rock/soul standard, eliciting superb cover versions by Solomon Burke, Arif Mardin,

Ike and Tina Turner(▶) and others. Checkmates Limited's version of song (masterminded by Phil Spector) was reputed to be most expensively produced single ever, several hundred musicians having been used on sessions.

Despite CCR's San Francisco origins, their spiritual home was deep in bayou country of the Southern states. Their songs like **Bad Moon Rising, Lodi, Born On The Bayou** and **Green River** were epics of swamp rock genre.

Fifth CCR album **Cosmo's Factory** included three gold singles (**Travellin' Band, Up Around The Bend** and **Lookin' Out My Back Door**) plus incisive 11-minute version of Marvin Gaye(▶)/Gladys Knight and the Pips'(▶) Motown classic **I Heard It Through The Grapevine.**

Produced, arranged and largely written by John Fogerty, CCR's music was amazingly tight. It relied almost entirely on band's own integral musicianship rather than depending on studio over-dubs (aside from occasional addition of saxophone). Musical togetherness was not matched on personal front, however. Tom Fogerty quit following differences with others. They continued as trio for world tour

**Creedence Clearwater Revival. Courtesy Fantasy Records.**

which yielded **Creedence—Live In Europe** album.

John Fogerty's increasing dominance caused further dissension. In what has come to be known as 'Fogerty's Revenge', he allowed Cook and Clifford equal creative participation in **Mardi Gras** album. Result was total disaster, lambasted by critics and leading to band's dissolution in October 1972.

Tom Fogerty went on to record moderately successful albums and his **Joyful Resur-**

**rection** single, cut with Cook and Clifford, was, he said, the story of CCR.

Clifford's solo outing was far less satisfactory. He continued working with Cook, however, as respected session rhythm team. They went on to join the Don Harrison Band.

Meanwhile, John Fogerty made low-key solo debut with **Blue Ridge Rangers** albums; he claimed it was made by group of that name but LP proved to be all his own work: he arranged, produced, played all instruments and sang. His re-make of Hank Williams'(▶) country oldie **Jambalaya** was US hit, as was version of **Hearts Of Stone**.

Protracted dispute with Fantasy Records caused three-year gap before he emerged with new Asylum deal, Top 30 hit single **Rockin' All Over The World** (covered in UK by Dave Edmunds)(▶) and applauded **John Fogerty** album. Excellent **Centrefold** set caused further legal wrangles over **Zanz Kant Danz** track—a dig at Fantasy's bossman. Fogerty's boundless enthusiasm certainly revived memories of CCR, despite that theirs was very much a 'sixties' sound. The advent of electro-pop has been given short shrift by this purveyor of traditional rock'n'roll.

**Final line-up:** John Fogerty; Cook; Clifford.

| Hit Singles: | US | UK |
|---|---|---|
| Suzie Q (Part 1), 1968 | 11 | — |
| Proud Mary, 1969 | 2 | 8 |
| Bad Moon Rising, 1969 | 2 | 1 |
| Green River, 1969 | 2 | 19 |
| Down On The Corner/Fortunate Son, 1969 | 3 | 31 |
| Fortunate Son/Down On The Corner, 1969 | 14 | — |
| Travellin' Band/Who'll Stop The Rain, 1970 | 2 | 8 |
| Who'll Stop The Rain/Travellin' Band, 1970 | 13 | — |
| Up Around The Bend, 1970 | 4 | 3 |
| Lookin' Out My Back Door, 1970 | 2 | — |
| Have You Ever Seen The Rain, 1971 | 8 | 36 |
| Sweet Hitchhiker, 1971 | 6 | 36 |

*John Fogerty Solo:*
| | | |
|---|---|---|
| Old Man Down The Road, 1985 | 10 | — |
| Rock And Roll Girls, 1985 | 20 | — |

**Albums:**
Creedance Clearwater Revival (Fantasy), 1968 **CD**
Bayou Country (Fantasy), 1969 **CD**
Green River (Fantasy), 1969 **CD**
Willy And The Poor Boys (Fantasy), 1969 **CD**
Cosmo's Factory (Fantasy), 1970 **CD**
Pendulum (Fantasy), 1971
Mardi Gras (Fantasy), 1972
Gold (Fantasy), 1972
More Gold (Fantasy), 1973
Live In Europe (Fantasy), 1973
Golliwogs (Fantasy), 1975.

*John Fogerty Solo:*
John Fogerty (Asylum), 1975
Centrefield (Warner Bros), 1985
The Collection (Impression), 1985

*Worth Searching Out:*
*Tom Fogerty:*
Tom Fogerty (Fantasy), 1972
*John Fogerty:*
Blue Ridge Rangers (Fantasy), 1973
*Doug Clifford:*
Doug 'Cosmo' Clifford (Fantasy), 1972

# Crosby, Stills, Nash & Young

US group formed 1968.

**Original/Current line-up:** David Crosby, guitar; Stephen Stills, vocals, guitar; Graham Nash, vocals, guitar.

**Career:** Band formed without Young(▶) as Crosby, Stills and Nash; Crosby came from Byrds(▶), Stills(▶) from Buffalo Springfield(▶) and Nash from UK 'beat group' The Hollies(▶). Debut album **Crosby Stills And Nash** released in 1969 to critical and commercial success. Semi-acoustic soft-rock with accent on vocal harmonies, music combined commercial appeal with 'sensitivity', occasional banality camouflaged by slickness. Album went gold and single from it, **Marrakesh Express**, charted in US and UK.

Looking to fill out sound, band recruited another ex-Buffalo Springfield alumnus, Neil Young(▶), then pursuing solo career. Young's chunky guitar and sombre vocals became major asset, and his songwriting ability gave authority to repertoire. **Deja Vu**, with added talents of bass-player Greg Reeves and drummer Dallas Taylor, also went gold. Critical plaudits tipped in favour of Young's contributions. Lyrical content was timely and in keeping with appearance at Woodstock festival.

Disappointing live set, **Four Way Street**, followed in 1971, but band members were already beginning to take individual directions and CSN & Y folded that year. Crosby and Nash continued to work as duo until late '70s; Stills took up threads of erratically successful solo career; and Young went on to become enigmatic rock superstar.

In 1977, Crosby, Stills and Nash cut reunion album **CSN**, before splitting and regrouping again in 1982.

Incarceration of Crosby for drug offence in 1985 should have sounded death knell for band. However, late 1987 saw yet another reformation, shortly after Crosby's release.

Old hippies never die, they simply fade away …and reform…and fade away…and reform again.

**Current line-up;** Crosby; Stills; Nash.

| Hit Singles: | US | UK |
|---|---|---|
| Marrakesh Express (without Young), 1969 | — | 17 |
| Woodstock, 1970 | 11 | — |
| Teach Your Children, 1970 | 16 | — |
| Ohio, 1970 | 14 | — |
| Just A Song Before I Go (without Young), 1977 | 7 | — |

**Albums:**
Crosby, Stills & Nash (Atlantic), 1969 **CD**
Deja Vu (Atlantic), 1970 **CD**
Four Way Street (Atlantic), 1972 **CD**
So Far (Atlantic), 1974 **CD**
CSN (Atlantic), 1977
Replay (Atlantic), 1980
Daylight Again (Atlantic), 1982
Allies (Atlantic), 1983 **CD**

*Crosby/Nash:*
Graham Nash & David Crosby (Atlantic), 1972
Wind On The Water (Polydor), 1975

*David Crosby Solo:*
If I Could Only Remember My Name (Atlantic), 1971

# Culture Club

UK group formed 1981.

**Original/Current line-up:** Boy George, (George O'Dowd) vocals; Jon Moss, drums, percussion; Roy Hay, guitar, keyboards; Michael Craig, bass.

**Career:** Modern-day Myra Breckinridge Boy George (ex-Bow Wow Wow(▶)) formed Culture Club with drummer Jon Moss (ex-Clash(▶), Damned(▶), Adam & Ants(▶)) from remnants of Praise of Lemmings. Recruiting Roy Hay

**Above: Boy George, singer, wit, raconteur, now developing a solo career.**

and Mickey Craig, band recorded debut **Kissing To Be Clever** set in 1982 and scored in US/UK single charts with **Do You Really Want To Hurt Me**, a slick piece of pop reggae.

Striving for missing link between soul and modern white electronic music, the Club came close with second single, **Time (Clock Of The Heart)**. Bizarre persona—though centred round George, rest of group was also highly visual—and extremely catchy material like

**Kissing To Be Clever, Culture Club. Courtesy Virgin Records.**

**Church Of The Poison Mind**, **Karma Chameleon** and **Victims** (haunting melodies surprisingly imaginative lyrics) made Culture Club the sensation of their time and proved there is always room in pop charts for good ballads.

Despite George's avowed bi-sexuality and his transvestite dress style, group managed to appear amazingly wholesome. Many were entertained but surprisingly few were outraged even in US. George's friendly nature and quick

**Below: Creedence Clearwater Revival, who enjoyed three-year tenure in US/UK pop charts. John Fogerty (centre) has revived bayou sound with mid-eighties albums.**

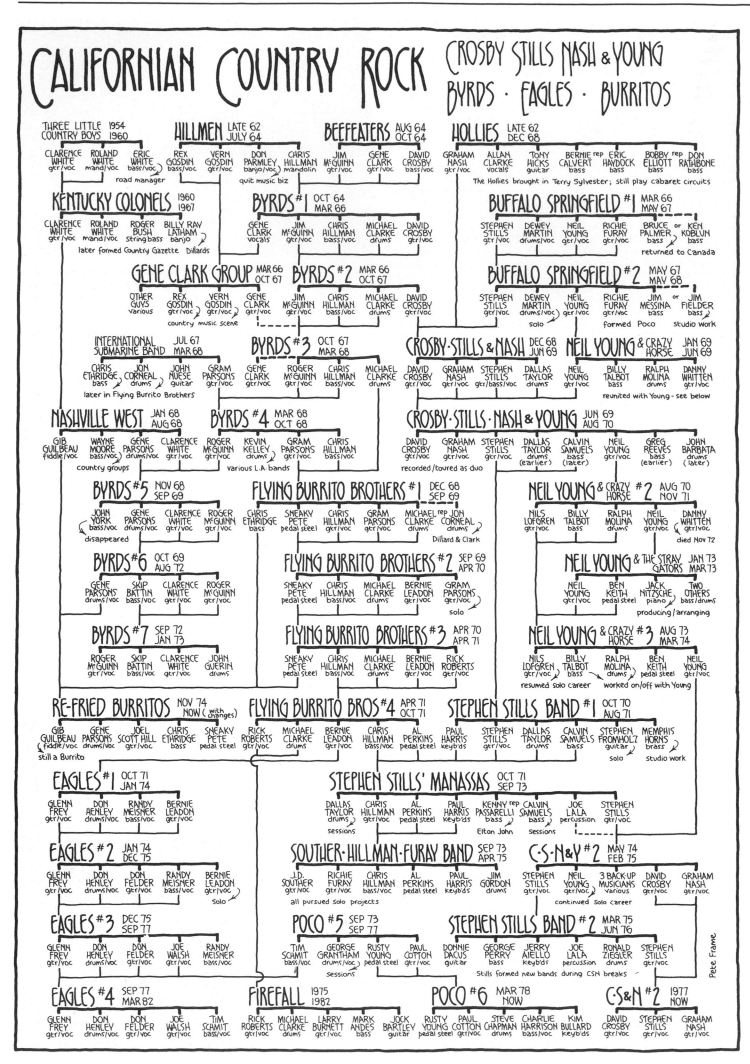

# CALIFORNIAN COUNTRY ROCK
## CROSBY STILLS NASH & YOUNG
## BYRDS · EAGLES · BURRITOS

wit—'I'd rather ahve a cup of tea than sex', he once quipped—won him friends.

Culture Club peaked out in 1984 with three Top Twenty US singles and two Top Ten UK singles. Fallow period in 1985 was broken by **From Luxury To Heartache** set, which spawned hit single **Move Away**.

But it seemed that glory years were over for band, as column inches were increasingly filled by stories concerning George's personal life, in particular his drug problems. Situation was exacerbated by death in George's home of US musician/friend Michael Rudetski, although singer was finally exonerated of all blame.

However, just when critics had written singer off, George bounced back with cover version of Ken Boothe's **Everything I Own** (itself a reggae cover of Bread's original hit.) Simple, catchy arrangement and George's heartfelt vocals made song a massive hit.

A major vocal talent, Boy George has also formed something of a reputation as a wit and raconteur — a kind of Quentin Crisp of the rock world. Provided he avoids tendency to self-destruct, Boy George seems likely to prove more durable than most.

| Hit Singles: | US | UK |
|---|---|---|
| Do You Really Want To Hurt Me, 1982 | 3 | 1 |
| Time (Clock Of The Heart), 1982 | 2 | 1 |
| I'll Tumble 4 U, 1983 | 9 | — |
| Church Of The Poison Mind, 1983 | 10 | 2 |
| Karma Chameleon, 1983 | 1 | 1 |
| Victims, 1983 | — | 3 |
| Miss Me Blind, 1984 | 5 | |
| It's A Miracle, 1984 | 13 | 4 |
| The War Song, 1984 | 17 | 2 |
| Sold, 1987 | — | 24 |
| To Be Reborn, 1987 | — | 13 |

*Boy George solo:*

| | | |
|---|---|---|
| Everything I Own, 1987 | — | 1 |

**Albums:**
Kissing To Be Clever (Epic/Virgin), 1982 **CD**
Colour By Numbers (Epic/Virgin), 1983 **CD**
Waking Up With The House On Fire (Virgin), 1984 **CD**
From Luxury To Heartache (Virgin), 1986
Sold (Virgin) 1987, **CD**

# The Cure

UK group formed 1977.

**Original line-up:** Robert Smith, vocals, guitar; Michael Dempsey, bass; Lol Tolhurst, drums.

**Career:** Signed originally to German label Hansa but dropped immediately, then released **Killing An Arab** single (based on 'The Outsider' novel by Camus) on indie label Small Wonder. Linked up with producer Chris Parry who signed them to his newly-formed Fiction Records, releasing **Three Imaginary Boys** debut LP and two sharp pop singles **Boys Don't Cry** and **Jumping Someone Else's Train**; both failed to chart.

Gained cult following for taut, angst-ridden, post-punk pop songs, but when Dempsey left, group expanded to four-piece (with Simon Gallup on bass and Matthieu Hartley on keyboards), gaining denser less concise sound. Second LP, **17 Seconds** was minor progression into complex arrangements but featured classic single of paranoia **A Forest**.

Subsequent LPs, **Faith** and **Pornography** found Smith dominating writing credits with dreary slabs of self-despairing dirges. First Hartley, then Gallup, left and Tolhurst decided to abandon drums and learn keyboards. Smith, meanwhile, joined Siouxsie & Banshees as guitarist, helping write and record **Hyaena** LP, as well as collaborating with Banshee bassist Severin on short-lived project The Glove. The Cure, it seemed, were dead.

But late 1982 saw Smith and Tolhurst re-unite for hypnotic **Let's Go To Bed** single, followed by **The Walk**, which charted. Recruited Andy Anderson (drums) and **Pornography** producer Phil Thornalley (bass) for **Lovecats**, a jazz-tinged fantasy single which destroyed Cure's reputation for gloom and established Smith as sexy pin-up star with smudged lipstick. **The Top** LP followed and Smith quit the Banshees to concentrate on revitalised Cure.

Line-up stabilised as Gallup returned on bass, Boris Williams joined on drums and extra guitarist Porl Thomson was added. Playfully disturbed **Head On The Door** LP boasted UK hit singles **In between Days** and **Close To Me** both showcased by delightfully zany videos.

**Kiss Me, Kiss Me, Kiss Me** double LP was a dazzling array of styles and content, crowning band's triumphant metamorphosis from pretentious pop philosophers to confident, teasing, beguiling contemporary artists, without sacrificing early punk ideals. Singles **Why Can't I Be You?** and **Catch** plus feature film 'The Cure In Orange' and sell-out tours confirm band's position as one of the most influential and vital of today's new underground pop establishment.

**Current line-up:** Smith, vocals, guitar; Tolhurst, keyboards; Simon Gallup, bass; Porl Thompson, guitar; Boris Williams, drums.

| Hit Singles: | US | UK |
|---|---|---|
| The Walk, 1983 | — | 12 |
| The Love Cats, 1983 | — | 7 |
| The Caterpillar, 1984 | — | 14 |
| In Between Days, 1985 | — | 15 |
| Close To Me, 1985 | — | 24 |
| Boys Don't Cry, 1986 | — | 2 |
| Just Like Heaven, 1987 | 40 | 29 |

**Albums:**
Three Imaginary Boys (Fiction), 1979
Faith (Fiction), 1980 **CD**
Seventeen Seconds (Fiction), 1980 **CD**
Japanese Whispers (Fiction/Sire), 1980
Pornography (Fictioh/A&M), 1982 **CD**
Boys Don't Cry (Fiction), 1983 **CD**
The Cure Live (Fiction), 1984 **CD**
The Top (Fiction/Sire), 1984 **CD**
The Hanging Garden (Fiction), 1985

**Below: The Cure, whose post-punk music seeks a wider audience towards the end of the '80s.**

Head On The Door (Fiction), 1985 **CD**
Standing On A Beach (Fiction/Elektra), 1986—the singles
Kiss Me Kiss Me Kiss Me (Fiction), 1987—double **CD**

# Cutting Crew

US band formed 1982.

**Original line-up:** Nick Van Eede, vocals, guitar; Kevin McMichael, guitar; Colin Farley, bass.

**Career:** First hit **(I Just) Died In Your Arms** on Siren elevated Cutting Crew to number 4 in the UK charts followed by **I've Been In Love Before** the same year. Four major tours in one year found them working with The Bangles, Huey Lewis and Starship.

Cutting Crew rapidly built up a strong European following, from Finland to Italy, and played both San Remo and Montreux festivals before flying to Japan to pick up an award for the best new rock band at the Tokyo Music Festival. Their appeal has even extended to China where they are one of the few Western rock acts to play live, appearing before an audience of 10,000 at one single gig.

Debut album **Broadcast** has notched up over 1m sales and Cutting Crew have had some 20 number one hit singles around the world including Canada and the US (which also gave Virgin its first US number one). Band now augmented by keyboards player Tony Moore, one-time member of Iron Maiden. With a

**Above: The phenomenal popularity of Cutting Crew around the world has given them more than 20 number 1 hit singles.**

capacity for haunting melodies and intelligent lyrics, Cutting Crew's worldwide success should continue to run a smooth course.

**Current line-up:** Van Eede; McMichael; Farley; Tony Moore, keyboards.

| Hit Singles: | US | UK |
|---|---|---|
| I Just Died In Your Arms, 1986 | 1 | 4 |
| I've Been In Love Before, 1986 | 9 | 24 |
| One for The Mockingbird, 1987 | 38 | — |

**Albums:**
Broadcast (Siren/Virgin), 1986 **CD**

**Broadcast, Cutting Crew. Courtesy Virgin Records.**

# Roger Daltrey

UK vocalist, actor.
Born London, March 1, 1944.

**Career:** Daltrey grew up in non-musical family in working-class neighbourhood of London's Shepherd's Bush. Around 12 he began playing self-made guitars. Thrown out of school at 15, he formed his own band, the Detours, later to become the Who(▶). After playing guitar in Detours for nearly two years, he became a singer and has remained so ever since, generally as lead vocalist with the Who.

Daltrey's first solo project was singing part of Tommy with Lou Reizner's London Symphony Orchestra production of the Who opera. His single **I'm Free** from this version went to No. 13 in UK. First completely solo venture came in 1973 when he sang compositions of then unknown writers such as Leo Sayer(▶) on **Daltrey,** his best solo effort to date. Produced by Adam Faith(▶) the album yielded a No.5 hit in UK, **Giving It All Away,** a great boost to Sayer. Away from the Who, Daltrey was able to expand his vocal range, abandoning screaming style he was best known for within band, and proving his ability to sing softer ballads. Daltrey was also interested in singing material written by other artists, as he'd been the vehicle for Pete Townshend's(▶) compositions/lyrics for 10 years.

1975 was a big year for Daltrey: he starred in his first film, the highly successful 'Tommy', and millions again identified the golden-maned Daltrey as the central character. To erase this impression, Daltrey starred in second Ken Russell film, 'Lisztomania,' portraying Franz Liszt as decadent 19th century pop star. Besides being heavily featured on the 'Lisztomania' and 'Tommy' soundtrack LPs, Daltrey also had another solo LP out that year, **Ride A Rock Horse.** Apart from award-winning cover, the LP broke no new ground, but was well-received. Daltrey again utilised unknown composers, giving them opportunities to expand. **One Of The Boys** (1977) was more of the same—a collection of songs sung quite well, but not surpassing his work with the Who.

Daltrey's other film roles included a ghastly performance in the low-budget horror flick 'The Legacy' in 1978 and the lead part in 'McVicar' in 1980 opposite Adam Faith, for which he received generally good reviews.

In 1983 Daltrey continues to record and

**Best Bits, Roger Daltrey. Courtesy Polydor Records.**

act, starring in the Jonathan Miller production of 'The Beggar's Opera' for British TV, and working on further solo albums and running business ventures includes a trout farm.

| Hit Singles: | US | UK |
|---|---|---|
| Giving It All Away, 1973 | — | 5 |
| I'm Free (London Symphony Tommy), 1973 | — | 13 |

Without Your Love, 1980      20      —

**Albums:**
Daltrey (MCA/Track), 1973
Ride A Rock Horse (MCA/Polydor), 1975
Lisztomania (A&M Ode/A&M), 1975
One Of The Boys (MCA/Polydor), 1977
McVicar (Soundtrack) (Polydor), 1980
Best Bits (Greatest Hits) (MCA/Polydor), 1983
Party Should Be Painless (Warner Bros), 1984
Under A Raging Moon (Ten), 1985 **CD**
Can't Wait To See The Movie (Ten), 1987 **CD**

# The Damned

UK group formed 1976.
**Original line-up:** Rat Scabies, drums; Captain Sensible, bass; Dave Vanian, vocals; Brian James, guitar.

**Career:** Close on heels of Sex Pistols(▶), Damned were in forefront of mid-'70s' assault on established rock. Line-up had settled down by May 1976 and signed to Stiff in September. **New Rose/Help** was released in October and revolution was on. First 'punk' album was **Damned, Damned, Damned** released in February 1977.

In August 1977, Lu Edmunds joined as second guitarist. Pink Floyd's(▶) Nick Mason produced second album, **Music For Pleasure.** Then band seemed to sink into superstar trauma but without reaching super success. Rat Scabies left in October 1977. Dave Berk sat in on loan from Johnny Moped for tour in November. Jon Moss joined as permanent drummer in late 1977. Loss of street creditbility and lack of sales resulted in Stiff dropping band in January 1978. Within month Captain Sensible and Brian James had usual musical differences and band folded. James eventually re-emerged with Deadboys' Stiv Bators as Lords Of The New Church.

Within six months of Rainbow farewell concert on April 8, 1978, Sensible and Vanian were back together. Sensible had talked Rat Scabies and Vanian into playing with him and Lemmy (from Motorhead(▶)) for one gig at Electric Ballroom. Damned alumni continued on with other musicians and appeared as the Damned while acquiring rights to old name.

In November 1978 re-vamped band appeared, with Sensible now on guitar, sharing vocals with Vanian. Rat Scabies on drums and Algy Ward from the Saints on bass completed line-up. Chiswick signed them and got a UK No.20 with **Love Song** in April 1979.

**Below: The Damned. Captain Sensible (far left) went on to solo success.**

**Machine Gun Etiquette** LP did not appear until November. Ward left in early 1980 to enter heavy-metal sweepstakes with Tank. His place was taken by Eddie and the Hot Rods' bass player Paul Gray. This line-up released critically acclaimed **The Black Album** in November 1980. Arguably album is stronger as single LP in US version. Band seemed

**Phantasmagoria, The Damned. Courtesy MCA Records.**

continually on road and new popularity prompted November 1981 release of **Best Of The Damned** which featured early work.

In early October 1982 Damned released excellent, but patchy, **Strawberries** album. Captain Sensible's vaudeville tendencies still sought other outlet. In July 1982 his cover of old Rodgers/Hammerstein tune **Happy Talk** was UK No.1 and second single as well as album followed. This schizoid approach plagued Damned from earliest days. Captain's success and band's relative commerical failure caused new label, Bronze, to drop Damned in April 1983 but they found new deal with MCA. Revised line-up won applause for **Phantasmagoria** and **Anything** albums.

**Current line-up:** Scabies, Vanian, Roman Jugg, guitar; Bryn Merrick, bass.

| Hit Singles: | US | UK |
|---|---|---|
| Love Song, 1979 | — | 20 |
| Eloise, 1986 | — | 5 |
| *Captain Sensible Solo:* | | |
| Happy Talk, 1982 | — | 1 |
| Glad It's All Over, 1984 | — | 6 |

**Albums:**
Damned, Damned, Damned (—/Stiff), 1977
Music For Pleasure (—/Stiff), 1977
Machine Gun Etiquette (—/Chiswick), 1979
The Black Album (—/Chiswick), 1980
The Best Of The Damned (—/Stiff), 1981
Strawberries (—/Bronze), 1982
Phantasmagoria (MCA), 1985
Mindless Directionless Energy, (ID) 1987
Best Of The Damned, (Big Beat) 1987

*Captain Sensible Solo:*
Women And Captains First (A&M), 1982
The Power Of Love (A&M), 1983
Sensible Singles (A&M), 1984

# Chris De Burgh

Irish vocalist, composer.

**Career:** Despite low-key image, Chris De Burgh has built worldwide audience and sold huge numbers of records over more than a decade of increasing reputation.

A student of Trinity College, Dublin, De Burgh (né Davison) was discovered by songwriter Doug Flett at a London party.

Flett and partner Guy Fletcher were working at A&M's publishing arm Rondor Music which led to publishing and recording deal for De Burgh in 1972. Flett and Fletcher hid De Burgh in a cupboard until A&M's A&R director Dave Margereson came into the room at which De Burgh burst into song.

Strong record company commitment and tours with A&M acts Supertramp and Gallagher and Lyle led to growing following. First number one came in Brazil with **Flying/Turning Round** double header while **Spanish Train And Other Stories** took him into North America via Canada.

When Sex Pistols spent four days of utter chaos signed to A&M it was De Burgh who wrote legendary 'There is life after the Sex Pistols' letter to label's UK boss, Derek Green.

De Burgh is now firmly established as Ireland's leading rock and pop singer.

De Burgh finally scored massive chart success with **Lady In Red**, his first hit action since signing with A&M some twelve years previously. Subsequent upsurge in acceptance led to concert appearances in UK and abroad.

| Hit Singles: | US | UK |
|---|---|---|
| The Lady In Red, 1986 | 8 | 1 |

**Below: Chris De Burgh, finally charting after all these years.**

**Albums:**
Far Beyond These Walls (A&M), 1975
Spanish Train & Other Stories (A&M), 1975 **CD**
At The End Of A Perfect Day (A&M), 1977
Crusader (A&M), 1979
Eastern Wind (A&M), 1980
Best Moves (A&M), 1981
The Getaway (A&M), 1982 **CD**
Man On The Line (A&M), 1984
The Very Best Of (Telstar), 1984 **CD**
Into The Light (A&M), 1986 **CD**

# Deep Purple

UK group formed 1968.
**Original line-up:** Rod Evans, vocals; Ritchie Blackmore, guitar; Jon Lord, keyboards; Nick Simper, bass; Ian Paice, drums.

**Career:** Formed in Germany from remnants of UK band Roundabout (Blackmore; Lord; Dave Curtis, bass; Chris Curtis, vocals; Bobby Clark, drums) as pop-rock outfit. First single (with line-up above), **Hush**, made Top 5 in US as did next two singles. First albums also achieved American success. However, band did not gain credibility in homeland until 1970 when Ian Gillan(▶) and Roger Glover replaced Evans and Simper for ambitious **Concerto For Group And Orchestra** album, recorded at Albert Hall with Royal Philharmonic Orchestra. New line-up also gained single success with **Black Night** in August of that year.

Pursuing a heavier rock direction, Purple

**House of Blue Light, Deep Purple.
Courtesy Polydor Records.**

quickly became one of the most successful and influential bands of early '70s; joined Black Sabbath(▶) and Led Zeppelin(▶) in spreading gospel of multi-decibel, piledriver British rock around the world. Main asset was Blackmore, who, although somewhat derivative, established reputation as guitar hero.

However, by 1972 band was beset by various ego problems; a year later Gillan left (later to achieve considerable success with his own band), followed shortly by Glover (who went into production). Glenn Hughes, bassist with moderately successful band Trapeze, replaced Glover, while Gillan was replaced by complete unknown David Coverdale. In 1975 Ritchie Blackmore also quit to form Rainbow(▶) (where he was later joined by Glover), and American Tommy Bolin, formerly of James Gang(▶), was recruited in his place.

By 1976, audience for Purple's music was beginning to diminish, and band died natural death that year. Coverdale, Lord and Paice eventually became three-fifths of Whitesnake(▶). Glenn Hughes recorded a solo album and undertook session work. Tommy Bolin died suddenly in Miami in 1976.

Fans were delighted when the group reformed in April 1984 with the classic line up of Gillan, Lord, Paice, Blackmore and Glover. Their reunion LP **Perfect Strangers** released

in November, was their first studio album in 11 years. It went platinum and their US tour was hailed as the second highest grossing of the year. They played to British fans at Knebworth in 1985 then began a world tour in 1987. With the highly successful **House Of Blue Light** released the same year, it seemed the revived Purple was not just a one night stand.

**Current line-up:** Blackmore; Lord; Paice; Ian Gillan, vocals; Roger Glover, bass.

| Hit Singles: | US | UK |
|---|---|---|
| Hush, 1968 | 4 | — |
| Black Night, 1970 | — | 2 |
| Strange Kind Of Woman, 1971 | — | 8 |
| Fireball, 1971 | — | 15 |
| Smoke On The Water, 1973 | 4 | 21 |

**Albums:**
Shades Of Deep Purple (Tetragrammaton/Harvest), 1968
Book Of Taliesyn (Tetragrammaton/Harvest), 1969
Deep Purple (Tetragrammaton/Harvest), 1969
In Concert (Portrait/Harvest), 1970
Concerto For Group & Orchestra (Warner Bros/Harvest), 1970
In Rock (Warner Bros/Harvest), 1970 **CD**
Fireball (Deep Purple/Harvest), 1971 **CD**
Machine Head (Warner Bros/Purple), 1972 **CD**
Made in Japan (Deep Purple/Purple), 1972
Who Do We Think We Are (Deep Purple/Purple), 1973 **CD**
Burn (Deep Purple/Purple), 1974
Stormbringer (Deep Purple/Purple), 1974
Come Taste The Band (Deep Purple/Purple), 1975
24 Carat Purple (—/Purple), 1975 **CD**
Purple Passages (Warner Bros), 1975
Made In Europe (Deep Purple/Purple), 1976
Powerhouse (—/Purple), 1977
Singles (—/Harvest), 1978
When We Rock We Rock (Warner Bros/—), 1978
Live In London (—/Harvest), 1982
Perfect Strangers (Mercury), 1984 **CD**
Knocking On Your Back Door (Polydor), 1985
The Anthology (Harvest), 1985
House Of Blue Light (Polydor), 1987 **CD**
Deepest Purple (Harvest), 1980 **CD**

# Def Leppard

UK group formed 1978.
**Original line-up:** Steve Clark, guitar; Rick Savage, bass; Pete Willis, guitar; Rick Allen, drums; Joe Elliot, vocals.

**Career:** Sheffield lads, Def Leppard cut an impressive debut album **On Through The Night** with twin guitar leads which owed as much to Wishbone Ash(▶) as new wave of British heavy metal.

Immediate attention brought by 'overnight success' caused problems. 1981 set **High 'n' Dry** sounded rather sedated, just another heavy metal album, and Pete Willis developed personal problems which resulted in his being

**Hysteria, Def Leppard.
Courtesty Vertigo Records.**

fired during recording of crucial third album. Band continued recording as foursome when Elliot heard that guitarist Phil Collen (ex-Girl) was available.

After 18 month delay, **Pyromania** LP (featuring Collen) released. Band then suffered cruel luck when drummer Rick Allen lost arm in car accident, although he remains with group.

Group spent four years perfecting their next album **Hysteria** released in 1987 and highly successful. It yielded a collection of hits including **Animal**, **Women**, **Hysteria**, **Pour Some Sugar On Me**, and **Armageddon It**.

The band toured with a specially adapted drum kit for Rick Allen whose drumming was as powerful as ever. In 1988 the band toured the world including Europe, Japan and America.

**Current line-up:** Clark; Savage; Allen; Elliot; Phil Collen, guitar.

| Hit Singles: | US | UK |
|---|---|---|
| Photograph, 1983 | 12 | — |
| Rock Of Ages, 1983 | 16 | — |
| Hysteria, 1987 | — | 26 |
| Animal, 1987 | 19 | 6 |
| Pour Some Sugar On Me, 1987 | — | 18 |

**Albums:**
On Through The Night (Mercury/Vertigo), 1980
High 'n' Dry (Mercury/Vertigo), 1981
Pyromania (Mercury/Vertigo), 1983 **CD**
Hysteria (Vertigo), 1987 **CD**

# Desmond Dekker

Jamaican vocalist, composer.
Born Kingston, Jamaica, 1943.

**Career:** Desmond Dekker was reggae's first superstar, responsible for carrying Jamaica's ethnic pop music to a massive white audience in both UK and US. Credit for his impact, however, must be shared with his guardian/mentor Leslie Kong who produced all Dekker's classic recordings from 1967 until 1971 when Kong died, aged 38, of heart attack.

Orphaned as small child, Dekker worked as welder before, in mid-'60s, joining the Aces, a studio group used by producers Duke Reid and Lloyd 'The Matador' Daley.

Portraying the Jamaican 'rude boy' cult, **007 (Shanty Town)** was one of the first rock-steady hits, bringing Desmond Dekker and the Aces to prominence not only in Jamaica but in UK, where record charted in 1967.

**007** was the first of more than 20 consecutive chart-toppers for Dekker in his home country. In 1969, he became first reggae artist to top UK charts, with **The Israelites** which also made No.9 spot in US, despite strange patois of its lyrics. **The Israelites** charted twice more on re-release in UK while **It Mek**, first released in Britain before **The Israelites**, also became a smash hit when given second chance.

**Pickney Gal**, **You Can Get It If You Really Want It** (featured in critically acclaimed Jimmy Cliff(▶) movie 'The Harder They Come') and, in 1975, **Sing A Little Song** were all UK hits but despite moving to London after Kong's death, Dekker's fortunes waned as Bob Marley assumed the title of reggae's numero uno.

In 1980 there were signs of new interest via the second generation of skinheads (he had been the original skinheads' cult hero) and an album with Stiff ensued, but neither that nor subsequent set produced by Robert Palmer(▶) made real impact.

| Hit Singles: | US | UK |
|---|---|---|
| 007 (Shanty Town), 1967 | — | 14 |
| The Israelites, 1969 | 9 | 1 |
| It Mek, 1969 | — | 7 |
| You Can Get It If You Really Want It, 1970 | — | 2 |
| The Israelites (re-issue), 1975 | — | 10 |
| Sing A Little Song, 1975 | — | 16 |

**Albums:**
Dekker's Sweet 16 Hits (—/Trojan), 1979
Black And Dekker (—/Stiff), 1980
Israelites (—/Cactus), 1980
Compass Point (—/Stiff), 1981

**Below: From the Steel City of Sheffield, Def Leppard.**

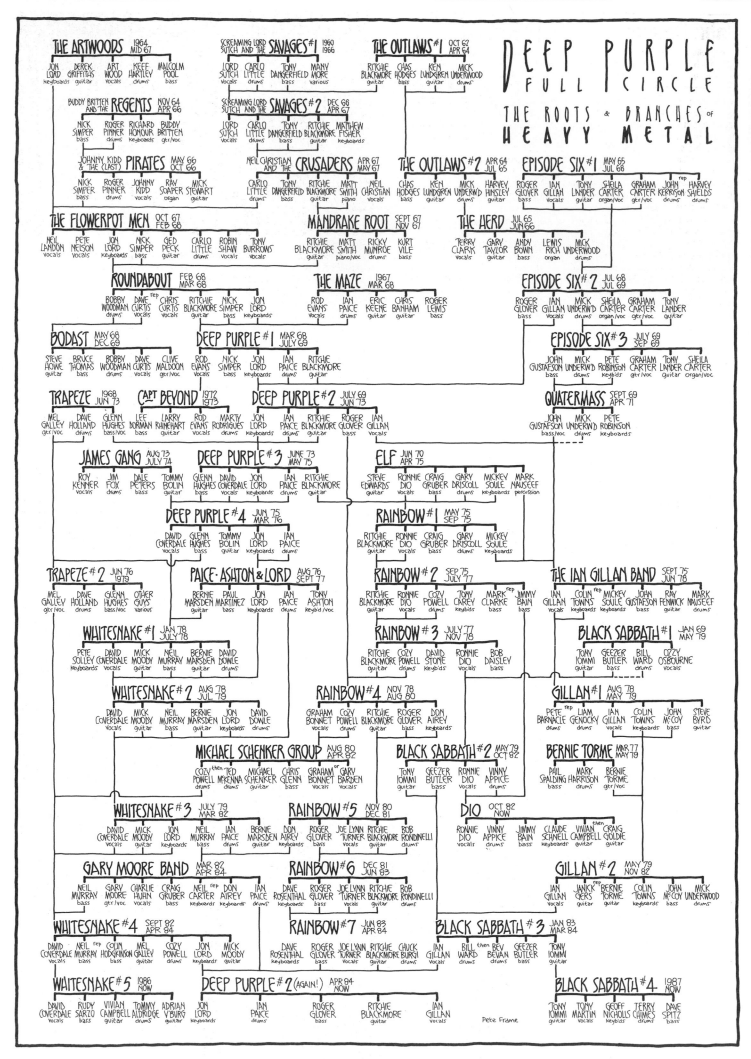

# John Denver

Singer, composer, guitarist.
Born John Henry Deutschendorf Jr., Rockwell, New Mexico, December 31, 1943.

**Career:** Son of USAF pilot who held three world aviation records, Denver spent youth moving from one base to another throughout America. First performed as folk singer in Lubbock, Texas, where he majored in architecture at college.

Moving to Los Angeles in 1964, he auditioned successfully as replacement for Chad Mitchell in Chad Mitchell Trio and toured with them for five years before going solo. First album in 1969 featured original composition **Leaving On A Jet Plane,** which became international hit for Peter, Paul and Mary(▶), the same year.

By 1971 Denver was major star thanks to million-selling **Take Me Home Country Roads** and gold album **Poems, Prayers and Promises.** Million-selling **Annie's Song** (1974) gave him UK chart debut and in 1975 he starred in series of major TV specials and in Lake Tahoe cabaret alongside Frank Sinatra.

**Windsong** album went gold on pre-release orders alone, while 'Rocky Mountain Christmas' TV special captured audience of 30 million. Film debut came in 1977 with 'Oh God', starring George Burns.

Country music's version of the All-American Boy, John Denver's ecology-minded material and easy-listening style have made him a show-business phenomenon and a major figure in field of country rock.

| Hit Singles: | US | UK |
|---|---|---|
| Take Me Home, Country Roads, 1971 | 2 | — |
| Rocky Mountain High, 1973 | 9 | — |
| Sunshine On My Shoulders, 1974 | 1 | — |
| Annie's Song, 1974 | 1 | 1 |
| Back Home Again, 1974 | 5 | — |
| Sweet Surrender, 1975 | 13 | — |
| Thank God I'm A Country Boy, 1975 | 1 | — |
| I'm Sorry, 1975 | 1 | — |
| Fly Away, 1976 | 13 | — |

**Albums:**
Poems, Prayers And Promises (RCA), 1971
Aerie (RCA), 1971
Rocky Mountain High (RCA), 1972
Farewell Andromeda (RCA), 1973
Greatest Hits (RCA/—), 1973 **CD**
Back Home Again (RCA), 1974 **CD**
Best Of (—/RCA), 1974
An Evening With (RCA), 1975
Windsong (RCA), 1975
Rocky Mountain Xmas (RCA), 1975
Spirit (RCA), 1976
Greatest Hits Volume II (RCA), 1977 **CD**
I Want To Live (RCA), 1977
Best Of Volume II (—/RCA), 1977
Autograph (RCA), 1980
Some Days Are Diamonds (RCA), 1981
Perhaps Love (with Placido Domingo) (Columbia/CBS), 1981
Seasons Of The Heart (RCA), 1984 **CD**
The John Denver Collection (Telstar), 1984 **CD**
Greatest Hits Vol 3 (RCA), 1985 **CD**
One World, 1986 (RCA)
It's About Time, 1986 (RCA)
Dreamland Express, 1987 (RCA)

# Depeche Mode

UK group formed 1980.

**Original line-up:** Andy Fletcher, guitar, vocals; Martin Gore, guitar, vocals; Vince Clarke, synthesisers, vocals; Dave Gahan, vocals.

**Music for the Masses, Depeche Mode. Courtesy Mute Records.**

**Career:** Formed by Fletcher, Gore and Clarke in Basildon, Essex, under forgotten name. Acquired Depeche Mode tag from French fashion magazine. In 1981, dispensed with guitars to become all-electronic band. Early demo tapes met with zero response, until group began to play 'futurist' nights at Bridge House pub in East London. Seen by group entrepreneur Stevo who included a track, **Photographic,** on semi-legendary **Some Bizzare** compilation LP; others on album included Soft Cell(▶), Blancmange, the The and Naked Lunch. Also approached by Daniel

**Below: The totally synthesised Depeche Mode have enjoyed incredible run of hit singles.**

Miller of Mute Records, who became group's svengali/record producer.

First Mute single, **Dreaming Of Me,** was minor hit in early 1981, since when numerous singles and albums have reached UK Top 10, despite departure, after release of first LP, of Vince Clarke, who had been main songwriter to this point. Martin Gore assumed this role and success continued unabated, while Vince Clarke formed Yazoo (or 'Yaz' in US) with Alison 'Alf' Moyet.

Early 1982 saw recruitment of ex-Hitmen synth operator Alan Wilder, and resulting quartet have maintained high chart profile despite absence of Clarke. Relationship with relatively low key Mute Records has worked to mutual advantage, although band may need to establish more distinctive image to maintain impetus. But, so far so good.

**Current line-up:** Gahan; Fletcher; Gore; Alan Wilder, electronics.

| Hit Singles: | US | UK |
|---|---|---|
| New Life, 1981 | — | 11 |
| Just Can't Get Enough, 1981 | — | 8 |
| See You, 1982 | — | 6 |
| The Meaning Of Love, 1982 | — | 12 |
| Leave In Silence, 1982 | — | 18 |
| Get The Balance Right, 1983 | — | 13 |
| Everything Counts, 1983 | — | 6 |
| *People Are People, 1984 | 13 | 4 |
| Master And Servant, 1984 | — | 9 |
| Somebody, 1984 | — | 16 |
| Shake The Disease, 1985 | — | 18 |
| It's Called A Heart, 1985 | — | 18 |
| Stripped, 1986 | — | 15 |
| A Question Of Time | — | 18 |
| Strangelove, 1987 | — | 16 |
| Never Let Me Down Again | — | 22 |
| Behind The Wheel | — | 22 |
| * 1985 in US | | |

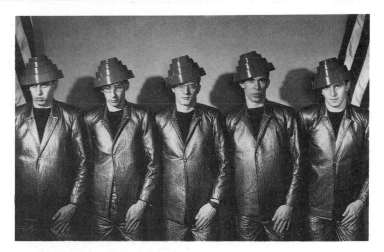

Oh No! philosphers of devolution, potatoes and flowerpots, Devo.

**Albums:**
Speak And Spell (Sire/Mute), 1981
A Broken Frame (Sire/Mute), 1982 **CD**
Construction Time Again (Sire/Mute), 1983 **CD**
Some Great Reward (Mute), 1984 **CD**
The singles 81-85 (Mute), 1985 **CD**
Music For The Masses (Mute), 1987

# Devo

US group formed 1976.

**Original/Current line-up:** Jerry Casale, bass; Mark Mothersbough, vocals, guitar, keyboards; Bob Casale, guitar; Bob Mothersbough, guitar; Alan Meyers, drums.

**Career:** Jerry and Mark met at Kent State in early '70s and began experimental non-musical approach to music mid-'70s upheaval provided chance for hearing. Bob Casale (brother of Jerry) and Bob Mothersbough (brother of Mark), and fellow Akron friend Myers completed line-up.

In 1977 Iggy Pop(▶), then David Bowie(▶), befriended band which won cult status. Self-released early singles (**Jocko Homo, Mongoloid,** and jerky, electronic cover of Stones' **Satisfaction**) with clinical, icy edge spread underground reputation. As befitting former Fine Art majors, Jerry and Mark marketed Devo with multi-media campaign incorporating masks, films, in-jokes about potatoes, philosophies of devolution, science and flower pots, as well as a self-developed language.

High Tech gloss was enhanced by Eno-produced first album. With Ken Scott-produced **Duty Now For The Future,** band took things more seriously, to its detriment, and **Freedom Of Choice** signified a shift to dance music with disco hit **Whip It.** Devo's electronic bop continued through quirky live mini LP and into precision beat of **New Traditionalists.**

LP **Oh No! It's Devo** sums up band; staccato synthesisers with at least one outstanding cut, but marketing and jokes wearing thin. First taste of Devo is disconcerting but interesting. Second bite is like undercooked spuds: hard and in need of warmth.

| Hit Singles: | US | UK |
|---|---|---|
| Whip It, 1980 | 14 | 51 |

**Albums:**
Q: Are We Not Men? A: We Are Devo (Warner Bros/Virgin), 1978
Duty Now For The Future (Warner Bros/Virgin), 1979

Freedom Of Choice (Warner Bros/Virgin), 1980
Live (mini-album) (Warner Bros/Virgin), 1981
New Traditionalists (Warner Bros/Virgin), 1981
Oh No! It's Devo (Warner Bros/Virgin), 1982
Shout (Warner Bros), 1984
Live: Devo (Virgin), 1987

# Dexys Midnight Runners

UK group formed 1978.

**Original line-up:** Kevin Rowland, vocals, guitar; Al Archer, guitar; Jimmy Paterson, trombone; Pete Saunders, organ; J.B., tenor saxophone; Steve 'Babyface' Spooner, alto saxophone; Pete Williams, bass; Andy Growcott, drums.

**Career:** Group's main-man Kevin Rowland (born Wolverhampton, August 17, 1953) started in Lucy and Lovers then joined the Killjoys. Made one record, **Johnny Won't Get To Heaven.** In July 1978 Birmingham-based Rowlands decided to form new band in '60s soul mould. Result was Dexys Midnight Runners. Image was based on New York '60s street gangs—inspired by movie 'Mean Streets'.

Former Clash(▶) manager Bernie Rhodes was called in to help; got group onto Specials' tour as support. Via his own Oddball label, Rhodes secured an EMI/Parlophone recording contract leading to release of **Dance Stance** in October 1979. Brass-laden record, with lyrics about bigotry towards Irish, made UK Top 40. This capitalised on small but dedicated following built via controversial 44-date 'Straight From The Heart' tour where Rowland's uncompromising attitude to audiences angered some, delighted others.

Having parted company with Rhodes, band issued second single. A-side **Geno** was tribute to '60s British soul club hero Geno Washington; flip-side was re-make of Johnny Johnson and the Bandwagon's soul oldie **Breaking Down The Walls Of Heartache.** On last day of recording debut LP, band snatched master-tapes from producer Pete Wingfield and refused to give them to EMI unless company came up with better contract; their nerve won out. Finally released in July 1980, **Searching For The Young Soul Rebels** stayed on charts for three months and was strong showcase for Rowland's stance—so strong that Rowland thought he would never be able to surpass it and made tentative plans to move into films. Third single **There There My Dear** was another hit.

Rowland continued to create controversy. Group took out full page adverts in which they slated music papers and rock writers as being 'dishonest and hippy'. They stated that in future they would communicate with fans by submitting their own essays to the press and by including written handouts with their records.

Band set off on aptly titled 'Midnight Runners Intense Emotion Revue Tour'. Tired from exhaustive recording sessions and under-rehearsed for the road, group met hostile reaction from audience. Rowland repaid compliment by abusing the crowd each night.

Massive row broke out in group during European tour. Rowland had decided to release **Keep It Part 2** as next single. Rest of band disagreed and when Rowland insisted on having own way they quit, with exception of Paterson.

Rowland returned to Birmingham to put together new line-up. (Rowland; Paterson;

Above: Kevin Rowland, chief Midnight Runner.

Micky Billingham, keyboards; Paul Speare, tenor sax; Brian Maurice, alto sax; Billy Adams, guitar; Seb Shelton, drums). He asked that group's recent recordings should not be exploited but EMI decided to release **Plan,** a song which they rightly thought would prove Dexys ability to come up with the goods. In protest, Rowland decided to walk out on contract. New manager Paul Burton spent two days studying small print before he found loophole that enabled Rowland to get away with it.

When group returned to stage there was whole new look. Hooded anoraks, tracksuit trousers and boxing boots replaced previous gang image. In keeping with this 'keep fit' style, group banned consumption of alcohol at their gigs. 'Midnight Runners Projected

Too-Rye-Ay, Dexy's Midnight Runners. Courtesy Mercury Records.

Passion Revue' climaxed with three nights at London's hallowed Old Vic theatre, the first rock band to play there.

New deal with Phonogram saw somewhat below par **Show Me** single make charts. Like image, the music was also changing direction. Rowland had been experimenting for some time with use of violins (playing riffs rather than as an orchestra). First result was **Liars A To E,** which was none too successful. Next time out, though, was the superb **The Celtic Soul Singers/Love Part Two.** On this, the fiddles of the Emerald Express—Helen O'Hara, Steve Brennan and Roger Macduff—replaced familiar Dexys brass sound. Record only reached lower limits of chart but die was cast.

Yet another new image emerged: dungarees, neckerchiefs and leather jerkins to fit almost folksy bent of much of the new music.

**Come On Eileen** (first US hit) shot group back to top in early summer 1982. **Too-Rye-Ay** album featured neat blend of acoustic guitar and violins with soft brass and included

brilliant brassy version of Van Morrison's(▶) **Jackie Wilson Said (I'm In Heaven When You Smile).**

After eighteen month hiatus, Rowland reappeared with **Don't Stand Me Down** set on Mercury, receiving mixed reviews. Although involved in a number of projects including TV theme tunes, Rowland has recently slipped from the public eye. However, mercurial talent could re-emerge at any time.

**Current line-up:** Rowland; Helen O'Hara, violin; Steve Brennan, violin; Billy Adams, guitar; Seb Shelton, drums.

| Hit Singles: | US | UK |
| --- | --- | --- |
| Geno, 1980 | — | 1 |
| There There My Dear, 1980 | — | 7 |
| Show Me, 1981 | — | 16 |
| Come On Eileen, 1982 | 1 | 1 |
| Because Of You, 1986 | — | 13 |

*As Kevin Rowland and Dexys Midnight Runners:*

| | US | UK |
| --- | --- | --- |
| Jackie Wilson Said,1982 | — | 5 |
| Let's Get This Straight (From The Start), 1982 | — | 17 |
| The Celtic Soul Brothers, 1983 (reissue)— | — | 20 |

**Albums:**
Searching For Young Soul Rebels (EMI/Fame), 1980
Too-Rye-Ay (Mercury), 1982
Geno (—/EMI), 1983
Don't Stand Me Down (Mercury), 1985

# Neil Diamond

US vocalist, composer, guitarist. Born Brooklyn, New York, January 24, 1941.

**Career:** Became staff songwriter with Sunbeam Music in New York City's legendary Brill Building 'hit factory' in early '60s. Earned biggest successes with **I'm A Believer** and **A Little Bit Me, A Little Bit You** for Monkees(▶).

Fellow writers Ellie Greenwich and Jeff Barry recognised Diamond's potential as artist and took him to Bert Berns' new Bang label in late 1965. Debut single **Solitary Man** (1966) set off train of hits, including **Cherry Cherry, Sweet Caroline** and **Cracklin' Rosie,** all cut after switch to Uni label. Meanwhile, **Kentucky Woman** (Elvis Presley(▶)) and Deep Purple(▶)) and **The Boat That I Row** (Lulu(▶)) gave Diamond further rewards as writer.

With **Tap Root Manuscript** album (1970), Diamond ventured beyond realms of pure pop

for imaginative (if trifle pretentious) **African Trilogy** song cycle.

Earlier projected as a clean-cut 'all-American boy', Diamond grew hair longer and cultivated new image as introspective folk-poet; built ever wider audience. In 1973, earned record multi-million dollar advance on signing to Columbia for conceptual **Jonathan Livingston Seagull** soundtrack album. This was followed by **Serenade** (1974), then two years of silence before superb **Beautiful Noise** set, produced by Band's(▶) Robbie Robertson, as was **Love At The Greek** live double album.

Teaming up with Barbra Streisand(▶) in late 1978, Diamond had huge hit with duet titletrack from **You Don't Bring Me Flowers** LP. (Diamond and Streisand had both recorded **Flowers** single; Colombia decided to record duet when they heard a DJ splice two versions together). Worked with Four Seasons' producer Bob Gaudio for follow-up set **September Morn** (1979).

The 1980 re-make of the classic Al Jolson movie 'The Jazz Singer', co-starring Sir Laurence Olivier, took Diamond to new heights and revealed his acting talents. Spine-tingling hit single **Love On The Rocks** from film showed his mastery of mood and innate soulfulness.

Perfunctory 'live' set preceded 1984 collection **Primitive,** although output has receded dramtically since prolific '70s decade. History may show this as his career 'high'.

In earlier times often dismissed as a purveyor of somewhat trite efforts at artiness, Diamond has emerged as a totally distinctive and creative songwriter, and a performer of major stature.

| Hit Singles: | US | UK |
| --- | --- | --- |
| Cherry Cherry, 1966 | 6 | — |
| I Got The Feelin' (Oh No No), 1966 | 16 | — |
| You Got To Me, 1967 | 18 | — |
| Girl, You'll Be A Woman Soon, 1967 | 10 | — |
| I Thank The Lord For The Night Time, 1967 | 13 | — |
| Sweet Caroline, 1969 | 4 | — |
| Holly Holy, 1969 | 6 | — |
| Cracklin' Rosie, 1970 | 1 | 3 |
| He Ain't Heavy—He's My Brother, 1970 | 20 | — |
| Sweet Caroline, 1971 | — | 8 |
| I Am. . . I Said, 1971 | 4 | 4 |
| Stones/Crunchy Granada Suite, 1971 | 14 | — |
| Song Sung Blue, 1972 | 1 | 14 |
| Play Me, 1972 | 11 | — |
| Walk On Water, 1972 | 17 | — |
| Longfellow Serenade, 1974 | 5 | — |
| If You Know What I Mean, 1976 | 11 | 35 |
| Beautiful Noise, 1976 | — | 13 |
| Desiree, 1978 | 16 | 39 |
| Forever In Blue Jeans, 1979 | 20 | 16 |
| September Morn, 1979 | 17 | — |
| Love On The Rocks, 1980 | 2 | 17 |
| Hello Again, 1981 | 6 | 51 |
| America, 1981 | 8 | — |
| Yesterday's Song, 1981 | 11 | — |
| Heartlight, 1982 | 5 | 47 |

*With Barbra Streisand:*

| | US | UK |
| --- | --- | --- |
| You Don't Bring Me Flowers, 1978 | 1 | 5 |

**Albums:**
(Excluding budget reissues)
The Feel Of Neil Diamond (Bang/—), 1966
Just For You (Bang/-), 1967
Greatest Hits (Bang/Joy), 1968
Velvet Gloves And Spit (MCA), 1968
Brother Love's Travelling Salvation Show (MCA), 1969
Touching You Touching Me (MCA), 1969
Gold (MCA), 1970

Shiloh/Solitary Man (Bang/—), 1970
Tap Root Manuscript (MCA), 1970
Do It (Bang/—), 1971
Moods (MCA), 1972 **CD**
Hot August Night (MCA), 1972
Double Gold (Bang/—), 1973
Rainbow (MCA), 1973
Jonathan Livingston Seagull (Soundtrack), 1973
Stones (MCA), 1974
Hits 12 Greatest Hits (Direct/MCA), 1974 **CD**
Serenade,(Columbia/CBS), 1974 **CD**
Beautiful Noise (Columbia/CBS), 1976 **CD**
And The Singer Sings His Song (MCA), 1976
Love At The Greek (Columbia/CBS), 1977 **CD**
20 Golden Greats (MCA), 1978
September Morn (Columbia/CBS), 1980 **CD**
The Jazz Singer (songs from the soundtrack) (Capitol), 1980 **CD**
Love Songs (Columbia/CBS), 1981
On The Way To The Sky (Columbia/CBS), 1981 **CD**
12 Greatest Hits, Volume II (Columbia/CBS), 1982 **CD**
Heartlight (Columbia/CBS), 1982 **CD**
Live Diamond (—/MCA), 1982
Classics (CBS), 1983 **CD**
Primitive (CBS), 1984
Headed For The Future (CBS), 1986 **CD**
Hot August Night II (CBS), 1987
I'm Glad You're Here With Me Tonight (CBS), 1987 **CD**
Sweet Caroline (MCA), 1987 **CD**
Sweet Caroline 2 (MCA), 1987 **CD**

*With Barbra Steisand:*
You Don't Bring Me Flowers (Columbia/CBS), 1978 **CD**

# Bo Diddley

US vocalist, guitarist, composer.
Born Ellas McDaniel, McComb, Mississippi, December 30, 1928.

**Career:** Raised by mother's cousin, Mrs Gussie McDaniel; taken to Chicago aged five. Studied classical violin for 12 years but also absorbed music of Baptist church services. Rhythm and blues influences were in complete contrast—balladry of Nat Cole(▶), humour of Louis Jordan, guitar of John Lee Hooker(▶). Streets of Chicago brought contact with Mississippi Delta blues style of Muddy Waters(▶) and Little Walter, who gigged in local clubs.

Given guitar by sister as teenager; taught himself to play and formed small group in early 1950s. Played on street corners: Diddley, vocals, guitar; Frank Kirkland, drums (Jerome Green, maraccas; Billy Boy Arnold sometimes on harp).

Earned money as boxer, then construction worker, before realising that music could also pay bills. Auditioned for Chess in 1954, cutting **I'm A Man** and **Bo Diddley,** a landmark with its throbbing jungle rhythm. Disc was released on Checker in spring 1955. A Top 10 R&B hit, it provided foundation for years of inimitable material. Regular band included half-sister 'The Duchess' on rhythm guitar. Diddley maintained phenomenal output of original, lyrically unorthodox material with strong humour content; **Cracking Up** provided Bo's first crossover pop hit in summer 1959; then **Say Man** became Top 20 smash. In early 1960s Diddley's repertoire was used by many British beat groups, songs like **Road Runner, Pretty Thing, Mona, Who Do You Love, I Can Tell** and **You Can't Judge A Book By The Cover** clocking up good mileage. Diddley released prodigious quantity of LPs, mainly during '60s. Material was still mainly original, often predictable, but artist's

humour and enthusiasm ooze from the grooves.

Distinctive pair of albums cut in 1967; **Super Blues,** with Bo, Muddy Waters and Little Walter, and **The Super Super Blues Band** with Bo, Muddy and Howlin' Wolf. Around 1970 Bo tried heavier musical context for LP **Another Dimension,** with uncomfortable results; similarly uninspiring was **Big Bad Bo** in 1974. In 1972 and 1973, his stage performance was filmed for **Let The Good Times Roll** and **Keep On Rockin'.**

Continued heavy schedule of live shows in US and Europe; disc career less active. With demise of Chess, signed with RCA; cut disappointing LP **20th Anniversary Of Rock 'n' Roll,** and **Not Fade Away,** a flop 45. Now tours with various revival packages.

Guitars: Various custom-bodied Gibsons.

| Hit Singles: | US | UK |
|---|---|---|
| Say Man, 1959 | 20 | — |

**Albums:**
Golden Decade (—/Chess),1973
Toronto Rock 'N' Roll Revival 1969 Volume 5 (Accord/—), 1981

*Worth Searching Out:*
Have Guitar Will Travel (Checker/—), 1962
Bo Diddley Is A Gunslinger (Checker/Pye), 1963
Black Gladiator (Checker/—), 1971
In The Spotlight (Chess), 1987
Bo Diddley (Vogue), 1987 **CD**

# Dion

US vocalist, songwriter.
Born Dion Di Mucci, Bronx, New York, July 18, 1939.

**Dion & the Belmonts' reunion LP. Courtesy B & C Records.**

**Career:** First professional appearance was at 15 on Paul Whiteman's 'Teen Club' TV show in Philadelphia. First group the Timberlanes formed 1957; recorded one single for Mohawk label without success. During 1958 formed new group the Belmonts, named after Belmont Avenue in NY; recorded further single for Mohawk, which also failed. Moved to Laurie label where **I Wonder Why** (released as Dion and the Belmonts) quickly became hit, followed by two Top 50 entries. Then, in 1959, had first Top 10 hit, **A Teenager In Love.** All were in pure, if 'white', doo-wop style.

Dion and the Belmonts became most popular white vocal group of rock 'n' roll era, although chart successes were somewhat erratic. Biggest hit **Where Or When** preceded Dion's departure from Belmonts in 1960, and first solo hit in similar style, **Lonely Teenager.** Despite failure of immediate follow-ups, achieved even greater success when **Runaround Sue** reached No. 1 in 1961, consolidating popularity in US and UK.

Moved to CBS Records in 1962. Continued to hit charts with singles still sounding like extension of Belmonts' style, until venture into MOR and, later, R&B, style failed to maintain popularity. Drugs problem forced semi-retirement during 1964 but returned in 1967 to re-unite with Belmonts, recording minor hit **My Girl The Month of May** for ABC; failed to equal past glories.

By 1969 had re-signed with Laurie Records and regained magic touch, with **Abraham, Martin & John** reaching No. 4 and heralding turn to 'folk-protest' style for remainder of Laurie output. Signed to Warner Bros in 1970. Apart from further reunion with Belmonts, which resulted in fine live LP (1972), recorded in contemporary singer-songwriter style without commercial success.

Despite highly regarded recordings with Phil Spector in late '70s and several attempts at comeback singles and albums, Dion has never equalled his early successes. Has recently started to record for **US** Christian label Dayspring.

| Hit Singles: | US | UK |
|---|---|---|
| No One Knows,* 1958 | 19 | — |
| A Teenager In Love,* 1959 | 5 | — |
| Where Or When*, Dion, 1960 | 3 | — |
| Lonely Teenager, 1960 | 12 | — |
| Runaround Sue, 1961 | 1 | 11 |
| The Wanderer, 1961 | 2 | 10 |
| Lovers Who Wander, 1962 | 3 | — |
| Little Diane, 1962 | 8 | — |
| Love Came To Me, 1962 | 10 | — |
| Ruby Baby, 1963 | 2 | — |
| Donna The Prima Donna, 1963 | 6 | — |
| Drip Drop, 1963 | 6 | — |
| Abraham, Martin & John, 1968 | 4 | — |
| The Wanderer, 1976 | — | 16 |

*With the Belmonts

**Albums:**
Dion's Greatest Hits (Laurie), 1964
Dion And The Belmonts Greatest Hits (Laurie), 1982.
Greatest Hits (Columbia/—), 1978.
I Put Away My Idols (Dayspring), 1985
Kingdom In The Streets (Dayspring), 1985

# Dire Straits

UK group formed 1977.

**Original line-up:** Mark Knopfler, Schecter, Fernandez guitars, vocals, producer; Dave Knopfler, guitar; John Illsley, bass; Pick Withers, drums.

**Communique, Dire Straits. Courtesy Vertigo Records.**

**Career:** Originally formed by Mark Knopfler with brother Dave on guitars, Illsley on bass, and Pick Withers on drums. Dire Straits burst on music scene with unlikely hit single, an affectionate rock song about a jazz band, **Sultans Of Swing.** In year dominated by punk in UK and arena-rock in US, record was surprising and refreshing, with simple arrangement and cool, silky Stratocaster solos by Mark Knopfler. Self-titled first album, released in 1978, was immediately successful, eventually going platinum in several countries, as did **Communique,** released later that year. Dave Knopfler then left band; replaced by Hal Lindes.

Mark Knopfler composes all Straits material and his husky, semi-spoken (Dylan-influenced) vocals, and instantly recognisable lead guitar are the Dire Straits sound, though he doesn't take limelight on stage. (Knopfler has played on sessions with, among others, Bob Dylan(▶) and Steely Dan(▶).

With third album **Making Movies,** band's sound expanded with effective addition of keyboards, played on record by E Street Band's Roy Bittan. Knopfler's songwriting also continued to grow, ranging from **Tunnel Of Love,** a lyrical carnival romance (introduced by a haunting few bars of Richard Rodgers' 'Carousel Waltz') to **Skateaway,** a chuckling appreciation of a city girl on rollerskates.

The next album, **Love Over Gold** (1982), went to top of US LP charts, remaining in Top 100 for months. With addition to permanent line-up of keyboardist Alan Clark, Dire Straits found neat, tight organisation with the flexibility of an orchestra. Knopfler's ever more powerful songs needed that flexibility. **Love Over Gold**

**Below: Dire Straits, led by Knopfler (bottom left) started the 1980s as one of the top groups in the world.**

took on more difficult subjects than personal passions. In it Knopfler explored, with some pain, not only states of the heart but state of the world, and the force of history. Album met with great critical approval, especially in UK. After **Gold**, respected drummer Terry Williams (ex-Man, Rockpile) joined as tour started.

Mark Knopfler is one of the new guitar heroes, a breed which almost perished in the first wash of the New Wave. In Dire Straits first appearance, he was a devoted user of the Fender Stratocaster; but recently he has been using several custom-made Schecter guitars with different pick-ups and tonal qualities, and a Japanese Strat copy, a Fernandez. His score for film 'Local Hero' earned him further plaudits for his ever-evolving technique in 1983.

After two-year sabbatical, group re-appeared in 1985 with **Brothers In Arms** album and video, and embarked on exhaustive world tour with a 13 keyboard combination to supplement Mark Knopfler's dexterous ability. As the man said: 'It's as if punk never ever happened'.

**Brothers In Arms** went on to achieve multi-platinum status, confirming Straits' status as supergroup on global scale. One of most successful acts of eighties, Dire Straits have wide constituency amongst baby-boomer rock fans. AOR appeal is reflected in band's success on compact disc format.

**Current line-up:** Mark Knopfler; Illsley; Hal Lindes, guitar; Alan Clark, keyboards; Terry Williams, drums; Jack Sonni, guitar.

**Hit Singles:**

| | US | UK |
|---|---|---|
| Sultans Of Swing, 1979 | 4 | 8 |
| Romeo And Juliet, 1981 | — | 11 |
| Private Investigations, 1982 | — | 2 |
| Twisting By The Pool, 1983 | — | 14 |
| So Far Away, 1985 | — | 20 |
| Money For Nothing, 1985 | 1 | 4 |
| Brothers In Arms, 1985 | — | 16 |
| Walk Of Life, 1986 | 13 | 2 |
| Your Latest Trick, 1986 | — | 26 |

**Albums:**
Dire Straits (Warner Bros/Vertigo), 1978 **CD**
Communique (Warner Bros/Vertigo), 1979 **CD**
Making Moves (Warner Bros/Vertigo), 1980 **CD**
Love Over Gold (Warner Bros/Vertigo), 1982 **CD**
Alchemy Live (Warner Bros/Vertigo), 1984 **CD**
Brothers In Arms (Warner Bros/Vertigo), 1985 **CD**

*Mark Knopfler Solo:*
Local Hero (soundtrack) (Vertigo), 1983

# Fats Domino

US vocalist, pianist, composer.
Born Antoine Domino, New Orleans, February 26, 1928.

**Career:** One of nine children in family with little musical background. Became interested in piano at early age; taught to play by his brother-in-law Harrison Verrett. Quickly gained proficiency; played and sang in local clubs. At 17, was in Billy Diamond's band; leader tagged him 'Fats' and it stuck. Played nights in juke-joints and worked days in factory when spotted by trumpeter/bandleader Dave Bartholomew.

Success began in 1949 with Imperial Records. December session yielded **The Fat Man,** a hit early in 1950. Fats had R&B hits for five years; style influenced by Albert Ammons, Meade Lux Lewis, Pleasant Joseph, Leon T. Gross (Archibald), Little Willie Littlefield.

Hit national charts in late 1955 with **Ain't**

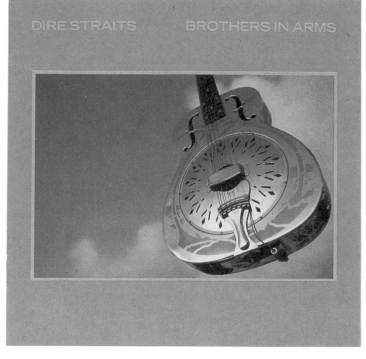

**Brothers In Arms, Dire Straits. Courtesy Vertigo Records.**

**That A Shame;** for next eight years was regular in US Top 50. Hits included **I'm In Love Again, Blueberry Hill, Blue Monday, Whole Lotta Loving, I'm Ready, Walking To New Orleans** and **Be My Guest.** Also had parts in rock movies 'Shake Rattle & Roll,' 'Disc Jockey Jamboree', 'The Big Beat,' 'The Girl Can't Help It'.

1960s saw dilution of music with occasional strings; material less convincing in aesthetic content. At end of 1962 declining sales brought parting with Imperial. Signed to ABC Paramount, output tailored to contemporary needs; **Red Sails In The Sunset** was Top 50 hit, combining piano triplets with swirling strings. A dozen releases yielded one more hit, **Heartbreak Hill;** by late 1964 Fats and Paramount had parted. Joined Mercury in 1965; brief association yielded a couple of abysmal singles.

Company taped Domino in Las Vegas, producing excellent 'live' LP. Made British debut at the Saville Theatre, March 1967. Following two years of recording inactivity formed own label, Broadmoor. Cut two singles before being signed by Reprise in 1968. Reprise album **Fats Is Back** was produced by Richard Perry; half-a-dozen singles had small sales; **Lady Madonna** made US charts.

Fats now seems content to live quietly at home with wife Rosemary and their eight children. Takes his pick of cabaret dates and occasional overseas tours; in 1978 went to Sea-Saint Studios to cut LP **Sleeping On The Job** for Sonet. Rumours of more new material in vintage New Orleans style have yet to be realised.

**Hit Singles:**

| | US | UK |
|---|---|---|
| Ain't That A Shame, 1955 | 10 | 23* |
| I'm In Love Again/My Blue Heaven, 1956 | 3 | 12 |
| My Blue Heaven/I'm In Love Again, 1956 | 19 | — |
| When My Dreamboat Comes Home, 1956 | 14 | — |
| Blueberry Hill, 1956 | 2 | 6 |
| Blue Monday, 1957 | 5 | 23 |
| I'm Walkin', 1957 | 4 | 19 |
| Valley Of Tears/It's You I Love, 1957 | 8 | 25 |
| It's You I Love/Valley Of Tears, 1957 | 8 | 25 |

| | | |
|---|---|---|
| The Big Beat, 1958 | 26 | 20 |
| Whole Lotta Loving, 1959 | 6 | — |
| Margie/I'm Ready, 1959 | 51 | 18 |
| I'm Ready/Margie, 1959 | 16 | — |
| I Want To Walk You Home/I'm Gonna Be A Wheel Someday, 1959 | 8 | 14 |
| I'm Gonna Be A Wheel Someday/I'm Gonna Walk You Home, 1959 | 17 | — |
| Be My Guest, 1959 | 8 | 11 |
| Country Boy, 1960 | 25 | 19 |
| Walking To New Orleans, 1960 | 6 | 19 |
| Three Nights A Week, 1960 | 15 | 45 |
| My Girl Josephine, 1960 | 14 | 32 |
| Let The Four Winds Blow, 1961 | 15 | — |
| *1957 in UK | | |

**Albums (selected):**
Million Sellers (Liberty), 1962
Fats Domino (Archive Of Folk And Jazz Music/—), 1966
Fats Domino Volume 2 (Archive Of Folk And Jazz Music/—), 1967
Legendary Masters (United Artists), 1972
The Fats Domino Story Volumes 1-6 (—/United Artists), 1977
Sleeping On The Job (Polydor/Sonet), 1979
The Best Of (Liberty), 1985 **CD**
16 Greatest Hits (Bescol), 1987 **CD**
Best Of (EMI/America)
Collection (Spectrum)
Fats Domino Collection (Deja Vu)

# Donovan

UK vocalist, guitarist.
Born Donovan Leitch, Glasgow, Scotland, May 10, 1946.

**Career:** Launched via ITV's 'Ready Steady Go' pop show (1965) as Britain's answer to Bob Dylan(▶), Donovan projected diluted version of then fashionable 'protest singer' image. His imitation extended to denim dungarees, flat denim hat, harmonica harness and acoustic guitar bearing legend 'This machine kills' (which Dylan himself had borrowed from Woody

**Donovan's Greatest Hits. Courtesy Epic Records.**

Guthrie(▶) who included the important extra word 'fascists'). Switching to flower-power in 1966 he became very much own man, with delightful results.

Signed to Pye Records, his first big hit, **Catch The Wind,** was still in Dylan mould, but by **Sunshine Superman** (1966) and **Mellow Yellow** (a US chart-topper in 1967) Donovan had evolved extremely catchy folk-pop sound, and consequent **Sunshine Superman** LP, produced by Mickie Most, was a gem, as was **A Gift From A Flower To A Garden** set. By this time Donovan had injected into his work a large measure of mysticism and colourful imagery.

After 1969 Jeff Beck(▶) collaboration on **Barabajagal** hit single, Donovan renounced drug culture, took up Eastern mysticism (following Beatles' lead) and retired to Ireland, emerging a year later to score movie 'If It's Tuesday This Must Be Belgium'.

In 1972 he scored 'The Pied Piper' (which he appeared in) and in '73 'Brother Sun, Sister Moon'. Also released in '73 was acclaimed **Cosmic Wheels** LP. However, most of Donovan's '70s LPs were poorly received in

**Below: The veteran rocker from New Orleans, Fats Domino.**

US, where the flower power image was 'out'.

Moving to US, he wrote stage show '7-Tease' in 1974 and cut concept album in Nashville before virtual retirement. Re-emerging at Edinburgh Festival, he toured Germany and France, and appeared on London Palladium charity Christmas show with Ralph McTell and Billy Connolly which led to 1981 UK concert tour and new album.

**Hit Singles:**

| | US | UK |
|---|---|---|
| Catch The Wind, 1965 | 23 | 4 |
| Colours, 1965 | — | 4 |
| Sunshine Superman, 1966 | 1 | 3 |
| Mellow Yellow, 1966 | 2 | 8 |
| Epistle To Dippy, 1967 | 19 | — |
| There Is A Mountain, 1967 | 11 | 8 |
| Jennifer Juniper, 1968 | 26 | 5 |
| Hurdy Gurdy Man, 1968 | 5 | 4 |
| Atlantis, 1969 | 7 | 23 |
| Barabajagal, 1969 | — | 12 |

**Albums:**

Catch The Wind (Hickory/Hallmark), 1965
Sunshine Superman (Epic/Pye), 1966
In Concert (Epic/Pye), 1968
Hurdy Gurdy Man (Epic/—), 1968
From A Flower To A Garden (Epic/Pye), 1968
Barabajagal (with Jeff Beck) (Epic/—), 1968
Greatest Hits (Epic/Pye), 1969
Colours (—/Hallmark), 1972
Cosmic Wheels (—/Epic), 1973
Donovan (—/Rak), 1977
The Donovan File (—/Pye), 1977
Greatest Hits (—/Embassy), 1979

# Doobie Brothers

US group formed 1970.

**Original line-up:** Tom Johnston, guitar, vocals; John Hartman, drums; Pat Simmons, guitar vocals; Dave Shogren, bass.

**Career:** Founded in San Jose, California, from remnants of band Pud; first line-up included Johnston, Hartman and bassist Gregory Murphy. Shogren quickly replaced Murphy, and with acquisition of Simmons group cut debut album for Warner Bros in 1971.

Additional drummer Mike Hossack joined soon after release of **The Doobie Bros;** Tiran Porter recruited for departing Dave Shogren (who joined Dave Gardner group). Quintet soon earned reputation on West Coast, basing themselves in San Francisco, latterly San Anselmo.

Twin guitars of Simmons and Johnston courted comparison with Allman Bros(▶). Doobies, however, were altogether lighter and less blues-influenced. Second album **Toulouse Street** introduced band to charts, both album and single (**Listen To The Music**) confirming hard-driving, but commercial, approach.

Now prominent concert attraction, band debuted in UK using new drummer Keith Knudsen (ex-Lee Michaels); Hossack moved to short-lived Bonaroo in 1975. Reviews were mixed but audiences enthusiastic. This line-up cut **The Captain & Me** LP, which followed **Toulouse Street** as second gold record. Band's long-time favourite **Long Train Running** was major single success from album.

**What Were Once Vices Are Now Habits** included session work from Jeff 'Skunk' Baxter, former Steely Dan(▶) guitarist. Baxter joined Doobies permanently shortly after album's release. Two-million seller **Black Water** (another band anthem) was US No. 1 culled from **Vices** set.

Another former Steely Dan member, keyboard player/vocalist Michael McDonald,

joined group in 1976; he had temporarily stood in for Johnston during '75 US tour. McDonald's inclusion took band into new era, with emphasis on R&B-styled rythms behind his high, impassioned voice—McDonald stands apart as one of the finest rock vocalist in the business (witness no. 1 single duet with Patti Labelle, **On My Own**).

Never the rock critic's favourite outfit, Doobies reversed opinion with stunning **Minute By Minute** album. With group now trimmed to six-piece (Johnston having left permanently in 1978), and McDonald and Simmons splitting lead vocal role, **Minute** earned four Grammy awards. Titletrack and **What A Fool Believes** are now rock classics, having been covered by various prominent performers (Aretha Franklin(▶) had minor US hit with **Fool**).

Doobies' ever-evolving line-up saw further changes in 1979, when Baxter and Hartman quit. Baxter is now producing (Nazareth(▶), Terry Boylan) and doing session work after stint with Four On The Floor (with Al Kooper(▶), Rich Schlosser, Neil Stubenhaus). Replacements were Cornelius Bumpus (ex-

**Stampede, The Doobie Brothers. Courtesy Warner Bros Records.**

**Below: The Doobie Brothers 'Takin' It To the Streets' in the late 1970s.**

Moby Grape(▶)), keyboards and sax; John McFee (ex-Clover, sessions for Steve Miller(▶) and Bill Wyman) guitar; and drummer Chet McCracken (ex-Don Randi Band, Nick Gilder). Seven-piece Doobies recorded **One Step Closer** in 1980, with long-time producer Ted Templeman still at helm. Album included Top 10 US hit **Real Love.**

Lack of studio recording since **Closer** (**Best of Volume 2** released in interim) has enabled McDonald to release debut solo album **If That's What It Takes** (1982) which features leading session players Steve Gadd, drums; Willie Weeks, bass; Dean Parks, guitar; Louis Johnson, bass; and Edgar Winter and Jeff and Mike Porcaro (Toto(▶)). McDonald has also recorded with Gary Wright, Elton John(▶), Jackie DeShannon, Christopher Cross(▶) and Kenny Loggins(▶) (with whom he wrote **What A Fool Believes**). Added keyboards to Tom Johnston's solo album **Everything You Feel Is True** (1979).

'Farewell Tour' album (1983) marked end of road for band with McDonald's solo work accelerating demise. Founder member Pat Simmons solo album **Arcade** (with Ted Templeman producing four tracks) released 1983 in attempt to maintain impetus. The Doobies were truly an institution and are certain inductees for a 'Rock Hall Of Fame'.

**Final line-up:** Simmons; Michael McDonald, keyboards, vocals; John McFee, guitar; Keith Knudsen, drums; Chet McCracken, drums, percussion; Tiran Porter, bass; Cornelius Bumpus, saxophones, keyboards.

**Hit Singles:**

| | US | UK |
|---|---|---|
| Listen To The Music, 1972 | 11 | 29 |
| Long Train Runnin', 1973 | 8 | — |
| China Grove 1973, | 15 | — |
| Black Water, 1975 | 1 | — |
| Take Me In Your Arms (Rock Me), 1975 | 11 | 29 |
| Takin' It To The Streets, 1976 | 13 | — |
| What A Fool Believes, 1979 | 1 | 31 |

**Best of, The Doobies. Courtesy Warner Bros. Records.**

| | | |
|---|---|---|
| Minute By Minute, 1979 | 14 | 47 |
| Real Love, 1980 | 5 | — |

**Albums:**

Doobie Brothers (Warner Bros), 1971
Toulouse Street (Warner Bros), 1972
The Captain And Me (Warner Bros), 1973 **CD**
What Were Once Vices (Warner Bros), 1974
Stampeded (Warner Bros), 1975
Takin' It To The Streets (Warner Bros), 1976
Best Of (Warner Bros), 1976 **CD**
Livin' On The Fault Line (Warner Bros), 1977
Minute By Minute (Warner Bros), 1979 **CD**
One Step Closer (Warner Bros), 1980
Best Of Volume 2 (Warner Bros), 1981

# Doors

US group formed 1965.

**Original line-up:** Jim Morrison, vocals; Ray Manzarek, keyboards; Robby Krieger, bass; John Densmore, drums.

**Career:** Leader and focus of band, Jim Morrison was born James Douglas Morrison in Melbourne, Florida, on December 8, 1943. Graduated from George Washington High

School in 1961, spent year at St Petersburg Junior College, then moved to Los Angeles to major in film techniques at UCLA. Met Chicago-born keyboard player Ray Manzarek who was running blues-flavoured band, Rick and the Ravens. They met LA native John Densmore, then playing with Psychedelic Rangers, and Robby Kreiger, at local meditation centre, and Doors opened career with gig at London Fog Club on Sunset Boulevard.

Early warning of subsequent tempestuous career came when they were banned from Los Angeles' prestigious rock club, Whiskey A Go-Go, for performance of **The End,** a half-spoken, half-improvised free-form epic song of apocalyptic imagery in which a young man murders his parents. A born rebel, Morrison claimed his own parents were dead and dropped one 's' from surname. His father was, in fact, a successful Rear Admiral from establishment family of long military standing.

The Doors' name was well chosen from William Blake: 'If the doors of perception were cleansed/All things would appear infinite'. Morrison's sense of theatrics aided him in acting out the fantasies, visions and fears of late '60s young America, from the innocuousness of flower power to the often frightening aspects of psychedelia and the self-destructiveness of drug culture. A charismatic figure on-stage, Morrison exuded animal sexuality with a mere glance.

Jack Holzman, who had been busy transforming his Elektra label from an esoteric folk outlet to major rock company, signed Doors; sensational debut album **Doors** included unedited version of **The End** as well as **Light My Fire,** which gave group US chart-topping single.

From sleeve art-work featuring various freaks, to bizarre lyrical content, second album, **Strange Days,** was archetypal Doors. Third set, **Waiting For The Sun,** yielded further No. 1 single **Hello I Love You** (only Doors recording which used a bass player — Doug Lubahn; Manzarek usually supplied bass lines through bass pedal of electric organ). Ray Davies of Kinks(▶)sued Doors, claiming **Hello** was rip-off of **All Day And All Of The Night;** UK royalties of **Hello I Love You** went to Davies instead of Doors. Featured on inner sleeve was full libretto of **The Celebration Of The Lizard King** but only small sampling, in form of **Not To Touch The Earth,** appeared on album, and plans for theatrical presentation were unfulfilled.

**Below: Morrison Hotel, The Doors. Courtesy Elektra Records.**

Morrison did venture into movie world via 'A Feast Of Friends' (in collaboration with two acquaintances from UCLA days) and two promotional films, 'Break On Through' and 'The Unknown Soldier'. He had also completed another screenplay (with novelist Michael McClure) shortly before his death.

Hippy generation felt Morrison's political and philosophical statements were diluted by an innate commercialism. Those in authority rated them anarchical heresies and when, on stage, he not only urged violent resistance to police repression but advocated blatant sexualism, he soon ran into trouble. He was arrested for using obscene language in New Haven, Connecticut, in December 1967, and for indecent exposure on stage in Miami in March 1969.

While court proceedings continued apace, rock critics alleged that Doors were merely pop outfit masquerading as leaders of youth revolution; this was confirmed in part when 1969 album **The Soft Parade** emerged with lightweight chart-style material and lack of direction. However, following album **Morrison Hotel** threw pretension to the wind, revealing hard and raw R&B. **Absolutely Live** set finally gave life to Morrison's reptilian fantasy (and alter-ego) via **The Celebration Of The Lizard.**

With **LA Woman** (1971), Doors reached creative zenith, blending brash rock 'n' roll with imagery of Morrison's lyrics in set which found them at most powerful and disturbing. From it came classic **Riders On The Storm**.

Four years of over-indulgence in sex, drugs, drink, philosophising, soul-searching and rock 'n' roll were taking their toll. An angry, depressed and world-weary Morrison quit group to live in Paris and write poetry (published as two books 'The Lords' and 'The New Creatures' in 1971).

Fittingly, Morrison's death is shrouded in mystery and there are even rumours that he still lives. According to official records he died of a heart attack in his bath on July 3, 1971. He is buried in Père Lachaise cemetery in Paris, which also houses remains of many of France's most famous artists, musicians, statesmen and legendary eccentrics. Morrison's tomb has become a point of pilgrimage for latter-day hippies.

Though lacking Morrison's touch of demented genius, **Other Voices** album was commendable effort from the three surviving Doors. **Full Circle** was sub-standard and trio broke up (though Manzarek made aborted effort to re-form group later with Iggy Pop(▶) as vocalist).

**Live at the Hollywood Bowl, The Doors. Courtesy Elektra Records.**

Manzarek continued career with solo albums for Mercury in 1975 — **The Golden Scarab** and **The Whole Thing Started With Rock 'N' Roll And Now It's Out Of Control,** a title that could well stand as most fitting epitaph for Jim Morrison.

Krieger and Densmore produced album for the Comfortable Chairs then formed short-lived Butts Band, Krieger re-emerging in 1977 with jazz/rock outfit for **Bobby Krieger And Friends** album on Blue Note. Manzarek continues to work in California as producer/manager for bands, notably LA group 'X'.

**Greatest Hits** (1980) went platinum in US, attesting to Doors dedicated following and new audience despite lack of new material or any chance of reunion.

**Final line-up:** Manzarek; Krieger; Densmore.

| Hit Singles: | US | UK |
| --- | --- | --- |
| Light My Fire, 1967 | 1 | 49 |
| People Are Strange, 1967 | 12 | — |
| Hello, I Love You, 1968 | 1 | 15 |
| Touch Me, 1969 | 3 | — |
| Love Her Madly, 1971 | 11 | — |
| Riders On The Storm, 1971 | 14 | 22 |

**Albums:**

Doors (Elektra), 1967* **CD**
Strange Days (Elektra), 1967 **CD**
Waiting For The Sun (Elektra), 1968 **CD**
The Soft Parade (Elektra), 1969
Morrison Hotel/Hard Rock Café (Elektra), 1970 **CD**
Absolutely Live (Elektra), 1970 **CD**
'13' (Elektra), 1971
LA Woman (Elektra), 1971 **CD**
Weird Scenes Inside The Goldmine (Elektra), 1971

Best Of (Elektra), 1973
An American Prayer (Elektra), 1978
Greatest Hits (Elektra), 1980**
Live At The Hollywood Bowl (Elektra), 1987 **CD**
*Re-mastered version available under same title (Mobile/—), 1982
**Includes remixed versions of singles.

*Worth Searching Out:*
Other Voices (Elektra), 1971
*Robbie Krieger Solo:*
Versions (—/Shanghai), 1984
*Ray Manzarek Solo:*
The Golden Scarab (Mercury), 1975
*Ray Manzarek Solo:*
Carmina Burana (A&M), 1983

# Dr John

US vocalist, multi-instrumentalist, composer. Born Malcolm John 'Mac' Rebennack, New Orleans, 1941.

**Career:** Son of model and record store owner; appeared in soap ads as baby. Learnt guitar from Sister Eustace at Temple Of The Innocent Blood in home city. Entered music business while teenager as session guitarist and producer with Johnny Vincent's Ace Records, working under Red Tyler. Local sax player Lee Allen, famed for work with Fats Domino and Little Richard, introduced him to regular session crew working on R&B product at Cosimo Matassa's New Orleans studio. Played guitar on sides for Ebb, Specialty, Ric and Ronn labels, and wrote and arranged, notably Jerry Byrne's rock 'n' roll hit **Lights Out.** Worked on road in bands of Byrne and Frankie Ford and cut instrumental single **Storm Warning** (Rex) leading to albums for Ace and Rex. Shot in finger in 1961, he switched to electric bass, working in Dixieland band, before learning organ; backed strippers in French Quarter. Returned to session work for Harold Battiste's AFO ('All For One') black co-operative (though white); cut organ album for AFO label.

With Battiste, split for Los Angeles in 1962, taking other musicians with them, including drummer John Boudreaux (later a mainstay of Dr John band) and Mel Lasty (who later played cornet with King Curtis(▶)). Detoured via Texas and became hung up on drugs. Companions became back-up team for Sam Cooke(▶) but by time Rebennack arrived on West Coast Cooke had been shot dead. Cooke's manager J.W. Alexander

helped Rebennack break into LA session scene; he was soon playing guitar on record and on stage for Sonny and Cher(▶) as well as working with other New Orleans exiles Jesse Hill, Alvin Robinson, Shirley Goodman). Also worked with such producer/arrangers as H.B. Barnum, Gene Page and Rene Hall.

Formed own bands, Grit's And Gravy (with Ronnie Barron), the Zu Zu Band (with Jessie Hill) and Morgus and the Three Ghouls. With Battiste's help, developed new mystic identity as Dr John Creux, The Night Tripper. This involved witch-doctor clothes, weird head dresses and self-proclamation as 'The Grand Zombie'. Image heightened by his vast bushy beard and considerable bulk.

Sonny Bono (of Sonny and Cher) financed first Dr John album, which was leased to Atlantic (1968) in one-off deal; included weird rhythms and hypnotic chants and eerie classic **Walk On Gilded Splinters**.

After further obscure album, Dr John joined Atlantic's regular roster thanks to producer Jerry Wexler, but he had become victim of drug abuse. A doctor from psychiatric ward of UCLA Medical Centre called Wexler who took him in hand; he was put on Atlantic staff as session musician, he cut organ for Aretha Franklin's (▶) **Spanish Harlem**.

Further Dr John recordings were cut and such musicians as Mick Jagger and Eric Clapton(▶) (who appeared on his 1971 album **Sun, Moon And Herbs**) helped spread the word.

Mixing voodoo, Creole, African and R&B influences, Dr John was one of pioneers of 'swamp rock' style (Doug Kershaw, Tony Joe White and Creedence Clearwater Revival(▶) were other exponents, though none sounded quite like him). In 1973 **Right Time, Wrong Place** single made big impact leading to major tours, including one of Europe backed by New Orleans' R&B giants the Meters. In 1978 recorded **City Lights** album for A&M.

Since that zenith, Dr John has maintained low profile, while guesting on albums; remains a revered session pianist.

**Hit Singles:**

| | US | UK |
|---|---|---|
| Right Place, Wrong Time, 1973 | 9 | — |

**Albums:**
City Lights (A&M), 1978
Love Potion (Accord/—), 1981
Plays (Clean Cuts/—), 1981

*Worth Searching Out:*
Gris Gris (Atco/Atlantic), 1968
Babylon (Atco/Atlantic), 1972
Cut Me While I'm Hot (—/DJM), 1976
Dr John Plays Mac Rebbenack (Edsel), 1982
I Been Hoodood (Edsel), 1984

# The Drifters

US vocal group formed 1953.

**Original line-up:** Clyde McPhatter; Gerhardt Thrasher; Andrew Thrasher; Bill Pinkney.

**Career:** More like a football side than a group, the Drifters have featured constantly changing line-up. More than 50 individuals have worked with the official group over past three decades. Several breakaway groups have exploited name, notably Bill Pinkney's Original Drifters.

Masterminded by manager George Treadwell, then husband of Sarah Vaughan, group was launched to showcase lead singer Clyde McPhatter. First six releases, via Atlantic, were R&B hits.

In 1955, McPhatter left for mililtary service, being replaced as lead singer briefly by David Baughn, then by Johnny Moore, who was in turn drafted. Bill Pinkney, Gerhardt

Thrasher and Bobby Hendricks also sang lead at various times but most records flopped. The best was **Flip Flop**, led by Moore, and **Drip Drop**, led by Hendricks. Significantly, both songs were penned by Jerry Leiber and Mike Stoller. When Treadwell sacked his group in 1958 and set about finding a new set of Drifters, he turned to Leiber and Stoller for material.

Group chosen—Ben E. King, Doc Green, Charlie Thomas, Elsbeary Hobbs—had been working with no real success as the Crowns. Moving King to lead singer and using Leiber/Stoller songs proved masterstroke and 1959 smash hit **There Goes My Baby** set in train whole gamut of big records.

King left for solo career, also with Atlantic, in 1960 and Rudy Lewis was brought in from Clara Ward Singers as new lead voice. Lewis held job for next three years. Rest of group was blended with female back-up quartet of Dionne and Dee Dee Warwick, Doris Troy and Cissy Houston. Arrangements by Phil Spector, Burt Bacharach, Bert Berns and Gary Sherman and songs from Gerry Goffin and Carole King(▶), Burt Bacharach and Hal David, and Barry Mann and Cynthia Weil added to potent format, producing classic hits like **Up On The Roof, Sweets For My Sweet** and **Let The Music Play**.

Lewis died on eve of session for **Under The Boardwalk** and Johnnie Moore, who had returned to group, stepped into breach as new lead singer. Though no longer with Drifters, Moore can claim to have sung lead on more than 80% of all their records to date.

Group had capitalised on coming together of black and white teenage tastes in early '60s, but subsequent polarisation of audiences saw their run of success subside. Then, in 1972, UK Atlantic started to score on charts with re-issues of their earlier classics.

Consequent recording deal with Bell, and link with British songwriters Roger Cook, Roger Greenaway and Tony Macauley, brought new run of hits, reviving the teen-ballad story-line themes of their Atlantic classics. **Saturday Night At The Movies** inspired **Kissin' In The Back Row Of The Movies**, and **Under The Boardwalk** and **Sand In My Shoes** provided theme for **Down On The Beach Tonight**.

With group now under management of Treadwell's second wife (and widow) Faye, a steady living was made playing cabaret venues around the world—helping people revive fond memories of their teens. Moore remained only constant factor in perpetually evolving line-up.

In 1980 Moore left for short-lived solo career. He rejoined for short spell then left again to form Slightly Adrift, with fellow Drifter Joe Blunt and former member Clyde Brown, when Faye Treadwell decided to sever 11-year business relationship with group's UK promoter Henry Sellers.

Treadwell brought Ben E. King back into Drifters as lead singer and he stayed on when Moore returned yet again in 1984.

Two developments in 1987 were The Drifters' introduction into Rock'n'Roll Hall Of Fame, and Ben E. King's topping of UK charts with **Stand By Me**. Latter event followed song's use in TV commercial for jeans.

**Current line-up:** Ben E. King, Johnnie Moore, Clyde Brown, Joe Blunt.

**Hit Singles:**

| | US | UK |
|---|---|---|
| There Goes My Baby, 1959 | 2 | — |
| Dance With Me, 1959 | 15 | 17 |
| This Magic Moment, 1960 | 16 | — |
| Save The Last Dance For Me, 1960 | 1 | 2 |
| I Count The Years, 1961 | 17 | 28 |
| Please Stay, 1961 | 14 | — |
| Sweets For My Sweet, 1961 | 16 | — |
| Up On The Roof, 1963 | 5 | — |
| On Broadway, 1963 | 9 | — |
| Under The Boardwalk, 1964 | 4 | 45 |
| Saturday Night At The Movies, 1964 | 18 | — |
| At The Club/Saturday Night At The Movies, 1972 | — | 3 |
| Come On Over To My Place, 1972 | — | 9 |
| Like Sister And Brother, 1973 | — | 7 |
| Kissin' In The Back Row Of The Movies, 1974 | — | 2 |
| Down On The Beach Tonight, 1974, | — | 7 |
| There Goes My First Love, 1975 | — | 3 |
| Can I Take You Home Little Girl, 1975 | — | 10 |
| Hello Happiness, 1976 | — | 12 |
| You're More Than A Number In My Little Red Book, 1976 | — | 5 |

**Albums:**
Golden Hits (Atlantic), 1966 **CD**
Greatest Recordings—The Early Years (Atco/—), 1960
Love Games (—/Bell), 1975
24 Original Hits (Atlantic), 1975
Juke Box Giants (—/Audio Fidelity), 1982
Drifters With Ben E. King (Entertainers), 1987 **CD**
Save The Last Dance For Me—The Definitive Collection (Atlantic), 1987 **CD**
20 Greatest Hits (Spectrum), 1987 **CD**

# Duran Duran

UK group formed 1980.

**Original/current line-up:** Simon Le Bon, vocals; Andy Taylor, guitar; Nick Rhodes, synthesiser; John Taylor, bass; Roger Taylor, drums.

**Career:** Nick (born 1962) and John (born 1960) formed early version of band (name taken from villain in Jane Fonda film 'Barbarella') with Steve Duffy (vocals) and Simon Colley (bass)—John played guitar at this point. Duffy and Colley left, replaced by Andy Wickett (vocals, ex-TV Eye) and Roger Taylor (born 1960, ex-Scent Organs). At this stage, band all from Birmingham area. Wickett left, John Taylor moved to bass, and Andy Taylor (born 1961) from Newcastle joined as a result of 'Melody Maker' advert. Simon (born 1958, Hertfordshire), then studying drama at Birmingham University, became final piece of jigsaw, assuming lyricist/vocal role.

In autumn 1980 band broke through to national attention touring as support to Hazel

**Below: The faces that cover teenage bedroom walls in '80s—Duran Duran.**

O'Connor, following up exposure with hit single **Planet Earth** in 1981. Album **Duran Duran** followed, spawning UK hit **Girls On Film**; hit also established Duran as video stars, status they would consolidate throughout their career.

From this point onwards band could do no wrong, garnering enormous commercial success both in UK and US. Somewhat mechanical formula made them less than favourites with critics, but teen buyers throughout world were convinced. Photogenic qualities of band members were no hindrance in conquest of pre- and post-pubescent females.

In mid-80s various dissatisfactions became

**Rio, Duran Duran. Courtesy EMI Records.**

apparent when Andy and John Taylor formed spin-off group Power Station with Robert Palmer, while remainder formed Duran-like outfit called Arcadia. Both aggregations enjoyed some success. Meanwhile, Simon Le Bon took up yacht racing and almost met a watery grave during transatlantic race.

Meanwhile Andy Taylor, persevered with his solo career. Duran got back together to record **Notorious** in 1986, enjoying renewed level of success.

Not always the most inspiring crew musically, Duran are nevertheless smart operators who know how to combine catchy songs and flashy visuals to irresistible effect. Not so much a band, more a triumph of eighties marketing expertise.

**Hit Singles:**

| | US | UK |
|---|---|---|
| Planet Earth, 1981 | — | 12 |
| Girls On Film, 1981 | — | 5 |
| My Own Way, 1981 | — | 14 |
| Hungry Like The Wolf, 1982 | 3 | 5 |
| *Save A Prayer, 1982 | 16 | 2 |
| Rio, 1982 | 14 | 9 |
| Is There Something I Should Know, 1983 | 4 | 1 |
| Union Of The Snake, 1983 | 3 | 3 |
| New Moon On Monday, 1984 | 10 | 9 |

| The Reflex, 1984 | 1 | 1 |
| Wild Boys, 1984 | 2 | 1 |
| A View To A Kill, 1985 | 1 | 2 |
| Notorious, 1986 | 2 | 7 |
| *1985 in US | | |

| The Power Station: | | |
| Some Like It Hot, 1985 | 6 | 14 |
| Get It On, 1985 | 9 | 22 |

| Arcadia: | | |
| Election Day, 1985 | 8 | 7 |

**Albums:**
Duran Duran (Harvest/EMI), 1981 **CD**
Rio (Harvest/EMI), 1982 **CD**
Seven And The Ragged Tiger (EMI) 1983 **CD**
Arena (EMI), 1984 **CD**
Notorious (EMI), 1986 **CD**

*The Power Station:*
Power Station (Parlophone), 1985

*Arcadia:*
So Red The Rose (Parlophone), 1985

# Ian Dury

UK vocalist, composer.
Born Billericay, Essex, 1942.

**Career:** Crippled by polio at age seven, Dury spent early youth at institution for disabled until going to grammar school. At 17 he went to Walthamstow Art College; then on to Royal College of Art for postgraduate course.

While teaching he formed band Kilburn and the High Roads, which cut a couple of albums and achieved considerable cult following. After Kilburn folded, Dury signed with Stiff Records and released **New Boots And Panties** with new band Blockheads (Chas Jankel, guitar; Mickey Gallagher, keyboards; Davey Payne, sax; Norman Watt-Roy, bass; Charley Charles, drums). Dury and co-writer/musical director Chas Jankel combined intriguing new blend of soul/disco musical feel with English music-hall lyrical approach.

**Boots** eventually sold almost half a million copies, mainly in UK, and spawned classic rock 'n' roll anthem **Sex And Drugs And Rock And Roll.**

By now Blockheads had established reputation as hot live act, and were touring in US and Europe. First major single hit came in 1978 with **What A Waste,** which was followed by No. 1 **Hit Me With Your Rhythm Stick.**

**Reasons To Be Cheerful Pt.3** was band's last big hit and label switch to Polydor in 1980 has so far proved unsuccessful. In 1986, Dury took up acting, playing title role in Mary O'Malley's 'Talk Of The Devil'.

| Hit Singles: | US | '''' |
| What A Waste, 1978 | — | 9 |
| Hit Me With Your Rhythm Stick, 1978 | — | 1 |
| Reasons To Be Cheerful, Pt. 3, 1979 | — | 3 |

**Albums:**
New Boots And Panties (Stiff), 1977
Do It Yourself (—/Stiff), 1979
Laughter (—/Stiff), 1980
Lord Upminster (Polydor), 1981
Sex & Drugs & Rock & Roll (Demon), 1978 **CD**

*Worth Searching Out;*
*Kilburn and the High Roads:*
Handsome (—/Pye), 1975
Wot A Bunch (—/Warner Bros), 1978

# Bob Dylan

US composer, vocalist, guitarist, harmonica player.
Born Robert Allen Zimmerman, Duluth, Minnesota, May 24, 1941.

**Career:** Quiet, serious Bobby Zimmerman got good grades, participated in school activities and graduated from Hibbing High in 1959. However, listened to blues and country music, and was more interested in becoming rock 'n' roll star. At University of Minnesota discovered remnants of beat era in nearby Dinkytown with its folk music coffee-houses. Seeing this as route to success, began playing at local folk clubs. Read Woody Guthrie's(▶) 'Bound For Glory', began calling himself Bob Dylan, and invented past as runaway with Okie roots.

With rambling boy image down pat, got blessing—and fare—from parents for December 1960 visit to Guthrie in hospital. Remained in New York, singing traditional songs in Greenwich Village clubs. 'Village Voice' and 'New York Times' predicted success, while others thought him Guthrie clone—but uncool, uncaring and mannered.

Played back-up harmonica on titletrack of Harry Belafonte's **Midnight Special** album, and for Carolyn Hester. Signed by Columbia Records' John Hammond in October 1961. First album **Bob Dylan,** including own compositions **Song To Woody** and **Talkin' New York,** plus traditional numbers, sold only 5,000 copies in first year.

Dylan predicted direction music was heading and took civil rights/anti-war stance, often using 'borrowed' tunes for self-righteous, moralising topical songs filled with brilliant imagery and caustic irony. By March 1963 reputation was growing, and **The Freewheelin' Bob Dylan** was released (after power struggle between Hammond and Dylan's manager Albert Grossman led to Hammond's departure in mid-recording, replaced by Tom Wilson).

Album includes **Blowin' In The Wind,** highlight of Newport Folk Festival that summer when Dylan sang it with Peter, Paul and Mary(▶). Trio's cover version became Top 10 hit, selling 320,000 copies in first eight days of release. Personal relationship developed with Joan Baez(▶) and Dylan appeared at her concerts. Becoming hot property, he headlined Carnegie Hall concert; **The Times They Are A-Changin'** album made him hero of protest movement. Because of public pressure, by February 1964 Dylan became recluse, using bodyguards and drugs as protection from outside world.

With success as folk singer achieved, Dylan began changing image. During British visits, he heard English rock (and had small role in BBC-TV play). As usual, he had eye on barometer: though acoustic, 1964 LP **Another Side of Bob Dylan** was first step toward rock. Self-pitying

Above: John Wesley Harding, Bob Dylan. Courtesy CBS Records.

Above: Knocked Out Loaded, Bob Dylan. Courtesy CBS Records.

and cruel, but vividly powerful, lyrics emphasised personal rather than political sentiments on songs like **All I Really Want To Do** and **It Ain't Me, Babe.** Folk fans and political protesters felt betrayed and album did not do as well as first two.

Spending much time in Woodstock, NY, Dylan wrote 18 new songs for 1965 **Bringing It All Back Home,** which completed switch from folk to rock, and from travelling to tripping. One side had four solo tracks, including **Mr Tambourine Man** and **It's All Over Now, Baby Blue;** other side with electric guitar and backup band featured **Subterranean Homesick Blues.** Released as single, this surreal, apocalyptic vision ultimately became Dylan's first gold record. The Byrds'(▶) two-minute version of **Mr Tambourine Man** went to No. 1 in US and UK, leading new folk-rock trend.

Although losing fans among protesters, Dylan gained wider audience of alienated young people who responded to funky music and sneering rejection of American Dream. May 1965 film 'Don't Look Back' showed on-stage and backstage dramas, including split with Baez, during Dylan's English tour. Returning to US, recorded **Like A Rolling Stone,** which gave him international stardom, with Mike Bloomfield(▶) on guitar and Al Kooper(▶) on organ. Single was released before rest of **Highway 61 Revisited,** produced by Bob Johnston.

Unveiling electric sound and Carnaby Street clothes at Newport and Forest Hills that summer, Dylan was booed by audience who saw prancing rock 'n' roller as sell-out. Next single **Positively 4th Street** was described as 'most vicious song ever to reach the Hit Parade'. Double album **Blonde on Blonde** was characterised by intense, poetic songs of drugs, dreams and nightmares about identity. Toured with the Hawks, later called the Band(▶); and married Sara Lowndes. Dylan admitted to being a millionaire with over 10 million records sold.

In July 1966, shortly after his 25th birthday, motorcycle crash led to 18-month disappearance; while recuperating in Woodstock from broken neck, rumours of death, disfigurement and drug addiction abounded. During this period Dylan recorded **Basement Tapes** with the Band (not officially released until eight years later). Early 1968 saw his

Above: Robert Allen Zimmerman circa 1963, a 'freewheelin' folkie.

Above left: Bob Dylan during the early '70s—the classic era.

appearance at benefit concert for Woody Guthrie, the birth of his first child, and release of **John Wesley Harding,** recorded in Nashville with country instrumentation. Voice had mellowed, lyrics were more accessible and gave hint of compassion, and tunes were melodic. **Nashville Skyline** continued songs in praise of living and gave last Top 10 single wilth **Lay Lady Lay.** During summer 1969 he split with Grossman; performed for huge crowds at Isle of Wight and Woodstock Festivals.

Moving back to Greenwich Village, released two disappointing records in 1970, although **Self Portrait** became seventh gold album. Over next two years kept low profile, while books, fanzines and Dylanology clubs interpreted his words and scavengers searched his garbage for significance. Meanwhile, bootleg records proliferated, Dylan's book Tarantula was published, and he visited Israel. Performed at Madison Square Garden benefit for Bangla Desh; recorded both electric and acoustic versions of **George Jackson** single, and did sessions for friends. **Greatest Hits II** was released.

Went to West Coast for small role in film 'Pat Garrett and Billy the Kid', and wrote score, including **Knocking On Heaven's Door.** When Columbia contract expired, recorded **Planet Waves** for Asylum; tour with the Band resulted in exciting live album **Before The Flood.** Re-signing with Columbia, recorded **Blood On The Tracks.** Filled with pain and bitterness (his marriage was breaking up), album was seen as return to form after recent simplistic good-time music. After recording new album **Desire,** toured with old friends and stars of 1960s in 1975-76 Rolling Thunder Revue. Dylan praised as charismatic entertainer; television special and live album **Hard Rain** released. During tour Dylan also created four-hour poetically rambling film 'Renaldo and Clara', screened in 1968.

At end of 1970s Dylan became born-again Christian. Somewhat self-righteously aimed moralising at non-believers (including fellow rock 'n' rollers). First post-conversion album **Slow Train Coming** (1979) featured talented instrumentalists. Later albums added gospel flavour, but didn't create much excitement.

Subsequent albums received patchy critical and commercial acceptance, but Dylan's live pulling power remained undiminished, as evidenced by 1986 tour with Tom Petty and the Heartbreakers and 1987 outings with fellow sixties legends The Grateful Dead(▶).

Latterly Dylan has appeared in slightly incongruous context of rock movie **Heats Of Fire**, playing eminence grise to English actor Rupert Everett's young rock star.

Above: Bob Dylan on stage during the late 1970s.

| Hit Singles: | US | UK |
| --- | --- | --- |
| Times They Are A-Changin', 1965 | — | 9 |
| Subterranean Homesick Blues, 1965 | 39 | 9 |
| Maggie's Farm, 1965 | — | 22 |
| Like A Rolling Stone, 1965 | 2 | 4 |
| Positively 4th Street, 1965 | 7 | 8 |
| Can You Please Crawl Out Your Window!, 1966 | 58 | 17 |
| Rainy Day Women, Nos 12 & 35, 1966 | 2 | 7 |
| I Want You, 1966 | 20 | 16 |
| Lay Lady Lay, 1969 | 7 | 5 |
| Knockin' On Heaven's Door, 1973 | 12 | 14 |
| Baby Stop Crying, 1978 | — | 13 |

**Albums:**
Bob Dylan (Columbia/CBS), 1962
Freewheelin' Bob Dylan (Columbia/CBS), 1963
Times They Are A-Changin' (Columbia/CBS), 1964
Another Side Of Bob Dylan (Columbia/CBS), 1964
Bringing It All Back Home (Columbia/CBS), 1965 **CD**
Highway 61 Revisited (Columbia/CBS), 1965 **CD**
Blonde On Blonde (Columbia/CBS), 1966 **CD**
Greatest Hits (Columbia/CBS), 1967
John Wesley Harding (Columbia/CBS), 1968
Nashville Skyline (Columbia/CBS), 1969 **CD**
Self Portrait (Columbia/CBS), 1970
New Morning (Columbia/CBS), 1970
Greatest Hits Volume II (Columbia/CBS), 1971
Pat Garrett & Billy The Kid (soundtrack) (Columbia/CBS), 1973
Dylan (Columbia/CBS), 1973
Planet Waves (Columbia/CBS), 1974
Before The Flood (Asylum/Island), 1974
Blood On The Tracks (Columbia/CBS), 1974 **CD**
Basement Tapes (CBS), 1975
Desire (Columbia/CBS), 1975
Hard Rain (Columbia/CBS), 1976
Street Legal (Columbia/CBS), 1978 **CD**
At Budokan (Columbia/CBS), 1978 **CD**
Slow Train Coming (Columbia/CBS), 1979 **CD**
Saved (Columbia/CBS), 1980
Shot Of Love (Columbia/CBS), 1981
Infidels (CBS), 1983 **CD**
Empire Burlesque (CBS), 1985 **CD**
Biograph (CBS), 1985 **CD**
Gaslight Tapes (The Compact Collection) (CBS) **CD**

**Right: Dylan as he appeared in the 'Rolling Thunder' Revue in 1976.**

The Times They Are A-Changin', Bob Dylan. Courtesy CBS Records.

**Above: Self Portrait, Bob Dylan. Courtesy CBS Records.**

**Above: Street Legal, Bob Dylan, Courtesy CBS Records.**

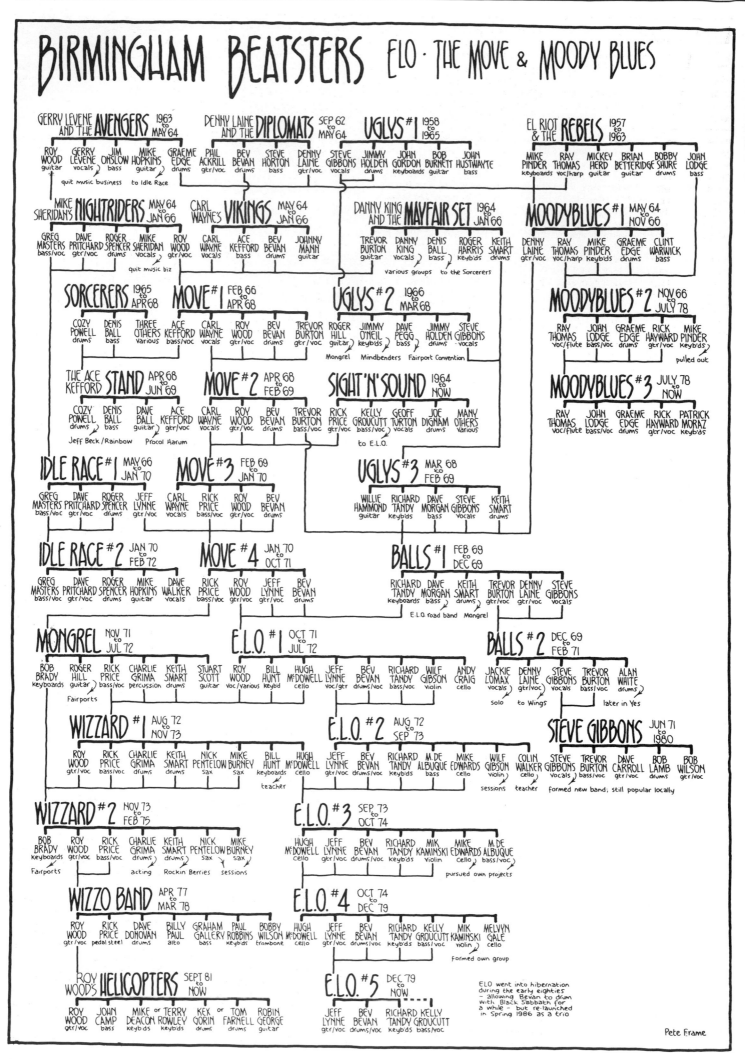

# BIRMINGHAM BEATSTERS ELO · THE MOVE & MOODY BLUES

Pete Frame

# ELO (Electric Light Orchestra)

UK group formed 1971.

**Original line-up:** Jeff Lynne, vocals, guitar; Roy Wood, vocals, guitar; Bev Bevan, drums, vocals.

**Career:** Band was formed out of remnants of Move(▶); idea was to expand boundaries of orchestral rock. First album, **Electric Light Orchestra**, was recorded over considerable period of time with various string players; yielded hit single in **10538 Overture**.

Although Roy Wood(▶) split to form Wizzard, Lynne decided to rebuild group from scratch, hiring motley collection of musicians, some with rock and some with classical backgrounds. **ELO II** was released in 1973 to critical indifference, but it yielded another hit single, an updated and highly orchestrated version of Chuck Berry's warhorse **Roll Over Beethoven**.

By this time recognisable style was being set, and it was proving to be commercially acceptable. Pop-orientated but with thick, dense texture overlaid by characteristic strings, ELO sound became mid-'70s winner. 1974 album **Eldorado** went gold in US, feat that most of following albums repeated or surpassed. At same time, band released almost unbroken string of Top 20 hit singles.

By end of decade it appeared that ELO could virtually do no wrong. Although involved in catastrophic movie 'Xanadu', band managed to walk away with massive hit single (with Olivia Newton-John(▶)), and retained most of their credibility. One time member violinist Mick Kaminski (1976) scored solo success in 1979 with **Violinski**.

After long period of inactivity, and temporary disbandment in 1983, Lynne resurrected group for excellent 1986 album **Balance Of Power**, with virtuoso violinist Kaminski back in the line-up.

Balance of Power, Electric Light Orchestra. Courtesy Epic Records.

Very much brainchild of Jeff Lynne, ELO exemplify bands who are able to flit in and out of rock business without harming reputation. Lynne's superb ear for melody is unquestionably the reason.

**Current line-up:** Lynne; Bevan; Richard Tannoy, keyboards; Melvyn Gale, cello; Kelly Groucutt, bass; Mick Kaminski, violin.

| Hit Singles: | US | UK |
|---|---|---|
| 10538 Overture, 1972 | — | 9 |
| Roll Over Beethoven, 1973 | 42 | 6 |
| Showdown, 1973 | 53 | 12 |
| Can't Get It Out Of My Head, 1975 | 9 | — |
| Evil Woman, 1976 | 10 | 10 |
| Strange Magic, 1976 | 14 | 38 |
| Livin' Thing, 1976 | 13 | 4 |
| Rockaria, 1977 | — | 9 |
| Telephone Line, 1977 | 7 | 8 |
| Turn To Stone, 1977 | 13 | 18 |
| Mister Blue Sky, 1978 | 35 | 6 |
| Sweet Talkin' Woman, 1978 | 17 | 6 |
| Wild West Hero, 1978 | — | 6 |
| Shine A Little Love, 1979 | 8 | 6 |
| The Diary Of Horace Wimp, 1979 | — | 8 |
| Don't Bring Me Down, 1979 | 4 | 3 |
| Confusion/Last Train To London, 1979 | — | 8 |
| Confusion, 1979 | 37 | — |
| Last Train To London, 1979 | 38 | — |
| I'm Alive, 1980 | 16 | 20 |
| All Over The World, 1980 | 13 | 11 |
| Hold On Tight, 1981 | 10 | 4 |
| Rock'n'Roll Is King, 1983 | 19 | 13 |
| Calling America, 1986 | — | 28 |

*With Olivia Newton-John:*
| | US | UK |
|---|---|---|
| Xanadu, 1980 | 8 | 1 |

**Albums:**
Electric Light Orchestra (Jet/Harvest), 1971*
ELO (Jet/Fame), 1973
On The Third Day (Jet), 1973
Face The Music (Jet), 1975
Eldorado (Jet), 1975
Olé ELO (Jet), 1976
New World Record (Jet), 1976 **CD**
Out Of The Blue (Jet), 1977
The Light Shines On (—/Harvest), 1977
The Light Shines On Volume 2 (—/Harvest), 1979
Discovery (Jet), 1979 **CD**
Greatest Hits (Jet), 1979 **CD**
A Box Of Their Best (Jet/—), 1980
Time (Jet), 1981
Secret Messages (Jet), 1983 **CD**
Balance Of Power (Epic), 1986 **CD**
'First Movement' (EMI), 1987 **CD**
*Titled **No Answer** in US

# The Eagles

US band formed 1971.

**Original line-up:** Glenn Frey, vocals, guitar; Randy Meisner, vocals, bass; Bernie Leadon, guitar, vocals; Don Henley, drums, vocals.

**Career:** Frey and Henley met as members of Linda Ronstadt's(▶) backing band. Following

Desperado, The Eagles. Courtesy Asylum Records.

recruitment of former Poco(▶) member Meisner and former Flying Burrito Brother(▶) Leadon, four flew to London to record first album as Eagles for Asylum.

Album **The Eagles** made major impact, as did single **Take It Easy**, co-written by Frey and stablemate Jackson Browne(▶). **Desperado** consolidated success, and crystallised Eagles' image as laid-back California outlaws. By now band had become major live attraction, adding large orchestra for some concerts.

Having contributed to sessions for third album **On The Border**, guitarist Don Felder added as fifth member. Band went from strength to strength, breaking British market for first time in 1975 with single **One Of These Nights**. Same year saw first No.1 single in US, **Best Of My Love**.

During mid-'70s band could do no wrong, achieving status of mega-group with across-board appeal. Heaped with gold and platinum records, garlanded with awards, only problem was meeting demand for product and live appearances. Strain proved too much for Bernie Leadon, who quit at end of 1975 to pursue unspectacular solo career. Slightly surprising choice of replacement was former James Gang(▶) guitarist Joe Walsh(▶), who had more recently been pursuing solo career; Walsh's songwriting/guitar work gave their 'laid-back' California sound a shot in the arm. In 1977 Randy Meisner also quit to go solo, and in came Timothy B. Schmidt, another former Poco stalwart.

By end of decade, by which time line-up had been further augmented by long-time friend Joe Vitale on keyboards, Eagles had become one of the most successful American recording acts of the '70s. Band has sold 40 million albums worldwide since inception; **Hotel California** sold nine million in year of release, **Greatest Hits** seven million. All concerts were immediate sell-outs.

1982 saw band in abeyance as both Glenn Frey and Don Henley had success with solo releases (Henley's **Dirty Laundry** (1982) in particular becoming major hit) but fans had consolation of **Greatest Messages Volume 2** album. The current split in ranks has lasted some years now, and band are unlikely to return as permanent unit.

Although criticised as epitome of unchallenging AOR, Eagles delivered impressively

consistent body of work and showed that genre doesn't have to be moronic. They combined songwriting abilities, musicianship and superb harmonies.

Eagles finally split when solo projects (see Frey separate entry) became increasingly time consuming.

**Final line-up:** Frey; Henley; Don Felder, guitar, vocals; Joe Walsh, guitar, vocals; Timothy B. Schmidt, bass, vocals; Joe Vitale, keyboards.

| Hit Singles: | US | UK |
|---|---|---|
| Take It Easy, 1972 | 12 | — |
| Witchy Woman, 1972 | 9 | — |
| Best Of My Love, 1975 | 1 | — |
| One Of These Nights, 1975 | 1 | 23 |
| Lyin' Eyes, 1975 | 2 | 23 |
| Take It To The Limit, 1976 | 4 | 12 |
| New Kid In Town, 1977 | 1 | 20 |
| Hotel California, 1977 | 1 | 8 |
| Life In The Fast Lane, 1977 | 11 | — |
| Please Come Home For Christmas, 1978 | 18 | 30 |
| Heartache Tonight, 1979 | 1 | 40 |
| The Long Run, 1979 | 8 | — |
| I Can't Tell You Why, 1980 | 8 | — |

*Don Henley Solo:*
| | US | UK |
|---|---|---|
| Leather And Lace, 1981* | 6 | — |
| Dirty Laundry, 1982 | 3 | — |
| The Boys Of Summer, 1985 | 5 | 12 |
| All She Wants To Do Is Dance, 1985 | 10 | 2 |
| *with Stevie Nicks | | |

*Randy Meisner Solo:*
| | US | UK |
|---|---|---|
| Hearts On Fire, 1981 | 9 | — |

**Albums:**
The Eagles (Asylum), 1972
Desperado (Asylum), 1973 **CD**
On The Border (Asylum), 1974 **CD**
One Of These Nights (Asylum), 1975 **CD**
Their Greatest Hits (Asylum), 1975 **CD**
Hotel California (Asylum), 1976 **CD**
The Long Run (Asylum), 1979 **CD**
Eagles Live (Asylum), 1980 **CD**
Greatest Hits Volume 2 (Asylum), 1982 **CD**
Best Of (Asylum), 1985 **CD**

*Don Henley Solo:*
I Can't Stand Still (Asylum/—),1982
Building The Perfect Beast (Geffen), 1985

*Randy Meisner Solo:*
Randy Meisner (Asylum), 1978
One More Song (Epic), 1980
Randy Meisner (Epic), 1982

*Joe Walsh Solo:*
(see separate entry)

# Sheena Easton

UK vocalist.
Born Bellshill, Glasgow, April 27, 1959.

**Career:** Chosen as subject for BBC television's 'The Big Time'—a documentary tracing aspiring singer's struggle for stardom— Sheena Easton lived out the part to establish herself as major international artist.

While studying at Royal Scottish Academy Of Music And Drama, she spent evenings working local pub/club circuit before auditioning for 'The Big Time'.

Signed to EMI, second single **9 To 5** became THE summer hit of 1980 and screening of 'The Big Time' in July focused attention on debut single **Modern Girl**, earlier a minor hit, which joined **9 To 5**, making her first British female singer to have two Top 10 hits at same time. In America she went one better: her first three singles all featured simultaneously in Top 50.

Easton's first year was topped off by Royal Variety Show appearance, while debut album quickly went gold in US and UK, and platinum in Japan and Canada, leading to awards as Best Female Singer of 1981 and Female Personality of Year in UK and Best Female Newcomer in US.

She not only sang theme to James Bond movie 'For Your Eyes Only' but appeared in opening sequence, and later performed song at 1982 Oscar ceremony.

Now carefully groomed with keen eye for fashion, Easton took advantage of US success, moving to California where she flourished on night club circuit.

Whilst chart success continued in US including unlikely duets with Kenny Rogers and, most recently, Prince, Easton's UK appeal dwindled. However, latterly US audience has increased to point where she has become established showbusiness personality. Astute management must take lion's share of credit for this metamorphosis, as artist's abilities remain essentially modest.

**Hit Singles:**

| | US | UK |
|---|---|---|
| 9 To 5*, 1980 | 1 | 3 |
| Modern Girl, 1980 | 18 | 8 |
| One Man Woman, 1980 | — | 14 |
| When He Shines, 1981 | — | 12 |
| For Your Eyes Only, 1981 | 4 | 8 |
| You Could Have Been With Me, 1981 | 15 | 54 |
| Telephone (Long Distance Love Affair), 1983 | 9 | — |
| Strut, 1984 | 7 | — |
| Sugar Walls, 1985 | 9 | — |
| *Sheena Easton (with Prince)* | | |
| U Got The Look, 1987 | 2 | 11 |

*Known as 'Morning Train' in US

**Albums:**
Take My Time (EMI), 1981
You Could Have Been With Me (EMI), 1981
Madness, Money And Music (EMI), 1982
Best Kept Secret (EMI), 1983
A Private Heaven (EMI), 1984 **CD**
Do You (EMI) **CD**
No Sound But A Heart (EMI) **CD**

**Below: Sheena Easton 'Modern Girl' of the '80s.**

# Duane Eddy
US guitarist, composer.
Born Corning, New York, April 28, 1938.

**Career:** Raised in Phoenix, Arizona, Eddy began playing guitar at five and at 16 was working in local dance bands before coming under influence of ace guitarist Al Casey.

After tuition from jazz guitarist Jim Wybele, Eddy was signed by local DJ Lee Hazlewood—later a recording star/producer himself—and Lester Sill in 1957. He cut debut **Movin' 'N' Groovin'** for Jamie with his backing band the Rebels (Larry Knechtel, Steve Douglas and Al Casey).

**Twangin' The Golden Hits, Duane Eddy compilation. Courtesy RCA Records.**

Eddy developed unique 'twangy' guitar sound by tuning normal six-string guitar down an octave and playing melody on bass rather than top strings. As much a part of his records' appeal were the raunchy saw solos of Steve Douglas and Jim Horn and the rebel yells of Ben De Moto. The overall effect was potent blend of rock'n'roll, R&B and Southern States' influences.

Second release **Rebel Rouser** (1958) went gold and led to string of big sellers (12 million records sold by 1963, total sales having now topped 30 million from some 25 singles, 21 of which made UK charts). More than half his hits were self-penned.

Eddy acted in TV western series 'Have Gun Will Travel', and movies 'Because They're Young' (his theme for which was 1960 million-seller), 'A Thunder Of Drums' and 'The Wild

Westerner'. He also composed the theme for 1961 movie 'Ring Of Fire'.

Eddy has continued to tour extensively, undertaking session work and moving into production. He is a frequent visitor to Europe. Recent unlikely teaming with Art Of Noise returned him to charts after 11 years.

**Hit Singles:**

| | US | UK |
|---|---|---|
| Rebel Rouser, 1958 | 6 | 19 |
| Cannon Ball, 1958 | 15 | 22 |
| Peter Gunn Theme, 1959 | — | 6 |
| Yep!, 1959 | 30 | 17 |
| 40 Miles Of Bad Road, 1959 | 9 | 11 |
| Some Kinda Earthquake, 1959 | 37 | 12 |
| Bonnie Come Back, 1960 | 26 | 12 |
| Shazam!, 1960 | 45 | 4 |
| Because They're Young, 1960 | 4 | 2 |
| Kommotion, 1960 | — | 13 |
| Peter Gunn Theme, 1960 | 27 | — |
| Pepe, 1961 | 18 | 2 |
| Theme From Dixie, 1961 | 39 | 7 |
| Ring Of Fire, 1961 | — | 17 |
| Drivin' Home, 1961 | — | 18 |
| Deep In The Heart Of Texas, 1962 | — | 19 |
| Ballad Of Paladin, 1962 | 33 | 10 |
| (Dance With The) Guitar Man, 1962 | 12 | 4 |
| Play Me Like You Play Your Guitar, 1975 | | 9 |
| Peter Gunn (With Art Of Noise), 1986 | | 8 |

**Albums:**
Have Twangy Guitar, Will Travel (Jamie/London), 1958
Especially For You (Jamie/London), 1958
Twang's The Thang (Jamie/London), 1959
Songs For Our Heritage (Jamie/London), 1960
$1,000,000 Worth Of Twang (Jamie/London), 1961
Girls, Girls, Girls (Jamie/London), 1961
$1,000,000 Worth Of Twang Volume 2 (Jamie/London), 1962
Twistin' (Jamie/—), 1962
In Person (Jamie/—), 1962
16 Greatest Hits (Jamie/—), 1962
Pure Gold (RCA), 1965
Best Of (RCA/Camden), 1965
Movin' 'N' Groovin' (—/London), 1970
Twangy Guitar (RCA), 1970
Duane Eddy Guitar Man (—/GTO), 1975
Legend Of Rock (—/Deram), 1975
Duane Eddy Collection (—/Pickwick), 1978
Greatest Hits Of (—/Ronco), 1979
20 Terrific Twangies (—/RCA), 1980
Duane Eddy (Capitol), 1987 **CD**

# Dave Edmunds
UK vocalist, guitarist, composer, producer.
Born Cardiff, Wales, April 15, 1944.

**Career:** Served eight-year musical apprenticeship in various local bands. Formed Love Sculpture with John Williams, bass, and Bob Jones, drums; their frenetic rock instrumental adaptation of Khatchaturian's **Sabre Dance** on Parlophone skated to six on UK chart in 1968 and was band's only hit. Love Sculpture broke up following American tour.

Edmunds signed as solo to Gordon Mills' MAM agency before moving back to South Wales with Kingsley Ward to build own Rockfield Studio in Monmouthshire. After months of experimentation, Rockfield developed unique sound, making it one of Britain's most active studios. Edmunds learned to exactly reproduce sounds of his favourite oldies. Re-make of Smiley Lewis's R&B classic **I Hear You Knocking** gave him three-million selling UK No.1 in 1970. Debut

album **Rockpile** (1972) featured John Williams and former Amen Corner leader Andy Fairweather-Low.

Besides own work, Edmunds produced Brinsley Schwarz, Ducks Deluxe, Flamin' Groovies, Shakin' Stevens(▶) and the Sunsets, and American legend Del Shannon(▶). Re-creating classic Phil Spector 'Wall Of Sound', had further hits of own with versions of Spector oldies **Baby I Love You** and **Born To Be With You.**

Appeared in 1975 David Essex(▶) movie 'Stardust'. He wrote much of the film score. Second album **Subtle As A Flying Mallet** appeared in 1975.

Former Brinsley Schwarz member Nick Lowe(▶) contributed to Edmunds' debut album with Led Zeppelin's Swan Song label, **Get It** (1975). Lowe also became member of Rockpile road band formed by Edmunds, and featured heavily on 1980 Rockpile LP **Seconds Of Pleasure**, a big US success. Rockpile included Edmunds (vocals, guitar), and Billy Bremner (vocals, guitar).

1979 **Repeat When Necessary** album included chart singles **Girls Talk, Queen Of Hearts** and **Crawling From The Wreckage.**

**Subtle As A Flying Mallet, Dave Edmunds. Courtesy RCA Records.**

Edmunds enjoyed further UK Top 30 hit with version of Guy Mitchell's **Singing The Blues** in following year.

During 80s Edmunds has maintained lower profile, continuing to record but also adding production and instrumental expertise to offerings by other artists (Stray Cats, Shaking Stevens amongst many others.)

A rock all-rounder, Edmunds will undoubtedly remain a force to be reckoned with for many years, although influence may be largely as backroom boy as he eventually becomes an elder statesman of rock.

Guitars: Gibson 335, also Gibson J200 acoustics, Fender Telecaster, Martin D45.

**Hit Singles:**

| | US | UK |
|---|---|---|
| I Hear You Knocking, 1970 | 4 | 1 |
| Baby I Love You, 1973 | — | 8 |
| Born To Be With You, 1973 | — | 5 |
| Girls Talk, 1979 | — | 4 |
| Queen Of Hearts, 1979 | — | 11 |

**Albums:**
*With Love Sculpture:*
Classic Tracks 68-72 (—/One-Up),1974
Singles, A's and B's (—/Harvest), 1980

*Solo:*
Subtle As A Flying Mallet (RCA), 1975
Get It (Swan Song), 1977
Tracks On Wax (Swan Song), 1978
Repeat When Necessary (Swan Song), 1979
Twangin' (Swan Song), 1981
Best Of (Swan Song), 1981
D.E. 7 (Columbia/Arista), 1982
Information (Swan Song), 1983
Live (Arista), 1987 **CD**
I Hear You Rockin (Arista), 1987 **CD**

**Above: The great Dave Edmunds, whose career stretches over three decades.**

*Rockpile:*
Seconds Of Pleasure (Columbia/F-Beat), 1980
Original Rockpile, The Volume II (Harvest), 1987 **CD**

*Worth Searching Out:*
Rockpile (NAM/Regal Zonophone), 1972

# Emerson, Lake And Palmer

UK group formed 1969.

**Original line-up:** Keith Emerson, keyboards; Greg Lake, bass, guitar, vocals; Carl Palmer, drums.

**Career:** Keith Emerson revealed classical background while with Nice and used that group to introduce knife-throwing, organ thrashing, musical mayhem act. Nice broke up in late '60s and Emerson began search for special talent to make up next venture.

He met Lake, then with the original King Crimson(▶), and convinced him to join. They then tried to enlist Randy Bachman, late of Guess Who(▶), and discussed union with Jimi Hendrix/Mitch Mitchell. Eventually Carl Palmer, whose background (ex-Chris Farlowe, Atomic Rooster and Arthur Brown) prepared him for Emerson's dynamic stage show, was recruited.

Band's live debut was 1970 Isle Of Wight festival followed shortly by first album. Both recordings and stage shows became grand-

**Right: Keith Emerson (left) and Greg Lake.**

iose and flamboyant displays of technical skill. But after third album, **Pictures**, sameness crept in. ELP could still sell albums, but could they come up with anything new? They released live set (**Welcome Back, My Friends, To The Show That Never Ends**) for fans and then disappeared: no tours and no recordings.

In 1977, **Works Volume 1** appeared. Large sales, despite album's overly pretentious base, seemed to indicate ELP's fans were still there, but ELP was apparently stranded in 1969/1970 time zone and grand orchestral style clashed with musical revolution of late '70s. Wise enough to know when to quit, ELP planned extravaganza farewell tour. Naturally, live set was recorded and **In Concert** appeared for the memories.

In 1985 Lake and Emerson reformed band, minus Palmer who was playing with supergroup Asia(▶). Replacing him with veteran session drummer and former Rainbow alumnus Cozy Powell, the new band released **Emerson, Lake and Powell** in 1986, supporting set with US tour. Moderate success of album showed that there was still life in essentially 70s concept.

| Hit Singles: | US | UK |
|---|---|---|
| Fanfare For The Common Man, 1977 | — | 2 |

**Albums:**
Emerson, Lake And Palmer (Cotillion/Island), 1970
Tarkus (Cotillion/Island), 1971
Pictures At An Exhibition (Cotillion/Island), 1971
Trilogy (Cotillion/Island), 1972
Brain Salad Surgery (Manticore), 1973
Welcome Back, My Friends, To The Show That Never Ends (Manticore), 1974
Works Volume I (Atlantic/Manticore), 1977
Works Volume II (Atlantic), 1978
Love Beach (Atlantic), 1978
In Concert (Atlantic), 1979
Best Of (Atlantic), 1980
The Best Of Emerson Lake And Palmer (Manticore), 1980 **CD**
Emerson Lake & Powell (Polydor), 1986 **CD**

# John Entwistle

UK bass player, vocalist, composer.
Born London, October 9, 1944.

**Career:** Entwistle pioneered new roles for bass players with lead runs on early Who(▶) singles. Developed now standard rotosound strings and was one of the first in rock to experiment with six and eight-string bass. Entwistle was only member of Who to undergo formal musical training (french horn), which led to brilliant terse horn work in Who from **Circles** through **Tommy** to solo efforts.

Nicknamed 'The Ox' and 'The Quiet One', Entwistle was known for fast-moving fingers accompanied by incongruous shock-still pose and general 'bored-with-it-all' look on stage. In fact, he lives to perform. As anchor man for Who, he also began writing B-sides of Who singles **In The City, I've Been Away, Doctor, Doctor, Someone's Coming.** He favoured humorous/macabre subjects on second Who LP, (**Boris The Spider, Whiskey Man**) but was pushed by Townshend to write **Cousin Kevin** and **Uncle Ernie** for **Tommy** project.

With '70s success of Who and slowdown in work schedule, Entwistle took chance to branch out in solo direction. **Smash Your Head Against The Wall** was first Who solo LP and met fair amount of support in States. **Whistle Rymes** (punning misspelt credits on Who recordings) showed promising musical developments. Next LP, **Rigor Mortis Sets In**, lamented state of rock in mid-'70s three years before punks, but did so by falling back on '50s style. **Made In Japan** is notable track.

His band Rigor Mortis went on road with overlarge production and failed to complete US tour. Entwistle compiled Who's **Odds'n' Sods** LP while rest of Who worked on 'Tommy' film. He next put together band Ox and released poorly received **Mad Dog** LP.

Death of Keith Moon spurred Who activity and Entwistle worked sporadically for next few years on **Too Late The Hero** with Joe Walsh. When released in 1981, it seemed too polished, too finished. Title cut was released in pic-disc, individually autographed by Entwistle. Issue disappeared in weeks from London shops but never charted.

Entwistle has also acted as music director on Who soundtracks (**Quadrophenia, Kids Are Alright**, both 1979).

With break-up of Who, Entwistle was able focus attention on solo career.

Bass: Fender Precision, Custom Alembic with spider web inlay (since 1975). (Entwistle has finest collection of antique guitars and basses in the UK.)

**Albums:**
Smash Your Head Against The Wall (Decca/Track), 1971

*Worth Searching Out:*
Whistle Rymes (Decca/Track), 1972
Rigor Mortis Sets In (MCA/Track), 1973
Mad Dog (MCA/Track), 1975
Too Late The Hero (ATCO/WEA), 1981

# David Essex

UK vocalist, composer.
Born London, July 23, 1947.

**Career:** During teens Essex played drums and sang in various semi-professional groups in East London. Lack of success in music led to change of direction in favour of acting, and stints in small-time theatre followed.

He landed leading role in American musical 'Godspell', and played in London's West End from 1971 to 1973. Attracting favourable attention from critics, he won central role in movie 'That'll Be The Day'. Movie's success prompted re-launch of singing career with self-composed **Rock On**. The record, a carefully crafted evocation of '50s atmosphere, became major hit in UK and US, establishing Essex as star.

Further hits and album successes followed, and in 1974 Essex starred in 'Stardust', sequel to 'That'll Be The Day'. By end of year Essex was attracting teenybopper attention comparable to Beatlemania, in UK and abroad.

Teenage fervour died down, and Essex's career has since alternated between well-crafted, listenable albums, hit singles of varying quality and film and theatre stints ('Evita', 'Silver Dream Racer', 'Childe Byron').

His ambitious 'Mutiny On The Bounty' stage musical was launched to critical and commercial acclaim at end of 1985.

**Hit Singles:**

| | US | UK |
|---|---|---|
| Rock On, 1973 | 5 | 3 |
| Lamplight, 1973 | — | 7 |
| Gonna Make You A Star, 1974 | — | 1 |
| Stardust, 1974 | — | 7 |
| Rollin' Stone, 1975 | — | 5 |
| Hold Me Close, 1975 | — | 1 |
| If I Could, 1975 | — | 13 |
| Oh What A Circus, 1978 | — | 3 |
| Silver Dream Machine (Part 1), 1980 | — | 4 |
| Me And My Girl, 1982 | — | 13 |
| A Winters Tale, 1982 | — | 2 |
| Tahiti, 1983 | — | 8 |

**Albums:**

Hold Me Close (Columbia/CBS), 1979
The David Essex Album (Columbia/CBS), 1979
Silver Dream Racer (Mercury), 1980
The David Essex Collection (—/Pickwick), 1980
Be-Bop The Future (Mercury), 1981
Stage Struck (Mercury), 1982
The Very Best Of David Essex (—/TV), 1982
Mutiny! (Mercury), 1983
This One's For You (Mercury), 1984

# Eurythmics

UK duo formed 1981.
David A. Stewart, guitar, keyboards, synthesiser, bass, composer; born Sunderland 1952.
Annie Lennox, vocals, composer, keyboards, flute, synthesiser; born Aberdeen, December 25, 1954.

**Career:** Duo were both members of the Tourists, promising pop-styled band 1977-80 scoring five hit singles, including Top 10 items **I Only Want To Be With You** (Dusty Springfield(▶) cover) and **So Good To Be Back Home Again,** plus three interesting LPs. Prior to forming Tourists, Stewart had worked in folk music, then had spell in Longdancer (early signing to Elton John's(▶) Rocket label). Lennox had studied at Royal Academy of Music (piano, flute) before working as part-time cabaret singer/waitress; met Stewart while

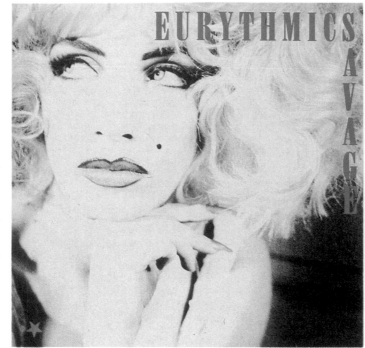

**Savage, Eurythmics.
Courtesy RCA Records.**

working in restaurant.

When Tourists folded, duo started writing (which neither had previously done seriously) and recorded first Eurythmics LP, **In The Garden,** in Cologne, produced by Tourists' mentor Conny Plank. Instrumental help provided by Clem Burke (drums) of Blondie(▶) plus members of Can and D.A.F. Although LP not huge success, it effectively laid ghost of Tourists. 1981-82 saw minor chart action but in 1983 duo came of age with two major hit singles, **Sweet Dreams Are Made Of This** (titletrack of second LP) and **Love Is A Stranger** (reissued after success of **Sweet Dreams**). In fact, 1983 saw duo sell more than six million records worldwide, and world tour in following year increased status and pulling power.

Controversy followed with film score for movie '1984'. Eurythmics-composed soundtrack was used to replace work of original composer, causing furious protest. Situation was no fault of Stewart and Lennox, and upside was hit single **Sex Crime (Nineteen Eightyfour)**.

In intervening years outfit has gone from strength to strength, confirming position as one of freshest and most talented pop/rock aggregations of 80s. Versatility was demonstrated by Lennox's 1985 teaming with Aretha Franklin on **Sisters Are Doing It For Themselves**, and Stewart's production duties for Feargal Sharkey, Lone Justice and others.

1987 proved best year yet, with album **Revenge** going triple platinum in UK and gold in US.

While Stewart provides musical and spiritual

**Below: Annie Lennox, once a Tourist—
more successful as a Eurythmic.**

support, Lennox is natural frontperson, displaying continuing invention and ingenuity in ever-changing visual personality. This theatricality and above average level of creativity make duo likely to remain major force, both separately and together.

**Hit Singles:**

| | US | UK |
|---|---|---|
| Love Is A Stranger, 1982 | 23 | 6 |
| Sweet Dreams Are Made Of This, 1983 | 1 | 2 |
| Who's That Girl, 1983 | 21 | 3 |
| Right By Your Side, 1983 | 29 | 10 |
| Here Comes The Rain Again, 1984 | 4 | 8 |
| Sexcrime (Nineteen Eightyfour), 1984 | — | 4 |
| Would I Lie To You, 1985 | 5 | 17 |
| There Must Be An Angel, 1985 | 22 | 1 |
| *With Aretha Franklin:* | | |
| Sisters Are Doing It For Themselves, 1985 | 18 | 9 |
| It's Alright (Babys Coming Back), 1986 | — | 12 |
| Thorn In My Side, 1986 | — | 5 |
| When Tomorrow Comes, 1986 | — | 30 |
| Missionary Man, 1987 | 16 | — |
| Beethoven (I Love To Listen To), 1987 | — | 25 |

**Albums:**

In The Garden (—/RCA), 1981 **CD**
Sweet Dreams (—/RCA), 1983 **CD**
Touch (—/RCA), 1983 **CD**
1984 For The Love Of Big Brother (Virgin), 1984 **CD**
Be Yourself Tonight (—/RCA), 1985 **CD**
Revenge (RCA), 1986 **CD**
Savage (RCA), 1987 **CD**

# The Everly Brothers

US vocal duo, guitarists, composers.
Don Everly born Brownie, Kentucky, February 1, 1937.
Phil Everly born Chicago, Illinois, January 19, 1939.

**Career:** Both Don and Phil had early experience appearing on parents Ike & Margaret's radio show in Knoxville, 1955, singing hillbilly gospel material. First recordings for US Columbia label in 1956 came as result of encouragement from family friend Chet Atkins(▶). First single **The Sun Keeps Shining** not successful but featured same harmonising later to bring them to charts. In 1956, auditioned for publisher Wesley Rose and soon signed to Cadence Records. First release in 1957, Felice and Boudleaux Bryant's **Bye Bye Love**, became major hit, followed by others in similar high-register harmony style. Rarely adventurous, material explored teen romance to limit with appropriately simple backing. Use of Gibson guitars prompted Gibson company to produce Jumbo style Everly model in limited quantities.

Everlys signed to newly formed Warner Bros Records at peak of career in 1960, quickly expanding musical horizons with material and accompaniment. Continued to reach charts throughout early and mid-'60s with imaginative and well-produced singles and albums, surviving where other '50s artists retired. Toured US and UK regularly even when singles failed to chart in late '60s.

Strain of touring contributed to growing friction between them which led to acrimonious split following on-stage row in 1973.

Both pursued solo careers and made fine records but these lacked commercial success of earlier efforts until Phil recorded in England with Cliff Richard, returning Everly name to charts with **She Means Nothing To Me**.

Differences settled, Don and Phil reunited after more than decade apart and enjoyed triumphant tours in 1985.

Influence of Everlys can be heard in many later groups which use harmony style including Beatles(▶), Beach Boys(▶), Hollies(▶), Simon and Garfunkel(▶) and the Eagles(▶). Everlys were in turn influenced by '50s bluegrass artists like Louvin Brothers and Lilly Brothers.

**Hit Singles:**

| | US | UK |
|---|---|---|
| Bye Bye Love, 1957 | 2 | 6 |
| Wake Up Little Susie, 1957 | 1 | 2 |
| All I Have To Do Is Dream, 1957 | 1 | 1 |
| Bird Dog/Devoted To You, 1958 | — | 10 |
| Devoted To You/Bird Dog, 1958 | 10 | — |
| Problems, 1958 | 2 | 6 |
| Take A Message To Mary, 1959 | 16 | 29 |
| ('Til) I Kissed You, 1959 | 4 | 2 |
| Let It Be Me, 1960 | 7 | 13 |
| Cathy's Clown, 1960 | 1 | 1 |
| When Will I Be Loved, 1960 | 8 | 4 |
| So Sad/Lucille, 1960 | 7 | 4 |
| Lucille/So Sad, 1960 | 21 | 4 |
| Like Strangers, 1960 | — | 11 |
| Walk Right Back/Ebony Eyes, 1961 | 7 | 1 |
| Ebony Eyes/Walk Right Back, 1961 | 8 | — |
| Temptation, 1961 | 27 | 1 |
| Don't Blame Me/Muskrat, 1961 | 20 | 20 |
| Cryin' In The Rain, 1962 | 6 | 6 |
| That's Old Fashioned/How Can I Meet Her, 1962 | 9 | 12 |
| No-One Can Make My Sunshine Smile, 1962 | — | 11 |
| The Price Of Love, 1965 | — | 2 |
| Love Is Strange, 1965 | — | 11 |

*Phil Everly (with Cliff Richard):*
| She Means Nothing To Me, 1983 | — | 9 |

**Albums:**
Very Best Of The Everly Brothers (Warner Bros), 1965
Golden Hits (Warner Bros), 1971
Walk Right Back With The Everlys (Warner Bros), 1975 **CD**
Rock'n'Roll Forever (Warner Bros), 1981

**Below: The Everly Brothers with their trademark Jumbo Gibsons.**

The Everly Brothers (Warner Bros), 1981
Rip It Up (Ace), 1983
Reunion Album (Impression), 1984 **CD**
The Everley Brothers (Mercury), 1984 **CD**
In The Studio (Ace), 1985
Born Yesterday (Mercury), 1985 **CD**
Instant Party (Warner Bros), 1986
Rocking In Harmony (Ace), 1986
Roots (Warner Bros), 1986
Susie Q (Magnum Force), 1987
20 Golden Love Songs (Spectrum) **CD**
20 Greatest Hits (Spectrum) **CD**
Bye Bye Love (Entertainers) **CD**
Great Recordings (Ace) **CD**

# Fabulous Thunderbirds
US group formed 1977.

**Original line-up:** Jimmy Vaughn, guitar; Ken Wilson, vocals, harmonica; Keith Ferguson, bass; Mike Buck, drums.

**What's The Word, Fabulous Thunderbirds. Courtesy Chrysalis Records.**

**Career:** Vaughn, Wilson and Ferguson formed nucleus of Texan band which played straight-ahead R&B with no pretentions and no adornment. Upheavals in establishment rock provided T-Birds with opportunity to record as part of new wave. First LP provided excellent example of band's stripped-down approach to basic rock music. Comparisons with George Thorogood(▶) come to mind as both expound simple, honest love of blues influence on rock music.

**What's The Word** saw departure of drummer Buck; half of LP has Fran Christina filling in as session drummer. Excellent **Butt Rockin'** included Christina as full-time member with Preston Hubbard now on bass. Nick Lowe(▶) indicated critical breakthrough of band by agreeing to produce strongest effort yet, **T-Bird Rhythm.**

Continued gigging consolidated band's reputation as exciting live band, and exposure on MTV expanded audience. By 1987, Fabulous Thunderbirds had become major band, with Top Ten chart album **Hot Number**. Success indicates continuing demand.

**Current line-up:** Vaughn; Wilson; Preston Hubbard, bass; Fran Christina, drums.

**Albums:**
Girls Go Wild (—/Chrysalis), 1979
The Fabulous Thunderbirds (Takoma/—), 1979
What's The Word (Chrysalis), 1980
Butt Rockin' (Chrysalis), 1981
T-Bird Rhythm (Chrysalis), 1982
Tuff Enuff (Epic) 1986
Portfolio (Chrysalis), 1987 **CD**
Hot Number (Chrysalis), 1987 **CD**

# The Faces
UK group formed 1968.

**Original line-up:** Rod Stewart, vocals; Ron Wood, guitar; Ronnie Lane, bass; Kenney Jones, drums; Ian MacLagan, keyboards.

**Career:** When lead singer Steve Marriott left Small Faces to form Humble Pie(▶) with Peter Frampton(▶) in 1968, his erstwhile partners, Jones, MacLagan and Lane, brought in Rod Stewart(▶) and Ron Wood from the Jeff Beck Group(▶) and became simply the Faces (though first LP was released as Small Faces to keep old audience). Wood switched back to lead guitar, having played bass with Beck.

Signed by Warner Bros in early 1969, band spent two years establishing themselves via UK university and club circuits. They turned out high-energy, if inconsistent albums. Repu-

**Ooh La La, The Faces. Courtesy Warner Bros Records.**

tation as a mischievous, free-boozing party band, plus growing success of Stewart's parallel solo career, made them one of the most popular on-stage outfits in UK/US during 1972-75.

Disappointing 1973 **Ooh La La** set was last album of fresh material Faces made together. Stewart's widely reported remarks that he didn't like it helped neither its commercial acceptability nor band's future as working unit.

Fed up with Stewart's dominance of band, Lane left (pursuing solo career) and was replaced by Japanese bass-player Tetsu Yamauchi (ex-Free); Stewart concentrated more on solo career. Wood released own solo effort **I've Got My Own Album To Do** (title meant as slap at Stewart's solo efforts) in 1974, guested on London dates with friends Keith Richard, Andy Newmark and Willie Weeks, and became increasingly involved with the Rolling Stones(▶). All this pointed to imminent demise of Faces. In 1975, Wood toured States as guest replacement for departed Mick Taylor in Rolling Stones and then joined Faces for their tour there. He also recorded second solo album **Now Look**, on which Bobby Womack and other names guested. In 1976 Wood and Lane recorded **Mahoney's Last Stand** (originally to be a soundtrack) with Jones and MacLagan sessioning on LP.

Having degenerated into a drinking club rather than a working band, Faces finally broke up December 1975 when Stewart announced his official departure for solo career.

Successful re-release of Small Faces' 1967 single **Itchycoo Park** led to temporary re-union of that outfit in 1977, while Wood became permanent member of Rolling Stones. Ronnie Lane made several solo LPs with his Slim Chance band. Kenney Jones joined the Who(▶) in 1979. Ian McLagan is now married to Keith Moon's ex-wife, Kim, while Ronnie Lane, himself a victim, has been active in rock music endeavours to raise funds for multiple sclerosis research and treatment.

**Final line-up:** Stewart; Wood; Jones; MacLagan; Testu Yamauchi, bass.

**Hit Singles:**
| | US | UK |
|---|---|---|
| Stay With Me, 1971 | 17 | 6 |

| | | |
|---|---|---|
| Cindy Incidentally, 1973 | 48 | 2 |
| Pool Hall Richard/I Wish It Would Rain,1973 | — | 8 |
| You Can Make Me Dance Or Sing Or Anything, 1974 | — | 12 |

**Albums:**
*Faces:*
First Step/Long Player (Warner Bros), 19⁻
A Nod Is As Good As A Wink. . .To A P'
   Horse (Warner Bros), 1971
Best Of (—/Riva), 1977
Faces (featuring Rod Stewart) (—/Pickwick),
   1980
Faces (Edsel), 1987

*Rod Stewart Solo:*
See separate entry.

*Ronnie Lane Solo:*
Rough Mix (with Pete Townshend) (MCA/
   Polydor), 1977

*Worth Searching Out:*
Anymore For Anymore (GM), 1974
Slim Chance (A&M/Island), 1975
One For The Road (—/Island), 1976
See Me (—/GEM), 1979

*Ron Wood Solo:*
Gimme Some Neck (Columbia/CBS), 1979

*Worth Searching out:*
Mahoney's Last Stand (Atco/Atlantic), 1976

*Ian McLagan Solo:*
Troublemaker (Mercury/—), 1979
Bump In The Night (Mercury/—), 1981
*Available as double album, UK only.
Originally 1970/1971.

# Fairport Convention

UK group formed 1967.
**Original line-up:** Simon Nichol, guitar,
vocals; Richard Thompson, guitar, vocals;
Ashley Hutchings, bass; Shaun Frater,
drums; Judy Dyble, autoharp, vocals.

**Career:** 12-year career of Fairport involved
14 different line-ups and 20 members.
Undoubtedly one of the most talented UK
musical ensembles, their repertoire extends
far beyond term 'folk-rock' to embrace rock 'n'
roll, blues, country, cajun and bluegrass.
   Original line-up (above) played debut gig in
spring 1967. By November, Martin Lamble
(drums) and lead singer Ian Matthews(▶)
were recruited for first album, **Fairport
Convention,** produced by manager Joe
Boyd. Early repertoire consisted of contemporary American folk-rock and original material. Dyble was replaced by the Strawbs'(▶)
Sandy Denny in 1968, and group began
eventual conversion to traditional British folk
music. **What We Did On Our Holidays**
revealed Thompson(▶) as major songwriting
talent, while demonstrating healthy balance
of original interpretations of traditional songs
and excellent Joni Mitchell(▶)/Bob Dylan(▶)
covers.
   Disillusioned by musical policy, Matthews
quit in January 1969, and was replaced by
established folkie Dave Swarbrick (violin/
vocals), who became Fairport's longest serv-
ing member. Traditionally based **Unhalfbricking** was succeeded by **Liege And Lief,**
the definitive British folk-rock album, generally
acknowledged as Fairport's finest work.
   In June 1969, following a Birmingham gig,
the group's van skidded from motorway and
Lamble was killed. By the end of the year,
Sandy Denny had quit to form Fotheringay,
while Ashley Hutchings left to start Steeleye
Span. New members Dave Mattacks (drums)

**First Step, (no longer Small) Faces.
Courtesy Warner Bros Records.**

and Dave Pegg (bass) kept unit stable for a
year during which **Full House** and **Live At
The L.A. Troubadour** were recorded. The
former, their first album without a female
singer, revealed Swarbrick/Thompson partnership at its best. By January '71, Richard
Thompson had gone on to pursue highly
acclaimed solo career, later duetting with
wife Linda. Following two more British folk/
rock albums, **Angel Delight** and **Babbacombe Lee,** the last of the original Fairports,
Simon Nichol left to form Albion Country Band
with Ashley Hutchings.
   From March-July 1972 group went through
unprecedented period of flux with line-up
changes involving Roger Hill (guitar), Tom
Farnell (drums), and David Rea (guitar),
before Trevor Lucas (guitar/vocals) and Jerry
Donahue (guitar) settled long enough to
complete two albums, **Rosie** and **Nine.**
Latter proved their best post-Thompson effort.
Group's somewhat fading credibility was
improved by dramatic return of Sandy Denny
in March 1974. The disappointing **Live
Convention** was followed by **Rising For
The Moon,** a showcase for Denny insuffi-
ciently integrated into group context.
   Mattacks left to join Etchingham Steam
Band, and in January 1976 Denny returned
to solo career. Lucas and Donahue also quit,
precipitating Fairport's demise. New members
were recruited, including Bruce Rowland
(drums), Bob Brady (piano), Dan Ar Bras
(guitar) and Roger Burridge (mandolin/fiddle).
Final Island album, **Gottle O'Geer,** originally
intended as Swarbrick solo, was recorded as
contractual filler. A brief period with Vertigo in
1977 resulted in two averge works, **The
Bonny Bunch Of Roses** and **Tipplers
Tales,** before anti-climactic **Farewell Farewell.** Former Fairports all succeeded at
various levels with spin off/solo ventures.
Sandy Denny died tragically of a brain haemorrhage on April 21, 1978, after falling down-
stairs at a friend's house.
   Although Fairport's later work was decidedly patchy in comparison with earlier
pioneering achievements, their influence on
development of British electric folk music is
inestimable.

**Right: Adam Faith, born Terry Nelhams,
succeeded as singer, actor and manager.**

**Final line-up:** Nichol; Bruce Rowland,
drums, vocals; Dave Swarbrick, violin, vocals;
Dave Pegg, bass, vocals;

**Albums:**
Fairport Convention (A&M/Polydor), 1968
What We Did On Our Holidays (—/Island),
   1969
Unhalfbricking (A&M/Island), 1969 **CD**
Liege and Lief (A&M/Island), 1969 **CD**
Full House (A&M/Island), 1970
Angel Delight (A&M/Island), 1971
Babbacombe Lee (A&M/Island), 1971
A History Of Fairport Convention (—/Island),
   1972
Rosie (A&M/Island), 1973
Nine (A&M/Island), 1973
Fairport Live—A Moveable Beast (Island),
   1974
Rising For The Moon (Island), 1974
Gottle O'Geer (Antilles/Island), 1976

Fairport Chronicles (A&M/—), 1976
Live At The LA Troubadour (—/Island),
   1976
The Bonny Bunch Of Roses (—/Vertigo),
   1977
Tipplers Tales (—/Vertigo), 1978
Farewell Farewell (—/Simons), 1979
Heyday (Hannibal), 1987 (BBC Radio Sessions)
Full House (Hannibal), 1987
In Real Time (Island), 1987 **CD**

# Adam Faith

UK vocalist, actor, manager, producer.
Born Terry Nelhams, London, June 23, 1940.

**Career:** A messenger in film business, at
Rank Screen Services, he joined workmates
in Worried Men skiffle group before TV pop
producer Jack Good suggested he go solo as
Adam Faith.
   After two '6.5 Special' TV appearances,
spell on road and flop HMV singles, he lost
heart and returned to Rank as assistant film
cutter before bandleader John Barry recommended him for TV series 'Drumbeat'. Faith
stayed for entire 22 week run and cut futher
flop single, for Top Rank, as well as appearing
in 'Beat Girl' teen movie.
   Raindrops' member and songwriter John
Worth offered Faith catchy song **What Do
You Want?** Exaggerating hiccupy style of
Buddy Holly(▶) over unusual John Barry-
arranged pizzicato string backing, Faith cut
song in late '59 and made it biggest selling
British record of 1960. However, although
one of biggest stars of '50s in UK, never had
US success. Exploiting same vocal treatment
and little-boy-lost lyrics, he had further chart-
topper with **Poor Me,** then charted **Someone
Else's Baby, Lonely Pup** and **Who Am I?**
   Becoming increasingly interested in acting,
he appeared in appalling 'What A Whopper'
before critically applauded dramatic role as
condemned man in 'Mix Me A Person'. In
1965, with recording career flagging, he
turned full-time to the stage, touring for two
years in relative obscurity of repertory, before
regaining national limelight as loser/tarnished
hero of 'Budgie' TV series.
   In 1973 produced Roger Daltrey's(▶) solo LP

Daltrey featuring Leo Sayer (whom Faith manages) compositions. He made recording comeback in 1974 with **I Survive** album (artistically far superior to earlier work). Returned to film in 1975 starring with David Essex in 'Stardust'. 1977 saw Faith produce comeback album of erstwhile skiffle idol Lonnie Donegan(▶) and in 1979 he starred with Roger Daltry in 'McVicar', while mid-'80s saw him appear in TV dramas including 'Minder'.

**Hit Singles:**

| | US | UK |
|---|---|---|
| What Do You Want?, 1959 | — | 1 |
| Poor Me, 1960 | — | 1 |
| Someone Else's Baby, 1960 | — | 2 |
| When Johnny Comes Marching Home/Made You, 1960 | — | 5 |
| How About That, 1960 | — | 4 |
| Lonely Pup, 1960 | — | 4 |
| This Is It/Who Am I, 1961 | — | 5 |
| Easy Going Me, 1961 | — | 12 |
| Don't You Know It?, 1961 | — | 12 |
| The Time Has Come, 1961 | — | 4 |
| Lonesome, 1962 | — | 12 |
| As You Like It, 1962 | — | 5 |
| Don't That Beat All, 1962 | — | 8 |
| The First Time, 1963 | — | 5 |
| We Are In Love, 1963 | — | 11 |
| Message To Martha, 1964 | — | 12 |

**Albums:**
24 Golden Greats (—/Warwick), 1981
Not Just A Memory (C For Miles), 1983

*Worth Searching Out:*
I Survive (Warner Bros/WEA), 1974

# The Fall

UK group formed 1977.
**Original line-up:** Mark Smith, vocals; Tony Friel, bass; Una Baines, keyboards; Martin Bramah, guitar; Karl Burns, drums.

**Career:** Formed Manchester, contemporaries of Joy Division, OMD and Human League, but with grittier approach and sound. Inspired and driven on by vocalist Mark Smith's blank verse rap/rant style, the music embraced punk, R'n'B and rockability in fierce rough'n'ready amalgam to create growling hybrid. Debut single on Step Forward, **Bingo Master's Breakout** was fast, direct and funny, while concerts were ramshackle and riveting — all preconceptions of rock'n'roll tradition and professionalism were jettisoned in favour of brutal realism and haphazard spontaneity. Two live tracks on **Short Circuit** compilation preceded the departure of bassist Tony Friel and keyboardist Una Baines, replaced by Marc Riley and Evonne Pawlett.

This line-up — still featuring original members Martin Bramah and Karl Burns—released ironic **It's The New Thing** single and ferocious **Live At The Witch Trials** debut album, which was recorded in a single day! Soon established as leading UK independent antirock cult group with European tours, second LP **Dragnet** and string of vitriolic but irresistible singles.

Bitter attack of both lyrics and music — especially after Pawlett left to be replaced by second guitarist — often masked scathing wit which bypassed critics and fans alike. But throughout following four years, continued to tour extensively with ever-changing line-up after Bramah left to form Blue Orchids with Baines.

Bassist Marc Riley took over on guitar and band released six further LPs before he too left, forming Marc Riley and the Creepers. Fall leader Smith met and married Californian blonde Brix, who then joined Fall as guitarist, adding both glamour and pop appeal. Joined Beggars Banquet records for **The Wonderful**

**And Frightening World Of The Fall** and **This Nation's Saving Grace** as they continued to evolve and adapt throughout numerous line-up changes, without losing sight of Northern roots. Eventually added second female American Marcia Schofield on keyboards/vocals and released surprise UK single with cover of **Ghost In My House**.

Durable yet unpredictable, The Fall are essential if difficult listening for any adventurous music fan.

**Current line-up:** Smith, vocals; Brix Smith, guitar/vocals; Craig Scanlon, guitar; Steven Hanley, bass; Marcia Schofield, keyboards/vocals; Simon Wolstencroft, drums.

**Albums**
Live At The Witch Trials
    (Step Forward/IRS/A&M), 1979
Grotesque (Roughtrade), 1980
The Fall Live (Roughtrade), 1980
Perverted By Language (Roughtrade), 1984
Total's Turns (Roughtrade), 1984
The Wonderful And Frightening World Of
    The Fall (Beggars Banquet/PVC), 1984
Hip Priests And Kamerads (Situation), 1985
This Nations Saving Grace (PVC), 1985
Bend Sinister (Beggars Banquet), 1986 **CD**

**This Nation's Saving Grace, The Fall. Courtesy Beggars Banquet Records.**

# Bryan Ferry

UK vocalist.
Born Washington, County Durham, September 26, 1945.

**Career:** Ferry had life-long interest in music groups. Upon graduation from Newcastle University, worked as teacher. By 1970 he had committed self to professional music with formation of Roxy Music(▶).

Band held his full-time attention until solo release in 1973 of **These Foolish Things**, featuring Ferry singing covers of his favourite rock songs. His second solo album featured original material which appeared to be Roxy cast-offs.

Inability to balance both careers resulted in dissolution of Roxy Music in 1976. Instead of waiting to produce proper release, Ferry offered strange collection from his earlier solo singles as well as reworked Roxy Music material. (The LP was really a compilation for US market.) Yet holding pattern of **Let's Stick Together** sounded interesting in comparison to next planned album, **In Your Mind**. Tours of UK/US failed to win any support for this material and made demise of Roxy Music all the more regrettable.

Just as public interest in Ferry reached low point, he produced superb **The Bride Stripped Bare** which reflected emotional trauma of break-up with girlfriend Jerry Hall. In August 1978 Ferry re-formed Roxy Music and

**Bête Noir, Bryan Ferry. Courtesy EG Records.**

began impressive return to public and critical favour.

Although many consider Roxy Music and Bryan Ferry to be one and the same, Ferry's fling at solo stardom shows they're not. Content to channel his creativity into group dynamics instead of controlling *everything*, Ferry is now in position to be lasting influence throughout '80s.

**Hit Singles:**

| | US | UK |
|---|---|---|
| A Hard Rain's Gonna Fall, 1973 | — | 10 |
| The In Crowd, 1974 | — | 13 |
| Smoke Gets In Your Eyes, 1974 | — | 17 |
| Let's Stick Together, 1976 | — | 4 |
| Extended Play (EP), 1976 | — | 7 |
| This Is Tomorrow, 1977 | — | 9 |
| Tokyo Joe, 1977 | — | 15 |
| Slave To Love, 1985 | — | 10 |
| Is Your Love Strong Enough, 1986 | — | 22 |
| The Right Stuff, 1987 | — | 37 |

**Albums:**
These Foolish Things (Atlantic/Island),
    1973
Another Time Another Place (Atlantic/Island),
    1974 **CD**
Lets Stick Together (Atlantic/Island), 1976 **CD**
In Your Mind (Atlantic/Polydor), 1977 **CD**
The Bride Stripped Bare (Polydor), 1978 **CD**
Boys And Girls (EG), 1985 **CD**
Bête Noir (EG), 1987 **CD**

# Fine Young Cannibals

UK group formed 1984.

**Current line-up:** Andy Cox, guitar; David Steele, bass/keyboards; Roland Gift, vocals.

**Career:** Formed by Cox and Steel (both ex-members of highly successful group The Beat who disbanded in 1983), who recruited soul-influenced vocalist Gift from little-known ska group The Akrylix.

On strength of impressive tape of self-composed songs, they secured deal with London Records, celebrating with appearance on influential UK TV show 'The Tube' and showcase gig at London's Wag Club.

Released debut single **Johnny Come Back**, to universal acclaim worldwide. Debut LP **Fine Young Cannibals**, relied on concise songwriting, immaculate musicianship and Gift's insistent, rasping vocal style as highlighted on second single **Blue** which was only a minor hit due to politically sensitive lyrical message.

Updating of Elvis Presley's **Suspicious Minds** re-established commercial success, coinciding with sell-out European tour. Further cover of Buzzcocks **Ever Fallen In Love?** (great choice of song, uninspired version) became minor hit before band disappeared from public view for 18 months.

Prior to second album Gift made acting debut in British film 'Sammy And Rosie Get Laid', while Cox and Steele combined for one-off disco project entitled Two Men, A Drum-Machine And A Trumpet, releasing the single **Tired Of Getting Pushed Around**.

**Hit Singles:**

| | US | UK |
|---|---|---|
| Johnnie Come Back, 1985 | — | 8 |
| Suspicious Minds, 1986 | — | 8 |
| Ever Fallen In Love, 1987 | — | 9 |

**Albums**
Fine Young Cannibals (London), 1985 **CD**
Candyman (ISR), 1986 **CD**

**Below: Roland Gift exercises his rasping vocal style on tour in 1987.**

# Fleetwood Mac

UK group formed 1967.

**Original line-up:** Peter Green, Gibson Les Paul guitar, vocals; John McVie, bass; Mick Fleetwood, drums; Jeremy Spencer, guitar, vocals.

**Career:** Peter Green(▶) formed band when he, McVie and Fleetwood quit (or were fired from) Mayall's(▶) Bluesbreakers. For short period McVie considered re-joining Mayall and Fleetwood Mac's debut performance at Windsor Festival (August 1967) featured temporary bassist Bob Brunning (who also recorded B-side on band's first single).

First LP featured straight-ahead blues and became instant steady seller for over a year. Green then added third guitarist, Danny Kirwan, for third album. Many consider this classic line-up to be band's best.

In UK, band released **Then Play On, Pious Bird Of Good Omen** and **Blues Jam At Chess** before Green left in May 1970 to join religious sect. From this period came No. 1 UK single **Albatross, Man Of The World,** and concert favourite **Oh Well.**

Spencer and Kirwan assumed leadership roles and produced excellent set **Kiln House**. For all practical purposes, McVie's wife, Christine Perfect (ex-Chicken Shack), joined as full-time member.

Band was beginning to recover self-confidence by February 1971 when Jeremy Spencer jolted Mac with conversion to religious cult, Children of God. Like Green, he renounced his past and swore to leave rock business. Green stepped in to help band complete US tour. Permanent guitar duties were assumed in April 1971 by Bob Welch and with him Mac released spotty **Future Games** and highly underrated **Bare Trees.**

Next casualty was Kirwan who was fired in summer 1972 because of growing disenchantment with road life. Welch's influence took Mac from blues-based rock towards softer California sound. This trend was accelerated by Kirwan's replacements, Americans Bob Weston (guitar, vocals) and Dave Walker (vocals). Walker had been lead singer with Savoy Brown and his addition was experiment to re-organise traditional frontman vocalist lines. Mac released **Penguin,** indicating McVie's fascination for the Antarctic bird which became band's symbol.

By June 1973 Walker had left to work with Kirwan, and band floundered. **Mystery To Me** was critically disappointing and is of interest only because original pressing included **Good Things (Come To Those Who Wait)** which was immediately replaced by cover of Yardbirds(▶) hit, **For Your Love.**

**Below: Christine McVie joined husband John in Fleetwood Mac in 1970.**

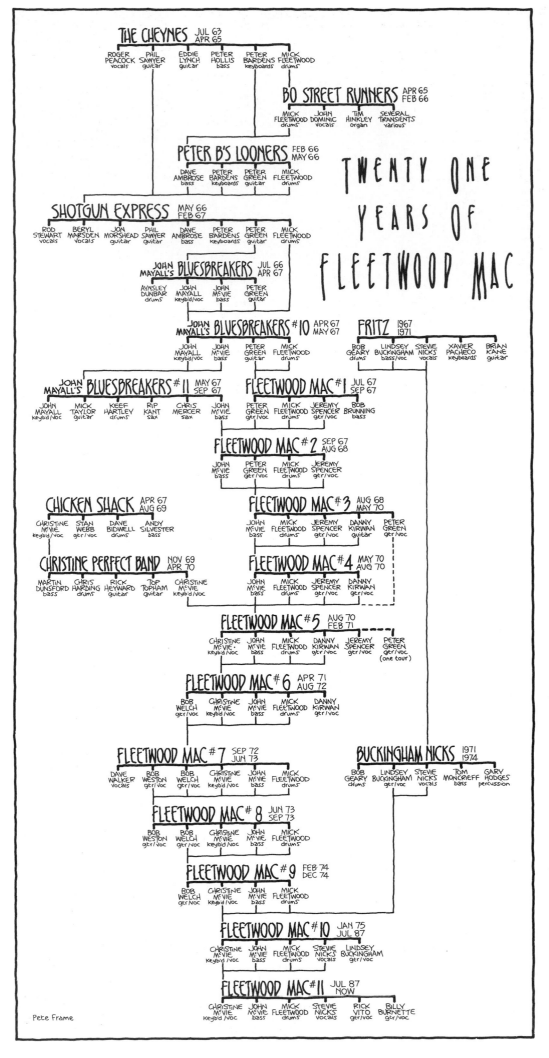

TWENTY ONE YEARS OF FLEETWOOD MAC

Pete Frame

Weston left after recording this LP and resulting internal upheavals caused band to cancel US autumn 1973 tour. Their manager formed bogus group to tour in their place at start of 1974. Band seemed to disappear for good as litigation ensued over various claims to name Fleetwood Mac. They reappeared with **Heroes Are Hard To Find** but seemed doomed to perennial flux as Bob Welch left shortly after.

Legend has it that Mick Fleetwood was checking out LA studio to record Mac's next album when he was introduced to Lindsey Buckingham, who was working next door with Stevie Nicks on their second album **Buckingham Nicks**. Fleetwood asked them to join his group. Somewhat reluctantly, duo accepted. Result was smash hit LP, **Fleetwood Mac**. Album maintained sales as nearly every track proved to be strong single in own right. Any doubts about Mac's ability to sustain this success was dispelled by even better and bigger hit, **Rumours**.

Mac's capacity to survive is evidenced by **Rumours** since it followed break-up of John and Christine McVie's marriage, as well as Fleetwood's. Buckingham and Nicks also broke off long-term relationship. **Rumours'** strength is its ability to convey hurt and loss without resorting to sentimentalism.

New success of Mac pushed band into realm of superstars. Certain air of self-indulgence appeared in long-awaited follow up, **Tusk. Fleetwood Mac Live** broke no new ground and Mac seemed to lose direction again as Nicks, Fleetwood and Buckingham all released solo offerings.

Demise of group looked permanent as individual careers took hold, particularly Nicks, but the lure of the dollar proved hard to resist, and 1987 saw release of brand new album **Tango In The Night**.

The never-ending story may not last much longer though, as Buckingham refused to tour with group, his place being taken by Billy Burnette (who appeared on Fleetwoods solo LP **I'm Not Me**) and West Coast session man Rick Vito who has recorded with Jackson Browne, John Mayall, Bonnie Raitt, Roger McGuinn, John Prine, Todd Rundgren, Rita Coolidge, etc, etc.

**Final line-up:** John McVie; Fleetwood; Christine McVie, keyboards, vocals; Lindsey Buckingham, guitar, vocals; Stevie Nicks, vocals.

| Hit Singles: | US | UK |
|---|---|---|
| Albatross, 1968 | — | 1 |
| Man Of The World, 1969 | — | 2 |
| Oh Well, 1969 | 55 | 2 |
| The Green Manalishi, 1970 | — | 10 |
| Albatross, 1973 | — | 2 |
| Rhiannon, 1976 | 11 | 46 |

Rumours, Fleetwood Mac. Courtesy Warner Bros Records.

| | | |
|---|---|---|
| Say You Love Me, 1976 | 11 | 40 |
| Go Your Own Way, 1976 | 10 | 38 |
| Don't Stop, 1977 | 3 | 32 |
| Tusk, 1979 | 8 | 2 |

Tango in the Night, Fleetwood Mac. Courtesy Warner Bros Records.

| | | |
|---|---|---|
| Sara, 1979 | 7 | 37 |
| Think About Me, 1980 | 20 | — |
| Hold Me, 1982 | 4 | — |
| Gypsy, 1982 | 12 | 46 |
| Oh Diane, 1982 | — | 9 |
| Big Love, 1987 | 4 | 9 |
| Little Lies, 1987 | 4 | 5 |
| Seven Wonders, 1987 | 19 | — |
| Everywhere, 1987 | 14 | — |

*Stevie Nicks with Don Henley:*

| | | |
|---|---|---|
| Leather And Lace, 1981 | 6 | — |

*Stevie Nicks with Tom Petty:*

| | | |
|---|---|---|
| Stop Draggin' My Heart Around, 1981 | 3 | — |

*Stevie Nicks Solo:*

| | | |
|---|---|---|
| Edge Of Seventeen, 1982 | 11 | — |
| Stand Back, 1983 | 5 | — |
| If Anyone Falls, 1983 | 14 | — |
| Talk To Me, 1986 | 11 | — |

*Christine McVie Solo:*

| | | |
|---|---|---|
| Got A Hold On Me, 1984 | 10 | — |

**Albums:**
English Rose (Epic/—), 1969
Then Play On (Reprise), 1969
Fleetwood Mac In Chicago* (Sire/Blue Horizon),1969
Kiln House (Reprise), 1970

The Original Fleetwood Mac (Sire/CBS), 1971
Black Magic Woman† (Columbia/CBS), 1971
Future Games (Reprise), 1971
Greatest Hits (Epic/CBS), 1971
Bare Trees (Reprise), 1972
Penguin (Reprise), 1973
Mystery To Me (Reprise), 1974
Heroes Are Hard To Find (Reprise), 1974
Fleetwood Mac (Reprise USA), 1975 **CD**
Vintage Years (Columbia/CBS), 1975
Albatross (—/Embassy), 1977
Rumours (Warner Bros), 1977 **CD**
Tusk (Warner Bros), 1979 **CD**
Live (Compact collection) (Warner Bros), 1980 **CD**
Mirage (Warner Bros), 1982 **CD**
History Of Vintage Years (CBS), 1984
Tango In The Night (Warner Bros), 1987 **CD**
Collection (Castle), 1987 **CD**
London Live '68 (Thunderbolt), 1968 **CD**
Rattlesnake Shake (Shanghai) **CD**
Tango In The Night (Warner Bros), 1988 **CD**
*UK title: Blues Jam At Chess
†Compilation of first two US LPs

*Selected Solo Albums:*
*Christine McVie:*
Christine Perfect (Sire/Blue Horizon), 1970
Christine McVie (Warner Bros), 1984 **CD**
*Jeremy Spencer:*
Jeremy Spencer (Reprise), 1970

**Below: An early line-up of Fleetwood Mac, with Peter Green in red robe.**

Jeremy Spencer & The Children Of God (Columbia/CBS), 1972
Flee (—/Alantic), 1979
*Lindsey Buckingham/Stevie Nicks:*
Buckingham Nicks (Polydor), 1973
*Stevie Nicks:*
Bella Donna (Modern/WEA), 1981
The Wild Heart (WEA), 1983
Rock A Little (EMI), 1985
*Lindsey Buckingham:*
Law & Order (Asylum/Mercury), 1982
Go Insane (Mercury), 1984
*Danny Kirwan:*
Second Chapter (DJM), 1975
Midnight In San Juan (DJM), 1976
Hello There Big Boy (DJM), 1979
*Mick Fleetwood:*
The Visitor (RCA), 1981
I'm Not Me (RCA), 1983
*Peter Green:*
(See separate entry)

# Foreigner

US/UK group formed 1976.

**Original line-up:** Mick Jones, guitar; Ian McDonald, guitar, keyboards; Dennis Elliot, drums; Lou Gramm, vocals; Al Greenwood, keyboards; Ed Gagliardi, bass.

**Career:** Formed in New York by two Englishmen — Jones (ex-Spooky Tooth, Leslie West Band) and McDonald (ex-King Crimson(▶), McDonald & Giles). Adding English drummer Elliot (also ex-King Crimson) and three Americans — Gramm, Greenwood and Gagliardi — band recorded debut album in 1977.

**Inside Information Foreigner. Courtesy Atlantic Records.**

**Foreigner** LP spawned hits **Feels Like The First Time** and **Cold As Ice**; established Gamm as premier rock vocalist and Jones as melodic composer in mêlée of heavy-metal outfits. After steady stream of chart singles and two further albums, Jones withdrew band from recording and touring in 1980.

With departure of McDonald, Greenwood and Gagliardi, Foreigner re-formed as four piece; Rick Wills (ex-Peter Frampton(▶)) took Gagliardi's bass spot. New line-up topped US album charts with **4** during winter 1981. Maintained single success, 1981 being most productive year since band's inception. Both **Urgent** (with stirring tenor solo by Junior Walker(▶)) and **Waiting For A Girl Like You** made US Top 5, the latter giving group first UK Top 20 chart entry.

Three years filled with sell-out concerts saw recording gap between **Best Of** in 1982 and massive selling **Agent Provocateur**. Tracks incuded Mick Jones' hit **I Want To Know What Love Is** which followed predecessors to platinum status.

1987 saw huge solo success for vocalist Lou

Gramm, with US Top Ten single **Midnight Blue** and chart-topping album **Ready Or Not**.

**Current line-up:** Jones; Elliot; Gramm; Rick Wills, bass.

**Hit Singles:**

| | US | UK |
|---|---|---|
| Feels Like The First Time, 1977 | 4 | 39 |
| Cold As Ice, 1977 | 6 | 24 |
| Long, Long Way From Home, 1978 | 20 | — |
| Hot Blooded, 1978 | 3 | 42 |
| Double Vision, 1978 | 2 | — |
| Blue Morning, Blue Day, 1979 | 15 | 45 |
| Dirty White Boy, 1979 | 12 | — |
| Head Games, 1979 | 14 | — |
| Urgent, 1981 | 3 | — |
| Waiting For A Girl Like You, 1981 | 2 | 8 |
| I Want To Know Want Love Is, 1985 | 1 | 1 |
| That Was Yesterday, 1985 | 8 | — |
| Say You Will, 1987 | 6 | — |

**Albums:**
Foreigner (Atlantic), 1977 **CD**
Double Vision (Atlantic), 1978 **CD**
Head Games (Atlantic), 1979 **CD**
4 (Atlantic), 1981 **CD**
Best Of (Atlantic), 1982
Records (Atlantic), 1983 **CD**
Agent Provocateur (Atlantic), 1985 **CD**
Inside Information (Atlantic), 1987 **CD**

---

# Four Seasons

US group formed 1962.
**Original line-up:** Frankie Valli, lead vocals; Bob Gaudio, vocals, keyboard; Nick Massi, vocals; Tommy De Vito, vocals.

**Career:** America's closest challengers to the Beatles(▶) (for short time both groups' records appeared on same US label, Vee-Jay). The Four Seasons' appeal hinged on unique falsetto-style lead vocals of Valli and song-writing talents of group member Bob Gaudio and producer Bob Crewe.

Record sales of more than 80 million copies, plus a career which outlasted that of their British rivals, make the Four Seasons arguably the greatest pop (as opposed to rock) group of all time.

Frankie Valli (born Francis Castelluccio, Newark, New Jersey, May 3, 1937) began career in 1953 joining local Variatone Trio (Nick and Tommy De Vito, Hank Magenski). Changing name to Four Lovers, group enjoyed minor hit in 1956 with **Apple Of My Eye** by black songwriter Otis Blackwell (who wrote several Presley hits).

Dropped by RCA in 1959 after three lean years, they met New York/Philadelphia based Bob Crewe. Four Lovers were intially used as back-up singers on sessions for Bob Crewe/Frank Slay-owned Swan label in Philly. Label had success with Freddy Cannon and launched careers of Mitch Ryder and the Toys (as well as being Beatles' first US label).

Nick Massi replaced Magenski and Nick De Vito was replaced by Charles Callelo, who in turn gave way to Bob Gaudio. A protégé of Crewe's, Gaudio (born Bronx, New York, November 17, 1942) had been member of the Royal Teens.

With new line-up and new name—the Four Seasons—group began to record, debut appearing on Gone. Signed to fast-rising Chicago-based independent Vee-Jay Records for second single **Sherry** (1962) for which Gaudio persuaded Valli to use his subsequent trademark falsetto sound.

Record shot to No. 1 in US, No. 8 in UK. **Big Girls Don't Cry** gave them second 1962 million seller followed in early 1963 by **Walk Like A Man**, making it three American chart-toppers in a row.

Four Seasons' emergence coincided with the 'Merseymania' explosion and they plus the equally nascent Beach Boys(▶) were the only groups able to challenge British domination of transatlantic charts.

Contractual arguments with Vee-Jay led to switch to Philips label in 1964. Vee-Jay, who also had US rights to Beatles material, issued lavish double album set featuring both acts and billed as 'The International Battle Of The Century'.

**Dawn (Go Away)** made No. 3, and **Rag Doll** (1964) saw the Four Seasons back at top of charts. 1965's **Let's Hang On** was fifth chart-topping million-seller and marked move into a blue-eyed soul flavoured style which made subsequent **Workin' My Way Back To You** such a classic. Song was successfully covered years later by black superstars the Detroit Spinners.

Parallel to group's continuing stardom, Valli issued solo record, scoring big with **The Proud One** and MOR slanted **Can't Take My Eyes Off You**. Group also recorded anonymously as the Wonder Who with quirky version of Bob Dylan's(▶) **Don't Think Twice It's Alright** with view to proving that it was their music and not their image which gave them hits; record went to Top 20 in US.

With both the Beatles and the Beach Boys veering towards progressive pop/rock and issuing concept albums, the Four Seasons came up with ambitious **Genuine Imitation Life Gazette** (1969) project in answer to **Sergeant Pepper** and **Pet Sounds**. Lavishly produced—reputedly one of most expensive recordings ever—it lacked conviction. Album failed dismally in commerical as well as artistic terms, leading to split with both Bob Crewe and Philips.

The Four Seasons spent some years in recording retirement, contenting themselves with playing cabaret venues and cashing in on nostalgia market. They were then signed by Berry Gordy for Motown's new West Coast label Mowest. **Chameleon** album and several singles passed relatively unnoticed at time though they have since become collectors' items.

Motown refused to release Valli's solo effort **My Eyes Adored You**, so he took it to Private Stock and was rewarded with massive transatlantic hit in late 1974. While Private Stock picked up Valli as solo artist and bought rights to all old Philips' material (re-packaged as hit album **The Four Seasons Story**), group itself signed new deal with Warner Bros. 1976 was good year for big comeback; cover versions of Four Seasons' oldies (**Bye Bye Baby** by the Bay City Rollers(▶), **Sherry** by Adrian Baker and Valli's **The Proud One** by the Osmonds(▶)) were peppering UK charts when their Motown oldie **The Night** was re-issued, reaching No. 3. Copies of the original pressing had been changing hands for £10 in British Northern Soul collectors' circles.

Classy Warner Bros album **Who Loves You** capitalised on both nostalgia of older audiences and emergent disco boom. The Four Seasons, albeit with much revised line-up, were right back on top. Follow-up single to **Who Loves You** was **December '63** on which new drummer Gerry Polci handled bulk of vocal; it became Four Seasons' first UK chart-topper. **Silver Star** also went Top 5 and resultant British tour was pure magic.

Though Bob Gaudio wrote all songs for **Who Loves You** album (with Judy Parker) he was no longer working member of group (except on record). Valli was still part-and-parcel of their greatness and the balance between his totally distinctive falsetto and the more gutsy voice of Polci added whole new dimension. Album's line-up comprised; Frankie Valli, vocals; Gerry Polci, drums, vocals; John Paiva, guitar; Lee Shapiro, keyboards; Don Ciccone, bass.

Spring 1976 saw same team, with more Gaudio songs, involved in **Hellicon** album. However, it lacked sparkle of its predecessor. In September 1977 Valli announced he was ending his long stint as leader of the Four Seasons to concentrate on solo projects. Had US No. 1, UK No. 3 in 1978 with theme from movie 'Grease'.

Like their erstwhile rivals the Beatles, the Four Seasons' appeal has remained strong through the years. They have consistently attracted new audiences. The group's shows have always been crowd-pullers even at times when they have had no chart success; in early '70s they filled Madison Square Gardens for eight shows in a row.

**Final line-up:** Valli; Gerry Polci, drums, vocals; John Paiva, guitar; Lee Shapiro, keyboards; Don Ciccone, bass.

**Hit Singles:**

| | US | UK |
|---|---|---|
| Sherry, 1962 | 1 | 8 |
| Big Girls Don't Cry, 1962 | 1 | 13 |
| Walk Like A Man, 1963 | 1 | 12 |
| Candy Girl, 1963 | 3 | — |
| Dawn (Go Away), 1964 | 3 | — |
| Stay, 1964 | 16 | — |
| Ronnie, 1964 | 6 | — |
| Rag Doll, 1964 | 1 | 2 |
| Save It For Me, 1964 | 10 | — |
| Big Man In Town, 1964 | 20 | — |
| Bye Bye Baby, 1965 | 12 | — |
| Let's Hang On, 1985 | 1 | 4 |
| Working My Way Back To You, 1966 | 9 | 50 |
| Opus 17 (Don't Worry 'Bout Me), 1966 | 13 | 20 |
| I've Got You Under My Skin, 1966 | 9 | 12 |
| Tell It To The Rain, 1967 | 10 | 37 |
| Beggin', 1967 | 16 | — |
| Come On Marianne, 1967 | 9 | — |
| Night, 1975 | — | 7 |
| Who Loves You, 1975 | 3 | 6 |
| December '63 (Oh What A Night), 1976 | 1 | 1 |
| Silver Star, 1976 | 38 | 3 |

*As The Wonder Who:*
| | US | UK |
|---|---|---|
| Don't Think Twice It's Alright, 1965 | 12 | — |

*Frankie Valli Solo:*
| | US | UK |
|---|---|---|
| Can't Take My Eyes Off You, 1967 | 2 | — |
| I Make A Fool Of Myself, 1967 | 18 | — |
| You're Ready Now, 1970 | — | 11 |
| My Eyes Adored You, 1975 | 1 | 5 |
| Swearin' To God, 1975 | 6 | 31 |
| Our Day Will Come, 1975 | 11 | — |
| Fallen Angel, 1976 | 36 | 11 |
| Grease, 1978 | 1 | 3 |

**Albums:**
Chameleon (Mowest), 1972
Who Loves You (Warner Bros), 1975
Greatest Hits (—/K-Tel), 1976
Story (Private Stock), 1976
Helicon (Warner Bros), 1977
Reunited Live (Warner Bros), 1981
Frankie Valli And The Four Seasons (K-Tel), 1982

*Frankie Valli Solo:*
Heaven Above Me (MCA), 1980
The Very Best Of (MCA), 1980

*Worth Searching Out:*
Sherry (Vee-Jay/Atlantic), 1963
Gold Vault (Philips), 1965
Working My Way Back To You (Philips), 1965

**Left: The Four Seasons, with the great Frankie Valli (centre).**

**Right: The Four Tops, one of Motown's most consistent acts of the '60s.**

# The Four Tops

US vocal group formed 1954.

**Original/Current line-up:** Levi Stubbs, lead vocals; Renaldo Benson, vocals; Abdul 'Duke' Fakir, vocals; Lawrence Payton, vocals.

**Career:** Formed as the Four Aims in Detroit, during period 1954-64, group signed to Chess, Singular, Riverside and Columbia without significant success. Eventually joined Motown in 1964, and changed name to Four Tops. Famed Motown team Holland/Dozier/Holland(▶) were assigned to writing and production duties; first release, **Baby I Need Your Loving**, was hit.

Success was consolidated in 1965 with **I Can't Help Myself**, US No.1, international hit and million-seller. Next few releases established Tops as major headlining act, much of spotlight falling on Levi Stubbs as particularly powerful and distinctive lead singer.

Group was forging style as fairly conventional Motown act, and thus surprised public and critics in 1966 with landmark record **Reach Out I'll Be There**. Superb production, with innovative rhythmic pattern and searing vocal by Stubbs, blasted record to No.1 spot on both sides of Atlantic. It established Motown as force in contemporary music as well as highly successful commercial company.

Further hits followed, continuing even after Tops lost Holland/Dozier/Holland when team split to form Invictus Records. By 1969 Tops began to feel overlooked among large number of acts now signed to Motown, particularly as musical supremo Norman Whitfield was concentrating on following rock-influenced directions with Temptations(▶). Tops split from Motown, apparently relatively amicably.

Group eventually signed with ABC/Dunhill in 1972, and achieved minor hits in early '70s. Their recorded output was not up to quality of Motown releases, but they continued to record throughout '70s with varying degrees of success. Meanwhile, they continued to tour steadily, being particularly popular in UK.

By end of '70s it seemed group were headed towards gold-plated semi-retirement on lucrative cabaret circuit, but events turned out differently. Having signed to Casablanca in 1981, they released **Tonight**, a classy collection of relaxed pop-soul songs that recaptured great deal of magic of Tops' great days. Album yielded hit singles which re-established act as credible force.

Now seems likely that Tops will go on forever as perennial mainstays of good black pop music. Although not overly innovative or sociologically significant, the Four Tops have in their time produced some superb and memorable music, much of which has achieved classic status.

**Hit Singles:**

|  | US | UK |
|---|---|---|
| Baby I Need Your Loving, 1964 | 11 | — |
| I Can't Help Myself, 1965 | 1 | 23 |
| It's The Same Old Song, 1965 | 5 | — |
| Something About You, 1965 | 19 | — |
| Shake Me Wake Me (When It's Over), 1966 | 18 | — |
| Reach Out I'll Be There, 1966 | 1 | 1 |
| Standing In The Shadows Of Love, 1966 | 6 | 6 |
| Bernadette, 1967 | 4 | 8 |
| Seven Rooms Of Gloom, 1967 | 14 | 12 |
| You Keep Running Away, 1967 | 19 | 26 |
| Walk Away Renee, 1967 | 14 | 3 |
| If I Were A Carpenter, 1968 | 20 | 7 |
| Yesterday's Dreams, 1968 | 49 | 20 |
| What Is A Man, 1969 | 53 | 16 |
| Do What You Gotta Do, 1969 | — | 20 |
| I Can't Help Myself (re-issue), 1970 | — | 10 |
| It's All In The Game, 1970 | 24 | 5 |
| Still Water (Love), 1970 | 11 | 10 |
| Simple Game, 1971 | — | 3 |
| Keeper Of The Castle, 1972 | 10 | 18 |
| Ain't No Woman (Like The One I've Got), 1973 | 4 | — |
| Are You Man Enough, 1973 | 15 | — |
| When She Was My Girl, 1981 | 12 | 3 |
| Don't Walk Away, 1982 | — | 16 |

*With Supremes:*

|  | US | UK |
|---|---|---|
| River Deep Mountain High, 1970 | 14 | 11 |

**Albums:**

Four Tops Second Album (Tamla Motown), 1966 CD
Reach Out (Tamla Motown), 1967
Greatest Hits (Tamla Motown), 1968
Still Waters Run Deep (Tamla Motown), 1970
Greatest Hits Volume 2 (Tamla Motown), 1971
The Magnificent Seven (with Supremes) (Tamla Motown), 1971
Keep Of The Castle (Dunhill/MFP), 1972
Four Tops Story (—/Tamla Motown), 1973
Main Street People (Dunhill/Probe), 1973
Shaft In Africa (Probe/Anchor), 1974
Live In Concert (Dunhill/Anchor), 1974
Night Lights Harmony (ABC/Anchor), 1974
Super Hits (—/Tamla Motown), 1976
Anthology (Tamla Motown), 1976
Catfish (ABC), 1976
The Show Must Go On (ABC/Anchor), 1977
Motown Special (—/Tamla Motown), 1977
At The Top (ABC), 1978
It's All In The Game (—/MFP), 1979
20 Golden Greats (—/Tamla Motown), 1980
Tonight (Casablanca), 1981 CD
Greatest Hits (ABC), 1982
Hits Of Gold (—/Pickwick), 1982
One More Mountain (Casablanca), 1982
Best Of The Four Tops (K-Tel), 1982
The Fabulous Four Tops (—/Pickwick), 1982
Main Street People (Charly), 1986
Reach Out/Still Waters Run Deep (Motown), 1967/1970 CD
Hot Nights (Motown), 1986 CD
Compact Command Performance (Motown) CD

# Peter Frampton

UK vocalist, guitarist, composer.
Born Beckenham, England, April 22, 1950.

**Career:** British pop music press traditionally seized cute faces to pump up, and cherubic-faced Peter Frampton was their choice for 'Face of '68' teen idol. He was then leader of the Herd who hit with **From The Underworld** (1967), **Paradise Lost** (1968) and **I Don't Want Our Loving To Die** (1968). But Frampton had other ideas, seeking recognition as talented musician rather than mere pin-up. He quit Herd to form highly rated Humble Pie(▶) with former Small Faces(▶) leader Steve Marriott, Greg Ridley (bass) and Jerry Shirley (drums), with hard-driving R&B-influenced style.

In 1971 Frampton left to pursue more melodic and romantic direction with increasing emphasis on tasteful guitar work and songs with potent hooklines. He also guested on George Harrison's(▶) **All Things Must Pass**, Harry Nilsson's(▶) **Son Of Schmilsson** and other projects.

First solo album, **Frampton**, featured Ringo Starr(▶), Billy Preston(▶), Klaus Voorman, former Herd cohort Andy Brown, ex-Spooky Tooth member Mike Kellie and Rick Wills from Cochise. Kellie and Wills were drafted into Frampton's new band Camel with Mick Gallagher, ex-Bell'n'Arc. Kellie soon moved back to re-formed Spooky Tooth, being replaced by American drummer John Siomos (ex-Voices of East Harlem and Mitch Ryder).

Camel toured US and concentrated on American market till break-up in 1974, Frampton continuing to record solo albums and tour with various back-up bands, scoring best-selling live album of all time (10 million) with 1976 **Frampton Comes Alive!** LP which included hit singles **Show Me The Way**, **Baby I Love Your Way** and **Do You Feel**. Mick Jagger, Stevie Wonder(▶) and other names helped on 1977 success **I'm In You**. Frampton's role in Stigwood's poorly received film 'Sgt. Pepper's Lonely Hearts Club Band', put him back to pre-**Comes Alive!** status.

A near-fatal car crash took him off road in 1978, and by mid-80s it seemed as though his solo career had gone into headspin. However, he returned to limelight with old chum David Bowie in 1987, as member of megastar's touring band.

**Hit Singles:**

|  | US | UK |
|---|---|---|
| Show Me The Way, 1976 | 6 | 10 |
| Baby I Love Your Way, 1976 | 12 | 43 |
| Do You Feel Like We Do, 1976 | 10 | 39 |
| I'm In You, 1977 | 2 | 41 |
| Signed, Sealed, Delivered (I'm Yours), 1977 | 18 | — |

**Albums:**

Wind Of Change (A&M), 1972
Frampton's Camel (A&M), 1973
Frampton (A&M), 1975
Comes Alive! (A&M), 1975
I'm In You (A&M), 1977
Where I Should Be (A&M), 1979
Super Disc Of Peter Frampton (—/A&M), 1979
Breaking All The Rules (A&M), 1981
The Art Of Control (A&M), 1982
Premonition (A&M), 1986 CD

Welcome to the Pleasuredome, Frankie Goes To Hollywood.
Courtesy ZTT Records.

# Frankie Goes To Hollywood

UK Band formed 1981.

**Original line-up:** Holly Johnson, vocals; Paul Rutherford, vocals; Peter Gill, drums; Mark O'Toole, bass; Gerard O'Toole, guitar.

**Career:** Named (so they say) after seeing poster announcing Frank Sinatra concert, Frankie and the lads formed in Liverpool towards the end of 1981.

First gig was at Liverpool pub 'Pickwicks'. This was an early highlight, as band was booked into an assortment of strip joints and gay haunts (London's Cha Cha's was a favourite).

Despite raw ability and poorly received Summer '82 concert in Liverpool's Sefton Park —Larks In The Parks—hometown following established.

Band's first studio venture was demos of **Relax** and **Two Tribes** for Arista Records, but company did not exercise option and group was also rejected by Phonogram. Brian Nash replaced Gerard O'Toole.

British TV appearance on pop programme 'The Tube' (January 1983), prompted producer Trevor Horn to sign them to his ZTT label for

£5,000 advance. Horn persuaded Chris Blackwell of Island Records and distributor of ZTT that, despite bizarre image, group would deliver the goods. Blackwell agreed and Horn went to work in studio.

First single **Relax**, released October 1983, quickly attracted notoriety, with lyrics expounding gay sex, although Holly Johnson denied this. Record banned by powerful BBC corporation, after DJ Mike Read refused to air record. Unavailability bred interest and single became number one in UK, having sold one million copies by March '84.

Frankie compounded success with second single **Two Tribes**, an instant number one. With **Relax** at number two, Frankie enjoy feat only previously accomplished by Presley, the Beatles and Lennon.

Debut album **Welcome To The Pleasuredome** went straight to the top of UK LP chart in October 1984, whilst third single **The Power Of Love** gave Frankie third consecutive number one single (emulating other Liverpool group Gerry and the Pacemakers(▶).

Brief visit to eponymous Hollywood in late 1984 paved way for US success in following year, although dissension in ranks was already apparent. Internal ranklings did not however prevent reprise of success in autumn 1986 with **Rage Hard** although single did not achieve heights attained by **Relax** and **Tribes**

Band eventually went critical, erupting into legal meltdown which involved ZTT seeking court injunction to stop Holly Johnson going solo. During long and messy court case it was revealed that none of band (except Johnson) had played on first two hit singles, impact of records being almost entirely result of Trevor Horn's production expertise.

At time of writing court case is still in progress. However, verdict is already in on Frankies' career: detention in maximum security home for the hitless.

**Current line-up:** Johnson; Rutherford; Gill; Mark O'Toole; Brian Nash, guitar.

**Hit Singles:**

| | US | UK |
|---|---|---|
| Relax, 1983 | 10 | 1 |
| Two Tribes, 1984 | — | 1 |
| Power Of Love, 1984 | — | 1 |
| Welcome To The Pleasuredome, 1985 | — | 2 |
| Warriors (Of The Wasteland), 1986 | — | 19 |

**Albums:**
Welcome To The Pleasuredome (ZTT), 1984 **CD**
Liverpool (ZTT), 1986 **CD**
Welcome To The Hippodrome (ZTT), 1987 **CD**

# Aretha Franklin

US vocalist, pianist, composer.
Born Memphis, Tennessee, March 25, 1942.

**Career:** 'Lady Soul' is daughter of Rev. C.L. Franklin, who has had more than 80 albums of sermons released in US. Along with sisters Erma and Carolyn—both subsequently successful soul artists—Aretha sang in choir at father's New Bethel Church in Detroit.

Her aunt was renowned gospel singer Clara Ward; legendary black singer Sam Cooke(▶) was family friend. With their encouragement she began recording career with local JVP label and Checker; then cut demos with Major Holly, bass player with jazz pianist Teddy Wilson. These brought her to attention of Columbia Records' A&R man John Hammond, who pronounced her 'Best natural singer since Billie Holiday'.

Debut Columbia album was mix of jazz, R&B and show-business standards. Entire six-year period of her stay with Columbia

**Above: Lady Soul circa 1960. Aretha Franklin has earned her title.**

showed lack of direction, though every album contained its share of gems.

When then husband/manager Ted White signed her to Atlantic in early 1967, Aretha's career took off. Atlantic vice president Jerry Wexler took personal charge of project. Debut album **I Never Loved A Man (The Way I Love You)**, hinged around single of same title, was masterpiece. Wexler had taken Aretha to Muscle Shoals, Alabama, for recordings, and classy studio team there were at best. By end of '67, further gold had

**Love All The Hurt Away, Aretha Franklin. Courtesy Arista Records.**

been mined with **Respect, Baby I Love You** and **Chain Of Fools**. Second album also sold over a million copies as did third LP **Lady Soul**, which used Atlantic's own New York session crew and featured masterful Eric Clapton(▶) guitar solo on **Good To Me As I Am To You**. LP helped earn Aretha accolade as 'R&B Singer Of The Year' in Grammy Awards.

1968 European tour—which yielded **Aretha In Paris** live album—helped **Think**, co-penned with her husband, to international hit status, but marriage was heading for rocks. After **Soul '69** album, Aretha was out of studios for more than a year before recording patchy **This Girl's In Love With You** LP in Miami and New York. Her stage shows too were less than satisfying as she reverted to mixing show-biz standards with solid soul.

Re-marriage and scrapping of large orchestra in favour of small, all-star combo led by King Curtis(▶), seemed to put fire back into the lady. By late 1970 Aretha was back on

top, thanks to some great records and exciting stage performances (one of which was captured on **Live At Fillmore West** album).

In 1972, Aretha returned to gospel roots for **Amazing Grace** album. This was recorded live at Temple Missionary Baptist Church in Los Angeles with gospel superstar James Cleveland and Southern California Community Choir.

Subsequent work saw gradual diminution in her magic. At her best when fronting a small Southern-soul flavoured combo, Franklin was recorded in increasingly sophisticated settings. While following general trend in soul music of the era, these were not the best frame for talent. Despite working with such redoubtable producers as Quincy Jones(▶), Van McCoy, Lamont Dozier and Curtis Mayfield (▶), vast majority of her mid-to-late '70s output was below par.

Switch of labels to Arista in 1980 began steady revival of fortunes. From first Arista album **Aretha** came frenetic version of Otis Redding's oldie **I Can't Turn You Loose**. This recalled feel of her '60s triumphs. Re-work of Sam and Dave's(▶) **Hold On, I'm Coming** from next album was even more potent. Also scored in duet with guitarist/vocalist George Benson on **Love All The Hurt Away**, the album's title cut. Appeared in 'Blues Brothers' film in 1980 (and on LP).

Although most critics would rate late 60s as classic period, Aretha has achieved greatest record sales in 80s. Pop-soul outings like **Freeway Of Love** and **Who's Zoomin' Who** have re-established chart potential, and she has regained pop credibility by recording with strictly 80s luminaries like Annie Lennox and George Michael. Franklin/Lennox collaboration led to smash **Sisters Are Doin' It For Themselves**, while effort with Michael produced UK number one, **I Knew You Were Waiting**, in 1987.

But although Aretha has revamped image and approach to fit in with slick eighties, she has not forgotten gospel roots. 1987 saw her returning to New Bethel Baptist Church in Detroit to cut first religious album in more than fifteen years. Straight gospel outing complete with homilies **One Lord, One Faith, One Baptism** is dramatic testament to swirling power of her voice.

Something of a reclusive personality, Aretha Franklin is nevertheless one of all-time great singers in any field. She looks set to continue

recording for years to come, and, even if greatest triumphs are in past, is assured of honoured place in rock/soul hall of fame.

**Hit Singles:**

| | US | UK |
|---|---|---|
| I Never Loved A Man (The Way I Love You), 1967 | 9 | — |
| Respect, 1967 | 1 | 10 |
| Baby I Love You, 1967 | 4 | 39 |
| A Natural Woman, 1967 | 8 | — |
| Chain Of Fools, 1968 | 2 | 43 |
| (Sweet Sweet Baby) Since You've Been Gone/Ain't No Way, 1968 | 5 | 47 |
| Ain't No Way/(Sweet Sweet Baby) Since You've Been Gone, 1968 | 16 | — |
| Think, 1968 | 7 | 26 |
| I Say A Little Prayer/The House That Jack Built, 1968 | 10 | 4 |
| The House That Jack Built/I Say A Little Prayer, 1968 | 6 | — |
| See Saw, 1968 | 14 | — |
| The Weight, 1969 | 19 | — |
| Share Your Love With Me, 1969 | 13 | — |
| Eleanor Rigby, 1969 | 17 | — |
| Call Me, 1970 | 13 | — |
| Don't Play That Song, 1970 | 11 | 13 |
| You're All I Need To Get By, 1971 | 19 | — |
| Bridge Over Troubled Water, 1971 | 6 | — |
| Spanish Harlem, 1971 | 2 | 14 |
| Rock Steady, 1971 | 9 | — |
| Day Dreaming, 1972 | 5 | — |
| Until You Come Back To Me (That's What I'm Gonna Do), 1974 | 3 | 26 |
| I'm In Love, 1974 | 19 | — |
| Freeway Of Love, 1985 | 3 | — |
| Sisters Are Doing It For Themselves (with Eurythmics), 1985 | 18 | 9 |
| Who's Zoomin' Who, 1985 | — | 7 |

*With George Michael:*

| | US | UK |
|---|---|---|
| I Knew You Were Waiting (For Me), 1987 | 1 | 1 |

**Albums:**
I Never Loved A Man (Atlantic), 1967
Aretha's Gold (Atlantic), 1969
Greatest Hits (Atlantic), 1971
Amazing Grace (Atlantic), 1972
Ten Years Of Gold (Atlantic), 1976
Aretha (Arista), 1980 **CD**
Sweet Bitter Love (Columbia/—), 1981
Love All The Hurt Away (Arista), 1981
Jump To It (Arista), 1982
The Legendary Queen Of Soul (Columbia/CBS), 1983
Get It Right (Arista), 1983
The Best Of (Atlantic), 1984
Who's Zoomin Who (Arista), 1985 **CD**
Soul Survivor (Blue Moon), 1986
The Aretha Franklin Collection (Castle Collectors), 1987
Never Grow Old Chess with Reverand Franklin, 1987
One Lord, One Faith, One Baptism (Arista), 1987 **CD**
The Aretha Franklin Collection (Castle) **CD**
20 Greatest Hits (WEA) **CD**

*Worth Searching Out:*
Aretha Arrives (Atlantic), 1967
Lady Soul (Atlantic), 1968
Soul '69 (Atlantic), 1969
Spirit In The Dark (Atlantic), 1970*
Live At Fillmore West (Atlantic), 1971

*Issued as **Don't Play That Song** in UK

# Free

UK group formed 1968.

**Original line-up:** Paul Kossoff, Gibson Les Paul guitar; Simon Kirke, drums; Andy Fraser, bass; Paul Rodgers, vocals.

**Career:** Kossoff and Kirke were in second division band Black Cat Bones. They saw Rodgers perform with Brown Sugar and asked him to join. Young Andy Fraser (then only 15) was in Mayall's(▶) Bluesbreakers but dissatisfied with jazz direction. Mutual friend contacted him and the four got together for jamming session; first evening produced four songs and group decided to make unit permanent.

Alexis Korner supported group and provided name from band he called Free At Last while with Ginger Baker(▶) and Graham Bond UK gigs impressed Island Records who signed band. First LP made substantial UK impact but second, **Free**, won massive US support; **All Right Now** single went Top 10 everywhere. Sudden success seemed to bring out friction as members strove for limelight. After **Highway** album, band split. Rogers' solo effort flopped as did Fraser's. Kossoff and Texan keyboards man Rabbit Bundrick for

**Free Live!**, Free. Courtesy Island Records.

**Kossoff, Kirke, Tetsu And Rabbit** LP.
In 1972 original band re-formed for **Free At Last** album. During tour Kossoff's drug habit and Rodgers/Fraser fights split group again. Kossoff and Fraser left, Tetsu and Rabbit replacing them. This line-up recorded **Heartbreaker** (Kossoff helped with guitar work). Single from LP, **Wishing Well**, prompted tour. Kossoff started but again collapsed and Wendell Richardson (ex-Osibisa) stepped in. At end of US tour, Free folded for good.

Fraser failed to follow up success with either Andy Fraser Band or Sharks. Kossoff died in 1976 of drug-induced heart failure shortly after setting up Back Street Crawler. Tetsu joined Rod Stewart's Faces(▶) and Rabbit did session work and two solo LPs before joining Who(▶) as tour 'member', 1978-'82. Rodgers and Kirke set up Bad Company(▶).

Certainly one of UK's finer bands, with understated, sparse arrangements and high energy spirit, Free has had far-ranging influence. Unfortunately, it is yet another story of talent which failed to reach its potential; drugs and egos doomed Free from the start.

**Final line-up:** Rodgers: Kirke; Wendell Richardson, guitar; Tetsu Kamauchi, bass; Rabbit Bundrick, keyboards.

**Hit Singles:**

| | US | UK |
|---|---|---|
| All Right Now, 1970 | 4 | 2 |
| My Brother Jake, 1971 | — | 4 |
| Little Bit Of Love, 1972 | — | 13 |
| Wishing Well, 1973 | — | 7 |
| All Right Now, 1973 | — | 15 |
| Free (EP), 1978 | — | 11 |

**Albums:**
Tons Of Sobs (A&M/Island), 1969
Free (A&M/Island), 1969
Fire And Water (A&M/Island), 1970 **CD**
Highway (A&M/Island), 1970
Live (A&M/Island), 1971
Free At Last (A&M/Island), 1972

Heartbreaker (A&M/Island), 1973
Best Of (A&M/—), 1975
Completely Free (A&M/Island), 1983*
*Compilation

# Glen Frey
US vocalist, guitarist.
Born Detroit, Michigan.

**Career:** One-time member of Linda Ronstadt's backing band, Frey was founding member of hugely successful Eagles (▶) penning many of their hits including classic **Hotel California**. On group's break-up he found niche as writer and performer of TV and movie themes, scoring with **The Heat Is On** from film 'Beverley Hills Cop' and **Smuggler's Blues** which was used in TV's 'Miami Vice' series in which Frey also made acting debut.

**Hit Singles:**

| | US | UK |
|---|---|---|
| The One You Love, 1982 | 15 | — |
| Sexy Girl, 1984 | 20 | — |
| The Heat Is On, 1985 | 2 | 12 |
| Smuggler's Blues, 1985 | 12 | 22 |
| You Belong To The City, 1985 | 2 | — |

**Albums:**
No Fun Aloud (Asylum), 1982
The Allnighter (MCA), 1984 **CD**

# Peter Gabriel
UK vocalist, composer, producer.
Born London, May 13, 1950.

**Career:** Musical career began at Charterhouse Public School in the Garden Wall, a short-lived unit featuring Tony Banks (piano) and Chris Stewart (drums). Group was formed

**Below: Since going solo in 1975, Peter Gabriel has experimented with ethnic sounds.**

**The second Peter Gabriel.
Courtesy Charisma Records.**

primarily as vehicle for Gabriel's songwriting; dressed in kaftan, beads and flowers he already revealed theatrical bent. Love of soul music, particularly Otis Redding(▶), James Brown(▶) and Nina Simone(▶), was major musical influence.

Garden Wall gradually evolved into Genesis(▶) and Gabriel systematically steered group's musical direction in early '70s; contributed much to their visual/theatrical appeal, as well as penning their best work. From 1970's **Trespass** through to 1974's **The Lamb Lies Down On Broadway,** Genesis emerged as one of UK's most popular groups. An elaborate tour to promote **Lamb Lies Down On Broadway,** featuring Gabriel playing album's leading character, proved enormously successful in both UK and US.

In May 1975, Gabriel shocked rock world by announcing his departure from band to pursue solo career. Debut **Peter Gabriel**, an intelligent and adventurous work, was well received and spawned hit single **Solsbury Hill**. For second album, replaced producer Bob Ezrin with Robert Fripp. A less accessible work, album showed collaboration to best effect on **Exposure**.

Third and fourth albums, also titled **Peter Gabriel**, showed growing confidence, with artist taking control of production. Two evocative hits from third album established reputation in singles charts. **Games Without Frontiers**, a scathing anti-jingoistic comment inspired by BBC television programme 'It's A Knockout', was followed by 33 rpm single **Biko**, about the controversial death of South African activist Stephen Biko.

Sometimes criticised for lack of spontaneity, Gabriel's work still shows greater adventure and experimentation than Genesis days. Freed from commercial restraints, he has frequently worked on rock/avant-garde fringe; allied himself closely with such contemporaries as Robert Fripp and Brian Eno(▶). In recent years has successfully broadened his musical and lyrical frames of reference

**So, Peter Gabriel.
Courtesy Virgin Records.**

encompassing a variety of contrasting ethnic sounds deriving from the Californian Indians, Central Africa and industrial Europe. Ever inventive, he has simultaneously incorporated unusual rhythms and sounds from factories, scrapyards, and even smashing television screens to complement his studio experimentation. Recently acclaimed for his role in organising WOMAD (World of Music, Arts and Dance) Festival which proved significant gathering of artists from all over the world. 1982 LP **Security** yielded successful US single **Shock The Monkey**; accompanying video, played frequently by MTV, is one of most imaginative and evocative ever made.

Following live double album and soundtrack for Alan Parker movie '**Birdy**', Gabriel released fifth studio album **So** in 1986. It achieved double platinum status in US, platinum in UK, and spawned huge hit single **Sledgehammer**. Latter picked up no fewer than nine MTV awards.

Always one of most innovative and least compromising figures in rock, Gabriel's work constantly surprises. Virtually immune to fads and fashions of rock, Gabriel seems likely to be successfully making music for years to come.

**Hit Singles:**

| | US | UK |
|---|---|---|
| Solsbury Hill, 1977 | — | 13 |
| Games Without Frontiers, 1980 | — | 4 |
| Sledgehammer, 1986 | — | 4 |
| Big Time, 1987 | 3 | 13 |
| In Your Eyes, 1987 | — | 19 |
| Sledgehammer, 1987 | — | 4 |

*With Kate Bush:*

| | | |
|---|---|---|
| Don't Give Up, 1986 | — | 9 |

**Albums:**
Peter Gabriel (Atco/Charisma), 1977 **CD**
Peter Gabriel (Mercury/Charisma), 1978 **CD**
Peter Gabriel (Charisma), 1980 **CD**
Peter Gabriel (Charisma), 1982 **CD**
Security (Geffen/—), 1982
Peter Gabriel Plays Live (Charisma), 1983 **CD**
Birdy (Charisma), 1985 **CD**
So (Virgin), 1986 **CD**

# Rory Gallagher

UK guitarist, vocalist, composer.
Born Ballyshannon, County Donegal, Ireland,
March 2, 1948.

**Career:** One of rock's true grafters. Raised in
Cork; played in local bands until 15. Joined
the Fontana Showband, an amalgam of brass
and guitars which played pop hits to enthusiastic dance-hall crowds.

With Charlie McCracken (bass) and John
Wilson (drums) formed Taste, high-energy
blues/rock trio. Band learned trade in Hamburg and home country before moving to UK
in 1969.

Polydor recording contract produced several
spirited albums. As live act, band headlined
throughout Britain and Europe. Earned ecstatic
reviews for Gallagher's dominant acrobatic
stage presence and dazzling guitar technique;
McCracken and Wilson provided energetic
rhythm section.

With Gallagher taking central role, dissension in group grew to extreme proportions, a
situation aggravated by unsympathetic management. Wilson often refused to take stage
for group encores, leaving Gallagher and
McCracken to appease audience. Trio split in
1971, Wilson and McCracken forming short-
lived Stud with Jim Cregan (future Family(▶),
Rod Stewart(▶) Band).

Gallagher took to road with Wilgar Campbell
(drums) and Gerry McAvoy (bass), using own
name as band title. Line-up completed three
successful albums before Campbell was
replaced by Rod De'Ath. Lou Martin was
added on keyboards.

Pursuing a hectic touring schedule, Rory
Gallagher Band secured reputation in Europe
and America. Steady album sales meant
considerable output, with several memorable
highlights. Live album **Irish Tour 74** captured
gregarious Gallagher at his best. Director
Tony Palmer filmed gigs for his movie 'Rory
Gallagher-Irish Tour '74' which premiered
at prestigious Cork Film Festival that year.

After '76 set **Calling Card**, De'Ath and
Martin quit. Drummer Ted Mckenna (ex-Alex
Harvey Band(▶)) joined for **Photo Finish**
(1978). 1980 world tour provided live cuts for
**Stage Struck** (1980). Album showed Gallagher still loved the road. '82 **Jinx** collection
maintained enthusiastic studio approach.

Complete absence from both UK/US singles
charts during recording career belies Gallagher's popular appeal. Steadfastly refusing
to 'commercialise' his work and rejecting
'pop' format TV shows, which he feels could
not do his work justice, Gallagher is secure in
knowledge that he is playing authentic
rock-based blues to undiminished ecstatic
audiences.
Guitar: Fender Stratocaster
Martin acoustic, also mandolin.

**Albums:**
*With Taste:*
Taste (Atco/Polydor), 1969
On The Boards (Atco/Polydor), 1970
Live Taste (—/Polydor), 1971
Live At The Isle Of Wight (—/Polydor), 1972
Taste (—/Polydor), 1977

*Solo:*
Rory Gallagher (—/Polydor), 1971
Deuce (—/Chrysalis), 1971
Live In Europe (Chrysalis), 1973*
Blueprint (Chrysalis), 1973
Tattoo (Chrysalis), 1973
Irish Tour '74 (Chrysalis), 1974*
In The Beginning (—/Emerald Gem), 1974
Against The Grain (Chrysalis), 1975
Calling Card (Chrysalis), 1976
Photo Finish (Chrysalis), 1978

Above: Rory Gallagher, the blues star
who refuses to compromise.

Top Priority (Chrysalis), 1979
Stage Struck (Chrysalis), 1980*
Jink (Chrysalis), 1982
Defender (Demon Solo), 1987
*Live

# Art Garfunkel

US vocalist, actor.
Born Forest Hills, New York, November 5,
1941.

**Career:** Although responsible for arranging
highly-praised two-part vocal harmonies as
well as being half of singing duo, Garfunkel
felt like junior partner of Simon and
Garfunkel(▶) as Simon(▶) wrote both words
and music and played guitar. Having acted in
one film, 'Catch-22', Art began moving in
independent direction. In light of Simon's
desire to attempt solo career split in 1970
seemed logical decision for duo.

After some time on Scottish farm, Garfunkel
returned to US West Coast to pursue both
acting and recording career. His performance
in films 'Carnal Knowledge' (1971) and 'Bad
Timing' (1979) (the latter more successful in
Europe than US) were critically well received.

Solo recording career began with 1973
**Angel Clare**, produced by Simon and
Garfunkel's Roy Halee, which went gold.
**Breakaway** in 1975, under influence of new
producer Richard Perry, surpassed it and
resulted in UK No. 1 with **I Only Have Eyes
For You**. Album included one-off reunion with
Paul Simon on **My Little Town** (also
released on Simon's LP **Still Crazy After All
These Years**).

Self-produced **Watermark** in 1978 featured James Taylor(▶) (for whom Garfunkel
had done session in 1976) and Paul Simon on
**(What A) Wonderful World**, one of few
tracks not by Jimmy Webb. **Fate For Breakfast**, partly recorded in London, featured Cliff

Richard(▶) hit **Miss You Nights**. Single
**Bright Eyes** from movie 'Watership Down'
gave him second UK No. 1 in 1979, and
**Since I Don't Have You** made charts same
year. **Scissors Cut** album was ignored.

Garfunkel returned to spotlight via Central
Park reunion concert with Paul Simon in 1981,
but latterly has kept relatively low profile.
Royalty income ensures that he is unlikely to
join breadline in foreseeable future.

Angel Clare, Art Garfunkel. Courtesy
Columbia Records.

**Hit Singles:**

| | US | UK |
|---|---|---|
| All I Know, 1973 | 9 | — |
| I Only Have Eyes For You, 1975 | 18 | 1 |
| (What A) Wonderful World (with James Taylor and Paul Simon), 1978 | 17 | — |
| Bright Eyes, 1979 | — | 1 |

**Albums:**
Angel Clare (Columbia/CBS), 1973
Breakaway (CBS), 1975 **CD**
Watermark (Columbia/CBS), 1977
Fate For Breakfast (Columbia/CBS), 1979
Scissors Cut (Columbia/CBS), 1981
The Art Garfunkel Album (CBS), 1984 **CD**
The Animal Christmas (CBS), 1986

# Marvin Gaye

US vocalist, composer, keyboard player,
drummer.
Born Marvin Pentz Gaye Jr, Washington DC,
April 2, 1939.

**Career:** Son of a minister, began singing in
church choir and learned organ. After spell in
US Air Force sang in various doo-wop bands
before joining seminal black vocal group
Rainbows. (Membership has also included
soul legends Don Covay and Billy 'Fat Boy'
Stewart.) Formed Marquis in 1957 with two
other former Rainbows. With help from Bo
Diddley, cut album for Okeh. In 1959, Harvey
Fuqua—later major figure at Motown
Records—invited Marquis to become his
backing group, the Moonglows. This new
line-up made two singles for Chess (some
years earlier, Gaye had won a Fuqua-judged
talent contest singing Moonglows' classic
**Ten Commandments Of Love**).

When Fuqua moved from Chicago to
Detroit in 1960, to set up his Tri-Phi and
Harvey labels, Gaye joined him. The labels
were soon to come into fledgling Motown
Records' fold. Fuqua married Gwen Gordy,
sister of Motown founder Berry Gordy Jr;
soon after Gaye married another Gordy sister,
Anna.

In 1961, Gaye's contract with Gwen
Gordy's label, Anna, was taken over by
brother Berry. While waiting for recording
career to flower, Gaye filled in time as
drummer for Motown sessions and for stage
appearances of Smokey Robinson and the
Miracles (for two years). He also sang back-up,
notably on Marvelettes' recordings, and
displayed talent as multi-instrumentalist.

Gaye's fourth single in own right, the
mid-tempo **Stubborn Kind Of Fellow** (1962),

Below: Art Garfunkel, owner of one of
the purest voices in rock music.

was breakthrough—first of nearly 30 Top 50 hits over next decade. First hit's producer Mickey Stevenson, was also involved in **Hitch Hike** and **Pride And Joy** successes before Berry Gordy, then the Holland/Dozier/Holland team, took over reins.

**Can I Get A Witness** (covered by Rolling Stones) and **You're A Wonderful One** were classics of Motown's Detroit Sound idiom. In 1964, Gaye was teamed with Mary Wells for duet album from which both sides of single scored. This was first of several successful Gaye partnerships with Motown ladies—Kim Weston, Tammi Terrell, Diana Ross.

Gaye/Terrell partnership was longest lasting (from 1967-70) and most fruitful. Terminated tragically when Tammi died following several operations for brain tumour. The then 24-year-old Gaye was deeply affected and became something of a hermit, dropping out of touring scene and rarely appearing in

**What's Going On, Marvin Gaye.**
**Courtesy Motown Records.**

studio. In 1971, he returned with introspective **What's Going On** album, a landmark in development of black music and, particularly, of the Motown Sound, being a conceptual LP rather than a collection of singles.Morever, Gaye produced/wrote album himself. Songs were covered by such major black artists as Diana Ross(▶) (**Save The Children**), Quincy Jones(▶) (**What's Going On**), Aretha Franklin(▶) (**Wholly Holy**) and Gil Scott-Heron (**Inner City Blues**).

1972 movie soundtrack **Trouble Man** continued vein as did sensual concept album **Let's Get It On**, before release of duo album with Diana Ross, **Diana And Marvin**.

By 1974, Gaye was established as leading solo vocalist in black music. Fronted 34-piece orchestra at Oakland Coliseum, California, for first stage appearance in four years.

Personal problems over break-up of his second marriage led to further stage/recording hiatus; and eventually to the self-pitying concept album **Here My Dear**.

Wife's affair with Teddy Pendergrass (one of Gaye's closest friends), troubles over alimony, tax arrears (which led to seizure of his recording studio) and disagreements with Motown resulted in inner turmoil and an increasingly unpredictable personality. Gaye even disappeared to Hawaii for time to live in a converted bread van.

Visit to UK for 1980 tour saw contrast between sensationally exciting performances and series of blown TV dates and late appearances.

Virtually unmanageable, Gaye was released by Motown; moved base to Belgium and lapsed into obscurity for a while.

New deal with CBS was fruit of two years of careful re-assessment; resultant 1982 album **Midnight Love** showed all his old mastery. Single (**Sexual**) **Healing** brought him back into charts with vengeance.

However, Gaye's turbulent life ended when his father shot him at the family home during a quarrel in April 1984.

**Above: The Legendary Soulster Marvin Gaye.**

**Hit Singles:**

| | US | UK |
|---|---|---|
| Pride And Joy, 1983 | 10 | — |
| You're A Wonderful One, 1964 | 15 | — |
| Try It Baby, 1964 | 15 | — |
| How Sweet It Is (To Be Loved By You), 1964 | 6 | 49 |
| I'll Be Doggone, 1965 | 8 | — |
| Ain't That Peculiar, 1965 | 8 | — |
| I Heard It Through The Grapevine, 1968 | 1 | 1 |
| Too Busy Thinking About My Baby, 1969 | 4 | 5 |
| That's The Way Love Is, 1969 | 7 | — |
| Abraham Martin And John, 1970 | — | 9 |
| What's Going On, 1971 | 2 | — |
| Mercy Mercy Me (The Ecology), (1971) | 4 | — |
| Inner City Blues (Make Me Wanna Holler), 1971 | 9 | — |
| Trouble Man, 1972 | 7 | — |
| Let's Get It On, 1973 | 1 | 31 |
| Got To Give It Up, Pt. 1, 1977 | 1 | 7 |
| (Sexual) Healing, 1982 | 3 | 4 |

*With Mary Wells:*

| | | |
|---|---|---|
| What's The Matter With You Baby, 1964 | 17 | — |
| Once Upon A Time, 1964 | 19 | 50 |

*With Kim Weston:*

| | | |
|---|---|---|
| It Takes Two, 1967 | 14 | 16 |

*With Tammi Terrell:*

| | | |
|---|---|---|
| Ain't No Mountain High Enough, 1967 | 19 | — |
| Your Precious Love, 1967 | 5 | — |
| If I Could Build My Whole World Around You, 1968 | 10 | 41 |
| Ain't Nothing Like The Real Thing, 1968 | 8 | 34 |
| You're All I Need To Get By, 1968 | 7 | 19 |

*With Diana Ross:*

| | | |
|---|---|---|
| You're A Special Part Of Me, 1973 | 12 | — |
| You Are Everything, 1974 | — | 5 |
| My Mistake (Was To Love You), 1974 | 19 | — |

**Albums**

M.P.G. Greatest Hits (Tamla Motown), 1970
What's Going On (Tamla Motown), 1971
Let's Get It On (Tamla Motown), 1973
Anthology (Tamla Motown), 1974
Best Of (Tamla Motown), 1976
I Want You (Tamla Motown), 1976
Here My Dear (Tamla Motown), 1979
Early Years (Tamla Motown), 1980
Motown Superstar Series Volume 15 (Motown/), 1981
In Our Lifetime (Tamla Motown), 1981
Magic Of (—/Pickwick), 1982
Midnight Love (Columbia/CBS), 1982
Whats Going On/Lets Get It On (Motown), 1971/1973 **CD**
I Heard It Through The Grapevine/I Want You (Motown), 1976 **CD**
Live At The London Palladium (Motown) **CD**
Marvin Gaye And His Women (Motown) **CD**
Trouble Man/MPG (Motown), 1970 **CD**
Compact Command Performances Vol 2 (Motown), 1987 **CD**

*With Tammi Terrell:*
United (Tamla Motown), 1966
Greatest Hits (Tamla Motown), 1969
Motown Superstar Series, Volume 2 (Motown/—), 1970

*With Diana Ross:*
Diana and Marvin (Motown), 1985 **CD**

*Worth Searching Out:*
How Sweet It Is (Tamla/MFP), 1964
Greatest Hits (Telstar), 1983
Dream Of A Lifetime (CBS), 1985

# Genesis

UK group formed 1967.

**Original line-up:** Anthony Phillips, guitar, vocals; Michael Rutherford, bass, guitar, vocals; Tony Banks, keyboards, vocals; Peter Gabriel, vocals; Chris Stewart, drums.

**Career:** Original members were attending Charterhouse public school when they met in

mid-'60s. Passing demo tapes to Charterhouse alumnus Jonathan King led to first contract, with Decca. King suggested name Genesis. Two early singles did little and Stewart was replaced with John Silver. King produced first album and when told to change group's name (because of American group of same name) he refused and worked up LP title **From Genesis To Revelations**. King's production muddled Genesis sound and as LP was poorly received, King and Decca lost interest.

Band almost broke up. Instead 'Melody Maker' ad found John Mayhew to take over drums and ex-school mate Richard MacPhail took over as road manager. Besides providing transportation, he rented cottage in October 1969 where band lived, wrote and rehearsed **Trespass** LP. Charisma boss Tony Stratton-Smith became interested in their live work and signed them in spring 1970; **Trespass** appeared in October.

Both Phillips and Mayhew quit soon after and another MM ad came up with Phil Collins (▶), who was added as drummer. It was not until December 1970 that band settled on Steve Hackett as guitarist. Band was still very 'art-rock' orientated, but 1971 **Nursery Cryme** showed sense of adventure and began to define mature Genesis sound. Gabriel(▶) had started wearing stage costumes, which were becoming more and more outrageous, but won favour with audiences. 1972 **Foxtrot** finally pushed them into major league and band started drawing larger crowds. 1973 **Genesis Live** is excellent account of band development at this point. Same year saw release of **Selling England By The Pound** and UK hit single **I Know What I Like**.

Band was clearly at forefront of progressive rock upon release of double LP, **Lamb Lies Down On Broadway**, with American interest sparked by elaborate stage show in which Gabriel acted out story-line. Rumours of Gabriel's loss of interest were confusing considering band's success, but were confirmed by shock announcement in June 1975 that he had quit.

Remaining members held many auditions to locate replacement. Eventual announcement puzzled fans and critics alike: Gabriel's replacement would be Phil Collins. Many backing vocals since 1971 had been by Collins, but at time it seemed unlikely Collins could replace Gabriel with any self-assurance. Even release of excellent **Trick Of The Tail** LP and two-month US tour (assisted by Bill Bruford (ex-Yes(▶) on drums) could not put down rumour band would completely fold. But within 11 months **Wind And Wuthering**

**Nursery Cryme, Genesis. Courtesy Charisma Records.**

was released and Genesis seemed permanently on road, this time with Chester Thompson (ex-Zappa(▶), Weather Report) assisting on drums. Paris dates were recorded and produced double live set **Seconds Out.**

**Abacab, Genesis. Courtesy Charisma Records.**

Mid-1977 brought more adjustments when Hackett left after 45-city US tour and three 'sold out' Earls Court, London, gigs, again raising speculation that band's days were over. But **And Then There Were Three . . .** became band's biggest seller and produced UK Top 10 hit, **Follow Me Follow You.** Supergroups seemed out of touch with musical upheavals of late '70s, and band wisely took recording break. Bank's 1979 solo LP **A Curious Feeling** and Rutherford's **Small Creeps Day** (1980) filled void. **Duke,** when released in 1980, proved Genesis could maintain energy levels, and if anything, become more accessible with rhythmic melodies. '70s pretensions disappeared as band successfully moved back into smaller venues on UK '80 and '82 tours (including surprise London Marquee gig).

Phil Collins' personal problems and ultimate divorce made up the content of highly successful solo LP, **Face Value.** 1981 also saw group release **Abacab** which continued healthy trend toward group compositions. Collins, resident workaholic, managed to record another solo LP, **Hello I Must Be Going,** which yielded No.1 hit with old standard **You Can't Hurry Love.** (A clever video with three Phil Collins' singing à la Supremes(▶) helped greatly.) Rutherford's **Acting Very Strange** was also solid but failed to attract as much attention.

**Three Sides Live** actually improved already high quality of **Duke** and **Abacab** tracks, demonstrating enthusiasm and energy of live Genesis even after 14 years on stage. As treat for (or exploitation of) fans, fourth side contains different material on US/UK versions. In recent years Collins has become massively successful solo artist, while continuing to lead band to ever greater success. His influence seems to have made Genesis more accessible to pop audience, and outfit has become almost permanent fixture in single and album charts. Similarly, live drawing power has grown and grown, to point where act is one of hottest concert tickets in world.

One of most soulful voices in rock, Collins is considerable asset to band which has become a rock institution, beloved by huge audience which even includes hipper members of Royal Family. Genesis are seventies survivors par excellence.

**Current line-up:** Collins, drums, vocals; Rutherford; Banks; Chester Thompson, drums (on tour).

| Hit Singles: | US | UK |
|---|---|---|
| Spot The Pigeon (EP), 1977 | — | 14 |
| Follow You Follow Me, 1978 | 23 | 7 |
| Misunderstanding, 1980 | 14 | 42 |
| Turn It On Again, 1980 | 58 | 8 |
| Abacab, 1981 | — | 19 |
| Paperlate (EP), 1982 | 32 | 10 |
| Mama, 1983 | — | 4 |
| That's All, 1983 | 6 | 16 |
| In Too Deep, 1986 | 3 | 19 |
| Invisible Touch, 1986 | 11 | 15 |
| Land Of Confusion, 1986 | 5 | 14 |
| Tonight Tonight Tonight, 1987 | 3 | 18 |
| Throwing It All Away, 1987 | 1 | — |

**Albums:**
Trespass (ABC/Charisma), 1970 **CD**
Nursery Cryme (Charisma), 1971 **CD**
Foxtrot (Charisma), 1972 **CD**
Genesis Live (Charisma), 1973
Selling England By The Pound (Charisma), 1973 **CD**
In The Beginning (1st LP retitled) (London/Decca), 1974
The Lamb Lies Down On Broadway (ATCO/Charisma), 1974 **CD**
A Trick Of The Tail (ATCO/Charisma), 1976 **CD**
Wind And Wuthering (ATCO/Charisma), 1976 **CD**
Seconds Out (ATCO/Charisma), 1977 **CD**
. . .And Then There Were Three . . .(ATCO/Charisma), 1978 **CD**
Duke (ATCO/Charisma), 1980 **CD**
Abacab (ATCO/Charisma), 1981 **CD**
Three Sides Live (ATCO/Charisma), 1982 **CD**
Released eponymous LP in 1983
Invisible Touch (Charisma), 1986 **CD**
When The Sour Turns To Sweet (Razor) mini LP, 1986 **CD**

*Mike Rutherford Solo:*
Mike And The Mechanics (WEA), 1985

**A Gerry & the Pacemakers compilation. Courtesy EMI Records.**

# Gerry And The Pacemakers

UK group formed 1961.

**Original/Final line-up:** Gerry Marsden, vocals, guitar; Freddie Marsden, drums; Leslie Maguire, piano; Les Chadwick, bass.

**Career:** After stints, often with brother Freddie, in various skiffle and rock'n'roll bands, Gerry Marsden formed Mars-Bars in hometown of Liverpool, playing local clubs for six months before break-up. Following split the Marsdens were joined by Les Chadwick to form Pacemakers trio.

After two months at Top Ten Club in Hamburg they returned to Merseyside, added Leslie Maguire and were signed by Beatles'(▶) manager Brian Epstein in June 1962.

Beatles' producer and Parlophone A&R chief George Martin saw performance at Birkenhead and chose to record Mitch Murray song **How Do You Do It?** which he had earlier tried to record with the Beatles (but they preferred to cut own material). Song climbed quickly to No. 1, as did another Mitch Murray song, **I Like It,** and their reading of Rodgers and Hammerstein ballad standard, **You'll Never Walk Alone,** making them only group ever to top charts with each of their first three records.

Belated Merseymania movie 'Ferry Cross The Mersey' ('65) gave group final top ten single with Marsden-penned theme.

Band was equally popular in US (after first US single success **Don't Let The Sun Catch You Crying,** their earlier singles were released there), but quickly faded from limelight and broke up in 1968. Marsden embarked on solo career which yielded no hits but five-year starring role opposite Anna Neagle in West End Musical production 'Charlie Girl'.

In 1975 Gerry and the Pacemakers reformed for triumphant 'Mersey Beat' revival tour of US and again for similar 'Sounds Of The Sixties' tour of UK in 1979.

Marsden has remained active in variety, pantomime and cabaret and led host of show business personalities on re-make of **You'll Never Walk Alone** to top of UK singles chart in 1985, as fund-raiser for Bradford Football Club fire disaster.

| Hit Singles: | US | UK |
|---|---|---|
| How Do You Do It? 1963 | 9 | 1 |
| I Like It, 1963 | 17 | 1 |
| You'll Never Walk Alone, 1963 | 48 | 1 |
| I'm The One, 1964 | — | 2 |
| Don't Let The Sun Catch You Crying, 1964 | 4 | 6 |
| Ferry Cross The Mersey, 1964 | 6 | 8 |
| I'll Be There, 1965 | 14 | 12 |

**Albums:**
Best Of (Capitol/Nut), 1977
Very Best Of (Mfp), 1984
The Singles Plus (EMI), 1987 **CD**
Hit Singles Album (EMI), 1986

# Gillan

UK group formed 1975.

**Original line-up:** Ian Gillan, vocals; Ray Fenwick, guitar; John Gustafson, bass; Mark Nauseef, drums.

**Career:** Ian Gillan was originally lead singer with Deep Purple; he left in 1973 and two years later formed Ian Gillan Band with above line-up and released **Child In Time** album. Band released two more albums under same name. Major personnel shake-up and shortening of name to Gillan heralded 1979 Top 20 album **Mr Universe.** Line-up on this album: Gillan; Steve Bird, guitar; John McCoy, bass; Pete Barnacle, drums; Colin Towns, keyboards.

Success was consolidated by 1980 signing to Virgin Records, although by this time personnel had changed again; Bernie Torme had replaced Steve Bird on guitar, and Mick Underwood had taken over drums. 1981 was successful year with two Top 20 LPs and Top 20 single, a version of Gary US Bonds' classic **New Orleans**. In the summer Torme quit and was replaced by Janick Gers.

By this time Gillan had established reputation as hard-working live act, undertaking gruelling tours in UK and abroad. 1982 saw consolidation of UK success with album **Magic**, but in 1983 Gillan disbanded; Ian Gillan joined Black Sabbath(▶) and, later, the re-formed Deep Purple(▶).

Ian enjoyed greater success and fulfilment with the new Purple than he had with his own band or Sabbath. He later revealed that while recording with Sabbath, he spent most time living in tent outside studio!

But after recording **Perfect Strangers** and **The House Of Blue Light** with Purple he began to get itchy solo feet again, and recorded an album with his old partner Roger Glover **Accidentally On Purpose** released in February 1988. Most of the tracks were played on keyboards, synthesisers and drum machines, and with a more relaxed vocal style, seemed like a determined effort to break away from heavy metal typecasting. He mooted plans to tour with his own band, dependent on successful sales of the album, to fit in between tours with Purple.

**Final line-up:** Gillan; Janick Gers, guitar; John McCoy, Fender Precision bass; Colin Towns, keyboards; Mick Underwood, drums.

| Hit Singles: | US | UK |
|---|---|---|
| Trouble, 1980 | — | 14 |
| New Orleans, 1981 | — | 17 |

**Albums:**
Clear Air Turbulence (Virgin), 1977
Scarabus (Virgin), 1977.
Live (—/Island), 1978
Mr Universe (—/Acrobat), 1979
Gillan (—/Flyover), 1979
Glory Road (—/Virgin), 1980
Future Shock (Virgin), 1981
Double Trouble (Virgin), 1981
Magic (Virgin), 1982
What I Did On My Vacation (Ten), 1986 **CD**

# Girlschool

UK group formed 1978.

**Original line-up:** Kim McAuliffe, vocals, guitar; Enid Williams, bass, vocals, Kelly Johnson, guitar, vocals; Denise Dufort, drums

**Career:** McAuliffe and Williams were in 1977 group Painted Lady. After several personnel shifts band had settled down by March 1978 with change of name to Girlschool, emphasising heavy-metal music (rather than Runaways image of girls playing at rock'n'roll game).

First single, **Take It All Away**, caught attention of Motorhead(▶) manager Doug Smith who put them on that band's 1980 tour and acquired Bronze recording deal. **Demolition** appeared in UK in June 1980 while band was on tour; within two weeks LP hit Top 30. Motorhead connection peaked with excellent **Saint Valentine's Massacre** EP, which includes superb cover **Please Don't Touch**. **Hit And Run** expanded audience and proved Girlschool's staying power.

Williams left in 1982 and was replaced by Gil Weston, following her recommendation by Motorhead bassist Lemmy. This line-up recorded band's best effort so far, **Screaming Blue Murder**. LP continued in thunder-and-swagger tradition of hard rock, but several cuts had touch of irony, humour and understanding.

After cutting **Play Dirty** set in US, band suffered loss of guitarist Kelly Johnson. Replacement was Chris Bonacci, from another all-girl HM crew She, whose vocalist Jackie Bodimead was also recruited. Termination of contract by Bronze caused further aggravation, but girls quickly secured deal with Phonogram.

In 1986 the girls recorded **Nightmare At Maple Cross** for GWR and in June that year they teamed up with Glam Rock veteran Gary Glitter with a new version of **I'm A Leader** which wasn't the hit they needed. In 1988 they toured extensively with Motorhead and began work on a new album with producer Andre Jacquamanin.

**Current line-up:** McAuliffe; Dutort, Tracy Lamb, bass; Chris Bonacci, guitar.

**Albums:**
Demolition (Bronze), 1980
Hit And Run (Bronze), 1981
Screaming Blue Murder (Bronze), 1982
Play Dirty (Bronze), 1983
Race With The Devil (Raw Power), 1986

# Gary Glitter

UK vocalist.
Born Paul Gadd, Banbury, Oxfordshire, May 8, 1940.

**Career:** As Paul Raven, he pursued undistinguished early career with string of unsuccessful solo singles for Decca and then Parlophone. In 1965 he joined TV pop show 'Ready Steady Go' as programme assistant and met writer/producer Mike Leander, later to become his mentor.

In 1967, again as Paul Raven, he signed with MCA and released yet more flop singles. Total lack of success continued until 1971 when he signed with teenybop specialists Bell Records and met up with Leander again.

Leander and Gadd set out to capitalise on then-current glitter-rock fad. Gadd created character 'Gary Glitter' and came up with sound to go with persona. First single, **Rock & Roll (Parts 1 & 2)**, was a spare, atmospheric opus, heavily reliant on bass and drums; public response was slow but eventually record made British charts, reaching No. 2 in June 1972. (It also became a No. 1 in US but remained his only major transatlantic success.)

Between June 1972 and June 1975 Glitter turned in 11 UK Top-10 hits, including three No.1s. All followed basic style set by **Rock & Roll**, and seemed to touch lucrative chord among pubescent Britons. Stranger perhaps than Glitter's long-awaited record success was his elevation to sex symbol. Apart from the

**Left: Girlschool, the acceptable face of female heavy metal music.**

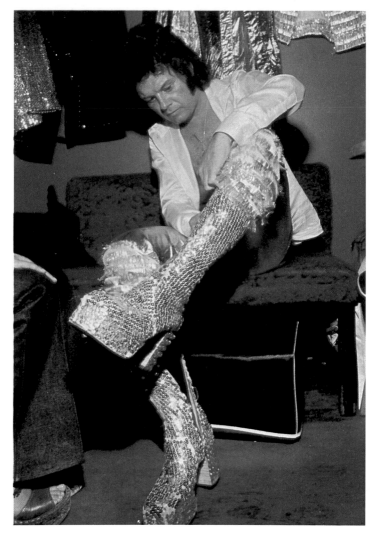

**Above: Gary Glitter was a superstar during the phase which bore his name,**

fact that his birthdate was rumoured to be considerably earlier than that given on his biography, he had something of a weight problem; stuffed into his shimmering jumpsuits and platform heels he often seemed more comic than sexy. (His backing group the Glitter Band also scored in UK during this period.)

In 1976 Glitter announced retirement 'for personal reasons', but returned to performing in December that year, and switched labels to Arista in 1977 for a couple more minor hits. During years of stardom he was a big spender, and profligacy took its toll when he was declared bankrupt. A circus tent tour with Gerry Cottle brought him back to the public but was a financial failure. Latterly he has been making strenuous efforts to re-establish himself as major attraction, and has become something of a father figure to post-punk musicians. (Joan Jett and the Blackhearts(▶) had a US hit with **Do You Wanna Touch Me** in 1982.) Never one to take himself too seriously, Glitter seems destined to be the rock equivalent of the 'old trouper', working on as long as audiences will turn out to see him.

Recently, Glitter has embarked on parallel career as "talking head" and all-round media personality, most notably as host of late night talk show for commercial television.

**Hit Singles:**

| | US | UK |
|---|---|---|
| Rock & Roll (Parts 1 & 2), 1972 | 1 | 2 |
| I Didn't Know I Loved You (Till I Saw You Rock'n'Roll), 1972 | 35 | 4 |
| Do You Wanna Touch Me (Oh Yeah), 1973 | — | 2 |
| Hello Hello I'm Back Again, 1973 | — | 2 |
| I'm The Leader Of The Gang (I Am), 1973 | — | 1 |
| I Love You Love Me Love, 1973 | — | 1 |
| Remember Me This Way, 1974 | — | 3 |
| Always Yours, 1974 | — | 1 |
| Oh Yes! You're Beautiful, 1974 | — | 2 |
| Love Like You And Me, 1975 | — | 10 |
| Doing Alright With The Boys, 1975 | — | 6 |
| Another Rock'n' Roll Xmas, 1984 | — | 7 |

**Albums:**
Remember Me This Way (Bell), 1974
G.G. (Bell), 1975
Greatest Hits (Bell), 1976
Gary Glitter's Golden Greats (—/GTO), 1977
I Love You Love Me Love (—/Hallmark), 1977
The Leader (—/GTO), 1980
Boys Will Be Boys (Arista), 1984 **CD**
Alive And Kicking (APK), 1985
Gary Glitter (The Collection), 1987 **CD**

# Go Gos

US group formed 1978.

**Original line-up:** Belinda Carlisle, vocals; Charlotte Caffey, lead guitar; Jane Wiedlin, rhythm guitar; Elissa, drums; Margot Olavera, bass.

**Career:** Formed to open for the Dickies, May 1978, in Los Angeles. Struggled around LA club scene under original name of the Misfits, before changing to Go Gos. Prior to this, Belinda invited to join the Germs (prevented from doing so by illness!); performed with Black Randy and the Metro Squad. Charlotte played with both the Eyes and Manual and the Gardeners, but rest of band were novices.

During 1980, signed one-off singles deal with Stiff for **We Got The Beat**, but expected major record deal failed to transpire. Shortly before single, Elissa was replaced by Gina

Shock; and shortly afterwards, Margot replaced by Kathy Valentine (ex-Textones).

By 1981, group signed with I.R.S. label and recorded **Beauty And The Beat** LP, from which came first hit single **Our Lips Are Sealed**, co-written by Jane and Terry Hall (then of Specials(▶)) — with whom Go Gos toured UK — now of Colourfield).

1982 was band's zenith, with two top 10 US singles, and album **Beauty And The Beast** topping American chart. Follow-up **Vacation** enjoyed similar success, although recognition out of their home country remained a problem.

Internal turmoil finished band in 1984, following illness of Caffey and heart surgery to Shock. Both Wiedlin and Carlisle pursued solo careers, the former in movies, most notably 'Star Trek IV (The Voyage Home)', whilst Carlisle enjoyed success on both sides of the Atlantic with her single **Heaven Is A Place On Earth**.

**Final line-up:** Carlisle; Caffey; Wiedlin; Kathy Valentine, Gina Shock, drums.

**Hit Singles:**

| | US | UK |
|---|---|---|
| Our Lips Are Sealed, 1981 | 20 | 47 |
| We Got The Beat, 1982 | 2 | — |
| Vacation, 1982 | 8 | — |

**Albums:**
Beauty And The Beast (IRS), 1981
Vacation (IRS), 1982
Talk Show (IRS), 1984

# Go West

UK group formed 1982.

**Original/current line-up:** Peter Cox, vocals; Richard Drummie, guitar, vocals.

**Career:** Two man outfit using regular session musician crew and producing sound which top US producer Arif Mardin has described as 'Modern Motown'.

1985 debut album **Go West** made number 10 in UK and videos made equal impact, especially that produced by Godley and Creme(▶) for first single **We Close Our Eyes**.

Early publishing deal with ATV Music saw Cox and Drummie co-writing with Peter Frampton and soul star David Grant and eventual major record deal with Chrysalis. Cox and Drummie specially wrote **One Way Street** for inclusion in 'Rocky IV' soundtrack after Sylvester Stallone heard and liked their album.

1985 world tour and subsequent acclaim should have established band as major force, but burgeoning line-up seems to have swamped straightforward vocal approach of main man Peter Cox. 1987 album **Dancing On The Couch** was received less than enthusiastically.

**Hit Singles:**

| | US | UK |
|---|---|---|
| We Close Our Eyes, 1985 | — | 5 |
| Call Me, 1985 | — | 12 |
| Don't Look Down — The Sequel, 1985 | — | 13 |
| Don't Look Down, 1987 | 39 | — |

**Albums:**
Go West (Chrysalis), 1985 **CD**
Bangs And Crashes (Chrysalis), 1986 **CD**
Dancing On The Couch (Chrysalis), 1987 **CD**

# Grand Funk

US group formed 1968.

**Original line-up:** Mark Farner, vocals, guitar; Mel Schacher, bass; Don Brewer, drums.

**Career:** Probably the most critically savaged successful band in rock history, Grand Funk

## Grand Funk (continued)

began as Grand Funk Railroad. Members played with various local bands around Michigan until formation of Grand Funk in late 1968. Crucial move was appointment of Terry Knight as business manager (Knight was lead singer of Brewer's former band the Pack).

Knight secured band a spot at Atlanta Pop Festival in 1969, where their brand of sledge-hammer rock went down a storm. Contract with Capitol followed, and first album **On Time** was released same year. Although ignored by radio stations and reviled by press, album reached top of American charts and achieved gold status. Two singles, **Time Machine** and **Mr Limousine Driver**, were also smash hits.

Two years of astounding success followed. Albums notched up mega-sales, and singles were equally successful. As live act, Funk became huge attraction nationwide, selling out massive venues such as New York's Shea Stadium.

In late 1971, however, band decided they could manage without Terry Knight and fired him. He counteracted with legal proceedings, but eventually lost. Once removed from Knight's Midas-like commercial influence, band sought 'artistic' respectability. Craig Frost (keyboards) joined at time of self-produced **Phoenix** album.

Of remainder of output, **We're An American Band** (1973) is notable in that it was produced by Todd Rundgren and yielded half-way decent hard-rock single in title track. **Good Singin' Good Playin'** featured production talents of Frank Zappa, but even he was unable to make much out of the unpromising material.

Grand Funk eventually folded in 1976 after the Zappa album. The theory 'right place, right time' goes some way towards explaining phenomenal success of this mediocre head-banging outfit. As a home-grown American band at time of invasion by British heavy rock outfits like Zeppelin(▶) and Black Sabbath(▶) they filled a lucrative if temporary gap. Re-formed in 1981 for **Grand Funk Lives** LP.

**Current line-up:** Farner; Brewer; Frost, keyboards; Dennis Bellinger, bass.

**Hit Singles:**

| | US | UK |
|---|---|---|
| We're An American Band, 1973 | 1 | — |
| Walk Like A Man, 1974 | 19 | — |
| Locomotion, 1974 | 1 | — |
| Shinin' On, 1974 | 11 | — |
| Some Kind Of Wonderful, 1975 | 3 | — |
| Bad Time, 1975 | 4 | — |

**Albums:**
On Time (Capitol/—), 1970
Grand Funk (Capitol), 1970
Closer To Home (Capitol), 1970
Live Album (Capitol), 1970
Survival (Capitol), 1971
E Pluribus Funk (Capitol), 1972
Mark, Don And Mel 1969-71 (Capitol), 1972
Phoenix (Capitol), 1973
We're An American Band (Capitol), 1973

**Good Singin', Good Playin', Grand Funk Railroad. Courtesy EMI Records.**

Shinin' On (Capitol), 1974
Masters Of Rock (—/EMI), 1975
Caught In The Act (Capitol), 1975
Good Singin' Good Playin' (MCA/EMI), 1976
Hits (Capitol), 1977
Lives (Full Moon), 1981
What's Funk (WEA), 1983

# Grateful Dead

US group formed 1966

**Original line-up:** Jerry Garcia, guitar; Phil Lesh, bass; Ron 'Pigpen' McKernan, keyboards Bob Weir, guitar; Bill Kreutzmann (aka Bill Sommers), drums; Robert Hunter, lyrics.

**Career:** Grateful Dead burst forth from San Francisco's hippy scene as amalgamation of several community bands. Garcia joined up with Hunter at San Mateo Junior College in early '60s. While playing blues in local spots, they came across Weir and Pigpen. Garcia met Kreutzmann when working in record store.

**Back of Europe '72, The Grateful Dead. Courtesy Warner Bros Records.**

Kreutzmann and Pigpen formed rock band Zodiacs, while Garcia and Hunter joined David Nelson (later New Riders of the Purple Sage(▶)) and Pete Albin (later Big Brother & The Holding Co.). This collection played bluegrass as Wildwood Boys and later as Hart Valley Drifters.

Garcia then formed Mother McCree's Uptown Jug Champions with Pigpen, Weir and John Dawson. Pigpen convinced band to change from ethnic music to electric blues and came up with name Warlocks. Dawson was replaced by Kreutzmann and after several gigs Phil Lesh joined on bass.

Warlocks were befriended by Tom Wolfe who documented the social milieu and cultural influences on band in his book 'The Electric Kool-Aid Acid Test'. In 1966 band chose name Grateful Dead and began the long, loose concert format so closely associated with group.

Garcia refused to commit himself to standard recording contract and band remained unsigned while other Bay area bands 'sold out' to commercial world. Finally signing with Warner Bros in 1967 and recording first LP in three days, Dead became known as band who did things their own way.

Unsatisfied with sound on first album, Garcia took six months to record follow-up, **Anthem Of The Sun.** Mickey Hart joined as second drummer for recording and soon after Tom Constanten added keyboards to band's sound. Third LP **Aoxomoxoa** put band even deeper into debt as Warner Bros had yet to recover studio costs for second release. Problem was inability to capture atmosphere of band on stage. Next effort attempted to correct that by presenting double live set, **Live Dead.**

Band now entered what many consider to be classic period. Constanten dropped out. Remaining line-up switched studio work from drawn-out jams to short, structured songs. **Working Man's Dead** and **American Beauty** reflect this care and attention and remain among Dead's best efforts.

Unfortunate incident involving embezzlement charges against manager (Hart's father), caused Hart to leave band. Drug charges after bust in New Orleans raised question of band's future. But Dead played in Europe and continued to perform from three to five hours per set. Fans of the band became known as 'Dead Heads' and were famous for their incredible loyalty—they would travel anywhere band was playing.

Growing reputation ensured success of **The Grateful Dead,** band's second live album; it marked peak which in many ways Dead has not regained. **Europe '72** was triple live set featuring some of Pigpen's last days with Dead and introduced Keith Godchaux (keyboards) and wife Donna Godchaux (vocals) who began filling in for Pigpen. Pigpen had liver disease which became serious and was shortly to force his retirement. He died in May 1973. Although outsiders might not appreciate his influence, this loss marked start of rough period for Dead.

Warners released **History Of The Grateful Dead, Volume I (Bear's Choice)** from February 1970 Fillmore East shows. It hardly seemed up to quality demanded when band had been with label. Yet band's own effort, **Wake Of The Flood,** did nothing to dispel concern about Dead's falling standards.

Continuing outside activities took attention away from group. However, excellent **Blues For Allah** LP proved Dead could still try for new sounds. It also marked Mickey Hart's return to fold.

In March 1976 Dead and Who(▶) were paired by Bill Graham for massive 100,000 strong two-day outdoor concert in Oakland, California. Although critically in same class, difference in styles seemed to make this a strange coupling, but it worked (and was repeated for 1981 gig in Essen, Germany).

Band continued to record and was willing to take new approaches; **Terrapin Station** was first Dead LP to use outside producer (Keith Olsen) and **Shakedown Street** was recorded at band's private studio, using producer Lowell George, in effort to get 'live' feel. This period also saw Warners release nostalgic restrospective, **What A Long Strange Trip It's Been.**

In 1978 Dead set up special night concert in front of Great Pyramid, Cairo, Egypt. **Go To Heaven** was last appearance of the late Keith Godchaux and wife Donna. Most artists who've been associated with Dead cannot be ruled out from future work. **Heaven** also featured keyboards by Brent Myland who has toured and recorded with band since. **Reckoning** is interesting side aspect of Dead which presents all-acoustic live work.

Somewhat surprisingly, Dead maintained huge drawing power into 80s, gigging to massive turnouts despite lack of new recorded material. When new studio album **In The Dark** did finally make appearance in 1987, it became one of biggest sellers of band's career with first ever hit single **Touch Of Grey.**

Dead's current fans are mixture of old faithfuls and second-generation aficionados, a huge constituency which seem likely to ensure outfit's survival into next century. Living proof that rock'n'roll is no longer solely province of the young, Dead are a legend.

**Current line-up:** Garcia; Weir; Lesh; Kreutzmann; Mikey Hart, percussion; Brent Myland, keyboards.

**Hit Singles:**

| | US | UK |
|---|---|---|
| Touch Of Grey, 1987 | 9 | — |

**Albums:**
Grateful Dead (Warner Bros/—), 1967
Anthem Of The Sun (Warner Bros), 1968
Aoxomoxoa (Warner Bros), 1969
Live Dead (Warner Bros), 1970
Workingman's Dead (Warner Bros), 1970
American Beauty (Warner Bros), 1970
The Grateful Dead (Warner Bros), 1971
Europe '72 (Warner Bros), 1972
History Of The Grateful Dead, Volume 1—Bear's Choice (Warner Bros), 1973
Wake Of The Flood (Grateful Dead), 1973 **CD**
Live From The Mars Hotel (Grateful Dead), 1974*
Blues For Allah (Grateful Dead), 1975 **CD**
Steal Your Face (Grateful Dead), 1976
Terrapin Station (Arista), 1977
What A Long Strange Trip It's Been (Warner Bros), 1977
Shakedown Street (Arista), 1978
Go To Heaven (Arista), 1980
Reckoning (Arista), 1981
Dead Set (Arista), 1981
Skeletons In The Closet (Thunderbolt), 1986
In The Dark (Arista), 1987 **CD**

*Available as double album in UK only

# Al Green

US vocalist.
Born Forrest City, Arkansas, April 13, 1946.

**Career:** Musical grounding came singing in family gospel group the Greene Brothers from age nine; family moved north to Grand Rapids, Michigan, in 1959. There Al made initial foray into secular musical styles, joining local group Creations (aged 17), recording some sides for Zodiac.

Progress was slow, until early 1967 when two group members, Palmer Jones and Curtis Rodgers, persuaded Al to sing a song of theirs so they could produce disc for Hot Line Music Journal label; thus emerged **Back Up Train**, a gently haunting love song, credited to Al Greene (with third 'e') and the Soul Mates, which climbed into R&B Top 10 early in 1968, crossing over to Top 50 in pop charts. Two subsequent singles in similar style, **Don' Hurt Me No More** and **Lover's Hideaway**, sold well enough locally, but failed to break nationally.

**Let's Stay Together, Al Green. Courtesy London Records.**

Group became unsettled at failure to maintain initial impact; Soul Mates split, leaving Al high and dry. Continued as solo performer; soon noticed at Texas gig by Willie Mitchell(▶), renowned R&B musician/writer/producer scouting for Hi Records in Memphis. Initial product dabbled in variety of styles from impassioned deep soul balladry **One Woman** and crisp funky **You Say It** to thumping power of **Right Now Right Now**. Also evident was blues influence (he cut version of Roosevelt Syke's vintage **Driving Wheel**); it was an interesting combination of blues and funk which yielded first major hit on Hi—Al Green's (now minus third 'e') powerful, ponderous treatment of **I Can't Get Next To You**, reviving Temptation's(▶) 1969 chart-topper.

In summer 1971, Al was back in upper reaches of charts with yet another change of musical direction; **Tired Of Being Alone** returned to Green's gospel roots—his tenor delivery, partly restrained, almost tearful, drawing on soaring emotional falsetto and crooning soulful melismatic sound lifted from Baptist choir heritage. Top 10 R&B, Top 20 pop was the result. Formula generated lengthy succession of smash hits over the next half-dozen years. **Let's Stay Together** topped R&B and pop charts in February 1972. Sound began to stagnate, slipping into predictable groove; main relief came with occasional burst of down-home gospel like **Have A Good Time**.

Al's vocals began to suffer from overkill of wistful introversion; became almost parody of himself. On stage he purveyed image of eternal romeo, playing heavily to female element in audience. Love-man image was to be his Waterloo however; a jealous female fan broke into Al's apartment while he was taking bath and tipped basin of boiling grits down his back; Al suffered severe skin burns, was unable to record or perform for some time. During lay-off, he 'found' religion again, and took to preaching around Memphis.

In 1977 cut highly-rated **Belle Album**; titletrack single, an intense soulful ballad, charted. 1978 brought fresh approach with LP **Truth'n'Time**. Ballad **To Sir With Love** had some chart action, while funky flip **Wait Here** had crisp, punchy beat; Al produced himself with more vigour than ever Willie Mitchell had generated.

By 1980 Green had forsaken R&B for gospel, recording fine albums in that idiom for Myrrh before returning to secular world for new A&M deal and fine **Going Away** album which also reunited him with Willie Mitchell's production genius.

| Hit Singles: | US | UK |
| --- | --- | --- |
| Tired Of Being Alone, 1971 | 11 | 4 |
| Let's Stay Together, 1972 | 1 | 7 |
| Look What You Done For Me, 1972 | 4 | 44 |
| I'm Still In Love With You, 1972 | 3 | 35 |
| You Ought To Be With Me, 1972 | 3 | — |
| Call Me (Come Back Home), 1973 | 10 | — |
| Here I Am (Come And Take Me), 1973 | 10 | — |
| Livin' For You, 1974 | 19 | — |
| Sha La La (Make Me Happy), 1974 | 7 | 20 |
| L.O.V.E., 1975 | 13 | 24 |

**Albums selected:**
Greatest Hits Volume 1 (Hi/—), 1976
Greatest Hits Volume 2 (Hi/—), 1978
Cream Of (Hi-Cream), 1980
Tokyo/Live (Hi-Cream), 1981
The Lord Will Make A Way (Myrrh/—), 1982
Precious Lord (Hi-Cream), 1982
Higher Plane (Hi-Cream), 1982
Explores Your Mind (Demon) **CD**
Greatest Hits Vol 2 (Hi), 1978 **CD**
Lets Stay Together (Hi), 1972 **CD**
Trust In God (Hi), 1985 **CD**

# Peter Green

UK guitarist, vocalist, composer.
Born Peter Greenbaum, London, October 29, 1946.

**Career:** In February 1966 Peter Bardens (later of Camel) finished short stint with

Them(▶) and returned to London to form new band. he contacted Mick Fleetwood who had drummed for him in previous local group and got young Peter Green to fill in on bass. The Peter Bees folded within months, but Green and Fleetwood stayed on to join Bardens and unknown Rod Stewart(▶) in Shotgun Express.

By now Green was playing guitar and playing well enough to gain the attention of John Mayall(▶). Green was given unenviable task of assuming Eric Clapton's(▶) place in Mayall's Bluesbreakers. He appeared on **A Hard Road** and put a halt to the cries 'bring back Eric'.

Fleetwood sat in with Mayall's band and shortly after, in rather unclear circumstances, Green, McVie and Fleetwood began forming what was to become Fleetwood Mac(▶). After brilliant run in that group, Green's history becomes difficult to pin down. He left Mac to join US fundamentalist religious group. His sincerity was beyond doubt as he began donating royalties to charity. **The End Of The Game** LP appeared in late 1970, but showed none of the ability expected of Green. He filled in awhile for Mac in 1971 after Jeremy Spencer left and did some one-off gigs around London.

Amid various rumoured activities, Green appeared in court in February 1977 following incident in which he belligerently renounced continued royalties from Fleetwood Mac. Following commitment to mental institution, he began recording again for first time in nearly 10 years. Unfortunately nothing has matched grace and style of his early years.

Guitar: Gibson Les Paul

**Albums:**
The End Of The Game (Reprise), 1970
In The skies (Sail/PVK), 1979
Little Dreamer (Sail/PVK), 1980
Whatcha Gonna Do? (Sail/PVK), 1981
Blue Skies (Sail/PVK), 1981
Kolors (Creole), 1983
A Case For The Blues (Nightflite), 1987
Legend (Creole), 1988 **CD**
A Case For The Blues (Compact Collection), 1986 **CD**
In The Skies (Creole), 1986 **CD**

# Sammy Hagar

US guitarist, vocalist, composer.
Born October 13, 1947.

**Career:** Son of a prizefighter, Hagar first came to prominence as guitarist in Montrose(▶). Left in 1975 to pursue solo career as heavy metal guitarist. Debut **Nine On A Ten Scale** showed promise with some interesting echobox phrasing, particularly on **Urban Gorilla**. 1977's eponymous album, recorded at Abbey Road, was less impressive and led to predictable mundane material on subsequent **Musical Chairs**. Within seven months **All Night Long** appeared, a rushed work seemingly bereft of new ideas.

His popularity having declined considerably, Hagar waited a year before releasing next work; **Street Machine** was distinct improvement, with Hagar taking control of production. Set included his paean to fast cars, **Trans-Am** which became great audience favourite. Fortunes continued to improve in 1979 and he enjoyed hugely successful appearances on Boston's(▶) US tour. A brief UK visit gained him some commendation and with resurgence there of interest in heavy metal he was pushed into limelight. Christmas single, **This Planet's On Fire/Space Station No. 5**, provided minor hit, and two months later **I've Done Everything For You** climbed into UK

Top 50, paving the way for a sell-out tour in April 1980.

Release of live **Loud And Clear** (March '80) was an inspired move, indicating that faulty earlier work could still sound impressive in live setting. Set included nine Hagar numbers, seven of which had originally appeared on swiftly deleted **All Night Long**; a version of Montrose's driving **Bad Motor Scooter** was another clever addition.

**Above: Sammy Hagar, on red street from 'Blow Up' film. Courtesy Capitol Records.**

Completed Capitol contract with **Danger Zone**, regarded by some as his finest album. Although limited by scope of heavy metal, Hagar's career has progressed surprisingly since 1978. In 1982, Hagar switched to megabuck Geffen label, a shrewd career move. Starting with Top 30 **Standing Hampton** album Hagar has gone on to huge success, culminating with chart-topping set in summer 1987.

Guitar: Various custom models

| Hit Singles: | US | UK |
| --- | --- | --- |
| Your Love Is Driving Me Crazy, 1982 | 13 | — |
| I Can't Drive 55, 1984 | 6 | — |
| Give To Love, 1987 | 23 | — |

**Albums:**
Nine On A Ten Scale (Capitol), 1976
Sammy Hagar (Capitol), 1977 **CD**
Musical Chairs (Capitol), 1978
All Night Long (Live) (Capitol), 1978
Street Machine (Capitol), 1979
Danger Zone (Capitol), 1979
Loud And Clear (Capitol), 1980
Standing Hampton (Geffen), 1982
Three Lock Box (Geffen), 1982
Voa (Geffen), 1984
Looking Back (Geffen), 1987

*Hagar, Schon, Aaronson &Shrieve:*
Through The Fire (Geffen), 1984

# Bill Haley

US vocalist, guitarist, composer.
Born William John Clifton Haley Jr., Detroit, July 6, 1927; died February 9, 1981.

**Career:** Bill Haley's career lived up to name of his backing group, the Comets. It was his classic single **Rock Around The Clock** (arguably the all-time anthem of rock music — and its biggest and most consistent selling single with total sales of more than 20 million copies) which really triggered off rock 'n' roll revolution when featured in 1955 movie 'The Blackboard Jungle'.

Moving to Booth-Winn Pennsylvania, at four and raised on parents' farm, Haley played hillbilly music at local country fairs as

teenager and spent two years in early '40s as guitarist in cousin Lee's band. Cut first solo record, **Candy Kisses**, in 1945 when 18.

After four years with various country and western bands, in 1949 Haley became DJ at Radio WPWA in Chester, Pennsylvania. Formed own group, the Four Aces Of Western Swing, to broadcast for station. Recorded for various labels (including one single on Atlantic) before signing to Dave Miller's Essex label in Philadelphia.

Jackie Brenston's 1951 R&B single **Rocket 88** has often been cited as first rock 'n' roll hit and Haley covered it for white audiences in rockabilly style, selling 10,000 copies, then notched 75,000 sales for follow-up, **Rock The Joint**, another R&B cover.

Sensing innate commercial potential of R&B/C&W hybrid, Haley stopped recording hillbilly material, changed band's name to Comets and made national charts in 1953 with **Crazy Man Crazy**, a pulsating record which formulated his successful and instantly recognisable style.

Already long past teens, his moon-shaped face crowned by a soon-to-be-famous kiss curl, Haley fronted band of seasoned musicians: John Grande, Al Reed, Francis Beecher, Billy Williamson, Don Raymond and Rudy Pompelli. Although belonging to different age group they touched chord of rising youth cult and suddenly became hottest property in music business.

**Rock Around The Clock**, recorded in April 1954 after move from Essex Records to Decca, was cut as favour to Haley's manager Dave Myers, who had written song 18 months earlier for Sunny Dae. Released late 1954, record reached No. 17 in UK in January 1955, then quickly dropped from chart. After follow-up **Shake Rattle And Roll** (re-make of Joe Turner R&B hit) scored on both sides of Atlantic, it was re-issued to top charts in June (US) and October (UK). It has subsequently been re-released several times, most recent chart revival being 1974 when it reached No. 12 in UK.

1955 saw no fewer than six Haley records scorch up charts. 1956 produced a further five hits with two final hit recordings in 1957.

Haley's American success was surpassed in UK where in February 1957 he was mobbed by many thousands of fans on arrival in a train specially chartered by the Daily Mirror newspaper at London's Waterloo Station. Cinema audience had rioted at showings of the two exploitation movies 'Rock Around The Clock' and 'Don't Knock The Rock' in which Haley starred. Concert tour produced similar scenes with theatre seats being ripped out and fans going into hysterics.

However, despite sometimes wild live act which saw Pompelli cavorting all over stage, playing saxophone flat on his back and the like, group couldn't hide fact that they were essentially middle-aged musicians pandering to kids. With arrival of Presley(▶), Haley's comet burned out, since these kids now had a hero of their generation. Haley's fate was sealed. A chubby-faced, rather sedate, happily married man, he could offer the excitement of his music but not the sex appeal of his younger rival. His music also soon lost its edge, later recordings lapsing into light-weight MOR genre.

Moving to Rio Grande Valley, Haley contented himself with occasional nostalgia-appeal tours with Comets. He was set for one such in Autumn 1980 but it was called off due to illness and in November he was admitted to an LA hospital with suspected brain tumour. Three months later the first hero of rock 'n' roll — a man who sold nearly 70 million records — was dead at early age of 54.

| Hit Singles: | US | UK |
|---|---|---|
| Crazy Man Crazy, 1953 | 12 | — |
| Shake Rattle And Roll, 1954 | 7 | 4 |
| Rock Around The Clock, 1955 | 1 | 1 |
| Dim, Dim The Lights, 1955 | 11 | — |
| Birth Of The Boogie, Mambo Rock 1955 | 17 | — |
| Mambo Rock, 1955 | 18 | 14 |
| Razzle-Dazzle, 1955 | 15 | — |
| Rock-A-Beatin' Boogie, 1955 | 23 | 4 |
| Burn The Candle, 1955 | 9 | — |
| See You Later Alligator, 1956 | 6 | 7 |
| R-O-C-K/The Saints Rock'n'Roll, 1956 | 16 | — |
| The Saints Rock'n'Roll, 1956 | 18 | 5 |
| Rockin' Thru The Rye, 1956 | — | 3 |
| Razzle-Dazzle, 1956 | — | 13 |
| Rock Around The Clock, 1956 | — | 5 |
| Rip It Up, 1956 | 25 | 4 |
| Rockin' Thru The Rye, 1957 | — | 19 |
| Rock The Joint, 1957 | — | 20 |
| Don't Knock The Rock, 1957 | — | 7 |
| Rock Around The Clock, 1968 | — | 20 |
| Rock Around The Clock, 1974 | 39 | 12 |

**Albums:**
Rock Around The Clock (Decca/MCA Coral), 1955
Twistin' Knights At The Round Table (Roulette/PRT), 1961
Rock The Joint (London/Roller Coaster), 1963
Greatest Hits (MCA), 1968
Rock 'n' Roll (GNP/—), 1970
On Stage (—/Hallmark), 1970
Rock Around The Country (GNP/Sonet), 1971
Golden King of Rock (—/Hallmark), 1972
Just Rock & Roll Music (—/Sonet), 1973
Mister Rock 'n' Roll (—/Ember), 1974
Golden Hits (MCA), 1974
Bill Haley Collection (—/Pickwick), 1976
R.O.C.K. (—/Sonet), 1976
Armchair Rock 'n' Roll (MCA), 1978
Everyone Can Rock 'n' Roll (—/Sonet), 1979
Golden Country Origins (—/Roller Coaster), 1979
20 Golden Pieces (—/Bulldog), 1979
Rockin' And Rollin' (Accord/Bear Family), 1981
Greatest Hits (Piccadilly/—), 1981
Tribute (—/MCA), 1981
The King Of Rock'N'Roll (Bellaphon), 1986 **CD**
The 16 Greatest Hits (Bescol), 1987 **CD**
Bill Haley Rarities (Ambassador), 1987

# Hall & Oates

US vocal/instrumental duo.
Daryl Hall, vocals, keyboards; born Phildephia, October 11, 1948; John Oates, vocals, guitar; born New York, April 7, 1949

**Career:** Hall doubled working with Philadelphia Orchestra and singing back-up for soul artists recording in the city. Made first record with the Romeos, a group led by Kenny Gamble. When Gamble and the Romeos' keyboard player Leon Huff started producing records, firstly for Jimmy Bishop's Arctic label then for their own Neptune and Philadelphia International labels, they used Hall as a regular back-up musician. As habitué of Sigma Sound Studios, Hall also worked on records by the Stylistics(▶), the Temptations(▶) and others.

Hall and Oates first met at teenage dance, later they sang together in various doo-wop outfits. While Oates went to college to get a

**Bigger Than Both Of Us, Hall & Oates. Courtesy RCA Records.**

degree in journalism, Hall teamed with singer/songwriter Tim Moore and producer Tim Sellers to record an album for Elektra as Gulliver. Oates occasionally played with band; he started to play regularly with Hall when it broke up. Duo landed contract with Atlantic in 1972, cutting folksy debut album in New York with Arif Mardin producing. 1973 saw them on US charts with soulful **She's Gone** from more R&B flavoured **Abandoned Luncheonette** album. Third Atlantic LP, the Todd Rundgren(▶)-produced **War Babies'** was in heavy-rock mould.

A more precise sense of direction came with move to RCA in 1975 for **Hall And Oates** set which yielded **Sara Smile** hit. Charted on both sides of Atlantic with **Bigger Than Both Of Us** LP (1976) from which came 1977 US chart-topper **Rich Girl**. 1980 found duo producing themselves, and next two albums, **Voices** and **Private Eyes**, contained eight hit singles of which **I Can't Go For That (No Can Do)** was an amazing crossover phenomenon, topping US pop, adult contemprary, R&B and dance charts.

In 1980 Hall had success with Robert Fripp-produced solo album **Sacred Songs**, while Oates wrote soundtrack for film 'Outlaw Blues'.

Moving ever closer to soul music—like a latter-day Righteous Brothers(▶)—Hall & Oates are prolific songwriters, often in collaboration with Sara and Janna Allen who penned Diana Ross's(▶) hit single **Swept Away** for which the Hall & Oates band laid down the backing tracks.

Hall & Oates have also worked apart,

**Private Eyes, Hall & Oates. Courtesy RCA Records.**

Hall staying on in London at end of tour to record a duet with Elvis Costello(▶), **The Only Flame In Town**.

In 1985 the pair was involved in one-off re-opening concert at Harlem's legendary Apollo Theatre, shrine of black music for 50 years. They sang on-stage with Eddie Kendricks and David Ruffin of The Temptations(▶) the ultimate accolade for two great exponents of 'blue-eyed soul' whose fifteen year partnership has produced rich crop of hit singles and albums.

1988 saw the end of a two-year split for duo when plans for a new album were announced.

| Hit Singles: | US | UK |
|---|---|---|
| Sarah Smile, 1976 | 4 | — |
| She's Gone, 1976 | 7 | 42 |
| Rich Girl, 1977 | 1 | — |
| It's A Laugh, 1978 | 20 | — |
| Wait For Me, 1979 | 18 | — |
| You've Lost That Lovin' Feeling, 1980 | 12 | 55 |
| Kiss On My List, 1981 | 1 | 33 |
| You Make My Dreams, 1981 | 5 | — |
| Private Eyes, 1981 | 1 | 32 |
| I Can't Go For That (No Can Do), 1981 | 1 | 8 |
| Did It In A Minute, 1982 | 9 | — |
| Maneater, 1982 | 1 | 6 |
| One On One, 1983 | 7 | — |
| Family Man, 1983 | 6 | 15 |
| Say It Isn't So, 1983 | 2 | — |
| Adult Education, 1984 | 8 | — |
| Out Of Touch, 1984 | 1 | — |
| Method Of Modern Love, 1985 | 5 | — |
| Some Things Are Better, 1985 | 19 | — |
| A Nite At The Apollo, 1985 | 20 | — |

**Albums:**
Whole Oates (Atlantic), 1972
Abandoned Luncheonette (Atlantic), 1973
War Babies (Atlantic), 1974
Hall & Oates (Atlantic), 1975
Bigger Than Both Of Us (RCA), 1976
Beauty On A Backstreet (RCA), 1977
Past Times Behind (Chelsea), 1977*
Live Time (RCA), 1978
Along The Red Ledge (RCA), 1978
X-Static (RCA), 1979
Voices (RCA), 1980 **CD**
Private Eyes (RCA), 1981 **CD**
H₂O (RCA), 1982 **CD**
Greatest Hits, Rockin' Soul Part 1 (RCA), 1984
Rock 'N' Soul Part 1 (RCA), 1984 **CD**

Big Bam Boom (RCA), 1984
Live At The Apollo (with Eddie Kendricks & David Ruffin) (RCA), 1985 **CD**
Hall And Oates Intertape **CD**
20 Classic Tracks (Meteor) **CD**

*Daryl Hall Solo:*
Sacred Songs (RCA), 1980

*Material from 1971-72

# Jan Hammer

US keyboard player, composer.
Born Prague, Czechoslovakia, 1950.

**Career:** Hammer's fledgling talent surfaced at age of four when he started playing piano. Studied at Prague Academy of Muse Arts during teenage years before leaving for the US following Russian invasion of native country in 1968.

Spent a year as keyboardist/conductor with Sarah Vaughan, moving on to work with Elvin Jones and Jeremy Steig in 1970. A year later joined the original line-up of the Mahavishnu Orchestra, who set the standard for rock and jazz fusion which has continued through to present day. After band split Hammer's solo career commenced with album **The First Seven days** followed by a successful tour of The Jan Hammer Group. Other albums followed **Oh Yeah?**, **Wired** (with Jeff Beck) which went platinum, and **Jeff Beck With The Jan Hammer Group Live**, certified gold.

Hammer returned to solo work with **Black Sheep**. In 1982 he recorded **Electric Rendezvous** with Al Di Meola. Early Eighties saw him working with the likes of James Young (ex-Styx), John Abercrombie, Mick Jagger's first solo **She's The Boss**, and Jeff Beck's **Flash** which included the song **Escape**, written by Hammer and winner of the 1985 Grammy for Best Rock Instrumental Performance.

**Escape from Television, Jan Hammer. Courtesy MCA Records.**

Mid-80s saw him moving into film and TV music and in 1984 he started scoring hit US TV series "Miami Vice". Following year saw "Miami Vice" Theme at the top of the Billboard Hot 100 chart, the first TV theme to do so since Henry Mancini's Theme From "Peter Gunn" in 1959. October 1985 "Miami Vice" soundtrack album with five instrumentals by Hammer also topped Billboard album chart.

Grammy Awards in 1986 for Best Pop Instrumental Performance and Best Instrumental Composition, plus two Emmy award nominations (1985, 1986) for Outstanding Achievement in Musical composition followed. **Crockett's Theme** from **Miami Vice II** album became a huge European hit in spring 1987, reaching number two in the UK. The album subsequently became a big seller. Hammer's prolific work as a producer, recording engineer, arranger, composer and performer seems sure to keep him involved in the lucrative area of TV/film music scoring.

**Hit Singles:**

| | US | UK |
|---|---|---|
| Miami Vice Theme, 1985 | 1 | 5 |
| Crocketts Theme, 1987 | — | 2 |

**Albums**
Escape From TV (MCA), 1987 **CD**
Miami Vice (MCA), 1987 **CD**

*With Neil Schon:*
Untold Passion (CBS), 1982

# Tim Hardin

US composer, vocalist, guitarist.
Born Eugene, Oregon, 1940; died December 29, 1980.

**Career:** One of rock's lost souls, Hardin was a sad, often pathetic figure whose writing/vocal talent has been undervalued.

An appearance at 1966 Newport Folk Festival prompted Verve to sign him, and he quickly established cult following, if only for interpretations of his songs by other performers. His best-known composition, **If I Were A Carpenter**, was hit for Bobby Darin(▶) in 1966 and for the Four Tops(▶) in 1968.

Hardin dismissed own recordings, particularly the Verve output, claiming overproduction and lack of sympathetic arrangements. He is said to have burst into tears upon hearing final master of **Tim Hardin 1** with additional strings.

Albums for Columbia and Antilles became increasingly maudlin, and it seemed that the talent which had produced songs like **Hang On To A Dream**, **The Lady Came From**

Below: Performing, composing, arranging, engineering, producing — the prolific Jan Hammer live.

**Baltimore**, **Don't Make Promises** and **Misty Roses** had evaporated.

Brief flirtation with success in the mid-'70s, prompted by the Rod Stewart(▶) recording of **Reason To Believe**, was spoiled by Hardin's increasing abuse of drugs. He died in 1980, leaving a fine legacy of material, but an underlying regret for 'what might have been'.

**Albums:**
Best Of . . . (Polydor), 1974
Nine (Antilles/GM), 1974
The Shock Of Grace (Columbia/—), 1981
Memorial Album (Polydor), 1982

**'Tim Hardin 1'. Courtesy Verve Records.**

# Emmylou Harris

US vocalist, composer guitarist.
Born Birmingham, Alabama, April 2, 1947.

**Career:** Developed early interest in country music; when family moved to Washington DC, played folk and country material in East Coast clubs and coffee-houses. 1969 album on Jubilee made little impression.

Break came at end of 1970 when Flying Burrito Brothers(▶) saw Harris performing at Cellar Door Club in Washington; Cellar Door was tiny club which has featured such local talent as Link Wray, Roy Buchanan, Nils Lofgren(▶) and Grin, and George Thorogood(▶). Met and went into partnership with Gram Parsons. Harris sang on his first solo album **G.P.**, shared vocal duties with him on next album **Grievous Angel**, and became member of his touring band.

On death of Parsons in September 1973, Harris returned to Washington and formed own outfit, Angelband. However, in 1974 she was offered contract by Reprise and recorded **Pieces Of The Sky**, a well-balanced and craftsmanlike album that immediately established her as important new voice in contemporary country music. On strength of LP success Harris formed appositely named backing group Hot Band. Members comprised legendary guitarist James Burton(▶), Glen D. Hardin on piano, Hank De Vito on pedal steel, Rodney Crowell(▶) on guitar and harmony vocals, Emory Gordy on bass and John Ware on drums.

During '70s Harris gained international success with series of albums that combined her plaintive voice with excellent choice of material and superlative instrumental back-up. (In 1976 James Burton left Hot Band to be replaced by another outstanding guitarist, Albert Lee.) Albums from **Luxury Liner** (1977) onwards show rock leanings, but in general Harris is true to her country roots. She appeals to rock audiences because she avoids sentimentality and redneck stance of straight country artists, keeping music appealingly honest and straightforward.

In 1980 Harris won Country Music Association award for best female vocalist, and during '80s has continued to crossover between country and rock with great success.

**Albums:**
Pieces Of The Sky (Reprise), 1975
Elite Hotel (Reprise), 1976
Luxury Liner (Reprise), 1977
Quarter Moon In A Ten Cent Town (Reprise), 1978
Profile (Warner Bros), 1978 **CD**
Blue Kentucky Girl (Reprise), 1979
Gliding Bird (Jubilee/Pye), 1979
Roses In The Snow (Reprise), 1980
Light Of The Stable (Reprise), 1980
Her Best Songs (—/K-Tel), 1980
Evangeline (Reprise), 1981
Cimarron (Reprise), 1981
Last Date (Reprise), 1982
White Shoes (Warner Bros), 1983 **CD**
The Ballad Of Sally Rose (Warner Bros), 1985

*With Ronstadt & Parton*
Trio (WEA), 1987 **CD**
13 (Warner Bros), 1987

# George Harrison

UK vocalist, guitarist, composer.
Born Liverpool, February 25, 1943.

**Career:** As youngest member of Beatles(▶) spent several years in shadow of Lennon(▶) and McCartney(▶) and in early days was rarely allowed to demonstrate not inconsiderable songwriting talent on Beatle records. In fact, achieved first single A-side for Beatles (**Something**) on last Beatle LP, **Abbey Road**. Even before that, Harrison had released solo Beatle record in shape of rather tedious soundtrack for film 'Wonderwall' first LP to be released on Apple label, in 1968. Also released experimental and similarly unlistenable LP, **Electronic Sounds**, before Beatles split up.

In late 1969, became involved with US white soulsters Delaney & Bonnie(▶), touring and recording with them. Perhaps curiously, Harrison was last of four Beatles to release genuinely musical album, triple set **All Things Must Pass**, in 1970. Set was immediate success, particularly **My Sweet Lord**, which was released as single, and topped charts around world. However, this song was to become notorious in view of court case over its similarity to **He's So Fine**, '60s hit for the Chiffons. Harrison lost case and in late '70s had to pay damages of more than half a million dollars to publishers of **He's So Fine**.

During later Beatle years, Harrison became besotted by India, leading to interest in transcendental meditation and the sitar. This aspect of his work was thankfully mostly absent from **All Things Must Pass**, but when leading Indian sitar player Ravi Shankar asked for help for starving people of Bangla Desh in form of charity concert, Harrison was delighted to oblige. With star-studded line-up, including Bob Dylan(▶), Eric Clapton(▶), Billy Preston, Leon Russell(▶) and Ringo Starr(▶), Harrison organised two concerts at Madison Square Garden, New York, which were recorded and filmed, with all proceeds theoretically going to assist Bangla Desh victims. In reality, prevarication on part of record companies to which other stars contracted meant long delays, although eventually substantial sum was donated.

By next LP, Harrison's interest in Eastern religion had largely changed musical direction, resulting in very poor LP. His marriage to '60s model Patti Boyd also fell apart; Patti moved in with Eric Clapton. 1974 LP, **Dark Horse**, was still overly religious and thus not popular;

Below: George Harrison either teaching or being taught how to use the studio.

next LP was no improvement.

In 1976, launched own Dark Horse label with A&M Records. By end of year, disagreements with A&M meant that Dark Horse (and George) moved to Warner Bros amid heavy lawsuits, although first Dark Horse LP by Harrison, 33 1/3 was best thing since Bangla Desh days. After long hiatus, next LP, **George Harrison** (1979), appeared to little success. Harrison is rarely seen in public, and only emerged following John Lennon's murder with tribute single **All Those Years Ago**, on which Paul McCartney and Ringo also guested. Follow-up LP, **Somewhere In England**, failed to improve much on previous few years' output, and most recent releases, **Gone Troppo** LP and **Wake Up My Love** single, were released almost secretly in late 1982.

**Cloud Nine, George Harrison. Courtesy Dark Horse Records.**

In 1976, launched own Dark Horse label with A&M Records. However, disagreements with that company led to early severance and move to Warner Bros, despite critical approval for Harrison's LP **33 1/3**.

Long hiatus followed and **George Harrison** failed to revive fortunes, whereupon ex-Beatle devoted energies to motor racing's Formula One circuits and film production. Involvement with Handmade Films led to credits as Executive Producer, most notably on 'Time Bandits', 'The Life Of Brian', 'The Long Good Friday', 'The Missionary' and 'Mona Lisa'.

A surprising late development has been Harrison's return to chart action with singles from his 1987 LP **Cloud Nine**, a pleasant and varied example of pop simplicity which featured Eric Clapton, Ringo Starr and ELO's Jeff Lynne. Simultaneously, Harrison has discarded low profile, and has become subject of media blitz with 20th anniversary of **Sgt. Pepper** and its corresponding CD release.

| Hit Singles: | US | UK |
|---|---|---|
| My Sweet Lord, 1970 | 1 | 1 |
| What Is Life, 1971 | 10 | — |
| Bangla Desh, 1971 | 23 | 10 |
| Give Me Love (Give Me Peace On Earth), 1973 | 1 | 8 |
| Dark Horse, 1974 | 15 | — |
| You, 1975 | 20 | 38 |
| Crackerbox Palace, 1977 | 19 | — |
| Blow Away, 1979 | 16 | 51 |
| All Those Years Ago, 1981 | 3 | 13 |
| Got My Mind Set On You, 1987 | 1 | 2 |

**Albums:**
Wonderwall (Apple), 1968
Electronic Sounds (Apple), 1969
All Things Must Pass (Apple), 1970
Concert For Bangla Desh (Apple), 1972
Living In The Material World (Apple), 1973
Dark Horse (Pathe), 1974
Extra Texture (Apple), 1975
33 1/3 (Dark Horse), 1976
Best Of (Capitol/Parlophone), 1977 **CD**
George Harrison (Dark Horse), 1979
Somewhere In England (Dark Horse), 1981

Gone Troppo (Dark Horse), 1982
Cloud Nine (Dark Horse), 1987 **CD**

# Hawkwind
UK group formed 1969.

**Original line-up:** Dave Brock, guitar, vocals; Huw Lloyd Langton, guitar; Terry Ollis, drums; Nik Turner, saxophone; John Harrison, bass; Dik Mik, electronics.

**Career:** Founded by Brock and Turner, unit emerged from Ladbroke Grove area of London as Group X, then Hawkwind Zoo and, finally, Hawkwind. Quickly established themselves as darlings of Notting Hill long-hair set. Manager Doug Smith negotiated recording contract with United Artists.

First album **Hawkwind** (1970) proved inauspicious, but strong live following boosted sales. Group's improvisational style was widely known after appearances at numerous festivals, including 1970 Isle Of Wight, where they played free for fans outside the site's fence. Even national press latched onto Nik Turner's silver-painted face, and publicity helped to increased devoted following.

Group soon emerged as heroes of underground, playing community gigs and benefit concerts at every opportunity. Reputation and/ or notoriety was further increased after newspaper reports about their apparent drug habits, prompting numerous police investigations.

In June 1971, played at Glastonbury Fayre Festival, aided by poet/painter/vocalist Bob Calvert, whose presence attracted interest from Sci-fi writer Michael Moorcock. This performance also introduced dancer Stacia, later to become regular feature at live gigs. Group's cosmic/space rock phase was evinced on 1971's **In Search Of Space**, which appeared with complex sleeve design by Barney Bubbles.

By early 1972, 'resident poet' Calvert joined as full-time member. In February, played London's Roundhouse alternative music spectacle, otherwise known as the 'Greasy Trucker's Party', later double album featured one side of Hawkwind performing **Masters Of The Universe** and **Born To Go**. Also played on triple album set **Glastonbury Fayre** with a host of celebrated rock heroes. Their highest single placing occurred during same period with No. 3 hit **Silver Machine**. Flushed with success, they financed their own Space Ritual Road Show which spawned **Space Ritual Live**, released following year.

As youthful following increased, group suffered series of personnel upheavals. Langton, Harrison and Ollis drifted away, replaced by Simon King (drums), Del Detmar (electronics) and a series of bassists: Thomas Crimble, Dave Anderson and, finally, Ian 'Lemmy' Kilminster. Keyboard player Dik Mik left as did Calvert for an on/off solo career. Detmar was himself replaced by Simon House (ex-Third Ear Band), who joined for spring 1974 US tour.

During Stateside jaunt, larger-than-life Lemmy was caught in possession of amphetamine sulphate, mistaken for cocaine by Canadian officials. Resulting fracas led to his dismissal and he flew back to England to form heavy-metal band Motorhead(▶). Pink Fairies' Paul Rudolph was selected as replacement, having previously played with group on ad-hoc basis. When King suffered an accident following soccer match, Alan Powell (ex-Chicken Shack/Vinegar Joe) was granted permanent membership.

In 1976, signed deal with Charisma Records, and **Astounding Sounds Amazing Music** was released shortly afterwards.

Further changes followed: Nik Turner left to form Sphinx and soon after Rudolph and Powell were fired because their playing was deemed 'too funky'.

While departing duo went on to Kicks, Adrian Shaw (bass/vocals) was recruited in time for **Quark, Strangeness And Charm**. Next album, **PXR5**, was not released until May 1979, by which time Hawkwind had effectively split. While Simon House went on to join Bowie's(▶) backing band, remaining members (with successive keyboards players Paul Hayles and Steve Swindells) met legal problems using group name. For brief period they became Hawklords, recording album under that title.

By September 1979, Hawklords had been replaced by revamped Hawkwind, comprising Dave Brock, Harvey Bainbridge, Simon King, Huw Lloyd Langton and Tim Blake. Played first gig at Futurama Festival in Leeds, introducing lasers to Hawkwind set for first time.

In 1980 signed to Bronze, releasing **Live '79**, which restored them to album charts. Ginger Baker(▶) replaced King on drums. Next album, **Levitation**, hit Top 20. Further line-up changes followed with departure of Blake (replaced by Keith Hale) and Baker (replaced by Martin Griffin).

In July '81, signed deal with RCA, producing three LPs for that company before switching to Flicknife label. Despite solo projects and personnel changes, band has retained hippy audience that may follow them forever.

**Current line-up:** Brock; Langton; Alan Davey, bass; Clive Deamer, drums.

| Hit Single: | US | UK |
|---|---|---|
| Silver Machine, 1972 | — | 3 |

**Albums:**
Hawkwind (Liberty/UA), 1970
In Search Of Space (Fame), 1971 **CD**
Greasy Trucker's Party (Liberty/UA), 1972
Doremi Fasol Latido (Liberty/UA), 1972
Space Ritual Live (Liberty/UA), 1973
Hall Of The Mountain Grill (Liberty/UA), 1974
Warrior On The Edge Of Time (Liberty/UA), 1975
Roadhawks (Liberty/UA), 1976
Astounding Sounds Amazing Music (—/Charisma), 1976
Masters Of The Universe (—/UA), 1977
Quark, Strangeness And Charm (Sire/Charisma), 1977
Hawklords (—/Charisma), 1978
PXR 5 (—/Charisma), 1979
Repeat Performance (—/Charisma), 1980
Hawkwind Live 1979 (—/Bronze), 1980
Levitation (Castle), 1980 **CD**
Sonic Attack (—/RCA), 1981
Church Of Hawkwind (—/RCA), 1982
Choose Your Masques (—/RCA), 1982
Bring Me The Head Of Yuri Gargarin (Demi-Monde), 1985
Space Ritual 2 (Magnum Force), 1985 **CD**

**Sonic Attack, Hawkwind. Courtesy RCA Records.**

Out And Intakes (Flicknife), 1987 **CD**
Collection (Castle) **CD**
Chronicle Of The Black Sword (Flicknife) **CD**
Anthology Vols 1 & 2 (Samurai), 1986 **CD**
Anthology Vols 1, 2 & 3 (Samurai), 1986
The Hawkwind Collection Parts 1 & 2 (Castle), 1986
Live 70/73 (Dojo), 1986
Angels Of Death (RCA), 1987
British Tribal Music (State Of The Art), 1987 **CD**

*With Various Artists:*
Glastonbury Fayre (—/Revelation), 1972

# Heart
US group formed 1973.

**Original line-up:** Ann Wilson, guitar, keyboards, vocals; Nancy Wilson, vocals, guitar; Michael Derosier, drums; Howard Leese, guitar, keyboards; Steve Fossen, bass; Roger Fisher, guitar.

**Career:** Wilson sisters grew up on British-influenced rock of '60s. Began playing Seattle bars when women's role in rock was strictly limited to vocals. They knocked this concept on the head by playing Led Zeppelin(▶) covers with flair and gusto. Despite growing popularity, band pulled up roots and moved to British Columbia, primarily to avoid draft problems of Roger Fisher. While in Canada, Heart signed with small new Mushroom label. **Dreamboat Annie** became word of mouth hit and Heart found it was picking up national radio play. Debut LP was unusual in that it ranged from easy, quiet ballads to heavy metal without sounding unfocused or without direction.

With new, larger audience, band returned to US and found that Mushroom's distribution system couldn't handle demand for first LP, so signed to Portrait Records. Mushroom promptly sued for breach of contract. Heart countersued over rights to recording for second LP, alleging Mushroom was about to release rough, unfinished demo work. While case was being settled in Seattle's Federal District Court, Portrait released excellent **Little Queen** LP.

Bootleg copies of second Mushroom LP began fetching ridiculous amounts and Mushroom released **Magazine** with its original mix outside US. With wisdom of Solomon, Seattle federal judge settled suit out of court by suggesting Heart had overstepped bounds in signing to Portrait but that Heart had the right to mix second Mushroom LP as they deemed artistically suitable; Mushroom finally released this new version of **Magazine** in US during 1978. Whether or not aesthetic differences between two versions make any sense outside of legal flail is questionable, but principle sets important precedent for other artists.

Next official LP, **Dog And Butterfly**, began with classic live cut, then seemed to fall apart. This time switch between hard rock and ballads didn't work as well and resulting confusion stalled band's career. **Bebe Le Strange** acknowledged break-up of Wilson/Fisher romance with Fisher's departure from band. His guitar work was missed and Heart's studio work seemed to continue downward. **Greatest And Live** compounded confusion by including a few new tracks, re-issuing some old selections, and adding nearly an entire LP's worth of live stage work; LP was cut down to single album a year later and released in UK as **Heart**. Taking time to re-organize their thoughts and ideas, Wilson sisters took two-year break before releasing

**Private Edition**. This marked a return to spirit of early band as well as making Top 30 in US LP charts. In 1982, both Fossen and Derosier quit, citing, ho hum, 'musical differences'. Replacements were ex-Jo Jo Gunne bassist Mark Andes, and drummer Denny Carmassi. New line-up supported Queen on '82 British tour, before cutting 1983 **Passion Works**. The Wilson Sisters' brand of raunch has kept the band in the first division of concert attractions, although, ironically, the melodic **These Dreams** single gave them major European success in 1988.

**Current line-up:** Ann Wilson; Nancy Wilson; Leese; Mark Andes, bass; Denny Carmassi, drums.

**Hit Singles:**

| | US | UK |
|---|---|---|
| Magic Man, 1976 | 9 | — |
| Barracuda, 1977 | 11 | — |
| Straight On, 1978 | 15 | — |
| Tell It Like It Is, 1980 | 8 | — |
| What About Love, 1985 | 10 | — |
| Never, 1985 | 4 | — |
| Alone, 1987 | 1 | 3 |
| Theres The Girl, 1987 | 12 | — |
| Who Will You Run To, 1987 | 7 | 30 |

**Albums:**
Dreamboat Annie (Mushroom/Arista), 1975 **CD**
Little Queen (Portrait), 1977 **CD**
Dog And Butterfly (Portrait), 1979
Bebe Le Strange (Epic), 1980
Greatest And Live (Epic/—), 1980
Private Audition (Epic), 1982
Passion Works (Epic), 1983
Heart (—/Epic), 1985 **CD**
Bad Animals (Capitol), 1987 **CD**

*Worth Searching Out:*
Magazine (Capitol), 1978 **CD**

# Jimi Hendrix

US guitarist/vocalist.
Born Johnny Allen Hendrix (name changed to James Marshall Hendrix in 1946), Seattle, Washington, November 27, 1942; died September 18, 1970.

**Career:** The most legendary guitarist in rock music, Jimi Hendrix spent early years, following military service, as back-up musician for R&B luminaries B.B. King(▶), Ike and Tina Turner(▶), Solomon Burke, Jackie Wilson, Tommy Tucker, Sam Cooke(▶), Little Richard(▶), Wilson Pickett(▶), the Isley Brothers(▶) and King Curtis(▶).

Settling in New York, Hendrix was heard playing in club by then girlfriend of Rolling Stone(▶) Keith Richard who persuaded former Animals'(▶) bass player turned manager, Chas Chandler, to check him out. Chandler decided to forgo own playing career and sold his bass guitars to buy equipment for Hendrix. He took the young black musician to London and embarked on major publicity campaign, bringing the Beatles(▶), Pete Townshend(▶) and Eric Clapton(▶) to 'in' clubs to see Hendrix's outrageously flashy performances.

A master showman, Hendrix exploited tricks learned from watching T. Bone Walker, Johnny Guitar Watson and other relatively unknown black American musicians, playing the guitar behind his neck or with his teeth, and experimenting with a whole new range of sound effects on his Fender Stratocaster. Polydor Records rushed to sign him and debut single **Hey Joe** stormed UK charts. In 1967 Hendrix debuted in his own country at the Monterey Pop Festival. His guitar-burning act (preserved

**Above: The unique Jimi Hendrix (foreground) with Noel Redding (left) and Mitch Mitchell — the Jimi Hendrix Experience.**

in film 'Monterey Pop') left the audience stunned.

Switching to associated Track label, Hendrix had further single success before becoming major album artist, reaching zenith of commercial success and artistic creativity in 1968 with classic **Axis Bold As Love** and **Electric Ladyland** LPs. (In the studio, session man Alan Douglas added to Hendrix's basic tracks and was later responsible for **Crash Landing**, **Midnight Lightning** and **I Go To The Universe**, released, like the vast majority of Hendrix LPs, after his death.)

After masterful appearance at Woodstock in August 1969, the Jimi Hendrix Experience (British musicians Noel Redding (bass); Mitch Mitchell (drums)) broke up amid welter of personal and business problems, as well as drug-linked difficulties with the authorities. Mostly, however, Hendrix felt cornered by the style of music.

Under some pressure from Black Power movement in US, Hendrix decided to form Band Of Gypsys (Billy Cox, bass; Buddy Miles, drums) but despite phenomenal powers as concert draw band was short-lived, Hendrix

walking out on 19,000 fans in middle of second number at Madison Square Garden gig in January 1970. That summer Hendrix played to nearly a quarter of a million people at the Isle Of Wight Festival, his last major concert and one which met with poor response from critics.

Three years of incredibly hard touring, recording and drink and drug abuse took their toll and on September 18, 1970, Hendrix was pronounced DOA at a Kensington Hospital, suffocated by his own vomit.

At times verging on the totally self-indulgent, Hendrix's guitar work nevertheless showed touch of sheer genius, opening up new musical horizons for a generation of rock musicians, while his vocals, despite their limited scope, oozed raw power.

Without a doubt Hendrix remains one of the most influential and popular artists in rock, as evidenced by the vast catalogue of his work still available.
Guitar: Fender Stratocaster.

**Hit Singles:**

| | US | UK |
|---|---|---|
| Hey Joe, 1967 | — | 6 |
| Purple Haze, 1967 | — | 3 |
| The Wind Cries Mary, 1967 | — | 6 |
| Burning Of The Midnight Lamp, 1967 | — | 18 |
| All Along The Watchtower, 1968 | 20 | 5 |
| Voodoo Chile, 1970 | — | 1 |

**Albums:**
Are You Experienced (Polydor), 1967 **CD**
Axis — Bold As Love (Reprise/Polydor), 1967
Smash Hits (Reprise/Polydor), 1968 **CD**
Electric Ladyland (Polydor), 1968 **CD**
Electric Ladyland 2 (—/Polydor), 1968
Band Of Gypsys (Capitol/Polydor), 1970 **CD**
Monterey (one side only; other side featured Otis Redding) (Reprise), 1970
Cry Of Love (Reprise/Polydor), 1971
Rainbow Bridge (Reprise), 1971 **CD**
Isle Of Wight (—/Polydor), 1971
Eternal Fire Of (—/Hallmark), 1971
Experience (soundtrack) (Mode/Bulldog), 1971 **CD**
Friends From The Beginning (with Little Richard) (—/Bulldog), 1971
In The West (Reprise/Polydor), 1972
Jimi Hendrix (—/Polydor), 1973
Loose Ends (—/Polydor), 1973
Jimi Hendrix Volume 1 (—/Pan), 1973
Jimi Hendrix Volume 2 (—/Pan), 1973
Jimi Hendrix Volume 3 (—/Pan), 1973
War Heroes (Reprise/Polydor), 1973

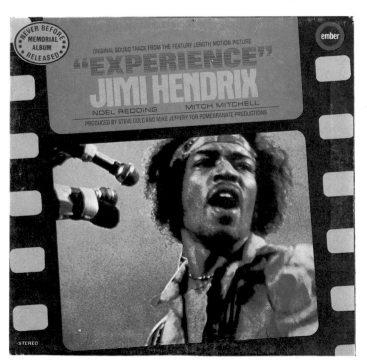

**Rainbow Bridge (soundtrack LP) Jimi Hendrix. Courtesy Reprise Records.**

The Wild One (with Curtis Knight) (—/Hallmark), 1973
Crash Landing (Reprise/Polydor), 1975
Rare Hendrix (Explosive/Enterprise), 1975
Jimi Hendrix 2 (—/Polydor), 1975
Midnight Lightning (Reprise/Polydor), 1976
For Real (—/DJM), 1976
The Essential (Reprise/Polydor), 1978

**Experience, Jimi Hendrix soundtrack album. Courtesy Ember Records.**

The Essential Volume 2 (Reprise/Polydor), 1978·
More Experience (—/Bulldog), 1979
Recordings From Jimi (—/Reprise), 1979
20 Pieces Of Jimi Hendrix (—/Bulldog), 1979
10th Anniversary Box (—/Polydor), 1980
9 To The Universe (Warner Bros/Polydor), 1980
Woke Up This Morning And Found Myself Dead (Red Lightnin'), 1980* CD
Hendrix '66 (—/President), 1980
Free Spirit (Accord/Phoenix), 1981
Cosmic Turnaround (—/AFE), 1981
Cosmic Feeling (Accord/—), 1982
The Jimi Hendrix Concerts (Reprise/CBS), 1982
Moods (—/Phoenix), 1982
Roots Of (—/Phoenix), 1982
Voodoo Chile (—/Polydor), 1982
20 Golden Pieces Of, Volume 2 (—/Bulldog), 1982
The Singles Album (Polydor), 1983 CD
Kiss The Sky (Polydor), 1984 CD
Jimi Plays Monterey (Polydor), 1986 CD
Live At Winterland (Polydor), 1987
The Best Of (EMI), 1987 CD

*Jam with Jim Morrison

# Herman's Hermits

UK group formed 1963.

**Original/Final line-up:** Peter Noone, vocals; Keith Hopwood, guitar; Derek Leckenby, guitar; Karl Green, bass; Barry Whitwarm, drums.

**Career:** with his little-boy looks, wide grin and big shiny teeth, Peter Noone (born November 5, 1947) was prototype for Donny Osmond(▶) , David Cassidy and other teeny-bopper pin-ups to come. Producer Mickie Most saw Noone's appearance as actor in massively popular 'Coronation Street' TV soap opera series and decided Noone's was to be the face of 1964.

Group had been formed a year earlier as

**Below: Peter Noone, who came to fame as Herman, leader of the Hermits, but later reverted to his real name.**

the Heartbeats; Most changed Noone's name to Herman and effectively projected him as front-man. Indeed, the Hermits didn't even play on most of their records (**Mrs Brown You've Got A Lovely Daughter, I'm Into Something Good** and **I'm Henry The VIII I Am** being exceptions). Instead he used such luminaries as Big Jim Sullivan and, later, Led Zeppelin(▶) founders Jimmy Page and John Paul Jones (Jones also did all the arranging).

Debut single **I'm Into Something Good** (1964) went to UK No. 1 and made low-key breakthrough in US where they eventually became far more popular than in home market.

Despite 10 entries in UK Top 20 in just three years, Herman's Hermits had un-obtrusive image there, and records made more impact than group. In America, however, Herman's return to clean-cut polite boy-next-door image of early Beatles days (while most British acts of era were into brash, rebellious R&B mould of Stones(▶),the Who(▶), et al) was a relief to parents, and just what American media were looking for. **Mrs Brown** and **I'm Henry The VIII** both sailed to No. 1 while Herman became TV and magazine personality of first order.

By 1967 American bubble had burst and title of US Top 20 entry **There's A Kind Of Hush** proved prophetic. However, UK hits continued before Noone went solo in 1970 (using real name).

He rejoined group briefly in 1973 for Richard Nader's English Invasion Revival tour while Hermits remained in America purveying their lightweight, happy style of innocuous pop. In 1979 Noone formed band the Tremblers (Noone, vocals, guitar, piano, bass; Gregg Inhofer, keyboards, guitar, vocals; Robert Williams, drums; George Williams, drums; George Connor, guitar, vocals; Mark Browne, bass) and in 1980 they recorded **Twice Nightly** LP. In 1983, Noone starred in new hit musical version of 'The Pirates Of Penzance'.

| Hit Singles: | US | UK |
|---|---|---|
| I'm Into Something Good, 1964 | 13 | 1 |
| Show Me Girl, 1964 | — | 19 |
| Can't You Hear My Heart Beat, 1965 | — | 2 |
| Silhouettes, 1965 | 5 | 3 |
| Mrs Brown You've Got A Lovely Daughter, 1965 | 1 | — |
| Wonderful World, 1965 | 4 | 7 |
| I'm Henry The VIII I Am, 1965 | 1 | — |
| Just A Little Bit Better, 1965 | 7 | 15 |
| A Must To Avoid, 1965 | 8 | 6 |
| Listen People, 1966 | 3 | — |
| You Won't Be Leaving, 1966 | — | 20 |
| Leaning On The Lamp Post, 1966 | 9 | — |
| This Door Swings Both Ways, 1966 | 12 | 18 |
| No Milk Today, 1966 | 35 | 7 |
| Dandy, 1966 | 5 | — |
| There's A Kind Of Hush, 1967 | 4 | 7 |
| Don't Go Out Into The Rain (You're Going To Melt), 1967 | 18 | — |
| I Can Take Or Leave Your Loving, 1968 | 22 | 11 |
| Sleepy Joe, 1968 | — | 12 |
| Sunshine Girl, 1968 | — | 8 |
| Something's Happening, 1968 | — | 6 |
| My Sentimental Friend, 1969 | — | 2 |
| Years May Come, Years May Go, 1970 | — | 7 |
| Lady Barbara, 1970 | — | 13 |

*Peter Noone solo:*

| | US | UK |
|---|---|---|
| Oh You Pretty Thing, 1971 | — | 12 |

**Albums:**

Greatest Hits (Abcko/—), 1973
20 Greatest Hits (—/K-Tel), 1977

# The Hollies

UK group formed 1962.

**Original line-up:** Allan Clarke, vocals; Tony Hicks, vocals, guitar; Graham Nash, vocals, guitar; Eric Haydock, bass; Don Rathbone, drums.

**Career:** Formed from members of two other Manchester groups, the Deltas and the Dolphins (Rathbone was almost immediately replaced by Bobby Elliot), like many British beat groups they took early material fr  JS R&B catalogue. First two singles were covers of Coasters(▶) hits, second of which, **Searchin'**, started long run of UK Top 20 hits.

Lacking positive image, band's appeal was based on Clarke's strong lead vocals, dis-tinctive harmonies and excellent choice of single material. Most early material came from outside band, from top writers like Graham Gouldman, but by 1966 they were writing own songs with considerable success. **But Stop** reached American Top 5, and established group as regular US hitmakers.

In 1966 Haydock left to be replaced by former Dolphins bass player Bernie Calvert.

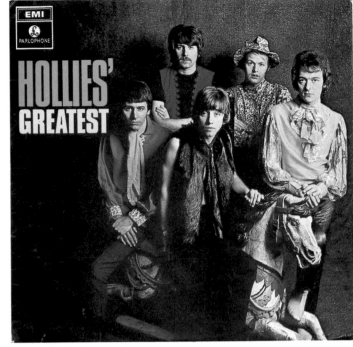

**Hollies' Greatest, The Hollies.
Courtesy Parlophone Records.**

As 'psychedelic' era dawned, problems over musical direction arose. While band were still massive singles sellers, they were unable to break LP market despite making several interesting albums at this time.

Disillusioned by band's failure to compete with newer, critically rated album bands, Graham Nash left in 1968 to join forces with David Crosby and Stephen Stills to form Crosby, Still and Nash(▶). Former Swinging Blue Jeans Terry Sylvester replaced Nash.

By 1971, band had reached something of a plateau; single releases were only moderately successful. Clarke left to pursue solo career. Replacement was Swedish singer Michael Rickfors. In 1972, however, single recorded with Clarke as lead singer, **Long Cool Woman In A Black Dress**, make No.1 spot in America (although strangely only 32 in UK). Rickfors was ousted and Clarke rejoined band, which signed new contract with Polydor. Last big hit was **The Air That I Breathe.**

Band continued to record throughout '70s, however, and found lucrative niche on cabaret circuit. In late 1981 **Holliedaze**, a single combining old hits in segued disco style, was minor hit in UK.

One of the longest-lasting pop-orientated British band, the Hollies can still turn in creditable performance, and given the right material, could still be chart force. As purveyors of finely crafted, memorable singles they probably have a more secure place in pop history than many of the more pretentious 'artists' they strove to emulate in late '60s.

**Current line-up:** Clarke; Hicks; Terry Sylvester, guitar, vocals; Bernie Calvert, bass; Bobby Elliot, drums.

| Hit Singles: | US | UK |
|---|---|---|
| Searchin', 1963 | — | 12 |
| Stay, 1963 | — | 8 |
| Just One Look, 1964 | — | 2 |
| Here I Go Again, 1964 | — | 4 |
| We're Through, 1964 | — | 7 |
| Yes I Will, 1965 | — | 9 |
| I'm Alive, 1ᴜ65 | — | 1 |
| Look Through Any Window, 1965 | 32 | 4 |
| If I Needed Someone, 1965 | — | 20 |
| I Can't Let Go, 1966 | 42 | 2 |
| Bus Stop, 1966 | 5 | 5 |
| Stop Stop Stop, 1966 | 7 | 2 |
| On A Carousel, 1967 | 11 | 4 |
| Carrie-Anne, 1967 | 9 | 3 |
| King Midas In Reverse, 1967 | 51 | 18 |
| Jennifer Eccles, 1968 | 40 | 7 |
| Listen To Me, 1968 | — | 11 |
| Sorry Suzanne, 1969 | 56 | 3 |
| He Ain't Heavy He's My Brother, 1969 | 7 | 3 |
| I Can't Tell The Bottom From The Top, 1970 | — | 7 |
| Gasoline Alley Bred, 1970 | — | 14 |
| The Air That I Breathe, 1974 | 6 | 2 |

**Albums:**

Hollies' Greatest (Capitol/Parlophone), 1968
Sing Dylan (Epic/Parlophone), 1969
Stop Stop Stop (Imperial/Starline), 1971
Greatest Hits (Epic/Polydor), 1974
I Can't Let Go (—/MFP), 1974
Another Night (Epic/Polydor), 1975
The Best Of The Hollies EPs (—/Nut), 1975
Russian Roulette (—/Polydor), 1976
Live Hits (—/Polydor), 1977
A Crazy Steal (—/Polydor), 1978
Sing Buddy Holly (—/Polydor), 1980
Long Cool Woman In A Black Dress (—/MFP), 1979
Five Three One-Double Seven O Four (—/Polydor), 1979
20 Golden Greats (EMI), 1979 CD

# Buddy Holly

US vocalist, guitarist, composer.
Born Charles Hardin Holley, Lubbock, Texas,
September 7, 1936. Died Feb. 3, 1959.

**Career:** During 1954-55 appeared on home-town radio station KDA, with partner Bob Montgomery. Played on package shows visiting towns who used local talent as warm-up acts to major artists. Spotted by Nashville talent scout on show headlined by Billy Haley(▶) and signed to Decca.

Dissatisfaction with company and producers encouraged Holly to record independently at Norman Petty's Clovis, New Mexico, studio. Master of **That'll Be The Day** made there subsequently sold to New York subsidiaries of Decca where group recordings as the Crickets (Joe B. Mauldlin, bass; Niki Sullivan, guitar (replaced by Tommy Allsop in 1959); Jerry Allison, drums) were released on Brunswick; Holly's solo efforts appeared on Coral. Resulting hits gave Holly dual career strengthened by own writing talents and those of Crickets, notably Allison.

Several US package tours and short visit to Australia preceded tour of UK in March 1958. Many UK musicians were impressed with his guitar style and then unkown Fender Stratocaster which, together with horn-rimmed glasses, became Holly's trademark.

Management problems and move to New York following marriage to Maria Elena Santiago in 1958 forced split with Crickets (who went on to record many more LPs without Holly). Recorded trendsetting session with Dick Jacobs Orchestra in New York and planned to record with Ray Charles(▶) Band.

Royalty disputes and lack of funds forced Holly into uncomfortable ballroom tour through frozen Mid-West states during early 1959. Halfway through tour chartered small plane with Ritchie Valens(▶) and Big Bopper to escape discomfort of tour buses. All three killed when plane crashed into snow-covered field.

Single coupling **It Doesn't Matter Anymore** and **Raining In My Heart** from orchestral session soon became biggest solo hit. Holly disappeared from US charts but had many further hits in the UK.

**Hit Singles:**

| | US | UK |
|---|---|---|
| That'll Be The Day*, 1957 | 1 | 1 |
| Peggy Sue, 1957 | 3 | 6 |
| Listen To Me, 1958 | — | 16 |
| Oh Boy*, 1958 | 10 | 3 |
| Maybe Baby*, 1958 | 17 | 4 |
| Rave On, 1958 | 37 | 5 |
| Think It Over*, 1958 | 27 | 11 |
| Early In The Morning, 1958 | 32 | 17 |
| It Doesn't Matter Anymore, 1959 | 13 | 1 |
| Peggy Sue Got Married, 1959 | — | 13 |
| Baby I Don't Care, 1961 | — | 12 |
| Reminiscing, 1962 | — | 17 |
| Brown Eyed Handsome Man, 1963 | — | 3 |
| Bo Diddley, 1963 | — | 4 |
| Wishing, 1963 | — | 10 |
| *With Crickets | | |

*Crickets:*

| | | |
|---|---|---|
| Don't Ever Change, 1962 | — | 5 |
| My Little Girl, 1963 | — | 17 |

**Albums:**
Buddy Holly (MCA), 1958
The Chirping Crickets (MCA), 1958
Legend (MCA), 1974
Greatest Hits (MCA), 1974 **CD**
The Nashville Sessions (MCA), 1975
20 Golden Greats (MCA), 1978
The Complete Buddy Holly* (MCA), 1979
Love Songs (MCA), 1981
For The First Time Anywhere (MCA), 1983 **CD**
Best Of (Grand Prix), 1986 **CD**
Buddy Holly — Historical Recordings Undubbed & Unreleased Versions (Nor-Va-Jak), 1987
*6 LP box set

The Complete Buddy Holly (6 LP boxed set), one of the most comprehensive collections ever released on record. Courtesy MCA Records.

# Bruce Hornsby and The Range

US group formed in 1982.

**Current/original line-up:** Bruce Hornsby, lead vocals, piano, accordion, synthesiser; David Mansfield, guitar, mandolin, violin; George Marinelli, electric, acoustic guitar; Joe Uperta, bass, vocals; John Molo, drums, percussion.

**Career:** After several years of paying dues and demands, Hornsby virtually shot to over-

Above: Million-selling The Way It Is has finally put the multi-instrumentalist Bruce Hornsby in the public eye on both sides of the Atlantic.

night success with debut album **The Way It Is**. LP sold more than 1m and the title track single topped the charts in US. Robbie Robertson, Bruce Springsteen and Steve Winwood are reckoned to be firm fans of Hornsby & The Range.

Brought up in Williamsburg, Virginia, Hornsby studied at the University of Miami School of Music before forming early incarnation of The Range that played throughout the South. 1980 found him writing formula pop tunes for 20th Century Fox in Hollywood followed by a two-year stint working with Sheena Easton's band. He continued to make demos though, and one tape featuring just piano, drums and accordion, was impressive enough to attract recording offers.

Hornsby's debut album for RCA included several tracks produced by Huey Lewis. The title track single charted in the UK. Hornsby's very accessible brand of rock should ensure that he doesn't go back to writing trite pop tunes.

**Hit Singles:**

| | US | UK |
|---|---|---|
| Every Little Kiss, 1986 | 11 | — |
| The Way It Is, 1986 | 1 | 15 |
| Mandolin Rain, 1987 | 4 | — |

**Albums**
The Way It Is (RCA), 1986 **CD**

# The Housemartins

UK group formed 1984.

**Original/Final line-up:** Paul (P.D.) Heaton, vocals; Stan Cullimore, guitar/vocals; Norman Cook, bass/vocals; Hugh Whittaker, drums/vocals.

**Career:** Formed in Hull, first as duo of Heaton & Cullimore, then expanding by stealing Whittaker and original bassist Ted Key from local rivals The Gargoyles. Won Viking Radio talent contest, leading to recording sessions for Radio One and support slot on tour with Billy Bragg who then recommended band to his label, Go! Discs.

Breezy style of English pop owing much to Buzzcocks, Squeeze and Smiths, they emerged as hybrid of 60s beat/skiffle influences with genuine love for gospel and soul. Early shows featured rousing version of Hollies'

**He Ain't Heavy, He's My Brother.** Released debut single **Flag Day** before Key quit, replaced by Cook; then released single **Sheep** and **Happy Hour Again**.

Debut album, **London 0 Hull 4** blended simple musical enthusiasm with clever lyrical subtleties, tackling social and political themes with surprising vehemence. Reinforced Christian stance with cover of Isleys' **Caravan Of Love**, topping UK chart Christmas 1986.

Continued to maintain down-to-earth image and devoted concert following before releasing second album, **The People Who Grinned Themselves To Death**.

The People Who Grinned Themselves To Death, The House Martins. Courtesy Go! Discs Records.

In January 1988, band shocked the rock world by announcing their dissolution when they seemed about to conquer America. Formal statement maintained they had achieved all they set out to do and there was nothing else left! Whittaker then rejoined Key in re-formed Gargoyles; Heaton, Cullimore and Whittaker delaying confirmation of future (separate) plans.

**Hit Singles:**

| | US | UK |
|---|---|---|
| Caravan Of Love, 1986 | — | 1 |
| Happy Hour, 1986 | — | 3 |
| Think For A Minute, 1986 | — | 18 |
| Five Get Over Excited, 1987 | — | 11 |
| Me And The Farmer, 1987 | — | 15 |
| Build, 1987 | — | 15 |

**Albums**
London 0 Hull 4 (Go! Discs/Elektra), 1986 **CD**
The People Who Grinned Themselves To Death (Go! Discs), 1987

Above: Down-to-earth Hull band The Housemartins just before they announced they were to split.

# Whitney Houston

US vocalist
Born New Jersey, 1963

If anyone was born for stardom, it was Whitney Houston. Blessed with startling combination of good looks, bubbly personality and major league vocal talent, she spent only a few years in the wings before breaking through as international megastar in 1986/87.

Daughter of near-legendary session singer Cissy Houston who, as member of Sweet Inspirations sang back-up on record and on stage for Elvis Presley and Aretha Franklin, Whitney started out as a top-ranking fashion model, earning description 'The woman every girl would like to be and every man would like to go out with'.

Showing talent as well as beauty, Whitney served musical apprenticeship singing backings on albums by Lou Rawls, Chaka Khan, Neville Brothers and others before being asked to duet with Teddy Pendergrass on US hit **Hold Me**. A further duet hit with Jermaine

**Whitney, from 1987.
Courtesy Arista Records.**

Jackson on **Take Good Care Of My Heart** led to solo contract with Arista and chart-topping single **Saving All My Love For You**.

However, 1987 was truly year of Whitney Houston, when second album **Whitney** went multi-platinum, with over 8 million copies sold

Below: Talented and beautiful, Whitney Houston is going to become one of the biggest stars of the '80s.

in US alone. Surefire combination of uptown soul and emotive Las Vegas-style ballads **Whitney** catapulted singer into international bigtime. Single **I Wanna Dance With Somebody** was *the* single of summer 1987, bouncy video showing singer's talents off to irresistible effect.

Despite lukewarn verdict from purist critics, Whitney looks likely to become one of biggest stars of late 80s, a Diana Ross for the Reagan generation. Like Ross, she may not be most powerful singer or most innovative stylist, but possesses indisputable star quality.

**Hit Singles:**

|  | US | UK |
|---|---|---|
| Saving All My Love For You, 1985 | 1 | 1 |
| How Will I Know, 1986 | 1 | 5 |
| Greatest Love Of All, 1986 | 2 | 8 |
| I Wanna Dance With Somebody, - 1987 | 1 | 1 |
| Didn't We Almost Have It All, 1987 | 1 | 14 |
| So Emotional, 1987 | 1 | 1 |

**Albums:**
Whitney Houston (Arista), 1985 **CD**
Whitney (Arista), 1987 **CD**

# Human League

UK group formed 1977.

**Original line-up:** Philip Oakey, vocals; Ian Craig Marsh, synthesisers; Martyn Ware, synthesisers; Adrian Wright, visual director, synthesisers.

**Career:** Computer operators Marsh and Ware and hospital porter Oakey made up original nucleus of band, formed in Sheffield

**Dare, The Human League. Courtesy Virgin Records.**

to explore possibilities of electronic music. Wright joined slightly later.

Almost immediately band began to gain reputation for innovation; first single **Electronically Yours** was released in June 1978 on independent Fast label. Following exposure on Siouxsie and Banshees(▶) tour, band was signed to Virgin in April 1979. First album **Reproduction** released in late 1979.

1980 saw beginnings of chart success with low placings for **Holiday '80** and **Empire State Human**, but in autumn of that year band broke up; Ware and Marsh left to establish Heaven 17 and British Electric Foundation. Oakey and Wright took new direction, recruiting old friend (actually bass-player) Ian Burden to play synthesisers, and adding two girl dancers, Joanne Catherall and Susanne Sulley (spotted by Oakey in Sheffield disco).

The girls quickly became vocalists; new sound was featured on first Top 50 single **Boys And Girls** at beginning of 1981. That year saw band go from strength to strength, with addition of guitarist Jo Callis (ex-Rezillos). Huge breakthrough came with single **Don't You Want Me** and album **Dare**. Both topped UK charts, and at beginning of 1982 repeated feat in territories all around world, most notably in US.

Human League had established themselves as stylish electronic pop outfit which combined irresistibly catchy tunes with lyrics of above average intelligence. In recent years Oakey has undertaken solo projects (film music, solo hit **Electric Dreams**) while maintaining band's position in public eye. 1986 album **Crash** contained major hit single **Human**.

**Final line-up:** Oakey; Wright; Ian Burden, synthesisers; Jo Callis, guitar; Joanne Catherall, vocals; Susanne Sulley, vocals.

**Hit Singles:**

|  | US | UK |
|---|---|---|
| The Sound Of The Crowd, 1981 | — | 12 |
| Love Action (I Believe In Love), 1981 | — | 3 |
| Open Your Heart, 1981 | — | 6 |
| Don't You Want Me, 1981 | 1 | 1 |
| Being Boiled, 1982 | — | 6 |
| Mirror Man, 1982 | — | 2 |
| Fascination, 1983 | 8 | 2 |
| The Lebanon, 1984 | — | 11 |
| Life On Your Own, 1984 | — | 16 |
| Louise, 1984 | — | 13 |
| Human, 1986 | 2 | 8 |

*Phil Oakey & Georgio Moroder:*

| Together In Electric Dreams, 1984 | — | 3 |
|---|---|---|

**Albums:**
Reproduction (—/Virgin), 1979
Travelogue (—/Virgin), 1980
Dare (A&M/Virgin), 1981 **CD**
Crash (Virgin), 1986 **CD**

*Phil Oakey & Georgio Moroder*
Hysteria (Virgin), 1986 **CD**

# Humble Pie

UK group formed 1969.

**Original line-up:** Peter Frampton, guitar, vocals; Steve Marriot, guitar, vocals; Greg Ridley, bass, vocals; Jerry Shirley, drums.

**Career:** Began in blaze of publicity as late '60s supergroup with Frampton(▶), 'the face of '68', from the Herd, and Marriot from the fashionable Small Faces(▶). Ridley (ex-Spooky Tooth) provided underground musical credibility to offset hype.

Arduous rehearsals at Marriot's house preceded release of first album, **As Safe As Yesterday,** on Small Faces' former label, Immediate. In spite of early Top 5 hit, **Natural Born Bugie,** Humble Pie were plagued by 'supergroup' publicity and LPs failed to fulfill critics' expectations. Much hoped-for early US success did not materialise and following liquidation of Immediate, group almost folded, but resurfaced on A&M, acquiring services of manager Dee Anthony.

Through extensive gigging, group gradually enlarged following in States, and record sales increased with each successive release. Marriot slowly achieved greater control of unit, moving away from Frampton's somewhat lightweight material towards heavy-metal sound. Policy proved commercially and aesthetically sound, with **Performance— Rockin' At The Fillmore** selling in vast quantities. Inevitably, Frampton quit to pursue lucrative solo career, replaced by more musically/socially compatible Dave 'Clem' Clempson from Colosseum.

Early '70s album **Smokin'** and live double **Eat It** revealed increasing move towards heavy rock. Group briefly experimented with soul during 1973, employing vocal trio the Blackbirds (Venetta Fields, Clydie King and Billie Barnum) for live revue.

With no new musical direction forthcoming, group gradually stagnated, in spite of some flattering gig reviews in States. Clempson quit to form Strange Brew, tolling death knell for Humble Pie, who finally broke up in July 1975. Marriot went on to form Steve Marriot All Stars, before involving himself in Small Faces reunion in 1978. Marriot then got involved in Humble Pie reunion with Bob Tench (guitar, vocals), Anthony Jones (bass, vocals) and Jerry Shirley (drums). This line-up released **On To Victory** LP in 1980.

**Final line-up:** Marriott; Ridley; Shirley; Dave Clempson, guitar.

**Hit Singles:**

| | US | UK |
|---|---|---|
| Natural Born Bugie, 1969 | — | 4 |

**Albums:**
Humble Pie (A&M), 1970
Rock On (A&M), 1971
Performance—Rockin' At The Fillmore (A&M), 1971
Smokin' (A&M), 1972
Eat It (A&M), 1973
Thunderbox (A&M), 1974
Lost And Found (A&M/—), 1976
Back Home Again (—/Immediate), 1976
On To Victory (A&M), 1980

# Janis Ian

US vocalist, composer, guitarist, pianist.
Born New York, April 7, 1951.

**Career:** At age 14 wrote **Society's Child,** dealing with racial discrimination, narrowness of educational system, parental pressure and hypocrisy. Released first as single, then included in first album **Janis Ian** which made charts in 1967. Sung in delicate, detached, almost alienated voice, it is often incorrectly assumed to be autobiographical. Based on observation, not experience, **Society's Child** was work of experienced songwriter; **Hair Of Spun Gold** (written at age 12½) was published in influential folk magazine 'Broadside'. Successful appearances at New York's Village Gate and Gaslight preceded first record.

Although beginning in Baez(▶)/Seeger(▶) folk tradition, even early albums used guitar, bass, organ, harpsichord and drums, including Richie Havens(▶) as drummer on **The Secret Life Of J. Eddy Fink** (1668). Critical enthusiasm waned until **Stars** in 1974, which once again added brilliance to skill and indicated new maturity. Title song has been recorded by Cher, Glen Campbell(▶) and Mel Torme, and **Jesse** was included on Joan Baez'(▶) **Diamonds And Rust.** Development confirmed by **Between The Lines** (1975) from which double-Grammy winner **At Seventeen** was US No. 1 single, going platinum in US and Japan. Renewed success, including Roberta Flack's(▶) version of **Jesse** which reached Top 10, led to 1976 re-issue of long-deleted early work.

Subsequent albums continued to show evidence of growing sophistication, incorporating jazz and blues into Ian's distinctive blend of vocals and instrumentation. **Night Rains** featured theme songs used by films 'The Foxes' and 'The Bell Jar', and highlights include solos by E Street Band saxophonist Clarence Clemmons and piano duet shared by Ian and Chick Corea.

Unhappy with increasing dependence on complex instrumentation, Ian's recent songs have been written to be performed by full band or simply with guitar or piano accompaniment. However, as recorded on 1981 **Restless Eyes,** backing musicians have been used to good effect.

**Hit Singles:**

| | US | UK |
|---|---|---|
| Society's Child, 1967 | 14 | — |
| At Seventeen, 1975 | 3 | — |

**Albums:**
Janis Ian (Polydor/Verve), 1967
Present Company (Capitol), 1971
Stars (Columbia/CBS), 1974
Between The Lines (Columbia/CBS), 1975
Aftertones (Columbia/CBS), 1975
Miracle Row (Columbia/CBS), 1977
Night Rains (Columbia/CBS), 1979
The Best Of (Columbia/CBS), 1980
Restless Eyes (Columbia/CBS), 1981

# Billy Idol

UK vocalist, guitarist, composer.
Born: Edgeware, London, November 30, 1955.

**Career:** Young, angry, aggressive and strikingly good looking, Billy Idol was a major figure on UK punk rock scene during heady days of 1977. One of the notorious 'Bromley Contingent' of punks, from which emerged the Clash(▶), Sex Pistols(▶), Siouxsie(▶) and others, Idol joined Generation X as lead singer in time for their historic gig on opening night of seminal club The Roxy in London's Covent Garden.

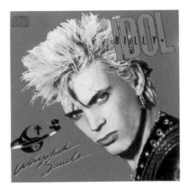

**Whiplash Smile, Billy Idol.
Courtesy Chrysalis Records.**

Generation X was first punk band to appear on 'Top Of The Pops' and logged several hits before, with punk rock wane, Idol left group in 1981. He rode into New York on wave of Gen. X's final hit **Dancing With Myself** which was featured on his debut solo EP **Don't Stop**.

Working with producer Keith Forsey and guitarist Steve Stevens, the expatriate Idol complete album **Billy Idol** which met with mixed response but single **Hot In The City** hit US Top 40 leading to album recovering from slow start to spend more than 80 weeks on chart.

This success was emulated by the re-released **Don't Stop** which was in Billboard listings for over 50 weeks.

The Idol/Stevens collaboration continued with **Rebel Yell** for which they co-wrote eight of the nine singles. Album went on to sell a couple of million copies, in process establishing Idol as bona fide teen icon.

Latterly Idol has gone from strength to strength, creating own genre of snarling, aggressive rock'n'roll with massive appeal. "Designer punk" image and elaborate (if hackneyed) videos have helped to consolidate him as pop star for late 80s, a kind of updated Rod Stewart.

**Hit Singles:**

| | US | UK |
|---|---|---|
| White Wedding, 1983* | 36 | 6 |
| Eyes Without A Face, 1984 | 4 | 18 |
| Rebel Yell, 1985 | — | 6 |
| To Be A Lover, 1986 | 5 | 22 |
| Sweet 16, 1987 | — | 17 |
| Hot In The City, 1987 | 48 | 13 |
| Mony Mony, 1987 | 1 | 7 |
| *1985 in UK | | |

**Albums:**
Billy Idol (Chrysalis), 1982 **CD**
Rebel Yell (Chrysalis), 1984 **CD**
Vital Idol (Chrysalis), 1985 **CD**
Whiplash Smile (Chrysalis) **CD**
Interview By Kris Needs (Lip Service), 1986

# Iggy Pop

US vocalist, composer.
Born James Jewel Osterberg, Ann Arbor, Michigan, April 21, 1947.

**Career:** Iggy Pop is a rock icon of sorts; can justifiably be called 'grandfather' of punk. Fans and critics alike are polarised by Pop; one either loves him or hates him. His personality can only be truly appreciated on stage, where he routinely rants, screams, falls down, knocks into the musicians and invites— or commands—the audience to perform unnatural acts. Has been known to flail about so desperately that he ends show dripping with blood. Audiences often respond by hurling not just abuse, but beer bottles and anything else that's handy.

Osterberg named himself Iggy in early days in Detroit, when he performed with band called the Prime Movers. When he joined the infamous pre-punk band the Stooges (Ron Asheton, guitar; Dave Alexander, bass; Scott Asheton, drums; Steve McKay, sax) became Iggy Stooge. Iggy and the Stooges were a band (and a philosophy) whose time had not yet come. Had moderate cult success, but lost inspiration and eventually fizzled out, leaving the albums **The Stooges** (1968), **Funhouse** (1969), and **Raw Power** (1973).

Iggy was rediscovered as an 'artist' by David Bowie(▶) in 1977. He changed his name symbolically to Iggy Pop, and toured with new mentor. This led to contract with RCA, for whom he recorded three albums in 1978. **The Idiot** and **Lust for Life** met with critical approval, but limited sales; switched to Arista in 1979, cutting two albums.
A further label-hopping ensued, while singer's reputation was enhanced by Bowie's 1983 hit cover version of Pop song **China Girl**. In 1986, after apparently winning protracted battle against toxic abuse, Pop emerged with new label (A&M) and successful album **Blah Blah Blah**. Album spawned UK single **Real Wild Child**, and Pop's career looked set to finally enter mainstream.

However, singer's general unpredictability and history of drug problems mean that he is unlikely to become elder statesman of rock in Elton John/Paul McCartney mould.

**Left: The Godfather of Punk, Iggy Pop. whose frenzied stage performances influenced a generation of new wave bands in the late '70s.**

**Albums:**
*With Stooges:*
The Stooges (Elektra), 1968
Funhouse (Elektra), 1969
Raw Power (Columbia/CBS), 1973
Metallic KO (Sky Dog/—), 1976

*Iggy Solo:*
The Idiot (RCA), 1976
TV Eye (RCA), 1978
Lust For Life (RCA), 1978
New Values (Arista), 1979
Soldier (Arista), 1979
No Fun (Elektra), 1980
Party (Arista), 1981
Zombie Birdhouse (Animal), 1982
Choice Cuts (RCA), 1984
Blah Blah Blah (A&M), 1986 **CD**

*Worth Searching Out:*
*With James Williamson:*
Killer City (Radar), 1977

# INXS

Australian group formed 1979.

**Original/Current line-up:** Michael Hutchence, vocals; Andrew Farriss, keyboards/guitar; John Farriss, drums; Tim Farriss, lead guitar; Kirk Pengilly, guitar; Garry Beer, bass.

**Career:** Formed Sydney 1977 by Andrew, John and Tim under name of The Farriss Brothers, expanding to six-piece immediately with line-up unchanged to this day.

Renamed group INXS in 1979; one year later they released debut album **INXS** on Deluxe Records and scored Australian hit single **Just Keep Walking**.

Second LP **Underneath The Colours** released via RCA, yielded two more Australian hits **Stay Young** and **Loved One**. INXS secured worldwide deal with WEA and released third album **Shabooh, Shoobah**, then toured US with Kinks and Adam Ant. Debut UK single **Don't Change** was accepted favourably.

Having built up loyal following for their brand of muscular yet melodic rock (comparisons include Simple Minds, David Bowie and Psychedelic Furs), they turned to Nile Rodgers to produce **Original Sin** single, hoping for US hit.

Eventually **Listen Like Thieves** LP broke band in America, released in UK 1986, promoted by UK tour, led to prestigious sell-out concert at London's Royal Albert Hall and two appearances supporting Queen at Wembley Arena. **Kick** album and **Need You Tonight** single firmly established band as rising stars.

Much of their success has been based on vocalist Hutchence's charismatic image (he also starred in low-budget Australian film, ('Dogs In Space') but their guitar-based driving rhythms and catchy repetitive songs take lots of credit too.

**Hit Singles:**

| | US | UK |
|---|---|---|
| What You Need, 1986 | 5 | — |
| Need You Tonight, 1987 | 1 | — |
| New Sensation, 1987 | — | 25 |

**Albums**
The Swing (Mercury/Atco), 1984 **CD**
Listen Like Thieves (Mercury/Atlantic), 1986 **CD**
Kick (Mercury), 1987 **CD**

**Right: Farriss and Pengilly of Australian rockers INXS, muscular yet melodic in their approach.**

# Iron Maiden

UK group formed 1977.

**Original line-up:** Steve Harris, bass, vocals; Paul Di'anno, vocals; Dave Murray, guitar; Doug Sampson, drums.

**Career:** Steve Harris formed Iron Maiden amid new wave/punk breeding ground of London's East End. Harris went for deliberate high-energy, power-driven sound. Taking name from medieval torture cage. Iron Maiden went through numerous personnel changes; settled down to line-up above by mid-1979.

Harris refused lucrative offer for gigs and record contract that required him to remould Maiden into fashionable new wave band. Instead, band released **Soundhouse Tapes** EP on own label which sold quite well via mail order. Sampson left to be replaced by Clive Burr (drums), and Dennis Stratton (guitar) joined, adding even stronger drive to band.

EMI signed group in December 1979 amid growing signs that new wave wasn't as all-pervasive as it had first seemed. **Running Free** made UK Top 30 which led to Maiden's historic live appearance on BBC TV's 'Top Of The Pops' — the first live gig since the Who in 1973. March 1980 found Maiden on road supporting Judas Priest(▶). Their impact was soon seen: debut album entered UK charts at No. 4. Album success led to headlining UK tour and European tour opening for Kiss(▶).

**Above: Iron Maiden may look like peaceful hippies — but definitely aren't when they're on stage...**

Stratton left at this point and Dave Murray brought in old friend Adrian Smith, to keep twin guitar sound.

**Killers** LP, released in January 1981, broke band internationally; extensive world tour took most of year. Band now seemed deservedly ready" for superstardom when departure of vocalist Di'anno was announced. What could have been devastating blow turned into even stronger line-up as Bruce Dickinson (ex-Samson) took over vocals. March 1982 saw release of excellent **Number Of The Beast** and another massive world tour.

Burr was replaced on drums by Nicko McBrain (ex-Pat Travers, Trust) for **Piece Of Mind** in 1983. A year later, group embarked on mammoth 'World Slavery' tour—200 performances spread over 322 days in 26 countries. This led to big-selling live album, live single **Running Free**, and hit video which captured their brand of sonic assault with added merit of interesting lyrics and, oftimes, strong melody.

Iron Maiden offer usual audio attack, but with degree of creativity. Forty gold and platinum discs are the testimony.

The band progressed further with the **Somewhere In Time** album released in 1986 when they played concerts in Yugoslavia as part of their world tour. The album was recorded in the Bahamas, Amsterdam and New York, resulting in different "feel" to the various tracks. In April 1988 they came up with a concept album **Seventh Son Of A Seventh Son** which ignored the trend towards thrash and resembled more 70s progressive rock. The songs were linked and told the story of a boy endowed with occult powers. The playing was excellent, Murray and Smith outstanding. The album yielded a UK top ten hit.

**Current line-up:** Harris; Murray; Bruce Dickinson, vocals; Adrian Smith, guitar; Nicko McBain, drums.

**Hit Singles:**

| | US | UK |
|---|---|---|
| Run To The Hills, 1982 | — | 7 |
| The Number Of The Beast. 1982 | — | 18 |
| The Flight of Icarus, 1983 | — | 11 |
| The Trooper, 1983 | — | 12 |
| 2 Minutes To Midnight, 1984 | — | 11 |
| Aces High, 1984 | — | 20 |
| Running Free, 1985 | — | 19 |
| Wasted Years, 1986 | — | 18 |
| Stranger In A Strange Land, 1986 | — | 22 |

**Albums:**
Iron Maiden (Harvest/EMI), 1980 **CD**
Killers (Harvest/EMI), 1981 **CD**
The Number Of The Beast (Capitol/EMI), 1982 **CD**
Piece Of Mind (Capitol/EMI), 1983 **CD**
Powerslave (EMI), 1984 **CD**
Live After Death (EMI), 1985 **CD**
Somewhere In Time (EMI), 1986 **CD**

# Isley Brothers

US group formed 1957.

**Original line-up:** Ronald Isley, vocals; Rudolph Isley, vocals; O'Kelly Isley, vocals.

**Career:** Began performing gospel around hometown of Cincinnati. Moved to New York in 1957, changed to more secular style and recorded for several small labels. Eventually signed with RCA in 1959, and released **Shout,** wild gospel-flavoured stomper that made Top 50 and spawned several later cover versions.

Although group continued to build up reputation as hot live act, no more hits were forthcoming until 1962 release of **Twist And Shout** on Wand. Record made US Top 20 and was later covered by Beatles(▶) (who were great Isley fans).

Slump again followed, during which time Isleys formed own label, T-Neck. This period also saw group employing Jimi Hendrix(▶) as session guitarist. Continued success only came after signing to Motown in 1965. First release, **This Old Heart Of Mine,** became US hit (and major hit in Britain two years later). Over course of four-year period, band notched up variety of single successes on both sides of Atlantic, with greater consistency in UK charts.

Nevertheless, group eventually felt constricted by Motown formula and split from company in 1969. Simultaneously they revived dormant T-Neck operation and signed distribution deal with Buddah. New business arrangements were matched by new approach to music, influenced by West Coast psychedelic bands, Hendrix and Sly and Family Stone(▶).

Ronald, Rudolph and O'Kelly recruited brothers Ernie on guitar and drums and Marvin on bass, plus cousin Chris Jasper on keyboards. Revitalised outfit exploded into new era of creativity and impact. Final barrier

to international pop success was crossed with records which carried them in mid'80s.

In 1985, Ernie, Marvin and Jasper cut acclaimed **Isley Jasper Isley** album and on Isley Brothers albums, the three originals reverted to trio format. Sadly, Kelly Isley died of heart attack in March 1986. However, Rudolph and Ronald made it clear that they intended to carry on as duo, and released album **Smooth Sailin'** in 1987. Jasper Isley fulfilled early promise with excellent **Caravan Of Love** and 1987 set **Different Drummer**.

**3 Plus 3, The Isley Brothers. Courtesy Epic Records.**

**Current line-up:** Ronald Isley; Rudolph Isley.

| Hit Singles: | US | UK |
|---|---|---|
| Twist And Shout, 1962 | 17 | — |
| This Old Heart Of Mine, (Is Weak For You), 1966 | 12 | 47 |
| This Old Heart Of Mine, (Is Weak For You), 1968 | — | 3 |
| I Guess I'll Always Love You, 1969 | — | 11 |
| Behind A Painted Smile, 1969 | — | 5 |
| It's Your Thing, 1969 | 2 | 30 |
| Put Yourself In My Place, 1969 | — | 13 |
| Love The One You're With, 1971 | 18 | — |
| That Lady, 1973 | 6 | 14 |
| Summer Breeze, 1974 | 60 | 16 |
| Fight The Power, 1975 | 4 | — |
| Harvest For The World, 1976 | — | 10 |
| It's A Disco Night (Rock Don't Stop), 1979 | — | 14 |

**Albums:**
Twist And Shout (Wand/DJM), 1962
This Old Heart Of Mine (Tamla Motown), 1966
3+3 (T-Neck/Epic), 1973
Live It Up (T-Neck/Epic), 1974
The Heat Is On (T-Neck/Epic), 1975
Harvest For The World (T-Neck/Epic), 1976
Super Hits (—/Tamla Motown), 1976
Go For Your Guns (T-Neck/Epic), 1977
Forever Gold (T-Neck/Epic), 1977

Showroom (T-Neck/Epic), 1978
Winner Takes All (T-Neck/Epic), 1979
Go All The Way (T-Neck/Epic), 1980
Grand Slam (T-Neck/Epic), 1981
Inside You (T-Neck/Epic), 1981
Motown Superstar Series Volume 6 (Motown/—) 1982
The Real Deal (T-Neck/Epic), 1982
Between The Sheets (Epic), 1983
Forever Gold (Epic), 1984
Smooth Sailin (Warner Bros), 1987

# J. Geils Band
US group formed 1967.

**Original line-up:** Peter Wolf, vocals; J. Geils, guitar; Magic Dick, harmonica; Danny Klein, bass; Stephen Bladd, drums.

**Career:** Formed in Boston, Massachusetts; originally known as J. Geils Blues Band. Dropped 'blues' tag in 1969, and added keyboards player Seth Justman. Gained strong local following playing no-nonsense synthesis of blues, R&B and rock.

Spotted by Atlantic Records on Dr John(▶) bill, band was signed, and released first album, **The J. Geils Band**, in 1971. Outfit showed direct approach reminiscent of Rolling Stones' (▶) attitude, which has persisted throughout recording career. **Bloodshot**, released in 1973, was band's first gold album, and also yielded first hit single, **Give It To Me**.

Further albums consolidated band's reputation, and **Monkey Island** (1977) took them qualitative step forward. Album showcased writing abilities of Justman and Wolf, and veered more towards hard rock ethos. It also heralded split from Atlantic and move to EMI America. (Changed name to simply Geils for **Monkey**, then went back to J. Geils.)

Shift seemed to revitalize band for they immediately produced 1978 gold album, **Sanctuary**. **Love Stinks** was equally successful, but it was only prelude to massive acceptance of album released at end of 1981, **Freeze Frame**. After 14 years of dues-paying, band reaped benefit of LP that topped charts all over the world, and yielded three hit singles, **Centrefold, Freeze Frame** and **Angel in Blue**. Nationwide US tour broke box-office records, and European tour with Rolling Stones(▶) brought wide acclaim.

Band had finally found formula to wed hardrocking approach to commercial appeal. They look set to continue successful career into foreseeable future. Possessing charismatic frontman in Peter Wolf (once gossip-column fodder during lengthy courtship of and short

**Below: J. Geils Band, with bare-chested, now ex-vocalist Peter Wolf.**

marriage to Faye Dunaway), and excellent musicians in Magic Dick and J. Geils, J. Geils Band are classic example of band who have made it through talent and sheer hard work.

The music world was shocked in 1983 when Wolf was kicked out of band after 16 years as focal point.

Ironically, Wolf's career has gone from strength to strength, culminating in massive success in summer 1987 for album **Come As You Are** and single of same name.

**Current line-up:** Geils; Magic Dick; Klein; Bladd; Seth Justman, keyboards.

| Hit Singles: | US | UK |
|---|---|---|
| Must Of Got Lost, 1974 | 12 | — |
| Centrefold, 1981 | 1 | 3 |
| Freeze Frame, 1982 | 27 | 4 |
| Do I Do, 1982 | 13 | — |

**Albums:**
J. Geils Band (Atlantic), 1971
The Morning After (Atlantic), 1971
Full House (Atlantic), 1972
Bloodshot (Atlantic), 1973
Ladies Invited (Atlantic), 1973
Nightmares And Other Tales From The Vinyl Jungle (Atlantic), 1974
Blow Your Face Out (Atlantic), 1976*
Monkey Island (Atlantic), 1977
Sanctuary (EMI), 1978
Love Stinks (EMI), 1980
Freeze Frame (EMI USA), 1981 **CD**
Showtime (EMI), 1982
You're Getting Even While I'm Getting Odd (EMI), 1984
Flashback—The Best Of (EMI USA) **CD**
*Live

# Joe Jackson
UK vocalist, pianist, composer. Born Portsmouth, 1956.

**Career:** Taught himself piano as child; undertook formal musical training at Royal Academy of Music. Early musical career included stints with various pub-rock outfits and Top 40 cover bands. While musical director of Portsmouth Playboy Club masterminded success of 'Opportunity Knocks' talent contest winners Coffee and Cream.

In meantime, Jackson was writing songs, and was signed to A&M in 1978. 1979 hit single **Is She Really Going Out With Him** showed emergence of distinctive new talent, combining deadpan vocal styling with wry lyric and strong melodic sense. Album **Look Sharp** confirmed success, gaining Top 20 chart placing in US.

Second LP **I'm The Man** won further acclaim, and early 1980 saw international success of single **It's Different For Girls**. Although superstardom was in sight, following year Jackson made bold decision to fold band and form new outfit, Jumpin' Jive. Band featured horns and was devoted to Louis Jordan-style swing and jump numbers from late '40s. Perhaps surprisingly, idea was successful. Jumpin' Jive played to full and ecstatic houses, and album of same name made UK Top 20 and US Top 60. However, Jackson had made it clear at outset that concept was one-off, and in due course folded band.

Ever ready to absorb new influences and environments, in 1982 Jackson left UK for New York. Album that resulted, **Night And Day,** became one of 1982's sensations, achieving No. 4 position in US charts. Single **Steppin' Out** was equally successful. Unusual in that it does not feature guitar, **Night And Day** shows jazz, funk and salsa

**I'm The Man, Joe Jackson, Courtesy A&M Records.**

influence and eclecticism typical of Jackson. At same time, album has wide AOR appeal. Jackson continued policy of musical exploration with even jazzier **Body And Soul**, which nevertheless yielded two US hit singles. Two years woodshedding followed, until release of 1986 set **Big World**, new material recorded live on stage onto two-track tape machine.

1987 release **Will Power** was described by one critic as "a soundtrack looking for a movie", and seemed to many to show an artist straying perilously far from commercial credibility. However, Jackson is intelligent and perceptive musician who seems content to go his own idiosyncratic way, and is likely to remain one of few genuinely **interesting** artists on pop and rock scene.

| Hit Singles: | US | UK |
|---|---|---|
| Is She Really Going Out With Him?, 1979 | 21 | 13 |
| It's Different For Girls, 1980 | — | 5 |
| Steppin' Out, 1982 | 6 | 6 |
| Breaking Us In Two, 1983 | 18 | — |
| You Can't Get What You Want, 1984 | 15 | — |

**Joe Jackson's Jumpin' Jive. Courtesy A&M Records.**

**Albums:**
Look Sharp (A&M), 1979 **CD**
I'm The Man (A&M), 1979
Beat Crazy (A&M), 1980
Jumpin' Jive (A&M), 1981
Night And Day (A&M), 1982 **CD**
Mike's Murder (A&M), 1983
Body And Soul (A&M), 1984 **CD**
Big World (A&M), 1986 **CD**
Willpower (A&M), 1987 **CD**

# The Jacksons
US group formed 1966.

**Original line-up:** Michael Jackson, lead vocals; Jackie Jackson, vocals, guitar; Tito Jackson, vocals, guitar; Marlon Jackson, vocals; Jermaine Jackson, vocals, bass.

**Career:** Black America's answer to the Osmonds, the Jackson Five proved to have international, multi-racial appeal. Sons of Joe Jackson, once guitarist with Falcons soul group, and clarinettist Kathy, family grew up in Gary, Indiana, where they were all born (Jackie, May 4, 1951; Tito, October 15, 1953; Jermaine December 11, 1954; Marlon, March 12, 1957; Michael, August 29, 1958; Randy, October 29, 1962), Boys have three sisters of whom two youngest, La Toya and Janet, have logged hits.

Tito had intense interest in music and persuaded others to form family group. Gigged in nearby Chicago and won several talent competitions, culminating in campaign benefit show for Gary's Mayor, Richard Hatcher. Diana Ross(▶) was in attendance

**Greatest Hits, Jackson Five. Courtesy Motown Records.**

and brought group to attention of Motown boss Berry Gordy. They had already recorded unsuccessfully for small local label, but Gordy saw them as major potential talent, especially with then nine-year-old Michael brought out front.

Debut single, **I Want You Back**, was immediate smash, Michael(▶) earning comparison with former child prodigy Stevie Wonder. **Diana Ross Presents The Jackson 5** album and group's inclusion in her 90-minute TV spectacular 'Diana' in 1971 helped build immediate fame. Following singles poured out at rapid rate giving them hits nearly every three months. Early material was all written and produced by 'The Corporation', i.e. Motown's multi-talented songwriting, arranging and production team.

Rivalry with Osmonds and resultant fan mania helped both groups; so did electric stage presence featuring colourful outfits and dazzling dance routines. The Jacksons were even made into a cartoon series.

Parallel—and ever more important—solo career for Michael began at 13 with 1972 hit **I'll Be There**. Tito and Jermaine also had solo releases but made less impact.

Steady flow of albums and singles led to multi-million dollar contract offer from Epic in 1976, which took group from Motown fold.

Having married Hazel, daughter of Motown boss Berry Gordy Jr, Jermaine opted to stay and left group. Name was changed to simply the Jacksons, addition of youngest brother Randy kept number at five.

First Epic album **The Jacksons** went gold; hit singles continued. In 1978 hit highest spot yet with superb **Destiny** album; smash singles **Blame It On The Boogie** and **Shake Your Body (Down To The Ground)** set world's discos alight. Album was self-produced, using cream of West Coast session musicians. During sell-out UK tour band played in front of the Queen at Silver Jubilee celebrations in Glasgow.

The phenomenal solo success of Michael has, of course, become pop history, but female siblings have begun to emulate their older brother. LaToya scored heavily with **If You Feel The Funk**, while former child actress Janet has gone on to become one of the biggest names of the late eighties with mega-selling album **Control** and slew of hit singles. Group has been dormant since problem-racked 1981 **Triumph** tour, although they did reform (including Jermaine) for Motown 25th Anniversary concert.

**Current line-up:** Michael; Jackie; Tito; Marlon; Randy Jackson, vocals.

| Hit Singles: | US | UK |
|---|---|---|
| *As Jackson Five:* | | |
| I Want You Back, 1970 | 1 | 2 |
| ABC, 1970 | 1 | 8 |
| The Love You Save, 1970 | 1 | 7 |
| I'll Be There, 1970 | 1 | 4 |
| Mama's Pearl, 1971 | 2 | 25 |
| Never Can Say Goodbye, 1971 | 2 | 33 |
| Maybe Tomorrow, 1971 | 20 | — |
| Sugar Daddy, 1972 | 10 | — |
| Little Bitty Pretty One, 1972 | 13 | — |
| Lookin' Through The Windows, 1972 | 16 | 9 |
| Corner Of The Sky, 1972 | 18 | — |
| Doctor My Eyes, 1973 | — | 9 |
| Hallelujah Day, 1973 | 28 | 20 |
| Dancing Machine, 1974 | 2 | — |
| I Am Love (Parts 1 & 2), 1975 | 15 | — |
| *As the Jacksons:* | | |
| Enjoy Yourself, 1977 | 6 | 42 |
| Show You The Way To Go, 1977 | 28 | 1 |
| Blame It On The Boogie, 1978 | 54 | 8 |
| Shake Your Body (Down To The Ground), 1979 | 7 | 4 |
| Lovely One, 1980 | 12 | 29 |
| Can You Feel It, 1981 | — | 6 |
| Walk Right Now, 1981 | — | 7 |
| State Of Shock, 1984 | 3 | 14 |
| Torture, 1984 | 17 | 26 |

**Below: The Jacksons, hitmakers (as the Jackson 5) on Motown, now on Epic.**

| *Jermaine Jackson solo:* | | |
|---|---|---|
| Daddy's Home, 1973 | 9 | — |
| Let's Get Serious, 1980 | 9 | 8 |
| Dynamite, 1984 | 15 | — |
| Do What You Do, 1985 | 13 | 6 |

*Michael Jackson solo:*
(See separate entry)

**Albums:**
*As Jackson Five:*
ABC (Tamla/Motown), 1970
Lookin' Through The Windows (Tamla/Motown), 1972
Greatest Hits (Tamla/Motown), 1972
Anthology (Tamla/Motown), 1977
20 Golden Greats (—/Motown), 1979
Motown Superstar Series Volume 12 (Tamla/—), 1981

*As The Jacksons:*
The Jacksons (Epic), 1976
Goin' Places (Epic), 1977
Destiny (Epic), 1978
Triumph (Epic), 1981
Live (Epic), 1982
Victory (Epic), 1984

*Jermaine Jackson solo:*
Jermaine (Tamla/Motown), 1980
Let's Get Serious (Tamla/Motown), 1980
I Like Your Style (Tamla/Motown), 1981
Let Me Tickle Your Fancy (Tamla/Motown), 1982
Dynamite (Arista), 1984 **CD**
Precious Moments (Arista) **CD**

# Michael Jackson
US vocalist, composer.
Born Gary, Indiana, August 29, 1958.

**Career:** Dominant brother of the Jacksons(▶), Michael was youngest in original line-up (before Randy joined) and was heralded as infant genius by his Motown mentors. Just as Little Stevie Wonder's(▶) early promise reached potential so Michael Jackson's talent has stood test of time.

Besides singing lead on the Jacksons' amazing run of hits, Michael has achieved enormous success in own right. He has earned reputed $40 million to date.

First solo hit was **Got To Be There** (1971). Other successes included theme from movie **Ben**, a ballad which contrasted with usual uptempo style of Jackson Five. Between 1971-1976 enjoyed six best-selling albums with Motown. His last collaboration with the company was starring as the scarecrow, opposite Diana Ross in 'The Wiz' black re-make of the classic movie 'The Wizard Of Oz'. The film was heavily criticised but Jackson won applause for his role. His duet with Diana Ross, **Ease On Down The Road**, was hit single.

Moving with his family to Epic label, Michael continued to front the Jacksons. He was also teamed up with producer Quincy Jones(▶) (whom he had met while both

**Below: Seemingly increasingly whacky in his private life, Michael Jackson has nevertheless seen his popularity reach new heights during the world tour of 1988.**

worked on 'The Wiz') for the appropriately epic **Off The Wall** solo album. This included superb material by Paul McCartney(▶), British writer Rod Temperton (ex-Heatwave(▶)) and Jackson himself. Claimed as biggest selling album by a black artist of all time, the Los Angeles-recorded album had no weak spots. In US a number of tracks were lifted as singles. In one week three singles from the LP were in US Top 10, a unique achievement. Cashing in on this phenomenal success, Motown reissued old track **One Day In Your Life** for 1981 UK chart-topper. In 1982 Michael scored US/UK duet hit with Paul McCartney on McCartney's composition **The Girl Is Mine**.

Follow-up album **Thriller** eclipsed success of **Off The Wall** with a raft of mega-singles including **Billie Jean** and **Beat It** (which featured Eddie Van Halen on guitar). Crucial feature of marketing campaign was video, 80s medium exploited to the full by ace movie director Jon Landis in ground-breaking mini-feature that showed Jackson's unique dancing off to stunning effect. At presstime, album had sold close to 30 million copies, leaving Jackson in awkward position of trying to maintain impossible level of success. However, an air of expectation hung over the music business for two years whilst Jackson and Quincy Jones recorded follow-up **Bad**.

Platinum upon release, album has sold in sufficient quantities to justify the pair's attention to detail, although unlikely to emulate the sales of **Thriller**.

1988 world tour saw popularity at a peak, despite Jackson's somewhat bizarre public persona. Rumours abound about star's regular visits to plastic surgeon and life-prolonging pure-air oxygen tent. He also maintains private zoo, upon which a series of stuffed animal toys called 'Michael's Pets' have been based.

**Bad, Michael Jackson.
Courtesy Epic Records.**

Speculation upon star's private life has not deterred hysterical following, nor inhibited Jackson's undoubted creative forces.

| Hit Singles: | US | UK |
|---|---|---|
| Got To Be There, 1971 | 4 | 5 |
| Rockin' Robin, 1972 | 2 | 3 |
| I Wanna Be Where You Are, 1972 | 16 | — |
| Ain't No Sunshine, 1972 | — | 8 |
| Ben, 1972 | 1 | 7 |
| Don't Stop Till You Get Enough, 1979 | 1 | 3 |
| Off The Wall, 1979 | 10 | 7 |
| Rock With You, 1979 | 1 | 7 |
| She's Out Of My Life, 1980 | 10 | 3 |
| One Day In Your Life, 1981 | 55 | 1 |
| Billie Jean, 1983 | 1 | 1 |
| Beat It, 1983 | 1 | 3 |
| Want To Be Startin' Somethin', 1983 | 5 | 8 |
| Human Nature, 1983 | 7 | — |
| PYT (Pretty Young Thing), 1983 | 10 | 11 |
| Thriller, 1984 | 4 | 10 |
| Farewell My Summer Love, 1984 | — | 7 |
| The Way You Make Me Feel, 1987 | 1 | 3 |
| Bad, 1987 | 1 | 3 |

| With Paul McCartney: | | |
|---|---|---|
| The Girl Is Mine, 1982 | 2 | 8 |
| Say Say Say, 1983 | 1 | 2 |

| With Siedah Garrett: | | |
|---|---|---|
| I Just Can't Stop Loving You, 1986 | 1 | 1 |

**Albums:**
Ben (Tamla Motown), 1972 **CD**
Got To Be There (Tamla Motown), 1972 **CD**
Best Of (—/Motown), 1975
One Day In Your Life (—/Motown), 1981
Off The Wall (Epic), 1979 **CD**
Thriller (Epic), 1982 **CD**
Ain't No Sunshine (—/Pickwick), 1982
Bad (Epic), 1987 **CD**
Got To Be There/Ben (Motown),1987 **CD**

# The Jam

UK group formed 1976.

**Original line-up:** Paul Weller vocals, bass; Steve Brookes, guitar; Bruce Foxton, guitar; Rick Buckler, drums.

**Career:** Above quartet got together while at school in Woking, Surrey, to play rock 'n' roll and R&B. Youth and social club gigs followed; after Steve Brookes left, Weller switched to guitar, Foxton to bass.

Line-up in this form made London debut in summer 1976, displaying image based on early '60s 'mod' look and playing sharp, well-crafted rock songs that showed songwriter Weller's debt to Pete Townshend(▶). Although band had little in common with most of 'New Wave' outfits, Jam won contract as part of mass record company signings that followed 'summer of punk'.

First single **In The City** hovered around bottom of chart, but follow-up **All Around The World** made No. 13. In meantime, debut album, also called **In The City**, made No. 20 in album chart. During next three years band became chart regulars with both singles and albums, establishing themselves as one of most interesting new outfits of late '70s. Weller (born May 25, 1958) set direction of band, and showed himself to be perceptive and socially aware writer and spokesman.

1980 saw further triumphs for band, with first No. 1 single **Going Underground/The Dreams Of Children** and title of 'Best Group' in the New Musical Express Readers' Poll. Next single, **Start**, also made No. 1 and group were not out of Top 10 until their their final demise.

**Above: The Jam, pictured before they split at the end of 1982.**

Despite massive success during 1982 — they swept board in all British polls and toured Britain and abroad to universal acclaim — Jam announced that band would fold at end of year. Apparently Weller found format too constricting and wished to move on to other things. During December band undertook farewell tour to usual ecstatic crowds, and retired from scene. 1982 LP **The Gift** entered UK charts at No. 1. Jam singles/sleeves are such collector's items that Polydor

**In The City, the first Jam album, with a very 'mod' sleeve. Courtesy Polydor Records.**

re-issued entire catalogue for third time.

Weller has already found further success with new band, the Style Council, and other acts such as Tracie on his own Respond label. Other members are involved with solo projects.

Although they never achieved more than cult status in US, Jam, always an intense live act, became one of most important bands in UK in '80s. Success was largely due to Paul Weller; his current projects and any future ones should be worth watching.

**Final line-up:** Weller, vocals, guitar; Foxton, bass; Buckler.

| Hit Singles: | US | UK |
|---|---|---|
| All Around The World, 1977 | — | 13 |
| Down In The Tube Station At Midnight, 1978 | — | 15 |
| Strange Town, 1979 | — | 15 |
| When You're Young, 1979 | — | 17 |
| The Eton Rifles, 1979 | — | 3 |
| Going Underground/The Dreams Of Children, 1980 | — | 1 |
| Start, 1980 | — | 1 |
| Funeral Pyre, 1981 | — | 4 |
| Absolute Beginners, 1981 | — | 4 |
| Town Called Malice/Precious, 1982 | — | 1 |
| Just Who Is The 5 O'Clock Hero, 1982* | — | 8 |
| The Bitterest Pill (I Ever Had To Swallow), 1982 | — | 2 |
| Beat Surrender, 1982 | — | 1 |

*German import

**Albums:**
In The City (Polydor), 1977
This Is The Modern World (Polydor), 1977*
All Mod Cons (Polydor), 1978*
Setting Sons (Polydor), 1979 **CD**
Sound Affects (Polydor), 1980
The Gift (Polydor), 1982
Dig The New Breed (Polydor), 1982†
Snap (Polydor), 1983
Compact Snap (Polydor), 1983 **CD**

*One track different on US/UK versions.
†Live

# Jan And Dean

US vocal duo formed 1958.
Jan Berry, born Los Angeles, April 3, 1941.
Dean Torrence, born Los Angeles, March 10, 1940.

**Career:** Major figures of California surf-music scene, Jan and Dean's career was abruptly terminated when a horrific car smash in 1966 left Jan with serious brain damage and considerable loss of mobility.

By no means originators, Jan and Dean were as much reliant on talents of their songwriters and producers as on own vocal abilities, but records like **Surf City, Little Old Lady From Pasadena** and **Dead Man's Curve** remain classics of their idiom — the totally unpretentious, fun-music West Coast sound of the early '60s.

They started singing together in shower room after football practice at Emerson Junior High School in Los Angeles, and recorded on a twin-track machine in garage with help from friend Bruce Johnston, later to become a Beach Boy(▶).

In 1958, Berry managed to place **Jenny Lee** (which featured Berry, Torrence and Arnie Ginsburg as trio but appeared as Jan and Arnie on label because Torrence was in Army and unavailable to sign contract), a song about a burlesque stripper, with Arwin, and it became US Top 10 hit. A year later Berry was back with Dean Torrence as Jan and Dean, with **Baby Talk**, produced by Lou Adler and Herb Alpert(▶). Concurrently, they attended college, Berry studying medicine, Torrence design.

Music soon took over, however, and after Top-30 hit on Challenge with **Heart And Soul** in 1961 they signed to Liberty the following year and started singing about their

**Golden Hits, Jan & Dean. Courtesy Liberty Records.**

big passion — surfing.

After a show with the Beach Boys, Brian Wilson played them demo of his composition **Surf City**. Their rendition went to No. 1 and was quickly followed by string of surf and hot-rod flavoured high-school epics, many of them written or produced by Brian Wilson. They repaid the favour, Jan Berry singing lead on the Beach Boys' live recording of **Barbara Ann**.

While filming 'Easy Come Easy Go' in spring 1966 Berry crashed his car into a parked truck. Since then it has been a long, slow path to partial recovery. Despite some sides recorded for A&M and recent stage appearances with erstwhile partner (where they were somewhat cruelly accused of going for sympathy market), Jan Berry's contribution to rock music remains rooted in his brief spell of '60s stardom. Dean Torrence was involved with the Legendary Masked Surfers and now runs a design studio which specialises in pop posters. 1978 movie 'Dead Man's Curve' chronicled duo's career.

**Hit Singles:**

| | US | UK |
|---|---|---|
| Jenny Lee (As Jan and Arnie), 1958 | 8 | — |
| Baby Talk, 1959 | 10 | — |
| Surf City, 1963 | 1 | 26 |
| Honolulu Lulu, 1963 | 11 | — |
| Drag City, 1964 | 10 | — |
| Dead Man's Curve, 1964 | 8 | — |
| Little Old Lady From Pasadena, 1964 | 3 | — |
| Ride The Wild Surf, 1964 | 16 | — |

**Albums:**

Dead Man's Curve (Liberty/—), 1964
Ride The Wild Surf (Liberty/Greenlight-Liberty), 1964
Little Old Lady From Pasadena (Liberty/—), 1964
Legendary Masters (Liberty/—), 1971
The Very Best Of (—/Sunset), 1974
Greatest Hits (MCS), 1987 **CD**
Silver Summer (Showcase), 1987 **CD**

# Jean-Michel Jarre

French composer, multi-instrumentalist. Born Lyon, France, August 24, 1948.

**Career:** Child prodigy from musical family, Jarre started to learn piano and guitar at five. Attended Conservatoire de Paris taking lessons in music structure and harmony. Heavily influenced by '60s English pop music during his latter school years. Played lead guitar in number of groups in western suburbs of Paris before moving on to more experimental music.

In 1968, Jarre enrolled at Group of Musical Research (GMR) and began thesis on non-European music (African, Amazonian and Oceanian). His increasing interest in synthesisers and free-form music conflicted with pursuits of GMR. Unsuited for classical career and disillusioned by clinical research, Jarre abandoned studies. Working in own recording studio with a number of technicians and sound engineers, Jarre built various instruments to own specification and worked out new ideas on the synthesiser.

For his debut in 1971, Jarre sensationally introduced electronic music to the opera; became youngest composer ever to have played at Palais Garnier. Impressed by public's reaction, Jarre sought wider acclaim. Extended activities to other areas: radio jingles, Pepsi commercials, and background music for department stores and airports.

Gradually, he succeeded in writing film and ballet music ('Dorian Gray' by Norbert Schmucki; 'Le Labyrinthe' by Joseph Lazzini).

More success followed with music and lyrical contribution for such artists as Gerard Lenorman, Christophe, Patrick Juvet and Françoise Hardy.

With such a long apprenticeship, Jarre was in perfect position to produce appealing, if undemanding, music for mass consumption. **Oxygene,** released in 1976, sold six million copies worldwide, as did successor **Equinoxe**. On July 14, 1979, Jarre erected an original spectacular show from **Oxygene** and **Equinoxe** at Place de la Concorde. The event attracted one million spectators (from the Etoile to the Tuileries) and 100 million telespectators (from Europe to Japan). In 1981, **Magnetic Fields** confirmed his position as one of the most commercially successful composers in his field. Played series of concerts in China in October 1981 which were broadcast to 500 million radio listeners and 30 million television viewers.

Latterly artist has consolidated success with series of international music/laser/video extravaganzas. Largely ignored by rock media as purveyor of expensively produced muzak, Jarre still turns in big-selling albums on a regular basis, and no doubt laughs all the way to the Left Bank. He is married to actress Charlotte Rampling.

**Hit Singles:**

| | US | UK |
|---|---|---|
| Oxygene Part IV, 1977 | — | 4 |

**Albums:**

Oxygene (Polydor), 1977 **CD**
Equinoxe (Polydor), 1978 **CD**
Magnetic Fields (Polydor), 1981 **CD**
The Concerts In China (Double) (Polydor), 1982 **CD**
Zoolook (Dreyfus/Polydor), 1984 **CD**
The Essential (Pacific), 1976-86 **CD**
Rendez Vous (Polydor), 1986 **CD**
In Concert Lyon/Houston (Polydor), 1987 **CD**
Jean-Michel Jarre In Concert (Dreyfus), 1987 **CD**

# Jason and the Scorchers

US group formed 1982.

**Original/current line-up:** Jason Ringenberg, vocals, harmonica; Warner Hodges, lead guitar, backing vocals; Jeff Johnson, bass; Perry Baggs, drums.

**Career:** Jason and the Scorchers' burning hot brand of country slanted rock music—branded 'cowpunk' by their admirers—made them US sensation of 1984.

Not unexpectedly, three of foursome are natives of Nashville—guitar hero Hodges being son of guitarist/singer team Ed and Blanche Hodges (Ed has played with Johnnie

**Fervor, Jason and the Scorchers. Courtesy EMI Records.**

Cash, Lefty Frizzell and others). Exception is Jason Ringenberg, son of Illinois hog farmer, who fronted various rockabilly, country and bluegrass (playing banjo) bands and worked as railroad labourer before heading for Nashville.

Two years' apprenticeship in Music City led to EP of garage/punkoid versions of country classics, titled **Reckless Country Soul**, three songs being recorded in Sam Phillips' Sun Studios in Memphis.

Breakthrough to mass acceptance was much lauded **Fervor**, mini-album, picked up from Proxis Records and re-released by EMI America. It included raw and rugged version of Dylan's **Absolutely Sweet Marie** to establish them as frontrunners in redneck rebel rock mould. British acceptance came via UK tour which took them to pub venues where such acts as the Boot Hill Foot Tappers, Helen and the Horns and Yip Yip Coyote had paved way for their brand of music.

'85 set **Lost And Found** earned prime time radio play, pushing these 'good young boys' closer to a mass market and unexpected chart success.

**Albums:**

Fervor (EMI), 1984
Lost And Found (EMI), 1985
Still Standing (EMI America), 1986

# Jefferson Airplane/Starship

US group formed 1965.

**Original line-up:** Marty Balin, vocals; Paul Kantner, guitar; Signe Anderson, vocals; Jorma Kaukonen, guitar; Jack Casady, bass; Skip Spence, drums.

**Career:** Balin and Kantner met on San Francisco's folk coffee-house circuit in early 1965. Balin felt it was time to return to his roots and explore rock 'n' roll of Elvis(▶), Jerry Lee Lewis(▶) and Little Richard(▶). Anderson joined, then Kaukonen. Balin called Washington, D.C., and asked long-time friend Casady to join on bass. Spence was recruited in mid-'65 and Airplane began building local reputation as band who played folk lyrics to rock beat. Bill Graham helped foster exciting,

**Red Octopus, Jefferson Starship. Courtesy RCA Records.**

vibrant image by providing priority booking at new Fillmore Hall. This lead to RCA contract, the first for Bay area band.

Spencer Dryden replaced Spence (later to form Moby Grape(▶)) while band recorded **Jefferson Airplane Takes Off**. National promotion helped 'folk-rock' sound achieve gold LP status and aroused industry interest in West Coast bands. Anderson left due to pregnancy and Kantner recruited Grace Slick (ex-Great Society) from band who used to open for Airplane.

This classic line-up scored big US hit with **Somebody To Love**. This song and **White Rabbit** were old Great Society songs. Slick's vocals made them, and whole of **Surrealistic Pillow** LP, haunting, emotive experience. To band's delight, critics and fans fell in love with album and it is marked as essential listening for understanding '60s.

Sudden success meant band could live in communal bliss, but community living also brought problems. **After Bathing At Baxter's** reflected this by reducing Balin's songwriting contributions and by trying new sounds and formats. Unlike previous LP, **Baxter's** experiments no longer hold interest upon re-hearing today.

Slick and Kantner had become lovers; when they began assuming full leadership roles, Balin backed off. **Crown of Creation** reduced Balin's role even further by including weak Slick song, **Lather**, and non-rock David Crosby song, **Triad**. Daring at time of release,

**Winds Of Change, Jefferson Starship Courtesy RCA 'Grunt Records. Still in the biz after nearly twenty years.**

and containing some good harmony, this LP is high point of early Airplane.

**Bless Its Pointed Little Head** is average live set. Next album, **Volunteers**, pushed band into forefront of counterculture's political stance. Considering shallow, preachy tone, LP has remained surprisingly interesting. Balin felt band was becoming too big and too smooth and left. Several US tours followed (including playing at Stones'(▶) Altamont concert), then band seemed to lose all sense of direction. Balin's loss, Slick's pregnancy with Kantner's child and Dryden's departure left Airplane grounded. Kaukomen and Casady began electric blues country band, Hot Tuna. At first a part-time affair, project eventually removed duo from Airplane altogether. In telling omen for the future, Slick and Kantner used several famous 'session' players (Jerry Garcia, David Crosby, Graham Nash) to record LP **Blows Against The Empire,** which they credited to 'Paul Kantner and the Jefferson Starship'.

Airplane returned with Joey Covington (drums) on **Bark** LP. State of Airplane is reflected by superior Slick-Kantner solo, **Sunfighter**, released at same time. With one more sub-par set, **Long John Silver**, Airplane finally crashed. David Frieberg, ex-Quicksilver Messenger Service(▶), added vocals on live but uninspired **Thirty Seconds Over Winterland**. Then with no formal announcement, Airplane disappeared. Casady and Kaukonen worked full time turning Hot Tuna into early heavy-metal band. Slick, Kantner and Frieberg produced weak solo effort, and Slick released unsatisfactory **Manhole** LP.

Two years later in 1974, Slick and Kantner decided to re-form band. Using Frieberg, 'Papa' John Creach (fiddler Hot Tuna had introduced to Airplane on **Bark**) ex-Turtles(▶) John Barbata (drums), Peter Sears (bass) and Craig Chaquico (guitar), new formation took name Jefferson Starship.

US tour, using early Airplane and solo material, convinced Slick and Kantner that band was viable proposition. **Dragon Fly** wasn't overly brilliant but sold well. More importantly, it had one Balin credit and indicated reunion with his creative influence; Balin began appearing with Starship and contributing efforts to recording sessions. However, he refused to sign with group or formally commit self to Starship. His **Miracles** became mammoth US hit in summer 1975 and pushed LP **Red Octopus** to US No. 1 (Airplane/Starship's first after 10 years of work).

The success of **Octopus** obviously influenced sales of next LP **Spitfire**, but album was inferior and seemed a sell-out/cash-in. **Earth** reflected growing personal problems and confusion over what to do next. Slick, Balin and Barbata all left and there seemed no reason to continue.

Kantner recruited Aynsley Dunbar (drums) and Mickey Thomas (vocals). **Freedom At Point Zero** was first Airplane/Starship line-up not to feature female lead vocals. Critically dismissed, Kantner pushed on to **Modern Times**; Slick provided some backing vocals. Having resolved bout with alcohol and various personal problems, she rejoined full time on **Winds Of Change** (after release of two solo LPs).

Break-up of Kantner/Slick's personal relationship led to Kantner leaving group June 1984 amid much acrimony, resultant law suits forcing band to abbreviate name in March 1985 to simply Starship for **Knee Deep In The Hoopla** album.

A near total lineup reshuffle resulted in international smash singles **We Built This City** and **Nothing's Gonna Stop Us Now**.

**Current line-up:** Slick; Elvin Bishop, guitar; Mickey Thomas, vocals; Craig Chaquico, guitar; Donny Baldwin, drums; Peter Sears, bass, keyboards.

| Hit Singles: | US | UK |
|---|---|---|
| *As Airplane:* | | |
| Somebody to Love, 1967 | 5 | — |
| White Rabbit, 1967 | 8 | — |
| *As Starship:* | | |
| Miracles, 1975 | 3 | — |
| With Your Love, 1976 | 12 | — |
| Runaway, 1978 | 12 | — |
| Count On Me, 1978 | 8 | — |
| Jane, 1979 | 14 | — |
| We Built This City, 1985 | 1 | 12 |
| Nothing's Gonna Stop Us Now, 1987 | 1 | 1 |
| Its Not Over, 1987 | 9 | — |

**Albums:**

*As Airplane:*
Jefferson Airplane Takes Off (RCA), 1966
Surrealistic Pillow (RCA), 1967
After Bathing At Baxter's (RCA), 1968
Crown Of Creation (RCA), 1968
Bless Its Pointed Little Head (RCA), 1969
Volunteers (RCA), 1969
The Worst Of The Jefferson Airplane (RCA), 1970
Bark (Grunt), 1971
Thirty Seconds Over Winterland — Live (Grunt), 1973
Surrealistic Pillow (RCA) **CD**
2400 Fulton Street — The CD Collection (RCA), 1987 **CD**

*As Starship:*
Dragon Fly (Grunt), 1974
Red Octopus (RCA), 1975 **CD**
Spitfire (Grunt), 1976
Earth (Grunt), 1978
Gold (Grunt), 1979
Freedom At Ground Zero (Grunt), 1980
Modern Times (Grunt), 1981
Winds Of Change (Grunt USA), 1982 **CD**
Nuclear Furniture (Grunt USA), 1984 **CD**
Knee Deep In The Hoopla (RCA), 1985

*Kantner-Slick:*
Blows Against The Empire (RCA), 1970
Sunfighter (Grunt), 1971

*Grace Slick:*
Dreams (RCA), 1980
Welcome To The Wrecking Ball (RCA), 1981

**Darklands, The Jesus and Mary Chain. Courtesy Blanco Y Negro Records.**

# The Jesus & Mary Chain

UK group formed 1982.

**Original/Current line-up:** Jim Reid, vocals; William Reid, guitars; Douglas Hart, bass; Murray Dalgleish, drums.

**Career:** Formed in 1982 in East Kilbride, near Glasgow (which also spawned Aztec Camera), and played mere handful of local gigs — being banned from one venue and rejected by Glasgow rock cognoscenti as being brash and tuneless — before releasing seminal debut single, **Upside Down**, on London indie label, Creation Records.

Early reputation based on low-key shambolic gigs highlighted by guitar feedback on stage and crowd trouble off. Series of singles via Blanco Y Negro licensing deal — **Never Understand**, **You Trip Me Up** and **Just Like Honey** — showed band moving into sweet

**Below: Jim Reid (left) and Douglas Hart of The Jesus and Mary Chain — below-the-line gothic rock enthusiasts.**

melodies with harsh arrangements, like Velvet Underground re-interpreting Beach Boys songbook. Debut LP, **Psycho Candy**, featured temporary drummer Bobby Gillespie and received critical acclaim before **Some Candy Talking** became a UK hit single.

Band then split from would-be Svengali manager Alan McGee and disappeared for year, experimenting with drum-machine and extra guitarist before re-emerging with **April Skies** and second LP **Darklands** which proved their talent for brooding ballads and atmospheric rock in vein of Echo & Bunnymen or the Cure.

Now regarded as leading purveyors of 80s gothic soundtracks, influencing new wave of young guitar-based rock bands.

| Hit Singles: | US | UK |
|---|---|---|
| Some Candy Talking, 1986 | — | 13 |
| April Skies, 1987 | — | 8 |
| Happy When It Rains, 1987 | — | 25 |
| Darklands, 1987 | — | 33 |

**Albums**
Psycho Candy (Blanco Y Negro), 1985 **CD**
Darklands (Blanco Y Negro), 1987 **CD**

# Jethro Tull

UK group formed 1968.

**Original line-up:** Ian Anderson, vocals, flute; Glenn Cornick, bass; Mick Abrahams, guitar; Clive Bunker, drums.

**Career:** Ian Anderson joined John Evan Band in native Blackpool in early 1966. Rapidly changing personnel brought him in contact with various musicians who would later work for him in Tull.

John Evan Band moved to London in winter 1967 and tried to break into club scene. Lack of success caused band's break-up, leaving Anderson and Cornick on their own. Abrahams and Bunker joined them in early 1968 and Anderson named band after 18th Century author/agriculturist Jethro Tull. Anderson's eccentric vocals and image caught attention of MGM records. Single **Aeroplane/ Sunshine Day** was fortunate flop in that

**Benefit, Jethro Tull.
Courtesy Island Records.**

band's name was misprinted as Jethro Toe. Island Records released next single, **Song For Jeffery,** which gathered bigger following and put band on road to success. Tull's albums began selling well as 'art-rock' in US and provided large, loyal following.

Abrahams left in late 1968 (forming Blodwyn Pig). Tony Iommi (later Black Sabbath(▶)) filled in for few weeks until Martin Barre was picked from auditions as permanent guitarist. This line-up recorded excellent **Stand Up** LP which was first indication of Anderson's true talent as songwriter. Adding old mate John Evan as session keyboard player, band recorded equally strong **Benefit** LP.

With flamboyant dress (usually like that of a mad jester) and leg-hopping antics, Anderson was now critical and popular success. Extended himself with rock opera **Aqualung** which took on typical early '70s targets (organised religion, society in general), but offered no substitute. Despite overblown, almost pretentious tone, LP **Aqualung** became huge US success and continues to sell well today. For this album John Evan became full member but co-founder Cornick was replaced by yet another Blackpool mate, Jeffery Hammond-Hammond. Cornick formed Wild Turkey; later he co-founded Paris with ex-Fleetwood Mac(▶) Bob Welch. By late 1971 Bunker had left and his place was taken by last ex-John Evan Band recruit, Barriemore Barlow.

Concept album ideas were extended in live show through use of stage props and pre-recorded films. After **Thick As A Brick,** Anderson threw caution to wind and presented **A Passion Play.** Rather than playing old hits or catering to any audience desire, Jethro Tull played new opera to astonished crowds.

Move proved to be rock'n'roll suicide as both fans and critics turned off. In retaliation Anderson announced break-up of group. He quickly realized his mistake explaining he really only meant group would take break from touring. Using same basic line-up from **A Passion Play,** Anderson recorded 'comeback' LP **War Child,** as part of film project. Finally realising rock opera and concept albums were passé, film was abandoned and LP was released by itself.

Despite this background, **War Child** recaptured early Tull flavour and seemed excellent indication for band's future. More surprising was LP's single, **Bungle In The Jungle,** which became big US hit, an event rare for Tull even when band played huge stadium concerts.

Unfortunately, it turned out to be Tull's last serious fling at critical or popular success. Using old line-up one more time, Anderson released disappointing **Minstrel In The Gallery.**

In 80s Jethro Tull became less than fashionable name, and Anderson concentrated on role as latter-day country squire while occasionally reconvening band to record albums.

Recent Tull works did not set world on fire,

although 1987 release **Crest Of A Knave** went some way towards rekindling public interest. In any event, Tull and in particular Anderson have already carved honourable niche in rock pantheon, as idiosyncratic practitioners of very British kind of rock.

**Final line-up:** Anderson; Peter Vettesse, keyboards; Martin Barre, guitar; Dave Pegg, bass; Doane Perry, drums.

**Hit Singles:**

| | US | UK |
|---|---|---|
| Living In The Past, 1969 | 11 | 3 |
| Sweet Dream, 1969 | — | 9 |
| The Witch's Promise/Teacher, 1970 | — | 4 |
| Life Is A Long Song/Up The Pool, 1971 | — | 11 |
| Bungle In The Jungle, 1974 | 12 | — |

**Albums:**
This Was (Reprise/Island), 1968 **CD**
Stand Up (Reprise/Island), 1969 **CD**
Benefit (Reprise/Island), 1970 **CD**
Aqualung (Chrysalis), 1971 **CD**
Thick As A Brick (Chrysalis), 1972 **CD**
Living In The Past (Chrysalis), 1972 **CD**
A Passion Play (Chrysalis), 1973
War Child (Chrysalis), 1974
M.U. The Best Of Jethro Tull (Chrysalis), 1975 **CD**
Minstrel In The Gallery (Chrysalis), 1975
Too Old Io Rock'n'Roll: Too Young To Die (Chrysalis),1976 **CD**
Songs From The Wood (Chrysalis), 1977 **CD**
Repeat: The Best Of Jethro Tull: Volume II (Chrysalis), 1976 **CD**
Heavy Horses (Chrysalis), 1978 **CD**
Live: Bursting Out (Chrysalis), 1978
Stormwatch (Chrysalis), 1979
A (Chrysalis), 1980
Broadsword And The Beast (Chrysalis), 1982 **CD**
Under Wraps (Chrysalis), 1984 **CD**
Crest Of A Knave (Chrysalis), 1987 **CD**
Original Masters (Chrysalis), 1986 **CD**

---

# Billy Joel

US vocalist, pianist, composer.
Born Long Island, New York, May 9, 1949.

**Career:** Encouraged by German-born father, Joel learnt piano from age four. In 1964,

joined first group, the Echoes, which later became Lost Souls. Further early aggregations included the Hassles, who recorded two albums for United Artists, and Attila, a duo which made one album for Epic.

In 1971, demo tape of own songs gained Joel contract with Family Productions, and year later first solo album, **Cold Spring Harbor,** was released. Record created some interest despite appalling production, but business problems led to Joel's exodus to California. During this time he performed in bars and hotels under name Bill Martin.

However, song called **Captain Jack** had come to attention of Columbia records, and company traced Joel to California and signed him. Album **Piano Man** was released in 1973, providing Top 30 single in titletrack. Album eventually went platinum.

Strangely, next album, **Street Life Serenade,** did not do as well, and Joel decided to return to familiar environment of New York. 1976 album **Turnstiles** reflected home town lifestyle and furthered Joel's reputation as writer of memorable melodies and often perceptive story-telling lyrics.

Massive breakthrough came with release of next album, **The Stranger.** It eventually became Columbia's biggest-selling album in US, surpassing even **Bridge Over Troubled Water.** LP also yielded instant standard in **Just The Way You Are,** covered by every artist from Englebert Humperdinck to Barry White(▶).

Since then Joel has alternated between effective ballads and more uptempo material. Somewhat lacking in identifiable image, Joel nevertheless appeals to enormous number of people, cutting across rock and MOR markets.

While recording **The Nylon Curtain** album, Joel had serious motorcycle accident on Long Island, resulting in fractures which needed extensive surgery. LP struck raw nerve in American consciousness, title song being hailed as first to express the experience of soldiers in Vietnam War. **Allentown** did same for steel workers and led 16,000 of its citizens to petition singer to include their town in his 1982 tour schedule.

For **Innocent Man,** Joel turned back to the music he loved as a teenager—the soul,

R&B and rock of late '50s early '60s. He recaptured the mood whilst avoiding being derivative, except in the case of the catchy hit **Tell Her About It** which came close to Frankie Valli and the Four Seasons' sound without inciting a 'passing off' action.

Now married to top model Christie Brinkley (the eponymous **Uptown Girl**) and immersed in family life, Joel continues as major concert attraction whilst remaining critically underrated. Recent Russian concerts had Soviet audiences singing along with his melodic and memorable repertoire.

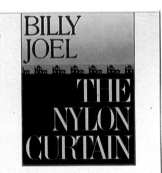

**The Nylon Curtain, Billy Joel.
Courtesy Columbia Records.**

**Hit Singles:**

| | US | UK |
|---|---|---|
| Just The Way You Are, 1978 | 3 | 19 |
| Movin' Out (Anthony's Song), 1978 | 17 | 35 |
| She's Always A Woman, 1978 | 17 | — |
| My Life, 1978 | 3 | 12 |
| Big Shot, 1979 | 14 | — |
| You May Be Right, 1980 | 7 | — |
| It's Still Rock And Roll To Me, 1980 | 1 | 14 |
| Say Goodbye To Hollywood, 1981 | 17 | — |
| Pressure, 1982 | 20 | — |
| Allentown, 1983 | 17 | — |
| Tell Her About It, 1983 | 1 | 4 |
| Uptown Girl, 1983 | 3 | 1 |
| An Innocent Man, 1984 | 10 | 8 |
| The Longest Time, 1984 | 14 | 25 |
| Keeping The Faith, 1985 | 18 | — |
| You're Only Human, 1985 | 9 | — |
| A Matter Of Trust, 1987 | 16 | — |
| This Is The Time, 1987 | 18 | — |

**Albums:**
Cold Spring Harbour (Columbia/CBS), 1972 **CD**
Piano Man (Columbia/CBS), 1973 **CD**
Street Life Serenade (Columbia/CBS), 1975 **CD**
Turnstiles (Columbia/CBS), 1976 **CD**
The Stranger (Columbia/CBS), 1977 **CD**
52nd Street (Columbia/CBS), 1978 **CD**
Glass Houses (Columbia/CBS), 1980 **CD**
Songs In The Attic (Columbia/CBS), 1981 **CD**
The Nylon Curtain (Columbia/CBS), 1982 **CD**
An Innocent Man (Columbia/CBS), 1983 **CD**
Greatest Hits Vols I&II (Columbia/CBS), 1985 **CD**
The Bridge (CBS), 1986 **CD**
Kohuept (CBS), 1987 **CD**

**Kohuept, Billy Joel.
Courtesy CBS Records.**

**Streetlife Serenade , Billy Joel. Courtesy Columbia Records. More melodies telling stories.**

# Elton John

UK vocalist, composer, pianist.
Born Reginald Kenneth Dwight, Pinner, Middlesex, March 25, 1947.

**Career:** Took piano lessons at early age. After leaving school in 1964, combined day job as messenger for music publisher with evening gig playing piano in pub. Following year joined local band Bluesology, which specialised in providing backing for visiting US soul stars like Billy Stewart, Patti Labelle and Major Lance. Band eventually became permanent backing outfit for Long John Baldry; this situation lasted until Baldry achieved pop stardom (albeit fleetingly) with **Let The Heartaches Begin** in late 1967.

By now John was collaborating as songwriter with lyricist Bernie Taupin, both having answered advertisement for talent placed by Liberty Records. Although Liberty lost interest, pair were signed by music publisher Dick James. After two years of attempting to write MOR material for other artists, John and Taupin concentrated on songs suitable for John's own voice. First single, **Lady Samantha**, was released in 1969 by Phillips.

Although it failed to chart, single created enough interest to boost first album, **Empty Sky**. Produced by DJM staffer Steve Brown on four-track machine, this in turn furthered John's growing reputation. But real breakthrough came with **Elton John**, more elaborately produced by Gus Dudgeon and featuring sensitive **Your Song**. Released as single, this became smash in UK and US.

A few months later, **Tumbleweed Connection** was released to almost universal acclaim. Atmospheric, evocative, filled with images of old American West, album made UK Top 20 and was soon joined in chart by earlier **Elton John**.

In meantime, John had formed Elton John Band with bass player Dee Murray and drummer Nigel Olsson. Outfit played Troubadour Club in Los Angeles to ecstatic audiences in August 1970; around same time **Elton John** and **Tumbleweed Connection** made US charts, and Elton John had made first steps towards huge American success.

Live album **17-10-70,** and **Friends,** soundtrack for obscure movie, were next two issues, but **Madman Across The Water**, released in October 1971, was regarded as next 'official' release. Top 10 album on both sides of Atlantic, it initiated period lasting until 1976 during which artist could virtually do no wrong. John became one of world's most famous and highest-paid solo rock performers, breaking records for sales and live performance audiences. Singles and albums met with equal success. He established reputation for elaborate stage shows and over-the-top costumes, becoming in many ways the 'Liberace' of rock.

During 1973 John set up own record company Rocket Records (although artist himself did not start releasing product on label until 1976 when contract with DJM ran out) When Elton asked Lennon(▶) for permission to record 1974 cover hit **Lucy In The Sky With Diamonds.** Lennon agreed to appear on stage with Elton if it reached No. 1; when it did Lennon joined Elton in NYC concert—Lennon's last public performance.

In 1975 Elton participated in Ken Russell's movie 'Tommy' as Pinball Wizard and in 1976 topped UK singles chart for first time, via duet with Rocket artist Kiki Dee, **Don't Go Breaking My Heart.**

Elton reached a peak in mid '70s; in late '70s began to keep a lower profile. In 1977 after years of punishing schedules and massive stage shows, played series of concerts accompanied only by percussionist Ray Cooper, an exercise he repeated in 1979 for tour of USSR.

**Above: Elton autographing Don't Shoot Me, I'm Only The Piano Player, 1973.**

**Above right: Captain Fantastic, still on top in the '80s.**

**Below: Elton with lyricist Bernie Taupin in the late '60s.**

**Below: In the '70s, Elton became the 'Liberace of Rock'.**

**Inset Below: Goodbye Yellow Brick Road. Courtesy MCA Records.**

In 1978 partnership with Bernie Taupin terminated, and John began new collaboration with lyricist Gary Osborne. Although many critics predicted that departure of Taupin would have significant effect on John's career, in fact he continued to turn out hits, albeit less spectacularly.

1982 saw Top 20 album in UK and US with **Jump Up**, as well as a handful of hit singles and reunion with Taupin.

His earlier visit to Russia inspired 1985 hit single **Nikita** and his music continued to develop, so too did his bank balance, thoughts of which led to huge court case against the late Dick James which ended in split decision. This enabled John and Taupin to regain control of their songs and squeeze some extra money but did not produce the asked-for damages.

One of rock's more endearing personalities, 'Our Elt' is never far from the news, whether it be football (although he is now trying to sell his beloved Watford FC), his receding hairline, increased paunch, photo opportunities (recently with Lech Walesa during his tour of Poland or marriage (to Renata Blauel in 1984). Career threatening throat surgery in Australia at the beginning of 1987 has thankfully not proved a problem, and John looks set for a further decade of success.

**Hit Singles:**

| | US | UK |
|---|---|---|
| Your Song, 1970 | 8 | 7 |
| Rocket Man, 1972 | 6 | 2 |
| Honky Cat, 1972 | 8 | 31 |
| Crocodile Rock, 1972 | 1 | 5 |
| Daniel, 1973 | 2 | 4 |
| Saturday Night's Alright For Fighting, 1973 | 12 | 7 |
| Goodbye Yellow Brick Road, 1973 | 2 | 6 |
| Bennie And The Jets, 1974 | 1 | 37 |
| Don't Let The Sun Go Down On Me, 1974 | 2 | 16 |
| The Bitch Is Back, 1974 | 4 | 15 |
| Lucy In The Sky With Diamonds, 1974 | 1 | 10 |
| Philadelphia Freedom, 1975 | 1 | 12 |
| Someone Saved My Life Tonight, 1975 | 4 | 22 |
| Island Girl, 1975 | 1 | 14 |
| Grow Some Funk Of Your Own/ I Feel Like A Bullet (In The Gun of Robert Ford), 1976 | 14 | — |
| I Feel Like A Bullet (In The Gun Of Robert Ford)/Grow Some Funk Of Your Own, 1976 | 18 | — |
| Pinball Wizard, 1976 | — | 7 |
| Sorry Seems To Be The Hardest Word, 1976 | 6 | 11 |
| Part Time Love, 1978 | 22 | 15 |
| Song For Guy, 1978 | — | 4 |
| Mama Can't Buy You Love, 1979 | 9 | — |
| Little Jeannie, 1980 | 3 | 33 |
| Empty Garden, 1982 | 13 | 51 |
| Blue Eyes, 1982 | 12 | 8 |
| I Guess That's Why They Call It The Blues, 1983 | 4 | 5 |
| I'm Still Standing, 1983 | — | 12 |
| Kiss The Bride, 1983 | 25 | 20 |
| Sad Songs (Say So Much), 1984 | 5 | 7 |
| Passengers, 1984 | — | 5 |
| Who Wears These Shoes, 1984 | 16 | — |
| Nikita, 1985 | — | 3 |
| Wrap Her Up, 1985 | 19 | 23 |
| Candle In The Wind, 1988 | — | 5 |

*With Kiki Dee:*

| | US | UK |
|---|---|---|
| Don't Go Breaking My Heart, 1976 | 1 | 1 |

**Albums:**

Empty Sky (MCA/DJM), 1969 **CD**
Elton John (MCA/DJM), 1970 **CD**
Tumbleweed Connection (MCA/DJM), 1970 **CD**
17-11-70 (MCA/DJM), 1971
Madman Across The Water (MCA/DJM), 1971 **CD**
Honky Chateau (MCA/DJM), 1972 **CD**
Don't Shoot Me, I'm Only The Piano Player (MCA/DJM), 1973 **CD**
Goodbye Yellow Brick Road (MCA/DJM), 1973 **CD**
Caribou (MCA/DJM), 1974 **CD**
Captain Fantastic And The Brown Dirt Cowboy (MCA/DJM), 1974 **CD**

**Below: The Piano Man, always excellent live in the early '70s.**

**Inset Below: Jump Up, Elton John. Courtesy MCA Records.**

Rock Of The Westies (MCA/DJM), 1975 **CD**
Greatest Hits (MCA/DJM), 1977 **CD**
Here And There (MCA/DJM), 1976
Blue Moves (MCA/Rocket), 1976
Single Man (MCA/Rocket), 1978 **CD**
Greatest Hits Volume 2 (MCA/DJM), 1979 **CD**
Victim Of Love (Rocket), 1979
Live Collection (—/Pickwick), 1979
21 at 33 (Rocket), 1980 **CD**
The Very Best Of Elton John (—/K-Tel), 1980
The Fox (Geffen/Rocket), 1981 **CD**
Jump Up (Geffen/Rocket), 1982 **CD**
Love Songs (—/TV), 1982 **CD**
Too Low For Zero (MCA/Rocket), 1983 **CD**
Breaking Hearts (MCA/Rocket), 1984 **CD**
Ice On Fire (Rocket), 1985 **CD**
Lady Samantha (DJM) **CD**
Leather Jackets (Rocket), 1986 **CD**
Live In Australia (Rocket), 1987 **CD**
Superior (Rocket), 1983 **CD**
Superior Sound Of Elton John (DJM), 1984 **CD**

# Grace Jones

West Indian vocalist, composer.
Born Jamaica, May 17, 1952

**Career:** Epitomising new genre of assertive sexually dominant women, Grace Jones embodies the bi-sexual, unisex concept. She has been dubbed 'The Dietrich of the new decade'.

Raised in Syracuse, New York, from age 12. Studied acting before becoming model for prestigious Manhattan agency and appearing in movie 'Gordon's War'. Followed twin brother to Paris and became top model, appearing on covers of 'Vogue', 'Elle' and 'Der Stern'. Earned worldwide assignments before turning to singing with a French label.

Switching to Island Records Grace capitalised on disco boom. Became darling of New York's jet set and first artist to perform live at Studio 54.

Bizarre conceptual stage act, with under-

**The Inside Story, Grace Jones.
Courtesy Island Records.**

tones of sado-masochistic fantasy, master-minded by French artist Jean-Paul Goude, outrageous outfits (though best known for sleek men's trousers and suit jacket look) and decadent sensuality made her cult figure. Records became increasingly more commercially successful. Her recordings, which incorporate semi-reggae rhythms, feature vocals often half-spoken or whispered, are provocative. In UK her infamous appearance on Russell Harty's TV chat show, when she attacked her interviewer, brought her nation-wide notoriety.

Grace's masterly theatrics more than compensate for any limitations in her singing voice. Her somewhat menacing image earned her role in a James Bond movie.

**Hit Singles:**

| | US | UK |
|---|---|---|
| Private Life, 1980 | — | 17 |
| Slave To The Rhythm, 1985 | — | 12 |
| Pull Up To The Bumper, 1986 | — | 12 |
| Love Is The Drug, 1986 | — | 35 |

**Albums:**
Portfolio (Island), 1977

**Below: Few rock stars of the 1980s have matched Grace Jones visually.**

Fame (Island), 1978
Warm Leatherette (Island), 1980 **CD**
Nightclubbin (Island), 1981 **CD**
Living My Life (Island), 1982
Slave To The Rhythm (Island), 1985 **CD**
Island Life (Island), 1985 **CD**
The Inside Story (EMI) **CD**

# Howard Jones

UK vocalist
Born: Southampton, Feb 23, 1955

**Career:** Jones was 28 before signing first recording contract but in following year had five hit singles and topped UK charts with debut album **Human's Lib**.

Previously employed as fruit and veg salesman, Jones gigged around pubs in native High Wycombe, using borrowed synthesiser, before compensation money from wife's injuries in a car smash enabled him to invest in proper equipment and take up music full-time.

Jones' songs, danceable but not disco, thought-provoking but not pretentious, struck immediate chord.

His technical brilliance reflects his early background in classical music and continued success seems certain.

**Hit Singles:**

| | US | UK |
|---|---|---|
| New Song, 1983 | 27 | 3 |
| What Is Love, 1983 | 33 | 2 |
| Hide And Seek, 1984 | — | 12 |
| Pearl In Shell, 1984 | — | 7 |
| Like To Get To Know You Well, 1984 | — | 4 |
| Things Can Only Get Better, 1985 | 5 | 6 |
| Look Mama, 1985 | — | 10 |
| Life In One Day, 1985 | 19 | 14 |
| All I Want, 1986 | — | 35 |
| No One Is To Blame, 1986 | — | 16 |
| You Know I Love You, 1987 | 8 | — |

**Albums:**
Human's Lib (WEA), 1984 **CD**
The 12'' Album (WEA), 1984
Dream Into Action (WEA), 1985 **CD**
One To One (WEA), 1986 **CD**

**Above: Southampton-born Howard Jones, who came to prominence with excellent 1983 hits New Song and What Is Love.**

# Quincy Jones

US conductor, composer, arranger, producer.
Born Chicago, 1934.

**Career:** When Ray Charles(▶) moved to Seattle in 1948 at age 16 he was befriended by local resident Quincy Jones. Jones was destined to play major role in the emergent soul star's future career but their paths diverged for a while as Jones chose to enrol in Berkley School of Music in Boston rather than go out with Charles on black club touring circuit.

Regular visits to New York furthered Jones' enthusiasm for jazz. Before graduation he landed job as trumpeter with the Lionel Hampton Big Band, which took him around world. Following visit to France he decided to settle in Paris to further his studies in writing and arranging, working under teacher Nadia Boulanger, who also counted classical genius Stravinsky among her pupils.

Jones worked for Discques Barclay and won numerous European awards for work as composer, arranger and conductor during six-year sojourn in Paris. Attempts to run 18-piece big band, however, brought him close to bankruptcy in 1961. On his return to US, Mercury Records employed him as musical director, and he became first black to hold job as Mercury's vice president in charge of A&R.

Lesley Gore's **It's My Party** in May 1963 gave Jones his first pop chart-topper as producer; his own album **Big Band Bossa Nova** charted at same time. Further success at Mercury came with productions for Brook Benton, Billy Eckstine, Sarah Vaughan and others, as well as run of own albums. Jones also undertook freelance work for Frank Sinatra(▶), Johnny Mathis(▶), Tony Bennett and Ray Charles (including his **Genius + Soul = Jazz** album, an R&B masterpiece).

The mid-'60s found Jones branching successfully into sphere of movie score writing, which was to take up most of his time for some seven years. Starting with music for 'The Pawnbroker' work included 'Bob And Carol And Ted And Alice', 'The Anderson Tapes', 'Cactus Flower', 'In The Heat Of The Night' (a particularly inventive effort which featured elements of country, pop, soul, jazz and electronic free-form, again working with Ray Charles), 'They Call Me Mr Tibbs', 'Mirage', 'Walk, Don't Run', 'Dollars' and 'The New Centurions'. Also scored TV series 'Ironside', 'I Spy' and, more recently 'Roots' (1977).

Moving back into popular music mainstream in 1969, Jones signed recording deal with A&M and began series of jazz-funk albums. Charted for first time since 1962 with **Walking In Space** LP, which won Grammy Award.

In early '70s, Jones was largely responsible for creating jazz-funk explosion, producing artists like fellow A&M act The Brothers Johnson and Chaka Khan-led Rufus. He also started association with Michael Jackson, masterminding **Off The Wall** at that time soul's biggest-selling album ever.

As mentor/producer/adviser, Jones also nurtured careers of, amongst others, songwriter Rod Temperton (former Heatwave keyboard player) and vocalists Patti Austin, James Ingram, Jim Gilstrap, Al Jarreau and Leon Ware.

But it is in the eighties that Jones has really come to the fore, most particularly as producer of Michael Jackson's **Thriller**, biggest seller of all time, and follow-up **Bad**. Reputation as rock and soul's premier backroom boy was also consolidated by production and organisational duties for megastar African aid single **We Are The World** in 1985.

| Hit Singles: | US | UK |
| --- | --- | --- |
| Ai No Corrida, 1981 | — | 14 |
| Razzamatazz, 1981 | — | 11 |
| Just Once (featuring James Ingram), 1981 | 17 | — |
| One Hundred Ways (featuring James Ingram), 1981 | 14 | — |

**Albums (selected):**
Smackwater Jack (A&M), 1974
Mellow Madness (A&M), 1975
I Heard That! (A&M), 1976
Quintessential Charts (Impulse/—), 1976
Sounds. . . And Stuff Like That (A&M), 1978
Body Heat (A&M), 1979
Great Wide World Of (Emarcy USA), 1981 **CD**
The Dude (A&M), 1981 **CD**
The Best (A&M), 1982 **CD**
Birth Of A Band (Emercy), 1984 **CD**
The Quintessence (MCA), 1985 **CD**

# Janis Joplin

US vocalist.
Born Port Arthur, Texas, January 19, 1943; died Los Angeles, October 4, 1970.

**Career:** An early fan of old Bessie Smith and Leadbelly blues records, Joplin started out in early '60s singing country and blues with bluegrass band in Texas. In 1966 she settled in hippy mecca of San Francisco and became lead vocalist of Big Brother and the Holding Company which featured James Gurley, guitar; Sam Andrew, guitar; Pete Albin, bass; and David Getz, drums.

Raucous, ill-disciplined, and, in some areas, musically inept, band nonetheless had rare brand of raw energy which showcased Janis to good effect, especially on her classic reading of Erma Franklin's soul opus **Piece Of My Heart**. This set, from the 1968 Columbia album **Cheap Thrills**, confirmed the promise shown on the band's earlier LP for Mainstream

(which Columbia re-released in 1970). **Cheap Thrills** sold more than a million copies and the management talents of Albert Grossman (man behind Dylan(▶) and others) made them Stateside superstars, though neither band nor Janis ever made it big in UK.

Janis Joplin's stature rapidly outgrew that of Big Brother (but band carried on for several years, Nick 'The Greek' Gravenites joining as vocalist in 1972) and in 1969 she went solo, earning immediate plaudits for **I Got Dem Ol' Kozmic Blues Again** set.

Her career was meteoric in its rapid rise, heights of adulation, and tragic fall. Seemingly trying to live up to her image, she became increasingly outrageous, drinking heavily, indulging in drug abuse and, in March 1970, being fined for using profane language on-stage. Seven months later she was found dead in a Hollywood hotel room of a heroine overdose. The album she had been working on with new backing outfit, the Full Tilt Boogie Band (comprising Richard Bell, piano; Ken Pearson, organ; John Till, guitar; Brad Campbell, bass; and Clark Pierson, drums), was issued under title **Pearl** (Janis' nickname) and included her memorable interpretation of Kris Kristofferson's(▶) **Me And Bobby McGee** which featured her vocals at their most spine-tinglingly soulful, and became posthumous US No. 1.

The 11-track album included two tracks for which she had not yet recorded vocals. Nick Gravenites was invited to sing them but declined so they appeared as instrumentals.

On her death, an immediate legend was created. A documentary titled 'Janis' was released in 1974, along with double-album soundtrack and biographies 'Buried Alive' by Myra Friedman and 'Going Down With Janis' by Peggy Caserta were widely read. Her tumultuous career and lonely private life were the inspiration for the film, 'The Rose', starring Bette Midler(▶) as Joplin. Both a product and a victim of the drug culture, Janis remains female personification of psychedelic/acid rock/hippie era.

| Hit Singles: | US | UK |
| --- | --- | --- |
| *With Big Brother And The Holding Company:* | | |
| Piece Of My Heart, 1968 | 12 | — |

**Above: Always a loner, Janis Joplin was on the verge of huge stardom when she tragically overdosed in 1970.**

| *Solo* | | |
| --- | --- | --- |
| Me And Bobby McGee, 1971 | 1 | — |

**Albums:**
Cheap Thrills (originally released as by Big Brother And The Holding Company) (Columbia/CBS), 1968
I Got Dem Ol' Kozmic Blues Again (Columbia/CBS), 1969
Pearl (Columbia/CBS), 1971 **CD**
In Concert (Columbia/CBS), 1972
Janis (Columbia/CBS), 1974
Anthology (Columbia/CBS), 1982
Farewell Song (Columbia/CBS), 1982
Janis Joplin In Concert (CBS), 1987

# Journey

US group formed 1973.

**Original line-up:** Gregg Rolie, vocals, keyboards, guitar; Neal Schon, guitar; George Tickner, guitar; Ross Valory, bass; Aynsley Dunbar, drums.

**Career:** Rolie and Schon were together in Santana(▶) when jazz influence created musical conflict of interest. They ran across Walter 'Herbie' Herbert who was attempting to assemble supergroup to play San Francisco area. Valory had played with Steve Miller(▶), and Dunbar with nearly every rock band with a drum kit — John Mayall(▶), Jeff Beck(▶), Zappa(▶) among others. Tickner was excellent session man.

For first gig, Journey played San Francisco's Winterland on last day of 1973. Interest from Columbia Records followed extensive touring, and first LP **Journey** appeared in spring 1975. Lack of response was discouraging and Tickner and Valory left band. Valory soon returned, however, and band continued year-round touring.

Next two albums (**Look Into The Future** and **Next**) were released in '75 and '76 with little notice. Manager Herbert suggested addition of lead vocalist Steve Perry, leaving

Rolie free to fill out band's sound. **Infinity** can be considered Journey's first real album with powerful vocals and synthesised riffs. Perry's contribution also earned band US Top 20 hit, **Lovin' Touchin' Squeezin'**.

Live shows shifted from interminable solos to tight format. Such restraint never fitted Dunbar's style and he quit. Steve Smith (who had played with Ronnie Montrose(▶) who opened **Infinity** tour) took Dunbar's place. Subsequent albums increased band's popularity, although not with critics, who still dismiss Journey as 'commercial product'.

Renewed interest in band's history resulted in compilation LP, **In The Beginning. Captured** is strong live set and **Escape** introduced keyboard player Johnathan Cain. He is also songwriter, and co-wrote hit single **Who's Crying Now**.

**Escape** eventually achieved multiplatinum status, setting pattern for all subsequent releases. In course of odyssey from guitar hard-rock to melodic AOR, Journey lost respect of many critics. However, American public has grasped band to its heart and put it up amongst megastars. Rest of world has not as yet been quite so impressed, but may yet succumb.

**Current line-up:** Schon; Valory; Steve Perry, vocals; Steve Smith, drums; Johnathan Cain, keyboards.

| Hit Singles: | US | UK |
| --- | --- | --- |
| Lovin' Touchin' Squeezin', 1979 | 16 | — |
| Who's Crying Now, 1981 | 4 | — |
| Don't Stop Believin', 1981 | 9 | — |
| Open Arms, 1982 | 2 | — |
| Still They ride, 1982 | 14 | — |
| Separate Ways (Worlds Apart), 1983 | 8 | — |
| Faithfully, 1983 | 12 | — |
| Only The Young, 1985 | 9 | — |
| I'll Be Alright Without You, 1987 | 11 | — |
| Girl Can't Help It | 11 | — |
| *Steve Perry with Kenny Loggins:* | | |
| Don't Fight It, 1982 | 17 | — |
| *Steve Perry Solo:* | | |
| Oh Sherrie, 1984 | 3 | — |
| Foolish Heart, 1985 | 18 | — |

**Albums:**
Journey (Columbia/CBS), 1975
Look Into The Future (Columbia/CBS), 1975

**Below: Lead singer Perry also writes for Journey.**

Next (Columbia/CBS), 1976
Infinity (Columbia/CBS), 1978
Evolution (CBS), 1979 **CD**
In The Beginning (Columbia/CBS), 1979
Departure (Columbia/CBS), 1980
Captured (CBS), 1980 **CD**
Escape (CBS), 1981 **CD**
Frontiers (Columbia/CBS), 1983
Raised On Radio (CBS), 1986 **CD**

*Steve Perry Solo:*
Street Talk (CBS), 1984

# Joy Division/ New Order

US group formed 1977.
**Original line-up:** Ian Curtis, vocals; Bernard Albrecht (né Dicken), guitar; Stephen Morris, drums; Peter Hook, bass.

**Career:** In 1977 Curtis, Albrecht, Morris came together and called themselves Warsaw. Early career consisted of nondescript playing throughout Manchester. They changed name to Joy Division, though there was never anything joyful about their sound, Curtis' flat voice being backed by depressing dirge-like instrumentals. Indications of things to come appear on live 10-inch compilation album **Short Circuit**. (**At A Later Date** is track by band while still Warsaw.)

Joy Division released four-track EP **An Ideal For Living** on own label Enigma. (Also released as 12-inch with vast improvement in sound quality on Anonymous Records.) Bands real potential for stark, sheer realism appeared first on new Factory label. **A Factory Sample** was EP to show off label's new talent. Two Joy Division tracks **Glass** and **Digital** were EP's high point.

National interest stirred by Martin Hannett-produced **Unknown Pleasures**, a bleak, troublesome, yet powerful debut album. Two out-takes given to Fast Records (Edinburgh) were released on **Earcom Two** compilation. Another two, **Atmosphere** and **DeadSouls**, appeared in 1,000 copy edition on small French Sordid Sentimentale label.

Joy Division's 1979 UK tour with Buzzcocks earned ecstatic response from critics and audience alike but the suicide of Curtis (in May 1980) curtailed planned US tour. Single **Love Will Tear Us Apart** and second album appeared after his death. Another out-take, **Komankino/Incubation**, appeared for awhile as free flexi-disc from Factory. Excellent **Still** release (1981) included live/studio material, covering the band's entire career.

Joy Division had agreed to 'kill' the name should any member leave the group, and remaining line-up thus became New Order.

By 1982 ethos of band had begun to change, with more dance-orientated sound coming to fore. New appeal was reflected in success of biggest single to date, top thirty entry **Temptation**. Further commercial progress was made in 1983 when band scored with **Blue Monday**, single which went on to sell more than a million worldwide.

Latterly New Order has built sizeable following while maintaining relatively low profile. Occasional chart entries and continuing super-cult status will doubtless keep band in business for some time to come.

**Current line-up (New Order):** Albrecht; Morris; Hook.

**Hit Singles:** | | US | UK
---|---|---|---
Love Will Tear Us Apart, 1980 | | — | 13

*New Order* | |
---|---|---
Blue Monday, 1983 | — | 9
Confusion, 1983 | — | 12
Thieves Like Us, 1984 | — | 18

**Albums:**
Unknown Pleasures (—/Factory), 1979
Closer (—/Factory), 1980
Still (—/Factory), 1981

*New Order*
Movement (Factory), 1981 **CD**
Power, Corruption & Lies (Factory), 1983 **CD**
Low Life (Factory), 1985 **CD**
Brotherhood (Factory), 1986 **CD**
Substance (Factory), 1987 **CD**

*Worth Searching Out:*
An Ideal For Living (12-inch EP) (Anonymous), 1977
The Ideal Beginning (EP, released 1981, as Warsaw (Enigma)

# Judas Priest

UK group formed 1973.
**Original line-up:** Rob Halford, vocals; Ken 'KK' Downing, Gibson Flying 'V' guitar; Ian Hill, bass; John Hinch, drums.

**Career:** One of Birmingham's local bands, Judas Priest always had extra spark setting them apart from usual heavy-rock treadmill. First album wears quickly but gained enough attention at the time to put group on first rung of ladder.

Initial change in drummers came as Alan Moore replaced Hinch; this line-up released second LP which got UK support but left band unknown in US. Simon Phillips played drums on band's debut CBS album **Sin After Sin**. Band spent 1978 in frenzied counter-attack on growing influence of new wave. **Stained Glass**, then **Killing Machine**, sounded the bombardment (Les Binks was now on drums).

Critics tended to dismiss band as outdated, but younger audience began picking up on TNWOBHM (The New Wave Of British Heavy Metal). This became apparent with single success of **Take On The World** in January 1979. Live recording from Japanese tour, **Unleashed In The East**, was 1979 LP and indicated band was rethinking direction. **British Steel** proved this to be true by providing balance of melody and vocal ballistics (with yet another new drummer, Dave Holland). Critics realised band was for real and sales finally improved in US. Appropriately titled album **Screaming For Vengeance** dispelled any doubt regarding band's commitment to heavy metal. It also became band's first platinum success in US which led to release of **Rocka Rolla**, nine years after UK release.

In May 1988 Judas Priest released their 11th studio album **Ram It Down** recorded at Puk Studios in Denmark, marking a determined effort to return to roots metal. A new version of Chuck Berry's 'Johnny B.Goode' was also released on Atlantic as part of a soundtrack for the movie of the same name.

1988 saw band cause a stir by recording Stock, Aitken and Waterman songs at a session in Paris, but Halford explained it was done as an experiment, "to see what would happen". But none of the songs made it on the album.

Aware of the need to experiment and to challenge audience, Judas Priest have proven long-lasting talent and have so far avoided becoming caricatures of themselves. Like Motorhead(▶) and Iron Maiden(▶), Judas Priest make narrow-minded heavy-metal category pointless.

**Current line-up:** Halford; Downing; Hill; Glen Tipton, Gibson SG guitar; Dave Holland, drums.

**Hit Singles:** | US | UK
---|---|---
Take On The World, 1979 | — | 14
Living After Midnight, 1980 | — | 12
Breaking The Law, 1980 | — | 12

**Albums:**
Rocka Rolla (—/Gull), 1974
Sad Wings Of Destiny (Janus/Gull), 1976 **CD**
Sin After Sin (Columbia/CBS), 1977
Best Of (Gull), 1978 **CD**
Stained Glass (Columbia/CBS), 1978
Killing Machine (Columbia/CBS), 1978
Unleashed In The East (Columbia/CBS), 1978
Hell Bent For Leather* (Columbia/—), 1979
British Steel (Columbia/CBS), 1980
Point Of Entry (Columbia/CBS), 1981
Screaming For Vengeance (Columbia/CBS), 1982
Defenders Of The Faith (CBS), 1984 **CD**
Hero Hero Line (W. Germany) **CD**
Turbo (CBS), 1986 **CD**
Priest Live (CBS), 1987 **CD**

*US version of **Killing Machine** with extra track

**Above: Nik Kershaw, multi-talented pop musician, who has appeared regularly in UK pop charts since 1984.**

# Nik Kershaw

UK vocalist, keyboards, composer.
Born Bristol, March 1, 1958.

**Career:** Nik Kershaw rose to quick stardom as 'pretty boy' pop singer but talents run deeper—he writes all his songs and plays most of the music on his records.

Son of a flautist and mother who runs a local choir in Ipswich, Suffolk, Kershaw did not become interested in music until a friend bought a guitar. After passing seven O levels, Kershaw decided to concentrate efforts on Half Pint Hog, a band formed with school friends. It quickly broke up and he spent three dispiriting years working at Department of Employment in home town before accepting job as guitarist with jazz-funk group Fusion.

When Fusion folded at beginning of 1982, Kershaw decided to concentrate on songwriting and learning other instruments. After six months, he felt he had sufficient material for record deal but met run of rejections before advertising in Melody Maker for a manager and linking with Mickey Modern who landed him deal with MCA.

Teamed with top producer Peter Collins, Kershaw put together debut album **Human Racing** which was previewed by his singles **I Won't Let The Sun Go Down On Me** and **Wouldn't It Be Good**. A well-received national tour followed using four-piece band comprising Keith Airey, guitar and keyboards; Tim Moore, keyboards; Dennis Smith, bass and Mark Price, a session drummer whose previous claim to fame was as the lad in the original Hovis bread TV commercial.

**Hit Singles:** | US | UK
---|---|---
Wouldn't It Be Good, 1984 | — | 4
Dancing Girls, 1984 | — | 13
I Won't Let The Sun Go Down On Me, 1984 | — | 2

**Sin After Sin, Judas Priest. Courtesy Columbia Records.**

| Human Racing, 1984 | — | 19 |
|---|---|---|
| The Riddle, 1985 | — | 3 |
| Wide Boy, 1985 | — | 9 |
| Don Quixote, 1985 | — | 10 |

**Albums:**
Human Racing (MCA), 1984 **CD**
The Riddle (MCA), 1984 **CD**
Radio Musicola (MCA), 1986 **CD**

# Chaka Khan

US vocalist.
Born Chicago, March 23, 1953.

**Career:** Consistently successful in field of black music, notably with 1978 mega-hits **I'm Every Woman** and **We Got The Love** (the latter a duet with guitarist/singer George Benson), Chaka Khan started out fronting multi-racial band which played mixture of soul, rock and pop.

Under name Rufus, band won major recording deal and made heavy impact as much for electric stage presence as for atmospherically classy, funk-slanted records like **Tell Me Something Good, You Got The Love** and **Once You Get Started**, which kept them in the US charts from 1972-7.

With her often bizarre stage outfits, belting vocals and stage charisma, the petite and curvaceous Chaka became focal point of Rufus and in 1978 group's then label, Warner Bros, offered her solo deal under production aegis of talented Turkish emigré Arif Mardin.

A succession of acclaimed albums and singles, and her participation in Lenny White's ambitious 1982 project **Echoes Of An Era** which recreated '50s jazz classics using contemporary artists, has kept Khan in musical forefront. She has also worked with Rick Wakeman, Ry Cooder and jazz legend Dizzy Gillespie on different projects, while her 1983 world tour took her to Carnegie Hall and similar prestigious venues. Her 1984 No.1 hit **I Feel For You** written by Prince, confirmed her as one of black dance music's leading figures.

**Hit Singles:** US UK

*With Rufus:*

| | US | UK |
|---|---|---|
| Tell Me Something Good, 1974 | 3 | — |
| You Got The Love, 1974 | 11 | — |
| Once You Get Started, 1975 | 10 | — |
| Sweet Thing, 1976 | 5 | — |

*Solo:*

| | | |
|---|---|---|
| I'm Every Woman, 1978 | 21 | 11 |
| I Feel For You, 1984 | 3 | 1 |
| This Is My Night, 1985 | — | 14 |
| Eye To Eye, 1985 | — | 16 |

**Albums (selected):**
*With Rufus:*
Rags To Rufus (MCA), 1974
Rufus Featuring Chaka Khan (MCA), 1975
*Solo:*
Chaka (Warner Bros), 1979
Naughty (Warner Bros), 1980
Whatcha' Gonna Do For Me (Warner Bros), 1981
Chaka Khan (Warner Bros/—), 1982
I Feel For You (Warner Bros), 1984

# Kid Creole And The Coconuts

US group formed 1979.

**Original line-up:** August Darnell, vocals; 'Sugar-coated' Andy Hernandez, aka Coati Mundi, percussion, vibraphone; Adriana Kaegi, Brooksie Wells, Lourdes Cotto, Fonda Rae, backing vocals.

**Career:** Band is brainchild of vocalist/guitarist/composer August Darnell, aka Kid Creole. Haitian-born, New York raised, Darnell first came to prominence with seminal mid-'70s disco outfit Dr Buzzard's Original Savannah Band, which cut pair of albums for RCA and one for Elektra.

Following collapse of Savannah Band amid litigation, Darnell and ex-Savannah Andy Hernandez recruited three female vocalists (including wife Adriana) to form Coconuts. Concept of outfit was fashionable version of pre-war tropical night-life — Darnell has said that his vision is based on night-club scenes in 'King Kong'.

Signed to hip East Coast label Ze, outfit released **Off The Coast Of Me** in 1980 to considerable critical enthusiasm but little public reaction. Album yielded minor hit in **Maladie D'Amour**. But it was not until release of 1982 album **Tropical Gangsters** that Creole and Coconuts started to gain commercial success, and then largely in UK.

Very much a personal creation of Darnell, he fronts stage full of props in '40s suits as playboy to three ladies, Creole and Coconuts offer originality, imagination and whimsical fantasy, all qualities which are not over-abundant on pop and rock scene. Nevertheless, Latin-based music has never enjoyed extended commercial success, and it remains to be seen whether outfit can sustain commercial appeal.

**Current line-up:** Darnell; Hernandez; Kaegi; Cheryl Poirier and Taryn Haegy, backing vocals.

**Hit Singles:**

| | US | UK |
|---|---|---|
| I'm A Wonderful Thing Baby, 1982 | — | 4 |
| Stool Pigeon, 1982 | — | 7 |
| Annie, I'm Not Your Daddy, 1982 | — | 2 |

**Albums:**
Off The Coast Of Me (Ze), 1980
Fresh Fruit In Foreign Places (Ze), 1981
Tropical Gangsters (Ze), 1982
Doppelganger (Ze), 1983
The Best Of (Island), 1984
In Praise Of Older Women/Other Crimes (Sire), 1985

**Tropical Gangsters, Kid Creole & the Coconuts. Courtesy Island Records.**

# B. B. King

US vocalist, guitarist, composer.
Born Itta Bena, Indianola, Mississippi, September 16, 1925.

**Career:** Truly living up to his name, Riley B. 'Blues Boy' King has majestically dominated the blues scene for more than 30 years, gigging an average of 300 days a year and spending most of the other 65 in the recording studio. Astute management and an ear for the modern has maintained enthusiastic concert crowds and undiminished reverence.

King has matched talents with finest of musicians, from black American greats the Crusaders(▶) to rock stars like Leon Russell(▶), Carole King(▶), Ringo Starr(▶) and Nicky Hopkins. He has recorded hits in a hotel room, in a garage, and in the world's foremost studios. His material has ranged from pure blues (both urban and rural), to country songs (his cousin is country blues legend Bukka White) rock numbers, pop songs and even Broadway material, though in every case transferred to the blues idiom.

His emergent style was heavily influenced by both T. Bone Walker and the jazz of Charlie Christian. Joining Radio WGRM in Greenwood, Mississippi, in late '50s, he was spotted by Sonny Boy Williamson (Rice Miller) who took him to the far more important Memphis station WDIA. King became resident DJ and was dubbed 'The Beale Street Blues Boy', later shortened to 'B.B.', by station manager Don Kearn.

King's recording debut came with **Miss Martha King** (1949). Then talent scout Ike Turner(▶) signed him to Modern Records' RPM subsidiary where he enjoyed 11-year stint, soaring to No. 1 on R&B charts in 1950 with **Three O'Clock Blues** which featured Turner on piano, Hank Crawford on saxophone and Willie Mitchell on trumpet.

Quickly becoming most in-demand artist on blues circuit, King quit WDIA. (His show was taken over by Rufus Thomas who went on to fame as a soul singer.)

King's flashy guitar lines with their torrent of notes were matched to the response of his highly emotive vocals, a mix of falsetto wailing and rich gospel-flavoured tenor. Despite a couple of quirks (he can neither play particularly good rhythm nor sing while playing) King has clearly been maestro of his chosen music, influencing countless other players, notably Buddy Guy, Otis Rush and Eric Clapton(▶).

In 1961 he switched to major ABC

**Below: The great B. B. King, pictured onstage in London during 1982 with his 'honey', Lucille.**

**Left: Chaka Khan, a 1980s black superstar in America.**

93

Paramount label who sought to broaden his appeal with a more sophisticated flavour.

Commanding an increasingly broad-based audience through '70s, his concerts drawing both white and black, young and old, King's recorded output became somewhat inconsistent. Often ill-matched with material and musicians as he tried to please wider following by diversity of music, at times he seemed in danger of sinking into MOR mire. Duets with Bobby Bland(▶) — an old friend adding a more sophisticated flavour to his music through lush arrangements by Johnny Pate (the Impressions(▶) producer) and Quincy Jones(▶) (who was concurrently working with Charles), and even adding string sections on several recordings.

In 1969, strings were used in stunning fashion for epic smash **The Thrill Is Gone**, and the **Completely Well** album, which included single, was arguably his best ever.

**Live At The Regal, Courtesy ABC Records.**

In 1985, he figured heavily on soundtrack of movie **Into The Night** and celebrated 50th album (there have actually been many more if compilations and re-workings of old material are included).

King's continually majestic stage performances now tend to surpass his recorded work and he remains king among the blues' Kings (neither Albert King nor the late Freddie King managed to reach his heights despite their undoubted class). In 1987, King was deservedly awarded a Lifetime Grammy for achievements in music.
Guitar: Gibson 335.

| Hit Singles: | US | UK |
|---|---|---|
| The Thrill Is Gone, 1970 | 15 | — |

**Albums (selected):**
Live At The Regale (MCA/HMV), 1965
His Best: The Electric B. B. King (MCA/ABC), 1969
Live And Well (MCA/ABC), 1970
Completely Well (MCA/ABC), 1970
Live At Cook County Jail (MCA/Probe), 1971
Back In The Alley (MCA/ABC), 1973
The Best Of B. B. King (—/Ace Cadet), 1981
Love Me Tender (MCA), 1982
Alive In London (with the Crusaders) (MCA), 1982
Midnight Believer (MCA), 1984

*With Pat Metheney, Dave Brubeck, Heath Bros:*
Live 1987 Kingdom Jazz **CD**
Spotlight On Lucille (Ace), 1986 **CD**
The Best Of BB King (MCA), 1987 **CD**
Completely Well (MCA), 1987 — Listed **CD**
One Nighter Blues (Ace), 1987
Rarest BB King (Blues Boy), 1987
Across The Tracks (Ace), 1987

*With Bobby Bland:*
Together For The First Time (MCA), 1974
Together Again (MCA), 1976

*Worth Searching Out:*
Indianola Mississippi (MCA/ABC), 1970

# Carole King

US composer, vocalist, pianist.
Born Carole Klein, Brooklyn, New York, February 9, 1942.

**Career:** Played piano from age four; smitten by rock 'n' roll in early teens, started hanging out at rock 'n' roll shows. Formed own group in high school. After school, attended Queen's College, where she met aspirant songwriter (later her husband) Gerry Goffin. Personal and musical collaboration followed, resulting in first hit **Will You Still Love Me Tomorrow**; recorded by Shirelles, song made No. 1 in US and No. 3 in UK.

Goffin and King then became part of 'Brill Building' stable of writers under aegis of entrepreneur/publisher Don Kirshner. During this period pair wrote seemingly endless series of classic hits, including **Up On The Roof** and **When My Little Girl Is Smiling** for Drifters(▶), **Take Good Care Of My Baby** for Bobby Vee(▶), **One Fine Day** for Chiffons (▶), **Halfway To Paradise** for Tony Orlando and Billy Fury(▶), **Every Breath I Take** for Gene Pitney(▶) and **The Locomotion** for little Eva (actually pair's babysitter, Eva Boyd).

Don Kirshner launched King as solo recording artist in 1962 with **It Might As Well Rain Until September**. Despite this international hit, follow-ups were not successful and King was not to make serious attempt to become artist as well as writer until end of decade. Having moved to West Coast, in 1970 King recorded first solo album, **Writer**.

Although not huge success, it paved way for next offering, **Tapestry**, which was to become one of most successful albums ever. Released in 1971, **Tapestry** stuck chord with post-psychedelic generation with its emphasis on simple life and values. Spawning clutch of hit singles, it went on to sell somewhere around 13 million units over course of next decade.

After **Tapestry**, King never quite achieved same heights. Despite recording and working live with varying success, she only had two further major hits as artist (**Jazzman** in 1974, **Nightingale** in 1975). However, **Tapestry** and equally valid body of work from early '60s ensure continued veneration among fans of good pop songs. Not one of the great singers, King is nevertheless convincing interpreter of self-penned material.

| Hit Singles: | US | UK |
|---|---|---|
| It Might As Well Rain Until September, 1962 | 22 | 3 |
| It's Too Late, 1971 | 1 | 6 |
| So Far Away, 1971 | 14 | — |
| Sweet Seasons, 1972 | 9 | — |
| Jazzman, 1974 | 2 | — |
| Nightingale, 1975 | 9 | — |

**Below. Carole King exchanged a career as a top notch songwriter for equal fame.**

| One Fine Day, 1980 | 12 | — |

**Albums:**
Writer (Ode), 1970
Tapestry (Ode), 1972
Music (Ode), 1972
Rhymes And Reasons (Ode), 1972
Fantasy (Ode), 1973
Wrap Around Joy (Ode), 1974
Thoroughbred (Ode), 1976
Simple Things (Capitol), 1977
Welcome Home (Capitol), 1978
Greatest Hits (Ode), 1978
Touch The Sky (Capitol), 1979
Pearls — Songs Of Goffin & King (Capitol), 1980
One To One (Atlantic), 1982
Speeding Time (Atlantic), 1983

# King Crimson

UK group formed 1969.

**Original line-up:** Robert Fripp, guitar, mellotron; Ian McDonald, reeds, keyboards; Greg Lake, bass, vocals; Peter Sinfield, lyricist; Mike Giles, drums.

**Career:** Evolved from Giles, Giles And Fripp, a pop-influenced trio from Dorset that recorded two singles and one barely noticed album, **The Cheerful Insanity Of Giles Giles And Fripp**. Group split in November 1968, Peter Giles temporarily quitting business; brother Mike and Fripp founded King Crimson. With new members McDonald and Lake (aided by lyricist Sinfield) rehearsals were completed below cafe in London's Fulham Road. Debut gig at Speakeasy (April 1969) established small cult following, dramatically increased following appearance at Rolling Stones'(▶) celebrated Hyde Park concert in July. First album **In The Court Of The Crimson King** received ecstatic response and established unit as one of most progressive of era. From this point on, group were dogged by series of personnel changes/upheavals.

An 11-day US tour in November/December 1969 took its toll; on return to London both Giles and McDonald quit. While seeking permanent line-up, Fripp employed a number of session men/friends to complete second LP **In The Wake Of Poseidon**. Giles returned as bassist, jazzer Keith Tippett played piano, Mel Collins added saxophone and Gordon Haskell contributed vocals. Sinfield was by this time credited as lyricist, light show operator and synthesiser player. Prior to album's release Fripp had declined invitations to join Yes(▶) and Aynsley Dunbar's Blue Whale. Lukewarm response afforded **Poseidon** meant that only Collins and Haskell were retained for third album, aided by drummer Andy McCullough. **Lizard** was noticeable improvement on predecessor, but following recording sessions Haskell and McCullough quit.

Fripp and Sinfield again restructured group, with Mel Collins, Ian Wallace (drums) and Boz Burrell, a singer whom Fripp taught to play bass. Following release of **Islands**, Sinfield left to reappear as Roxy Music's(▶) producer. Less than successful US tour killed off remaining members, leaving live **Earthbound** as final comment.

The ever-eccentric Fripp returned to England and, following period of hibernation, introduced another unit, comprising Bill Bruford (former Yes drummer), bassist John Wetton (ex-Family(▶)), percussionist James Muir and David Cross (violin/mellotron). The power and promise of line-up was fully revealed on excellent **Lark's Tongue In Aspic** and vindicated in concert performances. Unfortunately, Muir quit, leaving four-piece Crimson to record acceptable **Starless And Bible Black**.

In July 1974, Crimson closed tour with concert at NY's Central Park, captured for posterity on second live album, **USA**. In September, Fripp officially announced that Crimson no longer existed. A posthumous album, **Red**, was released in 1974 and saw return of original member Ian McDonald.

Few would disagree that Crimson split at the right time; they would have been in danger of losing credibility had they continued. Unlike their contemporaries, group managed to avoid worst excesses of self-indulgent '70s art rock. Their reputation as one of truly innovative progressive rock groups was aided by Fripp's forays into avant garde and ambient music. Between 1974-80, Fripp worked with number of artists, most notably Eno(▶) (collaborated on **No Pussyfooting** and **Evening Star**). Work with Peter Gabriel(▶) and David Bowie(▶) also attracted great interest, leading to new-found respect from previous detractors.

In 1981, Fripp took unusual step of re-forming King Crimson with Adrian Belew (guitar/lead vocal), Robert Fripp (guitar/devices!), Tony Levin (bass/vocals) and Bill Bruford (drums). Album **Discipline** was released in September 1981 amid critical arguments about whether Crimson were an anachronism, a seminal progressive rock band, or both. **Beat**, released following year, was first Crimson studio album to have same personnel on two consecutive releases. Since then, group have laid any misconceptions about a possible 'cash in' on the King Crimson name.

Fripp further developed outside ventures with self-produced albums including **I Advanced Masked** with Andy Summers and production work with Daryl Hall project **Sacred Songs** and two LPs for US band the Roches.

**Current line-up:** Fripp, guitar, keyboards; Bill Bruford, drums; Adrian Belew, guitar; Tony Levin, bass.

**Albums:**
In The Court Of The Crimson King (Island), 1969
In The Wake Of Poseidon (Island), 1970
Lizard (Island), 1970
Islands (Island), 1971
Earthbound (Island), 1972
Lark's Tongue In Aspic (Island), 1973
Starless And Bible Black (Island), 1974
Red (Island), 1974
USA (Island), 1975
A Young Person's Guide To King Crimson (Island), 1976
Discipline (EG/Polydor), 1981
Beat (EG/Polydor), 1982
Three Of A Perfect Pair (Polydor), 1984
The Compact King Crimson (EG), 1986 **CD**

*Robert Fripp with Andy Summers:*
I Advance Masked (A&M), 1982
Bewitched (A&M), 1984

# The Kinks

UK group formed 1964.

**Original line-up:** Ray Davies, vocals, guitar; Dave Davies, guitar, vocals; Peter Quaife, bass; Mick Avory, drums.

**Career:** Dressed in red huntsman's jackets and sporting mod haircuts, the Kinks were launched on British public as an image-heavy beat band. Debut Pye single **Long Tall Sally** was straight copy of Beatles' cover of Little Richard's(▶) classic; it bombed, as did follow-up **You Do Something To Me**, which only sold 127 copies. The rough, propulsive **You Really Got Me** was something quite different. Close in form to the Kingsmen's **Louie, Louie**, it had an R&B edge which British audiences were looking for at time and shot to No.1.

Producer Shel Talmy had found a golden vein and exploited it well over next 18 months with string of charters, mostly written by Ray Davies. From straightforward pop songs, Davies started composing ever more pictorial lyrics, strongly British in inspiration yet with a wide appeal. The humorous **Dedicated Follower Of Fashion** (taking off '60s fashion fanatics) the atmospheric **Waterloo Sunset** (which proved songs didn't have to have American locations to be effective), **Autumn Almanac** and others showed depth of his writing talent, which some rated on par with Lennon/McCartney.

As band began touring less, Ray Davies involved himself in solo projects, including score for 'The Virgin Soldiers'. Brother Dave had solo UK hit (backed by Kinks and issued as Kinks single in US) in 1967 with **Death Of A Clown**. This was included along with **Waterloo Sunset** and the funny yet perceptive **David Watts** on brilliant **Something Else By The Kinks** album, marking end of group's partnership with Shel Talmy.

With Ray Davies now producing, the Kinks followed Beatles and others into realms of concept albums, notably with **The Kinks Are The Village Green Preservation Society** and **Arthur (Or The Decline And Fall Of The British Empire)**; latter was originally commissioned as TV

soundtrack. By then Peter Quaife had been replaced by John Dalton. In 1970 group returned to singles' charts with controversial but excellent **Lola**, a song about transvestism and a hit on both sides of Atlantic. **Kinks Part 1: Lola Versus Powerman And The Moneygoround** had biting lyrics about rampant manipulation in pop music scene. Meanwhile, Ray Davies completed soundtrack of 'Percy' and had main role in television play 'The Long Distance Piano Player'.

Getting out of current management deal and Pye record contract, group pacted with RCA. Opening RCA album, **Muswell Hillbillies**, introduced John Gosling on keyboards plus brass section from the Mike Cotton Sound. Laurie Brown, Alan Holmes and John Beecham subsequently became regular members of the Kinks. Despite including **Alcohol** and **Skin And Bone**, two of most atypical Kink's classics, album sold poorly. Ironically, their following in America was burgeoning. Increasingly theatrical in concept, with strong roots in music-hall traditions, the Kinks' subsequent albums were often somewhat grandiose projects. **Sleepside** (1977) found group switching to Arista Records and album was another in string of Stateside successes.

In 1974 the Kinks had formed own Konk label, signing Claire Hamill. Ray Davies produced her **Stage Door Johnnies** album, and debut set by Cafe Society, also on Konk. 1977 label move to Arista saw departure of John Dalton; Davies then dropped horn section. Andy Pyle (ex-Savoy Brown(▶)) took up bass for a while but left by May 1978. Jim Rodford has filled spot since. John Gosling also left and was replaced on keyboards by Gordon Edwards, then Ian Gibbons. In 1979 group recorded **Low Budget**, their first venture in an American studio, and the following year issued **One For The Road**, a live double LP of their best-known material, recorded while on tour in US; a live version of **Lola** made US Hot 100 in 1980.

By 1983 and **Give The People What They Want** album, Ray Davies' writing abilities seemed in decline. However, that year also saw return to both UK and US singles charts with **Come Dancing**, and band's popularity in States was further consolidated. Most recent album **Think Visual** made US Top Twenty.

To many, however, Kink's finest hour came and went many years ago. Recent tributes to band's past glories have included Pretenders' versions of **Stop Your Sobbing** and **I Go To Sleep**, and, most recently, Stranglers' note-for-note cover of classic **All Day And All Of The Night**. Ultimately band deserves honoured place in pantheon of British rock, not least because of Ray Davies' idiosyncratic songs. Often as eccentric and British as George Formby's best, they are the legacy of an entirely individualistic talent.

**Current line-up:** Ray Davies; Dave Davies; Avory; Jim Rodford, bass; Ian Gibbons, keyboards.

| Hit Singles: | US | UK |
|---|---|---|
| You Really Got Me, 1964 | 7 | 1 |
| All Day And All Of The Night, 1964 | 7 | 2 |
| Tired Of Waiting For You, 1965 | 6 | 1 |
| Everybody's Gonna Be Happy, 1965 | — | 17 |
| Set Me Free, 1965 | 23 | 9 |
| See My Friend, 1965 | — | 10 |
| A Well Respected Man 1965 | 13 | — |
| Till The End Of The Day, 1965 | 50 | 8 |
| Dedicated Follower Of Fashion, 1966 | 36 | 4 |
| Sunny Afternoon, 1966 | 14 | 1 |
| Dead End Street, 1966 | — | 5 |
| Waterloo Sunset, 1967 | — | 2 |
| Autumn Almanac, 1967 | — | 3 |
| Days, 1968 | — | 12 |
| Lola, 1970 | 9 | 2 |
| Apeman, 1970 | 45 | 5 |
| Supersonic Rocket Ship, 1972 | — | 16 |
| Come Dancing, 1983 | 6 | 12 |

*Dave Davies Solo:*

| | US | UK |
|---|---|---|
| Death Of A Clown, 1967 | — | 3 |
| Susannah's Still Alive, 1967 | — | 20 |

**Albums:**
The Kinks (—/Hallmark), 1964 **CD**
You Really Got Me (Reprise/Pye), 1965
Live At The Kelvin Hall (Reprise/Pye), 1967 **CD**
Something Else (Reprise/Pye), 1967 **CD**
Village Green Preservation Society (Reprise/Pye), 1968 **CD**
Arthur (Or The Decline And Fall Of The British Empire) (Reprise/Pye), 1969 **CD**
Kinks Part 1: Lola Versus Powerman And The Moneygoround (Reprise/Pye), 1970 **CD**
Lola (—/Hallmark), 1971
Everybody's In Showbiz (RCA), 1972
Kink Kronikles (Reprise/—), 1972
Soap Opera (RCA), 1975
Schoolboys In Disgrace (RCA), 1975
Celluloid Heroes—The Kinks' Greatest (RCA), 1976
The Kinks File (—/Pye), 1977
Sleepwalker (Arista/Fame), 1977
Misfits (Arista), 1978
20 Golden Greats (—/Ronco), 1978
Low Budget (Arista), 1979
Second Time Around (RCA/—), 1979

**Above: The first LP released by The Kinks, back in 1964. Courtesy Pye**
**Below: The Kinks perform for British TV show 'Ready Steady Go'**

One For The Road (Arista), 1980*
Collection (—/Pickwick), 1980
Give The People What They Want (Arista),
1982
State Of Confusion (Arista), 1983
Dead End Street, Greatest Hits (PRT), 1983
Word Of Mouth (Arista), 1984
Greatest Hits, 1984 **CD**
Face To Face, 1986 **CD**
Kinks Kontroversy, 1986 **CD**
Percy (Soundtrack), 1986 **CD**
Think Visual, 1986 **CD**
Well Respected Men (PRT), 1987 **CD**
Hit Singles (PRT), 1987 **CD**

*Live double

*Worth Searching Out:*
Kinks-size (Reprise/—), 1965 **CD**
Kinda Kinks (Reprise/Pye), 1965
Muswell Hillbillies (RCA), 1971
The Great Lost Kinks Album (Reprise/—),
1973
Preservation Act I (RCA), 1973

# Kiss

US group formed 1973.

**Original line-up:** Ace Frehley, guitar; Paul Stanley, guitar; Gene Simmons, bass; Peter Criss, drums.

**Career:** Kiss began by taking Lou Reed(▶)/ David Bowie(▶) glitter rock and pushing it to extreme. Band obliterated members' past by hiding behind comic-book costumes and greasepaint. With first concerts, Kiss managed to alienate rock press, offend parents and win undying loyalty of New York's younger rock fans.

Albums emphasised gothic, bigger-than-life aspects of rock music. Live shows had massive drum kits rising 40 feet into air and explosives flashing everywhere, while Simmons spat fire (real) and blood (fake) or just rolled out his foot-long tongue. Critics wondered what this had to do with the music while kids made Kiss hottest selling band of decade.

Japan in particular took to Kiss early on and band showed appreciation by putting Japanese credits on second album in late 1974. **Alive** LP had giant **Rock And Roll All Nite** single and showed band was not all flash. Next LP, **Destroyer**, proved even more of surprise by including excellent ballad, **Beth**. Super hero/ hidden identity ploy enhanced by band's refusal to be photographed or interviewed without make-up, finally went over top by actually including comic-book history of band in **The Originals** (special re-issue of first three LPs). Next two album covers, **Rock And Roll Over** (1976) and **Love Gun** (1977), also had comic style covers instead of usual pictures.

By 1977, Kiss management had organised fans into Kiss Army and provided them with

**Rock And Roll Over, Kiss. Courtesy Casablanca Records.**

**Think Visual, The Kinks. Courtesy Arista Records.**

range of Kiss memorabilia and products. Disdain of other bands and managers had suspicion of jealousy. First sign that Kiss fans were possibly outgrowing their heroes came in 1978. Amid much publicity, four solo LPs, one from each member of Kiss, went platinum before day of release. All four began appearing in cut-out racks shortly after. **Dynasty** (1979) and **Unmasked** (1980) lacked outrageousness of early Kiss. Perhaps rock world found Kiss passé after Sid Vicious & Co. Peter Criss quit, claiming face could no longer cope with make-up; band had first photos taken without it.

Surprisingly, Criss's replacement Eric Carr not only filled position well, but band produced excellent **The Elder**. It seemed to be rock-opera soundtrack for non-existent movie. Such a concept would drag down any album in 1981 and **The Elder** flopped. **Creatures Of The Night** returned to old Kiss style; problem was finding audience for it. One puzzling aspect is why this most visual of bands hasn't translated well into video age, though **Creatures Of The Night** video is superb.

Personnel changes marked uncertain period

**Kiss Alive II, Kiss. Courtesy Casablanca Records.**

for band. Frehley left, with Bob Kulick depping, before Vince Cusano took permanent guitar spot. Cusano then quit after world tour, with Mark Norton added. But Norton, who works under stage name Mark St. John, suffered debilitating illness and ex-Blackjack guitarist Bruce Kulick took most temporary job in town.

In mid-80s band finally abandoned stage make-up, move which marked progress towards status of mainstream pop-rock hitmakers. At time of writing, band is as popular as ever. Despite continual critical misgivings, Kiss has weathered many stylistic storms to attain steady place near top of commercial league.

**Current line-up:** Stanley; Simmons; Eric Carr, drums; Bruce Kulick, guitar.

| Hit Singles: | US | UK |
|---|---|---|
| Rock And Roll All Nite (Live), 1976 | 12 | — |
| Beth, 1976 | 7 | — |
| Hard Luck Woman, 1977 | 15 | — |
| Calling Dr Love, 1977 | 16 | — |
| I Was Made For Lovin' You, 1979 | 11 | 50 |
| Crazy Crazy Nights, 1987 | — | 9 |
| Reason to Live, 1987 | — | 33 |

*Ace Frehley Solo:*

| | | |
|---|---|---|
| New York Groove, 1978 | 13 | — |

**Albums:**
Kiss (Casablanca), 1974
Hotter Than Hell, (Casablanca), 1974
Dressed To Kill (Casablanca), 1975
Alive (Casablanca), 1975 **CD**
Destroyer (Casablanca), 1977 **CD**
Rock And Roll Over (Casablanca), 1976
Love Gun (Casablanca), 1977
Kiss Alive II (Casablanca), 1977
Dynasty (Casablanca), 1979
The Best Of The Solo Albums (Casablanca),
1981
The Elder (Casablanca), 1981
Killers (Casablanca), 1982*
Creatures Of The Night (Casablanca), 1982
Lick It Up (Mercury), 1983 **CD**
Unmasked (Casablanca), 1983 **CD**
Animalize (Vertigo), 1984 **CD**
Double Platinum (Casablanca), 1985 **CD**
Asylum (Vertigo), 1985 **CD**
Crazy Crazy Nights (Vertigo), 1987 **CD**
*compilation

# Gladys Knight And The Pips

US vocal group formed 1952.

**Original line-up:** Gladys Knight; Merald (Bubba) Knight; Brenda Knight; William Guest; Elenor Guest.

**Career:** Gladys Knight (born Atlanta, Georgia, May 28, 1944) was child singing prodigy, winning talent contests and peforming with gospel groups; sang with Atlanta gospel group the Morris Brown Choir at four, won 'Ted Mack Amateur Hour' TV talent competition at seven. Gladys Knight and the Pips was formed following family celebration when Gladys was only eight; Bubba and Brenda were Gladys' brother and sister, William and Elenor Guest her cousins. Group were soon playing local gigs, and made first national tour (with Sam Cooke(▶) and Jackie Wilson) in 1956.

After unsuccessful releases on Brunswick, Brenda and Elenor left group, to be replaced by Edward Patten, another cousin, and Langston George. This line-up had major hit with **Every Beat Of My Heart** in 1961.

Further hits on Fury followed, and group became sought-after live attraction. George left group and current line-up stabilised. Signing to Maxx Records consolidated R&B success. Following label's demise group signed to Motown in 1966.

Motown started group off on route to international success; version of classic **I Heard It Through The Grapevine** went to No. 2 in US charts in 1967, and was followed by string of major hits. Nevertheless, when Motown deal expired in 1973 group moved to Buddah; period of unprecedented success followed.

First album, **Imagination**, produced three hit singles and made group America's most successful vocal outfit of 1973. Since then, acclaim and chart honours have been virtually automatic. Versatility and talent of group have received wide exposure in top venues and on TV. Vocal prowess of Gladys Knight ensures continued respect of black music fans. Unusually, Gladys and her family group manage to successfully straddle both cabaret/MOR and gutsier, more soul-orientated fields.

At end of '70s Gladys and Pips drifted apart temporarily, Pips making album on their own, but they soon reunited and signed new deal

with Columbia/CBS in 1980. Success continues, although hit singles have been less in evidence of late. Gladys and the Pips are one of the longest surviving acts, with over 30 years of showbiz behind them.

**Current line-up:** Gladys Knight; Bubba Knight; William Guest; Edward Patten.

| Hit Singles: | US | UK |
|---|---|---|
| Every Beat Of My Heart, 1961 | 6 | — |
| Letter Full Of Tears, 1962 | 19 | — |
| Take Me In Your Arms And Love Me, 1967 | — | 13 |
| I Heard It Through The Grapevine, 1967 | 2 | 47 |
| The End Of Our Road, 1968 | 15 | — |
| The Nitty Gritty, 1969 | 19 | — |
| Friendship Train, 1969 | 17 | — |
| If I Were Your Woman, 1971 | 9 | — |
| I Don't Want To Do Wrong, 1971 | 17 | — |
| Help Me Make It Through The Night, 1972 | 33 | 11 |
| Neither One Of Us (Can Be The First To Say Goodbye), 1973 | 2 | 31 |
| Daddy Could Swear, I Declare, 1973 | 19 | — |
| Midnight Train To Georgia, 1973 | 1 | — |
| I've Got To Use My Imagination, 1974 | 4 | — |
| The Best Thing That Ever Happened To Me, 1974 | 3 | 7 |
| On And On, 1974 | 5 | — |
| Try To Remember/The Way We Were, 1975 | 11 | 4 |
| Midnight Train To Georgia, 1976 | — | 10 |
| So Sad The Song, 1976 | 47 | 20 |
| Baby Don't Change Your Mind, 1977 | 52 | 4 |
| Come Back And Finish What You Started, 1978 | — | 15 |

**Albums (selected):**
Imagination (Buddah), 1973
Anthology (Tamla Motown), 1974
Best Of (Buddah), 1976
Thirty Greatest (—/K-Tel), 1977
Collection (Buddah), 1978
Memories Of The Way We Were (Buddah),
1979
Touch (Columbia/CBS), 1981
Looking Back — The Fury Years (—/Bulldog),
1982
Neither One Of Us (Motown), 1982 **CD**
Bless This House (Buddah), 1983
Life (CBS), 1985
Compact Command Performances (Motown),
1986 **CD**
All I Need (Motown) **CD**
About Love (CBS), 1987
Gladys Night & the Pips (Interpage), 1987 **CD**
The Early Years (Topline), 1987 **CD**

# Kool And The Gang

US group formed 1969.

**Original line-up:** Robert 'Kool' Bell, bass; Robert Mickens, trumpet; Michael Ray, trumpet; Dennis Thomas, alto saxophone; Ronald Bell, tenor saxophone; Clifford Adams, trombone; Amir Bayyan, keyboards; Charles 'Claydes' Smith, guitar; George Brown, drums.

**Career:** In 1964 Robert 'Kool' Bell formed band called Jazziacs in Jersey City. Band included brother Ronald Bell, Dennis Thomas and Robert Mickens, and played jazz-influenced dance music for local gigs.

During next five years they gained experience, tried out various names and expanded line-up. Eventually line-up as above signed as Kool And The Gang with De-Lite in 1969.

They continued policy of funky instrumental

R&B with jazz influence, gaining popularity without achieving spectacular success. But fifth album, **Wild And Peaceful**, spawned trio of big-selling singles — **Jungle Boogie, Funky Stuff** and **Hollywood Swinging**.

Although among progenitors of whole style, Kool And The Gang were not among main beneficiaries of mid-'70s disco boom. They did, howcvor, feature on best-selling **Saturday Night Fever** soundtrack album. Career finally took off in big way when band took on lead singer James 'J.T.' Taylor and combined forces with producer Eumir Deodato. Result was **Ladies Night**, major hit album which spawned several smash singles.

Since that time band has gone from strength to strength, conquering markets worldwide and becoming one of biggest attractions in black music. Slick but relaxed stage show is major strength, and band have found formula which cleverly combines dance potential with real musicality.

**Current line-up:** 'Kool' Bell; Mickens; Ray; Thomas; Ronald Bell; Adams; Bayyan; Smith; Brown; James 'J.T.' Taylor, vocals.

| Hit Singles: | US | UK |
| --- | --- | --- |
| Jungle Boogie, 1974 | 4 | — |
| Hollywood Swinging, 1974 | 6 | — |
| Ladies Night, 1979 | 8 | 9 |
| Too Hot, 1980 | 5 | 23 |
| Celebration, 1980 | 1 | 7 |
| Jones Vs. Jones, 1981 | 39 | 17 |
| Take My Heart (You Can Have It If You Want), 1981 | 17 | — |
| Take It To The Top, 1981 | — | 15 |
| Steppin' Out, 1981 | — | 12 |
| Get Down On It, 1982 | 10 | 3 |
| Big Fun, 1982 | 21 | 14 |
| Let's Go Dancin' (Ooh La La La), 1982 | 9 | 6 |
| Straight Ahead, 1983 | — | 15 |
| Joanna, 1983 | 2 | 2 |
| Tonight, 1984 | 13 | — |
| Fresh, 1985 | 9 | 12 |
| Misled, 1985 | 10 | — |
| Cherish, 1985 | 2 | 4 |
| Emergency, 1986 | 18 | — |
| Stone Love, 1987 | 13 | — |
| Victory, 1987 | 13 | — |

**Albums:**
Spin Their Top Hits (De-Lite/—), 1978
Ladies Night (De-Lite), 1979 **CD**
Everybody's Dancing (De-Lite/—), 1979
Celebrate (De-Lite), 1980 **CD**
Something Special (De-Lite), 1981 **CD**
As One (De-Lite), 1982 **CD**
Kool Kuts (De-Lite), 1982
Twice As Kool—The Hits of (De-Lite/Phonogram), 1983
In The Heart (De-Lite), 1983 **CD**
Emergency (De-Lite), 1984 **CD**
Forever (Club), 1986 **CD**
Victory (Club), 1986

# Al Kooper
US vocalist, keyboard player, guitarist, composer.
Born Brooklyn, New York, February 5, 1944.

**Career:** At 13 Kooper had Top 10 hit with **Short Shorts** (1958) as member of Royal Teens on ABC. In late teens worked as session guitarist. Left college at 19 to work as studio engineer and songwriter. Co-penned **This Diamond Ring** chart-topper for Gary Lewis and the Playboys in 1965, and began working folk club circuit.

Producer Tom Wilson invited Kooper to attend Bob Dylan(▶) session. He turned up with his guitar, but Mike Bloomfield(▶) had

been booked to play guitar. Determined to take part in session Kooper offered to lay down organ tracks though he hadn't played that instrument seriously before. Dylan was impressed with amateurish but fresh sound and used it on classic **Like A Rolling Stone** single; Kooper contributed to rest of **Highway 61 Revisited** album sessions.

Kooper joined Dylan's back-up band (basically Paul Butterfield(▶) Blues Band for controversial 1965 Newport Folk Festival set when when Dylan went electric to disapproval of folk purists, but approbation of rock fans. Kooper later worked on Dylan's **Blonde On Blonde** (1966) and **New Morning** (1970) sessions.

Through Tom Wilson, Kooper became involved in Blues Project. Featured on two live albums and studio set **Projections** before friction with guitarist Danny Kalb caused Kooper and Steve Katz to leave. They moved to Los Angeles to work on material for proposed new band; unveiled songs at 1967 Big Sur Folk Festival. Legend has it that band was formed solely to play one week at New York club to fund proposed trip to Britain. Band however, became more permanent unit as Blood, Sweat And Tears(▶). Kooper helped put line-up together and produced classic debut album **Child Is Father To The Man** (1969). Commercial success led to group moving in direction which did not suit Kooper; he quit to work as Columbia staff producer.

Kooper started trend for superstar jam sessions by recording **Super Session** album with Mike Bloomfield and Stephen Stills(▶) who had just left Buffalo Springfield, which led to series of concerts with Bloomfield and **Live Adventures Of Al Kooper And Mike Bloomfield** set (1969).

As session guitarist and keyboard player, Kooper appeared on Jimi Hendrix'(▶) **Electric Ladyland** and the Rolling Stones'(▶) **Let It Bleed**. Also recorded with Taj Mahal(▶) and B. B. King(▶), and did further Dylan sessions. Produced Don Ellis Band in jazz idiom and recorded series of solo albums of much-varied quality; **New York City You're A Woman**, largely recorded in London with members of Elton John's(▶) band, was among best. On 1969 **Kooper Session** he unveiled the emergent guitar talents of R&B veteran Johnny Otis's then 15-year-old son Shuggie Otis.

The '70s found Kooper concentrating increasingly on producing others, notably the Tubes(▶), Nils Lofgren(▶) and Lynyrd Skynyrd(▶). He moved base to Atlanta,

**Below: Notable country songwriter Kris Kristofferson has had his compositions covered by many.**

Georgia, to set up his own Sounds Of The South label. Published a highly enjoyable autobiography under title 'Backstage Passes'.

**Albums:**
Super Session (with Mike Bloomfield and Stephen Stills) (Columbia/CBS), 1969
Live Adventures (with Mike Bloomfield) (Columbia/CBS), 1969
Championship Wrestling (Columbia/—), 1981
(See also Blood, Sweat and Tears)

# Kris Kristofferson
US vocalist, guitarist, composer, actor.
Born Brownsville, Texas, June 22, 1936.

**Career:** Moved to California while in high school. After attending Pomona College went to England to take up Rhodes Scholarship at Oxford University. Started writing while at college; first fiction and later songs were under name of Kris Carson.

On return to US joined army and was eventually posted to Germany to fly helicopters. During German sojourn resumed songwriting and started to play in local clubs.

Back in US, joined West Point military academy for short period as English teacher, but made permanent move to Nashville in 1965.

For several years Kristofferson took menial jobs while songs (sent to Nashville publisher) made usual rounds. Eventually Roger Miller(▶) recorded some of his compositions, including **Me And Bobby McGee**, and Kristofferson was on his way. Janis Joplin's(▶) cover of **Bobby McGee** brought him to the youth/rock market.

In 1970 he was offered contract by Monument, and by time of marriage to Rita Coolidge(▶) in 1973 was major record seller. For next few years he and Coolidge ran careers together, using same band for touring, and cutting duet albums, **Full Moon** (1973) and **Breakaway** (1974). Dual appearance in Peckinpah movie 'Pat Garratt And Billy The Kid' started off Kristofferson's film career, which rapidly assumed major importance. Starring roles in movies like 'Alice Doesn't Live Here Anymore', 'A Star Is Born' (with Barbra Streisand) and 'Rollover' (with Jane Fonda) ensued.

Late '70s was bad period for Kristofferson personally, heavy drinking problems and break-up of marriage being widely publicised. However, latterly he has been as busy as ever, with both recording and film projects.

Although a passable singer and competent

actor, Kristofferson's real claim to fame lies in clutch of classic and much-covered songs. **Me And Bobby McGee, Help Me Make It Through The Night, Sunday Morning Coming Down, For The Good Times** and others ensure continuing reputation as songwriter.

| Hit Singles: | US | UK |
| --- | --- | --- |
| Why Me, 1973 | 16 | — |

**Albums:**
Me And Bobby McGee (Monument), 1970
The Silver Tongued Devil And I (Monument), 1971
Border Lord (Monument), 1972
Jesus Was A Capricorn (Monument), 1973
Spooky Lady's Sideshow (Monument), 1974
Songs Of Kristofferson (Monument), 1977
Easter Island (Monument), 1978
Shake Hands With The Devil (Monument), 1979
To The Bone (Monument), 1981
Repossessed (Mercury), 1987 **CD**

*With Rita Coolidge:*
Full Moon (A&M), 1973
Natural Act (A&M), 1978

*With Barbra Streisand:*
A Star Is Born (Soundtrack) (Columbia/CBS), 1977
*With Willie Nelson, Brenda Lee and Dolly Parton:*
The Winning Hand (Monument), 1983

# Cyndi Lauper
US vocalist, composer.
Born Queens, New York, June 20, 1953.

**Career:** 'If at first you don't succeed, etc . . .' could well stand as Cyndi Lauper's motto. Behind seeming instant 1984 success with platinum album **She's So Unusual** and superlative singles **Girls Just Want To Have Fun** and **Time After Time** lay years of heartbreak and trauma—the demise of her early band Blue Angel had led her to file for bankruptcy. All this and early background as convent schooled rebellious product of single-parent home was to shine through in her feminist but fun songmaking.

Perhaps biggest blow was in 1977 when, after several years fronting various poor cover-version bands, her voice failed and she was told she would never sing again. Help from vocal coach Katie Agresta made her singing better than ever and she bounced back from flop of Blue Angel's sole Polygram album in 1980 and $80,000 law suit loss against management company to find stardom with Portrait Records.

One of music business's true originals, Lauper combines real talent with quirky originality — after all, how many pop singers have had songs recorded by Miles Davis? (**Time After Time**). She continues to increase following with hits like **True Colours**, and may well demonstrate staying power when more glamorous stars begin to fade.

| Hit Singles: | US | UK |
| --- | --- | --- |
| Girls Just Want To Have Fun, 1984 | 2 | 2 |
| Time After Time, 1984 | 1 | 3 |
| She Bop, 1984 | 3 | 46 |
| All Through The Night, 1984 | 5 | — |
| The Goonies 'R' Good Enough, 1985 | 10 | — |
| True Colours, 1986 | 1 | 12 |
| What's Going On, 1987 | 11 | — |
| Change of Heart, 1987 | 4 | — |

**Album:**
She's So Unusual (Portrait), 1984 **CD**

# Led Zeppelin

UK group formed 1968.

**Original/final line-up:** Robert Plant, vocals; Jimmy Page, Gibson Les Paul guitar; John Paul Jones, keyboards, Fender Precision bass; John Bonham, drums.

**Career:** Formed by Jimmy Page upon demise of Yardbirds(▶) to complete scheduled dates in Northern Europe. Quartet completed by session bass-player John Paul Jones, Birmingham drummer John Bonham, and ex-Band Of Joy vocalist Robert Plant.

Page and Jones were both prominent studio players. Page's credits include Kinks(▶), Stones(▶), Georgie Fame(▶) and the Who(▶) (featured on **I Can't Explain**). Joined Yardbirds as replacement bass player for departing Paul Samwell-Smith; switched to guitar when Jeff Beck quit. Jones supplied bass/keyboards for Stones, Lulu, Dusty Springfield(▶) and many others; formerly bass player for Jet Harris/Tony Meehan, ex-Shadows(▶) duo.

As New Yardbirds, band fulfilled Swedish/ Finnish dates. With manager Peter Grant, group selected new name Led Zeppelin suggested by Keith Moon(▶) (John Entwistle(▶) has also been credited). Grant quickly secured recording contract with Ahmet Ertegun of Atlantic (originally turned down by Atlantic's distribution company in UK Polydor); Grant and Ertegun have since arrived at arm's length respect for each other.

First album **Led Zeppelin** was released in 1968; went gold early following year. Mixture of blues and orchestrated rock riffs filled in void left by Cream; superb musicianship and beginning of Plant's 'macho' bare-to-the-waist image saw them streets ahead of US contemporaries. Album's crisp production set it apart from myriad of ponderous, muddy-sounding heavy metal merchants. Single **Good Times Bad Times** culled from LP earned group first US Top 100 entry.

Reputation secured by **Led Zeppelin II** which included band's anthem **Whole Lotta Love**, a US Top 10. Band has never had singles success in UK, though **Love** was theme for BBC's 'Top Of The Pops' TV show for several years; band never officially endorsed singles culled by record company.

Zeppelin completed major tour of US in '73, compounding success of further albums **III** and **IV**. Tracks **Immigrant Song** (from **III**) and now all-time classic **Stairway To Heaven** (from **IV**) extracted phenomenal reaction from audiences. Band now at peak, with Grant turning down telephone number-size deals which conflicted with his long-term strategy.

Assuming Presley/Beatles-type publicity and sales, group spent over a year away from studio after release of **Houses Of The Holy** (1973). Returned in '75 with **Physical Graffiti**. Album was packaged in 'moveable' sleeve, revealing various objects/individuals in windows of tenement block, and was as impressive musically as visually, attracting more favourable critical reaction; band have always been at loggerheads with 'knowledgeable' music press.

Own label Swan Song launched with release of **Graffiti**; Bad Company(▶), Maggie Bell and Pretty Things also signed to label. Acts distributed by Atlantic and Island. Swan Song office in Kings Road, London, saw much frantic wheeling and dealing by Grant. Reportedly turned down one million pounds for worldwide satellite TV concert of band.

1975 saw Plant injured in car crash during Greek holiday. Second personal tragedy for group's singer occurred in 1977 when his son Karac died of virus infection. Plant's incapacity kept band off road for two years, although album **Presence** (1976) maintained momentum. LP had biggest advance orders ever in US, going platinum upon issue.

In 1976 movie/soundtrack album **The Song Remains The Same** released. Film captured explosive stage act to the full, despite some 'live' footage being shot at Pinewood Studios, England.

Massive US tour saw Zeppelin gross over one million dollars for New York dates (at Madison Square Garden) alone. 10 dates were cancelled, however, when Plant had to fly home on son's death. First rumours of break-up denied by Page. Band had meticulously worked schedule, with periods of inactivity which fuelled 'split' stories.

The turning cover of Led Zeppelin III.
Courtesy Atlantic Records.

Ninth album **In Through The Out Door** cut in Sweden at end of '78 for spring '79 release. Unlikely hosts in frozen North were Abba(▶), who had invited band to record in their studio.

Major outdoor concert at stately home Knebworth House in August 1979 saw band re-conquer homeland. **In Through The Out Door** LP was released shortly after. Album's unique packaging (wrapped in brown paper and featuring six different covers) won major marketing award in US.

Led Zeppelin II featured Whole Lotta Love. Courtesy Atlantic Records.

Coda the last Led Zeppelin album. Courtesy Atlantic Records.

After death of drummer John Bonham in 1980, another victim of rock excesses, band officially called it a day in cursory press release. In intervening years, Plant has forged successful solo career, employing young musicians in upbeat band which has captured spirit of '80s. (Despite anguished pleas from audiences, singer consistently refuses to warm over **Stairway To Heaven** and other Zep chestnuts.

1985 saw collaboration of Plant/Page in Honeydrippers, with Nile Rodgers and Jeff Beck; band made US number three with **Sea Of Love**. US success was also forthcoming for short-lived Page/Paul Rodgers band The Firm.

Three surviving members have always denied possibility of reformation, although at time of writing there was strong rumour that band would reconstitute for one-off charity gig with John Bonham's son Jason filling drum chair.

Coincidentally, Led Zeppelin's reputation is being rapidly rehabilitated in light of fashionable interest in early seventies. Classic sampled Zep riffs are now featured on many hip-hop tracks. What's more, group remain Atlantic Records' biggest-selling album artists bar none.

**Below: Led Zeppelin as they were at the height of their fame in the '70s. (Left to right) John Paul Jones, Robert Plant, Jimmy Page, John Bonham.**

**Above: Houses Of The Holy, Led Zeppelin. Courtesy of Atlantic Records.**

**Below: Jimmy Page of Led Zeppelin onstage with his Les Paul.**

**Hit Singles:**

| | US | UK |
|---|---|---|
| Whole Lotta Love, 1970 | 4 | — |
| Immigrant Song, 1971 | 16 | — |
| Black Dog, 1972 | 15 | — |
| D'Yer Mak'er, 1973 | 20 | — |

*Robert Plant Solo:*

| | US | UK |
|---|---|---|
| Big Log, 1983 | 20 | 11 |

*Honeydrippers* (Robert Plant, Jimmy Page, Jeff Beck & Nile Rodgers):

| | US | UK |
|---|---|---|
| Sea Of Love, 1985 | 3 | — |

**Albums:**
Led Zeppelin (Atlantic), 1968 **CD**
Led Zeppelin II (Atlantic), 1969 **CD**
Led Zeppelin III (Atlantic), 1970 **CD**
Led Zeppelin IV (Atlantic), 1971 **CD**
Houses Of The Holy (Atlantic), 1973 **CD**
Physical Graffiti (Swan Song), 1975 **CD**
Presence (Swan Song), 1976 **CD**
The Song Remains The Same (Swan Song), 1976 **CD**
In Through The Out Door (Swan Song), 1979 **CD**
Coda (Swan Song), 1982 **CD**
Chris Tetley Interviews Led Zeppelin 1987 (Music & Media)

*Robert Plant Solo:*
Pictures At Eleven (Swan Song), 1982 **CD**
The Priniciple Of Moments (Es Paranza), 1983 **CD**
Shaken'n'Stirred (Es Paranza), 1985 **CD**
*Jimmy Page Solo:*
Deathwish II Soundtrack (Swan Song), 1982 **CD**

*The Firm:*
The Firm (Atlantic), 1985 **CD**
Mean Business (Atlantic), 1986 **CD**

*Honeydrippers:*
Volume One (Es Paranza), 1984 **CD**

*Jimmy Page & Roy Harper*
Whatever happened to 1214 AD (Beggars Banquet), 1985

# Brenda Lee
US vocalist.
Born Brenda Mae Tarpley, Atlanta, Georgia, December 11, 1944.

**Career:** Lee's musical talent was already in evidence at age six when she won local talent contest in home town Nashville. Heard by country star Red Foley at 12, spot on his TV programme 'Ozark Jubilee Show' followed. Success was instantaneous, and further TV dates and Decca (later MCA) recording contract followed.

First releases were country-orientated and moderately successful, but when Lee turned to rock 'n' roll her career took off. **Dynamite** was first of several international hits that carried her into mid-'60s. Probably the best female white rock singer of her generation, she also showed winning style on pop ballads like **I'm Sorry** and **As Usual**.

When chart success began to die down, Lee, like many white '50s rock 'n' rollers (Bob Luman, Conway Twitty(▶)), turned back to roots and started recording country material again. In recent years career has been low profile, but she continues to undertake TV and live work.

Always a strong, distinctive singer, Brenda Lee combined genuine talent with appealing, chirpy personality. Her early '60s singles remain among some of most evocative discs of period.

**Hit Singles:**

| | US | UK |
|---|---|---|
| Sweet Nuthins, 1960 | 4 | 4 |

**Below: Mr. and Mrs. John Lennon at the time of the former's comeback.**

| | US | UK |
|---|---|---|
| I'm Sorry/That's All You Gotta Do, 1960 | 1 | 12 |
| That's All You Gotta Do/I'm Sorry, 1960 | 6 | — |
| I Want To Be Wanted, 1960 | 1 | 31 |
| Rockin' Around The Christmas Tree, 1960 | 14 | — |
| Let's Jump The Broomstick, 1961 | — | 12 |
| Emotions, 1961 | 7 | 45 |
| You Can Depend On Me, 1961 | 6 | — |
| Dum Dum, 1961 | 4 | 22 |
| Fool No. 1, 1961 | 3 | 38 |
| Break It To Me Gently, 1962 | 4 | 46 |
| Speak To Me Pretty, 1962 | — | 3 |
| Everybody Loves You But You, 1962 | 6 | — |
| Here Comes That Feeling, 1962 | — | 5 |
| Heart In Hand, 1962 | 15 | — |
| It Started All Over Again, 1962 | 29 | 15 |
| All Alone Am I, 1962 | 3 | 7 |
| Rockin' Around The Christmas Tree, 1962 | — | 6 |
| Losing You, 1963 | 6 | 10 |
| I Wonder, 1963 | 25 | 14 |
| The Grass Is Greener, 1963 | 17 | — |
| As Usual, 1964 | 12 | 5 |
| Is It True, 1964 | 17 | 17 |
| Too Many Rivers, 1965 | 13 | 22 |
| Coming On Strong, 1966 | 11 | — |

**Albums:**
Here's Brenda Lee (Vocalion/—), 1967
Let It Be Me (Coral/—), 1968
Brenda (MCA), 1973
Brenda Lee Story (MCA/Decca), 1974
Little Miss Dynamite (MCA/Warwick), 1976
Take Me Back (MCA), 1979
Even Better (MCA), 1980
16 Classic Tracks (-/MFP), 1982
25th Anniversary (MCA), 1982
Greatest Country Hits (—/MCA), 1982
Only When I Laugh (—/MCA), 1982
Very Best Of (MCA), 1985
Wiedersehen Ist Wunderschon (Bear Family), 1986

# John Lennon
UK composer, vocalist, guitarist.
Born John Winston Lennon, Liverpool, October 9, 1940; died December 8, 1980.

**Career:** After achieving worldwide success with the Beatles during the '60s, Lennon, under influence of second wife, Yoko Ono(▶), began recording without rest of group in 1968. First LP, recorded with Yoko, featured full frontral nude picture of duo, resulting in LP being sold in brown paper bag, while contents — avant-garde inspired non-music —

alienated Beatle fans around the world. Follow-up LP was no better, but in between, hit single by Plastic Ono Band (John, Yoko and friends), **Give Peace A Chance**, was substantial hit. Several follow-up singles were successful over years until 1976. LPs often unlistenable before **John Lennon/Plastic Ono Band**, released in 1970, in which John, under influence of primal therapy, tried to release all supposedly suppressed feelings about early life.

Next LP, **Imagine**, generally agreed to be Lennon's best solo album. Thereafter output was patchy—Lennon felt to be too easily influenced by those around him, leading to involvement with peace movement, exotic religions, and many other things which prevented him making classic rock'n'roll records of which everyone knew he was capable.

**The John Lennon Collection. Courtesy EMI Records/Geffen Records.**

On November 28, 1974, Lennon joined Elton John(▶) on stage at NY's Madison Square Gardens for three numbers (**Lucy In The Sky With Diamonds, I Saw Her Standing There,** and **Whatever Gets You Through The Night**); this turned out to be his last live performance.

On birth of second child (first by Yoko), Lennon vowed to cease recording for five years. On return to active service in 1980, produced half LP (other half by Yoko) spawning rather disappointing single hit **(Just Like) Starting Over**. As single began to descend chart, John was murdered by so-called fan outside New York apartment building. The entire world was shocked. Chart was soon deluged with Lennon/Beatles material for several months. While his post-Beatles work was very inconsistent, Lennon is regarded as most notable Beatle by majority of fans, making his quite senseless murder probably *the* ultimate tragedy of rock'n'roll. However the name lives on, not just in John's recorded legacy but in hits by his soundalike son Julian.
Guitar: Rickenbacker

| Hit Singles: | US | UK |
|---|---|---|
| Give Peace A Chance, 1969 | 14 | 2 |
| Cold Turkey, 1969 | 30 | 14 |
| Instant Karma, 1970 | 3 | 5 |
| Power to The People, 1970 | 11 | 7 |
| Imagine, 1971 | 3 | — |
| Happy Xmas (War Is Over), 1972 | — | 4 |
| Mind Games, 1973 | 18 | 26 |
| Whatever Gets You Thru The Night, 1974 | 1 | 36 |
| Number 9 Dream, 1975 | 9 | 23 |
| Stand By Me, 1975 | 20 | 30 |
| Imagine, 1975 | — | 6 |
| Happy Xmas (War Is Over) (3rd entry), 1980 | — | 2 |
| Imagine, 1980 | — | 1 |
| (Just Like) Starting Over, 1981 | 3 | 1 |
| Woman, 1981 | 2 | 1 |
| Watching The Wheels, 1981 | 18 | 30 |

| | | |
|---|---|---|
| Nobody Told Me, 1984 | 5 | 6 |

**Albums:**
Unfinished Music No.1—Two Virgins (Apple), 1968
Unfinished Music No.2—Life With The Lions, (Capitol/Parlophone), 1969
The Wedding Album (Capitol/Parlophone), 1969
Plastic Ono Band/Live Peace In Toronto, (Capitol/Parlophone), 1969
John Lennon/Plastic Ono Band (Capitol/Parlophone), 1970 **CD**
Imagine (Capitol/Parlophone) 1971 **CD**
Some Time In New York City (Capitol/Parlophone), 1972
Mind Games (Capitol/MFP), 1973 **CD**
Walls And Bridges (Capitol/Parlophone), 1974 **CD**
Rock'n'Roll (Capitol/Parlophone), 1975 **CD**
Shaved Fish (Collectable Lennon) (Capitol/Parlophone), 1975* **CD**
Double Fantasy (Capitol/Parlophone), 1980
The John Lennon Collection (Capitol/Parlophone), 1980*
Heartplay—Unfinished Dialogues (Polydor), 1983
Milk & Honey (with Yoko Ono) (Polydor), 1984
Live In New York City (Parlophone), 1986 **CD**
Menlove Ave (Parlophone), 1986 **CD**
*Compilations

# Level 42
UK group formed 1980.

**Original/current line-up:** Mark King, vocals, bass; Mike Lindup, keyboards, vocals; Phil Gould, percussion; Boon Gould, guitar.

**Career:** The early '80s found a number of UK bands exploiting the jazz-funk idiom then expanding own soul style to find major following for their white brand of black music. Level 42 was voted best British group for three years running in Blues & Soul magazine whose readers also cited Mark King as best bassist in world.

**World Machine, Level 42. Courtesy Polydor Records.**

Group's worldwide album sales of 1½ million confirm their credibility with dance music audience.

King and Gould brothers were friends from Isle of Wight days, linking up with Lindup and forming group after moving to London where they found record deal with Polydor.

1985 album **World Machine** went double platinum in UK, while later **Running In The Family** was equally successful. Mid 80s also marked band's development into major stadium filler.

Besides work in group, Mark King has played on records for M of **Pop Music** fame, Nik Kershaw(▶), Midge Ure(▶), Reflex and others, and handled re-mix work for Robert Palmer(▶) and Direct Drive.

| Hit Singles: | US | UK |
|---|---|---|
| The Sun Goes Down, 1983 | — | 10 |
| Hot Water, 1984 | — | 18 |
| Something About You, 1985 | — | 6 |
| Lessons In Love, 1986 | 14 | 3 |
| To Be With You Again, 1987 | — | 10 |
| Running In The Family, 1987 | — | 6 |
| It's Over, 1987 | — | 10 |
| Children Say, 1987 | — | 22 |

**Below: Level 42 live in 1986. White soul yet to have transatlantic appeal.**

**Albums:**
Level 42 (Polydor), 1981 **CD**
The Early Tapes (Polydor), 1982
The Pursuit Of Accidents (Polydor), 1982 **CD**
Standing In The Light (Polydor), 1983 **CD**
True Colours (Polydor), 1984 **CD**
Physical Presence (Polydor), 1985 **CD**
World Machine (Polydor), 1985 **CD**
Running In The Family (Polydor), 1987 **CD**

*Mark King Solo:*
Influences (Polydor), 1984

# Huey Lewis And The News
US group formed 1982.

**Original/current line-up:** Huey Lewis, vocals; Chris Hayes, guitar; Sean Hopper, keyboards; Johnny Colla, guitar, saxophone; Mario Cipollina, bass; Bill Gibson, drums.

**Career:** After graduation, Huey Lewis backpacked round Europe for several years, teaching himself harmonica while waiting for rides. Returning to Marin County, California, he joined country rockers Clover(▶) with whom he played London pub rock scene in late '70s, featuring on Elvis Costello's debut album **My Aim Is True** and also recording with Phil Lynott(▶).

On Clover's demise, he returned to San Francisco Bay Area to assemble News, Hopper also being ex-Clover while Colla, Cipollina and Gibson all came from local band Soundhole.

Signed worldwide to Chrysalis, group found instant success, quickly becoming biggest-grossing stage act in US and going five-times platinum with superlative **Sports** album (six million sales and 100 weeks on US chart).

**If This Is It** single brought UK recognition for group's R&B slanted brand of excitement but follow-up surprisingly flopped despite strong airplay.

Single **Power Of Love**, theme tune to blockbuster movie Back To The Future, made US

number one in 1985, and band has continued on to scale dizziest heights of commercial success. At time of writing, most recent album **Fore!** had achieved multiplatinum status,and looked set to follow **Sports** into commercial stratosphere.

**Hit Singles:**

| | US | UK |
|---|---|---|
| Do You Believe In Love, 1982 | 7 | — |
| Heart And Soul, 1983 | 8 | — |
| I Want A New Drug, 1984 | 6 | — |
| The Heart Of Rock'n'Roll, 1984 | 6 | — |
| If This Is It, 1984 | 6 | 7 |
| Walking On A Thin Line, 1984 | 18 | — |
| Power Of Love, 1985 | 1 | 11 |
| Hip To Be Square, 1986 | 1 | 41 |
| Stuck With You, 1987 | 1 | 12 |
| Jacob's Ladder, 1987 | 1 | — |
| I Know What I Like, 1987 | 8 | — |
| Doing It All For My Baby, 1987 | 6 | — |

**Fore! Huey Lewis and The News. Courtesy Chrysalis Records.**

**Albums:**
Huey Lewis & The News (Chrysalis), 1980
Picture This (Chrysalis), 1982 **CD**
Sports (Chrysalis), 1984 **CD**
Fore (Chrysalis), 1986 **CD**

**Below: Huey Lewis and The News, whose 1984 album 'Sports' stayed in the US charts for nearly two years.**

# Jerry Lee Lewis
US vocalist, pianist, composer.
Born Ferriday, Louisiana, September 29, 1935.

**Career:** Although Lewis made early start playing country style piano in bars and clubs, recording career did not commence until 1956 with signing to Sun Records in Memphis and first single **Crazy Arms**. Somewhat wilder style surfaced in 1957, with second single **Whole Lotta Shakin' Goin' On** becoming first hit and setting pattern for 'pumpin' piano' style, which rapidly became trademark.

Several hits and tours later, arrived in Britain in May 1958 for nationwide tour just as news broke of marriage to 13-year-old cousin, Myra. Resulting publicity effectively stalled career for over two years; made comeback with **What'd I Say** in 1961.

Began recording for Mercury in 1963 and style mellowed considerably over next five years as Lewis turned to country music with increasing success. New career followed with major hits in country charts and occasional excursions into rock 'n' roll.

Continued to tour US and UK regularly, and to appear in headlines as a result of lifestyle in keeping with reputation as wild man of rock. His various drug, booze and gun offences reached climax in 1976 when Lewis was arrested for brandishing a pistol outside Elvis Presley's(▶) home in Memphis.

Following signing to Elektra label in 1977, appeared to have adopted quieter lifestyle; relationship with label was strained, however, ultimately leading to lawsuits from both sides. During 1981 was rushed to hospital for extensive stomach surgery, reportedly close to death, but recovered sufficiently to resume stage appearances. The Killer suffered further serious illness in 1985, but recuperative powers were on hand once again. While ill-health has restricted recording during the '80s, Lewis is the favourite subject of indie labels in UK.

Recent concerts reveal only slightly reserved stage performance and the same self-confidence—Lewis has always asserted that 'The Killer' is the 'King of Rock 'n' Roll'. This title may have been hotly contested in the '50s, now it would appear to belong to Lewis alone, for he remains one of the few active rock 'n' roll exponents.

**Hit Singles:**

| | US | UK |
|---|---|---|
| Whole Lotta Shakin' Goin' On, 1957 | 2 | 8 |
| Great Balls Of Fire, 1957 | 3 | 1 |
| Breathless, 1958 | 7 | 8 |
| High School Confidential, 1959 | 21 | 12 |
| What'd I Say, 1961 | 30 | 10 |

**Albums:**
Whole Lotta Shakin' Goin' On (Sun), 1963
Live At The Star Club, Hamburg (Philips), 1964
Best Of The Country Music Hall Of Fame Hits (Mercury), 1969
Jerry Lee Lewis And His Pumping Piano (—/Charly), 1975
Rare Jerry Lee Lewis Volume 1 (—/Charly), 1975
Rare Jerry Lee Lewis Volume 2 (—/Charly), 1975
Good Rockin' Tonite (Sun), 1975
The Original Jerry Lee Lewis (—/Charly), 1976
Nuggets (—/Charly), 1977
Nuggets Volume 2 (—/Charly), 1977
The Essential Jerry Lee Lewis (—/Charly), 1978
Jerry Lee Lewis And Friends—Duets (Sun/Charly), 1978
Jerry Lee's Greatest (—/Charly), 1980
The Sun Years (12 LP Box Set) Sun), 1980
Killer Country (Elektra), 1980
Pumpin' Piano Cat (Sun), 1983
The Great Ball Of Fire (Sun), 1983
The Wild One (Sun), 1983
My Fingers Do The Talking (MCA), 1983
I Am What I Am (MCA), 1984
Milestones (Rhino), 1986
18 Original Sun Hits (Rhino), 1986 **CD**
20 Super Hits (Bellaphon), 1986 **CD**
Rare And Rockin (Sun), 1987 **CD**

The Killer (12 unit box set) (1963-1968, (Bear Family) **CD**
Up Through The Years (Bear Family), 1956-63 **CD**
The Session (Mercury), 1985 **CD**
Collection—Parts 1 & 2 (Castle), 1986
Complete London Sessions Vols 1 & 2 (Bear Family), 1986
Kickin' Up A Storm (Sun), 1987
Thirtieth Anniversary (Phonogram), 1987 **CD**

*With Carl Perkins and Johnny Cash:*
The Survivors (—/Hallmark), 1985

# Lindisfarne
UK group formed 1967.

**Original/Current line-up:** Alan Hull, vocals; Ray Jackson, guitar, mandolin, vocals; Simon Cowe, guitar, mandolin, vocals; Rod Clements, bass, violin, vocals; Ray Laidlaw, drums.

**Career:** Folk-rock band formed in Newcastle, had various names before signing as Lindisfarne to Charisma in 1969. First album, **Nicely Out Of Tune**, met with good reception, and steady gigging on college and festival circuit during 1969 and '70 paved way for commercial success.

Next album, **Fog On The Tyne**, was produced by Bob Johnston and became biggest-selling British album of 1970. Also spawned hit single **Meet Me On The Corner**. Earlier unsuccessful single **Lady Eleanor** was re-released and this time became major hit.

However, band faltered after this success and split in 1973. Clements, Laidlaw and Cowe formed Jack The Lad, whilst Hull and Jackson recorded moderate offerings.

Original line-up re-formed in late '70s, returning to club/festival circuit where they had enjoyed greatest success.

**Hit Singles:**

| | US | UK |
|---|---|---|
| Meet Me On The Corner, 1972 | — | 5 |
| Lady Eleanor, 1972 | — | 3 |
| Run For Home, 1978 | 33 | 10 |

**Albums:**
Fog On The Tyne (—/Charisma), 1971
Dingly Dell (—/Charisma), 1972
Lady Eleanor (—/Hallmark), 1976
Back And Forth (Atco/Mercury), 1978
The News (—/Mercury), 1979
The Singles Album (—/Charisma), 1981
Lindisfarne Live (—/Charisma), 1982
Sleepless Nights (—/LMP), 1982
Lindisfarne! Vol.2 (LMP), 1984
C'mon Everybody (Stylus), 1987 **CD**

# Little Feat
US group formed 1969.

**Original line-up:** Lowell George, guitar, harmonica, vocals; Bill Payne, keyboards, vocals; Richard Hayward, drums; Roy Estrada, bass.

**Career:** Lowell George (born 1945) played in mid-'60s folk rock group Factory (with Hayward and bassist Martin Kibbee) and, two years later, the Standells (**Dirty Water**), then Seeds (**Pushin' Too Hard**) briefly. George left to take over from singer Ray Collins in Mothers of Invention, playing on both **Weasels Ripped My Flesh** and **Hot Rats** (uncredited).

While in Mothers, wrote/recorded several demos, including **Willing** and **Truck Stop Girl**, the latter being picked up by Clarence White of the Byrds(▶) for inclusion on

(Untitled). Other covers followed by numerous US acts, including Seatrain, Linda Ronstadt(▶) and Commander Cody(▶).

During same period, George teamed up with Bill Payne, and both contributed to Fraternity Of Man's second LP, Get It On. Interest in George's demos eventually led to recording deal with Warners. Above line-up was assembled. (Group name apparently came from Mother's drummer Jimmy Carl Black and sarcastically refers to size of George's feet.)

First album Little Feat, released December 1969, was surprisingly mature work for debut and attracted some critical acclaim, though sales were poor. Same fate befell follow-up Sailin' Shoes, in spite of increased media coverage. Disillusioned, Estrada left to join

Captain Beefheart's Magic Band. The others re-grouped in new six-piece line-up, including Ken Gradney (bass), Sam Clayton (congas) and Paul Barrere (guitar). Third album Dixie Chicken also saw minimal success and members lost interest and drifted into other projects.

George was in constant demand as sessioneer/songwriter, but declined invitation to join projected group with John Sebastian and Phil Everly as well as similar request from Jackson Browne. Contributed to albums by the Meters(▶), Jimmy Webb, Carly Simon(▶), John Sebastian(▶), Kathy Dalton, Chico Hamilton, Nilsson(▶), Robert Palmer(▶) (Sneaking Sally Through The Alley), John Cale(▶) (Paris 1919) and Van Dyke Parks (Discover America). Payne, meanwhile,

Feats Don't Fail Me Now, Little Feat.
Courtesy Warner Bros Records.

went on road and appeared on albums with Doobie Brothers(▶) (Toulouse Street and The Captain And Me) and Bonnie Raitt(▶) (Taking My Time and Streetlights).

Little Feat re-formed in 1974 to cut excellent Feats Don't Fail Me Now. Followed with critically acclaimed tour of England as part of Warner Bros Music Show in early 1975. Returned to England in May 1976 to support the Who at Charlton Football Ground. Subsequently toured Europe with the Outlaws. During group's final years, Lowell George's role appeared to diminish. Contributed only three songs to The Last Record Album, including the memorable Long Distance Love.

Hepatitis precluded extensive involvement in next album, Time Loves A Hero, generally

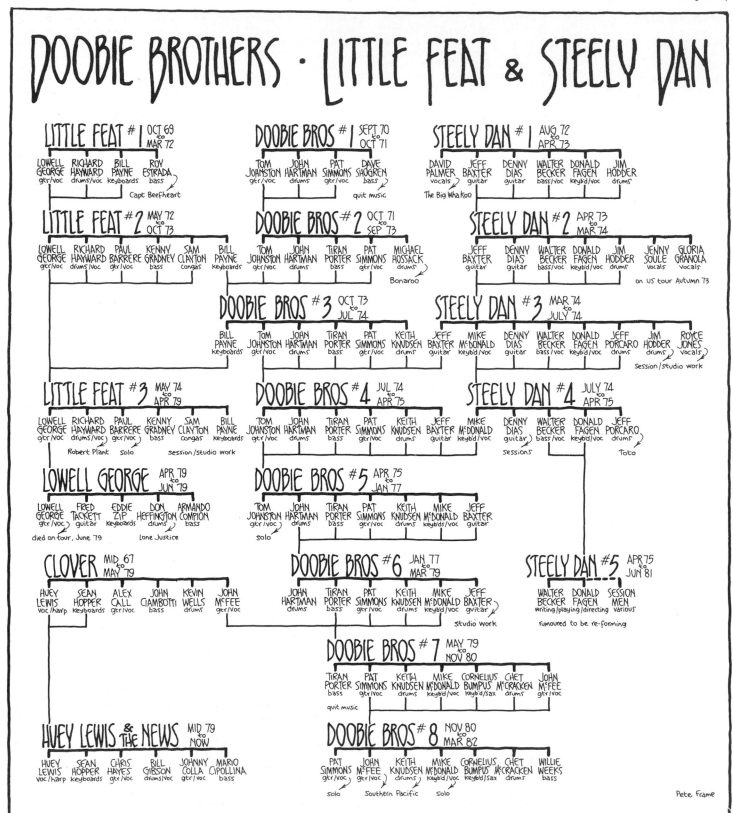

regarded as least impressive. Live double, **Waiting For Columbus** (1978), was also poor in relation to earlier work, which was hardly surprising since George was travelling separately during tours. Produced Grateful Dead's **Shakedown Street** same year.

Group finally split in April 1979 while recording final album. George, meanwhile, had begun solo career with average **Thanks I'll Eat It Here,** better work being anticipated in the future. On June 29, 1979, Lowell George died, age 34, from drug-induced heart failure in Arlington, Virginia; last gig had taken place at George Washington University in Washington DC the previous evening.

Ironically, posthumously released **Down On The Farm** revealed group's finest moments since early days. Since then, a further double album of new material has surfaced, **Hoy Hoy!.** Remnants of group were rumoured to be re-forming to promote work but, thankfully, idea was abandoned.

**Final line-up:** George; Hayward; Paul Barrere, guitar, vocals; Sam Clayton, vocals, percussion; Ken Gradney, bass; Bill Payne, keyboards, vocals, percussion.

**Albums:**
Little Feat (Warner Bros), 1971
Sailin' Shoes (Warner Bros), 1972
Dixie Chicken (Warner Bros), 1973
Feats Don't Fail Me Now (Warner Bros), 1974
The Last Record Album (Warner Bros), 1975
Time Loves A Hero (Warner Bros), 1977
Waiting For Columbus (Warner Bros), 1978
Down On The Farm (Warner Bros), 1979
Hoy Hoy! (Warner Bros), 1981
As Time Goes By (Warner Bros) compilation, 1986 **CD**

*Lowell George Solo:*
Thanks, I'll Eat It Here (Warner Bros), 1979

# Little Richard
US vocalist, composer, pianist.
Born Richard Wayne Penniman, Macon, Georgia, December 5, 1935.

**Career:** Family had strong religious ties; Richard was Seventh Day Adventist before leaving home for 'medicine show'. Adopted by white Macon couple Ann and Enotris Johnson, who featured as 'Miss Ann' (an intense blues) and as co-writer (Enotris) on **Long Tall Sally** in artist's later career.

Musical career began in 1951. Won talent contest in Atlanta as 'Little Richard'; the prize was a contract with RCA. Two sessions yielded eight songs, mostly ballads and frantic jump-blues. Richard's intense tenor voice was influenced by rich, throaty Roy Brown and gospelly blues-wailer Billy Wright.

Success was very limited, and by late 1953 he signed with Peacock Records. During three years recording with the Tempo Toppers vocal group, singles made only local sales. Richard sent demo tape to Art Rupe at Specialty Records. Rupe negotiated release from Peacock, and sent producer Robert 'Bumps' Blackwell to New Orleans to cut some sides with Richard. Results wrote new chapter in annals of rock'n'roll; debut **Tutti Frutti** charted in late 1955, followed by gems like **Long Tall Sally, Rip It Up, Ready Teddy, Lucille, Good Golly Miss Molly** and **The Girl Can't Help It**; latter also became a movie with Richard in cameo performance. ('Don't Knock The Rock' and 'Mr Rock And Roll' also featured him briefly.)

In 1957 Richard suddenly relinquished rock'n'roll and turned to religion. Career became patchy; Specialty lifted LP tracks for

**Above: The mercurial Lowell George, leading light of Little Feat, died on June 29, 1979.**

pop hits; he cut gospel songs for various labels, including Coral, End, Goldisc and Mercury (Mercury under the direction of Quincy Jones).

By 1962 Richard's vocals were heard on Little Star singles credited to his band the Upsetters. Then came Mercury single **He Got What He Wanted** with just gospel undertones. 1963 deal with Atlantic yielded gospel sides. 1964 took Richard back to Specialty with storming rocker **Bama Lama Bama Loo.** Moved to Vee Jay to record mixture of soul-tinged new material and crass re-hashes of Specialty classics. Among worthwhile singles were **Without Love** and **I Don't Know What You've Got But It's Got Me,** his only chart hit on Vee Jay.

Richard then made some interesting raunchy soul sides for Modern and Kent; moved on to Okeh in 1966. Debut **Poor Dog** charted briefly. Toured UK and recorded **Get Down With It,** his most torrid rocker in years. 

Lean times ensued—brash soul dancers on Brunswick, contemporary production on Reprise; subsequent discs appeared on Green

**The Georgia Peach, Little Richard. Courtesy Charly Records.**

Mountain, Manticore and Mainstream. Richard went from being a refreshingly original baggy-suited stand-up pianist and screamer to an embarrassing poseur in tight pink jumpsuits and effeminate make-up. He then suddenly found religion yet again and rejected his previous homosexuality: 'God made Adam and Eve, not Adam and Steve' he quipped in the best-selling biography 'The Quasar Of Rock'n'Roll', put together by English dentist and rock fan Chas 'Dr Rock' White.

Book put Richard back in limelight, and subsequent British TV programme about his chequered career showed him to be in good health and witty form. Richard's early hits were some of the alltime greatest rock'n'roll records, and influenced scores of rockers from the Beatles downwards. To many, Little Richard still personifies rebellious spirit of rock'n'roll, despite (or perhaps because of) gayness and continued religious leanings.

| Hit Singles: | US | UK |
|---|---|---|
| Tutti Frutti, 1956 | 17 | 29 |
| Long Tall Sally, 1956 | 6 | 3 |
| Rip It Up, 1956 | 17 | 30 |
| She's Got It, 1957 | — | 15 |
| The Girl Can't Help It, 1957 | 49 | 9 |
| Lucille, 1957 | 21 | 10 |
| Jenny Jenny, 1957 | 10 | 11 |
| Keep A Knockin', 1957 | 8 | 21 |
| Good Golly Miss Molly, 1958 | 10 | 8 |
| Baby Face, 1959 | 41 | 2 |
| By The Light Of The Silvery Moon, 1959 | — | 17 |
| Bama Lama Bama Loo, 1964 | — | 20 |

**Albums:**
His Biggest Hits (Specialty/London), 1957
The Fabulous Little Richard (Specialty/London), 1959
Well Alright (Specialty/—), 1959
Grooviest 17 hits (Speciality/—), 1960
The Original (—/Sonet), 1972
All Time Hits (—/Sonet), 1972
22 Original Hits (—/Warwick), 1977
Greatest Hits (—/Embassy), 1977
Tutti Frutti (Accord/—), 1981
Get Down With It (Edsel), 1982
His Greatest Recordings (Ace), 1985
20 Classic Cuts (Ace), 1986 **CD**
Lifetime Friend (WEA), 1986 **CD**
Little Richard The Collection, 1986 **CD**
The Sessions (Subway), 1987
Rip It Up (Topline), 1987 **CD**
Rock'n'Roll Resurrection (Charly), 1987 **CD**
Little Richard GreaTEST Hits (MCS), 1988 **CD**

# Nils Lofgren
US vocalist, composer, guitarist, pianist.
Born Chicago, 1953.

**Career:** Lofgren's parents moved to Maryland when he was a teenager. He and his brother began playng in local DC bands. Nils' talents came to attention of Crazy Horse(▶) who

featured him on their first album. (**Crazy Horse** remains strong upon hearing even today, thanks in part to Lofgren's lead runs.) This association led to work with Neil Young(▶) who used Lofgren on **After The Goldrush.**

18-year-old Lofgren returned to DC to set up own band, Grin. (From this era, LP **1+1** or compilation **The Best Of Grin** are worth a listen.) Grin had split by 1973 and Lofgren was happy to join Neil Young's(▶) **Tonight's The Night** tour.

Lofgren spent good part of 1974 re-forming Grin and watching it fall apart again. This background ensured modicum of interest when **Nils Lofgren** was released in 1975. Follow-up tour developed cult following and Lofgren seemed ready for stardom. Curious LP, **Back It Up,** appeared, which was 'authorised bootleg' pressed as promo only item. It became overnight collectors' item.

Despite this, even excellent 1976 **Cry Tough** and tour as opening act for Boston failed to gain expected results. Subsequent LPs are all of interest, **Night After Night** being live. 1979 LP **Nils** managed a lot of US

**I Came To Dance, Nils Lofgren. Courtesy A&M Records.**

airplay, but didn't chart well. Lofgren again played for Neil Young on 1982 **Trans** LP and joined Young's touring schedule. As expected, Lofgren played with great economy and style, which makes his only slightly successful solo career all the more perplexing the more so, his having played guitar for Bruce Springsteen(▶) on latter's acclaimed 1985 world tour.

Guitar: Fender Stratocaster

**Albums:**
1+1 (SpinDizzy/Epic), 1971
Nils Lofgren (A&M), 1975
Cry Tough (A&M), 1976
The Best Of Grin Featuring Nils Lofgren (Epic/CBS), 1976
I Came To Dance (A&M), 1977
Night After Night (A&M), 1977*
Nils (A&M), 1979
The Best Of (A&M), 1981
A Rhythm Romance (A&M), 1982
Night Fades Away (Backstreet), 1983
Wonderland (MCA), 1983
Code Of The Road (Towerbell), 1986 (Double)
*Live

# Los Lobos
**Current line-up:** Louis Perez, drums; David Hildago, guitar; Conrad Lozano, bass; Cesar Rosas and Frank Gonzales, vocals.

**Career:** Band began as a top 40 copy band in the US before switching in the early Seventies to exploring the sounds that have sprung up along the Rio Grande. After eclectic experiments playing traditional acoustic versions of classic Mexican-American tunes, the quintet

**By The Light Of The Moon, Los Lobos. Courtesy Splash Records.**

electrified their line-up and began winning a new following on the Los Angeles club circuit.

Signed to Splash Records in 1983, releasing **EP** and **Time To Dance**. One track **Anselma** won a Grammy award in 1984. First full-length album **How Will The Wolf Survive?** followed in October that year and band embarked on a tour of US, Europe, Japan and Australia. Recording work started in January 1986 on next album **By The Light Of The Moon** which included **Shakin' Shakin' Shakes, All I Wanted To Do Was Dance, Tears Of God** and **One Time One Night**.

Los Lobos' major commercial break came with their contributions to the film soundtrack "La Bamba", based on the life of Richie Valens and in which they also appeared. The title track alone soared to number 1 in the UK chart and was also a major Stateside hit while the soundtrack album has also been a big seller both sides of the Atlantic.

Main songwriters in Los Lobos are Louis Perez and David Hildago who manage to create a versatile mix of Tex-Mex, rock and R&B, country and ballads topped off with commercial appeal.

**Hit Singles:**

|  | US | UK |
|---|---|---|
| Bamba, 1987 | 1 | 1 |
| Come On Lets Go, 1987 | 21 | 18 |

**Albums:**
And A Time To Dance (Roughtrade/Splash), 1984
By The Light Of The Moon (Splash), 1987 **CD**
How Will The Wolf Survive (Splash), 1987 **CD**

**Below: David Hildago leads Los Lobos in their popular Tex-Mex brand of music, with R&B, country and ballads thrown in.**

# Love
US group formed 1965.

**Original line-up:** Arthur Lee, vocals, guitar, keyboards; Bryan Maclean, guitar, vocals; Ken Forssi, bass; Alban 'Snoopy' Pfisterer, drums; John Echols, guitar.

**Career:** Arthur Lee grew up in Memphis but moved to West Coast after British invasion (before it became de rigueur for aspiring American musicians). Was part of nascent music scene in California with several small groups like the LAGs (Los Angeles Group, a name inspired by his hometown success Booker T and the MGs(▶) — Memphis Group) and American Four. He saw Byrds(▶) perform and decided to explore their style. With Byrds' roadie Bryan Maclean he lined up Forssi, Echols and a drummer named Don Conka.

At first they called themselves the Grass Roots, but changed to Love when another band appeared with same name (later to become strong US singles band). At some point Conka was thrown out and 'Snoopy' brought in.

Live Love was always hit or miss and this edge of uncertainty made them a joy to watch. Loyal LA following (group had residency at Bido Lito's in Hollywood) provided strong local reputation. This led Jac Holzman to sign them when he decided Elektra labels should expand into growing rock field. First album was recorded late 1965 and released March 1966. Generally original material, Beatles-Byrds sound and cohesive impact presented very strong debut as well as sounding out growing American response to British rock. **My Little Red Book** became minor hit and **Signed D.C.** (a nod to Don Conka) got some FM play.

Lee already planned to push sound even further on next album. **Da Capo** had two additional players: Tjay Cantrelli (horns) and Michael Stuart (drums), with Snoopy on keyboards. They provided the fuller sound Lee sought. Heavy metal had not yet been invented but Lee laid some groundwork with **7 And 7 Is**. He can also take some blame for all magna opera of progressive rock for recording 19-minute **Revelation** over entire second side.

Big-time success failed to come. Uneven live performances and lack of proper tours kept Love an 'underground' (i.e. unknown) band. Love came to be appreciated more in

UK than at home (best evidenced by availability of Love albums in UK after US deletion). Size of band also became cumbersome and thrown together make-up took on 'hired hands' atmosphere as Snoopy was fired and Cantrelli disappeared. With remaining members, Lee recorded one of rock's finest albums, **Forever Changes**. It had everything: highs, lows, loud, soft, fast, slow — all mixed into symphonic excitement as fresh today as in 1967. Equally important then, it had lyrics and themes deep enough in year of Beatles(▶) **Sgt. Pepper** LP. Continued availability confirms its timelessness. However, it failed to win massive audience Lee felt his masterpiece deserved. Within months Love was gone.

In 1968 Lee produced new Love with Jay Donnellan (guitar), Frank Fayad (bass) and George Suranovich (drums). Lee again tried single-handedly to invent heavy metal. This Love lost British-influenced harmonies, replacing them with erratic volume on **Four Sail**. With this album's failure, Lee moved to Blue Thumb Records which later (1969) released double set, **Out Here**. Using recordings from same session as **Four Sail**, it hardly seemed auspicious start on new label.

**Da Capo, Love. Courtesy Elektra Records.**

1970 saw replacement of Donnellan (a.k.a. Jay Lewis) with Gary Rowles, and Love made rare visit to England. This line-up recorded **False Start**, unnotable but for one track, **The Everlasting First**, from Lee's collaboration with Jimi Hendrix(▶) during UK visit. (Supposedly an album's worth of material was recorded with Hendrix but results have never been released.) Weakness of **False Start** doomed Love; Lee broke up band before end of 1971. Using old mate Frank Fayad, he released solo album, **Vindicator** (1972), which showed some return to humour and enthusiasm of early Love, but still missed earlier standards and was generally ignored.

In 1973 Elektra released UK compilation **Love Masters,** worth finding for John Tobler's liner notes. Lee recorded another solo album in late '73 but financial problems prevented its appearance.

Love re-appeared in 1974; Lee, Melvan Whittington (guitars), John Sterling (guitars), Joe Blocker (drums), Sherwood Akuna (bass), Robert Rozelle (bass) and some guests/session musicians recorded the poor **Reel-To-Real**. Love deservedly disappeared again. Lee continued to play various one-off dates, trying to live down past.

One musician with whom he worked was John Sterling. In 1977 he got Lee and Maclean to re-form Love with himself, Kim Kesterton (bass) and George Suranovich (drums) from Love 2. Band tried recapturing the feel of early Love but perhaps should have been more inventive. (Bruce Gary (The Knack) drummed at some point for this version of Love.)

Interest in Love never died out as **Forever Changes** remained in Elektra catalogue, and Rhino Records sold a reasonable amount of 1980 compilation, **Best Of Love**. This led

Rhino to release **Arthur Lee** in 1981 — interesting but totally out of sync with times. MCA released curious LP in 1982 with one side featuring eight tracks from **Out Here** and live side from Fillmore East with no recording dates or personnel listed. The undying loyalty and unfailing interest in Love is justifiable since they were a brilliant band with several excellent albums, and classic **Forever Changes** LP is a must for any record collection.

**Final line-up:** Lee; Maclean; John Sterling, guitar; Kim Kesterton, bass; George Suranovich, drums.

**Albums:**
Love (Elektra), 1966
Da Capo (Elektra), 1967
Forever Changes (Elektra), 1967
Four Sail (Elektra), 1969
Out Here (Blue Thumb/Harvest), 1969
False Start (Blue Thumb/Harvest), 1970
Love Revisited (Elektra), 1970
Love Masters (—/Elektra), 1973
Reel-To-Real (RSO), 1974
Best Of Love (Rhino/—), 1980
Love Live (Rhino/—), 1982
Love (MCA/—), 1982

*Lee Solo:*
Vindicator (A&M), 1972
Arthur Lee (Rhino/Beggars Banquet), 1982

# Lovin' Spoonful
US group formed 1964.

**Original line-up:** John Sebastian, guitar, vocals, harmonica, autoharp; Zal Yanovsky, guitar; Joe Butler, drums; Steve Boone, bass.

**Career:** Sebastian and Yanovsky were together in folk group Mugwumps. Rest of band went on to form Mamas And Papas(▶); Sebastian travelled south. Upon return to New York in 1965, producer Eric Jacobson suggested Sebastian record his own songs. Lovin' Spoonful became New York club circuit favourites and record deal with Kama Sutra followed.

Band refused to dress or sound like popular English groups of time, although British invasion influence is obvious in band's rock fusion of folk and blues. Sebastian's **Do You Believe In Magic?** reflected excitement and energy of growing rock scene. **Daydream**

**Greatest Hits, The Lovin' Spoonful. Courtesy Kama Sutra Records.**

broke group in UK and **Summer In The City** became classic out-of-school, good time paean, as well as US No. 1. Establishment wanted to tap rock's enthusiasm and Sebastian found himself in demand for scoring 'with it' movies (Francis Ford Coppola's 'You're A Big Boy Now' and Woody Allen's 'What's Up Tiger Lily?').

Drug culture was still hidden side of rock music and Yanovsky's bust in 1967 proved devastating blow to popularity. Worse, Yanovsky went free by naming others involved and band's reputation within rock business was finished. Jerry Yester (brother of Association's Jim Yester) replaced Yanovsky for **Everything Playing** LP. By 1968, group had collapsed. Subsequent careers have been checkered. Sebastian appeared at Woodstock in 1969, and even got US hit with TV theme **Welcome Back, Kotter** in 1976, but generally failed to match expectations. Butler tried using Lovin' Spoonful name for flop 1969 LP. Yester has produced Tom Waits(▶).

With hindsight it can be said that there was little progression in band's career. Sebastian's songs seem lightweight now and it's hard to see what all the excitement was about. Still, their infectious sound influenced nearly everyone from the Beatles to Dylan. It is that widespread impact which makes up Lovin' Spoonful's legacy.

**Final line-up:** Sebastian; Butler; Boone; Jerry Yester, guitar.

**Hit Singles:**

| | US | UK |
|---|---|---|
| Do You Believe In Magic?, 1965 | 9 | — |
| You Didn't Have To Be So Nice, 1965 | 10 | — |
| Daydream, 1966 | 2 | 2 |
| Did You Ever Have To Make Up Your Mind, 1966 | 2 | — |
| Summer In The City, 1966 | 1 | 8 |
| Rain On The Roof, 1966 | 10 | — |
| Nashville Cats, 1966 | 8 | 26 |
| Darling Be Home Soon, 1967 | 15 | 44 |
| Six O'Clock, 1967 | 18 | — |

*John Sebastian Solo:*

| | | |
|---|---|---|
| Welcome Back, 1976 | 1 | — |

**Albums:**
The Best . . . Lovin' Spoonful (Kama Sutra/—), 1967
File (—/Pye), 1977

*Worth Searching Out:*
Hums (Kama Sutra), 1967
You're A Big Boy Now (Kama Sutra), 1967
Greatest Hits (Golden Hour), 1975
Golden Hour Of The Lovin' Spoonful's Greatest Hits (—/Golden Hour), 1977
Jug Band Music (Edsel), 1986
Collection (Masters), 1986 (Holland)

# Nick Lowe

UK vocalist, bassist, producer.
Born Woolridge, Suffolk, March 24, 1949.

**Career:** First significant group was Kippington Lodge, from Tunbridge Wells area; also included Brinsley Schwarz, guitar, Bob Andrews, keyboards. Recorded series of singles during second half of '60s without success, so decided at end of decade to change group name to Brinsley Schwarz. Management company Famepushers Ltd tried to launch 'new' group with debut gig at Fillmore East, New York, to coincide with release of first LP. This resulted in few taking group seriously, and career blighted thereafter, despite five more LPs, several of which were of above average quality, with many Lowe songs. Group folded in March 1975.

Lowe worked as songwriter and record producer (for Graham Parker(▶) & The Rumour, which included Schwarz and Andrews) and released pseudonymous singles, then joined new manager Jake Riviera (real name Andrew Jakeman) in launch of Stiff Records with ex-Brinsley manager Dave Robinson.

First Stiff release was Lowe's classic single **So It Goes**, and much of label's early output involved Lowe either as artist or producer (for

**Above: The much missed Lovin' Spoonful as they appeared on British TV show 'Ready Steady Go' in the 1960s.**

The Damned(▶), Wreckless Eric, etc) until Riviera signed Elvis Costello(▶), whose records Lowe produced for several years with great success. Also worked as producer for Dr Feelgood(▶), plus further Graham Parker album. Formed alliance with Dave Edmunds(▶) in group Rockpile, featured with Costello, Edmunds and Ian Dury in Stiff package tour at end of 1977.

Left Stiff with Riviera and Costello in late 1977, signed with Radar label; made UK Top 10 with first Radar release; had further hits by end of 1979. Continued to produce Costello, and recorded own albums and Edmunds albums using Rockpile musicians. Also produced first single by Pretenders(▶). Married Carlene Carter (step-daughter of Johnny Cash).

During 1980, contractual hassles which had prevented Rockpile recording under group name resolved, but this only resulted in group splitting up after single LP. Lowe made third solo album; produced LPs for Costello and Dr Feelgood, as well as for wife during 1981, and in 1982 formed band Noise To Go, with Paul Carrack (ex-Ace, Squeeze(▶)), who was achieving solo success on his own account. Also produced Carrack and Fabulous Thunderbirds(▶). Cut fourth LP. After much touring, spent time during first half of 1983 producing John Hiatt.

Nick Lowe is regarded as a man of many talents—producer, songwriter, singer, musician—but has only achieved major success consistently as record producer. He is well known around the world, but conceivably has yet to reach full artistic potential due to

**Jesus Of Cool, Nick Lowe. Courtesy Radar Records.**

diversification. At his best, his 'pure pop for now people' has few equals in history of rock music.

**Hit Singles:**

| | US | UK |
|---|---|---|
| I Love The Sound Of Breaking Glass, 1978 | — | 7 |
| Cruel To Be Kind, 1979 | 12 | 12 |

**Albums:**
*With Brinsley Schwarz:*
Nervous On The Road (Liberty), 1972
New Favourites Of Brinsley Schwarz (Liberty), 1974

*Solo:*
Jesus Of Cool (Columbia/Radar) (US title — Pure Pop For Now People), 1978
Labour Of Lust (Columbia/Radar), 1979
Nick The Knife (Columbia/F-Beat), 1982
The Abominable Showman (Columbia/F-Beat), 1983
Nick Lowe And His Cowboy Outfit (RCA), 1984
16 All-Time Lowes (Demon), 1984
Rose Of England (F-Beat), 1985

*With Rockpile:*
Seconds

*Worth Searching Out:*
*With Brinsley Schwarz:*
Fifteen Thoughts Of Brinsley Schwarz (compilation) (UA), 1978
Of Pleasure (Columbia/F-Beat), 1980

# Lynyrd Skynyrd

US group formed 1965.
**Original line-up:** Ronnie Van Zant, vocals; Gary Rossington, guitar; Allen Collins, guitar.

**Career:** Originally formed in Jacksonville, Florida, as high-school trio, named after their authoritarian PE teacher, Leonard Skinner. By 1972, full line-up completed with Leon Wilkeson (bass), Billy Powell (keyboards) and Robert Burns (drums). Discovered playing Southern bars and clubs by Al Kooper(▶), who immediately signed them to his Sounds of the South label. Session bassist Ed King (ex-Strawberry Alarm Clock) brought in by Kooper as full-time member. First album, **Pronounced Leh-nerd Skin-nerd**, received favourable response. Closing cut **Free Bird** later became group anthem, achieving minor chart placings following several re-releases.

Career boosted by playing support on Who's(▶) 1973 US tour. Quickly established themselves as one of America's most cele-

brated boogie bands, boasting three guitarists. Next album, **Second Helping**, went gold. Set included US hit single, **Sweet Home Alabama**, their famous riposte to Neil Young's(▶) scathing **Southern Man** and **Alabama** put downs. Third album, **Nuthin' Fancy** also went gold. Included US top 30 hit **Saturday Night Special.**

Extensive touring schedules consistently drained group's energies, prompting Burns' departure, replaced by Artimus Pyle. Not surprisingly, seasoned sessioneer Ed King left shortly afterwards. Undeterred, Skynyrd kept on boogieing and their increasingly raucous behaviour inspired strong, devoted following.

On October 20, 1977, a week after the release of the notable **Street Survivors** LP, Skynyrd embarked on lengthy US tour. Their private plane took off from Greenville, South Carolina, en route for Baton Rouge, Louisiana; approaching Gillsburg, Mississippi, the plane crashed in a wood, 200 yards from an open field. Casualties included Ronnie Van Zant, Steve Gaines, roadie Dean Kirkpatrick, and backing singer Cassie Gaines. The tragedy shook the rock world, for the group had always been much loved for their aggressive, uncompromising approach: MCA quickly stopped release of **Survivors** LP with its sadly prophetic cover. Even Neil Young sang **Sweet Home Alabama** at one of his concerts in their memory.

The Rossington Collins Band emerged with some remaining members of Skynyrd, retaining the spirit of the original group.

**Final line-up:** Van Zant; Rossington; Collins; Artimus Pyle, drums; Leo Wilkeson, bass; Billy Powell, keyboards; Steve Gaines, guitar.

**Hit Singles:**

| | US | UK |
|---|---|---|
| Sweet Home Alabama, 1974 | 8 | — |
| Free Bird, 1974 | 19 | — |

**Albums:**
Pronounced Leh-nerd Skin-nerd (MCA), 1974
Second Helping (MCA), 1974
Nuthin' Fancy (MCA), 1975
Gimme Back My Bullets (MCA), 1976
One More From The Road (MCA), 1976*
Street Survivors (MCA), 1977
First And Last (MCA), 1978
A Legend (MCA), 1987
Nuthin' Fancy (MCA), 1987 **CD**
*Double Live LP

# Madness

UK group formed 1978.

**Original/Final line up:** Suggs, (Graham McPherson), vocals; Chas Smash, vocals, compere, dancer; Chris Foreman, guitar; Lee 'Kix' Thompson, saxophone; Mark Bedford, bass; Dan Woodgate, drums.

**Career:** Formed in North London as the Invaders, changed name to Madness (after song by ska hero Prince Buster). In 1979, Specials(▶) launched 2 Tone records; Madness invited to cut single **The Prince/Madness**, which scored first hit. Group then signed by Stiff and became biggest act on label by far with 13 further consecutive UK hits and five Top 10 LPs by end of 1982, mostly composed within band.

With appealing mixture of ska (now largely abandoned), music hall, pop, R&B, visual comedy and biting yet amusing social comment, Madness have become most consistent UK hitmakers of '80s, guaranteed sell-out shows wherever they appear in UK, and to some extent in Europe. American success eluded them until 1983, perhaps because of curiously British lyrical content/humour and appearance. In 1981 made feature film financed by Stiff, 'Take It Or Leave It', which predictably achieved mammoth sales for video medium. **Complete Madness**, TV-advertised hits compilation, topped UK album charts for three weeks during 1982.

**Our House** (1983) marked US breakthrough, followed by five-week tour including dates as support for both Bowie(▶) and The Police(▶).

Following Christmas gig at London's Lyceum, in aid of Greenpeace, Mike Barson announced decision to quit band to live in Holland with Dutch wife Sandra.

As six-piece, the band greeted 1984 with **Michael Caine** single on which the actor "sang". Also opened own Liquidator studio in North London.

After five years and 18 consecutive hit singles, they left Stiff in May 1984 to form own Zarjazz label with Feargal Sharkey single as first release.

Pulling in members of UB40(▶), Specials(▶), General Public(▶), Pioneers and Afrodiziak, Madness put together admirable **Starvation** charity single as their contribution to African famine relief (see Band Aid/Live Aid entry) in 1985 but it peaked at 33 on national chart. Meanwhile, a band called the Wayfarers played to packed house at Bull and Gate pub in Kentish Town, London—and proved to be Madness rehearsing their new album prior to recording. Following hit single **Uncle Sam** showed band had lost none of its good humour.

That year band also released **Mad Not Mad** album which charted and spun off several hit singles. However, level of success was not as great as in previous years, and it began to seem as though band's time had come and gone. Madness finally split in 1986, leaving legacy of music which combined elements of British music-hall and Jamaican ska in peculiarly piquant blend. They are sorely missed.

| Hit Singles: | US | UK |
|---|---|---|
| The Prince, 1979 | — | 16 |
| One Step Beyond, 1979 | — | 7 |
| My Girl, 1980 | — | 3 |
| Work Rest And Play, 1980 | — | 6 |
| Baggy Trousers, 1980 | — | 3 |
| Embarrassment, 1980 | — | 4 |
| Return Of The Los Palmas 7, 1981 | — | 7 |
| Grey Day, 1981 | — | 4 |
| Shut Up, 1981 | — | 7 |
| It Must Be Love, 1981 | — | 4 |
| Cardiac Arrest, 1982 | — | 14 |
| House Of Fun, 1982 | — | 1 |
| Driving In My Car, 1982 | — | 4 |
| Our House, 1982 | — | 5 |
| Tomorrow's Just Another Day, 1983 | — | 8 |
| Yesterday's Men, 1985 | — | 18 |

**Albums:**
One Step Beyond (Sire/Stiff), 1980
Absolutely (Sire/Stiff), 1980

Seven (—/Stiff), 1981
Complete Madness (—/Stiff), 1982 **CD**
The Rise And Fall (—/Stiff), 1982
Keep Moving (Stiff), 1984
Mad Not Mad (Virgin), 1985
Utter Madness (Virgin), 1986 **CD**
Mad Not Mad (Zarjazz), 1987 **CD**

# Madonna

US vocalist.
Born Madonna Caccione, Detroit, Michigan, 1961.

**Career:** Sometimes the image is greater than the music. Madonna burst to superstardom in 1982 as much because of her widely reported allegedly outrageous behaviour as for the success of her records. It seemed the former bred the latter.

**Below: Madness, Stiff Records biggest hitmakers, live in London.**

**Above: Madonna looks set to see out the '80s as an all-round entertainer—singer, dancer, actress. Refreshing changes of image maintain the public's interest.**

That enigmatic mix of angel and seductress which has such dynamic appeal, Madonna encapsulated it all with her mega-hit **Like A Virgin**, topping the charts in 1984.

Raised in a huge Catholic family, Madonna studied dancing from early childhood, becoming proficient in ballet, modern and jazz dancing. Moving to New York in late '70s, she performed for two years with Pearl Lange and Alvin Ailey dance troupes then turned to acting and starred in underground movie 'Certain Sacrifice' and other films.

Turning to music, Madonna lived in Paris for a spell, returning to New York to work in various bands, learning to play drums, guitar and keyboards and develop sexy neo-punk image—sporting spiky hair-do and torn tights as well as prominent crucifix. Signed to Sire Records in 1982, she topped dance charts with **Everybody**, remixed by Rusty Egan for UK market.

Acclaimed **Madonna** album was followed two years later by potent **Like A Virgin** set produced by Chic's(▶) Nile Rodgers, and Madonna pursued parallel career as actress, working on first major starring role in 'Desparately Seeking Susan'. Married actor Sean Penn in 1985.

Latterly Madonna has continued to maintain hit output, while attempting to capitalize on relatively successful movie debut by making more films. Results have been less than earth-shattering however, with George Harrison-produced **Shanghai Surprise** (also starring husband Penn) being critical and commercial disaster, and **Who's That Girl?** faring little better.

However, singer has proved to be canny careerist in the past, and may be considerable contender in longevity stakes. Like long-running

rocker David Bowie, Madonna continually changes and updates her image, and has excellent understanding of her market. May yet develop into all-round entertainer.

| Hit Singles: | US | UK |
|---|---|---|
| Holiday, 1983* | 16 | 3 |
| Borderline, 1984 | 10 | — |
| Lucky Star, 1984 | 4 | 14 |
| Like A Virgin, 1985 | 1 | 3 |
| Material Girl, 1985 | 1 | 2 |
| Crazy For You, 1985 | 1 | 2 |
| Angel, 1985 | 5 | 5 |
| Into The Groove, 1985 | 1 | 1 |
| Dress You Up, 1985 | 5 | 5 |
| Gambler, 1985 | 4 | 4 |
| True Blue, 1986 | 3 | 1 |
| Live To Tell, 1986 | — | 2 |
| Open Your Heart, 1986 | 1 | 4 |
| Papa Don't Preach, 1986 | 1 | 1 |
| Who's That Girl, 1987 | 1 | 1 |
| La Isla Bonita, 1987 | 3 | 1 |
| Causing A Commotion, 1987 | 2 | 4 |
| Look Of Love, 1987 | — | 9 |

*1985 in UK

**True Blue, Madonna. Courtesy Sire Records.**

**Albums:**
Madonna (Sire), 1983 **CD**
Like A Virgin (Sire), 1984 **CD**
True Blue (Sire), 1986 **CD**
You Can Dance (Sire), 1987 **CD**

# The Mamas And The Papas

US vocal group formed 1965

**Original/Final line-up:** John Philips, Michelle Phillips, Cass Elliott, Denny Doherty.

**Career:** One of first aggregations to make freewheeling, California hippie image commercially acceptable, with series of records that combined strong, memorable melodies with soaring vocal harmonies and distinctive folk-rock sound.

Ex-folkie John Phillips and wife Michelle came together with Cass Elliott and Denny Doherty, former members of New York band the Mugwumps, in Virgin Islands. Almost immediately guiding light Phillips moved outfit to LA and arranged record deal with Lou Adler's newly formed Dunhill label.

First single was Phillips' **California Dreamin'**, a key flower-power cut almost as evocative as **San Francisco (Wear Some Flowers In Your Hair)** which Phillips also composed. Top 10 hit in US and substantial hit elsewhere, it set group on road to success, including three more major hits in 1966.

Despite single success and several gold albums, group was not destined for longevity. John and Michelle Phillips' marriage started teetering in 1966, and problems caused by this and other internal dissensions led to break-up in 1968. Subsequently John Phillips went into film production and took up lifestyle of California pop aristocrat. Michelle Phillips has sporadically surfaced as an actress ('Dillinger', 'Valentino'), while providing staple fare for gossip columns; Denny Doherty more or less disappeared from sight, while Cass Elliott died in 1974 of a heart attack, after patchy solo ventures.

Despite their brief career, the Mamas and the Papas had considerable influence on '60s music scene, paving way for more heavyweight protagonists of Aquarian age. Furthermore, they left behind cuts which have become much-played classics, particularly **California Dreamin'.**

**Hit Singles:**

| | US | UK |
|---|---|---|
| California Dreamin', 1966 | 4 | 23 |
| Monday Monday, 1966 | 1 | 3 |
| I Saw Her Again, 1966 | 5 | 11 |
| Words Of Love, 1966 | 5 | 47 |
| Dedicated To The One I Love, 1967 | 2 | 2 |
| Creeque Alley, 1967 | 5 | 9 |
| Twelve Thirty, 1967 | 20 | — |

**Albums:**
Farewell To The First Golden Era (Dunhill/—), 1968
The Papas And The Mamas (Dunhill/RCA), 1968
Hits Of Gold (ABC), 1969
A Gathering Of Flowers (Dunhill/Probe), 1970
Sixteen Of Their Greatest Hits (Dunhill/—), 1970
Twenty Golden Hits (Dunhill/Probe), 1972
The Best Of The Mamas And The Papas (—/Arcade), 1977
Golden Greats (MCA), 1985 **CD**

*Worth Searching Out:*
If You Can Believe Your Eyes And Ears (Dunhill/RCA), 1966 **CD**

**Hits Of Gold, The Mamas And The Papas. Courtesy ABC Records.**

# Manfred Mann

UK band formed 1962.
**Original line-up:** Manfred Mann, keyboards; Paul Jones, vocals, harmonica; Mike Vickers, reeds, guitar; Dave Richmond, bass; Mike Hugg, drums.

**Career:** South African-born Mann and Mike Hugg put together Mann-Hugg Blues Brothers in late 1962 and started gigging on burgeoning London blues circuit. Changing name to Manfred Mann, band signed with HMV and recorded first single, **Why Should We Not.**

Tom McGuinness replaced Dave Richmond on bass on release of third single, **5-4-3-2-1.** Track, which featured Paul Jones' harmonica, was adopted as theme tune for TV show 'Ready Steady Go' and became major hit. From that time until end of '60s, band were rarely out of singles charts, with succession of songs from wide variety of sources, particularly US soul material (**Doo Wah Diddy**

Diddy, **Oh No Not My Baby**) and Bob Dylan (**If You Gotta Go, Go Now; Just Like A Woman; Mighty Quinn**).

Changes took place during this period, however; Mike Vickers left at end of 1965, McGuinness switched to lead guitar and Jack Bruce joined on bass; six months later Jones left to pursue solo career as singer (and later actor), and Bruce quit to join supergroup Cream(▶). Their respective replacements were Mike D'Abo from Band Of Angels and Klaus Voorman (a Beatles(▶) cohort).

However, by end of decade, after 18 hit singles, members were tired of restrictions of pop formula. Mann folded band, and he and Hugg put together more ambitious Manfred Mann Chapter Three. More orientated towards albums, outfit lasted for couple of years. Mann then put together yet another outfit, Manfred's Mann's Earth Band. Original line-up comprised Mann, Colin Pattenden (bass), Mick Rogers (guitar), and Chris Slade (drums).

From beginning, band followed ambitious rock direction, backing album releases with heavy touring schedules in UK and US. In 1973 they had first hit single with **Joybringer**, based on theme from Holst's 'Planets', and in mid-'70s scored with cover of Bruce Springsteen's(▶) **Blinded By The Light.**
**Davy's On The Road Again** was also major hit, and since that time Earth Band has gone on recording and touring with continued moderate success. There have been several personnel changes, but the slightly enigmatic figure of Mann has given continuity.

Rarely less than interesting, Mann-led aggregations have provided much worthwhile music over last two decades.

**Current line-up:** (Manfred Mann's Earth Band); Mann; John Lingwood, drums; Chris Thompson, vocals; Steve Waller, guitar; Matt Irving, bass.

**Hit Singles:**

| | US | UK |
|---|---|---|
| *Manfred Mann:* | | |
| 5-4-3-2-1, 1964 | — | 5 |
| Hubble Bubble Toil And Trouble, 1964 | — | 11 |
| Doo Wah Diddy Diddy, 1964 | 1 | 1 |
| Sha La La, 1964 | 12 | 3 |
| Come Tomorrow, 1965 | 50 | 4 |
| Oh No Not My Baby, 1965 | — | 11 |
| If You Gotta Go, Go Now, 1965 | — | 2 |
| Pretty Flamingo, 1966 | 29 | 1 |
| Just Like A Woman, 1966 | — | 10 |
| Semi-Detached Suburban Mr James, 1966 | — | 2 |
| Ha! Ha! Said The Clown, 1967 | — | 4 |
| Mighty Quinn, 1968 | 10 | 1 |
| My Name Is Jack, 1968 | — | 8 |
| Fox On The Run, 1968 | — | 5 |
| Ragamuffin Man, 1969 | — | 8 |
| *Manfred Mann's Earth Band:* | | |
| Joybringer, 1973 | — | 9 |
| Blinded By The Light, 1976 | 1 | 6 |
| Davy's On The Road Again, 1978 | — | 6 |

**Albums:**
*Manfred Mann:*
The Best Of Manfred Mann (Mercury/Nut), 1977

*Manfred Mann Chapter Three:*
*Worth Searching Out:*
Chapter Three (Polydor), 1970

*Manfred Mann's Earth Band:*
Earth Band (Bronze), 1972
Glorified, Magnified (Bronze), 1972
Messin' (Bronze), 1973
Solar Fire (Polydor/Bronze), 1973
The Good Earth (Warner Bros/Bronze), 1974
Nightingales And Bombers (Warner Bros/Bronze), 1975
Mannerisms (—/Sonic), 1976

The Roaring Silence (Warner Bros/Bronze), 1976
Watch (Warner Bros/Bronze), 1978
Angel Station (Warner Bros/Bronze), 1979
The R&B Years (—/See For Miles), 1982
Semi-Detached Suburban (—/EMI), 1979
Chance (Warner Bros/Bronze), 1980
Somewhere In Afrika (—/Bronze), 1983
Budapest (—/Bronze), 1984
The Singles Plus (EMI), 1986 **CD**

# Manhattan Transfer

US vocal group formed 1969.
**Original line-up:** Tim Hauser; Janis Siegel; Alan Paul; Laurel Masse.

**Career:** Originally signed to Capitol Records in 1969; 1971 set **Jukin'** initially failed miserably; Re-vamped, re-styled and with only Hauser remaining, group earned reputation in early '70s in New York.

Hauser had been with R&B vocal group the Criterions in '50s; later worked as producer and actor. Paul (with BA in Music and Drama) was film and stage actor; appearing on Broadway in 'Camelot', 'The King & I' and 'Oliver'. Masse and Siegel had singing backgrounds — primarily jingles and session vocals. Siegel had recorded for Lieber & Stoller with the Young Generation on Red Bird R&B label.

**Extensions, Manhattan Transfer. Courtesy Atlantic Records.**

After period in gay bars and bath houses, quartet developed kitsch swing era image, but vocal ability partially swamped by grandiose stage act. Transfer, however, took good advice on album material; have charted sporadically since **Operator** (1975). Main success was in Europe, particularly France, and UK. Scored eight British Top 50 entries between 1976 and 1980. Lyrical ballad **Chanson D'Amour** made No. 1 in UK.

With Cheryl Bentyne replacing Masse, Transfer entered new era with '79 set **Extensions**. Produced by guitarist Jay Graydon, album had futuristic air while retaining strong jazz roots. Included stage favourite **Birdland** (used as jingle for Akai stereo), rock-flavoured **Nothin' You Can do About It** and electronic **Twilight Zone**, which returned outfit to US charts.

Reputation confirmed by Grammy awards and 'Downbeat' magazine honour of Best Vocal Group in 1980 poll. Chart status maintained with 1981 LP **Mecca for Moderns**, which made US Top 40. **Best Of** collection charted following year.

Unit's powerful live act has been refined in recent years; camp nostalgia 'feel' has in part been replaced by contemporary styling and design. Vocally, group use perfect mix of jazz, R&B and rock material. Paul's soulful reading of classic doo-wop numbers from '50s has

earned him comparisons with leading black performers.

**Current line-up:** Hauser; Paul; Siegel; Cheryl Bentyne.

**Hit Singles:**

| | US | UK |
|---|---|---|
| Chanson D'Amour, 1977 | — | 1 |
| Walk In Love, 1978 | — | 12 |
| On A Little Street In Singapore, 1978 | — | 20 |
| Boy From New York City, 1981 | 7 | — |
| Spice Of Life, 1984 | 40 | 19 |

**Albums:**
Jukin' (with Gene Pistilli) (Capitol/MFP), 1971
Manhattan Transfer (Atlantic), 1975
Coming Out (Atlantic), 1976
Pastiche (Atlantic), 1978
Live (Atlantic), 1978 **CD**
Extensions (Atlantic), 1979
Mecca For Moderns (Atlantic), 1981
Best Of (Atlantic), 1982 **CD**
Bodies And Souls (Atlantic), 1984 **CD**
Bop Doo Wop (Atlantic), 1985 **CD**
Brazil (WEA), 1987

# Barry Manilow

US vocalist, pianist, composer.
Born Brooklyn, New York, June 17, 1946.

**Career:** While studying at New York College of Music and Juilliard Academy, Manilow had part-time job in mail room at Columbia Records. After working on 'Callback' series of talent shows for WCBS-TV, in 1967 became conductor/arranger for Ed Sullivan TV specials. Met Bette Midler(▶) when working as pianist at New York's Continental Baths in 1972. Manilow arranged and co-produced her first two albums as well as joining her 1973 US tour as musical director and pianist. Tour gave him chance to showcase own talents as opening act, leading to own tour in 1974 and recording deal with Arista Records.

**Mandy** topped US charts in January 1975 within nine months of release, and was first of string of hits which showed crossover appeal between pop and MOR with audiences ranging from young girls to mums and dads.

Manilow's slick and rather schmaltzy stage shows—in the Liberace mould though not quite so over the top — have won him major international audience while at same time nauseating many critics. His records have been consistently well crafted and there is real talent behind the manufactured show-biz image.

Besides his records, Manilow has been prolific writer of TV and radio advertising jingles, including the famous 'You Deserve A Break Today' for McDonald's hamburgers.

He holds Broadway box-office record with $782,000 for one show.

**Hit Singles:**

| | US | UK |
|---|---|---|
| Mandy, 1975 | 1 | 11 |
| It's A Miracle, 1975 | 12 | — |
| Could It Be Magic, 1975 | 6 | 25* |
| I Write The Songs, 1976 | 1 | — |
| Tryin' To Get The Feeling Again, 1976 | 10 | — |
| Weekend In New England, 1977 | 10 | — |
| Looks Like We Made It, 1977 | 1 | — |
| Can't Smile Without You, 1978 | 3 | 43 |
| Even Now, 1978 | 19 | — |
| Copacabana, 1978† | 8 | 42 |
| Ready To Take A Chance Again, 1978 | 11 | — |
| Somewhere In The Night, 1979 | 1 | 42 |
| Ships, 1979 | 9 | — |
| When I Wanted You, 1979 | 20 | — |

| | US | UK |
|---|---|---|
| I Made It Through The Rain, 1980 | 10 | 6 |
| Bermuda Triangle, 1981 | — | 15 |
| Let's Hang On, 1981 | 32 | 12 |
| The Old Songs, 1981 | 15 | 48 |
| I Wanna Do It With You, 1982 | — | 8 |
| Read 'Em And Weep, 1983 | 18 | 17 |

*1978 UK.
†Double A-side in UK.

**Albums:**
Barry Manilow I (Arista), 1973
Barry Manilow II (Arista/—), 1974
Mandy (—/Arista), 1975
This One's For You (Arista), 1976
Trying To Get The Feeling (Arista/Fame), 1975
Manilow Magic—The Best Of (—/Arista), 1976
Greatest Hits (Arista), 1978
Even Now (Arista), 1978
One Voice (Arista), 1979
All The Best—Barry (Arista), 1980
If I Should Love Again (Arista), 1981
Here Comes The Night (Arista/—), 1981
Barry Live In Britain (Arista), 1982
Oh, Julie! (Arista), 1982
I Wanna Do It with You (Arista), 1982
A Touch More Magic (Arista), 1983 **CD**
2am Paradise Café (Arista), 1984
Manilow (RCA), 1985 **CD**

# Marillion

UK group formed 1982.

**Original line-up:** Fish, vocals; Mark Kelly, keyboards; Steve Rothery, guitar; Pete Trewavas, bass.

**Career:** Origins of Aylesbury-based quintet go back to 1979 when known as Silmarillion from a J.R.R. Tolkien novel. Name changed when various line-up changes saw Scotsman Fish join.

Exposure on Tommy Vance's BBC Radio One show led to extensive UK club tour, record deal with EMI and string of sell-out dates at Marquee club in London.

With just one minor hit single **Market Square Heroes** behind them, Marillion headlined at prestigious Hammersmith Odeon for two sell-out concert dates.

Debut album, **Script For A Jester's Tear** peaked at seven on UK chart, whilst original drummer was replaced by Ian Mosley, former drummer in 'Hair' and 'Jesus Christ Superstar' musicals and ex-member of Curved Air.

European and North American tours in 1984 helped build reputation while mushrooming market in Marillion bootlegs prompted release of budget-price **Real To Real** live album.

However, 1985 album **Misplaced Childhood** provided real breakthrough, spawning number two single **Kayleigh** and occupying upper end of UK charts for greater part of year.

Recent album **Clutching At Straws** made number two in album chart, confirming band as major force in UK rock. Condemned by many as throwback, Marillion has nevertheless obviously found UK niche. Idiosyncratic frontman Fish provides focus of attention, and outfit may well go on to international success.

**Current line-up:** Fish; Kelly; Rothery; Trewavas; Ian Mosley, percussion.

| Hit Singles: | US | UK |
|---|---|---|
| Garden Party, 1983 | — | 16 |
| Punch & Judy, 1984 | | 16 |
| Kayleigh, 1985 | — | 2 |
| Lavender, 1985 | — | 5 |
| Incommunicado, 1987 | — | 6 |
| Sugar Mice, 1987 | — | 22 |

**Albums:**
Script For A Jester's Tear (EMI), 1983 **CD**
Fugazi (EMI), 1984 **CD**
Real To Real (live) (EMI), 1984 **CD**
Misplaced Childhood (EMI), 1985 **CD**
Clutching At Straws (EMIR), 1987 **CD**
Besides Themselves (EMI), 1987 **CD**

# Richard Marx

US vocalist
Born Chicago, 1964.

**Career:** Marx recorded his first vocals at the age of five, thanks to his father a popular jazz pianist and top jingle writer and producer. His songwriting talents were influenced initially by Motown and Earth Wind & Fire and later Creedence Clearwater Revival and The Eagles. Early songwriting efforts came to the attention of Lionel Richie who had just left The Commodores and was working on his first solo album. Marx contributed vocals to several Richie hits including **You Are, All Night Long** and **Running With The Night**.

After introduction to David Foster, Kenny Rogers' producer, Marx started co-writing with Rogers. **And About Me** and **Crazy** were both US hits in 1985, and further songwriting credits included Chigago's **Good For Nothing**, Philip Bailey's **Love Is Alive** and Durrell Coleman's **Somebody Took My Love**.

Early 1986 Marx signed recording deal with EMI-Manhattan and thanks to his own talent and well-orchestrated marketing campaign has had two US top three hits, **Don't Mean Nothing** and **Should've Known Better**, a top 20 debut album, and a Grammy Nomination in the Best Rock Vocal Performance category alongside Joe Cocker, Bob Seger and Bruce Springsteen.

Eponymously-titled LP certified platinum in the US by February 1988. Big promotional push by EMI Records in UK and Europe has brought Marx's undoubted songwriting and recording talents to a growing section of the record-buying public.

| Hit Singles: | US | UK |
|---|---|---|
| Don't Mean Nothing, 1987 | 3 | — |
| Should've Known Better, 1987 | 3 | — |

**Albums:**
Richard Marx (Manhattan), 1987 **CD**

**Below: Talented songwriter Richard Marx—encouraged early in his career by Lionel Richie no less.**

# Bob Marley

Jamaican vocalist, composer.
Born Robert Nesta Marley, St Anns, Jamaica, 1945 (passport gave exact date as February 6, but Marley said this was inaccurate); died May 11, 1980.

**Career:** Son of an English army captain and Jamaican mother, Bob Marley was undoubtedly *the* giant figure in the evolution of reggae music.

While at Jamaica's Stepney School, became friendly with Winston Hubert McIntosh and Neville O'Reiley Livingstone; as Peter Tosh(▶) and Bunny Wailer they were later to join Marley in forming the Wailers.

At 16 cut debut record **Judge Not,** co-written with mentor Joe Higgs, at Ken Khouri's Federal Studio in Kingston. Then with Leslie Kong producing covered Brook Benton's **One Cup Of Coffee** after seeing the American star in concert with Dinah Washington.

Teaming with Tosh and Wailer, plus Junior Braithwaite and Beverly Kelso, Marley formed the Wailin' Wailers; signed to Clement Coxsone Dodds' Studio One label and sold more than 80,000 copies of first single **Simmer Down.**

Backed by studio band the Skatalites, quintet worked through ska and rock-steady eras towards dawn of reggae style. However, they broke up in 1966 following wrangles over payment for their recordings.

Marley joined his mother in Delaware, US, and worked in Chrysler car factory before returning to Jamaica to avoid service in Vietnam. Re-uniting with Tosh and Wailer, Marley recorded again with Leslie Kong who, via work with Desmond Dekker(▶), had become island's top producer. Following Kong's death from cancer, trio began work with Lee Perry who helped form Marley's distinctive style. Earned first international hit with **Small Axe.**

Espousing teachings of Jamaican politico/ folk legend Marcus Garvey, Marley and friends became devout Rastafarians. In 1968 Marley was busted for possession of marijuana, the first of many subsequent clashes with Jamaican establishment.

Quitting Perry's label, trio took his ace musicians, brothers Carlton and Aston 'Family Man' Barrett, with them and formed own short-lived Wailing Soul label.

When Wailer was sent to prison for year following another drugs bust, Marley signed as songwriter to American soul star Johnny Nash's(▶) Jad label. He helped Nash develop unique blend of soul and reggae which gave the American a UK No. 1 with **Stir It Up.**

Marley used resultant income to set up Tuff Gong label with Tosh and Wailer. Subsequent records won them an international deal with Island Records thanks to that company's Jamaican-born boss Chris Blackwell.

Blackwell's carefully orchestrated promotion put Bob Marley and Wailers in vogue with rock critics, musicians and audiences alike. **Catch A Fire** album (1973) led to well-received UK visit and Stateside tour with Sly and the Family Stone(▶). Though not quite so strong, follow-up set **Burnin'** did include **I Shot The Sheriff**, covered very successfully by Eric Clapton(▶).

Wailer and Tosh then quit group though they remained firm friends with Marley they were unhappy with Island deal.

Marley brought in his wife Rita plus Judy Mowatt and Marcia Griffiths (the I-Threes) as back-up vocalists and in 1975 recorded classic **Natty Dread** album. This set seal on his growing reputation as Jamaica's most important artist. Superb live LP, **Jah Live**, recorded at

**Above: Natty Dread, Marley and the Wailers. Courtesy Island Records.**

London's Lyceum, included version of **No Woman No Cry**, which became major UK pop hit, as well as brilliant **Lively Up Yourself**.

Marley's stature as spokesman for Jamaican masses — his songs were often full of social and political comment — made him target of political gangs. In December 1976 he was shot four times in the arm by a group who burst into his home on eve of concert he was to give for then ruling left-wing PNP party led by Michael Manley. Marley appeared in concert but immediately after went into exile in Miami for 18 months. Recorded 1976 album **Exodus** partly in that city, partly in London.

Marley's return to homeland was triumphant. Before 20,000 people at Kingston's National Stadium he joined Manley and political rival (now premier) Edward Seaga in symbolic handshake at concert which commemorated visit to Jamaica 12 years earlier by Emperor Haile Selassie of Ethiopia, figurehead of the Rastafarian movement. Marley also appeared in a special concert to celebrate birth of new African nation of Zimbabwe.

Towards end of his 1980 world tour he collapsed following performance at NY's Madison Square Gardens and was rushed to hospital. Three years earlier he had had cancerous toe removed, but now it seemed the cancer had spread. Despite treatment at famed Josef Issels Clinic in Bavaria, Marley's condition was incurable. He died during May 1980 at Cedars Lebanon Hospital in Miami where he had flown to visit his mother en-route for Jamaica.

During long stint with Island, Marley had recorded 10 albums; his music spanned whole gamut of Jamaican experience, both on national and international level. Material ranged from pure love songs to strident political statements. Marvellously evocative lyrics — even when full of patois they struck chord with both multi-national and multi-racial audiences — were matched by catchiest of melodies. His popularity and influence have not waned—if anything his impact is possibly stronger today.

**Below: Robert Nesta Marley, the number one figure in reggae.**

**Inset Below: Exodus, the 1977 album. Courtesy Island Records.**

| Hit Singles: | US | UK | Albums: |
|---|---|---|---|
| Exodus, 1977 | — | 14 | Catch A Fire (Island), 1972 |
| Jamming/Punky Reggae Party, | | | African Herbsman (—/Trojan), 1973 |
| 1977 | | | Burnin' (Island), 1973 |
| Is This Love, 1978 | — | 9 | Rasta Revolution (—/Trojan), 1974 |
| Could You Be Loved, 1980 | — | 5 | Natty Dread (Island), 1975 **CD** |
| No Woman No Cry, 1981 | — | 8 | Jah Live (Island), 1975 |
| Buffalo Soldier, 1983 | — | 4 | Rastaman Vibration (Island), 1976 **CD** |
| One Love, 1984 | — | 5 | Exodus (Island), 1977 **CD** |
| | | | Birth Of A Legend (Epic), 1977 |
| | | | Early Music (—/Embassy), 1977 |
| | | | Babylon By Bus (Island), 1978 **CD** |
| | | | Kaya (Island), 1987 **CD** |
| | | | Bob Marley And The Wailers (—/Hammer), |
| | | | 1979 |
| | | | Survival (Island), 1979 **CD** |
| | | | Uprising (Island), 1980 **CD** |
| | | | Soul Rebel (—/New Cross), 1981 |
| | | | Chances Are (Warner Bros), 1981 |
| | | | Confrontation (Island), 1983 |
| | | | Legend (Island), 1984 **CD** |
| | | | Live At The Lyceum (Island), 1984 **CD** |
| | | | Rebel Music (Island), 1984 **CD** |
| | | | Bob Marley Intertape, 1985 **CD** |
| | | | Mellow Mood (Topline), 1985 **CD** |

**Rasta Revolution, Bob Marley. Courtesy Trojan Records.**

**Inset Below: Uprising, Marley and the Wailers. Courtesy Island Records.**

# John Mayall

UK vocalist, guitarist, keyboard player, band-leader, composer.
Born Manchester, November 23, 1933.

**Career:** Mayall formed his first band, Power-house Four, at college after national service, building reputation backing US bluesmen John Lee Hooker(▶) and Sonny Boy Williamson(▶) on UK tours.

Encouraged by Alexis Korner to move to London in 1962, he formed Bluesbreakers with John McVie (bass) and Bernie Watson (guitar), cutting first album **Live At Klooks Kleek** 18 months later, Roger Dean replacing Watson and Hughie Flint joining on drums.

Succession of critically applauded singles and exhaustive club tours led to major breakthrough in 1966 when Eric Clapton of Yardbirds(▶) joined. **Bluesbreakers—John Mayall With Eric Clapton** won quick cult-status hitting No. 6 on UK album charts.

Mayall/Clapton/McVie/Flint line-up was arguably best British R&B band of all time. McVie was temporarily replaced by Jack Bruce and Clapton left to join emergent psychedelic movement, forming Cream(▶) with Bruce and Ginger Baker(▶). McVie re-joined. Peter Green coming in on guitar. Aynsley Dunbar on drums. Dunbar was soon replaced by Mick Fleetwood, the new line-up lasting till May 1967 when Fleetwood and Green left to form Fleetwood Mac(▶), soon to be joined by McVie.

The then unknown Mick Taylor joined Mayall from the Gods, staying till 1969 when he replaced late Brian Jones in the Rolling Stones(▶).

Changing musical direction, Mayall brought in Keef Hartley's powerhouse drumming and strong brass section for jazz-slanted sound. He also cut back-to-the-roots solo album, **The Blues Alone**.

Chris Mercer, who left for Juicy Luicy, Jon Hiseman and Dick Heckstall-Smith, who formed Colosseum, Andy Fraser, who became member of Free(▶), Jon Mark and Johnny Almond, who set-up Mark-Almond, all spent time with Mayall before July 1968 when he decided to go back to tighter backing group with new line-up of Mick Taylor, Stephen Thompson (bass) and Colin Allen (drums) from Zoot Money's band. This line-up cut **Blues From Laurel Canyon** set, inspired by brief holiday in Los Angeles. With Taylor leaving, Mayall moved to California, signed new deal with Polydor (after five years with Decca) and

**USA Union, John Mayall. Courtesy Polydor Records.**

put together first of many American line-ups.
In 1975, Mayall switched to ABC and later cut album with legendary New Orleans producer Allen Toussaint.

A charismatic catalyst of some of the finest white/multi-racial R&B line-ups ever, Mayall is remembered for knack of nurturing emergent major talents as much as for his own work.

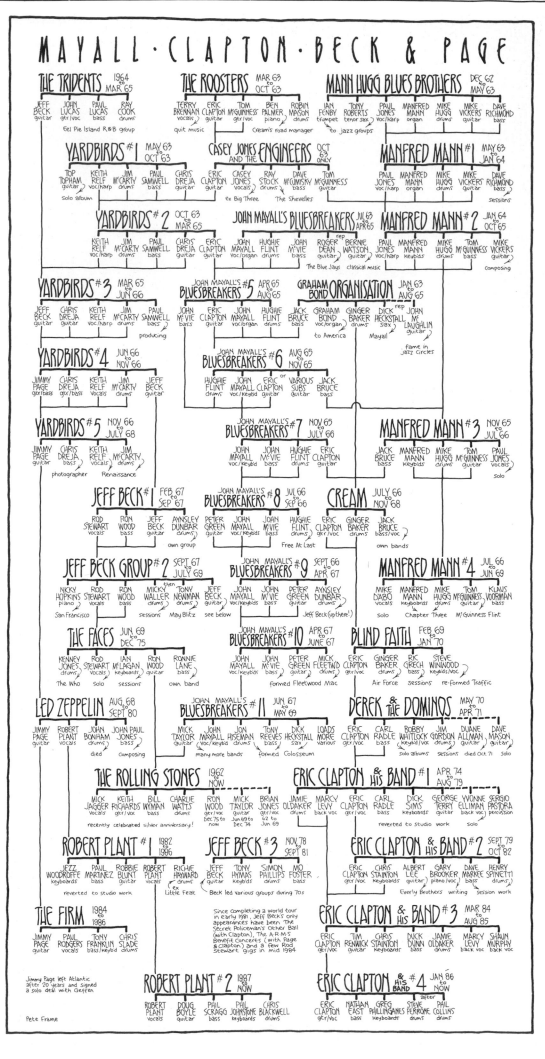

Above: A 1960s line-up of John Mayall's ever changing Bluesbreakers, which included John McVie and Mick Taylor.

**Albums:**
John Mayall Plays John Mayall (—/Decca), 1965
Bluesbreakers (London/Decca), 1965
A Hard Road (London/Decca), 1967 **CD**
Crusade (London/Decca), 1967
Blues Alone (London/Ace Of Hearts), 1967
Raw Blues (London/Ace Of Hearts), 1967
Bare Wires (London/Decca), 1968
Blues From Laurel Canyon (London/Decca), 1969
Diary Of A Band Volume 1 (—/Decca), 1968
Looking Back (London/Decca), 1969
Empty Rooms (Polydor), 1970
Turning Point (Polydor), 1970 **CD**
World Of Volume 1 (—/World Of), 1970
World Of Volume 2 (—/World Of), 1971
Beyond The Turning Point (Polydor/—), 1971
Diary Of A Band Volume 2 (—/Decca), 1972
Jazz Blues Fusion (Polydor), 1972
Through The Years (London/Decca), 1972
Best Of (Polydor), 1973
Notice To Appear (ABC), 1975
John Mayall (Polydor), 1976
A Hard Core Package (MCA/—), 1977
Primal Solos (London/—), 1977
Last Of The British Blues (MCA/—), 1978
No More Interviews (—/DJM), 1979
Bottom Line (—/DJM), 1979
Moving On (—/Polydor), 1985
Behind The Iron Curtain (PRT), 1986
Some Of My Best Friends Are Blues (Charly), 1986
The John Mayall Collection (Castle), 1986 **CD** (Double)

# Curtis Mayfield

US composer, vocalist, guitarist.
Born Chicago, June 3, 1942.

**Career:** Led own group, the Alphatones, as teenager. Met Jerry Butler in his grandmother's church choir. On moving to North Side of Chicago in 1956 renewed acquaintances with Butler, leaving Alphatones to link up with him and group known as the Roosters.

This team evolved into the Impressions(▶) with Butler as lead singer. Following **For Your Precious Love** smash, Butler went solo. Mayfield had stints as Butler's backing guitarist and wrote material for him while trying to hold the Impressions together. With Mayfield elevated to lead singer, the Impressions became one of most successful vocal groups in black music history.

In 1968 Mayfield formed own Curtom label and two years later left the Impressions, though he continued to produce them. Debut solo album went gold and single **Move On Up** took him into UK charts. His soundtrack for **Superfly** movie stood up in own right and spawned two gold singles, **Freddie's Dead** and **Superfly**. He also wrote and produced scores for 'Claudine' movie (performed by Gladys Knight(▶) and the Pips) and Staple Singers(▶) (**Let's Do It Again**). He appeared as actor in 'Short Eyes', writing the score, as he did for 'A Piece Of The Action' and 'Sparkle', which featured singing of Aretha Franklin(▶).

As record company boss, producer and songwriter, Mayfield continued to be active but Curtom folded (he switched to Epic) and his solo efforts lacked dynamism of Impressions days.

**Hit Singles:**

| | US | UK |
|---|---|---|
| Move On Up, 1971 | — | 12 |
| Freddie's Dead (Theme From Superfly), 1972 | 4 | — |
| Superfly, 1972 | 8 | — |

**Albums:**
Superfly (Buddah/RSO), 1974

**Curtis, Curtis Mayfield. Courtesy Buddah Records.**

Never Say You Can't Survive (Curtom), 1977
Honesty (Epic), 1983
Live In Los Angeles (Capital), 1986

*Worth Searching Out:*
Roots (Curtom), 1974
Curtis (Curtom), 1974

# Maze

US group formed 1976.
**Original line-up:** Frankie Beverley, vocals, composer; Sam Porter, keyboards; Roame Lowry, percussion; McKinley 'Bug' Williams, percussion; Wayne Thomas, lead guitar; Robin Duhe, bass; Joe Provost, drums.

**Career:** Nucleus of group which had worked from Philadelphia since 1971 as Raw Soul, went to San Francisco, pulled in extra members and signed to Capitol in 1976 as Maze.

Debut album, **Maze Featuring Frankie Beverley**, went gold after seven months and spawned hit singles while follow-up **Golden Time Of Day** sold far quicker and **Inspiration** LP established act with pop as well as black audience.

Much lauded **Joy And Pain** and **Live In New Orleans** albums broke band in UK and led to critically acclaimed Hammersmith concerts in 1982 since when, under Beverley's strong leadership, they have continued to triumph—the 19,000 tickets for their 1985 London concerts selling out in a day.

Maze successfully combine Sly Stone-inspired funk with high melodic content.

**Current line-up:** Beverley; Porter; Lowry; Williams; Thomas; Duhe; Wayne 'Ziggy' Linsey, keyboards; Michael White, drums.

**Albums (Selected):**
Live In New Orleans (Capitol), 1981 **CD**
Joy And Pain (Capitol), 1981
Can't Stop The Music (Capitol), 1985

# Paul McCartney

UK composer, vocalist, bass player.
Born James Paul McCartney, Liverpool, June 18, 1942.

**Career:** As half of the world-dominating Lennon/McCartney songwriting partnership (there were reportedly nearly 2,000 cover versions of their songs by 1965) seemed particularly alienated when Yoko Ono(▶) began exerting strong influence over Lennon(▶) in late '60s. Although not first member of Beatles(▶) to release solo record, McCartney sued for freedom from group contracts.

First solo LP released 1970, opening floodgates for virtual barrage of hit singles and inconsistent albums — indicating that break-up of group and particularly of songwriting team was major loss to rock 'n' roll — although singles especially not without controversy. **Give Ireland Back To The Irish** was banned by BBC, and **Hi Hi Hi** suffered the same fate.

In 1971, formed Wings (Paul, vocals, bass; wife Linda McCartney, keyboards, vocals; Denny Laine (ex Moody Blues(▶)), guitar, vocals; Denny Seiwell, drums), which first appeared on **Wild Life** LP. Various personnel changes took place during '70s — among members were guitarists Henry McCullough, Jimmy McCulloch (who died in January 1979 of drug related heart failure) and Laurence Juber, drummers Geoff Britton, Joe English and Steve Holley. However Paul, Linda and Denny Laine were ever present until Laine

**Back To The Egg, Paul McCartney & Wings. Courtesy Parlophone Records.**

left in 1980, after much publicised arrest of Paul on drug charges at start of planned Japanese tour. Best Wings LP was superb **Band On The Run**.

Subsequently, McCartney has recorded either completely solo, or with help from superstar friends, including Stevie Wonder(▶) and Michael Jackson(▶). His music has shown definite moves away from the hard rock of years with Beatles, but his praiseworthy organisation of annual events to commemorate Buddy Holly(▶) (whose music publishing is owned by McCartney) indicates continuing love for spirit of rock 'n' roll, if not for actual musical involvement. McCartney in '80s probably biggest AOR/pop star in world, and also now known for children's songs, as well as reputedly a multi-millionaire. Operates own company MPL from prestigious office in Soho Square in London's West End. However not everything McCartney touched turns to gold. His 1985 movie production 'Give My Regards To Broad Street' was panned by the critics and flopped commercially.
Bass: Höfner violin.

**McCartney II, Paul McCartney. Courtesy Parlophone Records.**

**Hit Singles:**

| | US | UK |
|---|---|---|
| *Solo:* | | |
| Another Day, 1971 | 5 | 2 |
| Uncle Albert/Admiral Halsey, 1971 | 1 | — |
| Wonderful Christmastime, 1979 | — | 6 |
| Coming Up, 1980 | 1 | 2 |
| Waterfalls, 1980 | — | 9 |
| Ebony And Ivory, 1982* | 1 | 1 |
| The Girl Is Mine, 1982† | 2 | 8 |
| Say Say Say, 1983† | 1 | 2 |
| Pipes Of Peace, 1983 | — | 1 |
| No More Lonely Nights, 1984 | 6 | 2 |
| We All Stand Together, 1984 | — | 3 |
| Spies Like Us, 1986 | 24 | 13 |
| Once Upon A Long Ago, 1987 | — | 10 |
| *With Steve Wonder | | |
| †With Michael Jackson | | |

*McCartney and Wings:*

| | US | UK |
|---|---|---|
| Give Ireland Back To The Irish, 1972 | 21 | 16 |

| | | |
|---|---|---|
| Mary Had A Little Lamb, 1972 | 28 | 9 |
| Hi Hi Hi/C Moon, 1972 | 10 | 5 |
| My Love, 1973 | 1 | 9 |
| Live And Let Die, 1973 | 2 | 9 |
| Helen Wheels, 1973 | 10 | 12 |
| Jet, 1974 | 7 | 7 |
| Band On The Run, 1974 | 1 | 3 |
| Junior's Farm, 1974 | 3 | 16 |
| Listen To What The Man Said, 1975 | 1 | 6 |
| Venus And Mars/Rock Show, 1975 | 12 | — |
| Silly Love Songs, 1976 | 1 | 2 |
| Let 'Em In, 1976 | 3 | 2 |
| Maybe I'm Amazed, 1977 | 10 | 28 |
| Mull Of Kintyre/Girls School, 1977 | 33 | 1 |
| With A Little Luck, 1978 | 1 | 5 |
| Goodnight Tonight, 1979 | 5 | 5 |
| Getting Closer, 1979 | 20 | 60 |

**Albums:**
*Solo:*
McCartney (Columbia/Parlophone), 1970 **CD**
Ram (Columbia/Parlophone), 1971 **CD**
(with Linda)
McCartney II (Columbia/Parlophone), 1980 **CD**
Tug Of War (Columbia/Parlophone), 1982 **CD**
Pipes Of Peace (Columbia/Parlophone), 1983 **CD**
Give My Regards To Broad Street (Columbia/Parlophone), 1984 **CD**
All The Best (Parlophone), 1987 (Compilation) **CD**

*McCartney and Wings:*
Wild Life (Columbia/Parlophone), 1971 **CD**
Red Rose Speedway (Columbia/Parlophone), 1973 **CD**
Band On The Run (Columbia/Parlophone), 1974 **CD**
Venus And Mars (Columbia/Parlophone), 1975 **CD**
Wings Over America (Capitol/Parlophone), 1976*
London Town (Capitol/Parlophone), 1978
Wings' Greatest (Capitol/Parlophone), 1978 (Compilation) **CD**
Back To The Egg (Columbia/Parlophone), 1979
*Triple live set

# Country Joe McDonald

US vocalist, composer, guitarist.
Born Joseph McDonald, El Monte, California, January 1, 1942.

**Career:** Named by leftist parents for Joseph Stalin. Grew up listening to country and folk. Served tour in US Navy and then began working as folk singer in Berkeley, California area. Recorded obscure, unknown solo in 1964, then met guitarist Barry Melton while working in folk band. Like many folk performers duo turned to rock, forming Country

**Here We Are Again, Country Joe & The Fish. Courtesy Vanguard Records.**

**All The Best, Paul McCartney. Courtesy Parlophone Records.**

Joe & the Fish with Barry Melton, guitar; David Cohen, keyboards; Bruce Barthol, bass; Chicken Hirsch, drums.

Band's first recordings were EPs made to accompany McDonald's self-produced magazine. Gigs at Fillmore attracted folk label Vanguard, who signed band in late 1966. Fish eventually recorded four LPs which at time were highly regarded for political stance, social satire and commitment to counter-culture. First LP, **Electric Music For The Mind And Body**, stands up best. Second (**Fixin' To Die**) is fondly remembered by nostalgists for Fish cheer ('Give us an 'F'. Give us a 'U', etc.')

Close identification with protest and Berkeley area ultimately backfired and band broke up for good in 1970. McDonald began variety of activities; he wrote music for several movies, briefly worked with Jane Fonda and

returned to early style of folk music. Moving to Paris, he played variety of venues and clubs, seeking support for ecological causes.

Late 1974 included brief reunion with Melton for UK gigs. After period in London, McDonald returned to San Francisco.

**Albums:**
*With Fish:*
Electric Music For The Mind And Body (Vanguard), 1967
I-Feel-Like-I'm-Fixin'-To-Die (Vanguard), 1967
Here We Are Again (Vanguard), 1969

*Country Joe Solo:*
Paradise With An Ocean View (Fantasy), 1975
Love Is A Fire (Fantasy), 1976
Goodbye Blues (Fantasy), 1977
Best Of Country (—/Golden Hour), 1977
Rock 'n' Roll Music From Planet Earth (Fantasy), 1978
Leisure Suite (Fantasy), 1979
The Early Years (Piccadilly/—), 1980
Animal Tracks (Animus), 1983

# Michael McDonald

US vocalist, keyboard player.
Born St. Louis, Missouri.

**Career:** Began his career as keyboardist with Steely Dan (▶) in the early 70s, before joining The Doobie Brothers' (▶) line-up for 1975 US tour. He became a fully-fledged member writing several of their hits including **Real Love** and **Minute by Minute**.

In 1980 received Grammy award for penning (with Kenny Loggins) **What A Fool Believes**, a composition that was also named Song Of The Year. Along with The Doobies he received two other Grammy awards for Record Of The Year and Best Group Vocal Performance for **Minute By Minute**. McDonald songs were by now being covered by Aretha Franklin, Carly Simon and Millie Jackson among others. First solo project (**If That's What It Takes**) included US hit single **I Keep Forgettin'**.

In 1985 released **No Lookin' Back** album which featured material co-written with Kenny Loggins, Ed Sanford and Chuck Sabatino. LP co-produced by McDonald with Ted Templeman. 1987 saw the release **Sweet Freedom: The Best of Michael McDonald**, digitally re-mastered by Lee Herschberg, which included 12 of his best recordings including **What A Fool Believes, Yah Mo B There** and his hit duet with Patti Labelle, **On My Own**.

**No Lookin' Back, Michael McDonald. Courtesy Warner Bros.**

| **Hit Singles:** | US | UK |
|---|---|---|
| *With James Ingram:* | | |
| Yah Mo B There, 1985 | 9 | 12 |
| Sweet Freedom, 1986 | 7 | 12 |
| *With Patti Labelle:* | | |
| On My Own, 1987 | 1 | 2 |

**Albums:**
If Thats What It Takes (Warner Bros), 1982 **CD**
No Lookin' Back (Warner Bros), 1985 **CD**
Best Of (WEA), 1986 **CD**
Sweet Freedom (Warner Bros), 1986 **CD**

# John McLaughlin

UK guitarist, composer.
Born Yorkshire, January 4, 1942.

**Career:** McLaughlin came from musical family. Self-taught, played first in trad jazz band of Big Pete Deuchar. Joined British R&B movement of mid-'60s working with Graham Bond, Herbie Goins and Brian Auger.

Shortly after emigrating to States in 1968 joined Tony Williams' Lifetime (Williams, drums; Larry Young (aka Khalid Yasin), keyboards.

Followed first solo album **Extrapolation** (1969), with **Devotion** (1971). Recorded in

**Left: Hit writer extraordinaire, Michael McDonald playing live in 1987.**

**Above: John McLaughlin, one of the fastest most accurate guitarists around.**

France, it included Buddy Miles(▶) on drums and Lifetime sideman Young.

Formed Mahavishnu Orchestra in 1971. Name suggested by guru Sri Chimnoy of whom McLaughlin was devotee. Band comprised Jerry Goodman (ex-Flock), violin; Billy Cobman(▶), drums; Jan Hammer, keyboards, and Rick Laird, bass. Goodman and Cobham had previously cut **My Goals Beyond** (1971) with McLaughlin, an acoustic album which explored Indian rhythms and scales.

Group's best work **Birds Of Fire** pushed jazz-rock genre to new heights; McLaughlin's flawless technique set yardstick for contemporaries. However, line-up split after three LPs, McLaughlin seemingly losing his spiritual inclination.

Recorded self-indulgent **Love Devotion Surrender** with fellow Chimnoy disciple Carlos Santana(▶) in 1973. Final Orchestra LP, **Between Nothingness And Eternity**, was cut live at NY's Central Park same year.

Anxious to work with larger unit, created multi-talented aggregation for 1974 LP **Apocalypse**. The 'new' Mahavishnu group featured Michael Walden (now 'Narada') drums; Ralph Armstrong, bass; Gayle Moran, keyboards, and French violin virtuoso Jean Luc-Ponty (ex-Mothers Of Invention). Recruitment of London Symphony Orchestra made **Apocalypse** a spectacular if cumbersome work.

Emerged from unwieldy unit after **Visions Of Emerald Beyond** (1975) for **Inner Worlds** (1976). Recorded at Château d'Heronville in France. Album retained Walden, Armstrong, Moran and added Stu Goldberg, keyboards.

McLaughlin had left Chimnoy in 1975 and future of MO was in doubt from that time. **Inner Worlds** proved last work from group. Free of responsibility of being band-leader/ focal point, McLaughlin settled quietly into Indian acoustic trio Shakti. Remained until 1978, cutting three LPs, **Shakti, Handful Of Beauty** and **Natural Elements**.

Now firmly entrenched in acoustic guitar, McLaughlin joined forces with Paco De Lucia and Larry Coryell — and later Al Di Meola(▶) — for 'supergroup' guitar trio, formed 1980. His phenomenal speed has been matched note for note by his partners in this definitive musical co-operative. That it remains melodic beyond the 100 mph phrases is a testimony to these guitar legends.
Guitars: Ovation acoustic/electric.

**Albums:**
*Mahavishnu Orchestra:*
Inner Mountain Flame (Columbia/CBS) 1971
Birds Of Fire (Columbia/CBS), 1973
Best Of (Columbia/—), 1980

*With Carlos Santana:*
Love Devotion Surrender (Columbia/CBS), 1973

*Solo:*
Extrapolation (Polydor), 1969
My Goals Beyond (Douglas/Elektra Musician), 1971
Inner Worlds (Columbia/CBS), 1976
Electric Guitarist (Columbia/CBS), 1978
Electric Dreams (Columbia/CBS), 1979
Music Spoken Here (Warner Bros/—), 1981
Belo Horizonte (Warner Bros), 1982
Best Of (Columbia/CBS), 1980
Adventures in Radioland (Polygram), 1987 **CD**

*Shakti:*
Shakti (Columbia/CBS), 1976
Handful Of Beauty (Columbia/CBS), 1977
Natural Elements (Columbia/CBS), 1978
(See also Al Di Meola)

*With Al Di Meola and Paco De Lucia:*
Friday Night in San Francisco (Columbia/CBS), 1981
Passion, Grace and Fire (Mercury), 1983

# Don McLean

US vocalist, guitarist, composer.
Born New Rochelle, New York, October, 2, 1945.

**Career:** Developed early interest in all forms of American music, particularly folk. On leaving school in 1963 started singing and playing in clubs.

By end of '60s MacLean had built up excellent reputation within his field and become a prolific songwriter. After spending two years knocking on record company doors, he made album **Tapestry** for small company which soon folded (although record was later re-released by United Artists, who signed him in 1971).

Breakthrough came with late '71 release of extraordinary single, **American Pie**. Despite McLean's folky background, record was symbolic 'history' of rock'n'roll, using evocative images tied to highly commercial hookline. Record was worldwide smash, catapulting McLean to instant stardom. Follow-up,

**Vincent,** a highly personal song celebrating genius of painter Vincent Van Gogh, was almost as successful. Both songs were excellent showcases for McLean's attractively plaintive voice.

Career received further boost in 1973 when MOR singer Perry Como had huge hit with **And I Love You So,** another McLean song. In meantime, McLean had become in-demand live performer, years of small-time gigs paying off in controlled, well-paced performances.

During remainder of '70s McLean consolidated career, although he was never elevated to 'bed-sit philosophy' status of singer-songwriters such as Cat Stevens(▶) and Leonard Cohen(▶). Perhaps strangely, he became more popular in UK than in homeland, and regular tours were always sellouts.

In 1980 McLean's career entered new phase with massive pop success of his cover of Roy Orbison's(▶) **Crying.** (True to form record became hit in UK well before it did in US.) However, he will no doubt always be best known for now classic **American Pie.**

| Hit Singles: | US | UK |
|---|---|---|
| American Pie, 1972 | 1 | 2 |
| Vincent, 1972 | 12 | 1 |
| Crying, 1980 | 5 | 1 |

**Albums:**
Tapestry (United Artists), 1972
American Pie (United Artists), 1972
Playin' Favourites (United Artists), 1973
Homeless Brother (United Artists), 1974
Solo (United Artists), 1976
Chain Lightning (Arista), 1979
Very Best Of (United Artists), 1980
Believers (Arista), 1982
Dominion (EMI), 1983

# Meat Loaf

US vocalist, actor.
Born Marvin Lee Aday, Dallas, Texas, September 27, 1948.

**Career: Bat Out Of Hell** was released in 1977 and very slowly began working way up through US/UK charts. Operatic, bombastic, with comic-book hero on cover, album seemed to combine pomp of early '70s with enthusiasm

of punk. As album settled in for what seemed permanent place in charts, interest grew in larger-than-life figure behind it.

Meat Loaf, it happened, had been around for sometime. He had released rather weak R&B album for Tamla in 1970; **Featuring Stoney And Meat Loaf** quickly disappeared. So did Meat Loaf as he ventured into theatre. In 1976 he appeared in cult film 'Rocky Horror Picture Show'. It was through acting that he met Jim Steinman. Meat Loaf liked Steinman's

**Bad Attitude, Meat Loaf.
Courtesy Arista Records.**

songs and together they began assaulting record companies with demo tapes. CBS eventually signed them.

After success of first CBS LP (produced by Todd Rundgren(▶)) **Bat Out Of Hell,** Meat Loaf toured (with back-up singers and band) until he ruined his voice. Wait for follow-up LP grew to point Steinman released separate opus **Bad For Good** in May 1981. Meanwhile Meat Loaf appeared in movie 'Roadie' after their first album.

**Dead Ringer** finally arrived in 1982 as continuation of gothic texture which made up **Bat.** Some claimed **Dead Ringer** was formalistic repeat while others called it brilliant return. Fans wondered if Meat Loaf really underwent rumoured exotic treatments (including drinking his own urine) to save his voice. Whatever the cure, it seems to have worked and **Bad Attitude,** which marked a label switch to Arista and featured a title cut vocal battle with ex-Who(▶) Roger Daltrey, contained some great songs.

**Below: Don McLean on stage in 1972.**

In recent years porcine star has continued to gig and make records with degree of success, but has yet to match level set by **Bat Out Of Hell**. By 1987 album had sold over 4 million copies in US alone.

**Hit Singles:**

| | US | UK |
|---|---|---|
| Two Out Of Three Ain't Bad, 1978 | 11 | 32 |
| Bat Out Of Hell, 1979 | — | 15 |
| Dead Ringer For Love, 1982 | — | 5 |
| Midnight At The Lost And Found, 1983 | — | 17 |
| Modern Girl, 1984 | 1 | 17 |
| Rock'n'Roll Mercenaries, 1986 | — | 31 |

**Albums:**
Featuring Stoney And Meatloaf (Prodigal), 1970
Bat Out Of Hell (Epic), 1978 **CD**
Dead Ringer (Epic), 1982 **CD**
Midnight At The Lost And Found (Epic), 1983
Bad Attitude (Arista), 1984 **CD**
Hits Out Of Hell (CBS), 1985 **CD**
Blind Before I Stop (Arista), 1986 **CD**
Live : Meatloaf (Arista), 1987 **CD**

# John Cougar Mellencamp

US vocalist, composer.
Born Seymour, Indiana.

**Career:** Married at 17, a father at 19, Mellencamp worked at various jobs before launching himself into music scene in 1975. On strength of demo tapes, was signed by Tony De Fries—then David Bowie's(▶) manager—who renamed him Johnny Cougar and signed him to MCA. First album **Chestnut Street Incident** combined new tracks with raw demos; split from De Fries swiftly followed.

Cougar then met up with Billy Gaff (then Rod Stewart's(▶) manager), head of Riva Records. Signed to Riva, Cougar achieved some impact with album **A Biography,** which yielded international chart single in **I Need A Lover,** and follow-up **Nothin' Matters And What If It Did,** which made US Top 50. Latter also provided two Top 40 singles, **This Time** and **Ain't Even Done With The Night.**

Steve Cropper produced **Nothin' Matters,** but Cougar decided that time had come to take full musical control. With Don Gehman co-producing, put together **American Fool;** album became one of the sensations of 1982, reaching No. 1 and achieving platinum status. Three singles which all received heavy MTV airplay were also hugely successful.

In meantime, Cougar had been touring regularly with band the Zones, and established himself as good live attraction. His music has wide appeal for rock and pop audiences, combining melodic sense, macho/boyish image, modicum of intelligence and evocative, quintessentially American lyrics. Now using his full name of John Cougar Mellencamp, career continues as rock star tailor-made for the mid-'80s.

In intervening years Cougar continued to build reputation as alternative Bruce Springsteen, straightahead all-American rocker concerned with subjects like girls, motorbikes and smalltown life. Artist reverted to real name of Mellencamp along the way.

1985 album **Scarecrow** was megaselling US number one, and finally established Mellencamp as superstar.

Recent album **Lonesome Jubilee** confirmed Mellencamp's songwriting talent, with convincing lyrics concerning ordinary Americans' hopes and aspirations, and many critics feel that artist is just reaching full potential. At time of writing UK tour is attracting sellout audiences and appreciative reviews.

**Hit Singles:**

| | US | UK |
|---|---|---|
| Ain't Even Done With The Night, 1981 | 17 | — |
| Hurt So Good, 1982 | 2 | — |
| Jack And Diane, 1982 | 1 | 25 |
| Hand To Hold On To, 1983 | 3 | 19 |
| Crumblin' Down, 1983 | 9 | — |
| Pink Horses, 1983 | 8 | — |
| Authority Song, 1984 | 15 | — |
| Lonely Ol' Night, 1985 | 6 | — |
| Small Town, 1985 | 6 | — |

**Albums:**
A Biography (Riva), 1978
John Cougar (Riva), 1979 **CD**
Nothin' Matters And What If It Did (Riva), 1980 **CD**
American Fool (Riva), 1982 **CD**
Uh-Huh (Riva), 1984 **CD**
Chestnut Street Incident (Mainman), 1984 **CD**
Scarecrow (Riva), 1985 **CD**

# George Michael

UK singer/songwriter.
Born Georgious Panayatiou, Finchley, North London, June 25, 1963.

**Career:** Met Andrew Ridgely at school, formed duo Wham! which achieved worldwide success from 1983 to 1986. Michael also scored solo hit singles with **Different Corner** and **Careless Whisper.**

Michael split Wham! partnership in mid-1985 and laid low for a year before launching solo career with controversial **I Want Your Sex** single, which immediately suffered media censorship. Lyrically it recommended sexual fidelity; musically it inspired sexual abandon, employing restrained rockabilly edge that would be more evident on **Faith** album and single.

Although Michael had quit Wham! to present a more mature style hence **Father Figure** a hit single in US, he had returned to simplistic 50s images and styles rather than relying on endless moody ballads.

As opposed to the wholesome image of Wham! — two clean-cut, fresh-faced young boys seeking instant fun — George Michael's solo career has been based on a more basic, earthy rock'n'roll image portraying a grown-up unshaven, leather-clad hero with hint of true rebellion. Musically and visually the influences are Gene Vincent, Eddie Cochran and John Lennon. His true talent so far has been adapting these influences to his own purpose to create convincing new style still deeply rooted in traditions of great songwriting and exciting stage performances. For that alone, George Michael deserves to be regarded as eighties superstar.

**Faith, George Michael.
Courtesy CBS Records.**

**Hit Singles:**

| | US | UK |
|---|---|---|
| Careless Whisper, 1984 | 1 | 1 |
| Different Corner, 1986 | — | 1 |
| Faith, 1987 | 2 | 1 |
| I Want Your Sex, 1987 | 2 | 3 |
| Father Figure, 1988 | 1 | 11 |

*With Aretha Franklin:*

| | US | UK |
|---|---|---|
| I Knew You Were Waiting For Me, 1987 | 1 | 1 |

**Album:**
Faith (CBS), 1987 **CD**

**Below: Talented George Michael looking forward to many more years at the top.**

# Steve Miller

US guitarist, vocalist, composer.
Born Milwaukee, Wisconsin, November 5, 1943.

**Career:** Began playing guitar at four under auspices of legendary Les Paul(▶) and T-Bone Walker, both friends of Miller's father. Formed first band before teens. This blues outfit, which included Boz Scaggs(▶), was known as the Marksmen Combo.

Returning from adopted home state of Texas, Miller enrolled at University of Wisconsin to study literature, playing guitar part-time in the Ardells and then the Fabulous Knight Train (re-uniting Miller with Scaggs).

After studying in Denmark for a year, Miller moved to Chicago's burgeoning blues scene. He got involved with fleeting projects — the Goldberg/Miller Blues Band (with Barry Goldberg) and the World War Three Blues Band — but spent most of his time jamming with blues greats Muddy Waters(▶), Buddy Guy, Junior Wells and Otis Rush.

A brief respite back in Texas introduced Miller to recording; working as janitor for a local studio, he cut demos in spare time, before heading for San Francisco in 1966.

Recruiting Lonnie Turner (bass), Tim Davis (drums) and James 'Curly' Cooke (guitar) he formed Steve Miller Band, debuting at the Matrix after frantic period rehearsing in basement of Berkeley University campus.

Band attained strong local following at Avalon Ballroom and Bill Graham's(▶) Fillmore Auditorium (where they backed Chuck Berry(▶) for a live album). In summer 1967 they appeared at Monterey Pop Festival.

With other San Franciscan outfits Mother Earth and Quicksilver Messenger Service(▶), they made recording debut with **Revolution** soundtrack album.

Signed with Capitol Records in 1967, band released first album **Children Of The Future** in May 1968, with Scaggs re-joining Miller (replacing Cooke) and Jim Peterman providing keyboards.

Stunning **Sailor** set (1968), produced by Glyn Johns, included classic material **Living In The USA, Gangster Of Love** and haunting **Song For Our Ancestors**, pushing Miller's band to top of West Coast pile.

Various personnel changes (a continuing feature of Miller's outfits) saw Scaggs go solo and Peterman turn to production. Subsequent Miller aggregations have included Nicky Hopkins, Ben Sidran (one-time member of Marksmen) and dextrous bassist Gerald Johnson.

Overcoming serious bout of hepatitis (one of several extended breaks due to health problems), Miller progressed steadily, if not prolifically, through '70s with gold albums **The Joker** and **Fly Like An Eagle**. A four-year hiatus from '77 to '81 ended with **Circle Of Love** Miller returning from extended period

**Children Of The Future, Steve Miller.
Courtesy Capitol Records.**

**Right: The king of comebacks, Steve 'Guitar' Miller, who survived a four year rest to return to the top.**

spent farming his estate in Oregon.

Maintaining that the best was yet to come, he set out to make '82 his own, with **Abracadabra** single storming US/UK charts.

Often dismissed as 'lightweight', Miller could be criticised for repetition, but his manipulation of memorable licks and sharp simple lyrics remain undisputedly close to heavyweight.

Guitars: Fender Stratocaster, Gibson Les Paul.

| Hit Singles: | US | UK |
|---|---|---|
| The Joker, 1974 | 1 | — |
| Take The Money And Run, 1976 | 11 | — |
| Rock'n Me, 1976 | 1 | 11 |
| Fly Like An Eagle, 1977 | 2 | — |
| Jet Airliner, 1977 | 8 | — |
| Swingtown, 1977 | 17 | — |
| Abracadabra, 1982 | 1 | 2 |

**Albums:**
Children Of The Future (Capitol), 1968
Sailor (Capitol), 1969
Brave New World (Capitol), 1969
Your Saving Grace (Capitol), 1970
Number Five (Capitol), 1970
Rock Love (Capitol), 1971
Recall The Beginning (Capitol), 1973
Living In The USA (Capitol), 1973
The Joker (Capitol), 1973
Anthology (Capitol), 1973
Fly Like An Eagle (Capitol/Mercury), 1976
Book Of Dreams (Capitol/Mercury), 1977
Best Of 1968-73 (Capitol), 1977
Greatest Hits '74-'78 (Capitol/Mercury), 1978 **CD**
Circle Of Love (Capitol/Mercury), 1981 **CD**
Abracadabra (Capitol/Mercury), 1982 **CD**
Steve Miller Band Live (Mercury), 1983
Italian X Rays (Mercury) **CD**
Living In The 20th Century (EMI), 1987 **CD**

# Mr. Mister

US group formed 1982.

**Current line-up:** Richard Page, vocalist/bass player; Steve George, keyboards; Steve Farris, guitar; Pat Mastelotto, drums.

**Career:** Band formed in Los Angeles after an initial meeting in a downtown rehearsal studio, although vocalist Page and keyboards player George had been working on same recording sessions before then (with Donna Summer,

Molly Hatchet and Quincy Jones et al). Guitar player Steve Farris spent three years touring with Eddie Money's band before joining Mr. Mister while drummer Pat Mastelotto had worked with producer Mike Chapman.

Band soon picked up a strong following on the LA club circuit prior to being signed by RCA. Debut album **I Wear The Face** followed by **Welcome To The Real World** in 1985. While touring with Tina Turner in the US, their debut single **Broken Wings** reached number one in the charts.

Their second single was **Kyrie** which also went to number one in US, giving Mr. Mister the rare accolade of the number one album, single and video in the US during the same week. Both singles were UK hits, the latter reaching the top five at the same time as they played their first London dates.

Their third album **Go On**, engineered, mixed and co-produced (with the band) by Kevin Killen, noted for his work with U2 and Peter Gabriel, was released March 1988.

| Hit Singles: | US | UK |
|---|---|---|
| Broken Wings, 1985 | 1 | 4 |
| Is It Love?, 1986 | 8 | — |
| Kyrie, 1986 | 1 | 11 |
| Something Real, 1987 | 29 | — |

**Albums**
Welcome To The Real World (RCA), 1985 **CD**
I Wear The Face (RCA), 1986 **CD**
Go On (RCA), 1987 **CD**

**Below: Masters of AOR Mr Mister led by Richard Page, standing on left.**

# Joni Mitchell

US vocalist, composer, guitarist, pianist. Born Roberta Joan Anderson, Fort McLeod, Alberta, Canada, November 7, 1943.

**Career:** Attended Alberta College of Art with intention of becoming commercial artist. Learned to play ukelele for personal enjoyment, then developed serious interest in folk music/songwriting. Securing gig at the Depression coffee-house, Joni gradually gained confidence. Following performance at Mariposa Folk Festival in Ontario, she wrote her first song, **Day After Day.** Professional career began in Toronto, where she quickly became a leading figure of the Yorktown set.

Married Chuck Mitchell in June 1965; couple moved to Detroit, achieving some acclaim as duo on local folk circuit. After break-up of marriage, Joni continued as soloist, securing engagements in New York; signed to Reprise in 1967. Under aegis of Elliot Roberts, she gained reputation as star songwriter with a series of covers by such artists as Judy Collins(▶), Gordon Lightfoot(▶), Johnny Cash(▶), Tom Rush(▶) and Fairport Convention(▶).

Employing services of ex-Byrd(▶) David Crosby as producer, Mitchell recorded **Songs To A Seagull**, a brilliant debut displaying talent as singer/songwriter. Early albums were essentially acoustic, melodic works, sharpened by poetic lyrics. Although a product of the singer/songwriter boom of the late '60s, Mitchell revealed a maturity and incisiveness that separated her from most of her contemporaries. While others wallowed in their own narcissism, Mitchell was careful to bring a cutting edge to many of her lines. She continually struggled to find meaning in her much-publicised broken relationships, without falling into self-indulgence.

Third album, **Ladies Of The Canyon**, provided the breakthrough that Mitchell needed for continued success in the '70s. Sales were boosted by surprise hit single, **Big Yellow Taxi,** and cover versions of **Woodstock** by Crosby, Stills, Nash & Young(▶) and Matthew's Southern Comfort (who took song to No. 1 in UK). More importantly, **Ladies Of The Canyon** included piano accompaniment to match her acoustic guitar work.

Successive albums, **Blue**, **For The Roses** and **Court And Spark**, showed greater confidence in her own writing and a willingness to explore new musical ideas. Introduction of Tom Scott on wind instruments on **For The Roses** LP revealed first recorded signs of an interest in jazz as possible avenue for later work. Significantly, the only non-Mitchell song of the set was a re-make of

Annie Ross' **Twisted**.

By 1975, Mitchell was moving too fast for many of her older fans. **The Hissing Of Summer Lawns**, in many respects her best work to date, featured an array of new musical effects, including synthesiser and the African drums of Burundi. The lyrics contained many of the old themes presented from different points of view. By this time, her songwriting talent was probably unmatched by any artist in rock, bar Dylan(▶). In spite of such achievements, her more myopic critics were crying for a return to the folky songs of the late '60s. Instead, Mitchell pushed forward; **Hejira** was another dense work, less tuneful than its predecessor, but still commercially successful.

Her attraction to jazz was fully expressed in late '70s LPs **Don Juan's Reckless Daughter** and, more noticeably, **Mingus**. Realising, perhaps, that her interests were becoming increasingly incompatible with the mainstream rock audience, Mitchell threatened to retire at the end of decade to devote more energy to her first love, painting. (Virtually all her albums feature her original paintings.)

Just as it seemed that her career was nearing a close, Mitchell returned in 1982 with **Wild Things Run Fast** on David Geffen's label. Surprisingly, it was a return to the more melodic work of the early '70s and fared well chart wise. Three year recording break was ended by release of 1985 set **Dog Eat Dog**, whose sharp lyrical content took swipes at everything from US evangelism to domestic bliss.

Now further enmeshed in painting "career", Mitchell again remained aloof from the recording studio before contractual obligations resulted in critically acclaimed 1988 album **Chalk Mark In A Rain Storm** which marked 20th anniversary of debut LP **Song For A Seagull**.

**Dog Eat Dog, Joni Mitchell. Courtesy Geffen Records.**

| Hit Singles: | US | UK |
|---|---|---|
| Big Yellow Taxi, 1970 | — | 11 |
| Help Me, 1974 | 7 | — |

**Albums:**
Joni Mitchell, aka Songs To A Seagull, (Reprise), 1968
Clouds (Reprise), 1969
Ladies Of The Canyon (Reprise), 1970
Blue (Reprise), 1971 **CD**
For The Roses (Asylum), 1972 **CD**
Court And Spark (Electra/Asylum), 1974 **CD**
Miles Of Aisles (Asylum), 1974
The Hissing Of Summer Lawns (Asylum), 1975 **CD**
Hejira (Asylum), 1976 **CD**
Don Juan's Reckless Daughter (Asylum), 1977
Mingus (Asylum), 1979
Shadows And Light (Asylum), 1980
Wild Things Run Fast (Geffen), 1982
Dog Eat Dog (Geffen), 1985 **CD**

**Above: Joni Mitchell casting a spell with her guitar — her unique talent is too little heard in the '80s.**

# Moby Grape

US group formed 1966.

**Original line-up:** Alexander 'Skip' Spence, guitar, vocals; Peter Lewis, guitar, vocals; Jerry Miller, guitar, vocals; Bob Mosely, bass, vocals; Don Stevenson, drums.

**Career:** Group formed by Peter Lewis (ex-Peter and the Wolves) and Bob Mosely (ex-Frantics) in conjunction with Jefferson Airplane(▶) manager Matthew Katz. Miller and Stevenson also former Frantics were brought in and quintet was completed with induction of Spence, who had recently quit Airplane. Debut at the Ark, Marin County, in 1966, led to prestigious and well-received gigs at San Francisco's Fillmore West and Winterland, during city's commercial heyday.

Moby Grape immediately gained small cult following, and won reputation for their vocal dexterity (particularly Moby's R&B styling) and imaginative guitar work. Attracted interest from Elektra, Kama Sutra and Columbia Records, who were all invited by Katz to see group play at the Fillmore, Columbia finally secured Grape, mainly through enthusiasm of producer David Rubinson.

Unfortunately, Rubinson was also responsible for masterminding mind-boggling publicity campaign to coincide with release of their debut, **Moby Grape**. A purple elephant paraded Sunset Strip, helium balloons bearing group's logo were hoisted in Golden Gate Park; a horse and cart delivered bunches of grapes to prominent Hollywood journalists. Most bizarre of all was the simultaneous release of five singles (none of them hits), consisting of every track from the album. Press were unimpressed and excellent debut

was buried amid cries of record company hype. Grape never truly recovered from this bitter blow.

Grape played extensively for next 12 months, determined to bury memory of promotional overkill. In 1968 released **Wow** which included a free album, **Grape Jam**, and featured services of supersessioneers Al Kooper(▶) and Mike Bloomfield(▶). It was inventive work, highlighting the distinctive guitar sound that had made debut a classic. Poor sales blighted group's chances and Skip Spence left shortly afterwards to record solo album **Oar**, a cult classic and collectors' item.

Now in artistic decline, group recorded **Moby Grape '69**, a distinctly lacklustre effort, and after a series of erratic gigs Mosely quit and joined the Marines, re-emerging later with an eponymous solo album. Remaining trio moved to Nashville to cut uninspired **Truly Fine Citizen** with Bob Moore on bass.

After dissolution in spring 1969, group re-formed in 1971 to complete disappointing **20 Granite Creek**. Miller, Mosely and Lewis re-formed Grape again in 1974, but that and subsequent attempts to relive halcyon '60s days were confined to local bar gigs around Santa Cruz, California. One late version of band, calling itself the Grape, released LP **Live Grape** on own label in 1978.

For all their early promise, Moby Grape failed to achieve the mass popularity for which they once seemed destined. Their rapid decline following brilliant start remains one of the saddest tales in the history of '60s American rock.

**Final line-up:** Mosely; Miller; Lewis; Stevenson; Spence; Gordon Stevens, viola, dobro, mandolin.

**Albums:**
*Worth Searching Out:*
Moby Grape (Columbia/CBS), 1967
Wow (Columbia/CBS), 1968

**Below: Mickey Dolenz, Peter Tork, Mike Nesmith, Davy Jones: The Monkees.**

# The Monkees

US group formed 1966.

**Original/final line-up:** Davy Jones, vocals; Mike Nesmith, guitar, vocals; Peter Tork, bass, vocals; Mickey Dolenz, drums, vocals.

**Career:** Following its conquest by the Beatles, Stones, Kinks and slew of lesser British talents like Herman's Hermits, by 1966 America was ready for home-grown pop phenomenon. What was needed was group along lines of the Limey invaders — mop-topped, cute and lovable — but *American*. British invasion had spawned imitators like Beau Brummells, but there was still a yawning gap. With typical transatlantic ingenuity, Americans decided to create their own Beatles from scratch — and the Monkees were born.

The Monkees phenomenon, although lasting a scant two years, was a brilliant exercise in marketing. The giant NBC-TV network was prime mover — what it wanted was a TV series that would tap same youth market as the Beatles' phenomenally successful 'A Hard Day's Night' and 'Help' featuring zany, vaguely anti-establishment 'beat group'. Music featured in the show could be marketed in its own right — the show could promote the records, and vice-versa. It was decided that existing groups could cause too many problems, so after auditioning hundreds of hopeful unknowns, NBC picked Dolenz and English-born Jones, former child actors, and small-time musicians Tork and Nesmith.

Considering how dire it could have been, the TV series was surprisingly entertaining as well as extremely successful. Music from the show was translated into a series of singles

in 1969. Mike Nesmith went on to forge successful career with own brand of country rock and is now a video/film producer. Dolenz eventually moved to England to become an in-demand commercials TV director. Attempt by Jones and Dolenz to re-create band with Tommy Boyce and Bobby Hart in 1975 was a failure, Jones going on to star in 1985/6 re-run of 'Godspell' stage musical.

Re-runs of group's TV series sparked phenomenal reformation in 1986 (minus Nesmith), and Jones, Tork and Dolenz enjoyed hysterical US tour, prompting memories nearly 20 years old. Hands up if you went to see them.

**Hit Singles:**

| | US | UK |
|---|---|---|
| I'm A Believer/(I'm Not Your) Steppin' Stone, 1967 | 1 | 1 |
| (I'm Not Your) Steppin' Stone/I'm A Believer, 1967 | 20 | — |
| Last Train To Clarksville, 1967 | 1 | 23 |
| A Little Bit Me, A Little Bit You, 1967 | 2 | 3 |
| Alternate Title, 1967 | — | 2 |
| Pleasant Valley Sunday/Words, 1967 | 3 | 11 |
| Words/Pleasant Valley Sunday, 1967 | 11 | — |
| Daydream Believer, 1967 | 1 | 5 |
| Valleri, 1968 | 3 | 12 |
| D. W. Washburn, 1968 | 19 | 17 |

**Albums:**
Monkees (—/Sounds Superb), 1974
The Best Of The Monkees (—/MFP), 1981 **CD**
The Monkees (Arista), 1981
20 Golden Greats (—/Ronco), 1982
Then And Now (Arista), 1986 **CD**
Pool It (Rhino), 1987 **CD**

**Pool It, The Monkees.
Courtesy Rhino Records.**

that were worldwide hits.

In fact, the Monkees' music, particularly the singles, stands up as an excellent example of superbly crafted mid-'60s pop — not so surprising perhaps considering that writing duties were in hands of people like Neil Diamond(▶), Tommy Boyce and Bobby Hart, and back-up production was taken care of by top talents of the day. (Needless to say, band resented not being allowed to play on their first few singles.) Nesmith penned several songs on their later LPs.

Ultimately, it was over as quickly as it had begun. Tork left after badly received movie 'Head', and the others split after hits dried up

# Montrose

US group formed 1974.

**Original line-up:** Ronnie Montrose, guitar; Sam Hagar, vocals; Denny Carmassi, drums; Bill Church, bass.

**Career:** Brainchild of Ronnie Montrose, a session musician from Bay Area of San Francisco. Having played on Beaver and

Krause's **Gandharva**, Montrose joined Van Morrison's(▶) backing group, playing on both **Tupelo Honey** and **St Dominic's Preview**. Stints with Boz Scaggs(▶) and Edgar Winter(▶) culminated in offer to join Mott the Hoople(▶); but Montrose preferred to form heavier group.

Debut LP **Montrose** revealed that unit could hold their own on US hard rock circuit. Basically a derivative boogie band, impetus was lost following departure of Hagar(▶) (replaced by Bob James) after 1974's **Paper Money**. Group made celebrated appearance in England as part of Warner Bros' Music Show with labelmates Doobie Brothers(▶), Little Feat(▶) and Graham Central Station. Jim Alcivar (keyboards) was recruited in 1975 to add musical depth, and following Church's departure, both Alan Fitzgerald and Randy Jo Hobbs did spells on bass. However, by this point, Montrose had already outlived their usefulness.

**Montrose. Courtesy Warner Bros Records.**

In 1976, they split, Montrose then forming Gamma, which cut three albums for Elektra. After European tour in 1982, Montrose broke up band to join forces with Gamma keyboards player Mitchell Froom in new combo.

**Final line-up (Montrose):** Montrose; Carmassi; Bob James, vocals; Jim Alcivar, keyboards; Randy Jo Hobbs, bass.

**Albums:**
Montrose (Warner Bros), 1974
Paper Money (Warner Bros), 1974
Warner Bros Presents Montrose (Warner Bros), 1975
Jump On It (Warner Bros), 1976
Territory (Pacific), 1978 **CD**

*Gamma:*
Gamma I (Elektra), 1980
Gamma II (Elektra), 1980
Gamma III (Elektra), 1982

# Moody Blues

UK group formed 1964.
**Original line-up:** Mike Pinder, vocals, keyboards; Denny Laine, vocals, guitar; Ray Thomas, flute, vocals; Clint Warwick, bass, vocals; Graeme Edge, drums.

**Career:** Line-up above formed R&B group in Birmingham; second single release, cover of classic Bessie Banks song **Go Now**, leapt to No. 1 in British charts, No. 10 in US.

Although band scored couple more minor hits, after two albums Laine and Warwick both quite (Laine later becoming mainstay of Paul McCartney's Wings(▶)). They were replaced by Justin Hayward and John Lodge. Following period of reappraisal, band came up with **Days Of Future Passed**, album which united group with London Symphony Orchestra. Total departure from pattern of previous work, album was heavy on portentous philoso-

phising, light on rock 'n' roll. However, it caught mood of time (1967) and proved to be total success, re-establishing group in big way and spawning classic single in **Nights In White Satin** (a hit several times over, and since covered by many artists).

From that time on Moodies cornered market in pomp-rock; albums generally repeated formula of pop philosophy dressed up in high-flown, often orchestral, arrangements. Occasional hit singles boosted sales, whch ran into multi-millions all over world. From 1969 Moodies' product was released on own Threshold label, which didn't alter winning formula.

After 1972 album **Seventh Sojourn**, group did not record any fresh material for six years, spending intervening period on various solo projects. Most viable of these was Lodge/Hayward album, **Blue Jays**, which spawned major hit single **Blue Guitar** in 1975.

Compilation album **This Is The Moody Blues** and collection of bits and pieces called **Caught Live And Five** kept Moodies' public simmering until their return in force in 1978 with **Octave**. Predictably successful album heralded further live work, with ex-Yes(▶) keyboard man Patrick Moraz taking place of Mike Pinder. **Long Distance Voyager** LP, featuring Moraz, took Moodies into '80s. It made No. 1 in US, No. 7 in UK, showing that market for group's particular brand of music was far from moribund.

Not always most critically praised band, Moody Blues nevertheless consistently give public what it wants. Skill and craft have never been in question, although it does seem that band could occasionally afford to introduce new ideas.

**Current line-up:** Thomas; Edge; Justin Hayward, vocals, guitar; John Lodge, bass, vocals; Patrick Moraz, keyboards.

| Hit Singles: | US | UK |
|---|---|---|
| Go Now, 1964 | 10 | 1 |
| Nights In White Satin, 1967 | — | 19 |
| Question, 1970 | 21 | 2 |
| Isn't Life Strange, 1972 | 29 | 13 |
| Nights In White Satin, 1972 | 2 | 9 |
| I'm Just A Singer (In A Rock And Roll Band), 1973 | 12 | 36 |
| Nights In White Satin, 1979 | — | 14 |
| Gemini Dream, 1981 | 14 | — |
| The Voice, 1981 | 16 | — |

**Albums:**
The Magnificent Moodies (London/Decca), 1966
Days Of Future Passed (Deram), 1967 **CD**
In Search Of The Lost Chord (Deram), 1968 **CD**
On The Threshold Of A Dream (Decca), 1969 **CD**

To Our Children's Children (Threshold), 1969 **CD**
A Question Of Balance (Threshold), 1970 **CD**
Every Good Boy Deserves Favour (Threshold), 1971 **CD**
Seventh Sojourn (Threshold), 1972 **CD**
This Is The Moody Blues (Threshold), 1974
Caught Live & Five (London/Decca), 1977
Octave (London/Threshold), 1978 **CD**
Out Of This World (K-Tel), 1979 **CD**
Long Distance Voyager (Threshold), 1981 **CD**
Present (Threshold), 1983 **CD**
Voices In The Sky (Decca), 1984 **CD**

*Worth Searching Out:*
*Moody Blues:*
Go Now (London/—), 1965

*Justin Hayward & John Lodge:*
Blue Jays (Threshold), 1975

*Graeme Edge Band with Adrian Gurvitz:*
Kick Off Your Muddy Boots (Threshold), 1975

*Ray Thomas Solo:*
Hopes, Wishes And Dreams (Threshold), 1976

*Michael Pinder Solo:*
The Promise (Threshold), 1976

*Justin Haywood Solo:*
Moving Mountains (Towerbell), 1985
Songwriter (Decca), 1987

# Keith Moon

UK drummer, actor.
Born London, August 23, 1946; died London, September 7, 1978.

**Career:** Moon began musical career in Harrow, playing with local friends in band not serious enough to merit name. Recorded obscure 1963 single, **Mad Goose/ You Can't Sit Down**, with the Beachcombers. Later joined Roger Daltrey(▶), John Entwistle(▶) and Pete Townshend(▶) in the Who(▶).

Moon quickly earned well-deserved reputation for being one of rock's most exciting, innovative drummers. Entirely self-taught, he had natural gift for using each arm and leg independently. Consequently, he was one of rock's first drummers to employ double bass drums and a myriad of cymbals. Unlike many later imitators with big flashy kits, Moon used all his equipment.

Equally deserved was Moon's growing reputation for crazy, over-the-top antics. His practical jokes, real-life adventures and deathy-defying feats are legendary .This aspect of Moon's life is detailed in personal manager/minder Peter 'Dougal' Butler's book (co-authored by Chris Trengove), 'Moon the Loon' ('Full Moon' in US). However, the larger-than-life image surrounding Moon not only

covered up some insecurity and personal unhappiness but also downplayed wide variety of unfortunate incidents which affected those who had to live or work with him. In 1967, the Who had to cancel studio sessions because of injuries suffered by Moon. He was directly involved in the death of his driver during a pub brawl. Such incidents were not nearly so isolated as suggested by the nothing-can-hurt me facade Moon was so fond of projecting.

Moon's growing party reputation soon jeopardised his private life. He had married in 1966, but kept the marriage secret for two years. By early '70s, he had moved his wife and daughter into country estate where they too were caught up with never-ending party atmosphere. Keith's mother, however, recalls his visits home to Harrow when he would

**Two Sides Of The Moon, Keith Moon. Courtesy Polydor Records.**

arrive alone, and ask only for tea and biscuits. After a few hours of quiet chatter Keith would leave and resume behaviour pattern expected by public.

By mid-1974, Moon's wife Kim could handle no more and left. In many ways, Moon never recovered from the loss. At this particular time, Who reached a two-year hiatus. While Townshend, Daltrey and Entwistle got involved in film or solo LPs, Moon, apart for brief role in 'Tommy' film, had nothing to do. In September 1974, Moon moved to Los Angeles to be near drinking partners Ringo Starr(▶) and Harry Nilsson(▶).

Moon convinced MCA he could be solo star, and managed to collect sizeable advance. Using money to party in studio, he began collecting every available LA musician he could and proceeded to record superstar session that defies description. MCA became concerned when single released in October 1974 proved a disaster. **Don't Worry Baby** was a cover of Moon's heroes the Beach Boys (▶) even expected hard core Who/Beach Boys fans weren't buying. Producer and former Beatles associate Mal Evans was replaced by Skip Taylor and John Stronack, who re-mixed entire album. Released in April 1975, LP's rapid appearance in cut-out bins announced end of Moon's party.

Moon returned to UK in 1978. His pudgy face and generally sloppy appearance were price of his relentless lifestyle. The death of possibly the greatest drummer in rock came as a kind of anticipated shock, but no surprise to those who knew him well. The Who continued with ex-Face(▶) Kenney Jones, but magic was lost.

Notable 'session' work includes: **Truth** (Jeff Beck(▶)), **Flash Fearless, Pussy Cats** (Nilsson(▶)), **All This & World War Two** soundtrack, **Sometime In New York** (John Lennon(▶)) and **The 20th Anniversary of Rock and Roll** (Bo Diddley(▶)).
Drums: Premier.

**Albums:**
*Worth Searching Out:*
Two Sides Of The Moon (MCA/Polydor), 1975

**Below: Keith Moon, rock's 'premier' drummer, and madman of the Who.**

# Van Morrison

UK vocalist, composer, guitarist.
Born George Ivan, Belfast, N. Ireland, August 31, 1945.

**Career:** Irish music played little part in Morrison's upbringing. Raised to the sounds of America's Deep South (his mother a blues and jazz singer, his father a fanatical record collector with love for rural blues), Morrison mastered guitar, saxophone and harmonica while at school, playing in skiffle bands from age 11 at local dance halls.

Leaving school in 1960 for career as professional musician, he joined Monarchs for tour of US air bases in Germany and in 1963 returned to Belfast to form Them with two Monarchs members and two other friends. Installed as house band at R&B club in Belfast's Maritime Hotel, Billy Harrison (guitar), Ronnie Millings (drums), and Eric Wicksen (piano), fronted by Morrison's vocals, built cult following for frenetic brand of blues-flavoured beat music.

A version of Slim Harpo's **Don't Start Crying Now** was Irish hit and, signed to Decca, band moved base to London and followed through with up-beat version of Big Joe Williams' classic **Baby Please Don't Go** which climbed high into UK national charts.

Ace American producer Bert Berns (co-writer of **Twist And Shout, Tell Him, Cry Baby** and other '60s soul classics) was brought in for Morrison's own composition **Here Comes The Night**, group's first transatlantic hit. Though never a UK hit, Them's **Gloria**, another Morrison original, helped establish band's reputation and is regarded as true classic. On debut album, session men, including guitarist Jimmy Page (later of Led Zeppelin(▶)), were brought in while Jackie McAuley replaced Wicksen.

**Astral Weeks, Van Morrison. Courtesy Warner Bros Records.**

By second album, band was on verge of collapsing and session men laid down most of tracks behind Morrison's vocals. Following unsatisfactory US tour Morrison disbanded Them and returned to Ulster.

Having formed own Bang label, Berns sent Morrison air ticket and took him into New York studios to cut solo sides from which sessions **Brown-Eyed Girl** was US hit in mid-'67. Them later re-formed for short period, but without Morrison, whose solo career took full flight.

Berns died of heart attack on December 1, 1967, and Morrison signed to Warner Bros, who gave him complete creative control. Resulting **Astral Weeks** album, cut in New York in just 48 hours, is one of all-time great rock albums, though with no obvious hit singles, it only sold modestly.

**Moondance** (containing hit single **Into The Mystic**) and **Van Morrison — His Band And Street Choir** (producing **Domino** hit) forged solid reputation and built Morrison

**Poetic Champions Compose, Van Morrison. Courtesy Mercury Records.**

---

**Them featuring Van Morrison. Courtesy Decca Records.**

into major US concert attraction, touring with large 11-piece band including strings. Close to the mike, eyes half-closed, lips barely parted, chubby face crowned by mass of rust-red hair, his vocals have always oozed soulfulness and personal conviction.

**Tupelo Honey** (1971), which included suite of love songs to wife Janet Planet, and further albums — especially the exceptionally strong **It's Too Late To Stop Now** live double LP (following hugely successful 1974 US and European tour) which was truly live with no over-dubs — brought Morrison to his zenith.

Personal and professional hassles continued, however. He divorced in 1973 and in 1974 suddenly broke up applauded Caledonia Soul Orchestra, carrying out next European tour with five-piece band, playing sax and harmonica himself.

Morrison had returned to Ireland in 1973 for first time in seven years and songs written there emerged as 1974 album **Veedon Fleece**, arguably his best work since **Astral Weeks**. Followed by several aborted album ventures (including one featuring the Crusaders(▶)), it was not till spring 1977 that **A Period Of Transition** surfaced (with Dr John(▶) guesting).

Despite guarded approach to media, Morrison appears approachable personality, whose annual tours and high-quality albums still attract maximum attention.

## Motorhead

UK group formed 1975.
**Original line-up:** Ian 'Lemmy' Kilminster; Larry Wallis, guitar; Lucas Fox, drums.

**Career:** Lemmy worked as roadie for Hawkwind(▶) and without prior experience took over group's bass spot. In 1974 he involved band with drug bust at US/Canadian border and got fired. Upon returning to UK, he formed Bastard. Journalist Mick Farren introduced him to ex-Pink Fairies Wallis, and then Fox.
Manager Doug Smith convinced trio to pick

---

| Hit Singles: | US | UK |
|---|---|---|
| *With Them:* | | |
| Baby Please Don't Go, 1965 | — | 10 |
| Here Comes The Night, 1965 | 24 | 2 |
| *Solo:* | | |
| Brown-Eyed Girl, 1967 | 10 | — |
| Domino, 1970 | 9 | — |

**Albums:**
Astral Weeks (Warner Bros), 1968 **CD**
Best Of (Bang/President), 1970
Moondance (Warner Bros), 1970 **CD**
His Band And Street Choir (Warner Bros), 1970
Tupelo Honey (Warner Bros), 1971
St Dominic's Preview (Warner Bros), 1972
Hard Nose The Highway (Warner Bros), 1973
It's Too Late To Stop Now (Warner Bros), 1974
Veedon Fleece (Warner Bros), 1974
Period Of Transition (Warner Bros), 1977
Wavelength (Warner Bros), 1978
Into The Music (Mercury), 1978 **CD**
Common One (Warner Bros/Mercury), 1980 **CD**
Beautiful Vision (Warner Bros/Mercury), 1982 **CD**
Inarticulate Speech Of The Heart (Mercury), 1983 **CD**
Live At The Grand Opera House Belfast (Mercury), 1984 **CD**
A Sense Of Wonder (Mercury), 1985 **CD**
No Guru No Method No Teacher (Mercury) 1986 **CD**
T.B. Sheets (Bellaphon) **CD**
Poetic Champions Compose (Mercury), 1987 **CD**

---

more viable name. Lemmy came up with Americanism for speed freak, Motorhead. Band debuted at Camden Town's Roundhouse on July 20, 1975 and promptly went on tour. Opening for Blue Oyster Cult's(▶) London October 1975 show they earned critical assessment as 'worst band in the world'. Motorhead never looked back.

Trio began recording LP for United Artists in December '75. Lemmy asked friend Phil Taylor for ride to Rockfield Studios and explained his dissatisfaction with Fox. Taylor volunteered to sit in and found himself re-recording entire album (except for one track). United Artists accepted tapes but refused to release LP. Phil introduced 'Fast' Eddie Clarke to band as second guitarist. Wallis left shortly afterwards and band was back to trio.

Giving up on United Artists, band recorded **White Line Fever/Leavin' Here** for Stiff Records in mid-1976. United Artists, although still refusing to support band, raised contractual objections and killed release. (Both cuts were eventually issued in 1977 on compilation LPs, **Bunch Of Stiffs** and **Hits Greatest Stiffs**.)

Band almost broke up but Ted Carroll of Chiswick Records asked them to record single and provided two days' studio time. Band worked around clock and presented Carroll with 13 backing tracks. He liked them and agreed for band to finish them off.

Single **Motorhead/City Kids** and album **Motorhead** both released Summer 1977.

**Overkill, Motorhead. Courtesy Bronze Records.**

Instead of finding success, Lemmy became involved in management problems with interloper Tony Secunda (ex-Move(▶)) and band found itself without label in spring 1978. Doug Smith stepped back in and arranged recording contract with Bronze Records. Single **Louie, Louie** was released and paved way for sonic assault of **Overkill** LP.

By now band was developing fanatical following whose loyalty rivals that of any group. Continuing tours opened up new audiences and **Bomber** album made No. 12 in UK charts. Tour supporting this release featured bomber lighting rig with replica of German airplane, and acrobats, which became exciting part of band's performance.

Not too surprisingly, United Artists noted Motorhead's growing stature and released band's first recordings as **On Parole**. Although hardly representative of band's current abilities, it provided insight into early days of Motorhead's history.

April 1980 saw release of live material on EP **The Golden Years**. Motorhead's live shows have always been strong point and EP became band's first Top 10 hit. **Ace of Spades** set became band's biggest seller so far and Motorhead was hot property. Chiswick released **Beer Drinkers** EP with four tracks recorded at time of **Motorhead** album.

Injury to Taylor caused cancellation of late 1980 tour, while Lemmy and Clarke joined

Girlschool(▶) to record **Valentines Day Massacre** EP. Year ended with band being voted No. 1 (as were **Ace of Spaces** LP and single) in Sounds Readers Poll.

Band returned to touring in March 1981, and while at Leeds Queen Hall/Newcastle City Hall recorded material for live LP, **No Sleep 'Til Hammersmith**. Described as guaranteed to melt speakers, fuse amps and short circuit turntables, album can claim to be best example of recorded high energy since Who's(▶) **Live at Leeds**. Hammersmith went to UK No. 1 within one week of issue. Just prior to its release, Motorhead opened Ozzy Osbourn's(▶) US Blizzard Of Oz tour. Band returned again in 1982 and seemed poised to crack US market. Instead, late May 1982 brought announcement that Clarke was leaving group in middle of tour (because of disagreement with Lemmy's ongoing plans for Motorhead's involvement in outside activities).

Lemmy's 'try anything once' attitude produced successful **Valentines Day Massacre** release as well as more bizarre single **Don't Do That** featuring himself, Nolan Sisters, Cozy Powell and others. But his disregard for convention reached new heights. He joined Wendy O. Williams of the Plasmatics to do send-up version of several-times-divorced Tammy Wynette's **Stand By Your Man**. This was too much for Clarke and he left (later to form Fastway). This crisis disrupted band's progression, although Brian Robertson (ex-Thin Lizzy(▶)) filled in so band could complete US tour.

Robertson stayed with band until end of 1983, featuring on big-selling album **Another Perfect Day**. Two years passed before release of next album **No Remorse**, and it featured entirely new line-up apart from Lemmy: Pete Gill, drums, and Michael "Wurzel" Burston and Phil Campbell, guitars, contributed to sonic mayhem.

In 1986 band signed with GWR, continuing with **Orgasmatron** to satisfy their legions of fans. About as subtle as a train crash, Motorhead offer a brand of lowdown, low-forehead musical overkill that to many is what rock is all about.

**Current line-up:** Lemmy; Phil Taylor, drums; Brian Robertson, guitar, vocals.

**Hit Singles:**

|  | US | UK |
|---|---|---|
| The Golden Years (EP), 1980 | — | 8 |
| Ace Of Spaces, 1980 | — | 15 |
| Motorhead (Live), 1981 | — | 6 |

**Albums (selected):**
Motorhead (—/Chiswick), 1977
Overkill (—/Bronze), 1979 **CD**

**Below: The very lovely Motorhead — (left to right) Phil Taylor, Lemmy, Brian Robertson.**

On Parole (—/United Artists), 1979
Bomber (—/Bronze), 1979 **CD**
Ace Of Spades (Mercury/Bronze), 1980 **CD**
No Sleep 'Til Hammersmith (Mercury/Bronze), 1981 **CD**
Iron Fist (Mercury/Bronze), 1982 **CD**
What's Words Worth (—/Big Beat), 1983*
Another Perfect Day (—/Bronze), 1983
No Remorse (Bronze), 1984
*Live At The Roundhouse, 1978
Anthology (Raw Power), 1986 **CD**
Orgasmatron (GWR), 1986 **CD**
Born To Lose (Dojo), 1986
Rock 'N' Roll (GWR), 1987

# Mott the Hoople

UK group formed 1969.

**Original line-up:** Mick Ralphs, guitar; Dale 'Buffin' Griffin, drums; Pete 'Overend' Watts, bass; Verden 'Phally' Allen, organ; Ian Hunter, vocals, guitar, keyboards.

**Career:** Evolved from Herefordshire group Silence, featuring Ralphs, Griffin, Watts, Allen and vocalist Stan Tippens. Signed to Island by A&R head Guy Stevens, who changed name to Mott the Hoople (from novel by Willard Manus). Following Stevens' suggestion, Tippens reverted to road manager, replaced by Ian Hunter(▶) (recruited from auditions).

Debut **Mott The Hoople** relied heavily on Hunter's rasping Dylanesque vocals, recalling sound of **Blonde On Blonde**. Next two albums, **Mad Shadows** (1970) and **Wildlife** (1971), revealed contrasting hard/soft rock styles of Hunter and Ralphs respectively. In spite of loyal following on London club circuit, album sales remained poor. **Brain Capers** (1971) was followed by barren period; group finally split in March 1972. Later that year, recent Hoople fan, David Bowie(▶), encouraged and nurtured re-formation. Following an introduction to Bowie's manager Tony De Fries, a new contract was signed with CBS. Bowie wrote/produced hit single **All The Young Dudes**, which climbed to No. 3. Success of fifth album gave group new lease of life and following Bowie's retreat as Svengali, they continued to chart until 1974. During interim, charismatic Hunter took over as leader, resulting in departure of Allen. Original leader Mick Ralphs left shortly afterwards to form Bad Company(▶).

New members were recruited: guitarist Ariel Bender (actually Luther Grosvenor of Spooky Tooth) and keyboards player Morgan Fisher, formerly of Love Affair. 1973 US summer tour proved particularly memorable with an array of costumes and theatrical effects; group subsequently played a week in a Broadway theatre. New line-up cut one

studio album, **The Hoople**, and a Top 50 single, **Saturday Gig**, before Grosvenor left, to be replaced by Bowie sideman Mick Ronson. Shortly afterwards, Hunter was hospitalised in New York suffering from exhaustion, and important British tour was cancelled. Amid rumour and confusion, Hunter and Ronson left to form new group just as **Live** LP was released and became band's biggest seller.

Six months later, renamed Mott regrouped with singer Nigel Benjamin and guitarist Ray Major. Two patchy albums appeared before Benjamin quit; CBS then dropped Mott from roster. Remaining members, minus Nigel Benjamin, teamed up with John Fiddler (ex-Medicine Head) for brief career as British Lions. Meanwhile, Hunter/Ronson liaison was short-lived. Hunter issued run of solo albums for Columbia/CBS and Chrysalis and became major influence on British New Wave, producing Generation X among others.

**Final line-up:** Watts; Griffin; Morgan Fisher, keyboards; Ray Major, vocals, guitar; Nigel Benjamin, vocals.

**Hit Singles:**

|  | US | UK |
|---|---|---|
| All The Young Dudes, 1972 | — | 3 |
| Honaloochie Boogie, 1973 | — | 12 |
| All The Way From Memphis, 1973 | — | 10 |
| Roll Away The Stone, 1973 | — | 8 |
| Golden Age Of Rock And Roll, 1974 | — | 16 |

**Albums:**
Mott The Hoople (Atlantic Island), 1969
Mad Shadows (Island), 1970
Wild Life (Island), 1971
Brain Capers (Island), 1971
All The Young Dudes (Columbia/CBS), 1972
Rock 'n' Roll Queen (Columbia/CBS), 1972

**Above: Head Hoopler Ian Hunter — after he left Mott The Hoople, group's commercial success soon departed.**

Mott (Columbia/CBS), 1973
Live (Columbia/CBS), 1974
Greatest Hits (Columbia/CBS), 1976

*As Mott:*
*Worth Searching Out:*
Drive On (CBS), 1975
Shouting And Pointing (CBS), 1976

**Mott, Mott The Hoople. Courtesy Columbia Records.**

# The Move

UK group formed 1965.

**Original line-up:** Carl Wayne, vocals; Roy Wood, guitar, vocals; Trevor Burton, guitar, vocals; Ace Kefford, bass; Bev Bevan, drums.

**Career:** Formed in Birmingham out of some of city's top musicians, the Move nevertheless first made their mark at London's Marquee Club in 1966. Their exciting stage show/pop-art image created much interest, and band was quickly signed to Deram Records. First single, Roy Wood's **Night Of Fear**, reached No. 2 in UK charts in January 1967.

A troupe of seasoned gigsters, the somewhat fey mantle of psychedelia sat uneasily upon them. However, helped by remarkable song-writing facility of Roy Wood, the Move took up flower-power banner and produced series of hits which to many sum up spirit of '60s.

From **Fire Brigade** onwards, Wood began handling lead vocals and it became obvious that band was coming more and more under his influence. 1968 saw first of series of personnel changes — Ace Kefford left, followed in early 1969 by Trevor Burton (who

**Something Else From The Move. Courtesy Harvest Records.**

later went on to Steve Gibbons Band). Rick Price, another Birmingham musician, joined on bass.

Hits continued through the late '60s and early '70s with **Curly, Brontosaurus, Tonight, Chinatown** and **California Man** all charting heavily in UK. Strangely, the Move never made much impact in US, being regarded as cult underground group rather than pop band.

By 1970, however, band was practically falling apart. Jeff Lynne came in to replace Carl Wayne, and by 1971 band was reduced to Wood, Bevan and Lynne. The stage was set for end of the Move and beginning of Electric Light Orchestra(▶), a concept which Wood had been kicking around for some time (Wood/Lynne originally planned to run Move and ELO simultaneously). Wood eventually left ELO to form Wizzard, and achieved considerable success with Spector-influenced sound up to mid-'70s.

Always plagued by problem of falling between several stools, not to mention personality clashes and wrangling over musical direction, the Move were never likely candidates in longevity stakes. However, they were important influence at a time when rock was beginning to emerge and become a separate form, and they leave behind collection of singles which stand up to repeated listening.

**Final line-up:** Roy Wood; Bevan; Jeff Lynne, guitar, vocals.

**Hit Singles:**

| | US | UK |
|---|---|---|
| Night Of Fear, 1967 | — | 2 |
| I Can Hear The Grass Grow, 1967 | — | 5 |
| Flowers In The Rain, 1967 | — | 2 |
| Fire Brigade, 1968 | — | 3 |
| Blackberry Way, 1968 | — | 1 |
| Curly, 1969 | — | 12 |
| Brontosaurus, 1970 | — | 7 |
| Tonight, 1971 | — | 11 |
| California Man, 1972 | — | 7 |

**Albums:**
The Best Of (A&M), 1974
The Greatest Hits (—/Hallmark), 1978
The Move (Shines On), 1979 (—/Harvest)
Platinum Collection (—/Cube), 1981
The Move Collection (Collectors), 1986 **CD** (Double)

*Worth Searching Out:*
Something Else (Live EP) (Regal/ Zonophone), 1968

# Alison Moyet

UK vocalist.
Born Basildon, Essex.

**Career:** In 10 years Alison Moyet has progressed from being a punk rock vocalist, through synth-dominated glam pop, to emerge as a fine jazz-slanted vocalist.

Drifted through series of jobs until she heard punk outfit X-Ray Spex and readily confessed to basing her initial vocal style entirely on Poly Styrene. A fan of soul and blues, she sang with the Vipers, the Vicars and the Screaming Abdabs and furthered her writing career—she had penned **Nobody's Diary**, later to be Yazoo's(▶) farewell single.

On point of advertising for new band when Vince Clarke, also from Basildon, left Depeche Mode, they teamed up and recorded **Only You** as a one-off.

£1,000 advance from Mute Records and immediate commercial success launched Moyet onto chart scene, sales topping 300,000 and establishing Yazoo overnight as new pop sensation—Moyet's roly-poly yet charismatic image combining admirably with

**Above: Birmingham beatsters The Move, with the great Roy Wood pictured second from left.**

Clarke's technical wizardry.

**Upstairs At Eric's** album hit number one and Yazoo seemed to be most inspiring of all synth bands which dominated 1982 pop but they had already decided to split before recording second album **You And Me Both** due to differences in character and approach to music, Moyet wishing to front real musicians rather than electronic machines.

After some delay, solo career got underway with instant smashes **Love Resurrection** and **All Cried Out** and million-selling debut album **Alf**, produced by Tony Swain and Steve Jolley, established her as one of Britain's premier girl singers.

Moyet contrasted herself with other girl singers: 'The way they sing is so . . . female. So submissive. They paint a picture of "lie back and think of England". I'd never sing submissive lyrics. That's what I like about a lot of black singers—the honesty. Women who are willing to show their ugliness and the ugly side of women. The possessiveness, the jealousy, the total lack of any scruples. If I'm singing a song I make myself feel really

**Below: Formerly Alf (in her punk days) is now the well-groomed Alison Moyet. Future international cabaret star?**

sad. I can make myself cry by singing . . .

Subsequent recording of Billie Holiday's **That Ol' Devil Called Love** and TV special fronting jazz big band signposts her probable direction. Not a soul singer, but she *is* a singer who is truly soulful.

**Raindancing, Alison Moyet. Courtesy CBS Records.**

In 1985 Moyet made bold move by releasing version of Billie Holiday classic **That Ol' Devil Called Love**, vindicated by record reaching charts. In that year, Live Aid duet with Paul Young was regarded by many as one of best moments of starry occasion.

Latterly singer seems to have been making concerted move towards mainstream, particularly with regard to slicked-up appearance, but continues to turn in classy vocal performances. Recent platinum album **Raindancing** confirms her position as one of UK's premier female talents.

**Hit Singles:**

| | US | UK |
|---|---|---|
| Love Resurrection, 1984 | — | 10 |
| All Cried Out, 1984 | — | 8 |
| That Ol' Devil Called Love, 1985 | — | 2 |
| Weak In The Presence Of Beauty, 1987 | — | 6 |
| Is This Love?, 1987 | — | 3 |
| Love Letters, 1987 | — | 4 |

**Albums:**
Alf (CBS), 1984 **CD**
Raindancing (CBS), 1987 **CD**

# Rick Nelson

US vocalist, guitarist, composer, actor. Born Eric Hilliard Nelson, Teaneck, New Jersey, May 8, 1940. Died January 31, 1985.

**Career:** Joined parents' radio show at four; made transition to television's 'Adventures of Ozzie and Harriet' in early '50s. Signed first record contract as Ricky Nelson with Verve in 1956, scoring first hit **I'm Walkin'**. Signed to Imperial Records 1957; consistently appeared in US and UK charts until early '60s.

Initial appeal was to young teens. He had same good looks as Presley(▶) but his clean-cut image was less threatening to middle-American morals. Records were somewhat subdued but well-crafted due to fine musicians, notably guitarist James Burton(▶), who contributed classic solos to sides that would have been classified as rockabilly had they been recorded in Memphis.

Change of image followed shortening of name to Rick in 1961 and recording deal with US Decca in 1963. Later material appealed more to young adults, including effective recording of Dylan's(▶) **She Belongs To Me** (1969). Formed own group, the Stone Canyon Band (1971), with leanings towards country rock. Had major hit in 1972 with autobiographical **Garden Party** summing up his feelings about audiences who regarded him as a rock'n'roller and nothing else. Since then Nelson failed to make chart contribution, despite several fine albums, including **Playing To Win** debut for Capitol.

Lack of hits did not diminish club and concert following (although audiences preferred older material). It was when en route to New Year's Eve gig in Iowa that Nelson was killed crashing his private aircraft.

**Hit Singles:**

| | US | UK |
|---|---|---|
| I'm Walkin'/A Teenager's Romance, 1957 | 2 | — |
| A Teenager's Romance/I'm Walkin', 1957 | 4 | — |
| Be Bop Baby, 1957 | 3 | — |
| Stood Up/Waitin' In School, 1958 | 2 | — |
| Waitin' In School/Stood Up, 1958 | 18 | — |
| My Bucket's Got A Hole In It/ Believe What You Say, 1958 | 12 | — |
| Believe What You Say/My Bucket's Got A Hole In It, 1958 | 4 | — |
| Poor Little Fool, 1958 | 1 | 4 |
| Lonesome Town/I Got A Feeling, 1958 | 7 | — |
| I Got A Feeling/Lonesome Town, 1958 | 10 | 27 |
| Someday, 1958 | — | 9 |

| | | |
|---|---|---|
| It's Late/Never Be Anyone Else But You, 1959 | 9 | 3 |
| Never Be Anyone Else But You/ It's Late, 1959 | 6 | 14 |
| Sweeter Than You/Just A Little Too Much, 1959 | 9 | 19 |
| Just A Little Too Much/Sweeter Than You, 1959 | 9 | 11 |
| I Wanna Be Loved, 1959 | 20 | — |
| Young Emotions, 1960 | 12 | — |
| Travelin' Man/Hello Mary Lou, 1961 | 1 | 2 |
| Hello Mary Lou/Travelin' Man, 1961 | 9 | 2 |
| Everlovin'/A Wonder Like You, 1961 | 16 | — |
| A Wonder Like You/Everlovin' 1961 | 11 | — |
| Young World, 1962 | 5 | 19 |
| Teenage Idol, 1962 | 5 | 39 |
| It's Up To You, 1963 | 6 | 22 |
| Fools Rush In, 1963 | 12 | 12 |
| For You, 1964 | 6 | 14 |
| Garden Party, 1972 | 6 | 41 |

**Albums:**
Ricky (Liberty/London), 1957
Decca Years (MCA/—), 1971
Intakes (Epic), 1977
The Rick Nelson Singles Album (Fame), 1978

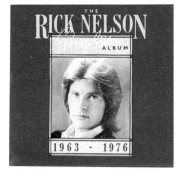

**The Rick Nelson Singles Album. Courtesy MCA Records.**

Rockin' Rock (MCA), 1979
Playing To Win (Capitol/—), 1981
The Best Of (Liberty), 1985 **CD**
More Songs By Ricky (EMI-Liberty) Holland
Comes Of Age (See For Miles), 1987
Sings Rare Tracks (United Factories), 1987

*Worth Searching Out:*
Garden Party (MCA), 1974

**Above: Late Rick Nelson, who proved more than just a pretty face.**

# New Model Army

UK group formed 1980.

**Current line-up:** Slade The Leveller, vocals, guitar, composer; Jason Harris, bass; Robb Heston, drums.

**Career:** Group took name from Cromwell's forces in English Civil War. Tense, restless yet melodic, New Model Army's music boasts lyrics which have emotive socio-political content—their album title track **Vengeance** was banned by Independent Broadcasting Authority in UK.

Formed in Bradford, Yorkshire, group reached no.17 on independent label chart with first release **Bittersweet** for Quiet Records. **Vengeance**, their third single, the second for Abstract label hit number one. **The Price** went straight into indie chart at number one and led to switch to EMI for **No Rest** which made number 28 on national chart, resultant album **No Rest For The Wicked** peaking at number 22.

Heavy touring schedule helped to make band one of leading "political" outfits of 80s. Recent album **The Ghost Of Cain** consolidated reputation.

**Albums:**
Vengeance (Abstract), 1984 **CD**
No Rest For The Wicked (EMI), 1985
Ghost Of Cain (EMI), 1986 **CD**

# Randy Newman

US composer, pianist, vocalist.
Born Los Angeles, November 28, 1943.

**Career:** Born into musical family, took piano lessons from age seven. Graduated from University of California in music composition.

Started career as arranger and songwriter and quickly gained reputation among fellow musicians as perceptive and unusually intelligent writer. Early supporters of his work included Judy Collins(▶), who recorded **I Think It's Going To Rain Today** in 1966, and Alan Price(▶) who hit in 1967 with **Simon Smith And His Amazing Dancing Bear.**

Newman signed with Warner Bros in 1968 and released **Randy Newman,** which featured his striking compositions with large orchestra. It created interest but had little commercial appeal, which could also be said about **Twelve Songs,** his next album (originally a collection of demos recorded before **Randy Newman**). This album contained **Mama Told Me Not To Come,** later a hit for Three Dog Night(▶).

After **Live,** concert versions of songs from first two albums, **Sail Away** and **Good Old Boys,** consolidated Newman's reputation as writer of pointed, oblique songs with sharp edge of satire. His subject matter—nuclear bombs, racism, pollution—although stuff of protest, was dealt with in wry, ambiguous manner that set Newman apart from run-of-the-mill protest singers. Rather than preaching, he has always preferred subtlety, creating miniature tableaux that make their own point.

In 1977 his album **Little Criminals** yielded hit single in **Short People,** a satire on bigotry which nevertheless was mistaken for bigotry itself by many people, including variety of organisations for midgets and dwarves. Despite controversy, **Little Criminals** won Newman much wider audience.

Never a prolific artist, Newman made further impact with **Born Again** in 1979, then released nothing until **Trouble In Paradise** in early 1983. Regarded by most critics as brilliant return to form of **Little Criminals,** album puts Newman's sardonic voice and spare piano accompaniment into context of LA session-rock ethos.

Although recorded work has become steadily more elaborate, Newman invariably undertakes live work accompanied only by his own piano. Complex, self-effacing man who is one of few truly original talents in rock, Randy Newman will probably eventually be regarded as one of most important artists of '70s and '80s.

| **Hit Singles:** | US | UK |
|---|---|---|
| Short People, 1978 | 2 | — |

**Albums:**
Randy Newman (Reprise), 1968
Twelve Songs (Reprise), 1969

Live (Reprise), 1971
Sail Away (Reprise), 1972
Good Old Boys (Warner Bros), 1974
Little Criminals (Warner Bros), 1977
Born Again (Warner Bros), 1979
Trouble In Paradise (Warner Bros), 1983 **CD**
Lonely At The Top (WEA), 1987 **CD**

# Olivia Newton-John

Australian vocalist.
Born Cambridge, England, September 26, 1948.

**Career:** British-born, Australian-raised, and now an American show-business institution, Olivia Newton-John has straddled the musical fields of pop, middle-of-the-road and country. Starred in movies 'Grease' and 'Xanadu' (for which she recorded title song, along with ELO, which hit No. 1 on UK charts).

Grandfather was Nobel prize winner, father was principal of Ormond College in Melbourne, where she grew up. Winning trip to England as first prize in talent contest at 16, she appeared in cabaret and on TV as one half of girl duo (with Pat Carrol) which broke up when partner's visa expired. She was also part of short-lived Toomorrow group, formed for abortive television series of same name.

Debut single, Dylan's **If Not For You,** made international noise and follow-up **Banks Of The Ohio** earned Grammy award. After touring Europe with Cliff Richard(▶), she became regular on his TV show. Third hit, **Let Me Be There,** won Grammy for Best Country Vocalist and America quickly became her strongest market.

Movie 'Grease' yielded her three huge hits: **You're The One That I Want** (a duet with co-star John Travolta(▶)), **Summer Nights** and **Hopelessly Devoted To You.** Re-united with Travolta for ordinary 1983 movie 'Two Of A Kind'.

**Below: Olivia Newton-John, whose looks only added to her vocal talent.**

From much criticised 'Xanadu', **Magic** was also international hit, while her '80s album **Physical** contained three hits and was accompanied by massive-selling video. Has also recorded successful duets with Bee Gees(▶), Andy Gibb and Cliff Richard.

**Hit Singles:**

| | US | UK |
|---|---|---|
| If Not For You, 1971 | 25 | 7 |
| Banks Of The Ohio, 1971 | — | 6 |
| What Is Life, 1972 | — | 16 |
| Take Me Home Country Roads, 1973 | — | 15 |
| Let Me Be There, 1974 | 6 | — |
| Long Live Love, 1974 | — | 11 |
| If You Love Me (Let Me Know), 1974 | 5 | — |
| I Honestly Love You, 1974 | 1 | 22 |
| Please Mr Please, 1975 | 3 | — |
| Something Better To Do, 1975 | 13 | — |
| Sam, 1977 | 20 | 6 |
| Hopelessly Devoted To You, 1978 | 3 | 2 |
| A Little More Love, 1978 | 3 | 4 |
| Physical, 1981 | 1 | 7 |
| Landslide, 1982 | 52 | 18 |
| Make A Move On Me, 1982 | 5 | 43 |
| Heart Attack, 1982 | 3 | 46 |
| Twist Of Fate, 1983 | 5 | — |
| Soul Kiss, 1985 | 20 | — |

*With John Travolta:*

| | | |
|---|---|---|
| You're The One That I Want, 1978 | 1 | 1 |
| Summer Nights, 1978 | 5 | 1 |

*With ELO:*

| | | |
|---|---|---|
| Xanadu, 1980 | 8 | 1 |

*With Andy Gibb:*

| | | |
|---|---|---|
| I Can't Help It, 1980 | 12 | — |

*With Cliff Richard:*

| | | |
|---|---|---|
| Suddenly, 1980 | 20 | 15 |

**Albums:**
Let Me Be There (MCA/—), 1973
If You Love Me Let Me Know (MCA/Pye), 1974
Long Live Love (MCA/EMI), 1974
First Impressions (MCA/EMI), 1974
Have You Never Been Mellow (EMI), 1975
Clearly Love (MCA/EMI), 1975
Come On Over (MCA/EMI), 1976
Don't Stop Believin' (MCA/EMI), 1976
Making A Good Thing Better (MCA/EMI), 1977
Greatest Hits (EMI), 1977 **CD**
Totally Hot (MCA/EMI), 1978
Grease Soundtrack (RSO), 1978
Xanadu Soundtrack (MCA), 1980
Physical (EMI), 1981
Greatest Hits (EMI), 1982
Soul Kiss (Mercury), 1986 **CD**

*With John Travolta:*
Two Of A Kind (EMI), 1984

# Harry Nilsson
US vocalist, composer.
Born New York, June 15, 1941.

**A Little Touch Of Schmilsson In The Night. Courtesy of RCA Records.**

**Right: The Motor City Madman mayhem merchant Ted Nugent.**

**Career:** Moved to California during teens, started writing songs. After some early success — he wrote **Cuddly Toy** for Monkees(▶) — he was signed by RCA in 1968.

Early albums showed Nilsson to be distinctive singer/writer of idiosyncratic promise, but first hit **Everybody's Talkin'** was theme tune of film 'Midnight Cowboy' (1969), written by Fred Neil. **Nilsson Schmilsson** became platinum album in US, yielding hit single (No. 1 in both US and UK) in Badfinger-composed song **Without You. Son Of Schmilsson** LP did nearly as well.

Next quirky turn in Nilsson's career came with release of **A Little Touch Of Schmilsson In The Night**, an album of cover versions of standard songs like **Makin' Whoopee**. Seemingly aimed somewhere between satire and tribute, album sold well to MOR audiences.

Since mid-'70s, however, artist seems to have been casting around for direction. In between bouts of well-publicised partying with friends like Ringo Starr(▶) he has continued to record with varying degrees of success. 'The Point', soundtrack of full-length animated film for TV, was adapted and presented successfully at London's Mermaid Theatre in 1976.

Latterly Nilsson has had success as songwriter while keeping generally low profile. Lack of discipline seems likely to remain obstacle to consistent achievement.

**Hit Singles:**

| | US | UK |
|---|---|---|
| Everybody's Talkin', 1969 | 6 | 23 |
| Without You, 1972 | 1 | 1 |
| Coconut, 1972 | 8 | 42 |

**Albums:**
Pandemonium Shadow Show (RCA), 1967
Aerial Ballet (RCA), 1968
Harry (RCA), 1969
Nilsson Sings Newman (RCA), 1970
Nilsson Schmilsson (RCA), 1971 **CD**
Son Of Schmilsson (RCA), 1972
Little Touch Of Schmilsson In The Night (RCA), 1973 **CD**
Du It On Mon Dei (RCA), 1975
Son Of Dracula (RCA), 1974
The Sandman (RCA), 1975
That's The Way It Is (RCA), 1976
Knillssonn (RCA), 1977
Early Times (Mercury/DSM), 1977
Greatest Hits (RCA), 1978 **CD**
Nilsson's Greatest Music (RCA), 1981

# Ted Nugent
US guitarist, bandleader, vocalist, composer.
Born Detroit, December 13, 1949.

**Career:** Self-styled 'wild man of rock', Nugent's antics (including hunting with bow and arrow and wearing a loin cloth) over his decade and a half of recording have almost justified epithet. He acquired first guitar at eight; joined first major band, Amboy Dukes, in 1965. Dukes played quasi-psychedelic music appropriate to times, but with extra Detroit metal quotient. Group scored US Top 20 hit in summer 1968 with **Journey To The Centre Of The Mind**, later included on notable **Nuggets** double LP. Early LPs became collectors' items when greater '60s consciousness returned in late '70s.

Group continued through '60s, eventually adopting name of Ted Nugent and the Amboy Dukes — Nugent in typical manner had altered nature of band from democracy to

dictatorship, with himself as dictator. Band's most famous member (other than Nugent) was probably Rusty Day, later in Cactus, although perhaps 10 people were members at one time or another. Despite label changes, group had little success and even two-year period without record deal. After signing with Epic in 1975, fortunes improved; Amboy Dukes tag dropped. First LP for new label was Nugent's first to make US Top 30, using quite long-lived band (by Nugent standards): Derek St Holmes, rhythm guitar, vocals; Rob Grange, bass; Cliff Davies. drums.

**Scream Dream, Ted Nugent. Courtesy Epic Records.**

1976 LP **Free For All** featured Meat Loaf(▶) (then less than household name) as guest vocalist and again reached Top 30. By 1978 LP **Weekend Warriors** band beginning to change again, although Cliff Davies remained as drummer and sometime producer through 1981 live LP **Intensities In Ten Cities**.

During 1982, Nugent changed labels after seven successful years with Epic, and formed new band of previous members Dave Kiswiney (bass) and Derek St Holmes (lead vocals), plus noted drummer Carmine Appice (ex-Vanilla Fudge(▶) etc.). With his lengthy experience and nearly 20 LPs behind him, Nugent is difficult to criticise, especially as his guitar playing is exemplary, if ear-splitting.

Nugent has continued to record throughout the 80s, hardly modifying his style. He maintains faithful fan following, although many of them may now be close to deafness (like Nugent himself). Although recently mad axeman has kept relatively low profile by his standards, his bank manager is no doubt comforted by recent achievement of multiplatinum status by Epic album **Ted Nugent**.

Guitar: Gibson Byrdland.

**Hit Single:**

| | US | UK |
|---|---|---|
| *With Amboy Dukes:* | | |
| Journey To The Centre Of The Mind, 1968 | 16 | — |

**Albums:**
*With Amboy Dukes:*
Marriage On The Rocks — Rock Bottom (Polydor), 1970

*Ted Nugent and the Amboy Dukes:*
Call Of The Wild, 1973*
Tooth, Fang & Claw, 1974*
Ted Nugent (Epic), 1975
Free For All (Epic), 1976
Cat Scratch Fever (Epic), 1977
Double Live Gonzo (Epic), 1978
Weekend Warriors (Epic), 1978
State Of Shock (Epic), 1979
Scream Dream (Epic), 1980
Intensities In Ten Cities (Epic), 1981
Great Gonzos The Best Of (Epic), 1981
Nugent (Atlantic), 1982
Penetrator (Atlantic), 1984
*Released as double album set (Discreet), 1977
Little Miss Dangerous (WEA), 1986 **CD**
Anthology (Raw Power), 1986 Double

*Worth Searching Out:*
*The Amboy Dukes:*
The Amboy Dukes (Mainstream/London), 1967
Journey To The Centre Of The Mind (Mainstream/London), 1968
Migration (Mainstream/London), 1969

*Ted Nugent and the Amboy Dukes:*
Survival Of The Fittest Live (Polydor), 1971

# Gary Numan
UK vocalist, instrumentalist.
Born Gary Anthony James Webb, London, March 8, 1958.

**Career:** Joined first band the Lasers, a punk outfit, in keeping with times in 1976. By 1977, had assumed control, renaming band Tubeway Army, with trio format: Numan front man (singer, writer, guitar, keyboards) and Paul Gardiner (bass) and Numan's uncle Jess Lidyard (drums). First single was **That's Too Bad**, recorded later that year. Signed with small Beggar's Banquet label in 1978.

Gigged around London, with drummer Bob Simmonds replacing Lidyard, then Barry

Benn replacing Simmonds; Sean Burke (guitar) added by mid-1978. Second single **Bombers** released, but Numan decided to disband group. Album's worth of demos (recorded before dissolution) impressed record company so much that these were released as debut LP in late 1978.

Early in 1979, Numan, Gardiner and Lidyard cut second and final Tubeway Army LP, **Replicas**, which included No. 1 single **Are Friends Electric?** — as a result, LP topped UK chart. After this, Numan decided to record under own name, and next LP **The Pleasure Principle** also topped chart, as did extracted single **Cars**. Numan's heavily synthesised sound and unworldly material, this time augmented by Chris Payne (keyboards, viola), captured public's imagination. During autumn 1979 first tour as star with stage set of fluorescent tubes was huge success.

In 1980 toured Europe, North America, Japan and Australasia. Hit with three more Top 10 singles in UK, as well as releasing one of earliest rock video cassettes. Cracked US Top 10 with **Cars** single (although American success remains comparatively limited). UK success tailed off, and during 1981, while still scoring hits, Numan was obviously less fashionable. By this time, drummer Cedric Sharpley (ex-Druid) had joined, replacing Lidyard. Halfway through year, Numan had decided to stop live work but two live LPs (issued separately and as boxed set) were released to coincide, but Numan was seemingly more interested in gaining private pilot's licence (he subsequently flew around the world). Released new LP **Dance** and single **She's Got Claws**, with help from numerous guest musicians, including Mick Karn (Japan(▶)), Roger Taylor of Queen(▶) and Canadian violinist (and Numan discovery) Nash the Slash. Wrote and produced hit single **Stormtrooper In Drag** for ex-colleague Paul Gardiner, as well as singing on hit single **Love Needs No Disguise** by Dramatis, group composed of his ex-band (Russell Bell, guitar; Dennis Haines, keyboards; Chris Payne, keyboards, viola; Cedric Sharpley, drums).

Success continued on into 80s with clutch of hit singles, Numan dividing his time between music and his hobby of flying World War II aeroplanes. 1985 album **The Fury** was panned by the critics (as have been many of his recorded efforts), but a couple of years later the former peroxide wonder returned with a vengeance with hit reworking of former biggies **Cars** and **Are Friends Electric?**; Sharpe/Numan duet likely to confirm renewal chart status.

Lightweight talent apparently bereft of sense of the ridiculous, Numan nevertheless has knack of long-term hitmaking.

**Hit Singles:**

| | US | UK |
|---|---|---|
| *With Tubeway Army:* | | |
| Are Friends Electric?, 1979 | — | 1 |
| *Solo:* | | |
| Cars, 1979 | 9 | 1 |
| Complex, 1979 | — | 6 |
| We Are Glass, 1980 | — | 5 |
| I Die; You Die, 1980 | — | 6 |
| This Wreckage, 1980 | — | 20 |
| She's Got Claws, 1981 | — | 6 |
| Music For Chameleons, 1982 | — | 19 |
| We Take Mystery, 1982 | — | 9 |
| White Boys And Heroes, 1982 | — | 20 |
| Warriors, 1983 | — | 20 |
| This Is Love, 1986 | — | 28 |
| I Can't Stop, 1986 | — | 27 |
| Cars (E Reg Model), 1987 | — | 16 |
| *Sharpe/Numan:* | | |
| Change Your Mind, 1985 | — | 17 |

**Albums:**

*With Tubeway Army:*
Tubeway Army (—/Beggar's Banquet), 1979
Replicas (—/Beggar's Banquet), 1979
The Plan (Beggar's Banquet), 1984

*Solo:*
The Pleasure Principle (—/Beggar's Banquet), 1979
Telekon (—/Beggar's Banquet), 1980
Dance (Atco/Beggar's Banquet), 1981
I Assassin (Atco/Beggar's Banquet), 1982
Warriors (Beggar's Banquet), 1983
White Noise (Numa), 1985
The Fung (Numa),1985
Exhibition (Beggars Banquet), 1987 **CD**
Strange Charm (Numa), 1986 **CD**
The Fury (Numa) **CD**
Numa Records Year 1 (Numa), 1986
Strange Charm (Numa), 1986
Exhibition (Beggars Banquet), 1987

**Below: Gary Numan, perhaps the first super-star of the synthesiser.**

# Billy Ocean
UK vocalist.
Born Trinidad, January 21, 1952.

**Career:** Growing up in London's East End, Ocean joined Shades Of Blue who played at local Bluecoat Boy pub. Signing solo, first off with Spark label, Ocean had various releases and supplemented income by working on Ford Motor assembly line. Sub-licence deal with GTO saw **Love Really Hurts Without You** kept off top of UK charts only by Brotherhood of Man's million-seller **Save Your Kisses For Me**. Further hits followed, including **Red Light Spells Danger** (1977) which also made number two. At this time Ocean signed new management deal with Laurie Jay but demise of GTO and switch to its distributors, CBS, saw Ocean pushed to back of long artist queue. Several frustrating years followed before Jay landed new deal for his artist with Clive Calder's Jive label.

Jay had worked tirelessly for years to make his artist overnight success in US and breakthrough came when Keith Diamond, a Trinidadian resident in US was brought in as writer and arranger.

Mutt Lange, successful with the Cars(▶), Foreigner(▶), AC/DC(▶) and Def Leppard(▶) was brought in to produce.

Released **African Queen** in Africa and **European Queen** in UK where it bombed at first, **Caribbean Queen** came out with different vocal track as well as title in US and was instant smash, crossing over from soul and dance charts to national listings. Reissued in UK in **Caribbean Queen** format, record was instant success and **Suddenly** album also yielded further hits, leading to 1985 American tour and Grammy award for Best Male Vocal Performance in R&B for **Caribbean Queen.**

**Hit Singles:**

| | US | UK |
|---|---|---|
| Love Really Hurts Without You, 1976 | 22 | 2 |
| L.O.D. (Love On Delivery), 1976 | — | 19 |
| Stop Me (If You've Heard It All Before), 1976 | — | 12 |
| Red Light Spells Danger, 1977 | — | 2 |
| Caribbean Queen, 1984 | 1 | 6 |
| Lover Boy, 1985 | 2 | 15 |
| Suddenly, 1985 | 4 | 4 |
| When The Going Gets Tough (The Tough Get Going), 1986 | 1 | 1 |

**Albums:**
City Limit (GTO), 1980
Inner Feelings (Epic), 1982
Suddenly (Jive), 1984
Billy Ocean (Epic), 1985
Love Zone (Jive), 1986

In 1986 Ocean had huge international hit with **When The Going Gets Tough, The Tough Get Going**, theme tune for Michael Douglas/Kathleen Turner movie Jewel Of The Nile. (Ocean's video, featuring Douglas, Turner and co-star Danny De Vito, was more entertaining than movie itself.) Now established as major star, Ocean is one of few 'black British' artists to have made international impact on large scale.

# Mike Oldfield
UK composer, multi-instrumentalist.
Born Reading, Berkshire, May 15, 1953.

**Career:** Started at age 14 in folk duo with sister Sally. Released acoustic **Sallyangie** in 1968 on Transatlantic. After forming short-lived Barefeet, joined Kevin Ayers and the Whole World as bassist/guitarist in 1970-71. Composed 50-minute demo, which was rejected by most major companies. Work was eventually chosen to launch Richard Branson's new label. Virgin. Oldfield overdubbed all the instruments in the studio, creating collage of melodies and instrumental lines that formed basis of **Tubular Bells**, released in May 1973. Album was critically acclaimed and sold in extraordinary quantities, much to amazement of the rock business. US success was assured when **Tubular Bells** was chosen as theme for film 'The Exorcist'.

The less instantly appealing **Hergest Ridge** covered similar ground. Oldfield received critical backlash but survived intact to produce best-selling **Ommadawn**, a more ambitious work incorporating African drums and Celtic pipes.

Friendship with avant-garde composer David Bedford, from Kevin Ayers days, led to work on **The Orchestrated Tubular Bells** with Royal Philharmonic Orchestra. In addition, Virgin released four-album set **Boxed**, which included all previous work, plus **Collaborations**. Meanwhile, Oldfield spent three years preparing **Incantations**, his most epic project to date.

Moving to London in '78, began experimenting with dance music, producing single **Guilty** with a New York rhythm section. First-ever tour followed, backed by 50 musicians, including string players and choir. Music was accompanied by set of films by Ian Eames; live double LP **Exposed** was culled from shows.

1980's **Platinum** was lighter work than its predecessors and included punk-rock parody **Punkadiddle**, juxtaposed alongside an Irish jig. To promote **Platinum,** Oldfield Music was formed; British debut (July '81) was followed by extensive European tour. New work, **QE2**, quickly followed and immediately went gold. World sales of **Tubular Bells** hit 10 million in 1981 and Oldfield was awarded The Freedom Of The City Of London in recognition of sales to exports and charity works. Further distinction came when he was entered in 'Who's Who', the only rock musician, bar McCartney(▶), to achieve recognition there. May 1982 saw formation of the Mike Oldfield Group (Maggie Reilly, vocals; Morris Pert, percussion/keyboards; Rick Fern, bass; Tim Cross, keyboards; and Pierre Moelen, drums). Eighth album **Five Miles Out** ended decade of extraordinary sales. In spite of criticism from mainstream rock press, Oldfield's popularity has never seriously waned, and seems likely to continue for many years, despite fluctuating 'live' audience.

**Hit Singles:**

| | US | UK |
|---|---|---|
| In Dulce Jubilo/On Horseback, 1975 | — | 4 |
| Portsmouth, 1976 | — | 3 |
| Blue Peter, 1979 | — | 19 |
| Moonlight Shadow, 1983* | — | 4 |

*with Maggie Reilly

**Albums:**
Tubular Bells (Virgin), 1973 **CD**
Gergest Ridge (Virgin), 1974 **CD**
Ommadawn (Virgin), 1975 **CD**
The Orchestrated Tubular Bells (Virgin), 1975 **CD**
Boxed (Virgin), 1975
Incantations (Virgin), 1978
Exposed (Virgin), 1979 **CD**
Platinum (Virgin), 1980 **CD**
QE2 (Virgin), 1980 **CD**
Five Miles Out (Virgin), 1982 **CD**
Crises (Virgin), 1983 **CD**
Discovery (Virgin), 1984 **CD**
The Killing Fields (Virgin), 1984 **CD**
The Complete Mike Oldfield (Virgin), 1985 **CD**
Islands (Virgin), 1987 **CD**

# Alexander O'Neal

US Vocalist
Born Mississippi, 23 January, 1955.

**Career:** Moved to Chicago in 1973 and then to Minneapolis where he first started singing professionally, most notably doing lead vocals for The Time whose line-up also included Jimmy Jam and Terry Lewis. The band has been helped up by rising star Prince Rogers Nelson (Prince) but following differences of opinion between him and O'Neal, the latter left the line-up.

O'Neal went on to sing with a variety of local groups, veering between rock, soul and funk. He met up with Jimmy Jam and Terry Lewis who had since left The Time and established themselves as producers/writers; a recording contract with CBS soon followed and an eponymously titled debut LP received excellent reviews from specialist and mainstream music press.

**Hearsay, Alexander O'Neal.
Courtesy Tabu Records.**

First UK hits were **If You Were Here Tonight** and **A Broken Heart Can Mend** but it was a soul **Saturday Love** duet with Cherrelle in 1985 that first introduced him to UK record buyers.

O'Neal's growing popularity in the UK was underlined by four sell-out concerts at London's Hammersmith Odeon in Novembr 1986 at a time when there was an absence of new product from him. His second album **Hearsay** spawned the hit single **Fake** while the follow-up single **Criticize** co-incided with more UK dates.

With richly expressive voice capable of tackling various styles of material and music, O'Neal is following in the respected footsteps of other great black music artists including Marvin Gaye and Teddy Pendergrass.

**Hit Singles:** | | US | UK
---|---|---|---
Criticize, 1987 | | — | 4
Fake, 1987 | | 25 | —

**Albums:**
Alexander O'Neal (—/Tabu), 1986
Hearsay (Tabu), 1987

# Roy Orbison

US vocalist, composer, guitarist.
Born Vernon, Texas, April 23, 1936.

**Career:** Formed first group, the Wink Westerners, at 13. Appeared on local radio talent shows, then formed the Teen Kings while at North Texas State University. First recordings made (after encouragement from college friend Pat Boone) at Norman Petty's Clovis, New Mexico, studio in 1955, including first version of **Ooby Dooby** released on Jewel. During 1956 recorded for Sun in Memphis; re-recording of **Ooby Dooby** reached lower part of US charts.

Encouraged by some success as songwriter, mostly stemming from Everly Brothers'(▶) version of **Claudette**, Orbison moved to Nashville and signed with RCA. Two singles failed to make impression and in 1959 signed

**Below: Alexander O'Neal finding much success this side of the Atlantic.**

with Monument Records, beginning long partnership with producer Fred Foster. Although first two releases were not hits, Orbison and Foster found right formula with **Only The Lonely** in summer 1960; many hits followed in similar style.

Orbison's records are characterised by romantic themes and vocal crescendos, making best use of distinctive voice. Dramatic stage performer despite lack of movement and tendency towards shyness, emphasised by dark glasses. Personal life marked by tragedy of wife Claudette's death in motorcycle accident (1966) and death of two sons in house fire (1968).

Popularity in US not maintained at quite the same level as in UK, but Orbison remains great performer, still touring to capacity audiences. His recent album for Elektra failed to match earlier material, although duet single with Emmylou Harris(▶), **That Loving You Feeling**, was moderate success in 1980.

**Hit Singles:** | US | UK
---|---|---
Only The Lonely, 1960 | 2 | 1
Blue Angel, 1960 | 9 | 11
Running Scared, 1961 | 1 | 9
Crying, 1961 | 2 | 25
Dream Baby, 1962 | 4 | 2
In Dreams, 1963 | 7 | 6
Falling, 1963 | 22 | 9
Blue Bayou/Mean Woman Blues, 1963 | 29 | 3
Pretty Paper, 1963 | 15 | 6
Mean Woman Blues/Blue Bayou, 1963 | 5 | 3
Borne On The Wind, 1964 | — | 15
It's Over, 1964 | 9 | 1
Oh Pretty Woman, 1964 | 1 | 1
Goodnight, 1965 | 21 | 14
Crawlin' Back, 1965 | 46 | 19
Lana, 1966 | — | 15

**Above: Roy Orbison, always capable of thrilling live audiences despite apparent shyness.**

Too Soon To Know, 1966 | — | 3
---|---|---
There Won't Be Many Coming Home, 1966 | — | 18

**Albums:**
Greatest Hits (Monument), 1972
All-Time Greatest Hits (Monument), 1973
The Big O (Charly), 1975
At The Rockhouse (Charly), 1980
Golden Days (Monument), 1981
Big O Country (Decca), 1983
The Roy Orbison Collection (Castle), 1986
In Dreams (Virgin), 1987 **CD**
Roy Orbison & Sonny James (Bear Family), 1987 **CD**
Go Go Go, (Charly) **CD**
The Other Side (Muskateer), 1987

# OMD (Orchestral Manoeuvres In The Dark)

UK group formed 1978.

**Original line-up:** Paul Humphreys and Andy McCluskey, various electronic instruments, vocals.

**Career:** Humphreys and McCluskey, both from Merseyside, formed first band, VCL XI, in 1976, when pair were 16. Interest stimulated by early German synthesiser bands like Kraftwerk(▶). Group never got beyond rehearsals, but duo joined Hitlers Underpantz, described as 'an assortment of musicians into doing things differently', although this band was no more successful than VCL XI. By end of 1977, duo became nucleus of the Id, an eight-piece band which soon folded.

In 1978, Humphreys and McCluskey adopted name of Orchestral Manoeuvres In The Dark (later abbreviated to OMD), using backing tapes played on tape recorder known as 'Winston'. Played debut gig in this formation at end of 1978 at 'Eric's' in Liverpool, then approached trendy independent label Factory Records of Manchester, who released single of **Electricity** as limited edition in June 1979. Signed by Virgin records subsidiary Dindisc, supported Gary Numan(▶) on UK tour. With proceeds built own recording studio, where they cut first LP, **Orchestral Manoeuvres In The Dark** (1980). After retiring 'Winston', expanded line-up by adding drummer Malcolm Holmes (ex-the Id) and David Hughes (ex-Dalek I) on bass and keyboards.

1980 saw two minor hit singles followed by first Top 10 single **Enola Gay** (titled after name of plane which dropped first atom bomb) from second LP **Organisation**. Hughes left during year, replaced by multi-instrumentalist (keyboards, saxophone) Martin Cooper. 1981 was big year for band — two Top 5 singles plus Top 3 LP, **Architecture And Morality**. Impetus continued into early 1982 with another Top 5 single. Rest of year spent recording fourth LP **Dazzle Ships**, which was less well received than earlier work; it seemed needlessly self-indulgent, although it contained another hit single, **Genetic Engineering**. OMD continued to turn out hits, but mid-80s output became increasingly self-indulgent, with over-reliance on effects. 1985 album **Crush** was return to simpler formula, but recent output has continued to attract critical obloquy. **The Pacific Age**, for example, was almost universally dismissed. At time of writing OMD are struggling to re-establish themselves as contenders in candyfloss-dominated UK pop scene, but European appeal remains undiminished.

**Current line-up:** Humphreys; McCluskey; Martin Cooper, keyboards; Malcolm Holmes, drums.

| Hit Singles: | US | UK |
|---|---|---|
| Enola Gay, 1980 | — | 8 |
| Souvenirs, 1981 | — | 3 |
| Joan Of Arc, 1981 | — | 5 |
| Maid Of Orleans, 1982 | — | 4 |
| Genetic Engineering, 1983 | — | 20 |
| Locomotion, 1984 | — | 5 |
| Talking Loud And Clear, 1984 | — | 11 |
| So In Love, 1985 | 16 | — |
| If You Leave, 1986 | — | 48 |
| Live and Die (Forever), 1986 | 19 | — |

**Albums:**
Orchestral Manoeuvres In The Dark (—/Virgin), 1980
Organisation (—/Virgin), 1980
Architecture And Mortality (Virgin-Epic/Virgin), 1981
Dazzle Ships (Virgin-Epic/Virgin), 1983
Junk Culture (Virgin), 1984 **CD**
Crush (Virgin), 1985
Pacific Age (Virgin) **CD**

# Ozzy Osbourne

UK vocalist.
Born John Osbourne, Birmingham, December 3, 1948.

**Career:** Ozzy Osbourne first won acclaim as Black Sabbath(▶) vocalist. Following departure in 1978 (under unpleasant terms) Sabbath

fans have been delighted with both sides trying to outdo each other professionally.

Formed permanent band called Blizzard of Ozz; signed to Jet on strength of past history. Strong debut album released in 1980 featured Lee Kerslake (ex-Uriah Heep(▶)) on drums, Bob Daisley on bass and Randy Rhoads on guitar; **Blizzard Of Ozz** showed Osbourne had no intention of avoiding confrontation with old mates. **Ozz** featured same hard rock approach of Sabbath and provided impetus for that band to re-form and work again.

**Diary Of A Madman** indicated Ozzy and Rhoads had special talent for creating exciting, riveting heavy metal. But just as it seemed as if Ozzy would leave Sabbath in the dust, his luck turned sour. Publicity stunt of biting the head of a dead bat thrown on stage backfired when Ozzy had to undergo painful rabies innoculations. Worse, Randy Rhoads was killed in freak airplane accident and Blizzard of Ozz crumbled around Osbourne. Kerslake and Daisley went to Uriah Heep.

Refusing to give in, Ozzy recruited Brad Gillis, guitar; Rudi Sarzo, bass; and Tommy Aldridge, drums. This line-up recorded blistering double live set **Talk of the Devil**, which included versions of early Sabbath material.

By 1982 Osbourne had become one of biggest headliners on American concert circuit.

Make-up artist Greg Cannon, who worked on movies 'The Howling' and 'American Werewolf In London' spent eight hours making Osbourne up for bizarre sleeve to 1983's **Bark At The Moon** album, artwork costing staggering £50,000 to produce. Platinum stature of album repaid investment and gave Osbourne first solo Top 30 singles in UK with title track and ballad **So Tired**.

Re-writing album twice helped account for two year delay before next album **The Ultimate Sin**, the first on which Osbourne has used an outside producer (ex-Led Zeppelin and Survivor man, Ron Nevison).

**Ultimate Sin** was Ozzy's most successful chart album. In 1987 he approved the issue of an album of five year old material featuring Randy Rhoads **Tribute**, originally intended for release on Jet.

The same year guitarist Jake E. Lee, who had contributed heavily to his last two studio albums, quit the band and Ozzy began a lengthy search for a replacement, settling on Zakk Wylde (21), from New Jersey, in time to start recording a new album in Hollywood in Spring 1988. After a battle against alcoholism, Ozzy took keep fit classes to prepare for a new round of touring.

| Hit Singles: | US | UK |
|---|---|---|
| So Tired, 1984 | — | 20 |
| Shot In The Dark, 1986 | — | 20 |

**Above:** Orchestral Manoeuvres In The Dark, who shortened name to OMD.

**Albums:**
Blizzard Of Ozz (Jet), 1980 **CD**
Diary Of A Madman (Jet), 1981 **CD**
Talk Of The Devil (Jet), 1982
Bark At The Moon (Jet), 1983
The Ultimate Sin (Epic), 1986 **CD**
Tribute (Epic), 1987 **CD**

# The Osmonds

US vocal group formed 1960.

**Original line-up:** Alan Osmond; Wayne Osmond; Merrill Osmond; Jay Osmond.

**Career:** Encouraged by parents, brothers were taught to sing and play several instruments. They first started performing at various Mormon Church functions. Professional career started with residency at Disneyland. Walt Disney TV show led to regular spot on Andy Williams show where they were mainly featured doing barber shop quartet type numbers, which lasted from 1962 to 1966. That group became regulars on Jerry Lewis Show, and younger brother Donny (then nine) joined group. Further TV work and worldwide touring followed.

In 1970 brothers signed with MGM, and following year scored US No. 1 with **One Bad Apple**. Record initiated string of hits (mainly cover versions) that lasted into mid-'70s, and elevation of group into 'teenybopper sensation' worldwide.

Success of group also spawned solo careers for Donny, younger brother Jimmy and sister Marie, as well as launching Donny and Marie as duo.

At best group were pale imitation of Jackson Five, although professionalism and polish could not be denied. Religious background ensured clean-living image, and in many quarters Osmonds became byword for safe, slick, showbiz approach to rock and pop.

Towards end of '70s appeal faded, and members pursued different career directions with varied success, Donny and Marie being the most successful with own TV show in late '70s. Jimmy has acted in films and TV, most recently featured in 'Fame' series.

In recent years family (without Donny) has regrouped as country-style outfit, swiftly becoming fixture at UK's Wembley Country Music Festival. Marie Osmond has also pursued career in country music with degree of success.

Donny has followed solo path, developing into stylish vocalist. However, success on scale he previously enjoyed continues to elude him.

**Final line-up:** Alan; Wayne; Merrill; Jay; Donny Osmond; Jimmy Osmond.

| Hit Singles: | US | UK |
|---|---|---|
| One Bad Apple, 1971 | 1 | 43 |
| Double Lovin', 1971 | 14 | — |
| Yo-Yo, 1971 | 3 | — |
| Down By The Lazy River, 1972 | 4 | 40 |
| Hold Her Tight, 1972 | 14 | — |
| Crazy Horses, 1972 | 14 | 2 |
| Going Home, 1973 | 36 | 4 |
| Let Me In, 1973 | 36 | 2 |
| I Can't Stop, 1974 | — | 12 |
| Love Me For A Reason, 1974 | 10 | 1 |
| The Proud One, 1975 | 22 | 5 |
| *Donny Osmond Solo:* | | |
| Sweet And Innocent, 1971 | 7 | — |
| Go Away Little Girl, 1971 | 1 | — |
| Hey Girl, 1971 | 9 | — |
| Puppy Love, 1972 | 3 | 1 |
| Too Young, 1972 | 13 | 5 |
| Why, 1972 | 13 | 3 |
| Twelfth Of Never, 1973 | 8 | 1 |
| Young Love, 1973 | 23 | 1 |
| When I Fall In Love, 1973 | 14 | 4 |
| Are You Lonesome Tonight, 1974 | 14 | — |
| Where Did All The Good Times Go, 1974 | — | 18 |
| *Marie Osmond:* | | |
| Paper Roses, 1973 | 5 | 2 |
| *Donny And Marie Osmond:* | | |
| I'm Leaving It All Up To You, 1974 | 4 | 2 |
| Morning Side Of The Mountain, 1974 | 8 | 5 |
| Make The World Go Away, 1975 | 44 | 18 |
| Deep Purple, 1976 | 14 | 25 |
| *Little Jimmy Osmond Solo:* | | |
| Long-Haired Lover From Liverpool, 1972 | 38 | 1 |
| Tweedle Dee, 1973 | 59 | 4 |
| I'm Gonna Knock On Your Door, 1974 | — | 11 |

**Albums:**
Our Best To You (MGM), 1974
Christmas Album (Polydor), 1976
Greatest Hits (Polydor), 1978

*Donny Osmond Solo:*
Donald Clark Osmond (Polydor), 1977

*Marie Osmond Solo:*
This Is The Way That I Feel (Polydor), 1977
There's No Stopping Your Heart (Capitol), 1986

*Donny And Marie Osmond:*
Growin' Coconuts (MGM), 1974
Deep Purple (Polydor), 1976
Winning Combination (Polydor), 1978

# Johnny Otis

US vocalist, composer, multi-instrumentalist. Born Johnny Veliotes, Vellejo, California, December 28, 1921.

**Career:** It may be paradoxical that a white man, son of Greek immigrant parents, should be known as 'The Godfather of Rhythm and Blues', but facts dictate that Johnny Otis is eminently worthy of the accolade. Inspired by big band jazz of Count Basie and Ellington, Otis learned to play drums then moved on to piano and vibes. Played in bands with Harlan Leonard and Count Matthews. By mid-1940s had own band; scored hit with **Harlem Nocturne** on Excelsior in 1946. After spell touring, settled down in Los Angeles to open Barrelhouse Club in 1948, partnered by late Bardu Ali. Venue featured local R&B acts and Johnny proved to have ear for talent, discovering the Robins and Little Esther (Phillips).

By 1950 Otis and protégés were scoring numerous hits on Savoy. Early '50s saw him form touring Revue of R&B talent; he also found time to produce hits for Johnny Ace and

Little Richard(▶) on Duke/Peacock Records in Houston, Texas. Travels took him to Detroit, where he spotted emergent singers Jackie Wilson(▶), Willie John and Hank Ballard.

Revue began recording for Capitol as rock 'n' roll years arrived. **Willie And The Hand Jive** was Top 10 smash for Otis in 1958. **Ma (He's Making Eyes At Me)** became popular for Marie Adams with the Revue. Further hits followed on Capitol for couple of years before Johnny moved to King; results were uninspiring and unsuccessful, so took break from performing.

Next Otis records were not until 1969; fine blues-based **Cold Shot** LP on Kent yielded R&B hit **Country Girl.** Featured his son Shuggie on guitar along with newer talents Delmar Evans and Gene Connors. Otis Band also connected with **Snatch And The Poontangs**, a risqué LP on Kent!

Success prompted Johnny to organise Revue to play 1970 Monterey Jazz Festival; featured veteran R&B giants Joe Turner, Little Esther and Roy Brown, among others. Show was committed to disc by Epic; label also signed Otis to contract. **The Watts Breakaway** appeared on Okeh.

In 1974 Otis launched own blues spectrum label, re-recording R&B greats like Charles Brown, Joe Turner, Pee Wee Clayton and Joe Liggins with his own combo, though not always with memorable results. After lull in activity, returned to disc with fresh Johnny Otis Show on Alligator in 1982.

**Hit Singles:**

| | US | UK |
|---|---|---|
| Ma He's Making Eyes At Me, 1957 | — | 2 |
| Bye Bye Baby, 1958 | — | 20 |
| Willie And The Hand Jive, 1958 | 9 | — |

**Albums:**
Original Show (Savoy), 1972
Original Show Volume 2 (Savoy/—), 1974
Johnny Otis (—/Bulldog), 1975
Rock 'n' Roll Hit Parade (—/Flyright), 1979

# Robert Palmer

UK vocalist, composer, guitarist.
Born Batley, Yorkshire, January 19, 1949.

**Career:** Developed taste for American R&B as teenager; first band (at 15) was Mandrakes. After year working as graphic designer Palmer decided to go for musical career. In 1968 he took vocalist job with Alan Brown Set; next year he moved on to group DaDa, which provided his first visit to US. DaDa eventually transformed into Vinegar Joe for whom he played rhythm guitar and shared vocals with Elkie Brooks. By 1974 Palmer and Brooks were off on solo careers.

Palmer approached Chris Blackwell (Island Records) with some of his demos and Blackwell immediately packed him off to New Orleans and New York to record first LP. **Sneakin' Sally Thru The Alley** was released in September 1974 and won Palmer enough US audience support to convince him to move to America. (In 1976 he transferred to Nassau.)

**Pressure Drop** was released little over a year later and was lead-in to Palmer's first US nationwide tour. True US success came in 1978-79 when singles **Every Kinda People** (from **Double Fun**) and **Bad Case Of Lovin' You** (from **Secrets**) won approval of national audience.

Palmer broadened his activities in 1980 by doing some production work but this led to a drastic reduction in his own output.

Palmer has so closely copied his US influences that many fans assume he is Philadelphia blue-eyed soul; his albums are

ultimately frustrating, however, because for every soulful classic there is another track which seems half-finished. His sound and LP covers project slick, almost dilettante, life style. Like any proper playboy, Palmer doesn't want to push himself too hard and every LP has air of casual under-achievement.

During 1985, Palmer became successfully involved in a new venture with moonlighting members of Duran Duran(▶) as The Power Station, as well as reviving own solo career with **Riptide** set.

**Below: Robert Palmer, aficionado of Philadelphia blue-eyed sole, in 1987.**

**Hit Singles:**

| | US | UK |
|---|---|---|
| Every Kinda People, 1978 | 16 | 53 |
| Bad Case Of Lovin' You (Doctor, Doctor), 1979 | 14 | — |
| Some Guys Have All The Luck, 1982 | — | 16 |
| Addicted To Love, 1986 | — | 5 |
| I Didn't Mean To Turn You On, 1986 | 3 | 9 |

*With Power Station:*

| | | |
|---|---|---|
| Some Like It Hot, 1985 | 6 | 14 |
| Get It On, 1985 | 9 | — |

**Rip Tide, Robert Palmer.**
**Courtesy Island Records.**

**Albums:**
Sneaking Sally In The Alley (Island), 1974 **CD**
Pressure Drop (Island), 1975 **CD**
Some People Can Do What They Like (Island), 1976
Double Fun (Island), 1978 **CD**
Secrets (Island), 1979
Clues (Island), 1980 **CD**
Maybe It's Alive (Island), 1982
Pride (Island), 1983 **CD**
Rip Tide (Island), 1985 **CD**
The Early Years 1987 (C5) with Alan Bown

*With Power Station:*
Power Station (Parlophone), 1985

# Alan Parsons Project

UK group formed 1975.
**Original/current line-up:** Alan Parsons, guitars, keyboards, vocals, producer, engineer; Eric Woolfson, keyboards.

**Career:** Parsons was assistant engineer at EMI studios in 1968 when he worked on Beatles' **Abbey Road**(▶). His involvement impressed Paul McCartney(▶) who used him to engineer several Wings LPs. Parsons also engineered various albums for the Hollies(▶) as well as Pink Floyds'(▶) **Dark Side Of The Moon.** Turning from engineering to production, cut Cockney Rebel, Pilot, and Al Stewart(▶).

Woolfson also worked at Abbey Road Studios where he met Parsons and together they began plans to create own music. Woolfson's previous experience had been as writer; became Project's idea man.

Woolfson's first idea seemed to borrow from Rick Wakeman(▶) who had begun electronic symphonic album concept in 1972 with **Six Wives Of Henry VIII.** Woolfson turned his attention to writing mood pieces to describe stories of Edgar Allen Poe. **Tales Of Mystery And Imagination** appeared in 1975 with highly innovative packaging scheme which almost caused music within to be overlooked.

Science fiction was motif of **I Robot** LP, while **Pyramid** was based on then popular pyramid power cult. **Eve** looked at relations with women, and bears close hearing as well as close look at surprising cover. **The Turn Of A Friendly Card** dealt with gaming and the role of fate in modern society. **Eye In The Sky** continued the concern with modern high-tech society by dealing with 1984 surveillance concepts.

Despite impeccable production and multi-talented session men, Project LPs tend to grate after repeated listenings. In spite of this drawback, any new Project LP is worth at least an initial listen to see where Parsons and Woolfson's imaginations have travelled.

**Hit Singles:**

| | US | UK |
|---|---|---|
| Games People Play, 1981 | | |
| Time, 1981 | | |
| Eye In The Sky, 1982 | 3 | — |
| Don't Answer Me, 1984 | | |

**Albums:**
Tales Of Mystery And Imagination (20th Century/Arista), 1975 **CD**
I Robot (Arista), 1977 **CD**
Pyramid (Arista), 1978 **CD**
Eve (Arista), 1979 **CD**
The Turn Of A Friendly Card (Arista), 1980 **CD**
Eye In The Sky (Arista), 1982 **CD**

Above: Alan Parsons (right) engineer of the Beatles' Abbey Road album.

Best Of (Arista), 1983 **CD**
Ammonia Avenue (Arista), 1984 **CD**
Vulture Culture (Arista), 1985 **CD**
Stereotomy (Arista) **CD**
Gaudi (Arista), 1987 **CD**

# Dolly Parton

US vocalist, guitarist, composer.
Born Locust Ridge, Tennessee, January 19, 1946.

**Career:** Born into large, poor rural family, showed early interest in music-making. Appeared on Grand Ole Opry at age 12; moved to Nashville after leaving high school at 18.

Contract with Monument Records led to little success, but break came when Parton formed partnership with country superstar Porter Wagoner in 1967. She became integral part of Wagoner's live show, and also recorded and made TV appearances with him. Under Wagoner's aegis Parton developed vivid 'blonde bombshell' persona that was to become her stock-in-trade.

In 1973 Parton left Wagoner show, although he continued to produce her solo records. In 1976 she split from Wagoner altogether, having signed contract with Los Angeles-based management company. In meantime, solo career began to take off, helped by endorsement of other female artists like Linda Ronstadt(▶), Emmylou Harris(▶) and Maria Muldaur(▶). (All three recorded Parton compositions on albums.)

Seeking to broaden appeal, Parton moved into rock territory with **New Harvest — First Gathering** in 1977. Featuring numbers like **My Girl** and **Higher And Higher**, album alienated country stalwarts but gained artist many new fans. Audience-widening process bore fruit when Parton scored platinum album with **Here You Come Again** in 1978. Elaborate West Coast production was far removed from country roots.

By beginning of '80s Parton had achieved dream of all-round stardom, with major role in successful movie '9 to 5' (self-penned title song from film was US No. 1), string of awards, and ability to draw capacity crowds at virtually any type of venue. A chat-show favourite, Parton showed that lively and witty intelligence lurked beneath spectacular Mae-West-meets-Barbie-Doll appearance.

Movie 'Best Little Whorehouse In Texas' (co-starring Burt Reynolds) provided further vehicle for Parton's acting talent, and in recent years artist has consolidated position as all-round entertainer.

Country aficionados and critics rate early

RCA recordings most appealing cuts, with **Best Of** compilations ideal showcases. Most recently, Parton has re-established Toots credentials with outstanding contribution to platinum-selling **Trio** album with Emmylou Harris and Linda Ronstadt.

| Hit Singles: | US | UK |
|---|---|---|
| Jolene, 1976 | 60 | 7 |
| Here You Come Again, 1978 | 3 | — |
| Two Doors Down, 1978 | 19 | — |
| 9 to 5, 1980 | 1 | 46 |

**Albums (selected):**
Best Of (with Porter Wagoner) (RCA), 1969
Best Of (RCA), 1970
My Tennessee Mountain Home (RCA), 1973
Jolene (RCA), 1974
Best Of Volume 2 (RCA), 1975
Love Is Like A Butterfly (RCA), 1975
Bargain Store (RCA), 1975
New Harvest—First Gathering (RCA), 1977
Here You Come Again (RCA), 1978
Both Sides Of (—/Lotus), 1979
The Dolly Parton Collection (Monument), 1980
9 to 5 And Odd Jobs (RA), 1981
The Very Best Of (RCA), 1981

Greatest Hits (RCA), 1982 **CD**
Heartbreak Express (RCA), 1982
The Winning Hand (with K. Kristofferson, W. Nelson & Brenda Lee) (Monument), 1983
The Great Pretender (RCA), 1984 **CD**
Once Upon A Christmas (with Kenny Rogers) (RCA), 1984
Real Love (RCA), 1985 **CD**
Just Because I'm A Woman (RCA), 1986
*With Ronstadt & Harris:*
The Trio (WEA), 1987 **CD**

# Les Paul

US guitarist, vocalist.
Born Lester Polfuss, Waukesha, Wisconsin June 9, 1923.

**Career:** Best remembered as creator of Gibson Les Paul model guitar, beloved of many musicians, which he developed in 1941 while in hospital recovering from car crash.

After apprenticeship playing hillbilly, then jazz, Paul formed first Les Paul Trio in late '30s before working as guitarist for Fred Waring, then Bing Crosby.

Above: Carl Perkins, composer of rock'n'roll gem Blue Suede Shoes.

Featuring a solid body and sustaining pick-ups, the Les Paul guitar appeared on the market in 1952. By this time Paul had made a series of unsuccessful singles for Decca and Columbia but then found major stardom in partnership with Mary Ford (born Colleen Summer, Pasadena, California, July 7, 1928). They married in 1948 and three years later sold a million copies of **Mockin' Bird Hill** (also a million-seller the same year for Patti Page) on Capitol.

The 'new sound', with Mary's voice matched to Paul's 'talking guitar' achieved by double track earned them two further million-sellers that year. **How High The Moon** and **The World Is Waiting For The Sunrise** and another in 1954 with **Vaya Con Dios** which topped Cashbox US charts for 11 weeks. Paul and Ford divorced in 1963, and Ford died in 1977. Paul subsequently entered 'guitar workshop' field as in-demand tutor.

| Hit Singles | US | UK |
|---|---|---|
| *With Mary Ford:* | | |
| Vaya Con Dios, 1953 | — | 7 |
| Hummingbird, 1955 | 7 | — |

**Albums:**
Multi-Trackin' / —), N/A
Trio (Glendale/—), N/A
New Sound Of, Volume 2 (Capitol/—), N/A
The World Is Waiting For The Sunrise (Capitol/EMI), 1979

*With Mary Ford:*
The Very Best Of Les Paul And Mary Ford (Capitol), 1974

*With Chet Atkins:*
Chester And Lester (RCA), 1977
Guitar Monsters (RCA), 1978

# Carl Perkins

US vocalist, guitarist, composer.
Born Lake City, Tennessee, April 9, 1932.

**Career:** Began performing country and blues material in Tennessee in late 1940s. By early '50s had evolved own style, apparent in first recordings for Flip and Sun labels in Memphis in 1955. At first encouraged to record country material by Sun's Sam Phillips, but turned to rockabilly and achieved distinction of first national rockabilly hit with own composition **Blue Suede Shoes** in 1956. Major setback to career came when hospitalised following

**Left: Dolly Parton, that 'cute bundle of fun' who outlasted infantile comment about busty physique, to become a successful movie and TV actress.**

serious injury in car crash on way to first major television appearance; unable to consolidate chart success.

Despite quality material and distinctive vocal and guitar style, Perkins was overshadowed by Elvis Presley(▶) (who covered **Blue Suede Shoes** with some success) and was neglected at Sun in favour of Jerry Lee Lewis(▶). Moved to US Columbia with fellow Sun artist Johnny Cash(▶) in 1958 in joint deal, only to find himself overshadowed again, this time by Cash ,and despite minor hit with **Pointed Toe Shoes**, star status eluded him.

Death of elder brother Jay in 1958 was further setback, and Perkins turned increasingly to drink. Signed to US Decca in 1963, toured Europe and recorded with Beatles(▶), who regarded him as hero. Cut good material for various labels during '60s and became integral part of Johnny Cash Road Show, touring extensively. Encouraged by Cash, turned towards Christianity and away from pills and booze. Split with Cash in 1976 in order to return to touring and recording independently.

Highly regarded as guitarist, Perkins still impresses with live performances and occasionally records, most recently for his own Suede label. In business where current competition plays major part, Perkins can be regarded as somewhat unlucky not to make greater chart impact.

Guitars: Gibson Switchmaster, later Fender Telecaster.

| **Hit Singles:** | US | UK |
|---|---|---|
| Blue Suede Shoes, 1956 | 2 | 10 |

**Albums:**
The Rocking Guitar Man (Charly), 1975
The Original Carl Perkins (Charly), 1976
Sun Sound Special (Charly), 1978
The Carl Perkins Dance Album (Charly), 1981 **CD**
The Sun Years (3 LP box set) (Sun), 1982
Survivors (with Johnny Cash and Jerry Lee Lewis) (CBS), 1982
Carl Perkins (MCA), 1986 **CD**
Dixie Fried (Charly) **CD**
Up Through The Years (Bear Family) **CD**

# Pet Shop Boys

UK vocal/instrumental duo formed 1983.
**Original line-up:** Neil Tennant, vocals, born London, 1954; Chris Lowe, instruments, born London 1959.

**Career:** Ex-UK pop magazine 'Smash Hits' music journalist Tennant and ex-architecture student Lowe met and discovered mutual love for Euro-disco rhythms in 1983. Contacted underground producer Bobby O, who produced debut single **West End Girls**; released as one-off deal and became minor hit in Europe, receiving extensive radio play in UK.

Spent all of 1984 extracting themselves from contract with Bobby O and unable to record elsewhere. Subsequently signed to

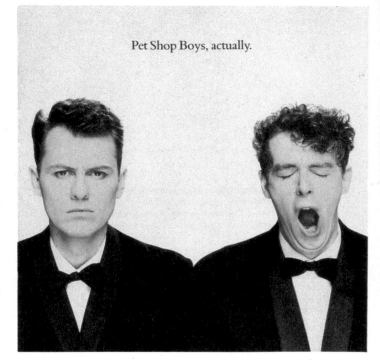

Parlophone Records and released **Opportunities Let's Make Lot's Of Money** produced by Art Of Noise which failed to chart. Re-recorded **West End Girls** with Stephen Hague, which became worldwide No 1.

**Pet Shop Boys, actually.**
**Courtesy Parlophone Records.**

**Below: Tennant (left) and Lowe without an audience.**

Debut album, **Please** featured both these plus **Love Comes Quickly** and **Suburbia**, also Top 20 hits, as PSB established winning formula that blended sardonic lyrics with hypnotic synthesiser melodies and stomping dancebeat.

**Disco** was specially remixed version of debut album. Next new release was **What Have I Done?** single featuring Tennant duet with 60s star Dusty Springfield, which reached No 2. Follow-up **It's A Sin**, reached No 1 despite allegations that it plagiarised Cat Stevens' 1970s hit 'Wild World'. Second album **Actually** contained both singles plus **Rent**, which became minor hit later in year. Album sleeve maintained PSB's image of refusing to smile for camera, even showing Tennant yawning!

Recorded electro-disco version of **Always On My Mind** for Elvis Presley TV special, which became surprise UK chart topper. Also produced single for Patsy Kensit & Eighth Wonder.

Despite refusing to play live concerts, Pet Shop Boys have proved to be a major British success story of 1987/88, taking over where previous synth-pop acts like Human League and Eurythmics once ruled supreme. Many critics find their low-profile approach too scheming and unemotional, but that is to miss their intuitive sense of what is both artistically subversive and commercially populist.

**Hit Singles:**

| | US | UK |
|---|---|---|
| West End Girls, 1985 | 1 | 1 |
| Opportunities, 1986 | 11 | 11 |
| Suburbia, 1986 | — | 8 |
| Love Comes Quickly, 1986 | — | 19 |
| Its A Sin, 1987 | 9 | 1 |
| What Have I Done To Deserve This, 1987 | 2 | 2 |
| Rent, 1987 | — | 8 |
| Always On My Mind, 1987 | — | 1 |

**Albums**
Disco (EMI) **CD**
Please (Parlophone/EMI America), 1986 **CD**
Actually (Parlophone), 1987 **CD**

# Peter, Paul And Mary

US group formed 1961.
Peter Yarrow, vocalist, guitarist; born New York City, May 31, 1938.
Paul (real name Noel) Stookey, vocalist, guitarist; born Baltimore, Maryland, November 30, 1937.
Mary Travers, vocalist; born Louisville, Kentucky, November 7, 1937.

**Career:** 'Antiseptic', complained those who thought trio's pretty harmonies and wholesome image diluted and softened impact of protest songs. 'Bringing message to mainstream', said others, noting that material was umcompromising and that group spoke out on civil rights and anti-war issues to wide audience, appearing on platform with Martin Luther King when civil rights leader made 1963 'I Have A Dream' speech.

Although P, P & M were manufactured in 1961 by Bob Dylan's(▶) manager Albert Grossman to emulate success of Kingston Trio, each had strong folk roots. Yarrow was exposed to folk scene at NY's High School of Music and Art, then studied and taught folklore while getting BA degree in psychology. Stookey led rock 'n' roll band while at school, compered and sang at student events at Michigan State, then came to NY for job in industry. Performing weekends as singer and comedian in Greenwich village clubs, met and was in-

fluenced by Tom Paxton(▶), Dave Van Ronk and others, becoming full-time performer in 1960. Travers grew up in progressive NY family, and at 14 belonged to Songswappers, a group which recorded three albums with Pete Seeger(▶).

With Milt Okun as musical director, trio's strong stage personality combined with intelligent material and arrangements to make them style-setters during 1960s. Programme mixed Yarrow/Stookey originals with traditional songs and compositions by others. First album **Peter, Paul and Mary** (1962) gave double-sided hit single of Seeger's **If I Had A Hammer** and **Lemon Tree**.

There were two 1963 albums, **Moving** and **In The Wind**, from which Dylan's **Blowin' In The Wind** went to No. 2 in US and No. 13 in UK, won Grammy and brought Dylan to public notice. Trio sang Dylan's song with him at memorable 1963 Newport Festival concert. Yarrow, member of Newport Folk foundation's initial board of directors, was compere when electric Dylan was booed off stage at 1965 Festival. 'He's gone to get his acoustic guitar,' he shouted, placating angry audience when Dylan stomped off.

Other major hits included **Puff The Magic Dragon** and John Denver's(▶) 1969 **Leaving On A Jet Plane**. Of ten albums, eight went gold; five of these were platinum. Then, after 1970 peace rally in Washington, DC, trio split.

Each made solo albums and each managed Top 100 single; but no spectacular success. Yarrow co-produced Mary MacGregor's 1976 album **Torn Between Two Lovers**, from which his titletrack composition became major 1977 chart topper. Stookey produced folk albums, then formed Neworld Media, running a recording studio and doing film editing. Travers hosted US radio chat show in 1975 and wrote her autobiography.

In 1978 trio reunited for anti-nuclear rally in California, then gradually began performing together more frequently. During 1983 they played a heavy schedule of concerts, including a European tour, and received high praise from critics and full-capacity audiences who found that old songs hadn't gone stale.

Now, almost thirty years after first formation, group can find considerable audience whenever it chooses to tour. An American institution, Peter, Paul and Mary remain one of the most distinctive exponents of commercial folk sound.

**Below: Guitarist/vocalist Tom Petty produced Del Shannon's 1982 album.**

**Hit Singles:**

| | US | UK |
|---|---|---|
| If I Had A Hammer, 1962 | 10 | |
| Puff The Magic Dragon, 1963 | 2 | |
| Blowin' In The Wind, 1963 | 2 | 13 |
| Don't Think Twice, It's Allright 1963 | 9 | |
| I Dig Rock And Roll Music, 1967 | 9 | |
| Leavin' On A Jet Plane, 1969 | 1 | 2 |

**Albums:**
Peter Paul & Mary (Warner Bros), 1962
In Concert (Warner Bros), 1965
Album 1700 (Warner Bros), 1967
Peter Paul & Mommy (Warner Bros), 1970
Ten Years Together (Warner Bros), 1974
Reunion (Warner Bros), 1978

# Tom Petty & The Heartbreakers

US group formed 1976.
**Original line-up:** Tom Petty, vocals, Fender Stratocaster, Rickenbacker 12-string guitars; Stan Lynch, drums, vocals; Mike Campbell, guitar; Benmont Tench, keyboards vocals; Ron Blair, bass.

**Career:** Petty grew up in Gainsville, Florida, and played for local group Epics in high school. He quit when band began posing instead of playing. After finishing high school he held variety of low-paid jobs while playing bass in Gainsville's premier band Mudcrutch, where he came across Campbell and Tench.

Mudcrutch elected to seek fortune in Los Angeles and moved there in April 1974. One single flopped and band folded. Trio kept in touch and in early 1976 were working on some of Tench's demos with Lynch and Blair (also from Gainsville) when they decided to try again. Group interested Shelter Records and released first LP, which received critical praise for Byrds(▶)-like feel with '70s technology. (Single from album, **American Girl**, ironically, was covered by Jim McGuinn.)

Exciting live shows and plenty of radio play ensured quick success for band, who responded by recording even stronger LP, **You're Gonna Get It!** Just as it seemed they were making it (**Don't Do Me Like That** single gave them first Top 10 hit), Shelter Records collapsed. Band became

deeply involved in legal problems (Petty himself filing bankruptcy) and lost momentum.

**Damn The Torpedoes** reflected band's tenacity and resilience in both title and sound. Doing much to pick up band again, album also brought approval of fellow musicians. Stevie Nicks, taking break from Fleetwood Mac(▶) used band on **Bella Donna** solo LP; Petty produced excellent, but obscure, Del Shannon(▶) LP; and Tench worked with Dylan(▶).

The double album **Pack Up The Plantation** emanated from band's gigs at Los Angeles' Wiltern Theatre but also included two vocal duets of Tom Petty with Stevie Nicks from an LA Forum dating back to 1981.

Petty continued to gather momemtum throughout 80s, albums like **Long After Dark, Southern Accents** and **Let Me Up, I've Had Enough** confirming position near top of rock tree. Recent double-header tour with Bob Dylan showed Petty's ability to hold his own against brightest starts of music firmament.

**Current line-up:** Petty; Campbell; Tench; Lynch; Howard Epstein, bass.

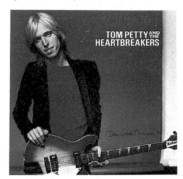

**Damn The Torpedoes, Tom Petty. Courtesy Backstreet Records.**

**Hit Singles:**

| | US | UK |
|---|---|---|
| Don't Do Me Like That, 1979 | 10 | — |
| Refugee, 1980 | 15 | — |
| The Waiting, 1981 | 19 | — |
| You Got Lucky, 1983 | 20 | — |
| Don't Come Around, 1985 | 13 | — |

*With Stevie Nicks:*

| | | |
|---|---|---|
| Stop Draggin' My Heart Around, 1981 | | 3 |

**Albums:**
Tom Petty & The Heartbreakers (Shelter/Island), 1976 **CD**
You're Gonna Get It! (Shelter/Island), 1978
Damn The Torpedoes (Backstreet), 1979 **CD**
Hard Promises (Backstreet), 1981 **CD**
Long After Dark (Backstreet), 1982 **CD**
Southern Accents (MCA), 1985 **CD**
Let Me Up (I've Had Enough) (MCA), 1987 **CD**

# Wilson Pickett

US vocalist, composer.
Born Prattville, Alabama, March 18, 1941.

**Career:** First made impression as lead singer for Detroit-based vocal group the Falcons; Falcons releases demonstrated full-blooded vocal style that was to become Pickett's stock-in-trade. After group split Pickett recorded **If You Need Me** and **It's Too Late** for Lloyd Price's Double L label; both were R&B hits.

Pickett signed with Atlantic in 1964 and after a couple of unsuccessful releases, company recorded him at Stax Studios in Memphis with Steve Cropper and Stax session mafia. Result was first major hit, the classic **In The Midnight Hour** (co-written by Cropper), which went to No. 21 in the US,

12 in the UK. **Hour**'s irresistible dance beat coupled with Pickett's cocky, macho vocalising established him as soul star on a par with '60s heroes like Otis Redding(▶).

The next four years saw slew of exciting soul hits, firmly based on solid dance beat (Pickett was underrated as an interpreter of soul ballads). He also toured extensively, with large soul revue show, and was particularly popular in UK.

Towards end of '60s Pickett's popularity waned as new flower-power ethos began to take effect (although strangely one of his biggest hits were cover of the Beatles(▶) mock gospel ballad **Hey Jude.** He signed with RCA in 1972, and has continued to record with varied success. Although there has been no diminution in the power of his voice, since the early '70s Pickett seems to have been searching for a direction that could open up a place for him in the era of Earth Wind and Fire(▶) and the Commodores(▶), but success has been only sporadic.

Pickett has continued to work live, but his aggressive personality has made him a less than bankable proposition; two recent trips to UK have been cancelled at last minute amid rumours of fisticuffs and/or ludicrous monetary demands.

One of the great soul performers of '60s, Wilson Pickett summed up for many what soul was all about. Sly, sexy, macho and aggressive, he had all the vocal equipment required to wring the last ounce out of a song. His hit singles collections demonstrate perfectly the raw exhilaration of '60s soul, and are essentials for any rounded record collection. Pickett recently signed to Motown, company well placed to engineer Tina Turner-style regeneration of career. **American Soul Man** was well received, and may signal new phase for veteran soulster.

**Hit Singles:**

| | US | UK |
|---|---|---|
| In The Midnight Hour, 1965 | 21 | 12 |
| 634-5789, 1966 | 13 | 36 |
| Land Of 1000 Dances, 1966 | 6 | 22 |
| Funky Broadway, 1967 | 8 | 43 |
| She's Lookin' Good, 1968 | 15 | — |
| Hey Jude, 1969 | 23 | 16 |
| Engine Number 9, 1970 | 14 | — |
| Don't Let The Green Grass Fool You, 1971 | 17 | — |
| Don't Knock My Love — Part 1, 1971 | 13 | — |

**Albums:**
If You Need Me (—/Joy), 1974
I Want You (United Artists), 1979
The Right Track (EMI), 1981
The Best Of (Atlantic), 1982

# Pink Floyd

UK group formed 1966.

**Original line-up:** Syd Barrett, vocals, guitar; Roger Waters, bass; Richard Wright, keyboards; Nick Mason, drums.

**Career:** Barrett and Waters attended Cambridge High School for boys, along with future member Dave Gilmour. Barrett moved to art college in London, playing in Geoff Mott and the Mottos and the Hollering Blues, before forming short-lived duo with Gilmour. Waters, meanwhile, was studying architecture in London and had formed Sigma 6 with Mason and Wright.

Group evolved into T. Set, Meggadeath and the Screaming Abdabs, finally bringing in jazz guitarist Bob Close and Barrett. Later dubbed group the Pink Floyd Sound, a name said to have been inspired by Georgia bluesmen Pink Anderson and Floyd Council. As they moved

towards psychedelic music, Close was ousted.

Group spent late 1966 playing at variety of early underground haunts, including the Marquee, the London Free School's Sound/Light Workshop in All Saint's Church Hall, Notting Hill and, most notably, the Roundhouse. By end of year they were regular headliners at UFO, London's foremost hippie club. With new managers Peter Jenner and Andrew King, secured contract with EMI, recording first single in January 1967. **Arnold Layne**, written by Barrett, was amusing tale of transvestite who steals underwear. Novel sound and theme ensured Top 20 placing in UK charts, establishing Floyd as most successful group to emerge from Britain's underground scene.

During May 1967, ambitious **Games For May** was staged at London's Queen Elizabeth Hall, complete with quadrophonic sound system. **Games For May**, retitled **See Emily Play**, was released as single and reached UK No. 6 in July.

In August, first LP **Piper At The Gates Of Dawn** demonstrated Barrett's dominant role in group. Songs were full of childlike images, subtly echoing work of Lewis Carroll, combining the innocent and the menacing. Barrett's lead guitar work was impressive, neatly complementing Wright's unusual keyboards style. Prior to first US tour, Barrett's behaviour became increasingly erratic, possibly a sideeffect of over-use of hallucinogens. In succeeding months, condition worsened; at some performances he would not play at all, remaining motionless on stage. By February 1968, Gilmour was brought in as replacement, Barrett finally leaving in April.

Without Barrett's lyrics, group had little chance of succeeding as singles act. Instead they concentrated on live work, appearing regularly at Middle Earth, and headlining free concert in London's Hyde Park in July. Second album, **A Saucerful Of Secrets**, demonstrated ability to survive. Used Waters instrumental/electronics/choral work to great effect, particularly during climactic **Set The Controls For The Heart Of The Sun**.

Subsequent concerts revealed increasing professionalism/imagination in use of lighting/sound. At Royal Festival Hall their presentation 'More Furious Madness From The Massed Gadgets Of Auximenes' featured the innovatory Azimuth Co-ordinator, a PA system that ingeniously projected the sound around auditorium. Increasing interest in soundtrack

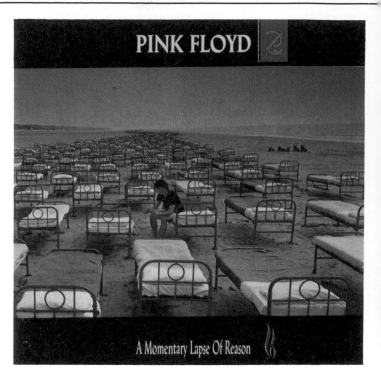

**A Momentary Lapse of Reason, Pink Floyd. Courtesy EMI Records.**

music led to scores for **More** (1969), **The Committee** (1969), **Zabriskie Point** (1970), **The Body** (1970) and **Obscured By Clouds** (1972).

Released double album **Ummagumma**, featuring two live sides (recorded at Mothers Club, Birmingham, and Manchester College of Commerce, in June 1969) backed by studio contributions from every member. Work was self-indulgent in parts and erratic in quality. A period of relative quiet ended with release of **Atom Heart Mother** (1970) which topped UK LP charts. In spite of commercial success, it was least impressive offering to date. Successful concerts followed, including free concert in Hyde Park that attracted 100,000 people.

Early in 1971, Floyd appeared at Crystal Palace Garden Party amid fireworks and rain. Premiered **Return To The Son Of Nothing**, an extended hard rock/melodic improvisation that finally emerged as **Echoes**, the key track on their 1971 LP **Meddle**. Extra-curricular work was undertaken frequently during early '70s. A film of group at Pompeii (directed by Adrian Maben) was premiered at Edinburgh Festival, while they worked industriously on next album.

**The Dark Side Of The Moon** LP, the culmination of various ideas over the years, centred on death and emotional breakdown caused by fear, loneliness and spiritual impoverishment. Work also underlined dark pessimism evident in Waters' songwriting, perhaps consciously rejecting the escapist romanticism that had characterised and destroyed Barrett. Bleakness of theme was offset by stunning production, unparalleled for its period. An aesthetically rewarding venture, album also became their biggest seller. Remained in UK lists for over two years; stayed in US charts for over a decade, making it the longest running LP in recording history.

Following album's release, group played London's Earls Court before 18,000 people, then retired for six months. Re-emerged briefly for Robert Wyatt benefit. For most of 1974 group members embarked on various projects, but they returned to the States for another tour in 1975, before playing badly received set at Knebworth.

**Wish You Were Here** finally appeared in September 1975 after two and a half years. Work was rather anticlimactic and press reaction proved unfavourable. Sales wise, it was another triumph. During 1976 group toured Europe and States, and completed work on **Animals**, released January 1977. Further solo projects followed amid rumours of impending dissolution. The release of **The Wall** in 1979 provided another phenomenal seller, including a Christmas single charttopper, **Another Brick In The Wall**. Spin-off film 'The Wall', starring Bob Geldof of Boomtown Rats(▶), received mixed review, but fared no worse than others in the genre.

Prophetically titled **The Final Cut** emphasised Waters' dominance of group with further bleak visions of present day society. From early underground following, group had gone on to worldwide acclaim but after Mason quit to pursue motor-racing fanaticism, they lapsed into inactivity.

**Piper At The Gates Of Dawn, Pink Floyd. Courtesy EMI/Columbia Records.**

Legal wrangles over use of group's name ensued, and in 1987 Wright, Gilmour and mason went on road with Floyd paraphernalia including famous inflatable pig. Waters also toured, using old Floyd film footage as visual back-up.

At presstime, legalities are unresolved, although success of Wright/Gilmour/Mason aggregation and solo Waters indicates continuing interest in Floydinia in all its forms.

**Final/Current line-up:** Waters; Wright; David Gilmour, guitar.

**Above: Original Pink Floyd line-up circa 1966, with (from left) Nick Mason, Richard Wright, Roger Waters and Syd Barrett.**

**Hit Singles:**

| | US | UK |
|---|---|---|
| Arnold Layne, 1967 | — | 20 |
| See Emily Play, 1967 | — | 6 |
| Money, 1973 | 13 | — |
| Another Brick In The Wall, 1979 | 1 | 1 |

**Albums:**
The Piper At The Gates Of Dawn (Columbia), 1967
A Sauceful Of Secrets (Columbia), 1968 **CD**
More (Columbia), 1969 **CD**
Ummagumma (Harvest), 1969 **CD**
Atom Heat Mother (Harvest), 1970 **CD**
Relics (Regal Starline), 1971
Meddle (Harvest), 1971 **CD**
Obscured By Clouds (Harvest), 1972 **CD**
The Dark Side Of The Moon (Harvest), 1973 **CD**
A Nice Pair (Harvest), 1973
Wish You Were Here (Harvest), 1975 **CD**
Animals (Harvest), 1977 **CD**
The Wall (Harvest), 1979 **CD**
The Final Cut (EMI), 1983 **CD**
Works (Capitol), 1983
A Momentary Lapse Of Reason (EMI), 1987 **CD**

*With Various Artists:*
Zabriskie Point (Soundtrack) (MGM), 1970
*Worth Searching Out:*
*Syd Barrett Solo:*
The Madcap Laughs And Barrett (Harvest), 1974
About Face (Harvest), 1984 **CD**
*David Gilmour Solo:*
David Gilmour (Columbia/CBS), 1978
*Nick Mason Solo:*
Fictitious Sports (Columbia/CBS), 1981

# Gene Pitney

US vocalist, composer.
Born Rockville, Connecticut, February 17, 1941.

**Career:** Began as songwriter; first record **I Wanna Love My Life Away** was made as song demo and only released after several music publishers had rejected song. Track featured Pitney playing all instruments and multi-track vocals; it reached No.39 in US charts, becoming first of many chart appearances throughout '60s.

Wrote several hits for other artists, including Roy Orbison(▶), Ricky Nelson(▶) and the Crystals. Most of own recordings were self-penned and later published by own company.

Pitney's distinctive tenor vocals made records immediately identifiable, and regular tours consolidated position in UK as major US solo artist of '60s, second only to Orbison(▶). The Beatles liked Pitney and they toured the UK with him. He never did as well in the US, where audiences considered him a bit square.

In late '60s Pitney turned to country music, dueting with George Jones(▶) for one US chart appearance, while retaining following in UK, which is still considerable.

**Hit Singles:**

| | US | UK |
|---|---|---|
| Town Without Pity, 1962 | 13 | — |
| (The Man Who Shot) Liberty Valance, 1962 | 4 | — |
| Only Love Can Break A Heart, 1962 | 2 | — |
| Half Heaven-Half Heartache, 1963 | 12 | — |
| Mecca, 1963 | 12 | — |
| 24 Hours From Tulsa, 1963 | 17 | 5 |
| That Girl Belongs To Yesterday, 1964 | 49 | 7 |
| It Hurts To Be In Love, 1964 | 7 | 36 |
| I'm Gonna Be Strong, 1964 | 9 | 2 |
| I Must Be Seeing Things, 1965 | 31 | 6 |
| Last Chance To Turn Around, 1965 | 13 | — |
| Looking Through The Eyes Of Love, 1965 | 28 | 3 |
| Princess In Rags, 1965 | — | 9 |
| Backstage, 1966 | — | 4 |
| Nobody Needs Your Love, 1966 | — | 2 |
| Just One Smile, 1966 | — | 8 |
| Something's Gotten Hold Of My Heart, 1967 | — | 5 |
| Somewhere In The Country, 1968 | — | 19 |
| She's A Heartbreaker, 1968 | 16 | — |

**Albums:**
(Not including repetitious budget compilations)
The Best Of (Piccadilly/—), 1981
Greatest Hits Of All Time (—/Phoenix), 1982
20 Golden Pieces Of (—/Bulldog), 1983
20 Greatest Hits (Spectrum) **CD**
22 Greatest Hits (Bescol) **CD**

# The Platters

US vocal group formed 1953.

**Original line-up:** Tony Williams; Alex Hodge; David Lynch; Herb Reed.

**Career:** Perhaps the best-known of many vocal harmony groups who trod fabled 'rags-to-riches' path during rock 'n' roll years of '50s, Platters climbed from obscurity of regional R&B charts to worldwide stardom. Original quartet met entrepreneur Buck Ram in Los Angeles in 1953; signed to Federal Records, but met little success. Ram made some inspired personnel changes, replacing Hodge with Paul Robi and recruiting Zola Taylor as contrasting female voice.

Continued to record for Federal, picking up local sales. Ram placed them with Mercury as virtual 'make-weights' in deal involving the Penguins, who had just scored pop hit with **Earth Angel**. Platters' first four records on Mercury all reached national Top 5 between fall 1955 and late 1956. **Only You, The Magic Touch, The Great Pretender** and **My Prayer** were fine, lyrical ballads; latter two topped charts, led by Tony Williams' clear, soaring tenor.

Hits continued to flow during next five years; chart-toppers **Twilight Time** and **Smoke Gets In Your Eyes** became 'pop' standards in Platters' distinctive ballad styling/lush orchestrations.

In 1961 Tony Williams quit to pursue solo career; auditions yielded Sonny Turner as replacement. Despite maintaining similar mode of performance, hits did not come as readily. Group made good living on cabaret circuit, though, and continued steady output of LPs until leaving Mercury in 1965.

Change of musical direction followed more personnel changes; Sandra Dawn replaced Zola, Nate Nelson took over from Paul Robi. Group pacted with Musicor in 1966, taking more soulful inclination and switching up-tempo; scored with lilting beaters like **I Love You 1000 Times** and **With This Ring**. Albums contained reworkings of their Mercury hits.

Subsequent years brought further personnel changes, record label switches, and profusion of lawsuits. 'Buck Ram Platters' are now touring minions of their ageing manager, who slaps injunctions on any original member who dares to quote Platters' name in show billings.

**Final line-up:** Lynch; Reed; Sonny Turner; Nate Nelson.

**Hit Singles:**

| | US | UK |
|---|---|---|
| Only You, 1955 | 5 | — |
| The Great Pretender, 1956 | 1 | — |
| The Great Pretender/Only You, 1956 | — | 5 |
| (You've Got) The Magic Touch, 1956 | 4 | — |
| My Prayer, 1956 | 1 | 4 |
| You'll Never Know/It Isn't Right, 1956 | 11 | 23 |
| It Isn't Right/You'll Never Know, 1956 | 13 | 23 |
| On My Word Of Honor/One In A Million, 1957 | 20 | |
| One In A Million/On My Word Of Honor, 1957 | 20 | |
| Only You, 1957 | | 18 |
| I'm Sorry/He's Mine, 1957 | 11 | 18 |
| He's Mine/I'm Sorry, 1957 | 16 | |
| Twilight Time, 1958 | 1 | 3 |
| Smoke Gets In Your Eyes, 1959 | 1 | 1 |
| Harbour Lights, 1960 | 8 | 11 |

**Albums (selected):**
Best Of Volume 1 (—/Philips), 1973
Best Of Volume 2 (—/Philips), 1973
Encore (Mercury/—), 1976
More Encore Of Greatest Hits (Mercury), 1976
19 Hits (King/—), 1977
20 Greatest Hits (Bescol) **CD**
Goldens Hits (Mercury) **CD**

# Pointer Sisters

US vocal group formed 1973.

**Original line-up:** Bonnie Pointer; Anita Pointer; Ruth Pointer; June Pointer.

**Career:** Four genuine sisters, daughters of church ministers; born Oakland, California. Started singing in church, and formed Pointer Sisters after leaving school.

Through acquaintance with producer David Rubinson, they became involved with session work on West Coast, singing behind such artists as Boz Scaggs, Grace Slick and Esther Phillips. Eventually they decided to pursue career in own right and Rubinson negotiated deal with ABC/Blue Thumb in 1973.

Initially the sisters concentrated on jazzy nostalgia material and featured close-harmony scat singing; '40s image was followed through in clothes and presentation. They achieved considerable success in this mode, and showed versatility by scoring country hit with Grammy award-winning **Fairy Tale.** Also featured in movie **Car Wash.**

Eventually musical frustration set in, and the sisters left ABC/Blue Thumb in 1977. They disbanded for short period, Bonnie branching out to pursue moderately successful solo career. Remaining three regrouped in 1978 and signed deal with producer Richard Perry's Planet label.

First album **Energy** and hit single **Fire** both achieved gold status and showed total change of direction, drawing on rock writers like Bruce Springsteen(▶) and Steely Dan's(▶) Becker and Fagen. Career since has concentrated on mainstream rock orientation, with considerable success.

One of very few black female vocal groups to follow rock direction, Pointer Sisters look set for career longevity through talent and individuality. Group commands wide following among AOR audience, with Perry's dynamic and commerical production transcending usual R&B/pop/rock barriers

**Retrospect, The Pointer Sisters. Courtesy MCA Records.**

**Current line-up:** Anita Pointer; Ruth Pointer; June Pointer.

**Hit Singles:**

| | US | UK |
|---|---|---|
| Yes We Can Can, 1973 | 11 | — |
| Fairy Tale, 1974 | 13 | — |
| How Long (Betcha' Got A Chick On The Side), 1975 | 20 | — |
| Fire, 1979 | 2 | 34 |
| Heaven Must Have Sent You, 1979 | 11 | — |
| He's So Shy, 1980 | 3 | 5 |
| Slow Hand, 1981 | 2 | 10 |
| Should I Do It, 1982 | 13 | 50 |
| American Music, 1982 | 16 | — |
| Automatic, 1984 | 5 | 2 |
| Jump (For My Love), 1984 | 3 | 6 |
| I'm So Excited, 1984 | 9 | 11 |
| Neutron Dance, 1985 | 6 | — |
| Dare Me, 1985 | 11 | 17 |
| Be There, 1987 | 42 | — |

**Albums:**
Live At The Opera House (ABC), 1974
Best Of . . . (Blue Thumb/ABC), 1976
Energy (Planet), 1978
Priority (Planet), 1979
Special Things (Planet), 1980
Black And White (Planet), 1981
Retrospect (MCA/—), 1981
So Excited (Planet), 1982
Greatest Hits (Planet), 1982
Black & White (Planet), 1984
Break Out (Planet), 1984 **CD**
Contact (RCA) **CD**
Hot Together (RCA), 1987 **CD**
Pointer Sisters (Planet) **CD**

**Below: The Pointer Sisters, now successful as a trio.**

# The Police

**UK group formed 1977.**

**Original line-up:** Sting (Gordon Sumner), vocals, Ibanez bass, Henri Padovani, guitar; Stewart Copeland, drums.

**Career:** Band was formed by drummer Copeland, previously with moderately successful UK outfit Curved Air. Idea was to combine post-punk principles of simplicity and spontaneity with coherence and melodic sense. Copeland recruited Sting from Newcastle jazz and rock scene, and pair pulled in Padovani on guitar.

Band's first single was **Fall Out**, released in January 1977 on Illegal Records, an independent label formed by Copeland with brother Miles. (Miles Copeland had also served as manager throughout band's career.) Padovani's tenure was short-lived; he left in August 1977 to form Flying Padovani Brothers; replacement was Andy Summers, veteran of Zoot Money's Big Roll Band, the Animals(▶), Soft Machine(▶), Kevin Ayers and Kevin Coyne

It was with re-release of **Roxanne** on A&M in 1979 that band started to attract attention. Combining reggae-styled verse with rocking harmony chorus, single eventually went silver. It was first of string of major hit singles, each distinctive yet recognisable Police. By end of 1980 band was firmly established in UK and was making major inroads into US and international market.

Albums were as successful as singles. **Outlandos D'Amour** went double platinum in UK and gold in US, **Regatta De Blanc** made triple platinum in UK and gold in US, and third album, **Zenyatta Mondatta**, had massive sales figures all over the world — it achieved triple platinum status in UK, platinum status in US and went either gold or platinum in virtually every other territory.

Meanwhile, band had gained reputation as exciting live act and toured throughout world to wild acclaim during 1980-81. **Six Pack**, a package of the first five Police singles plus new release **The Bed's Too Big Without You** on A&M, went to No. 17 in the UK singles charts, a rather unique accomplishment.

1982 saw **Ghost In The Machine** LP riding high in charts, and hit singles from album soaring; **Every Little Thing She Does Is Magic** gave them their fourth UK No. 1, and **Invisible Sun** reached No. 2 in the UK despite BBC banning of accompanying video which depicted troubled streets of Belfast. Band kept relatively low profile as members went about various solo projects. Sting, natural front man of band, had already had major acting parts in the Who(▶) film 'Quadrophenia' and BBC-TV film 'Artemis '81', and received further acclaim for his lead role in Dennis Potter-written movie 'Brimstone And Treacle'. As if that were not enough, he scored hit with **Spread A Little Happiness**, the '30s song featured in film. Andy Summers recorded moderately successful instrumental LP, **I Advance Masked,** with Robert Fripp in 1982.

Return to group work came in spring 1983. **Synchronicity** LP and single **Every Breath You Take** flew to No. 1 both sides of the Atlantic. **Synchronicity** was third Police LP in a row to enter UK album charts at No. 1.

Success continued and record sales soared but in recent times new releases ceased as trio concentrated on solo ventures, Sting featuring in movies 'Brimstone And Treacle', 'Dune',

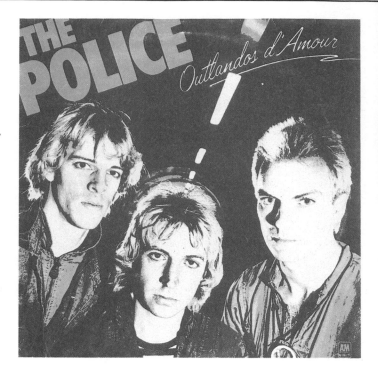

Outlandos d'Amour, the first Police album, which featured their first big hit, 'Roxanne'. Courtesy A&M Records.

'The Bride' and 'Plenty' then joining four American jazz musicians—Branford Marsalis, Daryl Jones, Kenny Kirkland and Omar Hakim—in a new concert and recording venture. He also scored with solo hit LP **The Dream Of The Blue Turtles**.

Solo output of Sting has been thoughtful, sophisticated and jazz-tinged, but has led to accusations of pretension and self-indulgence. Neither Copeland and Summers solo projects have achieved widespread success.

Although band have not officially split, their last gig together was Amnesty 86, and at presstime Police investigations had brought no new evidence to light.

**Current line-up:** Sting; Copeland; Andy Summers, Fender Stratocaster, Gibson 335 guitars, vocals.

The second album by the Police with a second enigmatic title. Courtesy A&M Records.

| Hit Singles: | US | UK |
|---|---|---|
| Roxanne, 1979 | 32 | 12 |
| Can't Stand Losing You, 1979 | — | 2 |
| Message In A Bottle, 1979 | — | 1 |
| Walking On The Moon, 1979 | — | 1 |
| So Lonely, 1980 | — | 6 |
| Six Pack, 1980 | — | 17 |
| Don't Stand So Close To Me, 1980 | 10 | 1 |
| De Do Do Do, De Da Da Da, 1980 | 10 | 5 |
| Invisible Sun, 1981 | — | 2 |
| Every Little Thing She Does Is Magic, 1981 | 3 | 1 |
| Spirits In The Material World, 1982 | 11 | 12 |
| Every Breath You Take, 1983 | 1 | 1 |
| Wrapped Around Your Finger, 1983 | — | 7 |
| Synchronicity II, 1983 | 16 | 17 |
| King Of Pain, 1984 | 3 | 17 |

*Sting solo:*

| | | |
|---|---|---|
| Spread A Little Happiness, 1982 | — | 16 |
| If You Love Somebody Set Them Free, 1983 | 3 | — |
| Fortress Round Your Heart, 1985 | 8 | — |
| Love Is The Seventh Wave, 1986 | 17 | — |
| The Russians, 1986 | — | 20 |
| We'll Be Together, 1987 | 7 | — |

**Albums:**
Outlandos D'Amour (A&M), 1978 **CD**
Regatta De Blanc (A&M), 1979 **CD**
Zenyatta Mondatta (A&M), 1980 **CD**
Ghost In The Machine (A&M), 1981 **CD**
Synchronicity (A&M), 1983 **CD**
Every Breath You Take — The Album (A&M), 1986 **CD**

*Sting Solo:*
Brimstone And Treacle (soundtrack) (A&M), 1982
The Dream Of The Blue Turtles (A&M), 1985 **CD**
Bring On The Night (A&M), 1987 Double **CD**
Nothing Like The Song (A&M), 1987 **CD**

*Andy Summers with Robert Fripp.*
I Advance Masked (A&M), 1982
Bewitched (A&M), 1984

*Andy Summers Solo:*
XYZ (A&M), 1987 **CD**

**Below: The Police in 1983 (left) Sting, Andy Summers and (front) Stewart Copeland.**

**Right: During their 1980 World Tour and (below) taking Western rock music to India where it has rarely been heard before their 1980 concert.**

A No. 1 album in both the US and UK. Courtesy A&M Records.

# Elvis Presley

US vocalist, guitarist, composer, actor: Born Tupelo, Misssissippi, January 8 - 1935; died Memphis, Tennessee, August 16, 1977.

**Career:** Early influences included gospel concerts, church singing, R&B radio shows in hometown, and country singers of '40s. In first public appearance at age 10, came second singing **Old Shep** in State Fair talent contest. Following family move to Memphis and some experience singing with gospel groups, visited Sun Studios to cut acetate as gift to mother.

Sun's Sam Phillips recognised potential and eventually in 1954 teamed Presley with Scotty Moore (guitar) and Bill Black(▶) (bass). Resulting first single, **That's All Right,** became big enough hit locally for trio to begin touring Southern US and eventually appear on 'Louisiana Hayride' radio show.

Further Sun singles consolidated popularity and reports of excitement generated at live appearances prompted Colonel Tom Parker to become manager and RCA-Victor Records to purchase contract from Sun for $35,000. In retrospect, sum paid seems minimal, but was astronomical in 1955.

With better distribution and promotion than Sun could provide, coupled with controversial television appearances, Presley rapidly became most important artist in rock 'n' roll field and major threat to 'establishment' singers. First major hit, **Heartbreak Hotel**, in summer 1956 was rapidly followed by succession of No. 1s in similar style, mostly introduced on major TV shows.

Fan fervour resulted in unprecedented merchandising of Presley products and hysterical scenes at concerts and public appearances. Although management policy was criticised later, Colonel Parker successfully promoted hysteria while building solid career for Presley, typified by first movie contract guaranteeing advances of $450,000 for first three films.

Career interrupted for two years by draft into US Army in 1958. However, Presley's popularity was scarcely affected by lack of public appearances thanks to stockpile of recordings and continuing publicity resulting from Colonel Parker's activities on his behalf. By 1960, when Presley returned from service in Germany, rock 'n' roll had ceased to rule the charts. Subsequent releases followed the pattern set by **It's Now Or Never**, an almost-MOR ballad.

First movies had shown some acting promise coupled with fairly natural musical content, but as demand for anything featuring Presley increased, less importance was placed on scripts. Aim was to maintain flow of glossy films with box-office appeal. Thus best films 'Love Me Tender', 'Jailhouse Rock' and 'Loving You' quickly degenerated to opportunist pap of 'Girls Girls Girls' and "Paradise Hawaiian Style".

Presley was undoubtedly capable of succeeding with better acting parts, as in 'Flaming Star', but more money could be made linking soundtrack album with teen-appeal films. Resulting 'assembly line' material bored Presley and accelerated decline as movie actor. At same time recorded material became less adventurous, with movie soundtrack providing singles releases to exclusion of stronger unrelated material; by late '60s singles had ceased to be automatic hits.

Following marriage in 1967 to Priscilla Beaulieu, daughter of Army officer, hoped-for return to former greatness confirmed by first TV appearance since 1960, 'NBC Special'. Both material and physical appearance raised hopes of fans who had watched their idol decline. Unfortunately, early promise of single **If I Can Dream** and live appearances in Las Vegas with distinguished band, including guitarist James Burton(▶), failed to sustain momentum. During '70s records and stage shows again declined, although faithful fans maintained following.

In mid-'70s Presley increasingly withdrew to safety of Graceland estate in Memphis with family and bodyguards. He became dependent on drugs to control basic functions, and gained weight. Record releases were irregular and stage appearances a parody of former self. Many were convinced that drugs were major factor in death from 'natural causes' at age 42. Presley's personal doctor is believed to be somewhat suspect.

**His Hand In Mine, Elvis Presley. Courtesy RCA Records. Presley holds the record for the most weeks at No. 1 in the UK.**

As news of death spread, there were hysterical scenes outside home in Memphis and at funeral. RCA was unable to cope with demand for Presley product as sales broke all previous records. Cult following since death has continued unabated. Books, articles, films and TV documentaries on Presley's life abound; many attempt to investigate cause of demise.

Despite criticism of later career, it is undeniable that Presley's influence on others has been and remains enormous. He was first rock 'n' roll artist to successfully blend black and white musical influences and retain appeal to broad audience. Presley holds nearly every rock record in UK, including Most Hits, Most Weeks In Charts and Most Top 10 Hits.

With his good looks, vocal talent and sex appeal, Presley was a 'natural' pop idol, and it is a measure of his greatness that he remains the most important and adulated oerformer of the rock 'n' roll era.

Tenth anniversary of artist's death in 1987 stimulated plethora of retrospectives and celebrations which showed that legend continued to grow.

| Hit Singles: | US | UK |
|---|---|---|
| Heartbreak Hotel/I Was The One, 1956 | 1 | 2 |
| Blue Suede Shoes (EP in US), 1956 | 20 | 9 |
| I Was The One/Heartbreak Hotel, 1956 | 19 | — |
| I Want You, I Need You, I Love You, 1956 | 1 | 14 |
| Don't Be Cruel/Hound Dog, 1956 | 1 | 2 |
| Hound Dog/Don't Be Cruel, 1956 | 1 | 2 |
| Love Me/When My Blue Moon Turns To Gold (EP), 1956 | 2 | — |
| When My Blue Moon Turns To Gold/Love Me, 1956 | 19 | — |
| Love Me Tender/Any Way That You Want Me, 1956 | 1 | 11 |
| Any Way That You Want Me/Love Me Tender, 1956 | 20 | — |
| Blue Moon, 1956 | — | 9 |
| Too Much, 1957 | 1 | 6 |
| All Shook Up, 1957 | 1 | 1 |
| (Let Me Be Your) Teddy Bear/Loving You, 1957 | 1 | 3 |
| Loving You/(Let Me Be Your) Teddy Bear, 1957 | 20 | — |
| Paralysed, 1957 | — | 8 |
| Party, 1957 | — | 2 |
| Got A Lot U' Livin' To Do, 1957 | — | 17 |
| Trying To Get To You, 1957 | — | 16 |
| Lawdy Miss Clawdy, 1957 | — | 15 |
| Santa Bring My Baby Back To Me, 1957 | — | 7 |
| Jailhouse Rock/Treat Me Nice, 1957 | 1 | 1 |
| Treat Me Nice/Jailhouse Rock, 1957 | 18 | — |
| Don't/I Beg Of You, 1958 | 1 | 2 |
| I Beg Of You/Don't, 1958 | 8 | — |

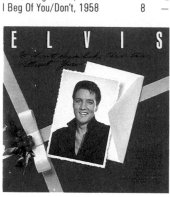

It Won't Seem Like Christmas Without You, just part of Elvis Presley's vast discography. Courtesy RCA Victor.

Below: Elvis Presley, the King of rock'n'roll, who will remain a true legend. Photo from the late '50s.

| Single | US | UK |
|---|---|---|
| Wear My Ring/Doncha Think It's Time, 1958 | 2 | 3 |
| Doncha' Think It's Time/Wear My Ring, 1958 | 15 | |
| Hard Headed Woman, 1958 | 1 | 2 |
| King Creole, 1958 | — | 2 |
| One Night/I Got Stung, 1958 | 4 | 1 |
| I Got Stung/One Night, 1958 | 8 | — |
| A Fool Such As I/I Need Your Love Tonight, 1959 | 2 | 1 |
| I Need Your Love Tonight/A Fool Such As I, 1959 | 4 | |
| A Big Hunk O'Love/My Wish Came True, 1959 | 1 | 4 |
| My Wish Came True/A Big Hunk O'Love, 1959 | 12 | — |
| Stuck On You/Fame And Fortune, 1960 | 1 | 3 |
| Fame And Fortune/Stuck On You, 1960 | 17 | — |
| It's Now Or Never, 1960 | 1 | 1 |
| A Mess Of Blues, 1960 | — | 2 |
| Are You Lonesome Tonight/I Gotta Know, 1960 | 1 | 1 |
| I Gotta Know/Are You Lonesome Tonight, 1960 | 20 | — |
| Surrender, 1961 | 1 | 1 |
| Wooden Heart, 1961 | — | 1 |
| Flaming Star (EP), 1961 | 14 | — |
| I Feel So Bad/Wild In The Country, 1961 | 5 | 1 |
| Wild In The Country/I Feel So Bad, 1961 | — | 4 |
| (Marie's The Name) His Latest Flame/Little Sister, 1961 | 4 | 1 |
| Little Sister/(Marie's The Name) His Latest Flame, 1961 | 5 | — |
| Can't Help Falling In Love/Rock A Hula Baby, 1962 | 2 | 1 |
| Rock A Hula Baby/Can't Help Falling In Love, 1962 | — | 1 |
| Good Luck Charm, 1962 | 1 | 1 |
| Follow That Dream (EP), 1962 | 15 | 34 |
| She's Not You, 1962 | 5 | 1 |
| Return To Sender, 1961 | 2 | 1 |
| One Broken Heart For Sale, 1963 | 11 | 12 |
| (You're The) Devil In Disguise, 1963 | 3 | 1 |
| Bossa Nova Baby, 1963 | 8 | 13 |
| Kiss Me Quick, 1963 | — | 14 |
| Viva Las Vegas, 1964 | 29 | 17 |
| Kissin' Cousins, 1964 | 12 | 10 |
| Such A Night, 1964 | 16 | 13 |
| Ask Me/Ain't That Loving You Baby, 1964 | 12 | — |
| Ain't That Loving You Baby/Ask Me, 1964 | 16 | 15 |
| Blue Christmas, 1964 | — | 11 |
| Do The Clam, 1965 | 21 | 19 |
| Crying In The Chapel, 1965 | 3 | 1 |
| Easy Question, 1965 | 11 | — |
| Tell Me Why, 1965 | 33 | 15 |
| I'm Yours, 1965 | 11 | — |
| Puppet On A String, 1965 | 14 | — |
| Love Letters, 1966 | 19 | 6 |
| All That I Am, 1966 | 41 | 18 |
| If Every Day Was Like Christmas, 1966 | — | 13 |
| Guitar Man, 1968 | 43 | 19 |
| US Male, 1968 | 28 | 15 |
| If I Can Dream, 1969 | 12 | 11 |
| In The Ghetto, 1969 | 3 | 2 |
| Clean Up Your Own Back Yard, 1969 | 35 | 2 |
| Suspicious Minds, 1969 | 1 | 2 |
| Don't Cry Daddy, 1970 | 6 | 8 |
| Kentucky Rain, 1970 | 16 | 21 |
| I've Lost You, 1970 | 32 | 9 |
| The Wonder Of You, 1970 | 9 | 1 |
| You Don't Have To Say You Love Me, 1970 | 11 | 9 |
| There Goes My Everything, 1971 | | 6 |
| Rags To Riches, 1971 | | 9 |
| I Just Can't Help Believin', 1971 | | 6 |
| Until It's Time For You To Go, 1972 | 40 | 5 |
| American Trilogy, 1972 | | 8 |
| Burning Love, 1972 | ? | 7 |
| Separate Ways/Always On My Mind, 1973 | 20 | |
| Always On My Mind/Separate Ways, 1973 | | 9 |
| Steamroller Blues/Fool, 1973 | 17 | |
| Fool/Steamroller Blues, 1973 | | 15 |
| If You Talk In Your Sleep, 1974 | 17 | 40 |
| Promised Land, 1974 | 14 | 9 |
| My Boy, 1975 | 20 | 5 |
| Girl Of My Best Friend, 1976 | | 9 |
| Suspicion, 1976 | | 9 |
| Moody Blue, 1977 | | 6 |
| Way Down, 1977 | 18 | 1 |
| My Way, 1977 | | 9 |
| It Won't Seem Like Christmas Without You, 1979 | | 13 |
| It's Only Love, 1980 | | 3 |

(In order of US release)

**Albums (selected):**
(Not including budget releases)

Rock 'n' Roll (RCA), 1956
Elvis Presley (RCA), 1956 **CD**
Elvis (RCA), 1956 **CD**
Loving You (RCA), 1957
King Creole (RCA), 1958 **CD**
For LP Fans Only (RCA), 1959
A Date With Elvis (RCA), 1959
Elvis Is Back (RCA), 1960
His Hand In Mine (RCA), 1960
Something For Everybody (RCA), 1961
Blue Hawaii (RCA), 1961 **CD**
Pot Luck (RCA), 1962
It Happend At The World's Fair (RCA), 1963
Roustabout (RCA), 1964
Harem Holiday (RCA), 1965
Paradise, Hawaiian Style (RCA), 1966
How Great Thou Art (RCA), 1967
Clambake (RCA), 1967
Double Trouble (RCA), 1967
Speedway (RCA), 1968
Elvis — NBC Special (RCA), 1968
That's The Way It Is (RCA), 1970
I'm 10,000 Years Old, Elvis Country (RCA), 1971
Elvis Sings The Wonderful World Of Christmas (RCA), 1971
Elvis Live At Madison Square Garden (RCA), 1972
Aloha From Hawaii (RCA), 1973 **CD**
Hits Of The '70s (RCA), 1974
Pictures Of Elvis (RCA), 1975
The Elvis Presley Sun Collection (RCA), 1975
Elvis In Demand (RCA), 1977
Elvis, Scotty and Bill — The First Year (Very Wonderful Golden Editions), 1979
Elvis Aaron Presley (RCA), 1980
Guitar Man (RCA), 1980
Elvis Presley Sings Leiber and Stoller (RCA), 1980
The Million Dollar Quartet (Sun), 1981
This Is Elvis (RCA), 1981
Rocker (RCA), 1983 **CD**
The Legend (RCA), 1983 **CD**
32 Film Hits (RCA), 1984
G.I. Blues (RCA), 1984 **CD**
Loving You (RCA), 1984 **CD**
Collection Vol. 3 (RCA), 1985 **CD**
Collection Vol. 4 (RCA), 1985 **CD**
Reconsider Baby (RCA), 1985 **CD**
Collection Vol. 1 (RCA), 1986 **CD**
Collection Vol. 2 (RCA), 1986 **CD**
Essential Elvis (RCA), 1986 **CD**

**Right:** The early Elvis Presley, whose brilliance was never surpassed by any other solo singer.

**Below right:** Elvis in decline—on stage during the 1970s.

**Below:** One of the few '60s artists who rivalled the Beatles in popularity.

# Pretenders

UK group formed 1978.

**Original line-up:** Chrissie Hynde, vocals; James Honeyman-Scott, vocals, keyboards, guitar; Pete Farndon, bass; Martin Chambers, drums.

**Career:** In 1974, American-born Chrissie Hynde quit job on London-based rock paper 'New Musical Express' to sing with French band, which flopped; returned to US to join R&B group Jack Rabbit. Giving France another try, she joined rock 'n' roll band the Frenchies before returning to London again. Then worked as back-up singer on Stiff Records' national tour.

Impressed with her work, bosses of Real label introduced her to group of musicians

on resultant double album.

Tours of Europe and America (received accolade as 'Best New Artists' in 'Rolling Stone' magazine) and release of another single, **Message Of Love**, and **Extended Play** (a five-track EP) preceded **Pretenders II** album (1981). Recorded in Paris and London and produced by Chris Thomas, nine of 12 songs were penned by Chrissie Hynde. She co-wrote two more with James Honeyman-Scott, but his death (drug-related) in mid-1982 put future of band in question. Soldiered on and late 1982 single **Back On The Chain Gang**, featuring Billy Bremner (guitar) and Tony Butler (bass), became Top 5 hit in US, with heavy airplay on MTV. Then suddenly, in April 1983, Farndon died. Two new members, Rob McIntosh (ex-Night) and Malcolm Foster (ex-Foster Brothers), were recruited in time for Pretenders performance at US Festival in

Above: Originals (from left), Farndon, Chambers, Hynde and Honeyman-Scott.

**Albums:**
Pretenders (Sire/Real), 1980 **CD**
Pretenders II (Sire/Real), 1981 **CD**
Learning To Crawl (Sire/Real), 1984 **CD**
Get Close (WEA), 1986 **CD**
The Singles (Real), 1987 **CD**

Above: The multi-talented Chrissie Hynde, soldiering on after the tragic deaths of Honeyman-Scott and Farndon.

from Hereford and groomed them as the Pretenders. Just cracking UK Top 30 with debut single, a re-make of Kinks' **Stop Your Sobbing**, band toured UK, released second single **Kid** (1979). With third record, catchy **Brass In Pocket** (highlighting Hynde's sensual vocals), topped chart.

**The Pretenders' classic first album. Courtesy WEA Records.**

Well-balanced debut album **Pretenders** went straight to No. 1. Appearance on all-star Kampuchean refugee charity concert heightened reputation; three of their songs appeared

May 1983 but in 1985 band broke up for good, Chrissie Hynde concentrating on raising family with Simple Minds' Jim Kerr, who she married in May 1984. She re-surfaced to join UB40 on 1985 hit re-make of Sonny and Cher's(▶) original **I Got You Babe**.

Most recently, Hynde has returned to touring with another edition of Pretenders, and has scored with US/UK top ten signle **Don't Get me Wrong** and gold album **Get Close**. Hynde has always been prime mover behind Pretenders, and renewed success will no doubt ensure survival of band for foreseeable future.

**Current line-up:** Hynde; Chambers; Rob McIntosh, guitar; Malcolm Foster, bass.

**Hit Singles:**

| | US | UK |
|---|---|---|
| Brass In Pocket, 1979 | 14 | 1 |
| Talk Of The Town, 1980 | — | 8 |
| Message Of Love, 1981 | — | 11 |
| I Go To sleep, 1981 | — | 7 |
| Back On The Chain Gang, 1982 | 5 | 17 |
| 2000 Miles, 1983 | — | 15 |
| Middle Of The Road, 1984 | 17 | — |
| Don't Get Me Wrong, 1986 | 5 | 10 |
| Hymn To Her, 1986 | — | 8 |

*Chrissie Hynde (with UB40):*

| | | |
|---|---|---|
| I Got You Babe, 1985 | 28 | 1 |

# Prince

US vocalist, guitarist.
Born Minneapolis, Minnesota, June 7, 1961.

**Career:** Christened Prince Rogers Nelson after jazz band leader father who used stage name Prince Rogers, Prince was fronting band, called first Grand Central then Champagne, at high school dances when only 12 years old.

Prince and Champagne's bass player André Cymone wrote bulk of group's material over five year period and when Champagne split, Prince went into studios to cut demos showcasing his material but trip to New York failed to yield record deal.

Undeterred, he cut further songs and took tape to Warner Bros in Los Angeles, securing long term contract.

A powerful catalyst for the Minneapolis music scene, Prince was quick to develop his charisma and individual flamboyant dress style, together with an extensive entourage which included the funky group Time, headed

by Champagne's one-time drummer Morris Day, and girlie group Vanity 6, later replaced by Apollonia 6.

Switch of management to high-powered Steve Fargnoli (who previously took Little Feat into big time) helped propel Prince's career into major league.

Debut album, which he wrote, produced, arranged and on which he sang and played all 27 instruments led to string of often outrageous LPs and eventually to semi-biographical movie 'Purple Rain' which showcased hit single **When Doves Cry**.

Album of movie showed signes of broadening of musical appeal, movement continued in 1985 set **Around The World In A Day**. Sixties/psychedelic influence now apparent, reflected in Sergeant Pepper-ish album sleeve.

Continuing to pursue celluloid ambitions, Prince then directed and starred in Under The Cherry Moon, one of most critically lambasted productions of all time. On music front, however, he further extended his horizons with 1987 double set **Sign 'O' The Times**, eclectic set which pleased critics and went on to achieve double platinum status.

Flamboyant yet enigmatic, Prince is truly star of eighties; broad base of capabilities enables him to retain full control of career. Likewise, he has acted as eminence grise to handful of ancilliary acts; as well as those mentioned above, he was important influence on producer Jimmy Jam, luscious songstress Sheila E. and several others. Genuine talent

Below: Prince of a broad range of musical skills, rapidly becoming the critics' favourite.

and charisma ensure long shelf-life for diminutive maestro.

| Hit Singles: | US | UK |
|---|---|---|
| I Wanna Be Your Lover, 1979 | 11 | — |
| 1999, 1983 | 12 | 25 |
| Little Red Corvette, 1983 | 6 | — |
| Delirious, 1983 | 8 | — |
| When Doves Cry, 1984 | 1 | 4 |
| Let's Go Crazy, 1984 | 1 | 7 |
| Purple Rain, 1984 | 2 | 8 |
| I Would Die 4 U, 1985 | 8 | — |
| Little Red Corvette/1999, 1985 | — | 2 |
| Raspberry Beret 1985 | 2 | 26 |
| Paisley Park, 1985 | — | 18 |
| Pop Life, 1985 | 7 | — |
| Kiss, 1986 | — | 6 |
| Mountains, 1986 | — | 45 |
| I Could Never Take The Place Of Your Man, 1987 | 10 | 29 |
| If I Was Your Girlfriend, 1987 | — | 20 |
| Sign The Times, 1987 | 6 | 10 |

*With Sheena Easton*
| U Got The Look, 1987 | 2 | 11 |

Sign Of The Times, Prince.
Courtesy Paisley Park Records.

Albums:
Prince (Warner Bros), 1980
Dirty Mind (Warner Bros), 1981 CD
Controversy (Warner Bros), 1982 CD
1999 (Warner Bros) (Double), 1983 CD
Purple Rain (Warner Bros), 1984 CD
Around The World In A Day (Warner Bros), 1985 CD
For You (Warner Bros), 1986 CD
Parade (Warner Bros), 1986 CD
Sign Of The Times (Paisley Park) (Double), 1987 CD
Lovesexy (Warner Bros), 1988 CD

# Procol Harum
UK group formed 1967.
**Original line-up:** Gary Brooker, vocals, piano; Ray Royer, guitar; Matthew Fisher, organ; David Knights bass; Bobby Harrison, drums.

**Career:** Brooker was singer with Southend R&B group the Paramounts, who worked club circuit between 1962-66 and had minor hit with re-working of Coasters'(▶) **Poison Ivy**. On break-up of group Brooker started collaboration with lyricist Keith Reid and recruited above line-up to record songs under name Procol Harum.
Under aegis of producer-entrepreneur Denny Cordell, band released **A Whiter Shade Of Pale** in summer 1967. This highly individualistic cut featuring surrealistic lyrics against cantata-like organ part struck chord with record buyers; **Pale** became enormous hit both sides of Atlantic.
Almost immediately line-up was re-shuffled; Royer and Harrison quit to form short-lived

Freedom, and were replaced by ex-Paramount Robin Trower(▶) on guitar and B. J. Wilson on drums. This line-up hit with **Homburg** and cut first three Procol albums.
In UK band was regarded as something of one-hit wonder, but US audiences took Procol to heart and American tours were successful. Meanwhile, Matthew Fisher quit band to pursue solo career, followed by David Knights. Bassist Chris Copping, another ex-Paramount, replaced latter and **Home** and **Broken Barricades** were made as quartet. Heavier rock direction was in evidence at this time.
Trower left in 1971, finding band too restricting for guitar heroics, and eventually formed highly successful Robin Trower(▶) Band. Copping switched to organ and in came bassist Alan Cartwright and guitarist Dave Ball. In November 1971 band went to Canada to gig with Edmonton Symphony Orchestra. Resulting live album was huge success, especially in US.
In 1973 Mick Grabham replaced Dave Ball, and line-up remained stable until 1976 when Cartwright left. Copping returned to bass and Pete Solley joined on organ.
Final albums suffered from lack of direction and provided only few gems compared to earlier output. Procol Harum eventually disbanded in 1977; Gary Brooker surfaced with solo album **Lead Me To The Water** in 1982.
Procol Harum always cut individualistic path through rock undergrowth, artistic stability being provided by Brooker's music and Reid's lyrics. Characteristic sound of organ and piano topped by Brooker's soul-influenced vocals are best in evidence on early albums. Band had considerable influence on development of self-consciously artistic strains of rock.

**Final line-up:** Brooker; Mick Grabham, guitar; Chris Copping, bass; Pete Solley, organ; B. J. Wilson, drums.

| Hit Singles: | US | UK |
|---|---|---|
| A Whiter Shade Of Pale, 1967 | 5 | 1 |
| Homburg, 1967 | 34 | 6 |
| A Whiter Shade Of Pale, 1972 | — | 13 |
| Conquistador, 1972 | 16 | 22 |
| Pandora's Box, 1975 | — | 16 |

Albums:
Procol Harum (A&M/Regal Zonophone), 1967†‡
A Salty Dog (A&M/Regal Zonophone), 1969† CD
Shine On Brightly (A&M/Regal Zonophone), 1969*
Home (A&M/Regal Zonophone), 1970*
Broken Baricades (A&M/Chrysalis), 1971
Live In Concert (A&M/Crysalis), 1972
Grand Hotel (Chrysalis), 1973
Exotic Birds And Fruit (Chrysalis), 1974
Ninth (Chrysalis), 1975
Platinum Collection (—/Cube), 1981
Procol Harum (Greatest Hits) (—/Impact), 1982
Collection (Collector) CD
*Gary Brooker Solo:*
Lead Me To The Water (Mercury), 1982
Echoes In The Night (Mercury), 1985

†Available as double set (—/Cube), 1975
‡Now known as **A Whiter Shade Of Pale**
*Available as double set (—/Cube), 1975

# Quarterflash
US group formed 1980.
**Original/current line-up:** Rindy Ross, vocals; Marv Ross, guitar; Jack Charles, vocals, guitar; Rich Gooch, bass; Rick DiGiallonardo, keyboards; Brian Willis, drums.

**Career:** Group formed by Mark and Rindy Ross, who had played music together since schooldays in Portland, Oregon, plus members

Left: **Quarterflash with their focal point, Rindy Ross (holding saxophone).**

of Pilot, another Portland band.
Signed by newly formed Geffen Records in early 1981; recorded eponymous debut LP, which reached US Top 10, as did single **Harden My Heart** which went platinum, topping charts in France, Italy, Australia and Japan. Three more singles charted in 1982 including theme from **Nightshift** movie. 1983 saw successful follow-up album **Take Another Picture** and Top Ten hit **Take Me To Heart** while Steve Levine was brought in to produce 1985's **Back Into The Blue** recorded at Studio Miraval in France.

| Hit Singles: | US | UK |
|---|---|---|
| Harden My Heart, 1981 | 3 | 49 |
| Find Another Fool, 1982 | 16 | |
| Take Me To Heart, 1983 | 14 | — |

Albums:
Quarterflash (Geffen), 1981 CD
Take Another Picture (Geffen), 1983
Back Into The Blue (Geffen), 1985

# Suzi Quatro
US vocalist, bass player, guitarist, actress. Born Detroit, June 3, 1950.

**Career:** Made debut at eight playing bongos in father Art Quatro's jazz band. Left school at 14 to appear on TV as go-go dancer Suzi Soul. Formed all-girl group Suzi and the Pleasure Seekers at 15 with sisters Patti, Nancy and

Greatest Hits, Suzi Quatro.
Courtesy RAK Records.

Arlene. They played all over US and even visited Vietnam for tour of US bases.
Changing name to Cradle, they performed at Detroit dance hall and were seen by British producer Mickie Most (in town to record Jeff Beck Group at Motown studios). Suzi's aggressive stage presence—despite her diminutive size—struck Most as star quality. He expressed interest in bringing her to Britain to sign for his Rak label.
Suzi toured UK working as support act. Most encouraged her songwriting and, after 1972 debut single **Rolling Stone** flopped, decided to call on services of then amazingly successful British songwriters Nicky Chinn and Mike Chapman.
Encased in black leather jump suit, blatantly sensual legs astride her bass guitar, she thumped away aggressively. Her small figure fronted band of tough guys; this image as trend-setting raunchy female rock star provided perfect showcase for Chinn and Chapman's propulsively direct rockers like chart-toppers **Can The Can, 48 Crash** and **Devil Gate Drive**.
Put together at time of her 1972 tour as

Left: **Suzi Quatro (foreground) on stage with bass and all male backing band.**

support for Slade, Quatro's band comprised Len Tuckey, guitar; Dave Neal, drums; and keyboard player Alastair McKenzie (soon replaced by Mike Deacon from Vinegar Joe).

Efforts to break in America—had a hit single there with **All Shook Up** and toured widely—caused her to lose grip on UK charts. She has, however, remained major personality of rock scene thanks to wide TV exposure via chart shows, variety shows, panel games and appearances as actress, inititally through 'Happy Days' comedy series as character based on self, Leather Tuscadero, friend of The Fonz and, more recently, as Annie Oakley in stage production of 'Annie Get Your Gun'.

Combines hectic work/domestic schedule with husband and guitarist Len Tuckey, with whom she has two children

Guitar Fender Precision bass

| Hit Singles: | US | UK |
|---|---|---|
| Can The Can, 1973 | 56 | 1 |
| 48 Crash, 1973 | | 3 |
| Daytona Demon, 1973 | | 14 |
| Devil Gate Drive, 1974 | | 1 |
| Too Big, 1974 | | 14 |
| The Wild One, 1974 | | 7 |
| If You Can't Give Me Love, 1978 | | 4 |
| She's In Love With You, 1979 | | 11 |

**Albums**
Suzi Quatro (Bell/Rak), 1973
Aggro-phobia (—/Rak), 1977
If You Knew Suzie (—/Rak), 1978
Greatest Hits (—/Rak), 1980
Main Attraction (—/Polydor), 1982

# Queen

UK group formed 1972.

**Original/Current line-up:** Brian May, self-made 'May Axe' guitar; Roger Meadows Taylor, drums; Freddie Mercury, vocals; John Deacon, bass.

**Career:** Evolved from college group Smile, featuring Brian May, Tim Staffell and Roger Meadows Taylor. Smile lasted long enough for series of gigs and one single, **Earth/Step On Me**, released only in US on Mercury. When group folded, Staffell persuaded flatmate Freddie Mercury to join May and Taylor in new venture Several months later Deacon was added

Group underwent strenuous rehearsals, playing occasionally at Imperial College, while Mercury masterminded flamboyant satin and silk image. Lucrative contract with EMI was quickly followed by debut single **Keep Yourself Mine**, which flopped. A month prior to its release, Mercury had recorded cover of Beach Boys'(▶) **I Can Hear Music** under pseudonym Larry Lurex, another rare cut.

First album **Queen** revealed group negotiating clever balance between early '70s glam rock and late '60s Zeppelin style heavy metal. With EMI publicity campaign in full swing, group eventually hit charts in early 1974 with **Seven Seas Of Rhye**. By end of 1974 two further LPs were issued, **Queen II** and **Sheer Heart Attack**. Latter attracted critical commendation from certain section of rock press, who praised group for aggressive rock and ingenious arrangements, courtesy of producer Roy Thomas Baker. Success of fifth single **Killer Queen** placed Queen in enviable position of achieving following from both Top 20 fans *and* heavy-metal enthusiasts.

Most of 1975 spent preparing **A Night At The Opera**, one of the most extravagant and expensive albums of era. Pilot single **Bohemian Rhapsody** was ultimate kitsch epic, an elaborate production brilliantly highlighting group's harmonies/guitar work and Mercury's falsetto vocal. Single became Christmas chart-topper for nine weeks, the longest stay at top since Paul Anka's **Diana** in 1957. From that point on, Queen were established as one of UK's most popular and enduring groups.

Success of **Bohemian Rhapsody** encouraged group to pursue more elaborate and grandiloquent works in complete contrast to their heavy-metal-tinged first three albums. Determined not to be dismissed as '70s glam rock refugees, group have changed image/style frequently in recent years, particularly on singles **Another One Bites The Dust** (penned by Deacon) and rockabilly **Crazy Little Thing Called Love**. Queen have been frequently castigated for pretentiousness and absurd posturings, but their cleverness deserves respect and in Brian May they have one of rock's more stylish guitarists.

Group's single success in recent years has been enhanced by imaginative use of video, for which their act seems particularly suited. Much-publicised 'Queen's Greatest Flix' has proved consistent No. 1 in video charts over last few years. Group also involved themselves in celluloid rock, writing soundtrack for film 'Flash Gordon' with lyrical/musical contributions from all four members.

International appeal of Queen has increased since late '70s, following gruelling tours of South America and the Far East, often visiting cities not normally associated with rock concerts. Their 75-ton gear and 30-strong road crew continue to provide one of rock's most expensive and spectacular live shows— their 1981 São Paulo, Brazil concert drew 131,000, the largest paying audience ever for one group.

**A Kind of Magic, Queen.
Courtesy Elektra/EMI Records.**

Band show no sign of faltering, despite numerous solo activities of members. Mercury in particular has enjoyed chart action, most recently with enjoyable pastiche of Platters' classic **The Great Pretender**.

| Hit Singles: | US | UK |
|---|---|---|
| Seven Seas Of Rhye, 1974 | — | 10 |
| Killer Queen, 1974 | 12 | 2 |
| Now I'm Here, 1975 | — | 11 |
| Bohemian Rhapsody, 1975 | 9 | 1 |
| You're My Best Friend, 1976 | 16 | 7 |
| Somebody To Love, 1976 | 13 | 2 |
| Queen's First EP, 1977 | — | 17 |
| We Are The Champions, 1977 | 18 | 2 |
| Bicycle Race/Fat Bottomed Girls, 1978 | — | 11 |
| Don't Stop Me Now, 1979 | — | 9 |
| Crazy Little Thing Called Love, 1979 | — | 2 |
| Save Me, 1980 | — | 11 |
| Play The Game, 1980 | — | 14 |
| Another One Bites The Dust, 1980 | 1 | 7 |
| Flash, 1980 | — | 10 |
| Las Palabras de Amor, 1982 | — | 17 |
| Body Language, 1982 | 11 | 25 |
| Radio Ga-Ga, 1984 | 16 | 2 |
| I Want To Break Free, 1984 | — | 3 |
| It's A Hard Life, 1984 | — | 6 |
| Hammer To Fall, 1985 | — | 13 |
| One Vision, 1985 | — | 7 |
| Who Wants To Live Forever, 1986 | — | 24 |
| Friends Will Be Friends, 1986 | — | 14 |
| A Kind Of Magic, 1986 | — | 3 |
| *With David Bowie:* | | |
| Under Pressure, 1981 | 29 | 1 |
| *Freddie Mercury Solo:* | | |
| Love Kills, 1984 | — | 10 |
| I Was Born To Love You, 1985 | — | 11 |
| Great Pretender, 1987 | — | 4 |
| *Freddie Mercury and Montserrat Caballe:* | | |
| Barcelona, 1987 | — | 8 |

**Albums:**
Queen (Elektra/EMI), 1973 **CD**
Queen II (Elektra/EMI), 1974 **CD**
Sheer Heart Attack (Elektra/EMI), 1974 **CD**
A Night At The Opera (Elektra/EMI), 1975 **CD**
A Day At The Races (Elektra/EMI), 1976 **CD**
News Of The World (Elektra/EMI), 1977 **CD**
Jazz (Elektra/EMI), 1978 **CD**

**Left: Queen (from left) Brian May, Freddy Mercury, John Deacon and Roger Taylor.**

Live Killers (Elektra/EMI), 1979 **CD**
The Game (Elektra/EMI), 1980 **CD**
Flash Gordon (Soundtrack) (Elektra/EMI), 1980 **CD**
Greatest Hits (Elektra/EMI), 1981 **CD**
Hot Space (Elektra/EMI), 1982 **CD**
The Works (Elektra/EMI), 1984 **CD**

*Freddie Mercury Solo:*
Mr Bad Guy (CBS), 1985 **CD**

*Brian May Solo:*
Star Fleet Project (EMI), 1983

# Quicksilver Messenger Service

US group formed 1965.

**Original line-up:** David Freiberg, bass; John Cipollina, guitar; Jim Murray, vocals; Casey Sonoban, drums; Alexander 'Skip' Spence, guitar, vocals.

**Career:** Individual members were either folksingers or refugees from prototype San Franciscan groups. Dino Valente was poised to join original line-up but was arrested and jailed on drug charges. By mid-1965, Sonoban and Spence had left, replaced by Gary Duncan (guitar/vocal) and Greg Elmore (drums). Establishing sizeable reputation following free concert appearances, group were wooed by record company A&R men. Resisted signing contract until Capitol coughed up large advance. Initially heard singing two songs on soundtrack of movie 'Revolution'. By October 1967 Murray had quit (later to re-emerge in Copperhead) and group continued as quartet.

Debut **Quicksilver Messenger Service** (May 1968) was seminal San Franciscan rock album, ably demonstrating complementary guitar work of Cipollina and Duncan. Follow-up **Happy Trails** (March 1969) was even better and is generally acknowledged as quintessential San Franciscan acid-rock album. The 25-minute re-working of Bo Diddley's(▶) R&B chestnut **Who Do You Love** remains finest recorded moment.

By January 1968, newly released Valente enticed Duncan away to join the Outlaws(▶), a group that never emerged. Meanwhile, British session-pianist Nicky Hopkins was drafted for less impressive **Shady Grove**. (Band had shortened name to simply 'Quicksilver' by this time.) Following New Year's Eve gig, Valente and Duncan returned, completed Stateside tour and recorded **Just For Love** as six-piece. With Valente assuming dominant role, Hopkins quit (replaced by Mark Naftalin) and group entered period of disillusionment. Cipollina then quit, along with manager Ron Polte, and next album **What About Me** was completed by session musicians.

While recording sixth album, Freiberg was convicted on marijuana charge and imprisoned for two months in July 1971. Following release, reverted to session work before joining Jefferson Starship(▶); replacement was Mark Ryan. During interim Naftalin also left; Chuck Steaks brought in on organ. Succeeding albums **Quicksilver** and **Comin' Thru** displayed little sign of artistic renaissance. A long period of inactivity only brought further line-up changes, involving John Nicolas (bass), Harold Acevas (drums), Bob Hogan (keyboards), Bob Fluria (bass) and Skip Olsen (bass).

Like many San Franciscan groups, Quicksilver's original energy and spark were dissipated amid succession of line-up changes as members sought vainly to recapture old

spirit. By mid-'70s even the most die-hard enthusiasts were left with feeling that Quicksilver should have split after 1969 peak.

Attempting to rekindle past glories, a re-formed Quicksilver with Duncan, Cipollina, Freiberg, Elmore and Valente cut **Solid Silver**, a bitter disappointment. Failure of this grand design prompted final dissolution, though occasionally news filters through of Quicksilver re-formations. Valente and Duncan apparently teamed up with Rick Wetzel and Chris Myers in preparation for September 1977 Breman Festival, but failed to appear.

**Final line-up:** Freiberg; Cipollina; Gary Duncan, guitar; Greg Elmore, drums; Dino Valente, vocals.

**Albums:**
Quicksilver Messenger Service (Capitol), 1968
Happy Trails (Capitol), 1969
Shady Grove (Capitol), 1969
Just For Love (Capitol), 1970
What About Me (Capitol), 1971
Quicksilver (Capitol), 1971
Anthology (Capitol), 1973
Solid Silver (Capitol), 1975
Maiden Of The Cancer Moon (Pycho), 1983
1st LP (Edsel) **CD**

# Gerry Rafferty

UK vocalist, composer, guitarist.
Born Paisley, Scotland, April 16, 1947.

**Career:** Original member of Scottish folk trio Humblebums (with Billy Connolly and Tam Harvey), cutting two albums for ethnic UK label Transatlantic.

Debut solo album **Can I Have My Money Back**, released 1971, featured Joe Egan and Rab Noakes (guitars), and Roger Brown (bass), founding members of Stealers Wheel (with bassist Ian Campbell). Unit quickly disbanded. Rafferty and Egan then recruited Paul Pilnick, guitar, Tony Williams, bass, and Rod Coombes, drums, to supply additional instrumentation for 1973 **Stealers Wheel** album.

LP included **Stuck In The Middle**, a US/UK Top 10 single, and excellent example of legendary producers Leiber/Stoller's(▶) ear for a hit. Still under aegis of Leiber/Stoller, band recorded **Ferguslie Park** (1974) and then **Right Or Wrong** (1975), a Mentor Williams production which marked end of Rafferty/Egan partnersnip.

Shackled by legal problems resulting from **Stealers Wheel**, Rafferty did not re-surface until 1977, when **City To City** album was released. His melodic, easy-going approach is best demonstrated by **Baker Street**, the million-selling single culled from LP, featuring explosive tenor sax solo by Raphael Ravenscroft.

Sporadic album releases and reluctance to tour have made introverted Rafferty an enigmatic character, but a talent worth persevering with. Joe Egan's solo career has been less satisfactory, despite two acceptable albums for Ariola.

| Hit Singles: | US | UK |
|---|---|---|
| Baker Street, 1978 | 2 | 3 |
| Right Down The Line, 1978 | 12 | — |
| Days Gone Down, 1979 | 17 | — |
| Night Owl, 1979 | — | 5 |

*With Stealers Wheel:*

| | | |
|---|---|---|
| Stuck In The Middle, 1973 | 6 | 8 |

**Albums:**
Can I Have My Money Back (Blue Thumb/Transatlantic), 1971

Gerry Rafferty Revisited ( —/Transatlantic), 1974
Gerry Rafferty (Visa/Logo), 1978
City To City (Liberty/United Artists), 1978 **CD**
Night Owl (Liberty/United Artists), 1979
Snakes And Ladders (Liberty/United Artists), 1980 **CD**
Sleepwalkin (Liberty), 1982 **CD**
Early Collection (Transaltantic) **CD**

# Rainbow

UK group formed 1975.

**Original line-up:** Ritchie Blackmore, Fender Stratocaster guitar; Ronnie James Dio, vocals; Mickey Lee Soule, keyboards; Craig Gruber, bass; Gary Driscoll, drums.

**Career:** Virtuoso guitarist Blackmore was founder-member of Deep Purple(▶), but left amid much speculation in 1975. Joined forces with New York band Elf to form first version of Rainbow. Eponymous album released 1975.

Summer of 1976 saw first of succession of personnel changes. Blackmore sacked entire band except Dio, and brought in Jimmy Bain on bass, Tony Carey on keyboards and Cozy Powell on drums. Line-up released **Rainbow Rising**, including tracks with Munich Philharmonic Orchestra. For **Long Live Rock 'n' Roll** LP, group added bassist Bob Daisley and keyboards man was David Stone.

The next album heralded reunion with former Purple bassist Roger Glover, while Don Airey replacing Stone and former half of Marbles hit-making duo Graham Bonnet taking over on vocals. This line-up was the most successful so far, scoring two major hit singles. These showed Rainbow to be masters of pop-metal sub-genre, able to combine heavy rock power with commercial melody lines. By now (1980) band had also become top-line live attraction, headlining that summer's hugely successful Castle Donington Festival.

However, further personnel changes were in store. Powell and Bonnet left to pursue solo careers and were replaced by Bob Rondinelli on drums and Joe Lynn Turner on vocals. Run of success continued with album **Difficult To Cure** and hit singles **I Surrender** and **Can't Happen Here**.

Record success continued throughout 1982, with **Straight Between The Eyes** making US album charts. After American tour in same year, Roninelli quit, being replaced by Chuck Burgi.

UK tour in 1983 preceded rumblings of

Gerry Rafferty Revisited

**Above: One of the numerous Rainbow line-ups led by Ritchie Blackmore (second from right).**

group's demise. This was confirmed with re-formation of Deep Purple(▶), with Blackmore as instigator.

**Final line-up:** Blackmore; Roger Glover, bass; Chuck Burgi, drums; Dave Rosenthal, keyboards; Joe Lynn Turner, vocals.

| Hit Singles: | US | UK |
|---|---|---|
| Since You've Been Gone, 1979 | 57 | 6 |
| All Night Long, 1980 | — | 5 |
| I Surrender, 1981 | — | 3 |
| Can't Happen Here, 1981 | — | 20 |

**Albums:**
Ritchie Blackmore's Rainbow (Polydor), 1975 **CD**
Rainbow Rising (Polydor), 1976 **CD**
On Stage (Polydor), 1977 **CD**
Long Live Rock 'n' Roll (Polydor), 1978
Down To Earth (Polydor), 1979 **CD**
Difficult To Cure (Polydor), 1981 **CD**
Jealous Lover (Polydor/—), 1981 **CD**
The Best Of (Polydor), 1981 **CD**
Straight Between The Eyes (Polydor), 1982 **CD**
Bent Out Of Shape (Polydor), 1983 **CD**
Finyl Vinyl (Polydor), 1986 **CD**

# Bonnie Raitt

US guitarist, vocalist, composer.
Born Los Angeles, California, November 8, 1949.

**Career:** Grew up in musical family in LA, moved to Cambridge, Boston, area in 1967. Raitt selected Dick Waterman as manager because of his association with various blues artists, her childhood heroes.

1971 debut LP set pattern of using wide variety of material and musicians for each recording. Subsequent LPs showed maturity, understanding and warmth in Raitt's reading of good contemporary material. Notable examples are: Jackson Browne's(▶) **Under The Falling Sky** and Eric Kaz's **Love Has No Pride** from second LP; Allen Toussaints'(▶) **What Is Success** on **Streetlights** LP; and Hayes-Porter's (▶) **Your Good Thing** from **Glow** album.

Raitt's performances and regular touring finally earned US success with **Sweet Forgiveness** album (1977). **The Glow** was carefully prepared as follow-up and included more original material than previous LPs. It failed to push Raitt towards bigger audience, which may be just as well since some artists have special flair for creating excitement in smaller, more intimate atmosphere. Raitt is a master who is true descendant of her blues heroes.

**Albums:**
Bonnie Raitt (Warner Bros), 1971
Give It Up (Warner Bros), 1972
Takin' My Time (Warner Bros), 1973
Streetlights (Warner Bros), 1974
Home Plate (Warner Bros), 1975
Sweet Forgiveness (Warner Bros), 1977
The Glow (Warner Bros), 1979
Green Light (Warner Bros), 1982
Nine Lives (Warner Bros), 1986

# Ramones
US group formed 1974
**Original line-up:** Joey Ramone (Jeffrey Hyman), drums; Dee Dee Ramone (Douglas Coldin), bass; Johnny Ramone (John Cummings), guitar

**Career:** Began as a trio, first appearing at New York's Performance Studio in March 1974. Four months later, manager Tommy Ramone (Tommy Erdelyi) became drummer with Joey switching to lead vocals (original and later members all changed from real names to 'Ramone'). Residency at CBGBs (new wave club in NY's Bowery) in summer allowed group to develop stage act, but on first attempt to spread wings—opening Johnny Winter(▶) concert—were booed from stage. Danny Fields took over management in late 1975, having already worked with MC5(▶), the Stooges and Lou Reed(▶)

Record deal with Sire led to recording of debut **Ramones**, released in April 1976. Album served as catalyst by encouraging other companies to sign many of New York's up-and-coming young acts. Prototype new wave rockers, group received rapturous welcome in UK in summer of '76, heavily influencing emerging punk movement with their distinctive dress (leather jackets and torn jeans) and high-speed minimalist rock (17 song sets played in half an hour!).

Next two albums, **Leave Home** and **Rocket To Russia**, established familiar pattern of high-powered rock based on late '50s/early '60s themes. Singles were uniformly impressive, but neither **Sheena Is A Punk Rocker** nor **Swallow My Pride** cracked Top 20. Having championed pinheads, cretins and glue sniffing during 1977, group were swiftly becoming redundant following first flowering of punk. In May 1978, Tommy departed to become producer, playing memorable farewell gig at CBGBs. New drummer Marc Bell (Marty Ramone) debuted on 1978's **Road To Ruin** and LP proved most commercially successful to date, though met mixed response from critics, disturbed by mid-tempo material. Following in England was underlined by release of double **It's Alive** from Rainbow gigs of 1979.

Very much the spirit of CBGBs, Ramones have modified original formula to a minimal degree over the years, though union with producer Phil Spector resulted in less raucous material in **End Of The Century**. Group only finally broke into UK charts late in 1980 with uncharacteristic but memorable violin-steeped cover of Ronettes' 1964 hit, **Baby I Love You**, a complete contrast to earlier headbanging material. 1980 also saw release of first feature film 'Rock 'n' Roll High School', the title of a track from **End Of The Century**.

Often dismissed as unintelligent and

ephemeral, Ramones have survived '70s intact. 1981 album, **Pleasant Dreams**, a return to basics with 12 self-penned songs, showed group's astuteness in employing professional hitmaker Graham Gouldman (Mindbenders, 10 cc) as producer. 1983 album, **Subterranean Jungle**, received strong support from critics, several of whom compared it favourably with the best of group's early work. Since recording the album, drummer Bell has been replaced by ex-Velveteen Richard Beau (now Ricky Ramone). By mid '80s Joey Ramone had found additional career producing various acts.

**Current line-up:** Joey; Dee Dee; Johnny; Ricky Ramone, drums.

| **Hit Single:** | US | UK |
|---|---|---|
| Baby I Love You, 1980 | — | 8 |

**Albums:**
Leave Home (Sire), 1977
Rocket To Russia (Sire), 1977
Road To Ruin (Sire), 1978
It's Alive (—/Sire), 1979
End Of The Century (Sire), 1980
Pleasant Dreams (Sire), 1981
Subterranean Jungle (Sire), 1983
Too Tough To Die (Beggar's Banquet), 1985
Animal Boy (Beggar's Banquet), 1986

*Worth Searching Out:*
Ramones (Sire), 1976

# Johnnie Ray
US vocalist, pianist, actor.
Born John Alvin Ray, Dallas, Oregon, January 10, 1927.

**Career:** First professional appearance at age 15 with Jane Powell on Portland, Oregon, radio talent show. Moved south to California in 1949 and for next two years worked night clubs and bars in Hollywood. Moved to Detroit in 1951; discovered by DJ Robin Seymour who obtained record deal with Columbia Records. Following success of double-sided hit **Cry/The Little White Cloud That Cried**, many presumed singer was black as single was released on Columbia's R&B subsidiary Okeh.

Ray's vocal histrionics earned him nickname 'The Prince of Wails', and he rapidly became one of the most popular artists of early '50s. Inspired a fanatical, sometimes hysterical, fan following; near-riots resulted when he toured Britain just prior to the rock 'n' roll explosion.

First film with Ethel Merman, 'There's No Business Like Show Business', led to further film roles and major US theatre productions. Record sales waned in US but hits continued into rock 'n' roll era in UK, with **Yes Tonight Josephine** almost making permanent transition.

Since age 15 has worn hearing aid and has devoted much time to raising funds in aid of deaf children. In recent years has toured while continuing charity work and occasionally recording.

| **Hit Singles:** | US | UK |
|---|---|---|
| Cry/The Little White Cloud That Cried, 1951 | * | * |
| Please Mr Sun/Here I Am Brokenhearted, 1952 | * | * |
| What's The Use, 1952 | * | * |
| Walking My Baby Back Home, 1952 | * | * |
| Faith Can Move Mountains, 1952 | * | * |
| Somebody Stole My Gal, 1953 | * | * |
| Such A Night, 1954 | * | * |
| If You Believe, 1955 | — | * |
| Paths Of Paradise, 1955 | — | 20 |
| Hey There, 1955 | — | 5 |

*Left: Johnnie Ray who has worn a hearing aid since 15, hands out presents at one of the schools for deaf children to which he gives financial aid.*

| | US | UK |
|---|---|---|
| Song Of The Dreamer, 1955 | — | 10 |
| Who's Sorry Now, 1956 | — | 17 |
| Ain't Misbehavin', 1956 | — | 17 |
| Just Walkin' In The Rain, 1956 | 2 | 1 |
| You Don't Owe Me A Thing/ Look Homeward Angel, 1957 | 10 | 12 |
| Look Homeward Angel/You Don't Owe Me A Thing, 1957 | 36 | 7 |
| Yes Tonight Josephine, 1957 | 12 | 1 |
| Build Your Love (On A Strong Foundation), 1957 | 58 | 18 |

**Albums:**
Best Of (—/Hallmark), 1968
Greatest Hits (Columbia/Embassy), 1977
An American Legend (—/Embassy), 1979
20 Golden Greats (—/MSD), 1979
Yesterday, Today And Tomorrow (RCA), 1981

# Chris Rea
UK vocalist, songwriter.
Born Middlesbrough, 1951.

**Career:** Sometimes cited as 'the English Springsteen', Rea has likeable, down-to-earth personality and knack for writing evocative songs.

Of half-Irish half-Italian decent, he entered music business after hearing a Joe Walsh record and in 1975 formed Magdelene which quickly changed name to Beautiful Losers and won Melody Maker 'Best New Band' award. David Coverdale, who later fronted Whitesnake, was also in group.

Signed to Magnet as solo in 1976, Rea wrote **Fool If You Think It's Over** for his sister. His recording charted both sides of Atlantic while Elkie Brooks' cover was also big UK hit.

Advent of punk made his style unfashionable but he came back strongly in 1983 with

**Below: Chris Rea, 'the English Springsteen', in 1982.**

I Can Hear Your Heartbeat hit and half-million selling Watersign album.

Having in 1979 partnered Pete Wingfield and Rod Argent on Deltics LP, he became involved with Rolling Stone(▶) Bill Wyman, working on Willie and the Poor Boys' project in mid-'80s.

Watersign in fact proved to be watershed, and further albums put Rea up into million-selling class. Success was clinched by Let's Dance single.

Unassuming artist who has always relied on well-crafted records and continuous touring to spread word, Rea offers high-class brand of AOR that seems likely to display good staying power.

| Hit Singles: | US | UK |
|---|---|---|
| Fool If You Think It's Over, 1978 | 12 | 30 |
| Lets Dance, 1987 | — | 12 |

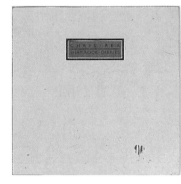

Shamrock Diaries, Chris Rea.
Courtesy Magnet Records.

Albums:
Whatever Happened To Benny Santini (Magnet), 1978 CD
Deltics (Magnet), 1979 CD
Tennis (Magnet), 1980 CD
Chris Rea (Magnet), 1982 CD
Watersign (Magnet), 1983 CD
Shamrock Diaries (Magnet), 1985 CD
Wired To The Moon (Magnet), 1985 CD
On The Beach (Magnet), 1986 CD
Dancing With Strangers (Magnet), 1987 CD

# Otis Redding

US vocalist, composer.
Born Macon, Georgia, September 9, 1941; died December 10, 1967.

Career: All-time soul great, Redding started musical career in time-honoured fashion, singing in local church choir and at gigs around his home town of Macon. Through school-friend Phil Walden (later to head up Capricorn Records), Redding was introduced to local band Johnny Jenkins and the Pinetoppers, and in 1959 joined them on the road as general assistant and occasional vocalist.

Redding recorded various sides over the next few years for several small labels, but did not taste success until 1962 when he cut These Arms Of Mine and Hey Hey Baby at the end of a Jenkins recording session at Stax Studios. Stax boss Jim Stewart was impressed by Redding's style and composing talent, releasing These Arms Of Mine in November 1962.

The single made impression on US charts, and paved way for succession of successful singles over next few years. Master of the soul ballad, Redding was particularly affecting on slow numbers like Pain In My Heart, That's How Strong My Love Is, the classic I've Been Loving You Too Long and the much-loved My Girl, but was capable of whipping up a storm of excitement on

uptempo material. Classic Redding stompers include Respect, I Can't Turn You Loose, Sam Cooke's(▶) Shake, Hard To Handle and Love Man.

Many soul albums feature one or two hits and a lot of mediocre padding, but Redding's albums were of consistently high standard. The definitive Redding album is Otis Blue, a superbly balanced set of ballads and uptempo material which includes a magisterial version of B. B. King's Rock Me Baby.

Otis Redding also excelled as live performer, and toured regularly between 1964 and 1967. He headed the 1965 Stax-Volt tour of Europe and made other trips to UK with own band, and during this period was probably appreciated more in Britain than in his native country. Never giving less than 100% of himself, Otis Redding was the performer for whom the term 'soul' might have been invented. Dancing, dropping to his knees, running on the spot, urging on members of his band, he radiated energy and emotional commitment.

In 1967 Redding's career looked set to achieve new levels of success. His appearance at Monterey Pop Festival, recorded on 1970 Reprise LP Monterey International Pop Festival: Otis Redding/The Jimi Hendrix Experience, on bill which featured heavy rock acts like Jimi Hendrix(▶) and the Who(▶), was hailed by critics and fans alike, European tour later the same year won him more friends, so much so that he was voted top international male singer by Melody Maker readers. But just as everything seemed to be coming together for the soul star, Redding was killed when his plane crashed into Lake Monona in Wisconsin in 1967. Several members of his band, the Bar-Kays, also perished.

As often happens, Redding's tragic death seemed to improve his marketability. Posthumous single Dock Of The Bay reached top of American charts and became a million-seller, and made No. 3 in Britain. It was easily his biggest hit.

One of the most important and best-loved of the '60s soul heroes, Redding had an

inimitable vocal style and ability to get to the heart of a song, particularly ballads. Scorned during the psychedelic and 'heavy rock' eras, he is now revered as one of the major influences of black music.

| Hit Singles: | US | UK |
|---|---|---|
| My Girl, 1965 | — | 11 |
| Tramp (with Carla Thomas), 1967 | — | 18 |
| Dock Of The Bay, 1968 | 1 | 3 |
| Hard To Handle, 1968 | 51 | 15 |

Albums:
Otis Blue (Atco/Atlantic), 1966
Otis Redding Live In Europe (Volt/Atlantic), 1966
The Immortal Otis Redding (Atco/Atlantic), 1968
Love Man (Atco/Atlantic), 1969
History Of Otis Redding (Atco/Atlantic), 1969
History Of Otis Redding (Volt/Atlantic), 1970
Best Of (Atco/Atlantic), 1972 CD
Pure Otis (Atco/Atlantic), 1979
Recorded Live (Atlantic), 1982
The Dock Of The Bay — The Definitive Collection (Atlantic), 1987 CD

Worth Searching Out:
Pain In My Heart (Atco/Atlantic), 1965
Dictionary Of Soul (Volt/Atlantic), 1966
Sings Soul Ballads (Atco/Atlantic), 1970

# Lou Reed

US vocalist, guitarist, composer.
Born Long Island, New York, March 2, 1943.

Career: Born into rich middle-class family. Spent much of adolescence 'rebelling' in various punk/garage groups (Pasha and the Prophets, the Eldorados, the Shades and the Jades). Later attended Syracuse University; dropped out; dabbled in journalism, acting and music. Record companies refused songs because of their bizarre nature, so for time he wrote conventional love songs, but eventually organised new group with another disenchanted performer, John Cale/(▶). Velvet Underground(▶) achieved some measure of fame and notoriety, mainly in New York, but

albums were too controversial for mass consumption; group eventually folded in 1970, after which their influence was increasingly felt.

Reed drifted for a year, even taking up employment at father's accountancy firm in Long Island, before signing RCA contract in late 1971. Moved to Britain to work on solo debut with aid of New York writer Richard Robinson. Lou Reed was effective in parts, but spoiled by uninspired production.

Luck changed when David Bowie(▶) took interest in Reed's career. With Bowie in producer's chair, sessions were completed for Transformer; Reed was invited to appear at

Live and Loud, 1975. Courtesy RCA Records.

Royal Festival Hall alongside the androgenous one. Album received great publicity, sold well, and spawned memorable and controversial hit Walk On The Wild Side. The appearance of Reed in eye liner, singing deliberately risqué songs, yet minus the true menace of his Velvet Underground work, led to accusations of commercial sell-out. Reed was clearly parodying himself, and has continued to do so frequently over the years. Berlin was attempt to recapture power of Velvets' work, but in spite of some critical approbation, failed commercially. Nevertheless it remains Reed's most harrowing album in its analysis of sado/masochism and suicide.

Following Berlin sessions, Reed assembled touring group comprising Dick Wagner (guitar), Steve Hunter (guitar), Prakash John (bass) and Whitey Glan (drums). One of their better performances, at NY's Academy Of Music, released as Rock 'n' Roll Animal. Having partially restored credibility, Reed faltered with next work, Sally Can't Dance, his least inspired to this point. Another average effort followed before horrendous Metal Machine Music, a double album of 'electronic music', consisting almost entirely of tape hum. Rock's premier candidate for 'the worst album ever made', Metal Machine Music was ultimate example of artistic suicide.

Coney Island Baby was reasonable, yet hardly sufficient to repair damage done to career. Since then, Reed has had mixed fortunes, and Arista albums, including Street Hassle (co-produced by Richard Robinson), The Bells and Growing Up In Public, received merely lukewarm response from critics and public. In October 1981, recorded a new work with producer Sean Fuller at RCA's New York studios; The Blue Mask, released in 1982, proved surprise return to form.

Recent bizarre collaboration with Sam Moore (of sixties soul superstars Sam and Dave) exposed Reed's vocal limitations but pointed up his devil-may-care attitude.

| Hit Singles: | US | UK |
|---|---|---|
| Walk On The Wild Side, 1973 | 16 | 10 |

Albums:
Lou Reed (RCA), 1072

Below: One of the original members of the Velvet Underground, Lou Reed, in the 1970s.

Transformer (RCA), 1972 **CD**
Berlin (RCA), 1973 **CD**
Rock 'n' Roll Animal (RCA), 1973 **CD**
Sally Can't Dance (RCA), 1974 **CD**
Lou Reed Live (RCA), 1975 **CD**
Coney Island Baby (RCA), 1976 **CD**
Rock And Roll Heart (Arista), 1976
Walk On The Wild Side — The Best Of Lou Reed (RCA), 1977 **CD**
Street Hassle (Arista), 1978
Live — Take No Prisoners (Arista), 1978
The Bells (Arista), 1979
Growing Up In Public (Arista), 1980
Rock 'n' Roll Diary 1967-1980 (Arista). 1980 **CD**
The Blue Mask (RCA), 1982
Legendary Hearts (RCA), 1983
New Sensations (RCA), 1984 **CD**
Mistrial (RCA), 1986 **CD**

# REM

US band formed in 1981

**Original/current line-up:** Bill Berry, drums, backing vocals; Peter Buck, guitars; Mike Mills, bass, backing vocals, keyboards; Michael Stipe, vocals, words

**Career:** Band started in Macon, Georgia when Mike Mills and Bill Berry teamed up at High School. Together they moved to Athens to attend university and there met up with Peter Buck and Michael Stipe, fellow students.

The four formed REM, playing gigs in Athens performing covers of **Needles And Pins**, The Sex Pistols' **God Save The Queen** and **California Sun**. After dropping out of university made an independent single **Radio Free Europe/Sitting Still**, on the strength of which IRS signed the band and released the already-recorded EP **Chronic Town**.

**Reckoning** followed in 1984, and in 1985 the band arrived in London to record their third album **Fables Of The Reconstruction**, produced by Joe Boyd. The harder-edged **Life's Rich Pageant** followed.

REM's fifth album **Document**, recorded in Nashville and mixed in Los Angeles, released autumn 1987 coinciding with their sole UK gig at Hammersmith Odeon. Band co-produced with Scott Litt and LP achieved strong reviews

**Life's Rich Pageant, REM. Courtesy IRS Records.**

| Hit Singles: | US | UK |
|---|---|---|
| The One I Love, 1987 | 9 | — |

**Albums:**
Reckoning (IRS), 1984
Chronic Town (IRS), 1984
Fables Of Reconstruction (IRS), 1985 **CD**
Lifes Rich Pageant (IRS), 1986 **CD**
Dead Letter Office (IRS), 1987 **CD**
Document (IRS), 1987 **CD**

# REO Speedwagon

US group formed 1971.

**Original line-up:** Gary Richrath, Gibson Les Paul guitar, vocals; Neil Doughty, keyboards; Alan Gratzer, drums; Gregg Philbin, bass; Barry Luttnell, vocals.

**Career:** Formed in Champaign, Illinois, REO Speedwagon began years of local, then national, touring. Owing as much to Ted Nugent(▶) and Bob Seger(▶) as any English influence, REO played highly competent rock with no frills.

Stripped-down sound underwent various changes: Luttrell left after first album and Kevin Cronin brought more laid-back almost country feel when he took over vocals. (He was replaced by Michael Murphy in 1974-75 before returning to resume lead vocals.)

**You Get What You Play For** was live recording and attempted to translate energy of live REO onto vinyl. Widespread success

continued to elude band until self-produced **Nine Lives** LP. With new bass player Bruce Hall, REO consolidated its growing popularity through another live album **A Decade Of Rock And Roll 1970-1980**.

Nothing suggested REO would ever produce massive hit, but **Hi Infidelity** roared to top of US charts and became REO's ticket to headlining large concerts. Unexpected success took REO by surprise and band spent over two years following up with next release. It could hardly match its predecessor and **Good Trouble** attracted criticism that REO was Frampton-like one-LP wonder.

Like Foghat, Journey(▶) and Styx(▶), REO suffers from faceless, 'corporate' band image. No individual stands out to grasp fans' attention although Richrath is a fine guitarist. When long years of hard work earned 'overnight success', band was in quandary on how to follow up. Playing hard rock on stage, but owing chart success to ballad-like singles, REO's problem is pleasing two audiences.

**Current line-up:** Richrath; Doughty; Gratzer; Kevin Cronin, vocals; Bruce Hall, bass.

| Hit Singles: | US | UK |
|---|---|---|
| Keep On Lovin' You, 1981 | 1 | 7 |
| Take It On The Run, 1981 | 5 | 19 |
| Keep The Fire Burnin', 1982 | 7 | — |
| Can't Fight This Feeling, 1985 | 1 | 16 |
| One Lonely Night, 1985 | 19 | — |
| That Ain't Love, 1987 | — | 15 |
| In My Dreams, 1987 | — | 19 |

**Albums:**
REO Speedwagon (Epic), 1971
R.E.O. T.W.O. (Epic), 1972
Ridin' The Storm Out (Epic), 1973
Lost In A Dream (Epic), 1974
This Time We Mean It (Epic), 1975
REO (Epic), 1976
You Get What You Play For (Epic), 1977*
You Can Tune A Piano But You Can't Tuna Fish (Epic), 1978
Nine Lives (Epic), 1979
A Decade Of Rock 'n' Roll 1970-1980 (Epic), 1980*
Hi Infidelity (Epic), 1980

**Below: REM (from left) Mike Mills, Bill Berry, Michael Stipe and Peter Buck.**

Good Trouble (Epic), 1982
Speedwagon (Epic), 1984
Wheels Are Turnin (Epic), 1984 **CD**
Best Foot Forward (Epic), 1985,
*Live
Life As We Know It (CBS), 1987 **CD**
REO Grande (Epic) **CD**

**The debut album. Courtesy Epic Records.**

# Cliff Richard

UK vocalist, guitarist, composer.
Born Harry Rodger Webb, Lucknow, India, October 14, 1940.

**Career:** Spent childhood in colonial India where English father worked for catering company; returned to UK in 1948. Following early racial problems due to sunburnt skin, soon became integrated into post-war British life, discovering rock 'n' roll via Bill Haley(▶) and especially Elvis Presley(▶); played in local skiffle groups. Formed the Drifters in 1958, which included Terry Smart (drums), Norman Mitham (guitar) and Richard himself (guitar, vocals). Mitham then replaced by Ian Samwell. After impressing agent with neo-Presley style, signed to EMI's Columbia label in August 1958. First single **Move It**, written by Samwell, recorded with session musicians, is now regarded as first British rock 'n' roll record.

Booked to appear on national tour, recruited new band — Smart, Samwell (bass), plus guitarists Hank B. Marvin (real name Brian Marvin) and Bruce Welch, both from Newcastle. After tour, Smart and Samwell were replaced by Jet Harris (bass) and Tony Meehan (drums) — entire band (including Cliff) was spawned by early London rock 'n' roll coffee bar, the '2Is'. Cliff and the Drifters became original British rock superstars, with ten Top 10 singles; by end of 1960, Drifters (changing name to Shadows to avoid confusion with black US vocal group) were chart-topping act in own right.

Cliff and Shadows appeared in several very popular films during '60s, including 'Expresso Bongo', 'The Young Ones', 'Summer Holiday', 'Wonderful Life' and 'Finder's Keepers'. By mid-1962 Harris and Meehan had left group for short-lived solo success, replaced by Brian Bennett (drums) and first Brian Locking, later John Rostill (bass). Hits continued in UK: 43 for Cliff, including eight No. 1's, plus 24 for Shadows, including five No. 1's, by 1968. Still very little US success. By end of '60s, Shadows had disbanded, but Cliff's success continued; his early rock 'n' roll was toned down to become 'family entertainment' and withstood Merseybeat/R&B crazes of early and mid-'60s. However, conversion to Christianity in '66 blunted his pop sensibility.

Continued (sometimes with re-formed Shadows, including Marvin, Welch and Bennett) as prime cabaret attraction with own TV series, but seemed generally out of touch with youth during progressive rock years,

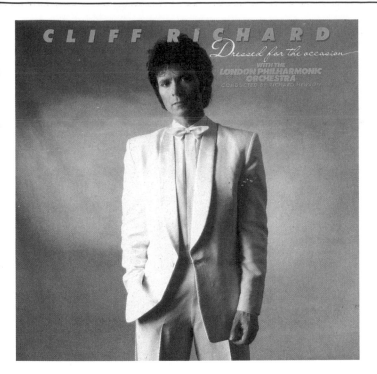

**Dressed for the Occasion, 1983 LP by Cliff. Courtesy EMI Records**

although twice representing UK in Eurovision Song Contest. Rostill died in November 1973 from accidental electrocution. John Farrar, member of an Australian group based on Shadows, joined Marvin, Welch and Farrar group in 1970 and cut two albums. Farrar joined Shadows in 1972.

Cliff appeared close to retirement by mid-'70s; returned with strong material and arrangements **Miss You Nights** and **Devil Woman** in 1976; latter was first US Top 10 hit. 1977 compilation LP **40 Golden Greats** was a huge seller which topped UK charts. Rest of '70s continued with 20th Anniversary celebrations by Cliff and Shadows, with end of decade providing Cliff's tenth No. 1 single, **We Don't Talk Anymore** (first chart topper since 1968), and growing US following.

In 1980 Richard was awarded OBE by Queen Elizabeth II. Charted with duet **Suddenly** from film 'Xanadu', with Olivia Newton-John(▶), whom he had helped to fame via his early '70s TV series. In 1983, Cliff celebrated 25 years as a rock star, having scored over 80 British hit singles, including ten No. 1's, plus numerous big-selling LPs. His appeal as clean, well-spoken boy next door seems undiminished by passage of time, and his fans range from eight to 80.

1986 has proved to be highly successful thus far with a comic collaboration with TV's The Young Ones taking **Living Doll** to No. 1 in UK, and a starring role in Dave Clark's West End musical 'Time'.

His appeal continues undiminished, with starring role in Dave Clark's hit musical Time and almost permanent residence in UK singles charts. Dorian Gray-like youthful appearance possibly demonstrates benefits of Christian lifestyle as opposed to usual rock'n'roll debauchery.

| Hit Singles: | US | UK |
|---|---|---|
| Move It, 1958* | — | 2 |
| High Class Baby, 1958* | — | 7 |
| Livin' Lovin' Doll, 1959* | — | 20 |
| Mean Streak/Never Mind, 1959* | — | 10 |
| Living Doll, 1959* | 30 | 1 |
| Travellin' Light, 1959† | — | 1 |
| Dynamite, 1959† | — | 16 |
| Expresso Bongo (EP), 1960† | — | 14 |
| A Voice In The Wilderness, 1960† | — | 2 |
| Fall In Love With You, 1960† | — | 2 |
| Please Don't Tease, 1960† | — | 1 |
| Nine Times Out Of Ten, 1960† | — | 3 |
| I Love You, 1960† | — | 1 |
| Theme For A Dream, 1961† | — | 3 |
| Gee Whiz It's You, 1961† | — | 4 |
| A Girl Like You, 1961† | — | 3 |
| When The girl In Your Arms Is The Girl In Your Heart, 1961 | — | 3 |
| The Young Ones, 1962† | — | 1 |
| I'm Looking Out The Window/ Do You Wanna Dance, 1962 | — | 2 |
| It'll Be Me, 1962† | — | 2 |
| The Next Time/Bachelor Boy, 1962† | — | 1 |
| Summer Holiday, 1963† | — | 1 |
| Lucky Lips, 1963† | — | 4 |
| It's All In The Game, 1963 | 25 | 2 |
| Don't Talk To Him, 1963† | — | 2 |
| I'm The Lonely One, 1964† | — | 8 |
| Constantly, 1964 | — | 4 |
| On The Beach, 1964† | — | 7 |
| The Twelfth Of Never, 1964 | — | 8 |
| I Could Easily Fall, 1964† | — | 9 |
| The Minute You're Gone, 1965 | — | 1 |
| On My Word, 1965 | — | 12 |
| Wind Me Up (Let Me Go), 1965 | — | 2 |
| Blue Turns To Grey, 1966† | — | 15 |
| Visions, 1966 | — | 7 |
| Time Drags By, 1966† | — | 10 |
| In The Country, 1966† | — | 6 |
| It's All Over, 1967 | — | 9 |
| The Day I Met Marie, 1967 | — | 10 |
| All My Love, 1967 | — | 6 |
| Congratulations, 1968 | — | 1 |
| Good Times (Better Times), 1969 | — | 12 |
| Big Ship, 1969 | — | 8 |
| Throw Down A Line, 1969** | — | 7 |
| With The Eyes Of A Child, 1969 | — | 20 |
| Goodbye Sam, Hello Samantha, 1970 | — | 6 |
| Sunny Honey Girl, 1971 | — | 19 |
| Sing A Song Of Freedom, 1971 | — | 13 |
| Living In Harmony, 1972 | — | 12 |
| Power To All Our Friends, 1973 | — | 14 |
| (You Keep Me) Hangin' On, 1974 | — | 13 |
| Miss You Nights, 1976 | — | 15 |
| Devil Woman, 1976 | 6 | 9 |
| I Can't Ask For Anything More Than You Babe, 1976 | — | 17 |
| My Kinda Life, 1977 | — | 15 |
| We Don't Talk Anymore, 1979 | 7 | 1 |
| Carrie, 1980 | 34 | 4 |
| Dreamin', 1980 | 7 | 8 |
| A Little In Love, 1981 | 11 | 15 |
| Wired For Sound, 1981 | — | 4 |
| Daddy's Home, 1981 | 23 | 2 |
| The Only Way Out, 1982 | — | 10 |
| Little Town, 1982 | — | 11 |
| True Love Ways, 1983 | — | 8 |
| Never Say Die, 1983 | — | 15 |
| Please Don't Fall In Love, 1983 | — | 7 |
| She's So Beautiful, 1985 | — | 17 |
| Living Doll (with the Young Ones), 1986 | — | 1 |

*With Olivia Newton-John*
| Suddenly, 1980 | 20 | 15 |

*With Phil Everly:*
| She Means Nothing To Me, 1983 | — | 9 |

*Single With Sarah Brightman:*
| All I Ask Of You, 1986 | | 3 |

| Some People, 1987 | — | 3 |
| My Pretty One | — | 6 |

*with Shadows (As Drifters)
†with Shadows
**with Hank Marvin

**Albums (selected):**
The Young Ones (—/Columbia), 1961
Summer Holiday (Epic/Columbia), 1963
I'm Nearly Famous (Rocket/EMI), 1976
40 Golden Greats (—/EMI), 1977
Rock 'n' Roll Juvenile (—/EMI), 1979
Wired For Sound (EMI America/EMI), 1981 **CD**
Dressed For The Occasion (—/EMI), 1983
Silver (EMI), 1983 **CD**
Now You See Me Now You Don't (EMI), 1985 **CD**
Walking In The Light (Myrrh), 1985
Always Guaranteed (EMI), 1987 **CD**
Best Of (Maybelline), 1987 **CD**
Cliff (EMI), 1987 **CD**

**Always Guaranteed, Cliff Richard. Courtesy EMI Records.**

# Lionel Richie
US vocalist, composer, producer
Born June 20, 1949.

**Career:** Former economics major at Alabama's Tuskegee Institute who had considered career as Episcopal priest, Richie was founder member, saxophonist and subsequent lead singer of Commodores(▶). Developed writing/

**Below: Cliff with three-quarters of the Shads circa 1960?**

production talents while with band, penning and producing **Lady** for Kenny Rogers(▶), cut **Endless Love** duet with Diana Ross(▶) from Franco Zeffirelli film of same title - single stayed at top of US single charts for nine weeks.

In 1981 released first solo album **Lionel Richie**. Set included hit singles **Truly You Are** and **My Love**

Richie combined soul music background with a healthy regard for easy-listening country flavoured ballads to emerge as one of Motown's solo megastars. Such crossover appeal was rewarded with country music as well as black music awards

In 1983, cheerful calypso-flavoured sound of **All Night Long (All Night)** showed further dimension to Richie's talents and was that year's major dance-floor success, propelling subsequent album to number one on both sides of Atlantic

Hit single **Say You, Say Me** was taken from 'An Officer And A Gentleman' director Taylor Hackford's subsequent movie 'White Nights'.

**Can't Slow Down** LP became Motown's all-time best seller, logging more than 14 million sales worldwide, spawning no fewer than five Top 20 singles in UK where he has consistently commanded strong following.

His efforts for African famine relief with the Grammy award-winning **We Are The World** (co-written with Michael Jackson) showed a further dimension to an artist who is amongst a select handful of "bankable" music stars

**Above: Lionel Richie, who has enjoyed unbroken run in US/UK charts for Motown since leaving Commodores.**

**Dancing On The Ceiling, Lionel Richie. Courtesy Motown Records.**

| Hit Singles: | US | UK |
| --- | --- | --- |
| My Love, 1983 | 5 | |
| All Night Long, 1983 | 1 | 2 |
| Running With The Night, 1983 | 7 | 9 |
| Hello, 1984 | 1 | 1 |
| Stuck On You, 1984 | 3 | 12 |
| Penny Lover, 1984 | 8 | 18 |
| Say You, Say Me, 1985 | 1 | 8 |
| Ballerina Girl 1986 | 9 | 17 |
| Love Will Conquer All, 1987 | 9 | 45 |
| Dancing On The Ceiling, 1987 | 1 | |

**Albums:**
Lionel Richie (Motown), 1982 **CD**
Can't Slow Down (Motown), 1983 **CD**
Say You, Say Me (Motown), 1986
Dancing On The Ceiling (Motown) 1987 **CD**

# The Righteous Brothers

US vocal duo formed 1962
Bill Medley born Los Angeles September 19 1940
Bobby Hatfield born Wisconsin August 10 1940

**Career:** Bill Medley and Bobby Hatfield came together as blue-eyed soul duo in 1962. They

undertook club gigs around Southern California, and had small hit in 1963 with Medley-penned **Little Latin Lupe Lu** on Moonglow. Originally called 'The Paramounts', changed name because early black fans called their music 'righteous'.

Although increasingly popular on home ground, they didn't gain national prominence until noticed by TV producer Jack Good who gave them regular spot on pop show 'Shindig'. At this point Phil Spector stepped in. Already hot, with big hits by Crystals and Ronettes under his belt, Spector took the Brothers into the studio and worked with them for three solid weeks on one song. The result of this concentrated effort was **You've Lost That Loving Feeling**.

**Feeling** was released on Spector's own Philles label, and by January 1965 had reached No. 1 spot on both sides of Atlantic. The combination of Bill Medley's Ray Charles-influenced baritone, Bobby Hatfield's impassioned high tenor and Spector's inspired production provided pop masterpiece and perennial favourite. A slew of successful, if not quite so brilliant, singles followed.

The Brothers eventually parted company in 1968 after farewell concert in Los Angeles. Bill Medley pursued solo career, making series of undistinguished and not particularly successful albums. Bobby Hatfield recorded solo and also attempted to keep the Brothers act together with new partner, Billy Walker, but with little success

In 1974, however, Medley and Hatfield got together again and scored US Top 10 hit with **Rock 'n' Roll Heaven**, a novelty death disc, following it with **Give It To The People**. A couple of albums also ensued before they split again

Without doubt, their best testimony is early work, particularly of re-issued **You've Lost That Loving Feeling,** magnificent **Unchained Melody** and underrated **Ebb Tide.**

Rare among blue-eyed soul artists in that their delivery was 100% convincing, the Righteous Brothers offered unique, instantly recognisable sound with perfect harmonies and helped to assimilate 'soul' approach into mainstream of pop music.

A surprise postscript to the Brothers' career was provided by Bill Medley's re-emergence in 1987, duetting with Jennifer Warnes on hit movie cut **Time Of My Life**.

| Hit Singles: | US | UK |
| --- | --- | --- |
| You've Lost That Loving Feeling, 1965 | 1 | 1 |
| Just Once In My Life, 1965 | 9 | — |
| Unchained Melody, 1965 | 4 | 14 |
| Ebb Tide, 1965 | 5 | 48 |
| (You Are My) Soul And Inspiration, 1966 | 1 | 15 |
| He, 1966 | 18 | — |
| You've Lost That Loving Feeling, 1969 | — | 10 |
| Rock 'n' Roll Heaven, 1974 | 3 | — |
| Give It To The People, 1974 | 20 | — |

**Albums:**
Greatest Hits (MGM), 1987* **CD**

*Worth Searching Out:*
Soul And Inspiration (Verve), 1966
Two By Two (MGM), 1973*
*Originally issued on Verve label

# Marty Robbins

US vocalist, composer, guitarist.
Born Glendale, Arizona, September 26, 1925; died December 8, 1982.

**Career:** A genuine country & western performer, with emphasis on western. Robbins came from musical family, including harmonica virtuoso father. Had aspirations to emulate 'singing cowboys' of the '30s/'40s. Started singing in bars and clubs in legendary cowboy town of Phoenix, Arizona, following term in Navy.

Quickly earned local reputation, appearing on own TV show in area. Signed to Columbia after guest on his show Little Jimmy Dickens recommended him to company. First single **Love Me Or Leave Me Alone** released in 1952. After regular period in country charts, made Billboard 100 in 1956 with **Singing The Blues** (covered by Guy Mitchell in States and Tommy Steele in UK). Impressive run of crossover hit singles continued until 1962 and included definitive cowboy ballad **El Paso**.

Appeared in several western 'B' movies and maintained hold on country charts throughout '60s and '70s. Re-entered US Top 60 in 1970 with powerful **My Woman, My Woman, My Wife**, a love opus which pulled at heart strings of middle America.

Robbins' dominant tenor voice and casual guitar playing made him a concert favourite. He was an Opry regular for nearly 30 years. Sadly, this prominent country performer died in 1982 after long battle with heart disease. His influence will endure as long as the saddled stars he worshipped.

| Hit Singles: | US | UK |
| --- | --- | --- |
| Singing The Blues, 1956 | 17 | — |
| A White Sport Coat (And A Pink Carnation), 1957 | 2 | — |
| The Story Of My Life, 1957 | 15 | — |
| El Paso, 1960 | 1 | 19 |
| Don't Worry, 1961 | 3 | — |
| Devil Woman, 1962 | 16 | 5 |
| Ruby Ann, 1962 | 18 | 24 |

**Albums (selected):**
Gunfighter Ballads And Trail Songs (Columbia/CBS), 1962
El Paso (Columbia/Hallmark), 1962
Greatest Hits (Columbia/CBS), 1966
The Legend (Columbia/CBS), 1981
Come Back To Me (Columbia/CBS), 1981
A Lifetime Of Song 1951-1982 (CBS), 1984

# Robert Cray Band

US band formed 1983.

**Current line-up:** Robert Cray, vocals, guitar; Richard Cousins, bass; Peter Boe, keyboards; David Olson, drums.

**Career:** Born in Georgia, US, son of a serviceman, spent his formative years moving from place to place. Robert Cray Band formed by Cray with bassist Richard Cousins and inspired by blues hero Albert Collins. Worked initially

**Below: Heir apparent to Blues Legends, Robert Cray, on the verge of huge things.**

in the Eugene, Oregon area playing club and college dates.

First record deal with Tomato which produced album **Who's Been Talkin'** (released in UK on Charly). Four years later came a deal with Hightone Records and two albums **Bad Influence** and **False Accusations** (UK release on Demon). Albums and UK appearances helped increase UK profile of the band (both Demon LPs topped in the indies chart). In 1986 they signed a lucrative recording deal with PolyGram

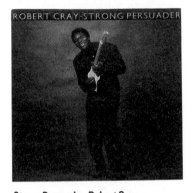

**Strong Persuader, Robert Cray.**
**Courtesy Hightone Records.**

(Mercury in UK) and recorded the **Strong Persuader** album.

Cray guested with Tina Turner on her Break Every Rule TV special, and toured in the US with Huey Lewis & The News and Eric Clapton. **Strong Persuader** climbed the US charts to become the most successful blues album in American chart history.

Cray has been described as the heir apparent to such blues legends as B B King and Albert King — lofty accolades to live up to but his band of soul and white rock and roll has won him a huge following which seems set to grow even larger.

**Albums:**
Whos Been Talking (Charly), 1985 **CD**
False Accusation (Demon/Hightone), 1986 **CD**
Strong Persuader (Mercury/Hightone), 1986
Bad Influence (Demon/Hightone), 1986 **CD**

# Smokey Robinson

US vocalist, composer, executive.
Born William Robinson, Detroit, February 19, 1940.

**Career:** Formed Miracles (then called the Matadors) as high-school vocal group in 1955 with Bobbie and Emerson Rogers and Warren 'Pete' Moore; when Claudette Rogers replaced brother, became the Miracles. Met up with Berry Gordy in 1957 while latter was still working as independent producer. Collaboration led to release of **Got A Job**, through End Records, and **Bad Girl**, through Chess. Moderate success encouraged Gordy to set up Tammie — later Tamla — Records, with Robinson and Miracles as first signing. Group consisted of Robinson (lead vocals), Claudette and Bobbie Rogers (first and second tenors), Ronnie White (baritone), Warren More (bass) and Marvin Tarplin (guitar).

1960 saw first major success for Miracles and Tamla. **Shop Around**, written by Gordy and Robinson, reached No. 2 in US charts. Group was on its way, and next few years saw clutch of hit singles that included classics like **You've Really Got A Hold On Me** (covered by Beatles(▶)) and **Mickey's Monkey** (actually written by Holland/Dozier/Holland(▶)).

At the same time Robinson started writing for and producing other artists. Mary Wells scored with **Two Lovers** and **What's So Easy For Two**, and had her finest hour with **My Guy** in 1964. That same year Robinson began two-year collaboration with Temptations(▶), which resulted in memorable classics such as **Get Ready, The Way You Do The Things You Do, It's Growing, Since I Lost My Baby** and evocative **My Girl** (covered by Otis Redding(▶) and many others). Incredibly, Robinson found time to work with other Motown artists like Marvin Gaye(▶) (**I'll Be Doggone, Ain't That Peculiar**) and the Marvelettes.

During second half of '60s Miracles continued to release hit after hit, including **Tracks Of My Tears**, considered one of all-time great singles. Robinson was by now regarded as important creative force, attracting particular attention for his lyrics. Although most of his songs (apart from straight dance tunes) were about hackneyed subject of love, unrequited or otherwise, fresh, vivid imagery, and felicitous turn of phrase ensured memorable impact. At same time, Robinson had established himself as one of pop's great voices, his plaintive high tenor providing some of its most moving moments. Group became known as Smokey Robinson and the Miracles.

However, Motown's impetus was being provided more and more by writing/production team of Holland/Dozier/Holland and their artists Supremes(▶) and Four Tops(▶), and by end of decade Robinson was thinking of leaving Miracles. In 1971, after series of farewell concerts, he did split from group, and started to concentrate on position as Vice-President of Motown Records with special responsibility for new talent.

Initially, Robinson continued to produce Miracles, but they were soon handed over to other Motown 'house' producers and eventually left label for Columbia. Robinson himself worked on series of solo albums, which continued to make impression on black American market while being largely ignored by general pop audience. Often more experimental than his previous output, Robinson's '70s album repay listening and contain gems that are worth searching out.

However, in 1981 Robinson made return to pop spotlight with **Cruisin'** a US Top 10 hit This was only foretaste of 1981 success of **Being With You**, a romantic Robinson composition originally intended for Kim Carnes(▶). No. 1 both sides of the Atlantic, it brought Robinson to attention of new generation of record buyers and provided momentum for new career in '80s.

Writer of over 60 hit songs, possessor of one of pop's great voices, consistently successful for more than a quarter of a century, Smokey Robinson is a key figure of modern music. Superb 1987 album **One Heartbeat** shows that he is far from a spent force, and Robinson looks set to influence popular music for another twenty-five years.

| Hit Singles: | US | UK |
|---|---|---|
| *Smokey Robinson and the Miracles:* | | |
| Shop Around, 1961 | 2 | — |
| You Really Got A Hold On Me, 1963 | 8 | — |
| Mickey's Monkey, 1963 | 8 | — |
| Ooo Baby Baby, 1965 | 16 | — |
| Tracks Of My Tears, 1965 | 16 | — |
| My Girl Has Gone, 1965 | 14 | — |
| Going To A Go-Go, 1966 | 11 | 44 |
| (Come 'Round Here) I'm The One You Need, 1966 | 17 | 37 |
| The Love I Saw In You Was Just A Mirage, 1967 | 20 | — |
| I Second That Emotion, 1967 | 4 | 27 |
| If You Can Want, 1968 | 11 | 50 |
| Baby Baby Don't Cry, 1969 | 8 | — |
| Tracks Of My Tears, 1969 | — | 9 |
| Tears Of A Clown, 1970 | 1 | 1 |
| (Come 'Round Here) I'm The One You Need, 1971 | — | 13 |
| I Don't Blame You At All, 1971 | 18 | 11 |
| *Miracles* | | |
| Do It Baby, 1974 | 13 | — |
| Love Machine, 1976 | 1 | 3 |
| *Solo:* | | |
| Being With You, 1981 | 1 | 1 |
| Just To See Her, 1987 | 9 | — |
| One Heartbeat, 1987 | 10 | — |

**Albums:**
*Smokey Robinson and the Miracles:*
Anthology (Motown), 1974
Greatest Hits (Tamla/Motown), 1977
18 Greatest Hits (Motown)
Compact Command Performances Vol. 4 (Motown)
Going To A Go-Go/Tears Of A Clown (Motown)

*Smokey Robinson:*
Smokey (Tamla/Motown), 1973
Smokin' (Tamla/—), 1978
Being With You (Motown), 1981
Yes It's You Lady (Motown), 1982
Essar (Motown), 1984
22 Greatest Hits (Motown) **CD**
Greatest Songs (Motown) **CD**
Smoke Signals (Motown/Ace), 1986 **CD**
One Heartbeat (Motown), 1987 **CD**

**Below: The sublime, yet electrifying, Smokey Robinson (right) onstage with the Miracles in 1965. Smokey has few equals as a songwriter of sensitive and soulful lyrics.**

# Rolling Stones

UK group formed 1963.

**Original line-up:** Mick Jagger, vocals; Keith Richard, guitar, vocals; Brian Jones, guitar, vocals; Bill Wyman, bass; Ian Stewart, piano; Charlie Watts, drums.

**Career:** Jagger and Richard first met at primary school in Kent, then went their separate ways. In 1960, when Richard was attending Dartford Art School and Jagger the London School of Economics, they discovered mutual interest in blues and R&B. Pair moved in and out of ever-changing group line-ups that made up London's infant blues scene.

Line-up that was to become first version of Rolling Stones came together around Alexis Korner's Blues Incorporated, pioneer British blues outfit that had regular gig at Ealing Blues Club. Occasional sitter-in with outfit was Cheltenham-born guitarist Brian Jones. By early 1962 Jagger was regular singer with band, and was also rehearsing with Jones, Richard, and other like-minded musicians such as pianist Ian Stewart.

In June 1962 Blues Incorporated were booked for radio broadcast; budget only allowed for six players, so Jagger stepped down and instead deputised for Blues Incorporated at gig at London's Marquee Club; band was billed as Brian Jones and Mick Jagger and the Rollin' Stones. Line-up as above did not coalesce until following year when Charlie Watts made move from Blues Incorporated, and Bill Wyman joined on bass after audition.

Turning-point was residency at Crawdaddy Club in Richmond. Reputation quickly spread by word of mouth, and band came to attention of former PR man Andrew Loog Oldham; he became band's manager and negotiated record contract with Decca. (First move was to oust pianist Stewart on the grounds that he looked too 'normal'—although he was to remain 'sixth Stone' throughout band's career, playing on records and at gigs.)

First release, version of Chuck Berry's(▶) **Come On,** came out in June 1963, and although not a major hit brought band to notice of public and, particularly, of media. Oldham pushed Stones as 'bad boys' compared to 'lovable moptop' Beatles(▶), and band swiftly became cult figures among youth. First album **The Rolling Stones**, largely covers of R&B material, reached top of UK charts in April 1964. June that year saw first US tour and first UK chart-topper, their version of Bobby Womack's **It's All Over Now**.

From this time onwards band quickly gathered momentum. From 1965 all singles were Jagger/Richard compositions, and band developed distinctive pop/rock style that still kept strong blues undertones. **The Last Time** made US Top 10, and paved way for first No. 1 on both sides of the Atlantic, the classic **(I Can't Get No) Satisfaction** (yet to be released in full stereo version).

By end of '60s Stones had become international attraction, second only to Beatles(▶) in importance. They were surrounded by almost permanent aura of publicity and notoriety: **Let's Spend The Night Together** was censored by the Ed Sullivan TV show; Jagger, Richard and Jones were all busted for drugs; Jagger's relationship with Marianne Faithfull provided gossip-column titillation; and virtually every 'pillar of decency' from Bournemouth to Wagga

**Below: Mick Jagger onstage at Leeds in 1982, proving that he can still excite a crowd 20 years later.**

**Right: An impressive stage setting at Wembley Stadium, 1982, for the return to London of the Stones.**

**Above: Mick Jagger (left) and Ron Wood onstage, 1976.**

**Inset above: Goat's Head Soup. Courtesy Rolling Stones Records.**

Wagga denounced band as corrupters of youth, tramplers on moral values, etc. End of decade also saw tragedy of Brian Jones' death, following his exit from group. Mick Taylor, formerly with John Mayall Band(▶), replaced him.

Musically, apart from 1967 flirtation with psychedelia manifested by **Their Satanic Majesties Request** album and **We Love You** single, band had gone from strength to strength. **Beggars Banquet** and **Let It Bleed** were both classic rock albums, regarded by many critics as together making up Stones' finest hour.

In '70s Stones became something of a rock 'n' roll institution, living life of jet-setting tax exiles and establishing new records for massively attended live performances. In 1974 Mick Taylor quit, to be replaced by Ron Wood, a member of Faces(▶). There was some toning down of former 'rebel' image, as members eased into mature years, their former 'two-fingers-to-the-world' stance being taken over by '70s punk outfits like Sex Pistols(▶). Record-wise, band continued to put out worthwhile albums (after 1971 on their own Rolling Stones label) that generally contained a couple of classics each, and maintained standard of singles with releases like **Brown Sugar** and **It's Only Rock And Roll.**

Although it might be assumed that band would be happy to coast into '80s, or even think about throwing in towel, 1981 saw US tour that broke all box-office records, while album **Tattoo You** made No. 1 in US charts, No. 2 in UK. **Still Life**, live album of '81 tour, was almost equally successful in following year and momentum has continued since, added interest coming from Jagger's solo album and hit duet with David Bowie on re-make of Martha and the Vandellas' **Dancing In The Street** in 1985.

Whilst Jaggar pursues uneven solo career (1987 album **Primitive Cool** received mixed reviews) and interest from gossip coumnists, including frantic first week of 1987 in Barbados, when Jerry Hall was arrested for possession of Marijuana (charges later dropped), other Stones have kept busy as well. Charlie Watts formed his own jazz band, Ronnie Wood had a one-man exhibition of his painting in London during the Autumn of '87, whilst Keith Richard (now signed to Virgin Records) maintained a high profile in the pop papers suggesting that "Mick should stop trying to be like Peter Pan and grow up." The end? We hope not.

**Current line-up:** Jagger; Richard; Wyman; Watts; Ron Wood, guitar, vocals.

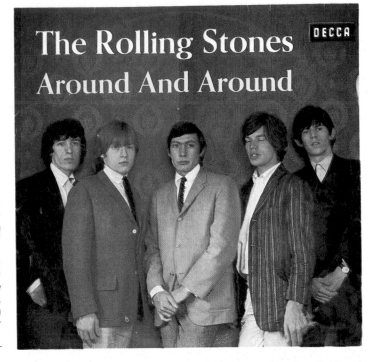

Above: An early album sleeve reproduced courtesy of Decca Records.
Below: The controversial sleeve for 1978's Some Girls, which resulted in several law suits. Courtesy of Rolling Stones Records.

**Hit Singles:**

| | US | UK |
|---|---|---|
| I Wanna Be Your Man, 1963 | — | 12 |
| Not Fade Away, 1964 | 48 | 3 |
| It's All Over Now, 1964 | 26 | 1 |
| Little Red Rooster, 1964 | — | 1 |
| Time Is On My Side, 1964 | 6 | — |
| Heart Of Stone, 1965 | 19 | — |
| The Last Time, 1965 | 9 | 1 |
| (I Can't Get No) Satisfaction, 1965 | 1 | 1 |
| Get Off My Cloud, 1965 | 1 | 1 |
| As Tears Go By, 1966 | 6 | — |
| 19th Nervous Breakdown, 1966 | 2 | 2 |
| Paint It Black, 1966 | 1 | 1 |
| Mother's Little Helper, 1966 | 8 | — |
| Have You Seen Your Mother Baby (Standing In The Shadows), 1966 | 9 | 5 |
| Ruby Tuesday/Let's Spend The Night Together, 1967 | 1 | 3 |
| Let's Spend The Night Together/ Ruby Tuesday, 1967 | 55 | 3 |
| We Love You/Dandelion, 1967 | 14 | 8 |
| Jumping Jack Flash, 1968 | 3 | 1 |
| Honky Tonk Women, 1969 | 1 | 1 |
| Brown Sugar/Bitch/Let It Rock, 1971 | 1 | 2 |
| Tumbling Dice, 1972 | 7 | 5 |
| Angie, 1973 | 1 | 5 |
| Doo Doo Doo Doo Doo (Heartbreakers), 1974 | 16 | — |
| It's Only Rock And Roll, 1974 | 16 | 10 |
| Ain't Too Proud To Beg, 1974 | 17 | — |
| Fool To Cry, 1976 | 10 | 6 |
| Miss You/Far Away Eyes, 1978 | 1 | 3 |
| Beast Of Burden, 1978 | 8 | — |
| Emotional Rescue, 1980 | 3 | 9 |
| Start Me Up, 1981 | 2 | 7 |
| Waiting On A Friend, 1982 | 13 | 50 |
| Hang Fire, 1982 | 20 | — |
| Undercover Of The Night, 1983 | 9 | 11 |
| Just Another Night, 1985 | — | 9 |
| Harlem Shuffle, 1986 | — | 13 |

*Mick Jagger (with David Bowie):*
| | | |
|---|---|---|
| Dancing In The Street, 1985 | 7 | 1 |

*Bill Wyman Solo:*
| | | |
|---|---|---|
| Si Si Je Suis Un Rock Star, 1983 | — | 14 |

**Inset above: The classic Aftermath. Courtesy Decca Records.**

**Left: 'Thank Your Lucky Star' TV show, 1965. (From left) Brian Jones, Mick Jagger, Bill Wyman, Charlie Watts and Keith Richard.**

**Inset left: Still Life LP (1982). Courtesy Rolling Stones Records.**

**Albums:**
The Rolling Stones (London/Decca), 1964 **CD**
12x5 (London/—), 1965 **CD**
The Rolling Stones Now (London/—), 1965
Out Of Our Heads (London/Decca), 1965 **CD**
Decembers Children (London/—), 1965
Aftermath (London/Decca), 1966 **CD**
Big Hits (High Tide And Green Grass) (London/Decca), 1966
Got Live If You Want It (London/—), 1967
Between The Buttons (London/Decca), 1967 **CD**
Flowers (London/Decca), 1967
Their Satanic Majesties Request (London/ Decca), 1967 **CD**
Beggars Banquet (London/Decca), 1968 **CD**
Let It Bleed (London/Decca), 1969 **CD**
Through The Past Darkly (Big Hits Volume 2) (London/Decca), 1969
Get Yer Ya Yas Out (London/Decca), 1970
Sticky Fingers (Rolling Stones), 1971 **CD**

Stone Age (—/Decca), 1971
Gimme Shelter (—/Decca), 1971
Milestones (—/Decca), 1971
Exile On Main Street (Rolling Stones), 1972 **CD**
Hot Rocks: 1964-71 (London/—), 1972 **CD**
More Hot Rocks (Big Hits And Fazed Cookies) (London/—), 1972 **CD**
Goats Head Soup (Rolling Stones), 1973 **CD**
No Stone Unturned (—/Decca), 1973
It's Only Rock'n'Roll (Rolling Stones), 1974 **CD**
Rolled Gold (—/Decca), 1975
Metamorphosis (London/Decca), 1975
Made In The Shade (Rolling Stones), 1975 **CD**
Black And Blue (Rolling Stones), 1976 **CD**
Love You Live (Rolling Stones), 1977 **CD**
Some Girls (Rolling Stones), 1978 **CD**
Emotional Rescue (Rolling Stones), 180 **CD**
Sucking In The Seventies (Rolling Stones), 1981 **CD**

Tattoo You (Rolling Stones), 1981 **CD**
Still Life (Rolling Stones), 1982 **CD**
Undercover (Rolling Stones), 1983 **CD**
Dirty Work (CBS), 1986 **CD**

*Mick Jagger Solo:*
She's The Boss (CBS), 1965 **CD**
Primitive Cool (CBS), 1987 **CD**

*Bill Wyman (with Buddy Guy &Junior Wells):*
Drinkin' T.N.T. 'N' Smokin' Dynamite (Red
  Lightnin'), 1983

*Bill Wyman Solo:*
Bill Wyman (A&M), 1982

*Worth Searching Out:*
Monkey Grip (Rolling Stones), 1974
Stone Alone (Rolling Stones), 1976

*Ron Wood Solo:*
(See Faces entry.)

# Linda Ronstadt

US vocalist.
Born Tucson, Arizona, July 15, 1946.

**Prisoner In Disguise. Courtesy Asylum
Records.**

**Career:** Daughter of guitar player; had
musical upbringing. After attending Arizona
State University, headed for California in
1964 to try luck in music business. She
teamed up with old friend Bob Kimmel and LA
musician Ken Edwards to form folk-rock group
Stone Poneys. Band made three albums for
Capitol between 1966 and 1968, scoring hit

**Get Closer. Courtesy Asylum Records.**

single with Mike Nesmith's **Different Drum**.
 Encouraged by Capitol, Ronstadt decided
to go solo in 1969. First two albums created
considerable interest, and second, **Silk
Purse**, provided first solo hit single **Long,
Long Time**.
 In 1971 she recruited Don Henley, Glenn
Frey and Randy Meisner to form new backing
band. All played on **Linda Ronstadt**, but split
within six months to form Eagles(▶).
 Career really began to take off when
Ronstadt joined country-rock orientated West
Coast label Asylum in 1973. Debut album
**Don't Cry Now**, co-produced by Peter Asher,
made US album charts. (Asher became
manager and has produced all albums since.)
1974 album **Heart Like A Wheel** (con-
tractually obligated to Capitol) eventually
went platinum, spawning three gold singles
inlcuding No. 1's **You're No Good** and **When
Will I Be Loved**. At end of year Ronstadt
had become top-selling female artist in US.
 Further albums confirmed superstar status
and Ronstadt also became huge concert
attraction. In meantime, private life provoked
much rumour and comment. Relationship with
California Governor Jerry Brown elicited most
column inches.
 Although sometimes criticized for lack of
passion and power Ronstadt has made much
fine music during course of career. Latterly
has gained sufficient technical mastery to tackle
material outside rock canon.
 Recently took lead role in hit version of
Gilbert and Sullivan's **Pirates Of Penzance**
on Broadway, also appeared in film version. In
further change of direction, collaborated with
late Nelson Riddle (Sinatra's favourite accom-
panist and veteran of a million film scores) in a
series of albums featuring standard songs by
Gershwin, Rodgers and Hart, Irving Berlin and
others. 1987 marked something of return to
roots with **Trio**, platinum-selling album collaboration with Emmylou Harris and Dolly Parton.

| Hit Singles: | US | UK |
| --- | --- | --- |
| *Linda And The Stone Poneys:* | | |
| Different Drum, 1968 | 13 | — |
| *With James Ingram:* | | |
| Somewhere Out There, 1987 | 9 | 18 |
| *With Ronstadt & Parton:* | | |
| Trio (WEA), 1987 **CD** | | |
| *Solo:* | | |
| You're No Good, 1975 | 1 | — |

**Above: Motown superstars (from left) Diana Ross, Marvin Gaye, Stevie Wonder.**

| | | |
| --- | --- | --- |
| When Will I Be Loved, 1975 | 1 | — |
| Heat Wave, 1975 | 5 | — |
| That'll Be The Day, 1976 | 11 | — |
| Blue Bayou, 1977 | 3 | 35 |
| It's So Easy, 1977 | 5 | — |
| Back In The USA, 1978 | 16 | — |
| Ooh Baby Baby, 1979 | 17 | — |
| How Do I Make You, 1980 | 10 | — |
| Hurt So Bad, 1980 | 8 | — |

**Albums:**
Hand Sown, Home Grown (Capitol), 1969
Silk Purse (Capitol), 1970
Linda Ronstadt (Capitol), 1972
Don't Cry Now (Asylum), 1974
Heart Like A Wheel (Capitol), 1974
Different Drum (Capitol), 1975
Stone Poneys Featuring Linda Ronstadt
  (Capitol), 1975
Prisoner In Disguise (Asylum), 1975
Hasten Down The Wind (Asylum), 1976
Greatest Hits (Asylum), 1976 **CD**
Simple Dreams (Asylum), 1977 **CD**
Retrospective (Capitol), 1977
Living In The USA (Asylum), 1978
Greatest Hits Volume 2 (Asylum), 1980 **CD**
Mad Love (Asylum), 1980
Beginnings (Capitol/—), 1981
Get Closer (Asylum), 1982 **CD**
Lush Life (Asylum), 1984 **CD**
What's New? (Asylum) **CD**
For Sentimental Reasons (Asylum), 1986 **CD**
Canciones De Mi Padre (Asylum), 1987

# Diana Ross

US vocalist, actress.
Born Detroit, March 26, 1944.

**Career:** Following endless speculation, Ross
left record-breaking vocal group Supremes(▶)
in December 1969. First solo single, **Reach
Out And Touch**, was released in June 1970
and started string of hits which has continued
to present.
 Right from beginning, however, Ross and
Motown label boss Berry Gordy collaborated
to project Ross as more than merely successful
pop singer. Pair envisaged all-round superstardom à la Streisand(▶). To this end Ross
was presented as centrepiece of series of
elaborately staged concerts and TV specials,
at same time making debut in 'Lady Sings The
Blues', a Motown-produced film about Billie
Holiday.
 While movie was not universally critically
well received, it was commercially successful
and Ross won general acclaim for her
portrayal of the tragic jazz singer. Second
foray into film acting was in the less suc-

cessful 'Mahogany' (1975), although film did
give Ross opportunity to wear variety of
high-fashion costumes.
 In meantime, hits continued apace —
generally highly arranged ballads which
allowed Ross to emote to good effect. In
1976, however, she surprised everyone with
**Love Hangover**, a genuinely exciting upbeat
disco stomper.
 For third film, Ross played part of Dorothy in
re-make of 'Wizard Of Oz' called 'The Wiz'.
Again, movie was less than ecstatically
received by critics but Ross herself garnered
generally good reviews.
 By 1980 relations with Motown were
becoming strained, and Ross split from the
company, signing with RCA for US and with
Capitol for rest of world. However, this was not
before artist had reasserted her dancefloor-
filling credentials with Chic(▶)-produced album
**Diana**, which yielded three hit singles.
 Since changing companies Ross has gone
from strength to strength, producing herself
and continuing to chart heavily. (Although
ironically one of her biggest hits of the 80s has
been her duet from film soundtrack with
Lionel Richie(▶) **Endless Love**, her swansong
for Motown.) Like all survivors, Ross has
adapted well, handling pop, soul, disco and
rock masterfully. Now a major superstar who
can fill world's largest venues many times
over, Ross looks set to endure.

| Hit Singles: | US | UK |
| --- | --- | --- |
| Reach Out And Touch (Somebody's | | |
| Hand), 1970 | 20 | 33 |
| Ain't No Mountain High Enough, | | |
| 1970 | 1 | 6 |
| Remember Me, 1970 | 16 | 7 |
| I'm Still Waiting, 1971 | — | 1 |
| Surrender, 1971 | 38 | 10 |
| Doobedoob'ndoobe | | |
| Doobedood'ndoobe, 1972 | — | 12 |
| Touch Me In The Morning, 1973 | 1 | 9 |
| All Of My Life, 1974 | | 9 |
| Last Time I Saw Him, 1974 | 14 | 35 |
| Do You Know Where You're Going | | |
| To (Theme from 'Mahogany'), | | |
| 1976 | 1 | 5 |
| Love Hangover, 1976 | 1 | 10 |
| The Boss, 1979 | 19 | 40 |
| Upside Down, 1980 | 1 | 2 |
| My Old Piano, 1980 | — | 5 |
| I'm Coming Out, 1980 | 5 | 13 |
| It's My Turn, 1981 | 9 | 16 |
| Why Do Fools Fall In Love?, 1981 | 7 | 4 |
| Mirror Mirror, 1982 | 8 | 36 |
| Work That Body, 1982 | 44 | 7 |
| Muscles, 1982 | 10 | 15 |
| Swept Away, 1984 | 19 | — |
| Missing You, 1985 | 10 | — |

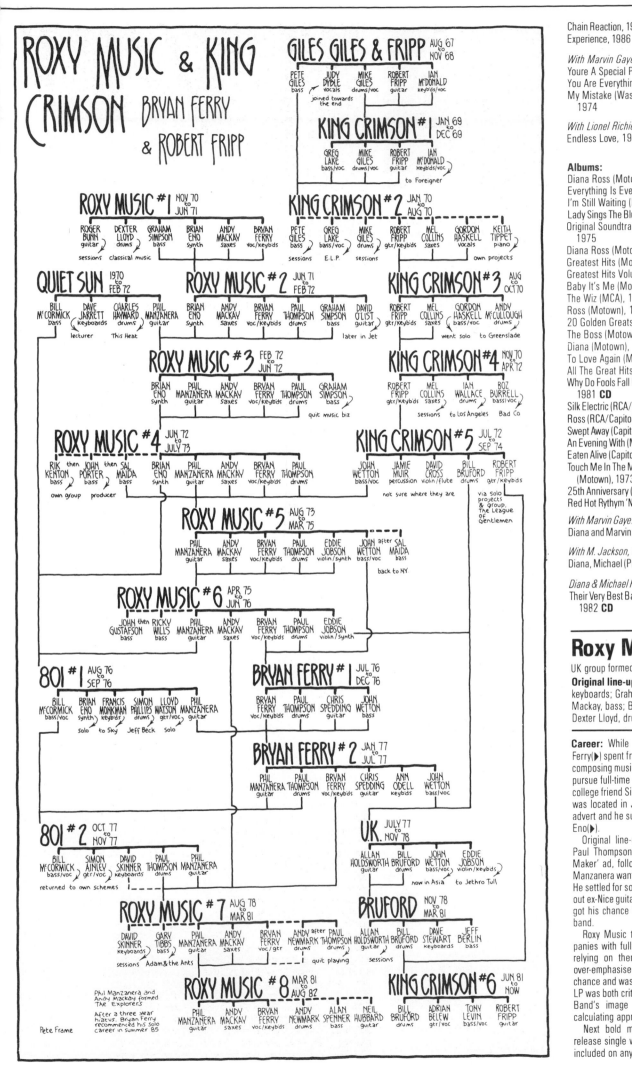

| Chain Reaction, 1986 | — | 1 |
| Experience, 1986 | — | 47 |

*With Marvin Gaye:*

| Youre A Special Part Of Me, 1973 | 12 | — |
| You Are Everything, 1974 | — | 5 |
| My Mistake (Was To Love You), 1974 | 19 | — |

*With Lionel Richie:*

| Endless Love, 1982 | 1 | 7 |

**Albums:**

Diana Ross (Motown), 1970
Everything Is Everything (Motown), 1971
I'm Still Waiting (Motown), 1971
Lady Sings The Blues (Motown), 1972 **CD**
Original Soundtrack Of Mahogany (Motown), 1975
Diana Ross (Motown), 1976
Greatest Hits (Motown), 1976
Greatest Hits Volume 2 (Motown), 1976
Baby It's Me (Motown), 1977
The Wiz (MCA), 1978
Ross (Motown), 1978
20 Golden Greats (Motown), 1979
The Boss (Motown), 1979
Diana (Motown), 1981
To Love Again (Motown), 1981
All The Great Hits (Motown), 1981
Why Do Fools Fall In Love? (RCA/Capitol), 1981 **CD**
Silk Electric (RCA/Capitol), 1982
Ross (RCA/Capitol), 1983
Swept Away (Capitol), 1984 **CD**
An Evening With (Motown), 1985
Eaten Alive (Capitol), 1985 **CD**
Touch Me In The Morning/Baby Its Me (Motown), 1973/1977 **CD**
25th Anniversary (Motown), 1986 Double
Red Hot Rythym 'N' Blues (EMI), 1977

*With Marvin Gaye:*
Diana and Marvin (Motown), 1974 **CD**

*With M. Jackson, G. Knight & S. Wonder:*
Diana, Michael (Priority), 1986 **CD**

*Diana & Michael Ross:*
Their Very Best Back To Back (Priority), 1982 **CD**

## Roxy Music

UK group formed 1970.

**Original line-up:** Bryan Ferry, vocals, keyboards; Graham Simpson, bass; Andy Mackay, bass; Brian Eno, synthesiser; Dexter Lloyd, drums; Roger Bunn, guitar.

**Career:** While working as teacher, Bryan Ferry(▶) spent free-time learning, playing and composing music. By 1970 he had decided to pursue full-time music career and sought out college friend Simpson to form band. MacKay was located in January 1971 through trade advert and he subsequently introduced Brian Eno(▶).

Original line-up lasted only few months. Paul Thompson (drums) answered 'Melody Maker' ad, following Lloyd's departure. Phil Manzanera wanted to join as second guitarist. He settled for sound-mixer when Ferry sought out ex-Nice guitarist, David O'List. Manzanera got his chance when Bunn, then O'List, left band.

Roxy Music tried to interest record companies with fully textured sound rather than relying on then standard lead guitar and over-emphasised bass. Island finally took chance and was rather surprised when debut LP was both critical and commercial success. Band's image and sound projected cool, calculating approach to rock as yet unseen.

Next bold move for early '70s was to release single which was not intended to be included on any LP. **Virginia Plain** made UK

No. 4 and won band broad audience. This release also featured first of many new bass players, Rik Kenton. Within a few months, his place was taken by John Porter who lasted only first two months of 1973 while band recorded **For Your Pleasure.** During 1973 Europe/UK tours, Sal Maida filled in on bass.

Roxy Music took vacation for second half of 1973 due to Eno's departure for solo career and Ferry's growing interest in developing parallel solo venture. Eddie Jobson (ex Curved Air) assumed Eno's spot on keyboards and Roxy Music returned to stage work in autumn 1973. This time Ferry pushed 'cool' image to extreme by cutting long hair and wearing tuxedo on stage.

Roxy's live efforts helped boost **Stranded** LP to UK No. 10. John Gustafson played bass on this album (and next two) but did so as session player and didn't tour with Roxy. John Wetton took on this role from autumn 1974 until April 1975 when he suddenly left for Uriah Heep(▶), and Gustafson at last went on the road. In late 1975 he was replaced by Rick Wills (later Small Faces(▶)).

Although **Country Life** and **Siren** were big success in UK and garnered critical praise in US, Ferry wanted to try solo tour. Roxy Music's break-up was never formally announced but band no longer existed after June 1976. Various solo projects failed to produce new careers for Roxy members but public interest in band remained high, as seen by UK chart success of live LP **Viva,** and then **Greatest Hits.**

In late 1978 Ferry gathered nucleus of MacKay, Manzanera and Thompson for Roxy Music re-union. Using ex-Vibrator Gary Tibbs (bass) and ex-Ace Paul Carrack (keyboards), band recorded **Manifesto.**

After extensive touring, Roxy Music entered new stage of career with **Flesh**

Greatest Hits. Courtesy Polydor.

**And Blood.** Although not radically different from past, this album marked new level of sophisticated lyrics with melodic background. Somehow Roxy achieved sound which fitted into '80s without destroying roots from '60s; they reworked classic old John Lennon(▶) song, **Jealous Guy,** and produced moving tribute for Lennon in early 1981.

By now Roxy Music had lost Thompson and remaining core used various session players to produce their finest effort, **Avalon. More Than This** and **Take A Chance With Me** are two classic cuts from LP which surpass bounds of rock and encourage hope that, though Roxy Music has split, its work will remain strong influence on today's newer bands.

**Final line-up:** Ferry; Manzanera; Mackay.

**Hit Singles:**

|  | US | UK |
|---|---|---|
| Virginia Plain, 1972 | — | 4 |
| Pyjamarama, 1973 | — | 10 |
| Street Life, 1973 | — | 9 |
| All I Want Is You, 1974 | — | 12 |
| Love Is The Drug, 1975 | 30 | 2 |

The first album, Roxy Music. Courtesy Island Records.

|  | US | UK |
|---|---|---|
| Virginia Plain, 1977 | — | 11 |
| Dance Away, 1979 | — | 2 |
| Angel Eyes, 1979 | — | 4 |
| Over You, 1980 | — | 5 |
| Oh Yeah (On The Radio), 1980 | — | 5 |
| The Same Old Scene, 1980 | — | 12 |
| Jealous Guy, 1981 | — | 1 |
| More Than This, 1982 | — | 6 |
| Avalon, 1982 | 27 | 13 |

**Albums:**
Roxy Music (Reprise/Island), 1972 **CD**
For Your Pleasure (Warner Bros/Island), 1973 **CD**
Stranded (Atco/Island), 1973 **CD**
Country Life (Atco/Island), 1974 **CD**
Siren (Atco/Island), 1975 **CD**
Viva Roxy Music (Live), (Atco/Island), 1976 **CD**
Greatest Hits (Polydor), 1977 **CD**
Manifesto (Polydor), 1979 **CD**
Flesh And Blood (Polydor), 1980 **CD**
The First Seven Albums (Polydor), 1981*
Avalon (Polydor), 1982 **CD**
The High Road (Polydor), 1983†
The Atlantic Years 1973-80 (EG), 1983

*Boxed set
†Live mini-LP

*Andy Mackay Solo:*
In Search Of Eddie Riff (—/Island), 1974
Resolving Contradictions (—/Bronze), 1978

*Phil Manzanera Solo:*
Diamond Head (Atco/Island), 1975
Quiet Sun: Mainstream (Antilles/Island), 1975
801: Live (Polydor/Island), 1976
Listen Now (Polydor), 1977
K Scope (Polydor), 1978

*Bryan Ferry Solo:*
(See separate entry)

# Todd Rundgren

US vocalist, composer, producer, guitarist. Born Upper Darby, Pennsylvania, June 22, 1948.

**Career:** Greatly influenced by 'British Invasion' spearheaded by Beatles and Rolling Stones; acquired first electric guitar at 17. First band was Woody's Truck Stop (for less than a year); by 1968 had left to form the Nazz, legendary Philadelphia band who made three LPs between 1968 and 1970, now regarded as prime collectors' items (reissued in 1983 by Rhino Records, Los Angeles). However, Todd left group by mid-1969 to perfect ability as producer/engineer.

Produced only minor acts early on, but engineered for such as the Band(▶), Paul Butterfield(▶) Blues Band and Jesse Winchester, as well as embarking on personal solo career.

Had great success with 1972 LP

**Something/Anything?**, plus production of debut LP by Sparks(▶) (then known as Halfnelson) and Badfinger.

1973 productions included New York Dolls, Grand Funk Railroad(▶) and Fanny. In 1974 he formed Utopia (longest-lived line-up: Rundgren, guitar, vocals; Roger Powell, keyboards, vocals; Kasim Sulton, bass, vocals; Willie Wilcox, drums, vocals). Since 1974, group and Todd's solo LPs effectively interleaved. Musically and vocally, Rundgren has experimented with several styles: equally proficient backed solely by own guitar or piano. His lyrics are also varied, sometimes poignant, often witty, but always perceptive.

During '70s, probably best known as producer, while own performing/recording career has largely retreated into cult status. Among notable productions during this period are those for Hall & Oates(▶), Tom Robinson(▶), Tubes(▶), Patti Smith(▶) and **Bat Out Of Hell** by Meat Loaf(▶).

During early '80s, somewhat less active as producer; also cut down on live performances, due to major involvement in videos. Awardwinning **Time Heals** must be seen.

**Hit Singles:**

|  | US | UK |
|---|---|---|
| We Gotta Get You A Woman, 1971 | 20 | — |
| I Saw The Light, 1972 | 16 | 36 |
| Hello It's Me, 1973 | 5 | — |

**Albums:**
*With The Nazz:*
*Worth Searching Out:*
Nazz (Screen Gems-Columbia/—), 1968
Nazz Nazz (Screen Gems-Columbia/—), 1969
Nazz III (Screen Gems-Columbia/—), 1970

*Solo and with Utopia:*
Something/Anything (Bearsville), 1972
A Wizard, A True Star (Bearsville/Island), 1973
Todd (Bearsville), 1973
Todd Rundgren's Utopia (Bearsville), 1974
Initiation (Bearsville), 1975
Another Life (Bearsville), 1975
Faithful (Bearsville), 1976
Ra (Bearsville), 1977
Oops! Wrong Planet (Bearsville), 1977
Hermit Of Mink Hollow (Bearsville/Island), 1978

A Wizard, A True Star, Todd Rundgren. Courtesy Bearsville Records.

Back To The Bars (Bearsville), 1978
Adventures In Utopia (Bearsville), 1980
Deface The Music (Bearsville), 1980
Healing (Bearsville), 1981
Swing To The Right (Bearsville), 1982
Utopia (Bearsville), 1982
The Ever Popular Tortured Artist Effect (Bearsville), 1983
A Cappella (Warner Bros), 1985

*Worth Searching Out:*
Runt (Bearsville), 1970
The Ballad Of Todd Rundgren (Bearsville), 1971

# Rush

Canadian group formed 1973.

**Original line-up:** Alex Lifeson, guitar; Geddy Lee, bass, keyboards, vocals; John Rutsey, drums.

**Career:** Band began playing bars in Toronto, using hard rock/heavy metal sound to project

**Hemispheres, Rush. Courtesy Mercury Records.**

gothic images of sci-fi future. Privately produced first LP was rejected by major labels but received extensive airplay in Seattle. This led to some American bookings in Pacific Northwest and group caught attention of Mercury Records who had promoted fellow Canadians Bachman-Turner Overdrive(▶) to stardom.

Mercury released first album and set up national tour when Rutsey decided to leave. Neil Peart joined and expanded band's potential by adding lyric-writing abilities and vocal talents.

**Right: Rush frontmen Alex Lifeson (left) and Geddy Lee.**

Next two LPs spread band's reputation for hard rock; more importantly began expounding Rush's vision of the individual winning out against high-tech in some distant society. This approach culminated in extended work covering entire first side of **2112,** which tells the tale of a young man who discovers an electric guitar and suddenly finds himself an outlaw for inventing music to go with it.

At this point, band stepped back and released live set **All The World's A Stage**. Subsequent LPs have continued to dabble in sci-fi motifs or space age trappings (excellent **Countdown** on **Signals** LP is good example). Group managed to avoid taking itself too seriously and have won over ever-growing audience with extensive touring. **Exit: Stage Left** indicates Rush's unwillingness to stray too far from studio sound when performing live which tends to make a Rush concert somewhat predictable.

Rush consolidated their worldwide following without any spectacular hit singles or making sensational headlines. Their music continued to develop and in late 1987 they released another fine album **Hold Your Fire**, and toured the world in 1988.

**Current line-up:** Lifeson; Lee; Neil Peart, percussion, vocals.

| Hit Singles: | US | UK |
|---|---|---|
| Spirit Of Radio, 1980 | — | 13 |

**Albums:**
Rush (Mercury), 1974 **CD**
Fly By Night (Mercury), 1975 **CD**
Caress Of Steel (Mercury), 1975 **CD**
2112 (Mercury), 1976 **CD**
All The World's A Stage (Double live),
   (Mercury), 1976 **CD**
A Farewell To Kings (Mercury), 1977 **CD**
Archives (Mercury), 1978*
Hemispheres (Mercury), 1978 **CD**
Permanent Waves (Mercury), 1980
Rush Through Time (Mercury), 1980†
Moving Pictures (Mercury), 1981 **CD**
Exit: Stage Left (Live) (Mercury), 1981 **CD**
Signals (Mercury), 1982 **CD**
Grace Under Pressure (Vertigo), 1984 **CD**
Power Windows (Vertigo), 1985 **CD**
Hold Your Fire (Mercury), 1987 **CD**

*Re-issue of first three LPs
†Picture disc of previous material

# Leon Russell

US composer, vocalist, pianist, guitarist.
Born Lawton, Oklahoma, April 2, 1941.

**Career:** Studied classical piano from early age; at 14 took up trumpet and formed own band. Other experience included playing with Ronnie Hawkins(▶) and Jerry Lee Lewis(▶).

In 1958 Russell moved to Los Angeles and became session musician, working with artists like Glen Campbell(▶), Byrds(▶), Herb Alpert(▶), Crystals(▶) and Righteous Brothers(▶). In late '60s became friendly with blue-eyed soul duo Delaney and Bonnie(▶), and in 1969, along with numerous other West Coast session luminaries, joined Delaney and Bonnie's Friends for touring and recording.

Most of Friends eventually became part of Joe Cocker's(▶) touring band, Mad Dogs And Englishmen, which Russell led. Exposure made him cult figure, and solo career started to take off in 1970 with **Leon Russell** (released on his own Shelter label, formed with English producer Denny Cordell).

Next few years saw enormous popularity for artist. Although technically limited singer, Russell made up for this with excellent production, superstar session line-ups and good, largely self-penned material. Already renowned for Joe Cocker hit **Delta Lady** — originally written for Rita Coolidge(▶), Russell came up with several much-covered classics, notably **A Song For You, Superstar** and **This Masquerade**. Recording career peaked with gold album **Carney** (1972) and triple album **Live** (1973).

Despite striking stage personality — wispy grey hair and beard, stove-pipe hat — and evident talent, Russell's career quietened down in late '70s. Following an earlier country album in 1973—tribute to Hank Williams' **Hank Wilson's Back — Volume I** in recent years artist has turned to country roots with albums like **One For The Road** with Willie Nelson(▶) and **New Grass Revival Live**. Somewhat enigmatic figure, Russell has made much good music and earned honourable place in rock pantheon.

| Hit Singles: | US | UK |
|---|---|---|
| Tight Rope, 1972 | 11 | — |
| Lady Blue, 1975 | 14 | — |

**Albums:**
Leon Russell (MCA), 1970
Leon Russell And The Shelter People (MCA),
   1971
Carney (MCA), 1972
Will O' The Wisp (MCA), 1975
Best Of Leon Russell (MCA), 1976
Leon Russell And New Grass Revival Live
   (Paradise), 1981

*With Marc Benno:*
Asylum Choir (MCA), 1968

*With Willie Nelson:*
Willie And Leon (Columbia/CBS), 1979

# Sade

UK group formed 1982.

**Original/Current line-up:** Sade Adu, vocals; Stuart Matthewman, saxophone; Paul Denman, bass; Andrew Hale, keyboards.

**Career:** Though singer Sade Adu holds the spotlight, Sade insist they are not an individual but a four-strong group, augmenting itself with such extra musicians as drummer Dave Early and percussionist Martin Ditchman to produce 'soul with a jazz feel'.

Asked by manager Lee Barrett if she could sing, Sade auditioned for London funk band Pride.

When Matthewman and Denman came down from Hull to join Pride they instantly got on with Adu and ballads penned by her and Matthewman soon became high spot of

Pride's otherwise pungent funk set. Sade developed into first an opening act for Pride then a separate band in own right.

Adding Hale and linking with producer Robin Millar, act signed to Epic and re-worked old Pride number **Smooth Operator** into smash hit, concurrent **Diamond Life** album also making major impact, with group's total sales figures topping six million before release of second, chart-topping album **Promise**.

From debut at Ronnie Scott's Jazz Club through concerts at Montreux and prestigious concert halls to Live Aid appearance, Sade have carved special niche, with the lady herself emerging as most successful black singer yet produced by British music scene.

| Hit Singles: | US | UK |
|---|---|---|
| Your Love Is King, 1984 | — | 6 |
| Smooth Operator, 1984 | 5 | 19 |

**Albums:**
Diamond Life (Epic), 1984 **CD**
Promise (Epic), 1985 **CD**
Stronger Than Pride (Epic), 1987

**Santana (the first album). Courtesy CBS Records.**

# Santana

US guitarist, bandleader, composer.
Born Carlos Santana, Autlan, Jalisco, Mexico, July 20, 1947.

**Career:** Emerged as major local rock musician during San Francisco's Haight-Ashbury flower-power era; guested on seminal **The Live Adventures Of Mike Bloomfield And Al Kooper** album, then put together own band. Brought Latin flavour to rock through use of conga player Mike Carrabello and award-winning Central American percussionist José 'Chepito' Areas alongside Gregg Rolie, keyboards, vocals, David Brown, bass, and Mike Shrieve, drums.

Reputation was already made before 1969 debut album **Santana** which sold a million copies (most after Woodstock) in US alone. Band's appearance in 'Woodstock' concert and film, performing **Soul Sacrifice**, was one of the great moments of rock.

**Oye Como Va**, penned by Latin-music great Tito Puente, helped second album **Abraxas** (1970) to equally big sales. **Santana 3** (1972) brought Santana's guitarist protégé Neil Schon and Coke Escovedo into band. Live album jamming with Buddy Miles was less satisfying. Its realease co-incided with disbanding of original Santana group in wake of Santana's espousal of teachings of guru Sri Chinmoy at instigation of friend Mahavishnu John McLaughlin(▶). Santana adopted name Devadip.

Latin/jazz/rock fusion **Caravanserai** album used Rolie and Schon, along with studio musicians; they were not included in new band in 1973. This placed Santana originals

**Promise, Sade. Courtesy Epic Records.**

**Right: Carlos Santana, one of the finest guitarists to emerge from San Francisco in the '60s.**

Areas and Shrieve alongside Tom Coster, keyboard, James Mingo Lewis and Armando Peraza, percussion, and Doug Rauch, bass. Besides own band's work, Santana recorded **Love, Devotion, Surrender** album in partnership with McLaughlin, and **Illuminations** with Alice Coltrane.

Various line-up changes saw Santana band return from heady experimentation to simpler roots, which put albums back among bestsellers.

In 1977, Santana ditched existing band, except Coster; Schon and Rolie formed Journey(▶). Santana came under management of former Fillmore and Woodstock promoter Bill Graham, which led in 1977 to CBS Records' first 'Crystal Globe' Award for sale of five million units in Europe. 1982 brought Santana's output to 14 albums in 15 years, his guitar work remaining distinctive for its pure tone, and providing fluid solos to enhance his always melodic material. Carlos Santana is the Latin voice of rock.
Guitar: Gibson 335.

**Hit Singles:**

| | US | UK |
|---|---|---|
| Evil Ways, 1970 | 9 | — |
| Black Magic Woman, 1970 | 4 | — |
| Oye Como Va, 1971 | 13 | — |
| Everybody's Everything, 1971 | 12 | — |
| She's Not There, 1977 | 27 | 11 |
| Winning, 1981 | 17 | — |
| Hold On, 1982 | 15 | — |

**Albums:**
Santana (Columbia/CBS), 1969 **CD**
Abraxas (Columbia/CBS), 1970 **CD**
Santana III (Columbia/CBS), 1971 **CD**
Caravanserai (Columbia/CBS), 1972
Welcome (Columbia/CBS), 1973
Greatest Hits (Columbia/CBS), 1974 **CD**
Borboletta (Columbia/CBS), 1976
Amigos (Columbia/CBS), 1976 **CD**
Moonflower (Columbia/CBS), 1977
Inner Secrets (Columbia/CBS), 1978 **CD**
Marathon (Columbia/CBS), 1979 **CD**
Swing Of Delight (Columbia/CBS), 1980
Zebop! (Columbia/CBS), 1981 **CD**
Shango (Columbia/CBS), 1982 **CD**
Havana Moon (Columbia/CBS), 1983
Beyond Appearances (CBS), 1985 **CD**
Freedom (CBS), 1987 **CD**

# Saxon

UK group formed 1977.
**Original line-up:** Peter 'Biff' Byford, vocals; Paul Quinn, guitar; Graham Oliver, guitar; Steve Dawson, bass; Pete Gill, drums.

**Career:** Yorkshire lads who, refusing to cash in on punk or new wave syndrome, played power chord riffs with a vengeance few others could attain. Carrere signed band in 1979 and released **Saxon** LP same year. Despite typical heavy-metal posing (i.e., standardised logo, long hair, lots of leather), Saxon actually played decent, but loud, songs with tight arrangements and above-average lyrics.

**Wheels Of Steel** was released in May 1980 and became long-running hit. Next album saw Gill replaced by Nigel Glockler. It was no surprise when fourth LP, **Denim And Leather,** became international hit and proved band to be excellent example of hard rock at its best.

Extensive touring interfered with recording schedule, so band released commendable live set, **The Eagle Has Landed.** But this

was only filler, as good as it was. With **Power And The Glory** (1983) band has picked up again and provided another superb studio set.

Ambitious **Crusader** album project in 1984 was accompanied by mammoth tour which used a castle set to stunning effect and gave Saxon's brash, rugged sound its US breakthrough.

Legal battles with Carrere Records enforced one year lay-off before **Innocence Is No Excuse** appeared.

Steve Dawson quit the band and was replaced by Paul Johnson (bass) in August 1986 when the band released **Rock The Nations** album. In April 1987 Nigel Glockler left to join GTR featuring Steve Hackett and Steve Howe, and Saxon recruited Nigel Durham, from Barnsley, resulting in a line up of 100 per cent Yorkshiremen.

1988 saw new album **Destiny** released, produced by Stephan Galfas and featuring a version of the Christopher Cross song **Ride Like The Wind** issued as a single. **I Can't Wait Anymore** was released on single to coincide with a UK tour. Saxon's music has now become more AOR based to broaden their appeal.

**Current line-up:** Byford; Quinn; Oliver; Paul Johnson, bass; Nigel Durham, drums.

**Hit Singles:**

| | US | UK |
|---|---|---|
| Wheels Of Fire, 1980 | — | 20 |
| 747 (Strangers In The Night), 1980 | — | 13 |
| And The Bands Played On, 1981 | — | 12 |
| Never Surrender, 1981 | — | 18 |

**Below: Saxon in concert and full flight at full volume.**

**Albums:**
Saxon (—/Carrere), 1979
Wheels Of Steel (—/Carrere), 1980
Strong Arm Of The Law (Carrere), 1980
Denim & Leather (Carrere), 1981 **CD**
The Eagle Has Landed (—/Carrere), 1982
Power And The Glory (—/Carrere), 1983
Crusader (—/Carrere), 1985
Greatest Hits (—/Carrere), 1985
Innocence Is No Excuse (Parlophone), 1985
Rock The Nations (EMI), 1986 **CD**

# Leo Sayer

UK vocalist, composer.
Born Gerard Sayer, Shoreham, Sussex, May 21, 1948.

**Career:** After period as busker, was discovered in 1972 by musician/agent Dave Courtney and singer/actor Adam Faith(▶) Courtney and Sayer formed songwriting partnership, with Faith managing Sayer. First break came when Faith produced Roger Daltrey's(▶) first solo album **Daltrey** in 1973, Sayer's composition from LP **Giving It All Away** became UK Top 5 single.

First album **Silver Bird** made UK charts, helped by success of single **The Show Must Go On.** Sayer's strong material and idiosyncratic singing style often employing falsetto quickly established him as successful new contender in pop-rock field, with string of hit singles. His chirpy personality (he originally wore clown make-up) also ensured TV exposure as guest on various shows.

In 1975 Sayer ended his association with Courtney (although he worked with him again later), and in 1976 joined forces with ace producer Richard Perry for album **Endless Flight.** Project was great success, resulting in huge disco-orientated hit single **You Make Me Feel Like Dancing,** which broke Sayer in US market. Collaboration with Perry continued successfully into late '70s, with Sayer spending much of his time in US.

Sayer has starred in his own show on UK TV, which has showcased his likeable unassuming personality and distinctive musical talents. Although not a major artist, Sayer provides pleasant music in lightweight vein and has talent to sustain career into foreseeable future either as performer or songwriter.

**Hit Singles:**

| | US | UK |
|---|---|---|
| The Show Must Go On, 1973 | — | 2 |
| One Man Band, 1974 | — | 6 |
| Long Tall Glasses, 1974 | 9 | 4 |
| Moonlighting, 1975 | — | 2 |
| You Make Me Feel Like Dancing, 1973 | 1 | 2 |
| When I Need You, 1977 | 1 | 1 |
| How Much Love, 1977 | 17 | 10 |
| I Can't Stop Loving You, 1978 | — | 6 |
| More Than I Can Say, 1980 | 2 | 2 |
| Have You Ever Been In Love, 1982 | — | 10 |
| Orchard Road, 1983 | — | 16 |

**Albums:**
Silverbird (Warner Bros/Chrysalis), 1973
Just A Boy (Warner Bros/Chrysalis), 1974
Another Year (Warner Bros/Chrysalis), 1975
Endless Flight (Warner Bros/Chrysalis), 1976
Thunder In My Heart (Warner Bros/Chrysalis), 1977
Leo Sayer (Warner Bros/Chrysalis), 1978
The Very Best Of (Chrysalis), 1979 **CD**
Here (Chrysalis), 1979
The Show Must Go On (—/Pickwick), 1979
Living In A Fantasy (Chrysalis), 1980
When I Need You (—/Hallmark), 1982
World Radio (Warner Bros/Chrysalis), 1982 **CD**
Have You Ever Been In Love (Chrysalis), 1983

# Boz Scaggs

US vocalist, guitarist, composer.
Born William Royce Scaggs, Ohio, June 8, 1944.

**Above: The sophisticated Boz Scaggs pictured on stage.**

**Career:** William 'Boz' Scaggs was brought up in Texas, and met Steve Miller(▶) at high school in Dallas. Joined Miller's band the Marksmen in 1959.

Scaggs and Miller moved on to University of Wisconsin; formed band (the Ardells) to play local gigs. Scaggs quit college in 1963 to return to Texas and put together short-lived outfit called the Wigs, playing R&B. From 1964 to 1966 Scaggs was in Europe, scraping living as solo act (as folk singer). First album, **Boz**, recorded in Stockholm.

In 1967 Scaggs returned to America to join Steve Miller in San Francisco, collaborating on two highly acclaimed albums, **Children Of The Future** and **Sailor**. Left in late 1968, citing musical differences.

After one Atlantic album, Scaggs signed with CBS and started to move towards R&B stylings that would eventually make his name. During early '70s Scaggs continued to build following with albums like **My Time** and **Slow Dancer**; but it was not until 1976 release of **Silk Degrees** that he hit big time.

Featuring musicians now famous as members of Toto(▶), **Degrees** was soul-influenced without being slavishly imitative, and full of memorable songs. Album contained several hit singles, including much-covered semi-standard **We're All Alone**, and went on to sell over five million copies.

**Two Down Then Left** followed similar musical pattern and scored comparable success. Scaggs consolidated position by touring extensively (material performed even better live) throughout US and rest of world. 1980 album **Middle Man** featured guest guitarist Carlos Santana, and was followed by compilation **Hits**!

At time of writing, Scaggs was keeping relatively low profile. He is thoughtful artist with real facility for combining intelligent commercial songs with R&B feel. Well-crafted and played on only best musicians, Scaggs' music appeals to extremely wide audience, ensuring longevity.

| Hit Singles: | US | UK |
| --- | --- | --- |
| Lowdown, 1976 | 3 | 28 |
| What Can I Say, 1977 | 42 | 10 |
| Lido Shuffle, 1977 | 11 | 13 |
| Breakdown Dead Ahead, 1980 | 15 | — |
| Jojo, 1980 | 17 | — |
| Look What You've Done To Me, 1980 | 14 | — |
| Miss Sun, 1980 | 14 | — |

**Albums:**
Boz Scaggs (Atlantic), 1969
Moments (Columbia/CBS), 1971
Boz Scaggs And Band (Columbia/CBS), 1971
My Time (Columbia/CBS), 1972

**Silk Degrees, Boz Scaggs. Courtesy CBS Records.**

Slow Dancer (Columbia/CBS), 1974
Silk Degrees (Columbia/CBS), 1976 **CD**
Two Down Then Left (Columbia/CBS), 1977
Middle Man (Columbia/CBS), 1980
Hits! (Columbia/CBS), 1980

# Michael Schenker Group

European group formed 1980.

**Original line-up:** Michael Schenker, guitar; Gary Barden, vocals; Simon Phillips, drums; Mo Foster, bass; Don Airey, keyboards.

**Career:** Schenker (born Saustedt, West Germany, January 10, 1955) joined brother's band, Scorpions(▶), who opened for UFO(▶) on one of their early German tours. UFO was impressed enough to ask Schenker to join them. From 1974 until 1979, helped develop UFO into excellent hard rock band, culminating in brilliant live LP, **Strangers In The Night**.

By time of its release in early 1979, Schenker had left group. Briefly touring with Scorpions again, he then guested on their **Long Drive** LP before finally going solo.

Following jamming sessions with Aerosmith (▶) in September 1979, Schenker was free to work on solo LP. Rehearsals began with Gary Barden and Denny Carmassi (ex-Montrose(▶)) on drums, as well as Billy Sheehan on bass. Schenker then went into hospital because of personal problems and project fell apart.

Within a year, had formed line-up above; hired Roger Glover as producer, and released first solo LP. (Phillips' previous notable work included sessions for Jack Bruce(▶), Nazareth(▶), Roger Glover, Art Garfunkel(▶), Jeff Beck(▶), Roxy Music(▶), and Pete Townshend(▶).

Although strong, line-up was never meant to be permanent and Schenker recruited touring unit of Barden; Chris Glen, bass; famous session drummer Cozy Powell (Jeff Beck(▶) and Rainbow(▶) among many others); and his own replacement in UFO, Paul Raymond.

In 1981, this line-up struggled to produce second studio LP. **MSG** was expensive flop and, as expected, line-up again changed. However, old line-up was featured on double-live LP, **One Night At Budokan**.

Raymond left for full-time duties with UFO and Graham Bonnet stepped in for vocalist Barden. Bonnet helped band present a very strong Reading Festival performance, then recorded **Assault Attack**. For some reason, Bonnet's vocals failed to live up to either his earlier solo work or live efforts with Schenker. Barden returned on vocals and Ted McKenna replaced Cozy Powell. Further dissension in group saw quick fire changes — Barden returned, Andy Nye joined on keyboards and, after **Built To Destroy** LP, guitarist Derek St. Holmes was recruited. Barden was then replaced by Ray Kennedy, and then bassist Chris Glen said goodbye, with Dennis Feldman taking his place. In epitaph to the upheavals, Nye, McKenna and Feldman all then left. At time of writing, Schenker, no longer with Chrysalis, was recruiting yet again.

MSG broke up in 1984, and then Michael forged a new working relationship with Irish singer/songwriter Robin McAuley formerly of Grand Prix and Far Corporation. The new McAuley Schenker Group featured German drummer Bodo Schopf bassist Rocky Newton and second guitarist Mitch Perry. After several months of rehearsal the band made their debut at the European Monsters Of Rock Festival in 1987 and released their album **Perfect Timing** in October, with a subsequent single **Love Is Not A Game**. The band toured America, uncomfortably billed with Rush and later toured the UK with Whitesnake. Schenker was happy to reduce his 'guitar hero' role to allow room for McAuley to develop as writer and performer.

**Current line-up:** Schenker; Robin McAuley, vocals; Bodo Schopf, drums; Rocky Newton, bass; Mitch Perry, guitar.

**Albums:**
The Michael Schenker Group (Chrysalis), 1980 **CD**
MSG (Chrysalis), 1981
One Night At Bukodan (Chrysalis), 1981
Dancer (Chrysalis), 1982

Assault Attack (Chrysalis), 1983
Built To Destroy (Chrysalis), 1983
Portfolio (Chrysalis), 1987 **CD**

# Scritti Politti

UK group formed 1981.

**Original line-up:** Green Gartside, vocals, guitar; Tom Morley, drum programmer; Matthew K. programmer organiser.

**Career:** Originally a bunch of enthusiastic amateurs led by Welsh-born Gartside, Scritti Politti (condensed from Italian phrase meaning 'political writings') evolved through punk era to official first line-up in 1981.

Signed to Rough Trade, first 12-inch single was accompanied by frenetic and anarchic gigs. In 1983, a now restrained Gartside signed with Virgin in the UK and Warner Bros for the US market, and recruited American sidemen David Gamson and Fred Maher, to replace departed Morley and Matthew K. Mellower outlook resulted in chart action with Arif Mardin-produced material.

**Current line-up:** Gartside; David Gamson; Fred Maher.

| Hit Singles: | US | UK |
| --- | --- | --- |
| Wood Beez (Pray Like Aretha Franklin), 1984 | — | 10 |
| Absolute, 1984 | 1 | 17 |
| The Word Girl, 1985 | — | 6 |
| Perfect Way, 1985 | 11 | — |

**Albums:**
Songs To Remember (Rough Trade), 1982 **CD**
Cupid And Psyche (Virgin), 1985 **CD**

# The Searchers

UK group formed 1962.

**Original line-up:** Mike Pender, vocals, guitar; John McNally, vocals, guitar; Tony Jackson, vocals, bass; Chris Curtis, drums.

**Career:** On Merseyside in early '60s the Searchers were second only to Beatles in terms of local popularity; they specialised in high, keening harmonies and immaculate stage presentation.

National attention came after signing to Pye in 1963; group's cover of Drifters' **Sweets For My Sweet** soared to No. 1 spot and made group integral part of Merseybeat boom.

Group did not write own material and generally relied on covering suitable American hits like Jackie De Shannon's **Needles And Pins** (co-written by Sonny Bono of Sonny and Cher(▶)), Orlons' **Don't Throw Your Love Away** and **When You Walk In The Room**, also a hit for De Shannon. Group had considerable American success on Kapp label, making Top 40 on five occasions in 1964.

By 1965 group seemed unable to find right material and hits dried up. Jackson left to form Tony Jackson and the Vibrations (one minor hit), and was replaced by Frank Allen, formerly with Cliff Bennett's Rebel Rousers. At this time band started to move into lucrative club and cabaret circuit, where they continue to make substantial living to this day.

In their time the Searchers were one of the best-loved British 'beat groups', appealing to

**Left: Guitar star Michael Schenker, who worked with both the Scorpions and UFO before embarking on his own successful career.**

wide audience with their soaring harmonies and jangling guitar sound. In musical approach if not image they anticipated later folk-rock harmony outfits like Byrds(▶) and Mamas and Papas(▶). In early 1983 group celebrated 21 years in the music business with a series of special concerts, and look set to continue for another 21 years.

**Current line-up:** Pender; McNally; Frank Allen, bass; Bob Jackson, keyboards; Billy Adamson, drums.

| Hit Singles: | US | UK |
| --- | --- | --- |
| Sweets For My Sweet, 1963 | — | 1 |
| Sugar And Spice, 1963 | 44 | 2 |
| Needles And Pins, 1964 | 13 | 1 |
| Don't Throw Your Love Away, 1964 | 16 | 1 |
| Some Day We're Gonna Love Again, 1964 | 34 | 11 |
| When You Walk In The Room, 1964 | 35 | 3 |

**Golden Hour Of The Searchers. Courtesy Golden Hour/Pye Records.**

| | | |
| --- | --- | --- |
| Love Potion No. 9, 1964 | 3 | — |
| What Have They Done To The Rain, 1964 | 29 | 13 |
| Goodbye My Love, 1965 | 52 | 4 |
| He's Got No Love, 1965 | — | 12 |
| Take Me For What I'm Worth, 1966 | — | 20 |

**Albums:**
Meet The Searchers (Kapp/Pye), 1963
Sugar And Spice (—/Pye), 1963
When You Walk In The Room (—/Pye), 1964
It's The Searchers (—/Pye), 1964
Sounds Like The Searchers (—/Pye), 1964
Take Me For What I'm Worth (—/Pye), 1965
The Searchers (Sire), 1980
Needles And Pins (—/Hallmark), 1971
The Searchers File (—/Pye), 1977
100 Minutes (—/Pye), 1982
Loves Melodies (Sire/—), N/A
Silver Searchers (Nouveou), 1986 **CD**
Hits Collection (PRT), 1987 **CD**

# Neil Sedaka

US vocalist, composer, pianist.
Born Brooklyn, New York, March 13, 1939.

**Career:** Piano prodigy at eight, this son of a taxi driver studied at prestigious Juilliard School and had promising future as classical pianist. At 13 began writing songs with neighbour Howard Greenfield, who remained lyric-writing partner for over 20 years (until replaced by Phil Cody after 1973). Sedaka and Greenfield were one of several teams working at Brill Building in New York, turning out high-quality music which bridged gap between Tin Pan Alley and rock'n'roll for teen market's top performers. Then, in 1958, Connie Frances(▶) had hit with their **Stupid Cupid**.

Sedaka began recording own songs and between 1959 and 1963 hits like **The Diary, Calendar Girl, Oh Carol** (dedicated to friend and fellow Brill Building writer Carole King(▶)), **Stairway To Heaven, Breaking Up Is Hard To Do** and **Happy Birthday Sweet Sixteen** sold over 20 million copies. Never succumbing to pitfalls of stardom, Sedaka lived and worked in father's unpretentious Brooklyn apartment, writing over 500 songs before Beatles-influenced music caused his popularity as performer to fade. Composing talent was still in demand, however, and he wrote for Tom Jones, the Fifth Dimension and Andy Williams.

Always popular in Britain (his second record, **I Go Ape**, made No. 5 in UK), Sedaka was persuaded in 1971 to do come-back concert at Albert Hall in London; show successfully combined new songs with oldies. While in Britain he recorded two albums with group called Hot Legs (who became 10cc(▶)), then returned to Los Angeles to record third album—all for Britain. When Elton John(▶) realised Sedaka had no US record company, he signed him to own label, Rocket Records. Gold-rated **Sedaka's Back** and **The Hungry Years,** combining songs from three British

**Oh Carol, Neil Sedaka. Courtesy RCA Records.**

LPs, was well received in US and Sedaka had his first US No. 1 hit single in ten years with **Laughter In The Rain** (1975) followed by hit **Bad Blood,** which featured Elton John on backing vocals. **Breaking Up Is Hard To Do** returned to charts in 1976 after 14 years.

Sedaka's songs for Captain and Tenille, **Love Will Keep Us Together** and **You Never Done It Like That,** further enhanced revived reputation. First NBC-TV special in 1976 received both critical and popular acclaim. Since then, Sedaka has continued to write, record, appear on television and play to full houses in Las Vegas, Lake Tahoe and around the world. A star at 20 and a has-been at 25, Sedaka has accepted ups and downs with equanimity. His new songs remain fresh and original, and his music is enjoyed by widest possible audience.

**Hit Singles:**

| | US | UK |
|---|---|---|
| The Diary, 1959 | 14 | — |
| I Go Ape, 1959 | 42 | 5 |
| Oh! Carol, 1959 | 9 | 3 |
| Stairway To Heaven, 1960 | 9 | 8 |
| You Mean Everything To Me, 1960 | 17 | 45 |
| Calendar Girl, 1961 | 4 | 8 |
| Little Devil, 1961 | 11 | 9 |
| Happy Birthday, Sweet Sixteen, 1961 | 6 | 3 |
| Breaking Up Is Hard To Do, 1962 | 1 | 7 |
| Next Door To An Angel, 1962 | 5 | 29 |
| Alice In Wonderland, 1963 | 17 | — |
| Oh Carol/Breaking Up Is Hard To Do/Little Devil, 1972 | — | 19 |
| That's When The Music Takes Me, 1973 | 27 | 18 |
| Laughter In The Rain, 1974 | 1 | 15 |

| | | |
|---|---|---|
| Bad Blood, 1975 | 1 | — |
| Breaking Up Is Hard To Do, 1976 | 8 | — |
| Love In The Shadows, 1976 | 16 | — |

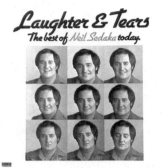

**Laughter And Tears, Neil Sedaka. Courtesy Polydor Records.**

*With Daria Sedaka:*
Should've Never Let You Go, 1982  19  —

**Albums:**
Oh Carol (—/Camden), 1970
Stupid Cupid (—/Camden), 1972
Tra-La Days Are Over (Polydor), 1974
Live At The Royal Festival Hall, With The Royal Philharmonic Orchestra (Polydor), 1974
Laughter In The Rain (Polydor), 1974
Let's Go Steady Again (—/Pickwick), 1975
Laughter And Tears (Polydor), 1976 **CD**
And Songs—A Solo Concert (Polydor), 1977
Sedaka '50s and '60s (RCA), 1977
A Song (Elektra/Polydor), 1977
All You Need Is The Music (Polydor), 1978
Many Sides Of (RCA), 1979
Neil Sedaka's Greatest Hits (RCA), 1980
In The Pocket (Elektra/Polydor), 1980
Now (Elektra/Polydor), 1981
Singer, Songwriter, Melody Maker (Accord/—), 1982
20 Golden Pieces Of (—/Bulldog), 1982
Good Times (PRT), 1986 **CD**

# Bob Seger

US vocalist, composer, guitarist. Born Detroit, Michigan, 1947.

**Career:** Seger grew up in Detroit and played in local band, Last Heard. 1966 saw release of solo material. Several tracks received good critical notice or became regional hits (**Heavy Music** (1966), **2+2=?** (1967) and **Ramblin' Gamblin' Man** (1968)). After four LPs and many, many mid-Western gigs, Seger quit music in 1969 and went to college. By 1971 he was on the road again, with same results; critical praise, regional hits—and always just out of the running.

Third phase of career began when he formed permanent backing group, the Silver Bullet Band. This aggregation produced **Beautiful Loser,** but again national success just eluded Seger. He decided to try Frampton's(▶) approach of using live LP to sell sound rather than collection of old hits.

**Live Bullet** proved to be key and Seger was sudden overnight success some 12 years after first attempts. He quickly followed up with **Night Moves** and both albums stayed in US charts for some time, (**Night Moves** went platinum).

Anxious to give fans same musical diet Seger finally found time in heavy touring schedule to record **Stranger In Town,** which went triple platinum.

**Against The Wind** went to No. 1 in US LP charts, but seemed to suffer from platinum overdosage. Seger sensed this and offered another live set, **Nine Tonight,** a collection

of old hits, giving him time to rejuvenate his creative forces for his personal masterpiece, **The Distance.**

Last few years have seen Seger maintaining relatively low profile, broken by **Shakedown** contribution on platinum 'Beverley Hills Cop II' soundtrack.

**Hit Singles:**

| | US | UK |
|---|---|---|
| Ramblin' Gamblin' Man, 1969 | 17 | — |
| Night Moves, 1977 | 4 | — |
| Still The Same, 1978 | 4 | — |
| Hollywood Nights, 1978 | 12 | 42 |
| We've Got Tonite, 1979 | 13 | 41 |
| Fire Lake, 1980 | 6 | — |
| Against The Wind, 1980 | 5 | — |
| You'll Accomp'ny Me, 1980 | 14 | — |
| Tryin' To Live My Life Without You, 1981 | 5 | — |
| Shame On The Moon, 1983 | 2 | — |
| Even Now, 1983 | 12 | — |
| Understanding, 1985 | 17 | — |
| Shakedown (From Beverley Hills Cop II), 1987 | 1 | — |

**Albums:**
Ramblin' Gamblin' Man (Capitol), 1969
Noah (Capitol/—), 1969
Mongrel (Capitol), 1970
Smokin' O.P.'s (Reprise), 1972
Seven (Reprise), 1974
Beautiful Loser (Capitol), 1975
Live Bullet (Capitol), 1976
Night Moves (Capitol), 1976
Stranger In The Town (Capitol), 1980

**Stranger In Town, Bob Seger. Courtesy Capitol Records.**

Against The Wind (Capitol), 1980 **CD**
Nine Tonight (Capitol), 1982
The Distance (Capitol), 1983 **CD**
Greatest Hits (Capitol), 1984
Like A Rock (Capitol), 1986

# The Sex Pistols

UK group formed 1975.

**Original line-up:** Steve Jones, guitar, vocals; Glen Matlock, bass; Paul Cook, drums; Johnny Rotten, vocals.

**Career:** Jones, Cook and Matlock used to hang around Malcolm McLaren's clothes store; there they met John Lydon whom McLaren suggested as band's vocalist. McLaren became manager and began developing strong image by encouraging tough, ragged street dress (which rebelled against decadent glam look of '70s acts). He renamed Lydon 'Rotten' and coined moniker Sex Pistols.

Early gigs were hardly professional but full of explosive energy. McLaren capitalised on group's inexperience and used it to promote image of angry young men only refused to copy established rock stars (megabands in particular).

1976 gigs not only enhanced band's reputation for being 'anti' everything but began involving audience in violence on regular basis. November 1976 turned Sex Pistols loose on centre of rock world. A few days after signing EMI contract, and readying **Anarchy In The UK** single, Pistols were provoked into swearing on live Thames TV programme. Uproar made them front page items of all newspapers, not just music weeklies. Kids loved it and the 'punk' revolution was on.

EMI dropped band in January 1977, losing £40,000 advance. A&M stepped in to sign band, but gave up £75,000 advance a few days later. By time Virgin offered £50,000 advance in May 1977, band had collected over £150,000 for one single.

In interim, Rotten replaced Matlock with friend Sid Vicious. Pistols were banned practically everywhere which meant there was no way to follow up notoriety with a little rock'n'roll. Subsequent recordings ensured Pistol's place in chart histories, but on concluding first American tour, Rotten announced group's break up. Other three carried on temporarily, even using infamous Great Train Robber Ronald Biggs for vocal or two. All this was pointless; it became macabre when Vicious was arrested for murder of girlfriend. He died in ugly overdose incident while awaiting trial.

Several post-Pistols solo projects (Rich Kids, Professionals, Public Image Ltd.) have

**Never Mind The Bollocks, Sex Pistols. Courtesy Virgin Records.**

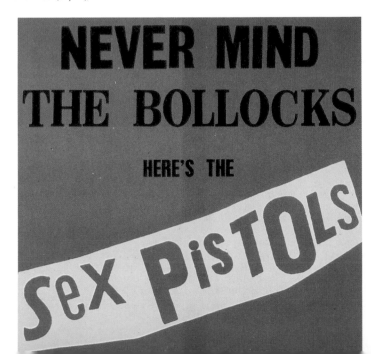

all failed to win either wide critical acclaim or the popular support afforded Pistols. Ironically, Pistols influenced entire rock industry but accomplished little musically. Band's assault on established rock heroes forced these stars to question their secure status and make more of an effort to remain fresh.

The Sex Pistols raw style inspired many young musicians/singers, previously inhibited by lack of money or finesse, to form back-to-the-basics bands. The Pistols were not only a shot in the arm to the music industry, but (with McLaren's foresight, which he continues to demonstrate) helped bring back the fashion/music connection that had been so exciting in the '60s. Most importantly, the Sex Pistols encouraged audiences and performers to question the music scene.

Very much a creation of manager Malcolm McLaren's publicity hype machine, the Sex Pistols lived out their role as punk radicals to the fullest extent and are likely to be remembered more for their image and their charisma than for their musical contribution.

Tenth anniversary of 'summer of punk' in 1986 brought resurgence of interest in proto-typical punksters, as did well-received Vicious biopic Sid And Nancy.

**Final line-up:** Jones, guitar, vocals; Cook, drums; Sid Vicious, bass, vocals.

| Hit Singles: | US | UK |
|---|---|---|
| God Save The Queen, 1977 | — | 2 |
| Pretty Vacant, 1977 | — | 6 |
| Holidays In The Sun, 1977 | — | 8 |
| No One Is Innocent/My Way, 1978 | — | 7 |
| Something Else/Friggin' In The Riggin', 1979 | — | 3 |
| Silly Thing/Who Killed Bambi, 1979 | — | 6 |
| C'mon Everybody, 1979 | — | 3 |

**Albums:**
Never Mind The Bollocks, Here's The Sex Pistols (Warner Bros/Virgin), 1977* **CD**
The Great Rock'n'Roll Swindle (—/Virgin), 1978 **CD**
Some Produce (—/Virgin), 1979
Carry On Sex Pistols (—/Virgin), 1979
Flogging A Dead Horse (—/Virgin), 1979 **CD**
Original Pistols Live (Dojo), 1986 **CD**
*Only LP released while band was working unit.

# The Shadows
UK group formed 1959.

**Original line-up:** Hank Marvin, Fender Stratocaster guitar; Bruce Welch, Fender Telecaster guitar; Jet Harris, bass; Tony Meehan, drums.

**Career:** In 1958 Marvin and Welch were members of Cliff Richard's(▶) backing group the Drifters. By following year personnel had stabilised as above, and group had changed name to Shadows to avoid confusion with American Drifters(▶).

Although band continued to back Richard, they started to record independently from 1959. During a 1960 British tour, Jerry Lordan, artist on same bill, gave them instrumental piece he had written called **Apache**. Their version of song reached No. 1 in July 1960, and set pattern for instrumental hits that would last until psychedelia era of 1967. Formula was simple yet effective; Marvin's guitar would carry melody, while others provided clipped, efficient backing.

Almost completely arranged, Shadows music could be clinical; yet it provided example for thousands of young instrumentalists, especially, of course, guitar players. Image-wise, Shadows relied on matching mohair suits and laid-back non-chalance; wildness of ensuing beat and R&B era was in many cases reaction to their uniformed neatness.

During this period several personnel changes took place. Tony Meehan left in 1961 to be replaced by Brian Bennett. Jet Harris quit in 1962 and almost immediately joined up with Meehan again — duo produced three Top 10 singles in 1963 before Harris retired from scene due to ill health. For short while Harris was replaced in Shadows by Brian 'Licquorice' Locking; he in turn was followed by John Rostill.

In 1968, after hits had dried up, outfit ceased to exist as regular working aggregation. During '70s members got involved in other musical activities; among many other projects, Bruce Welch wrote for and produced Cliff Richard(▶), John Farrar produced Olivia Newton-John(▶), and Brian Bennett became in-demand session musician. However, band continued to record and work together sporadically, with various bass players.

In 1977 **Twenty Golden Greats** compilation album topped UK charts, and following year group returned to singles chart in big way with version of show tune **Don't Cry For Me Argentina**. Since that time group has made sporadic chart appearances, and tours continue to be guaranteed sell-outs.

Although their music has not been that influential — few rock guitarists actually play like Hank Marvin — Shadows encouraged generation of young men to take up instruments and make music for themselves. Many current axe heroes point to Hank Marvin as their first role model. Now elder statesmen of rock and pop, Shadows will undoubtedly clock up more hits before drawing final curtain.

**Current line-up:** Marvin; Welch; Brian Bennett, drums.

| Hit Singles: | US | UK |
|---|---|---|
| Apache, 1960 | — | 1 |
| Man Of Mystery/The Stranger, 1960 | — | 5 |
| F.B.I., 1961 | — | 6 |
| Frightened City, 1961 | — | 3 |
| Kon-Tiki, 1961 | — | 1 |
| The Savage, 1961 | — | 10 |
| Wonderful Land, 1962 | — | 1 |
| Guitar Tango, 1962 | — | 4 |
| Dance On!, 1962 | — | 1 |
| Foot Tapper, 1963 | — | 1 |
| Atlantis, 1963 | — | 2 |
| Shindig, 1963 | — | 6 |
| Geronimo, 1963 | — | 11 |
| Theme For Young Lovers, 1964 | — | 12 |
| The Rise And Fall Of Flingel Bunt, 1964 | — | 5 |
| Genie With The Light Brown Lamp, 1964 | — | 17 |
| The Next Time I See Mary Anne, 1965 | — | 17 |
| Stingray, 1965 | — | 19 |
| Don't Make My Baby Blue, 1965 | — | 10 |
| War Lord, 1965 | — | 18 |
| Let Me Be The One, 1975 | — | 12 |
| Don't Cry For Me Argentina, 1978 | — | 5 |
| Theme From The Deer Hunter (Cavatina), 1979 | — | 9 |
| Riders In The Sky, 1980 | — | 12 |

**Albums:**
The Shadows (—/Columbia), 1962
Greatest Hits (—/Columbia), 1963
Dance With The Shadows (—/Columbia), 1964
The Sound Of The Shadows (—/Columbia), 1965
More Hits (—/Columbia), 1965
Shadow Music (—/Columbia), 1966
Jigsaw (—/Columbia), 1967
Established 1958 (—/Columbia), 1968
Something Else (—/Columbia), 1969
Shades Of Rock (—/Columbia), 1970
Rockin' With Curly Leads (—/EMI), 1973
Specs Appeal (—/EMI), 1975
The Shadows (—/Ember), 1975
Live At Paris Olympia (—/EMI), 1975
Rarities (—/NUT), 1976
Tasty (—/EMI), 1977
20 Golden Greats (—/EMI), 1977
At The Movies (—/MFP), 1978
String Of Hits (EMI), 1979 **CD**
Change Of Address (—/Polydor), 1980
Another String Of Hot Hits (—/EMI), 1980 **CD**
Hits Right Up Your Street (—/Rollover), 1981
Live (—/MfP), 1981
Life In The Jungle (—/Polydor), 1982

**Left: The surviving Shadows (left to right) Bruce Welch, Brian Bennett and Hank B. Marvin, in the 1980s.**

Guardian Angel (Roll Over Records), 1984 **CD**
Compact Shadows (Polydor) **CD**
Moonlight Shadows (Polydor) **CD**
Simply Shadows (Polydor), 1987 **CD**
XXV (Polydor), 1987 **CD**
20 Golden Greats (EMI), 1987

**Albums:**
The Del Shannon Hit Parade (--/London), 1980
Live In England (—/Fame), 1982
Drop Down And Get Me (Elektra/Demon), 1982
Runaway Hits (Elektra/Demon), 1984 **CD**
I Go To Pieces (Edsel), 1986

# Del Shannon

US vocalist, composer.
Born Charles Westover, Grand Rapids, Michigan, December 30, 1939.

**Career:** Shannon took up singing and guitar in early teens. First real experience was gained in US Army, where he performed on Armed Forces Network's 'Get Up and Go' programme. After discharge returned to his home state, and began singing professionally in local clubs.

Discovered by Detroit agents Harry Balk and Irving Micahnik, Shannon was soon signed to Big Top Records. His first and biggest hit, **Runaway**, was recorded almost immediately. Shannon and keyboard player Max Crook had worked out song in clubs with an electric organ called the Musitron. Single made No. 1 in US in early 1961, remaining on chart for 17 weeks; hit in UK during June of that year, staying on charts for 22 weeks. Shannon had further Top 20 singles, including **Hats Off To Larry, Little Town Flirt** and **Keep Searchin'**.

**The Greatest Hits, Del Shannon. Courtesy Line Records.**

Chart success declined after 1965, although English duo Peter and Gordon scored with his **I Go To Pieces**. Shannon's sharp, early '60s sound was considered dated by 1967; he tried varying sound by recording album with producer Andrew Loog Oldham; though interesting, it was a commercial failure. Shannon produced other artists with considerable success; Brian Hyland's Shannon-produced **Gypsy Woman** was No. 1 in UK, Top 5 in US. Continued to tour, particularly in England; a fine live album was released in 1972.

In '70s Shannon released singles produced by Jeff Lynn (of ELO(▶) and Dave Edmunds(▶)), again with little commercial success. In 1982 signed with Elektra records who released album produced by long-time admirer Tom Petty(▶), **Drop Down And Get Me**, which met with critical approval and lead to crop of reissues.

| Hit Singles: | US | UK |
|---|---|---|
| Runaway, 1961 | 1 | 1 |
| Hats Off To Larry, 1961 | 5 | 6 |
| So Long Baby, 1961 | 28 | 10 |
| Hey Little girl, 1962 | 38 | 2 |
| Swiss Maid, 1962 | — | 2 |
| Little Town Flirt, 1963 | 12 | 4 |
| Two Kinds Of Teardrops, 1963 | 50 | 5 |
| Keep Searchin' (We'll Follow The Sun), 1965 | 9 | 3 |

# Simon & Garfunkel

US duo formed 1957.

**Career:** During late '50s, a bouncy little guy named Paul Simon(▶) was hustling for fraternity party gigs around Forest Hills High School in New York. Unfashionable and uncool, his vocal harmony duo Tom and Jerry had few takers. (When he and partner Art Garfunkel(▶) became famous in 1965 as Simon and Garfunkel, lots of people were kicking themselves.) As Paul and Jerry they actually reached No. 54 in charts with late 1957 **Hey Schoolgirl** but, despite appearance on 'American Bandstand', follow-ups failed to take off. They went separate ways, Paul Simon to Queens College and Art Garfunkel to New York's Columbia University.

While at college, Simon and fellow-student Carole King(▶) made demo tapes for publishers, which taught him techniques like overdubbing. Single **The Lone Teen Ranger** (recorded in 1962 as Jerry Landis) got to 97 in US charts. Dropping out of law school in 1964, Simon left for England to perform on folk circuit. Another single **He Was My Brother** (recorded as Paul Kane) was heard in New York by Columbia Records, who agreed to produce Simon and Garfunkel album. Simon returned to US where **Wednesday Morning 3 AM** was recorded under real names. Garfunkel had recorded for Octavia, then Warwick as Arty Garr. Mixing traditional and modern folk songs plus original numbers by Simon, album was less than successful. Simon therefore returned to UK, where he recorded solo album **The Paul Simon Songbook**, containing own material, including **I Am A Rock** and, like **3 AM**, using only guitar accompaniment.

Producer Tom Wilson, who had helped electrify Dylan, saw possibilities in one track on **3 AM**. Adding electric guitar, bass and drums, Wilson released **Sounds Of Silence** as single, which shot to US No. 1. Hearing of success while in Europe, Simon again returned to US. In 1966 he and Garfunkel recorded **Sounds Of Silence** album, including material from **Songbook**, but with rock backing. **Homeward Bound**, written while waiting for train in Lancashire, became duo's first UK hit single, reaching No. 9 (No. 5 in US).

Simon's literate, poetic yet aggressive lyrics, filled with introspection, isolation and

**Greatest Hits, Simon And Garfunkel** '60s classics. **Courtesy CBS Records.**

ironic protest, combined perfectly with Garfunkel's delicate vocal arrangements to create a sound that appealed to increasingly sophisticated young listeners. Tour of US and UK was followed by **Bookends**, then **The Graduate** soundtrack album which won Grammy for Best Original Motion Picture Score. Also received Grammy for **Mrs Robinson** (Best Record), supposedly written almost by accident while working on film score: new song had gap which, by chance, had same number of beats as name of character in Mike Nichols' film, so Simon jokingly used her name to fill gap. When Nichols heard there was song called Mrs Robinson, he demanded to hear it, and it went straight into film.

By now Simon and Garfunkel were so popular that **3 AM** was finally released in UK. In 1970 **Bridge Over Troubled Water** became extraordinarily successful, title track reaching No. 1 in US and UK, and album selling over 9 million copies. Despite success, duo felt constrained by partnership, so split up after final concert in Garfunkel's home town of Forest Hills. Although Garfunkel occasionally did guest numbers with Simon, it was 11 years before they reunited for 1981 free concert in New York's Central Park. Nearly half a million people, including the Mayor, gathered there to be reminded of, as New York

**Below: Art Garfunkel (left) and his partner Paul Simon, who remain one of the most popular duos in the history of rock music.**

Times said, 'distinct musical identities that complement each other in a very special way'. Double-record, video and six-week European tour followed, giving much-needed boost to stagnating solo careers.

| Hit Singles: | US | UK |
|---|---|---|
| The Sounds Of Silence, 1966 | 1 | — |
| Homeward Bound, 1966 | 5 | 9 |
| I Am A Rock, 1966 | 3 | 17 |
| A Hazy Shade Of Winter, 1966 | 13 | — |
| At The Zoo, 1967 | 16 | — |
| Scarborough Fair (Canticle), 1968 | 11 | — |
| Mrs Robinson, 1968 | 1 | 4 |
| Mrs Robinson (EP), 1969 | — | 9 |
| The Boxer, 1969 | 7 | 6 |
| Bridge Over Troubled Water, 1970 | 1 | 1 |
| Cecilia, 1970 | 4 | — |
| El Condor Pasa, 1970 | 18 | — |
| My Little Town, 1975 | 9 | — |

**Albums:**
Wednesday Morning 3 AM (Columbia/CBS), 1966 **CD**
The Sounds Of Silence (Columbia/CBS), 1966 **CD**
Parsley, Sage, Rosemary And Thyme (Columbia/CBS), 1966 **CD**
Bookends (Columbia/CBS), 1968 **CD**
The Graduate (Soundtrack) (Columbia/CBS), 1968 **CD**
Bridge Over Troubled Water (Columbia/CBS), 1970 **CD**
Greatest Hits (Columbia/CBS), 1972 **CD**

Collected Works (Columbia/—), 1981
Collection (—/CBS), 1981 **CD**
Concert In Central Park (Warner Bros), 1982

# Carly Simon

US vocalist.
Born New York, June 25, 1945.

**Career:** Carly emerged on New York folk scene in mid-'60s with sister Lucy as the Simon Sisters. Enjoyed minor hit on Kapp in 1964 with **Winkin', Blinkin' And Nod** while still studying at exclusive Sarah Lawrence College.

When Lucy got married, Carly went to France; did not return to singing until she met Bob Dylan's manager Albert Grossman. He brought in Dylan's producer Bob Johnson, and his regular backing musicians, including the Band(▶), Al Kooper(▶) and Mike Bloomfield(▶). He persuaded Dylan(▶) himself to write one song for 1966 New York session aimed at establishing Carly as 'The female Dylan'.

The pair fell out, however, and tracks were never released. Carly was re-discovered by Elektra Records' boss Jac Holzman at party in late 1969.

**Coming Around Again, Carly Simon. Courtesy Arista Records.**

'Esquire' magazine film critic and screenplay writer Jacob Brackman had been writing material with her for some time. This provided content for debut album which included smash single **That's The Way I've Always Heard It Should Be**, a pensive song about difference between childhood dreams and adult realities. Theme was fully exploited in subsequent albums, notably on follow-up set **Anticipation**.

1972s **No Secrets** album made Simon international star thanks to classic single **You're So Vain** (featuring Mick Jagger on backing vocals). Reportedly, its anonymous non-hero was film star Warren Beatty though Carly refused to confirm this.

Married to singer/songwriter James Taylor(▶) in 1973, the couple duetted on 1974 hit single **Mockingbird**, a mirror copy of Inez and Charlie Foxx's original. Following that year's **Hotcakes** album, had 18-month hiatus before appearance of **Playing Possum**, Simon's third LP with ace producer Richard Perry. After **Another Passenger** album (produced by Ted Templeman in 1976) returned to Richard Perry in following year for Oscar and Grammy nomination song **Nobody Does It Better**, theme for James Bond film 'The Spy Who Loved Me'.

Carly finished long contract with Elektra in 1979, then sojourned briefly with Warner Bros and Epic before settling at Arista in 1987. **Coming Around Again** album and single revitalised career which had been flagging since break up with James Taylor.

**Hit Singles:**

| | US | UK |
|---|---|---|
| That's The Way I've Always Heard It Should Be, 1971 | 10 | — |
| Anticipation, 1972 | 13 | — |
| You're So Vain, 1972 | 1 | 3 |
| The Right Thing To Do, 1973 | 17 | 17 |
| Haven't Got Time For The Pain, 1974 | 14 | — |
| Nobody Does It Better, 1977 | 2 | 7 |
| You Belong To Me, 1978 | 6 | — |
| Jesse, 1980 | 11 | — |
| Why, 1982 | — | 10 |
| Coming Around Again, 1987 | — | 10 |

*With James Taylor:*

| | US | UK |
|---|---|---|
| Mockingbird, 1974 | 5 | 34 |

**Albums:**
Carly Simon (Elektra), 1971
Anticipation (Elektra), 1971
No Secrets (Elektra), 1972
Hot Cakes (Elektra), 1974
Playing Possum (Elektra), 1975
Best Of (Elektra), 1976 **CD**
Another Passage (Elektra), 1976
Boys In The Trees (Elektra), 1978
Spy (Elektra), 1979
Come Upstairs (Warner Bros), 1980
Torch (Warner Bros), 1981
You're So Vain (—/Hallmark), 1981
Spoiled Girl (Epic), 1985 **CD**
Hello Big Man (Elektra), 1986 **CD**
Coming Around Again (Arista), 1987 **CD**

# Paul Simon

US composer, vocalist, guitarist
Born Newark, New Jersey, October 13, 1941.

**Career:** Musical career began as schoolboy with, in 1964, startlingly successful partnership of Simon and Garfunkel(▶). Far from remaining with Garfunkel throughout early years, Simon recorded on his own as Paul Kane, Jerry Landis and True Taylor, toured European folk circuit and made solo album of own material in London before duo's hit single **Sounds Of Silence** became US No. 1 in 1966. Pair then continued to record and toured together until splitting up amicably in 1970, at height of success.

Freed from constraints of partnership, Simon became more musically complex, incorporating variety of influences, including South American group Los Incas, jazz violin of Stephane Grapelli and Jamaican reggae. 1972 album **Paul Simon** not only provided US/UK hit single **Mother And Child Reunion**, but reached No. 1 in UK. Dixie Hummingbirds gospel group and top quality session musicians were added to second LP **There Goes Rhymin' Simon**. Lyrically more relaxed, simpler and funkier, album gave Simon hit singles on both sides of Atlantic. Concert album **Live Rhymin'** from 1973 tour featured Jesse Dixon gospel group and South American band Urubamba performing new versions of his old songs.

In 1975, **Still Crazy After All These Years** blended musical changes with starkly precise personal songs. Containing US No. 1 single **50 Ways To Leave Your Lover**, album won two Grammys (Best Album And Best Male Pop Vocal Performance), bringing Simon's Grammy award total to 12. Disappointed that critical attention still focused on lyrics rather than musical ideas. Simon toured again with top-rated session musicians.

**One Trick Pony, Paul Simon. Courtesy Warner Bros Records. Simon scored and starred in film.**

Following acting debut in Woody Allen's 'Annie Hall' (1980), Simon produced, starred-in and scored disappointing **One Trick Pony** the same year. Film soundtrack, artist's first original release in five years, fared as badly as the movie.

Temporary re-union with Garfunkel for Central Park Concert seemed to give Simon new impetus, although 1983 release **Heart And Bones** failed to generate prolonged appeal.

Simon's interest in indigenous music resulted in classic 1987 **Graceland** album, an anthema to certain anti-apartheid organisations because of it's involvement with South African musicians. Subsequent world tour prompted audience to remember the stature of this giant of pop music.

**Hit Singles:**

| | US | UK |
|---|---|---|
| Mother And Child Reunion, 1972 | 4 | 5 |
| Me And Julio Down By The Schoolyard, 1972 | 22 | 15 |
| Take Me To The Mardi Gras, 1973 | — | 7 |
| Kodachrome, 1973 | 2 | — |
| Love Me Like A Rock, 1973 | 2 | 39 |
| 50 Ways To Leave Your Lover, 1976 | 1 | 23 |
| Slip Slidin' Away, 1977 | 5 | 36 |
| (What A) Wonderful World (with Art Garfunkel and James Taylor), 1978 | 17 | — |
| Late In The Evening, 1980 | 6 | — |
| Boy In The Bubble, 1986 | — | 33 |

**Albums:**
Paul Simon (Columbia/CBS), 1972*
There Goes Rhymin' Simon (Columbia/CBS), 1973* **CD**
Live Rhymin' (Columbia/CBS), 1974 **CD**
Still Crazy After All These Years (Columbia/CBS), 1975* **CD**
Greatest Hits (Columbia/CBS), 1977 **CD**
One Trick Pony (soundtrack) (Warner Bros), 1980 **CD**
Hearts And Bones (Warner Bros), 1983 **CD**
Graceland (Warner Bros), 1986 **CD**

*Available as 5 LP set **Collected Works** (Columbia/—), 1981, with **Paul Simon Songbook** LP.

# Nina Simone

US vocalist, pianist.
Born Eunice Wayman, Tryon, North Carolina, February 21, 1933.

**Career:** By age of seven Nina Simone had taught herself piano and organ. She sang in church choir, but received formal music training at high school in Asheville, Carolina, and at famed Juilliard School of Music.

When her family moved to Philadelphia, Simone began working East Coast clubs. She gained contract with Bethlehem Records, which led to million-selling version of **I Loves You Porgy** in 1959. On moving to Colpix in 1960 numerous albums and couple of minor hits followed. A period with Philips between 1965 and 1967 resulted in hits **Don't Let Me Be Misunderstood** and Screamin' Jay Hawkins' **I Put A Spell On You**. Latter established Simone internationally.

In 1967 Simone switched labels again, to RCA, and entered her most productive and commercially successful period with further hit singles, and number of albums which combined high-quality material with classy, often jazz-influenced arrangements.

In '70s, she began to devote more time to political work, and from mid-'70s to present day she has worked and recorded only sporadically. Superb 1978 album **Baltimore** showed that her talent remained undimmed, although recent reports of serious financial and personal problems give cause for concern.

In late 1987 scored major hit in UK with reissued **My Baby Just Cares For Me**; financial situation was not improved, however, as artist had sold rights to recording many years previously.

**Hit Singles:**

| | US | UK |
|---|---|---|
| I Loves You Porgy, 1959 | 18 | — |
| Ain't Got No/I Got Life, 1968 | — | 2 |
| To Love Somebody, 1969 | — | 5 |
| My Baby Just Cares For Me, 1987 | — | 5 |

**Albums:**
Here Comes The Sun (RCA), 1969
Best of Nina Simone (RCA/—), 1972 **CD**
I Loves You Porgy (Bethlehem/CBS), 1977
Baltimore (CTI), 1978
Cry Before I Go (—/Manhattan), 1980
My Baby Just Cares For Me (Charly), 1982 **CD**
Artistry Of Nine Simone (—/RCA), 1982
Nina Simone (—/Dakota), 1982
Lady Midnight (Connoisseur Collection), 1987

**Baltimore, Nina Simone. Courtesy CTI/Polydor Records. Simone became more political in the '70s.**

# Simple Minds

UK group formed 1977

**Original line-up:** Jim Kerr, vocals; Charlie Burchill, guitar; Brian McGee, drums; Mick MacNeil, keyboards; Derek Forbes, bass.

**Career:** Scottish outfit now reaping commercial rewards after nearly nine years building following on pub, club and university tour circuit. Formed from remains of punk outfit Johnny and the Self-Abusers, band was quickly signed by Arista for national distribution of Edinburgh label Zoom.

Three albums later, Arista and band parted company, with Virgin promptly offering quintet new contract. 1981 LP **Sons And Fascination/Sister Feelings Call**, produced by Steve Hillage, entered UK top 20, before McGee left to be replaced (temporarily) by Kenny Hyslop. Mike Ogletree the took drum chair for '82 set **New Gold Dream (81-82-83-84)**.

With percussionist Mel Gaynor recruited early '83, band undertook series of festival gigs to further broaden ever-widening market. US tour in 1984 (supporting Pretenders(▶)) provided sufficient media attention—not least the marriage of Pretenders' vocalist Chrissie Hynde and Jim Kerr—to spur single **Don't You** to one million sales. Band subsequently featured in Live Aid concert at Philadelphia.

Growing confidence and more mature material has since edged group ahead of contemporaries such as Duran Duran(▶), OMD(▶) and Spandau Ballet(▶).

**Current line-up:** Kerr; Burchill; MacNeil; Mel Gaynor, drums; John Giblin, bass.

**Hit Singles:**

| | US | UK |
|---|---|---|
| Promised You A Miracle, 1982 | — | 13 |
| Glittering Prize, 1982 | — | 16 |
| Waterfront, 1983 | — | 13 |

| | | |
|---|---|---|
| Speed Your Love To Me, 1984 | — | 20 |
| Don't You Forget About Me, 1985 | 1 | 7 |
| Alive And Kicking, 1985 | 11 | 7 |
| All The Things She Said, 1986 | — | 9 |
| Ghostdancing, 1986 | — | 13 |
| Promised You A Miracle, 1987 | — | 19 |

**Albums:**
Sons And Fascination/Sister Feelings Call (Virgin), 1981 **CD**
New Gold Dream (81-82-83-84) (Virgin), 1982 **CD**
Life In A Day (Virgin), 1982 **CD**
Real To Real Cacophony (Virgin), 1982 **CD**
Empire And Dance (Virgin), 1983 **CD**
Celebration (Virgin), 1983
Sparkle In The Rain (Virgin), 1984 **CD**
Once Upon A Time (Virgin), 1985 **CD**
In The City Of Light (Virgin), 1987 **CD**

# Simply Red

UK group formed 1982.

**Original/Current line-up:** Mick "Red" Hucknall, vocals; Chris Joyce, drums; Tony Bowers, bass; Tim Kellet, keyboards/trumpet; Fritz McIntryre, keyboards/vocals; Sylvan Richardson, guitars.

**Career:** Brought up in Manchester, ex-art student Hucknall formed excellent indie punk band called Frantic Elevators, who released 3 singles including early version of **Holding Back The Years**.

Formed first version of soul-influenced Simply Red in 1982 and was immediately offered a million-dollar deal by Seymour Stein, who owned Sire Records, to turn solo. Hucknall refused and Stein signed an unknown called Madonna instead! Three months later, Hucknall fired the rest of the band anyway. Recruited Joyce, Bowers and Kellet from fellow Manchester band Durutti Column, added McIntryre and later Richardson, before recording impressive demoes and securing deal with Elektra Records in early 1985.

Teamed up with soul producer Stewart Levene and recorded version of **Money's Too Tight** by Valentine Brothers as first single, which created media interest but failed to chart in US. Released second single **Come To My Aid**, supported James Brown in London and recorded debut album **Picture Book** which featured further near-miss singles **Jericho** and **Red Box**. Then came hit single — firstly in US, then worldwide — with new version of slow, yearning ballad **Holding Back The Years**.

Supported UB40 on UK tour, then headlined own world tour throughout 1986. Hucknall, with instant image of curly red hair and walking cane, became media personality, writing songs for Diana Ross and co-composing with Motown legend Lamont Dozier.

Recorded second album **Men And Women** with late Alex Sadkin, covering songs by Sly Stone, Bunny Wailer and Cole Porter! Musically, the blend was both melodic and rhythmic, topped off by Hucknall's distinctive 'white soul' vocals.

Further hits followed — notably the remarkably cool version of Porter's **Ev'ry Time We Say Goodbye** — and band played another sell-out world tour through 1987, despite Hucknall suffering throat problems which caused cancellation of London Shows. Assuming Hucknall doesn't lose his voice, Simply Red will continue to be simply massive.

| Hit Singles: | US | UK |
|---|---|---|
| Holding Back the Years, 1985 | 1 | 2 |
| Moneys Too Tight, 1985 | — | 13 |
| The Right Thing, 1987 | — | 11 |
| Ev'ry Time We Say Goodbye, 1987 | — | 11 |

**Picture Book, Simply Red. Courtesy Elektra Records.**

**Albums**
Picture Book (Elektra), 1985 **CD**
Men and Women (WEA/Elektra), 1987 **CD**

# Siouxsie And The Banshees

US group formed 1976.

**Original line-up:** Siouxsie Sioux, vocals; Steve Severin, bass; Sid Vicious, drums; Marco Pirroni, guitar.

**Career:** Siouxsie had closely followed Sex Pistols(▶) attack on polished, professional

sound of established rock bands; without rehearsal formed above line-up for one gig. Within two months Vicious and Pirroni were gone, Vicious to infamy with latter-day Sex Pistols and Pirroni to play in the Motels, then with Adam and the Ants(▶). Kenny Morris took over drums and Peter Fenton assumed guitar.

Refusal to sign standard recording contract meant band was ignored by major firms. Plans to sign with Kit Lambert's Track label (Who(▶)) fell through when Track folded. By July 1977 Fenton was replaced by John McKay.

Polydor finally signed Siouxsie and promptly found itself in confrontation with band. ('I wouldn't piss on our record company if their building was on fire', was widely quoted as indication of band's regard for their label.)

Following release of two LPs, McKay and Morris quit in autumn 1979 just as band started extensive tour. Ex-Slits member 'Budgie' was quickly taken on as permanent drummer. Cure guitarist Robert Smith was 'loaned' to meet tour dates. John McGeoch (ex-Magazine) then joined as permanent guitarist. **Kaleidoscope** LP also featured great guitar work from Steve Jones (ex-Pistols, Professionals), yet studio work did not seem to quite fit band's no-compromise approach; never matched live enthusiasm of Siouxsie on stage. Despite strong LP **Ju Ju**, spirit of band is best experienced on **Once Upon A Time/The Singles**.

Despite parallel venture The Creatures, featuring Siouxsie and Budgie, the Banshees have remained a viable proposition up to the time of writing. Individualistic approach has withstood fads and fashions of 80s scene, although no doubt further hits would be welcome.

**Current line-up:** Siouxsie; Severin; Budgie, drums.

| Hit Singles: | US | UK |
|---|---|---|
| Hong Kong Garden, 1978 | — | 7 |
| Happy House, 1980 | — | 17 |
| Dear Prudence, 1983 | — | 3 |
| Candyman, 1986 | — | 34 |
| This Wheel's On Fire, 1987 | — | 14 |

*Creatures:*

| | | |
|---|---|---|
| Right Now, 1983 | — | 7 |

**Albums:**
The Scream (—/Polydor), 1978
Join Hands (—/Polydor), 1979
Kaleidoscope (Gem/Polydor), 1980
Ju Ju (Gem/Polydor), 1981
Once Upon A Time/The Singles (Gem/Polydor), 1981
A Kiss In The Dreamhouse (Polydor), 1982

*Siouxsie & Budgie as the Creatures:*
Wild Thing EP (—/Polydor), 1981
Feast (—/Polydor), 1983
Hyeana (Polydor), 1984 **CD**
Tinderbox (Wonderland), 1986 **CD**
Through The Looking Glass (Wonderland), 1987 **CD**

# Ricky Skaggs

US vocalist, multi-instrumentalist, composer. Born Cordell, Kentucky July 18, 1954.

**Career:** Despite comparative youth, Skaggs has enjoyed long and varied career as sideman, band member and now solo performer.

Made TV debut aged seven on Flatt and Scruggs(▶) show, and in early teens became member of legendary banjo player Ralph Stanley's group. Later worked with Country Gentlemen and J.D. Crowe and the New South, having temporarily abandoned music to work in boiler room for a power company.

Formed own group Boone Creek in 1975, and then joined Emmylou Harris's Hot Band for three year stay.

Equally adept on guitar, fiddle, banjo and mandolin, Skaggs signed to Epic Records in 1980, where he has recorded a succession of Gold albums. Is the recipient of several Country Music Association awards.

**Instruments:**
Martin D-28, D-18, 000-21 and Washburn (vintage 1934) guitars, Fender Telecaster, Gibson F-5 Lloyd Loar mandolin, Arthur Connor fiddle, Mandocaster electric mandolin.

**Albums (selected):**
Waitin' For The Sun To Shine (Epic), 1981
Highways And Heartaches (Epic), 1982
Don't Cheat In Our Home Town (Epic), 983
Country Boy (Epic), 1984
Favourite Country Songs (Epic), 1985
Live In London (Epic), 1985
That's It (Rebel), 1985 **CD**
Family and Friends (Rounder/Sundown), 1985* **CD**
Sweet Temptation (Sugar Hill/Ritz), 1985*
Loves Gonna Get Ya! (Epic), 1986 **CD**

*With Boone Creek:*
Boon Creek (Rounder), 1977
*UK release date

**Left: Mick "Red" Hucknall of Simply Red during the band's hugely successful 1987 tour.**

Above: Slade on stage (left to right) Jimmy Lea, Noddy Holder, Dave Hill and Don Powell. Their succession of hits in the early '70s tells its own story.

# Slade

UK group formed 1966.

**Original/Current line-up:** Noddy Holder vocals, guitar; Dave Hill, guitar; Jimmy Lea, bass, piano; Don Powell, drums.

**Career:** Group started out playing routine material in Midlands clubs as 'N Betweens. Changed name to Ambrose Slade; discovered in 1969 at Rasputin's Club in London's Bond Street by Chas Chandler, during era of original skinhead cult. Chandler, who had been member of Animals(▶) and had already turned Jimi Hendrix(▶) into a superstar, decided on cash-in image. Short-cropped hair, 'bovver boots', rolled-up jeans etc. were adopted. Audiences saw it as pure marketing ploy and gambit failed.

Chandler persevered, hanging on to Polydor contract while shortening band's name to Slade. Re-make of Bobby Marchan's **Get Down And Get With It,** also a US R&B hit for Little Richard, got them into chart. Image now was of aggressive glitter, heavy stomping and loud guitar. Adopting gimmick of misspelt song titles, band were projected as teen working-class heroes. **Look Wot You Dun, Take Me Bak 'Ome, Mama Weer All Crazee Now, Cum On Feel The Noize** and others made them Britain's top pop band of 1972-74. Between October 1971 and October 1974 released 12 singles, all of which made UK Top 5, six of them reaching No 1. 1973 Christmas hit **Merry Xmas Everybody** also made No. 1 and charted again in December 1980, '81 '82 and '83.

Songwriting partnership of Lee and Holder now mentioned in same breath as Lennon/McCartney, while band were touted as new Beatles(▶) However, despite success, songs elicited few cover versions and Slade never showed Beatles' diversity of musical talent.

Attempts to broaden base of appeal served only to dampen fires of Slade fever. Spent tail-end of 1974 working on 'Flame' movie project in which they starred as mythical band. Despite some flair for acting and good script, movie made little impact though yielded hit semi-ballad **Far Far Away.** Time spent trying to crack Stateside market served only to further weaken grasp on UK. 1975 was bad year, but Slade bounced back in 1976 with stomping **Let's Call It Quits.** Title was somewhat prophetic as emergence of new wave pushed them into background. Slade didn't listen to own message and revived career on back of heavy metal boom with big 1981 hit **Lock Up Your Daughters.**

1983/4 proved particularly successful chartwise and band celebrated 20th anniversary on April 1, 1986.

**Hit Singles:**

| | US | UK |
|---|---|---|
| Get Down And Get With It, 1971 | — | 16 |
| Coz I Luv You, 1971 | — | 1 |
| Look Wot You Dun, 1972 | — | 4 |
| Take Me Bak 'Ome, 1972 | — | 1 |
| Mama Weer All Crazee Now, 1972 | — | 1 |
| Good Buy T' Jane, 1972 | — | 2 |
| Cum On Feel The Noize, 1973 | — | 1 |
| Skweeze Me Pleeze Me, 1973 | — | 1 |
| My Friend Stan, 1973 | — | 2 |
| Merry Xmas Everybody, 1973 | — | 1 |
| Everyday, 1974 | — | 3 |
| Bangin' Man, 1974 | — | 3 |
| Far Far Away, 1974 | — | 2 |
| How Does It Feel, 1975 | — | 15 |
| Thanks For The Memory (Wham Bam Thankyou Mam), 1975 | — | 7 |
| In For A Penny, 1975 | — | 11 |
| Let's Call It Quits, 1976 | — | 11 |
| We'll Bring The House Down, 1981 | — | 10 |
| My Oh My, 1983 | 37 | 2 |
| Run Run Away, 1984 | 20 | 7 |
| All Join Hands, 1984 | — | 15 |

**Albums:**
Slade Alive (Polydor), 1972
Slade Alive Volume 2 (—/Barn), 1978
Return To Base (—/Barn), 1979
We'll Bring The House Down (—/Cheapskate), 1981
Lock Up Your Daughters (—/RCA), 1981
Slade On Stage (—/RCA), 1982
The Amazing Kamikaze Syndrome (RCA), 1983
Slade's Greats (Polydor), 1984
Crackers (Telstar), 1985
Rogues Gallery (RCA), 1985
You Boyz Make Big Noise (RCA), 1987 **CD**

# Sly And The Family Stone

US group formed 1966.

**Original line-up:** Sly Stone, vocals, keyboards, guitar; Freddie Stone, guitar; Cynthia Robinson, trumpet; Jerry Martini, saxophone; Rosie Stone, piano, vocals; Larry Graham, bass; Greg Errico, drums.

**Career:** The history of Sly and the Family Stone is virtually the history of founder and guiding light Sly Stone. Born Sylvester Stewart in 1944 in Dallas, Texas, he played in various bands with brother Freddie after family had moved to California. As lead singer for group called the Viscanes, he made his recording debut with **Yellow Moon,** which became small local hit.

In late teens and early twenties Sly gained experience in many areas of the music

business, writing and producing successfully for artists like Bobby Freeman, the Mojo Men and the Beau Brummels, and working as DJ on San Francisco radio. In 1966 he put together own band, the Stoners, which was forerunner of Family Stone.

Formation of Family Stone coincided with upsurge of psychedelia centred in San Francisco. An inter-racial, male and female band, Family Stone pioneered acid-soul-rock, combining punch brass riffs and stinging rock guitar with wild vocal harmonies and an irresistible dance beat. Finding their audience among newly liberated white kids rather than in black dance halls, band was in tune with the times.

Success came in early 1968. Signed to Epic, band released LP **A Whole New Thing,** and single **Dance To The Music. Dance** was an exhilarating rock/soul amalgam that brought breath of fresh air to charts both sides of Atlantic.

Follow-up single **M'Lady** did better in UK than US, where it only just made Top 100, but third single, **Everyday People,** topped American charts. **Stand,** the album from which it was taken, went gold, and titletrack was also hit.

Sly and the Family Stone become in-demand concert act, and were a high point of 1969 Woodstock Festival. Sly's **I Want To Take You Higher** became Festival's anthem, but the Festival turned out to be zenith of band's career. More record success was still to come, but personality clashes and drug problems led to band (in particular Sly, who often failed to show up at scheduled concerts) becoming increasingly unreliable. Sly's darker side was reflected in pessimistic vision of 1971 album **There's A Riot Going On.**

Following years saw band undergo various personnel changes (with Larry Graham carving successful solo career). Subsequent albums were less than convincing. Collection of Sly's old hits, **Back On The Right Track,** was issued in 1979, and in 1982 he surfaced in partnership with George Clinton. Seminal cultural figure of his time, Sly Stone showed that rock could be funky as well as heavy, and that there was still a place for dance music in '60s and early '70s.

---

**Final line-up:** Sly Stone; Freddie Stone; Cynthia Robinson; Rusty Allen, bass; Bill Lordan, drums; Rosie Stone; Jerry Martini; Pat Rizzo, saxophone; Sid Page, violin.

**Hit Singles:**

| | US | UK |
|---|---|---|
| Dance To The Music, 1968 | 8 | 7 |
| Everyday People, 1969 | 1 | 36 |
| Hot Fun In The Summertime, 1969 | 2 | - |
| Thank You Falettinme Be Mice Elf Agin, 1970 | 1 | — |
| Family Affair, 1971 | 1 | 15 |
| Runnin' Away, 1972 | 23 | 17 |
| If You Want Me To Stay, 1973 | 12 | — |

**Albums:**
Dance To The Music (Epic/Direction), 1968 **CD**
Life (Epic), 1968
A Whole New Thing (Epic), 1970
High Energy (Epic), 1975
Back On The Right Track (Warner Bros), 1979
Recorded 64/67 (Sculpture), 1979
Greatest Hits (Epic), 1981
Ain't But The One Way (Warner Bros), 1983
Fresh (Edsel), 1987 **CD**
Free (Edsel), 1987

*Worth Searching Out:*
Stand (Epic), 1969
There's A Riot Going On (Epic), 1971

# Small Faces

UK group formed 1965.

**Original line-up:** Steve Marriott, vocals, guitar; Jimmy Winston, organ; Ronnie 'Plonk' Lane, bass; Kenny Jones, drums.

**Career:** The Who(▶) were group that adopted mod image as sales ploy; the Small Faces were mods who became a group.

Formed in London's East End, Small Faces (so called because of members diminutive size, 'faces' being flash mods) were built round lead singer, former child actor Marriott. Wearing razor-sharp clothes group initially set out to re-create the American R&B soul music espoused by fellow mods. Borrowing riff from Solomon Burke's **Everybody Needs Somebody To Love** they came up with potent **Watcha Gonna Do About It?** to crash chart in September 1965. Ian MacLagan replaced Winston for follow-up **I've Got Mine,** which flopped but was quickly followed by successes, **Sha La La La Lee, Hey Girl,** the chart-topping **All Or Nothing** and **My Mind's Eye.** All were co-written by Marriott and Lane (one

**Greatest Hits, a Small Faces reissue. Courtesy Immediate Records.**

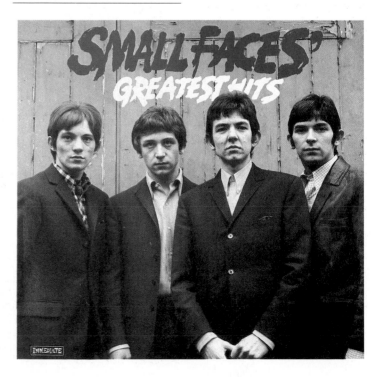

159

of the strongest songwriting duos of the '60s), moving increasingly into straight pop vein.

Switching to Immediate label, set up by Rolling Stones(▶) manager Andrew Loog-Oldham, and Tony Calder, Small Faces came up with more interesting material with clever and evocative **Itchycoo Park** (1967), their only US Top 20 record, and the perceptive **Lazy Sunday** (1968). Then came superlative **Ogden's Nut Gone Flake** album (1968), its classic circular fold-out sleeve a replica of the familiar UK tobacco brand.

**The Small Faces' 1966 debut album. Courtesy Immediate Records.**

Marriott left in early 1969 to join Peter Frampton(▶) in formation of Humble Pie(▶). Lane, Jones and MacLagan soldiered on. Went through very rough patch but turned down offers to work as backing band for solo artists, linking up with Jeff Beck Group emigrés Rod Stewart(▶) and Ron Wood later the next year as the Faces(▶). Wood was eventually invited to join Rolling Stones(▶) and Stewart concentrated increasingly on solo image, leading to Faces' early demise.

Small Faces re-formed in 1976 with following line-up: Marriott; Jones; MacLagen; Rick Wills (Roxy Music(▶)) bass. Cut two mediocre LPs **Playmates** and **78 In The Shade** in attempt to cash in on then extant mod revival but, despite new generation following, Small Faces' fortunes could not be regenerated.

Lane, a multiple sclerosis victim, formed Slim Chance and in 1985 was catalyst for charity record to help fellow sufferers.

**Final line-up:** Marriott; Jones; Ian MacLagan, organ; Rick Wills, bass.

| Hit Singles: | US | UK |
| --- | --- | --- |
| Watcha Gonna Do About It?, 1965 | — | 14 |
| Sha La La La Lee, 1966 | — | 3 |
| Hey Girl, 1966 | — | 10 |
| All Or Nothing, 1966 | — | 1 |
| My Mind's Eye, 1966 | — | 4 |
| Here Comes The Nice, 1967 | — | 12 |
| Itchycoo Park, 1967 | 16 | 3 |
| Tin Soldier, 1967 | — | 9 |
| Lazy Sunday, 1968 | — | 2 |
| Universal, 1968 | — | 16 |
| Itchycoo Park, 1975 | — | 9 |

**Albums:**
Small Faces (—/Decca), 1966
Ogdens Nut Gone Flake (Immediate), 1967 **CD**
Rock Roots: The Small Faces (—/Decca) 1976*
Greatest Hits (—/Immediate), 1977
Playmates (Atlantic), 1977
78 In The Shade (Atlantic), 1978
Big Hits (—/Virgin), 1980
For Your Delight (—/Virgin), 1981
By Appointment (Accord/—), 1981

**Right: Too precious to lose forever? Internal disharmony means that future is likely to be turbulent.**

Sha La La La Lee (—/Decca), 1981
Collection (Collector), 1985 **CD**
*Features all Decca A&B sides.

*With Amen Corner:*
Amen Corner And Small Faces (—/New World), 1975

*Worth Searching Out:*
There Are But Four Small Faces (Immediate), 1967
Autumn Stone (Castle), 1969 **CD**

# The Smiths
UK group formed 1982.
**Original/Current line-up:** Johnny Marr, guitar; Stephen Morrisey, vocals; Andy Rourke, bass; Mike Joyce, drums.

**Career:** Some would say wimpish and fragile, others poetic and concise, but while opinion is divided the Smiths have quickly established a loyal and substantial following.

After a handful of gigs, group signed to Rough Trade, who fought off (so their press office says) six-figure offers from several major record companies. First single **Hand In Glove** (May '83) preceeded sessions for debut album produced by ex-Teardrop Explodes/Fashion member Troy Tate. Tate's efforts were subsequently dumped when group met John Porter, who re-recorded material for **The Smiths**.

Extensive UK tour hurried LP to instant number 2 position in Britain, with gold status quickly following.

Bizarre coupling of Smiths with Sandie Shaw (Morrisey's favourite female singer) earned **Hand In Glove** single a UK top thirty entry in Spring '84.

Following year saw **Meat Is Murder** album expound band's vegetarian lifestyle; LP entered UK charts at No. 1. Succession of British hit singles following **What Difference Does It Make** (1984) seemed certain to establish Smiths at forefront of pop circus, but rumblings of discontent within group placed a question mark over their future.

**Meat Is Murder, The Smiths. Courtesy Rough Trade Records**

In 1987, Morrisey/Marr conflict split band. Marr has since gigged with the Pretenders, whilst Morrisey swiftly embarked upon solo career; debut single **Suedehead** issued February 1988, taken from session which promised album release one month later.

**"Strangeways, Here We Come", The Smiths. Courtesy Rough Trade Records.**

| Hit Singles: | US | UK |
| --- | --- | --- |
| What Difference Does It Make, 1984 | — | 12 |
| Heaven Knows I'm Miserable Now, 1984 | — | 10 |
| William It Was Really Nothing, 1984 | — | 17 |
| The Boy With The Thorn In His Side, 1985 | — | 15 |
| Ask, 1986 | — | 14 |
| Panic, 1986 | — | 11 |
| Girlfriend In A Coma, 1987 | — | 13 |
| Shoplifters Of The World, 1987 | — | 12 |
| Sheila Take A Bow, 1987 | — | 10 |
| I Started Something I Couldn't Finish, 1987 | — | 23 |

*Morrisey solo:*
| | | |
| --- | --- | --- |
| Suedehead—Nowhere | — | 28 |

**Albums:**
The Smiths (Rough Trade), 1983 **CD**
Meat Is Murder (Rough Trade), 1984 **CD**
Hatful Of Hollow (Rough Trade), 1985 **CD**
Louder Than Bombs (Rough Trade), 1987 **CD**
The World Won't Listen (Rough Trade), 1987 **CD**
Sheila Take A Bow (Pacific), 1987 **CD**
The Queen Is Dead (Rough Trade), 1987 **CD**
Big Mouth Strikes Again (Rough Trade), 1987 **CD**
Strangeways Here We Come (Rough Trade), 1987 **CD**

*Morrisey solo:*
Viva Hate! (Parlophone), 1988 **CD**

# Sonny And Cher
US vocal duo formed 1963.
Sonny, born Salvatore Bono, Detroit, Michigan, February 12, 1935;
Cher, born Cherilyn Sakasian La Pierre, El Centro, California, May 20, 1946.

**Career:** Sonny wrote his first song in 1951, and by early '60s was making inroads into music business as writer, and as house producer for Specialty Records. In 1963, he co-wrote **Needles And Pins**, later to become huge international hit for the Searchers(▶), and started work as assistant to Phil Spector.

Cher moved from her home town to Hollywood to be an actress and took up session singing to pay for acting lessons. She met Sonny at a Ronettes' recording session, and the duo's professional and personal partnership started. They married in 1963.

Recording as Caesar and Cleo for Reprise and as Sonny and Cher for Vault, the pair eventually landed contract with Atco in 1965,

**Above: Accomplished star of film, Oscar winner Cher in 1988.**

which was to prove the turning point. In summer 1965 **I Got You Babe** was released and raced to No. 1 spot both sides of the Atlantic. Written, arranged and produced by Sonny, it contained every ingredient needed for success in '65, a strong melody, lyrics that were vaguely anti-authoritarian yet romantic, and a catchy, easily recognisable oboe riff.

Visually, Sonny and Cher came on as the acceptable face of hippiedom — colourful but not totally outrageous, groovy but not threatening. The combination proved irresistible, and their career took off. However, despite their long hair and 'flower-child' appearance, Sonny and Cher, weren't particularly interested in substance of '60s 'alternative' ethos, and veered increasingly towards 'all round entertainer' position.

Following career lull in late '60s, they began to move into supper-club work, and started own TV show in 1972. Meanwhile, a couple more hit singles kept their names before the pop public.

Despite foundering of duo's personal and professional relationship, they still recorded

**Cher's most recent album. Courtesy Geffen Records.**

together, and featured on each other's supposedly 'solo' singles. In 1974, however, Sonny & Cher split permanently to follow diverse career paths.

Whilst Sonny struggled to maintain impetus, Cher soon achieved mega stardom, which had been threatened since the powerful **Gypsies, Tramps And Thieves** single.

Relationships with Gregg Allman, Gene Simmonds and Les Dudek stimulated interest in gossip columns, and the lady moved almost effortlessly (and convincingly) into movies, making her debut in 'Come Back To The Five And Dime Jimmy Dean, Jimmy Dean' (1982).

Normally the death knell for most other pop performers, films have enveloped Cher, and

she has subsequently featured in: 'Silkwood', with Meryl Streep (1983), 'Mask' (1985), 'The Witches Of Eastwick', 'Suspect' and 'Moonstruck' (all 1987), the latter rewarding her with an Oscar at the 1988 ceremony for Best Actress. Recording interest has been maintained by singles like 'I Found Someone', a US hit at the beginning of 1988.

Sonny's spluttering movie career was somewhat revived by the 1988 release 'Hairspray', although his major impact in recent years was on the David Letterman TV show, when he was re-united with Cher for a generous dollop of nostalgia. The following week, Newsweek magazine featured Cher on it's front cover, emphasising the relative impact of their separate careers.

**Hit Singles:**

| | US | UK |
|---|---|---|
| I Got You Babe, 1965 | 1 | 1 |
| Baby Don't Go, 1965 | 8 | 11 |
| Just You, 1965 | 20 | — |
| But You're Mine, 1965 | 15 | 17 |
| What Now My Love, 1966 | 14 | 13 |
| Little Man, 1966 | 21 | 4 |
| The Beat Goes On, 1967 | 6 | 29 |
| All I Ever Need Is You, 1971 | 7 | 8 |
| A Cowboy's Work Is Never Done, 1972 | 8 | — |

**Sonny:**

| | | |
|---|---|---|
| Laugh At Me, 1965 | 10 | 9 |

**Cher:**

| | | |
|---|---|---|
| Bang Bang, 1966 | 2 | 3 |
| You Better Sit Down Kids, 1967 | 9 | — |
| Gypsys, Tramps, and Thieves, 1971 | 1 | 4 |
| The Way Of Love, 1972 | 7 | — |
| Half-Breed, 1973 | 1 | — |
| Dark Lady, 1974 | 1 | 36 |
| Take Me Home, 1979 | 8 | — |
| I Found Someone, 1987 | 10 | 5 |

**Albums:**
The Very Best Of Sonny And Cher (—/Hallmark), 1981

*Cher Solo:*
Take Me Home (Casablanca), 1979
Prisoner (Casablanca), 1980
Gypsies Tramps And Thieves (MFP), 1981
Golden Greats (MCA), 1985
Best Of (Liberty/EMI America), 1985
Cher (Geffen), 1987 **CD**

*With Greg Allman:*
Two The Hard Way (Warner Bros), 1977

---

# Southside Johnny & The Asbury Jukes

US group formed 1975.

**Original line-up:** Johnny Lyon, vocals; 'Miami' Steve Van Zandt, guitar, vocals; Kevin Kavanaugh, keyboards, vocals; Billy Rush, guitar; Alan Berger, bass; Kenny Pentifallo, drums, vocals; Carlo Novi, tenor sax; Ricky Gazda, trumpet; Deacon Earl Gardner, trumpet; Bob Malach, tenor sax; Louie Parente, trombone; Bill Zacagni, baritone saxophone.

**Career:** 'Southside' Johnny Lyon (born December 4, 1948) was besotted by blues and R&B from an early age. Lyon joined Sonny Kenn Blues Band at 16, then various other groups until early '70s, when he, Bruce Springsteen(▶) and Miami Steve Van Zandt were all in Sundance Blues Band and then in Dr. Zoom and the Sonic Boom (where Lyon acquired 'Southside' epithet). March 1972 saw Lyon plus others from Asbury Park, New

Jersey, moving to Richmond, Virginia, to join Studio B — band failed to conquer world.

In 1973, back in New Jersey, formed acoustic blues duo, Southside Johnny and the Kid (Van Zandt), then Bank Street Blues Band, which also included Kevin Kavanaugh. Van Zandt left in 1974 to play with Dovells, where he met Alan Berger, while Lyon joined Blackberry Booze Band, which included Kenny Pentifallo. BBB became resident band at now legendary Asbury Park night spot Stone Poney in December 1974. Van Zandt returned to co-lead in early 1975, and name changed to Asbury Jukes in mid-1975, although soon afterwards Van Zandt joined Springsteen's E Street Band; during time off from Springsteen, Van Zandt produced demos with Asbury Jukes.

First LP soon followed, featuring guest spots from Ronnie Spector and Lee Dorsey. Group's impressive R&B sound indicated major success to follow, but live shows seemingly made more impact than records, despite inclusion of unreleased Springsteen material. Second LP featured guest tracks from Drifters(▶), Coasters(▶) and five Satins, but still no hits; ditto third album. In 1979, moved to Mercury label (from Epic) and discontinued use of Van Zandt as producer. At this point, band line-up included Lyon, Kavanaugh, Rush, Berger, Gazda, plus Steve Becker, drums; Ed Manion, baritone sax; Richie 'La Bamba' Rosenberg, trombone; Joel Gramolini, guitar; Bob Muckin, trumpet; Stan Harrison, tenor sax. Material, now written by Lyon, Rush and Berger, noticeably inferior, although first LP for new label produced minor hit single.

For 1980 LP, Rush and Lyon took over production, to no great improvement — band still hot, but material sadly lame. After impressive double live LP (using some of earlier material), group appear to have vanished, possibly returning to New Jersey circuit — Lyon himself perhaps unable to accept that his undoubted talent as R&B singer/front man did not extend to songwriting or production. Nevertheless, destined for semi-legendary status on basis of early recordings.

**Current line-up:** Lyon; Rush; Kavanaugh; Richie Rosenberg, trombone; Steven Becker, drums; Joel Gramolini, guitar; Rick Gazda, trumpet; Ed Manion, saxophones; Steve Buslowe, bass.

**Albums:**
I Don't Want To Go Home (Epic), 1976
This Time It's For Real (Epic), 1977
Hearts Of Stone (Epic), 1978
The Jukes (Mercury), 1979

Havin' A Party With Southside Johnny (Epic/CBS), 1979*
Love Is A Sacrifice (Mercury), 1980
Reach Up And Touch The Sky (Mercury), 1981
I Don't Want To Go Home (Epic), 1982
In The Heat (Polydor), 1984
*compilation

---

# Spandau Ballet

UK group formed 1979.

**Original/Current line-up:** Tony Hadley, vocals; Gary Kemp, guitar; Martin Kemp, bass; Steve Norman, saxophone; John Keeble, drums.

**Career:** Formed by young Londoners to provide soundtrack for 'futurist'/'new romantic' activities in ultra fashion-conscious London night-clubs. Early on managed by Steve Strange, before latter formed Visage. Band refused to publicise early gigs other than by word of mouth, creating elitist image which led to exposure on TV documentary about London scene. Played gig on HMS Belfast moored on River Thames.

Signed with Chrysalis Records in mid-1980, given own label identity, Reformation Records — such a distinction for unknown band that success was assured. First single and album both made Top 5. First single showed that band could provide more than 'futurist' sound. One side, **Glow**, using jazz funk, provided new direction for next single, **Chant No. 1**, which reached Top 3, using black London horn section Beggar and Co. Bubble seemed to be bursting in early 1982, but second LP was released in normal form and as boxed set of 12in singles. Worked live in Europe and America, while **Instinction** and **Lifeline** were both remixed from LP to become Top 10 singles.

Success continued in 1983 with release of third LP **True**; title track topped singles chart in first half of year. Despite having been dismissed as shallow hype in early days, Spandau Ballet have persevered; they now rank with Duran Duran(▶) as major attraction in Britain.

Long-term million dollar deal with CBS in 1986 provided solid platform for continued development.

**Below: Spandau Ballet in the early '80s, dismissed as hype at the start, but who later came through with numerous hits.**

| Hit Singles: | US | UK |
|---|---|---|
| To Cut A Long Story Short, 1980 | — | 5 |
| The Freeze, 1981 | — | 17 |
| Muscle Bound/Glow, 1981 | — | 10 |
| Chant No. 1 (I Don't Need This Presure On), 1981 | — | 3 |
| Instinction, 1982 | — | 10 |
| Lifeline, 1982 | — | 7 |
| Communication, 1983 | — | 12 |
| True, 1983 | — | 1 |
| Gold, 1983 | 29 | 2 |
| Only When You Leave, 1983 | 34 | 3 |
| I'll Fly For You, 1984 | — | 9 |
| Highly Strung, 1984 | — | 15 |
| Round And Round, 1985 | — | 18 |
| Fight For Ourselves, 1986 | — | 15 |

**Albums:**
Journeys To Glory (Chrysalis), 1981 **CD**
Diamond (—/Chrysalis), 1982
True (—/Chrysalis), 1983
Parade (Chrysalis), 1984 **CD**
Singles Collection (Chrysalis), 1985 **CD**
Through The Barricades (CBS), 1986 **CD**
Twelve Inch Mixes (Reformation), 1986 **CD**
Best Of (Chrysalis) **CD**

# The Specials

UK group formed 1977.

**Original line-up:** Terry Hall, vocals; Lynval Golding, guitar, vocals; Jerry Dammers, keyboards; Roddy Radiation, guitar; Horace 'Gentleman' Parker, bass; Neville Staples, percussion, vocals; John Bradbury, drums.

**Career:** Exploited Jamaican ska style, which pre-dated reggae; the Specials struck a chord with British youth—black and white—and especially, the unemployed. Dubbed their up-dated and racially integrated dance music style 'Two-Tone'. Band, formed in Coventry mid-'77, seemed set to lead nationwide ska revival with **Message To You Rudy** hit. Instead they evolved own lyrically strong 'lounge music' style, featuring veteran Jamaican trombone player Rico Rodriguez as regular guest.

**Too Much Too Young, Rat Race, Do Nothing** and other hits showed way for UB40(▶), Madness(▶), Bad Manners(▶), and others like-conceived groups. As keyboard player Jerry Dammers increasingly dominated proceedings as songwriter and producer, discontent flared. In summer 1981 singers Neville Staples and Terry Hall and guitarist Lynval Golding were already preparing to split and form Fun Boy Three(▶). They laid down tracks for debut album while the Specials' superb **Ghost Town** — which summed up riot-torn summer — was soaring to UK No. 1.

Remnants of the Specials now totally Dammers-dominated, revived earlier name, Specials AKA. Backed girl singer Rhoda on controversially acidic **The Boiler** before re-emerging in chart with effective **Free Nelson Mandela** single.

With Dammers now more and more involved with individual projects, including **Starvation** benefit single and **Winds Of Change** 45 with Robert Y Wyatt, Specials AKA gradually drifted apart.

**Current line-up:** Dammers; Bradbury; Stan Campbell, vocals; Rhoda Dakar, vocals; Gary McManus, bass; John Shipley, guitar.

| Hit Singles: | US | UK |
|---|---|---|
| Gangsters, 1979 | — | 6 |
| A Message To You Ruby/Nite Club, 1979 | — | 10 |
| Too Much Too Young (EP), 1980 | — | 1 |
| Rat Race/Rüde Boys Outa Jail, 1980 | — | 5 |

**Above: The Specials on stage, with Terry Hall (left) and Jerry Dammers (extreme right).**

| | | |
|---|---|---|
| Stereotype/International Jet Set, 1980 | — | 6 |
| Do Nothing/Maggies Farm, 1981 | — | 4 |
| Ghost Town, 1981 | — | 1 |
| Free Nelson Mandela, 1984 | — | 9 |

**Albums:**
Specials (Chrysalis), 1979
More Specials (Chrysalis/Two Tone), 1980

# Dusty Springfield

UK vocalist.
Born Mary O'Brien, London, April 16, 1939.

**Career:** First made impression as part of pop-folk trio the Springfields which had handful of hits in early '60s. Group broke up in September 1963, and Springfield embarked on solo career. Forsaking folksiness for more soulful style (then being popularised by Motown), she was responsible for series of hit singles which combined commercial catchiness with distinctive vocalising. More than any other British female singer of the time she made an impression on the US market; five singles made US Top 20.

Well thought of by critics and fellow professionals, Springfield was better equipped vocally than most of her contemporaries, and could make creditable job of more demanding soul material. This ability was best displayed on 1969 LP **Dusty In Memphis**, produced by Jerry Wexler, featuring Memphis session mafia. Although in retrospect not as brilliant as made out to be at the time, it remains one of the best blue-eyed soul efforts of this era.

**Son Of A Preacher Man** in late 1968 was Springfield's last major chart success; she then began to fade from sight amid rumours of personal problems. During '70s she lived somewhat reclusively in America, occasionally recording and acting as back-up for other singers. A flurry of activity in 1978/79 resulted in couple of LPs and promotional appearances.

Latterly, Springfield has returned to the public eye in a number of incarnations, most particularly as guest vocalist on Pet Shop Boys' UK/US top ten single **What Have I Done To Deserve This**.

An appearance with other sixties notables on a British TV commercial reminded current audiences of her panda-eyed charm, and subsequent 'greatest hits' collection made chart impact in UK. Pot-pourri of promotional appearances may lead to major comeback.

| Hit Singles: | US | UK |
|---|---|---|
| I Only Want To Be With You, 1963 | 12 | 4 |
| Stay Awhile, 1964 | 38 | 13 |
| I Just Don't Know What To Do With Myself, 1964 | — | 3 |
| Wishin' And Hopin', 1964 | 6 | — |
| Losing You, 1964 | — | 9 |
| In The Middle Of Nowhere, 1965 | — | 8 |
| Some Of Your Lovin', 1965 | — | 8 |
| Little By Little, 1966 | — | 17 |
| You Don't Have To Say You Love Me, 1966 | 4 | 1 |
| Going Back, 1966 | — | 10 |
| All I See Is You, 1966 | 20 | 9 |
| I'll Try Anything, 1967 | 40 | 13 |
| I Close My Eyes And Count To Ten, 1968 | - | 4 |
| Son Of A Preacher Man, 1968 | 10 | 9 |
| Am I The Same Girl, 1969 | — | 9 |

**Born In The U.S.A., Bruce Springsteen. Courtesy CBS Records.**

*With Pet Shop Boys:*
| | | |
|---|---|---|
| What Have I Done To Deserve This?, 1987 | 2 | 2 |

**Albums:**
Golden Hits (Philips), 1966
This Is Dusty Springfield Volume 2—The Magic Garden (—/Philips), 1973
You Don't Have To Say You Love Me (—/Contour), 1976
It Begins Again (Liberty/Mercury), 1978
Greatest Hits (Mercury/Phonogram), 1979
Living Without Your Love (Liberty/Mecury), 1979
Memphis Plus (Mercury), 1980
The Very Best Of Dusty Springfield (—/K-Tel), 1981
Whiteheat (Casablanca/—), 1982

*Worth Searching out:*
Dusty In Memphis (Atlantic/Philips), 1969
Love Songs (Philips), 1984 **CD**
Beautiful Feelings (Mercury), 1985 **CD**
Dusty—The Silver Collection (Phillips), 1988

# Bruce Springsteen

US composer, vocalist, guitarist.
Born Freehold, New Jersey, September 23, 1949.

**Career:** Springsteen grew up watching Beatles(▶) revolutionising rock 'n' roll and decided he wanted to be a rock star. Started gigging in New York clubs, formed various bands, went to California, returned to East Coast, and missed completely.

In 1972 he hired Mike Appel to manage him. Appel took him to John Hammond of Columbia Records who supposedly was as impressed with Springsteen as he had been years ago with Bob Dylan(▶) Result was recording of folkish **Greetings From Asbury Park, New Jersey.** Bruce still missed.

Second LP, **The Wild, The Innocent And The E-Street Shuffle,** carried the seeds for developing back-up group, the E Street Band. It also marked Springsteen as original talent rather than another Dylan soundalike.

Live shows began to take on marathon proportions of epic tales, true-life ballads, whispered intimacies and buckets of sweat. If it seemed as pre-arranged as a James Brown(▶) stage faint, it was still exciting, warm and sincere.

East Side Story, Squeeze. Courtesy A&M Records.

American critic Jon Landau had become acquainted with Springsteen and liked his shows. In May 1974 he wrote review citing Springsteen as 'rock and roll future'. The phrase caught on, and aided by Columbia, pushed Springsteen into glare of mass media publicity.

Landau and Springsteen became friends and when sessions for next LP bogged down, Springsteen asked Landau to help out production. **Born To Run** finally justified media hype and deservedly became instant success. It also continued maturation process begun on second album, while holding on to bravado and immediacy of garage bands.

The LP ensured sell-out tours for 1975, during which Springsteen honed down live act to professional perfection. It was obviously time to start on follow-up album. Instead, Springsteen's career came to halt when he and Appel became involved in contract dispute. This delayed new releases until 1978, when **Darkness On The Edge Of Town** appeared. It naturally reflected loss of innocence, but expressed hope for some ultimate workable future.

Springsteen's vision of everyman's future continued on excellent album **The River**. His willingness to continue to take chances was proved by 1982 release **Nebraska.**

Deciding that studio tapes had lost raw edge, Springsteen instead released demos. Decision vindicated when **Nebraska** hit number one in US charts. With Miami Steve van Zandt, revived Gary 'US' Bonds career with raw-edged LPs in early '80s.

Van Zandt (now Little Stevie) instigated anti-Apartheid **Sun City** disc, one of two charity efforts (with the awesome **Live Aid** Springsteen associated with. These and massive 1985 world tour (with Nils Lofgren(▶) on guitar) confirmed Bruce 'The Boss' Springsteen as (almost) every man's favourite rock'n'roll son.

Now married to model Julie-Anne Philips, Springsteen spent last couple of years confirming status as rock's biggest money-spinner. Boxed set of live performances went multiplatinum in 1987.

**Hit Singles:**

| | US | UK |
|---|---|---|
| Hungry Heart, 1980 | 5 | — |
| Fade Away, 1981 | 20 | — |
| Dancing In The Dark, 1984 | 2 | 4 |
| Cover Me, 1984 | 38 | 16 |
| Born In The U.S.A., 1985* | 9 | — |
| I'm On Fire, 1985* | 6 | 5 |
| Glory Days, 1985 | 5 | 17 |
| I'm Going Down, 1985 | 9 | — |
| Santa Claus Is Coming To Town, 1985 | — | 9 |
| My Home Town, 1986 | 16 | — |
| War, 1986 | 12 | 18 |
| Brilliant Disguise, 1987 | 5 | 20 |
| Tunnel Of Love, 1987 | 9 | — |
| *Double A side in UK | | |

**Albums:**
Greetings From Asbury Park, New Jersey (Columbia/CBS), 1973 **CD**
The Wild, The Innocent and The E-Street Shuffle (Columbia/CBS), 1973 **CD**
Born To Run (Columbia/CBS), 1975 **CD**
Darkness On The Edge Of Town (Columbia/CBS), 1978 **CD**
The River (Columbia/CBS), 1980
Nebraska (Columbia/CBS), 1982 **CD**
Born In The U.S.A. (Columbia/CBS), 1984 **CD**
Live (1975-85) (CBS), 1986 **CD**
Tunnel Of Love (CBS), 1987 **CD**

*Clarence Clemons Solo:*
Hero (CBS), 1985

# Squeeze
UK group formed 1974.

**Original line-up:** Jools Holland, keyboards; Harry Kakoulli, bass; Gilson Lavis, drums; Chris Difford, guitar, vocals; Glenn Tilbrook, guitar, vocals.

**Career:** Until their demise in autumn 1982, Squeeze (band known as UK Squeeze in US until American band of same name split up) had successfully re-written teenage anthem songbook expounding love in the back seat.

The enterprising South East London quintet first recorded for independent Deptford Fun City label with EP **Packet Of Three** in 1974, carving out a solid local reputation.

First album **Squeeze** released on A&M in 1978 contained hit single **Take Me I'm Yours**, first in series of cockney, adolescent anecdotes from pens of Difford and Tilbrook. Personnel changes (John Bentley replacing Kakoulli, Paul Carrack (ex-Ace) coming in for Holland) established line-up which scored with singles **Up The Junction, Another Nail In My Heart** and **Pulling Mussels**.

Fourth album **East Side Story** earned group breakthrough in States, and included new keyboard player Don Snow (ex-Sinceros) following departure of Carrack to Carlene Carter's band. Carrack then toured with Nick Lowe(▶) and pursued solo career.

Ironically, soon after American success, band went into swift demise. Difford and Tilbrook cut album together, and wrote play 'Labelled With Love' in which they featured. Jools Holland formed Millionaires and became popular front man for UK TV music show 'The Tube'.

Band reformed in 1985, with bass player Keith Wilkinson (who had played in the Difford-Tilbrook aggregation).

However, after fifth album **Sweets From A Stranger** band announced surprise split. Difford and Tilbrook continued to work together, while Holland became presenter of UK TV rock show 'The Tube'. Band reformed in 1985, and renewed effort for chart status was rewarded in late 1987 with hit single **Hourglass**. Despite quality material, band's laid-back jocular approach has restricted further chart success, although **Hourglass** made US top 40 at end of 1987.

**Current line-up:** Lavis; Difford; Tilbrook; Holland; Keith Wilkinson, bass.

**Hit Singles:**

| | US | UK |
|---|---|---|
| Take Me I'm Yours, 1978 | — | 19 |
| Cool For Cats, 1979 | — | 2 |
| Up The Junction, 1979 | — | 2 |
| Another Nail In My Heart, 1980 | — | 17 |
| Labelled With Love, 1981 | — | 4 |
| Hour Glass, 1987 | 15 | 16 |
| 853-5937, 1987 | 32 | — |

**Albums:**
Squeeze (A&M), 1978
Cool For Cats (A&M), 1979
Argy Bargy (A&M), 1980
East Side Story (A&M), 1981

Singles (A&M), 1982 **CD**
Sweets From A Stranger (A&M), 1982
Cosi Fan Tutti Frutti (A&M), 1985 **CD**
Babylon And On (CDA), 1987 **CD**

*Difford & Tilbrook:*
Difford & Tilbrook (A&M), 1984

# Ringo Starr
UK drummer, vocalist, composer, actor. Born Richard Starkey, Liverpool, July 7, 1940.

**Career:** The only member of the Beatles(▶) to have played in other bands (notably Rory Storme and the Hurricanes) before Beatles; Ringo only joined most famous group of all immediately before first Parlophone recording session (which produced **Love Me Do**). Throughout Beatles era, was never taken seriously as writer, although occasional songs were set aside for him to sing, like **Honey Don't** on **Beatles For Sale** LP and especially singalong **Yellow Submarine**. Shortly before Beatles split, he released extremely poor LP of standards **Sentimental Journal**, supposedly recorded because his mother liked such songs as **Night And Day** and **Bye Bye Blackbird**.

Ringo continued to work with both John Lennon(▶) and George Harrison(▶) after split, appearing on most of their early solo records. In 1970 released second solo effort, country & western flavoured **Beaucoups Of Blues**, produced by Nashville star Pete Drake. It was major improvement over debut, if still somewhat obscure. During this period, made several appearances in films, including Frank Zappa's(▶) '200 Motels', 'Blind Man' and 'Born To Boogie' starring Marc Bolan(▶), but best of all, 'That'll Be The Day', which launched David Essex(▶) as major movie star. Next LP, excellent **Ringo**, produced by Richard Perry, was incredibly successful, spawning two US chart-topping singles, plus participation from other three ex-Beatles (although not altogether). Follow-up LP, **Goodnight Vienna**, used same recipe, but with fewer hits.

1976's **Ringo's Rotogravure** LP was far less interesting; subsequent LPs show little sign of return to mid-'70s form. Own label Ognir proved unsuccessful. Seemingly, Ringo has now outlived the advantages of being a Beatle, and while his drumming remains object lesson in unostentatious brilliance, as a vocalist he is now regarded as merely adequate. He looks unlikely to return to chart contention unless he teams up with Richard Perry (or someone like him). Movie career has continued with appalling 'Cave Man', co-starring Barbara Bach, whom Ringo married in 1982.

Latterly Starr has remained in public eye in number of ways, jamming at 'Prince's Trust' concert and other gigs, usually with venerable rock notables like Eric Clapton and George Harrison. He has also advertised beer on US

TV, and seems doomed to spent rest of career as odd-job man of rock.

**Hit Singles:**

| | US | UK |
|---|---|---|
| It Don't come Easy, 1971 | 4 | 4 |
| Back Off Boogaloo, 1972 | 9 | 2 |
| Photograph, 1973 | 1 | 8 |
| You're Sixteen, 1974 | 1 | 4 |
| Oh My My, 1974 | 5 | — |
| Only You, 1974 | 6 | 28 |
| No No Song, 1975 | 3 | — |

**Albums:**
Sentimental Journey (Apple), 1970
Beaucoups Of Blues (Apple), 1970
Ringo (Apple), 1973
Goodnight Vienna (Apple), 1974
Blast From Your Past (Apple), 1975* **CD**
Ringo's Rotogravure (Atco/Polydor), 1976
Ringo The 4th (Atco/Polydor), 1977
Bad Boy (Portrait/Polydor), 1978
Stop And Smell The Roses (Boardwalk/RCA), 1981

*Compilation

# Status Quo
UK group formed 1967.

**Original line-up:** Rick Parfitt, guitar, vocals; Francis Rossi, guitar, vocals; Alan Lancaster, bass, vocals; John Coghlan, drums, Roy Lynes, organ, vocals.

**Career:** Rossi (originally known as Mike) met Lancaster at school in spring 1962. As young 12-year-olds, they formed first band, Scorpions. Within four months, band's guitarist quit. Rossi and Lancaster recruited another schoolmate to carry on. This second band came across Coghlan in September 1962 when his own group was practising next door.

Going through several personnel changes in the merge, the Spectres, as they called themselves, began playing holiday camps. In April 1965 Roy Lynes took over organ spot. The line-up of Rossi, Lancaster, Coghlan and Lynes actually recorded three flop singles for Pye. Parfitt was added in May 1967

Group changed name to Traffic, then to Traffic Jam because of Winwood's group. Another single flopped and to earn living band had to assume backing duties for US artists.

In August 1967, group took new name of Status Quo. They recorded Rossi number, **Pictures Of Matchstick Men,** and quietly resumed duties as back-up band. Early 1968 found Status Quo sudden pop stars as single became international hit, but subsequent work failed to maintain success.

Lynes left in 1970 when Quo was at nadir of career. A year later band moved to Vertigo Records with no noticeable change in fortunes. Instead, they began building up following by

**Below: Status Quo as was: (from left) Andy Bown (keyboards), Rossi, Parfitt, Kirchner, Lancaster.**

**In The Army Now, Status Quo.
Courtesy Vertigo Records.**

playing relentless (some say, repetitious) boogie. Despite critical write-off, Status Quo's audience put band back in UK Top 10 with **Paper Plane. Piledriver** LP charted shortly after and everything band did seemed to go gold. Single **Down, Down** went to No. 1 in UK and album **On The Level** charted in late '74. Andy Bown played keyboards on and off from 1974-79. Since 1974 every new LP on Vertigo has made UK Top 5.

The long tours and hard work seemed to have no effect on rock's longest established line-up. So it was surprising that 1982 began with announcement of Coghlan's retirement. Pete Kirchner (ex-Original Mirrors) stepped in and Quo promptly released two further chart albums, before announcing final European tour in 1984. Band Aid concert appearance in '85 was billed as the end, but band reappeared in mid-'86 with Andy Bown on keyboards and ex-Climax Blues Band Jeff Rich and John Brown on drums and bass.

**Current line-up:** Parfitt; Rossi; Andy Bown; John Brown; Jeff Rich.

**Hit Singles:**

| | US | UK |
|---|---|---|
| Pictures Of Matchstick Men, 1968 | 12 | 7 |
| Ice In The Sun, 1968 | — | 8 |
| Down The Dustpipe, 1970 | — | 12 |
| Paper Plane, 1973 | — | 8 |
| Mean Girl, 1973 | — | 20 |
| Caroline, 1973 | — | 5 |
| Break The Rules, 1974 | — | 8 |
| Down, Down, 1974 | — | 1 |
| Roll Over Lay Down, 1975 | — | 9 |
| Rain, 1976 | — | 7 |
| Mystery Song, 1976 | — | 11 |
| Wild Side Of Life, 1976 | — | 9 |
| Rockin' All Over The World, 1977 | — | 3 |
| Again And Again, 1978 | — | 13 |
| Whatever You Want, 1979 | — | 4 |
| Living On An Island, 1979 | — | 16 |
| What You're Proposing, 1980 | — | 2 |
| Lies/Don't Drive My Car, 1981 | — | 11 |
| Something 'Bout You Baby I Like, 1981 | — | 7 |
| Rock'n'Roll, 1981 | — | 8 |
| Dear John, 1982 | — | 10 |
| Caroline (live), 1982 | — | 13 |
| Ol' Rag Blues, 1983 | — | 9 |
| A Mess Of Blues, 1983 | — | 15 |
| Marguerita Time, 1983 | — | 3 |
| Going Downtown Tonight, 1984 | — | 20 |
| The Wanderer, 1984 | — | 7 |
| Dreamin', 1986 | — | 15 |
| In The Army Now, 1986 | — | 2 |

**Albums:**
(not including various repetitious compilations)
Ma Kellys Greasy Spoon (PRT), 1970 **CD**
Dog Of Two Heads (PRT), 1971 **CD**
Piledriver (A&M/Vertigo), 1973
Hello (A&M/Vertigo), 1973
Quo (A&M/Vertigo), 1974
On The Level (Capitol/Vertigo), 1975

Blue For You (—/Vertigo), 1976
Status Quo Live (Capitol/Vertigo), 1977
Rockin' All Over The World (Capitol/Vertigo), 1977
Status Quo File (—/Pye), 1977
If You Can't Stand The Heat (—/Vertigo), 1978
Whatever You Want (—/Vertigo), 1979
Twelve Gold Bars (Vertigo), 1980 **CD**
Just Supposin' (—/Vertigo), 1980
Never Too Late (—/Vertigo), 1981
1982 (Vertigo), 1982 **CD**
'From The Makers Of...' (—/Vertigo), 1982
Twelve Gold Bars Vols I & II (Vertigo), 1984
In The Army Now (Vertigo), 1986 **CD**
Spare Parts (PRT) **CD**
Back To Back (Vertigo) **CD**
Best Of (PRT) **CD**

# Steely Dan

US group formed 1972.

**Original line-up:** Donald Fagen, keyboards, vocals; Walter Becker, bass, vocals; Denny Dias, guitar; Jeff 'Skunk' Baxter, guitar, pedal steel guitar; Jim Hodder, drums; David Palmer, vocals.

**Can't Buy A Thrill, first album for Steely Dan in their own right. Courtesy MCA Records.**

**Career:** Formed around dual writing/performing talents of Fagen and Becker, both former students at Bard College, New York. First band included Denny Dias; joined Jay And Americans back-up band when group split. First recorded work was soundtrack for off-beat Zalman King movie 'You Gotta Walk It Like You Talk It (Or You'll Loose That Beat)'. Took name Steely Dan from a William Burroughs novel.

**Below: Donald Fagen (right) and Walter Becker, late of Steely Dan.**

Moved to West Coast at insistence of producer Gary Katz; signed as writers to ABC/Dunhill Records. Katz/Fagen/Becker assembled group comprising Dias, fellow New Yorker Palmer, and Bostonians Baxter and Hodder.

Debut album **Can't Buy A Thrill** (1972) set pattern for jazz-structured melodies and succinct, Runyonesque lyrics. Singles from LP **Do It Again** and **Reelin' In The Years** made US Top 20.

Palmer quit (forming Wha Koo in 1977) before second album **Countdown To Ecstasy**, leaving vocals exclusively to Fagen. Quintet completed **Pretzel Logic** (with notable session musicians such as Michael Omartian, Jeff Porcaro (now in Toto(▶)), Chuck Rainey, Dean Parks, Vic Feldman and Crusaders'(▶) Wilton Felder). Album included classic **Rikki Don't Lose That Number**, a US Top 10 single.

With Fagen and Becker deriving more pleasure from recording than touring, Baxter and Hodder departed; Baxter subsequently joined Doobie Brothers(▶). For **Katy Lied**, group added Michael McDonald (also later to join Doobies), vocals, and Jeff Porcaro, drums. McDonald had previously toured both US and UK with band.

By now almost permanent studio unit, group cut **The Royal Scam** with addition of session players but without departed Dias. Chart success maintained with track **Haitian Divorce**.

**Aja** (1977) saw Fagen/Becker firmly in control; musicians included drummer Bernard Purdie(▶) guitarists Larry Carlton(▶) and Lee Ritenour, and guest appearance by Dias; veteran Feldman on percussion and keyboards, and surprisingly Chuck Rainey on bass, depriving Becker of his role for all but one track. McDonald supplied back-up vocals.

Steely Dan's final album to date, **Gaucho** (1980), returned duo to singles chart with track **Babylon Sisters**. Becker again limited on bass contribution, with Rainey and Anthony Jackson (a Simon & Garfunkel(▶) favourite) stepping in.

Band's tenuous story further confused by Donald Fagen solo set **Nightfly** (1982); songs were exclusively Fagen's (except Leiber/Stoller's **Ruby Baby**) but sound was definitive Steely Dan.

**Nightfly** explored fantasies of teen America; sound complemented by Porcaro, Brecker Bros (trumpet and sax), Carlton, Hugh McCracken, guitar, and bassist Rainey Jackson, Marcus Miller, Abe Laboriel and Will Lee. Becker could take heart from the talent it took to replace him.

1985 double album set **Best Of** was best seller and fuelled rumours that duo would reform. Becker and Fagen did in fact appear together again in 1986, when featured on Rosie Vela's debut LP **Zazu**, although both have since concentrated on solo projects, with Fagen now turning his attention to movie scores.

**Current/Final line-up:** Fagen; Becker; plus session players.

**Hit Singles:**

| | US | UK |
|---|---|---|
| Do It Again, 1973 | 6 | 39 |
| Reelin' In The Years, 1973 | 11 | — |
| Rikki Don't Lose That Number, 1974 | 4 | — |
| Haitian Divorce, 1976 | 3 | 17 |
| FM (No Static At All), 1978 | 7 | 49 |
| Peg, 1978 | 11 | — |
| Deacon Blues, 1978 | 19 | — |
| Babylon Sisters, 1980 | 2 | |

**Albums:**
You Gotta Walk It (Visa/—), 1969
Can't Buy A Thrill (MCA), 1972
Countdown To Ecstasy (MCA), 1973
Pretzel Logic (MCA), 1974
Katy Lied (MCA), 1975
The Royal Scam (MCA), 1976
Aja (MCA), 1977 **CD**
Greatest Hits (MCA), 1979
Gaucho (MCA), 1980 **CD**

**Steely Dan's Gaucho, featuring hit single Babylon Sisters. Courtesy MCA Records.**

Gold (MCA), 1982
Reelin' In The Years (MCA), 1985
Best Of (MCA), 1985 **CD**
Berry Town (Bellphon), 1986 **CD**
Old Regime (Thunderbolt), 1987 **CD**

*Donald Fagen Solo:*
The Nightfly (Warner Bros), 1982 **CD**

# Steppenwolf

US group formed 1967.

**Original line-up:** John Kay, guitar, vocals; Jerry Edmonton, drums; Goldy McJohn, organ; Michael Monarch, guitar; Rushton Moreve, bass.

**Career:** East German-born John Kay and his family fled to Canada when he was 14. There he discovered Western music and formed blues group Sparrow. Realising limited chances in Toronto, Kay took band to New York, then California.

Sparrow began adapting style to blues-based gritty rock made popular by English bands. By mid-1967 they had become Steppenwolf and the first of many bass player changes occurred as John Russell Morgan replace Moreve.

When band recorded debut LP in late '67, they had several years of road experience and original material stored up. **Born To Be Wild** single was released as crisis in Czechoslovakia led to Russian invasion. Rough vocals, outrageous lyrics and grinding music epitomised political atmosphere of tanks in the street and worldwide call to break free. **Magic Carpet Ride,** released barely three months later, enhanced image of bold, creative force at large.

Albums by Steppenwolf were patchy and uneven until 1969 release, **Monster.** This represented band at its most political as well as its most cohesive musically. Instead of pushing ahead, frenzied past few years caught up and group began more extensive personnel changes. Monarch's guitar spot was taken by Larry Byrom, then Kent Henry. Bass player duties were handed over to Nick St. Nicholas, then to George Biondo. This caused break-up of tight-knit sound forged by early band, and in February 1972 came announcement of Steppenwolf's demise.

When Kay's solo career failed to take hold, he reorganised band in 1974 with McJohn, Edmonton, Biondo and guitarist Bobby Cochran. After **Slow Flux** LP Wayne Cook replaced McJohn. **Hour Of The World** album proved band could sometimes recapture old sound, but Kay failed to come up with

**Above: John Kay, lead singer of US hard rock band Steppenwolf.**

material that matched magic days of 1967-1969. Despite further efforts, band never regained old form.

Steppenwolf's place in rock history depends as much on political climate of '60s as on music. As memories fade, band's music seems less potent, less a call to arms. Nevertheless, underlying sound still has powerful hold as seen by many successful greatest hits and compilation releases.

**Final Line Up:** Kay; Edmonton; Bobby Cochran, guitar; George Biondo, bass; Wayne Cook, keyboards.

**The first Steppenwolf album. Courtesy RCA Records.**

| Hit Singles: | US | UK |
|---|---|---|
| Born To Be Wild, 1968 | 2 | 30 |
| Magic Carpet Ride, 1968 | 3 | — |
| Rock Me, 1969 | 10 | — |

**Albums:**
Steppenwolf (Dunhill/Stateside), 1968 **CD**
Steppenwolf The Second (Dunhill/Stateside), 1968 **CD**
Live Steppenwolf (Dunhill/Probe), 1970
Steppenwolf 7 (Dunhill/Probe), 1970
Steppenwolf Gold (MCA), 1971
16 Greatest Hits (ABC), 1973
Gold (MCA), 1981
Golden Greats (MCA), 1985

# Cat Stevens

UK vocalist, composer, guitarist.
Born Steven Georgiou, London, July 21, 1947.

**Career:** Son of a Greek restauranteur father and Swedish mother, Stevens enjoyed two distinct musical careers, first as straightforward folk-influenced pop artist then, following time off scene seriously ill, as folk-rock album star experimenting heavily with ethnic Greek instruments which gave his style unique dimension.

He became involved in folk scene while studying at Hammersmith College and met former Springfields' folk group member Mike Hurst, then working as independent record producer. Instead of emigrating to America as intended, Hurst invested his savings in recording Stevens' own composition, **I Love My Dog,** which he then licensed to Tony Hall for Decca's newly formed Deram (progressive music subsidiary) as label's debut release. The record charted and follow-up **Matthew And Son** did even better, reaching No. 2 in early 1967.

Stevens toured with both Jimi Hendrix(▶) and Englebert Humperdinck and his perceptive songs were snapped up by other recording stars (notably P.P. Arnold with **The First Cut Is The Deepest** and the Tremeloes with **Here Comes My Baby).** In early 1968 he scored third Deram hit with **I'm Gonna Get Me A Gun.**

After contracting TB, Stevens spent year recuperating, using the time to develop new ideas and songs in almost classical manner. Taking time to get everything just right, Stevens eventually signed to Island and released the landmark **Mona Bone Jakon** in 1970. From that set, **Lady d'Arbanville** (written about a former girlfriend) emerged as hit single, but Stevens had truly matured into album artist and subsequent sets made him a superstar both sides of Atlantic.

Massive earnings from records and concerts led to tax exile in Brazil during which time he became heavily involved with UNESCO and various charities.

By mid-'70s, Stevens had become very much the recluse, developing a passionate interest in mysticism. He converted to Moslem faith and married girl he had seen at a London mosque but never spoken to.

**The Old School Yard** (1977) was his last hit single; subsequently he retired completely from music scene, devoting himself to religious studies and adopting the name Yusef Islam.

| Hit Singles: | US | UK |
|---|---|---|
| Matthew And Son, 1967 | — | 2 |
| I'm Gonna Get Me A Gun, 1967 | — | 6 |
| A Bad Night, 1967 | — | 20 |
| Lady D'Arbanville, 1970 | — | 8 |
| Wild World, 1971 | 11 | — |
| Peace Train, 1971 | 7 | — |
| Morning Has Broken, 1972 | 6 | 9 |
| Can't Keep It In, 1972 | — | 13 |
| Sitting, 1972 | 16 | — |
| Oh Very Young, 1974 | 10 | — |
| Another Saturday Night, 1974 | 6 | 19 |

**Above: Cat Stevens, a chart star of two decades, but now retired.**

**Albums:**
Matthew And Son (—/Deram), 1967
New Masters (—/Deram), 1968
World Of (—/Decca), 1970
Mona Bone Jakon (A&M/Island), 1970 **CD**
Tea For The Tillerman (A&M/Island), 1971 **CD**
Teaser & The Fire Cat (A&M/Island), 1971 **CD**
Catch Bull At Four (A&M/Island), 1972 **CD**
Foreigner (A&M/Island), 1973
Buddha & The Chocolate Box (A&M/Island), 1974
View From The Top (—/Deram), 1974
Numbers (A&M/Island), 1975
Greatest Hits (A&M/Island), 1975 **CD**
Izitso (A&M/Island), 1977
Back To Earth (A&M/Island), 1978
The First Cut Is The Deepest (—/Decca), 1980

# Shakin' Stevens

UK vocalist, composer.
Born Michael Barratt, Ely, Wales, March 4, 1948.

**Career:** Formed first band, the Sunsets, in 1969; toured pubs/clubs establishing reputation as premier rock 'n' roll revivalist. Signed to Parlophone records in 1970; first album **A Legend** produced by Dave Edmunds(▶).

Over next six years recorded for variety of major and minor labels mostly in same 'revival' style with some success, notably in Europe. Similarity to Presley(▶) resulted in starring role in London musical 'Elvis', followed by regular spot on revived 'Oh Boy!' TV show.

Signed to Track Records during Elvis show for first album without Sunsets; moved to Epic following 'Oh Boy' appearances. First singles on Epic unsuccessful but fourth single became Top 30 hit in February 1980. **Marie, Marie** fared better. Finally consolidated popularity in 1981 with **This Ole House.**

Although initially regarded as rockabilly artist, Stevens has since softened image somewhat, at same time retaining obvious affection for '50s music, carefully produced by Stuart Coleman.

| Hit Singles: | US | UK |
|---|---|---|
| Marie, Marie, 1980 | — | 19 |
| This Ole House, 1981 | — | 1 |
| You Drive Me Crazy, 1981 | — | 2 |
| Green Door, 1981 | — | 1 |
| It's Raining, 1981 | — | 10 |
| Oh Julie, 1982 | — | 1 |
| Shirley, 1982 | — | 6 |
| Give Me Your Heart Tonight, 1982 | — | 11 |
| I'll Be Satisfied, 1982 | — | 10 |
| Blue Christmas (EP), 1982 | — | 2 |
| It's Late, 1983 | — | 11 |
| A Love Worth Waiting For, 1984 | — | 3 |
| A Letter To You, 1984 | — | 2 |
| Teardrops, 1984 | — | 10 |
| Breaking Up My Heart, 1985 | — | 14 |
| Lipstick Powder & Paint, 1985 | — | 11 |
| Merry Christmas Everyone, 1985 | — | 1 |
| Turning Away, 1986 | — | 15 |
| Because I Love You, 1986 | — | 14 |
| A Little Boogie Woogie, 1987 | — | 12 |
| Come See About Me, 1987 | — | 24 |
| What do You Want To Make Those Eyes At Me For, 1987 | — | 5 |

**Albums:**
Shakin' Stevens (—/Polydor), 1978
Shakin' Stevens & The Sunsets — A Legend (—/Nut), 1979
Shakin' Stevens & The Sunsets — Tiger (Everest), 1980
Marie Marie (—/Epic), 1980

**This Ole House, Shakin' Stevens. Courtesy Epic Records.**

Take One (—/Epic), 1980
Shakin' Stevens & The Sunsets at The Rockhouse (—/Magnum), 1981
Shakin' Stevens & The Sunsets (—/Mint), 1981
Manhattan Melodrama (—/Mint), 1981
Shakin' Stevens (—/Hallmark), 1981
Rock On With A Legend (—/MFP), 1981
Shatterin', Volume II (—/Contour), 1981
Shaky (—/Epic), 1981
This Ole House (Epic), 1981
You Drive Me Crazy (Epic/—), 1981
Get Shakin' (Epic/—), 1982
Hot Dog (—/Epic), 1982
Give Me Your Heart Tonight (—/Epic), 1982
The Bop Won't Stop (Epic), 1983 **CD**
Greatest Hits (Epic), 1984
Lipstick Powder And Paint (Epic), 1985
Collection (Collector Series) **CD**
Lets Boogie (Epic), 1987

# Al Stewart

UK vocalist, composer, guitarist.
Born Glasgow, Scotland,

**Career:** Public school drop out, originally studied guitar with Robert Fripp and played lead in Bournemouth group Tony Blackburn & the Sabres. Moved to London, establishing small following after solo folk club appearances at Bunjies and Les Cousins in mid-'60s. Signed to CBS, recorded Dylan-influenced **Bedsitter Images**, a slight work, sweetened by orchestral backing. Grand attempt to launch Stewart at Festival Hall with elaborate accompaniment proved premature.

**Love Chronicles** continued artist's near obsession with unrequited love as major theme. 18-minute titletrack gained some notoriety for 'artistic' use of swear word 'fucking' and established Stewart as troubadour of London's bedsitter land. 1970's **Zero She Files** followed familiar self-analytical style of predecessors as Stewart gradually won favour on college circuit. Transitional **Orange** hinted at possible development, not fully realised until 1974's **Past, Present And Future,** his most ambitious work to date. Concept album, inspired by Erika Cheetham's book **The Centuries Of Nostradamus,** featured series of songs based on important historical events of 20th century. Two of longer cuts, **Roads To Moscow** and **Nostradamus,** highlighted Stewart's talent as writer/guitarist/arranger.

**Past, Present And Future** was first work to be released in US, prompting an ambitious March '74 tour, for which backing group was assembled from recently defunct Home. Mid-'70s albums **Modern Times** and RCA debut **Year Of The Cat** revealed Stewart attempting to shed old folkie image in favour of more contemporary sound.

His preoccupation with time as theme continued in **Time Passages,** which included songs focusing on French Revolution, 16th century England and contemporary America. Incorporation of jazz/reggae elements along-side familiar acoustic work proved sufficiently successful to secure breakthrough into US mainstream where all Stewart's RCA albums have sold well — **The Year Of The Cat** climbing to Top 5.

In spite of recent American successes, Stewart is often dismissed in his home country for lack of aggression and conservatism. His early self-indulgence has alienated most British critics but at his rare best he deserves greater respect.

**Hit Singles:**

| | US | UK |
|---|---|---|
| Year Of The Cat, 1977 | 8 | 31 |
| Time Passages, 1978 | 7 | — |

**Albums:**

Love Chronicles (—/RCA), 1969
Orange (CBS), 1972
Past, Present And Future (Arista/CBS), 1974
Modern Times (Arista/CBS), 1975
Year Of The Cat (Arista/RCA), 1976 **CD**
The Early Years (Arista/RCA), 1978
Time Passages (Arista/RCA), 1978 **CD**
24 Carrots (Arista/RCA), 1980
Live; Indian Summer (Arista/RCA), 1981
24 Carrots (RCA), 1981
Russians And Americans (RCA), 1984

# Rod Stewart

UK vocalist, guitarist.
Born London, January 10, 1945.

**Career:** London born, but eternally proud of Scottish ancestry (his brothers were born North of the border). Attended same school as Ray and Dave Davies of the Kinks.

After spells as fence-erector and grave-digger, signed apprentice forms with Brentford Football Club but was soon disillusioned by poor pay and having to clean boots of senior players. However, he is still a soccer fanatic.

While travelling around Europe, met folk singer Wizz Jones in Spain who taught him to play harmonica. Repatriated as destitute Stewart learned guitar and joined Birmingham outfit Jimmy Powell and the Dimensions; sang and played harmonica.

In 1964 Stewart recorded obscure but superb version of R&B clasic **Good Morning Little Schoolgirl** for Decca. Joined Long John Baldry's band the Hoochie Coochie Men as second vocalist. Fronted Soul Agents for while before joining Brian Auger, Julie Driscoll and Reginald Dwight (better known as Elton John(▶)), in Steampacket in mid-'65. Also had spell in Steampacket's next form, Bluesology. Backed by Auger's organ playing, Stewart cut version of his hero Sam Cooke's(▶) **Shake** for Columbia in 1966. Quit to sing alongside Beryl Marsden in Shotgun Express with Peter Green(▶) (guitar), Peter Bardens (keyboards); Dave Ambrose (bass) and Mick Fleetwood (drums). Despite classy line-up, band failed. While continuing as-yet-unsuccessful solo recording career, Stewart joined Jeff Beck Group(▶).

After disastrous London concerts, band found feet in America. Stewart featured on lauded albums **Truth** (1968) and **Beck-Ola** (1969). This led to solo contract with Mercury in 1969.

Stewart quit Beck's band when latter wanted to fire Ronnie Wood with whom Stewart had struck up friendship and strong working relationship. Soon after, Stewart and Wood were added to line-up of the Faces(▶).

While Faces, with Stewart singing lead, turned out patchy albums, Stewart's solo efforts for Mercury were outstanding. After initial break in US via **An Old Raincoat Won't Ever Let You Down** (the **Rod Stewart Album** in US) and **Gasoline Alley** LP in 1970, he quickly built similar reputation in homeland. Hit big with **Maggie May** from dynamic 1971 album **Every Picture Tells A Story**. In September 1971, Stewart achieved distinction of topping both album and single charts on both sides of the Atlantic in same week.

Fronting Faces for live appearances, Stewart built band into massive concert attraction. Generated frenetic atmosphere and built legion of fanatical followers who followed him in adopting the tartan symbol — and espousing football. Group regularly kicked footballs into audience and Stewart always took time out to attend major games.

In 1972, **Never A Dull Moment** LP and **You Wear It Well** single struck gold. An astute minor label dug out an old track Stewart had recorded, for session fee alone, with studio group Python Lee Jackon back in 1968. They could not use Stewart's name but his reputation was enough and **In A Broken Dream** made No. 3 in UK charts.

Recording material first made famous by his heroes in rock 'n' roll, soul and R&B (ranging from Jerry Lee Lewis to Chuck Berry to Sam Cooke), Stewart always added his own inimitable touch. Cover versions and new material alike showed enormous creativity and fully exploited merits of his gravelly vocals.

Court wrangles between Mercury and Warner Bros (to whom Faces were signed) led to delays in release of next album. Time was filled in by **Sing It Again, Rod**, a compilation set of old tracks which also included Stewart's version of **Pinball Wizard** from Lou Reizner's Rainbow Theatre stage presentation of Pete Townshend's rock musical 'Tommy' in which Stewart had appeared. Ever the ligger, Stewart indulged in notorious boozing sessions with Elton John and other cohorts.

Issued late in 1974, Stewart's **Smiler** album was disappointing. In December 1975 he announced he was leaving Faces to give

**Left: Rod Stewart, a chart topping artist from 1973 onwards, and one of the biggest stars still active.**

**Best Of Rod Stewart, '70s hits from the highly adaptable 'Rod The Mod'. Courtesy Mercury Records.**

solo career more impetus. Debut Warner Bros' album Tom Dowd-produced **Atlantic Crossing**, recorded largely in Muscle Shoals, Alabama (he had moved home base to Hollywood), was good start. 1976 follow-up, **A Night On The Town**, appeared on manager Billy Gaff's Riva label (through Warner Bros) and was hugely successful, yielding three US chart-topping singles: **Tonight's The Night, The Killing Of Georgie** and **The First Cut Is The Deepest.** The first equalled achievement of the Beatles' **Hey Jude** in topping US charts for eight weeks.

**Sailing** brough another UK number one, but on personal front Stewart had problems. His long-standing but tempestuous relationship with actress Britt Ekland broke up amid acrimony and 'kiss and tell' stories. He later married actor George Hamilton's ex-, Alana, but they also parted company. Stewart also severed partnership with manager Gaff, relinquishing his one third share of Riva records.

Stewart seemed happier and more confident as undisputed leader of own band rather than as member of a group. Strutting in front of classy but disciplined musicians like Phillip Chenn (bass), Carmine Appice (drums) and Jim Cregan (guitar), he oozed extrovert showmanship and throughout subsequent line-up changes he has managed to maintain equilibrium. With his tight leopard-skin pants, spiky blond hair and emaciated yet sensual looks, he can rest assured that fans from the '70s to the '80s have given a resounding yes to his recorded question **Do You Think I'm Sexy?**

**Hit Singles:**

| | US | UK |
|---|---|---|
| Reason To Believe/Maggie May, 1971 | — | 19 |
| Maggie May/Reason To Believe, 1971 | 1 | 1 |
| You Wear It Well, 1972 | 13 | 1 |
| Angel/What Made Milwaukee Famous, 1972 | 40 | 4 |
| Oh No Not My Baby, 1973 | 59 | 6 |
| Farewell/Bring It On Home To Me/ You Send Me, 1974 | — | 7 |
| Sailing, 1975 | 58 | 1 |
| This Ole Heart Of Mine, 1975 | — | 4 |
| Tonight's The Night, 1976 | 1 | 5 |
| The Killing of Georgie, 1976 | 30 | 2 |
| Get Back, 1976 | | 11 |
| I Don't Want To Talk About It/ The First Cut Is The Deepest, 1977 | 21 | 1 |
| You're In My Heart, 1977 | 4 | 3 |
| Hotlegs/I Was Only Joking, 1978 | 28 | 5 |
| Ole Ola (Muhler Brasileira), 1978 | — | 4 |
| Do Ya Think I'm Sexy?, 1978 | 1 | 1 |
| Ain't Love A Bitch, 1979 | 22 | 11 |
| Passion, 1980 | 5 | 9 |
| Tonight I'm Yours (Don't Hurt Me), 1981 | — | 8 |
| Young Turks, 1981 | 5 | 11 |
| Baby Jane, 1983 | 15 | 1 |

| | | |
|---|---|---|
| What Am I Gonna Do, 1983 | 35 | 3 |
| Infatuation, 1984 | 6 | 27 |
| Some Guys Have All The Luck, 1984 | 10 | 15 |
| Every Beat Of My Heart, 1986 | — | 2 |
| Love Touch, 1987 | 5 | — |

**Albums:**
An Old Raincoat Won't Ever Let You Down (Vertigo), 1970* **CD**
Gasoline Alley (Mercury/Vertigo), 1970 **CD**
Every Picture Tells A Story (Mercury), 1971 **CD**
Never A Dull Moment (Mercury), 1972 **CD**
Sing It Again Rod (Mercury), 1973 **CD**
Smiler (Mercury), 1974 **CD**
Atlantic Crossing (Warner Bros/Riva), 1975 **CD**
A Night On The Town (Warner Bros/Riva), 1976
Foot Loose & Fancy Free (Warner Bros/Riva), 1977
Best Of (Mercury), 1977†
Best of, Volume II (Mercury), 1977†
Blondes Have More Fun (Warner Bros/Riva), 1978
Greatest Hits (Warner Bros), 1979 **CD**
Foolish Behaviour (Warner Bros/Riva), 1980
Tonight I'm Yours (Warner Bros/Riva), 1981
Rod The Mod (Accord), 1981
Maggie May (—/Contour), 1981
Absolutely Live (Warner Bros/Riva), 1982 **CD**
Body Wishes (WEA), 1983 **CD**
Camouflage (Warner Bros), 1984 **CD**
Greatest Hits Vol. 2 (CBS), 1986 **CD**
Every Beat Of My Heart (Warner Bros), 1987 **CD**

*Titled **Rod Stewart Album** aka **Thin** (Mercury) in US.
†Double compilations

# Stephen Stills

US guitarist, vocalist, songwriter.
Born Dallas, Texas, January 3, 1945.

**Career:** Moved about Southern US as child, attending variety of schools, eventually entering University of Florida. After playing part-time in local folk circles, Stills quit college and moved to New York for its reputed folk scene. Perceiving changing musical climate, he left for Los Angeles. After several projects (one of which was to fail audition for Monkees(▶)), he helped found Buffalo Springfield(▶). Stills wrote band's major hit, **For What It's Worth.**

Following Buffalo's demise, Stills recorded **Supersession** with Al Kooper(▶) and Mike Bloomfield(▶), toured with girlfriend Judy Collins(▶), played on one of her albums and did sessions for Joni Mitchell(▶).

End of 1968 brought announcement of Crosby, Stills and Nash(▶) supergroup (CSN). Still's ode to Judy Collins became their first hit, **Suite: Judy Blue Eyes.** When CSN reunited Stills with old Buffalo Springfield mate Neil Young(▶), band became top heavy with egos, and Stills began working on first solo LP, recorded while he was living in London. Stills employed number of major musicians, including Jimi Hendrix(▶), who died before album's release; LP was dedicated to him. Second solo album used CSN&Y sidemen whom Stills organised into loose confederation he called Manassas. After two releases, part of band left with Chris Hillman who was to form Souther-Hillman-Furay Band.

Stills reorganised back-up band but broke off activity for 1974 CSN&Y reunion tour.

**Right: The Stranglers (from left) Dave Greenfield, Jet Black, Jean-Jacques Burnel, Hugh Cornwell.**

Since then Stills has released several LPs, most notable being joint venture with Neil Young as Stills-Young Band. He has also rejoined CSN, whenever that happens along, but of late his influence is diminishing as '60s recede.

| **Hit Singles:** | US | UK |
|---|---|---|
| Love The One You're With, 1971 | 14 | 37 |

**Albums:**
Stephen Stills (Atlantic), 1970
Stephen Stills II (Atlantic), 1971
Stills (Columbia/CBS), 1975
Stills Live (Atlantic), 1976
Illegal Stills (Columbia/CBS), 1976
The Best Of Stephen Stills (Atlantic), 1976
Long May You Run (with Stills-Young Band) (Reprise), 1976
Thoroughfare Gap (Columbia/CBS), 1978
Right By You (WEA), 1984

*Manassas:*
Manassas (Atlantic), 1975
Down The Road (Atlantic), 1973

*Worth Searching Out:*
Supersession (with Al Kooper and Mike Bloomfield) (Columbia/CBS), 1968

# The Stranglers

UK group formed 1975.

**Original/Current line-up:** Hugh Cornwell, vocals, Fender Telecaster guitar; Jean-Jacques Burnel, vocals, bass; Dave Greenfield, keyboards; Jet Black, drums.

**Career:** Following formation in village near Guildford, Surrey, supported Patti Smith(▶) on 1975 UK tour. During 1976 played more than 200 gigs, mainly around London, and built up reputation as powerful live act. Benefited from interest in 'new wave' despite having little in common with punk outfits.

Two years live work paid off with release of first album **Rattus Norvegicus**, which leapt to No. 4 in UK charts. Simultaneously, single **Peaches/Go Buddy Go** reached No. 8 in singles charts.

Winning streak continued throughout 1977 and 1978, but from 1979 to beginning of 1981 band seemed to slip from limelight somewhat. Had no major singles success during this time, but continued touring regularly. Low point came when, following series of legal wrangles, band was imprisoned in Nice, France.

**All Live And All Of The Night, The Stranglers. Courtesy Epic Records.**

Although successful within their field, band seemed destined to remain something of unknown quantity to average record buyer. Some were already beginning to dismiss Stranglers as 'punk revivalists' when band bounced back in 1981 with two major albums, **The Meninblack** and **La Folie.** More surprising was single from **La Folie, Golden Brown.** In contrast to tough black leather visual image and usual output it was gentle, floating summery waltz that appealed to many who had never before bought Stranglers records. Single was huge hit all over world, few months later band followed with almost as succesful **Strange Little Girl** single.

Latterly, 'unpredictable' tag has worn thin, as band has become increasingly reliant on clichéd philosophising and rentamouth media shenanigans. At time of writing, band is relying on uninspired copy of Kinks' classic **All Day And All Of The Night** for renewed chart status. Although live set **All Live And All Of The Night** demonstrates band's true strengths, American success continues to elude them.

| **Hit Singles:** | US | UK |
|---|---|---|
| Peaches/Go Buddy Go, 1977 | — | 8 |
| Something Better Change/Straighten Out, 1977 | | 9 |
| No More Heroes, 1977 | — | 8 |
| Five Minutes, 1978 | — | 11 |
| Nice 'n' Sleazy, 1978 | | 18 |
| Duchess, 1979 | | 14 |
| Golden Brown, 1982 | — | 2 |
| Strange Little Girl, 1982 | | 7 |
| European Female, 1983 | | 9 |
| Skin Deep, 1984 | | 15 |
| Always The Sun, 1986 | | 30 |
| Nice In Nice, 1986 | | 30 |
| Big In America, 1986 | | 49 |
| All Day And All Of The Night, 1988 | | 7 |

**Albums:**
Rattus Norvegicus (A&M/United Artists) 1977 **CD**
No More Heroes (A&M/United Artists), 1977
Black And White (A&M/United Artists), 1978
Live (X Cert) (A&M/United Artists), 1979
The Raven (A&M/United Artists), 1979 **CD**
The Meninblack (EMI), 1981
La Folie (EMI), 1981
The Collection 1977-1982 (—/Liberty) 1982 **CD**
Feline (Epic), 1983
Dreamtime (Epic), 1986 **CD**
Off The Beaten Track (Liberty), 1986
Aural Sculpture (Epic), 1987
All Live And All Of The Night (Epic) 1988 **CD**

# Barbra Streisand

US vocalist, actress
Born Barbara Joan Streisand, Brooklyn, New York, April 24, 1942.

**Career:** Worked as switchboard operator and theatre usherette before winning talent competition in Greenwich Village night club. Played cabaret circuit before joining an off-Broadway revue. Made Broadway debut in 1962 in 'I Can Get It For You Wholesale' playing Yetta Tessye Marmel Stein opposite Elliot Gould whom she later married (and later divorced). Barbra stole show with her singing and clowning, winning New York critics' award and becoming star overnight.

In 1964 she played/sang role of Fanny Brice in Broadway muscial 'Funny Girl'. Same year signed multi-million dollar recording contract with Columbia. Soon had first hit record with **People**.

Film debut was 1968 film version of 'Funny Girl': tied with Katharine Hepburn for an Academy Award as Best Actress.

In 1977 Streisand won an Oscar for her music for song **Evergreen** (co-written with Paul Williams) featured in re-make of movie 'A Star Is Born' in which she starred as a rock singer, opposite Kris Kristofferson(▶).

Other notable movie appearances have included 'Hello Dolly' (with Louis Armstrong), 'The Owl And The Pussycat' (with George Segal), 'What's Up Doc' and 'The Main Event' (with Ryan O'Neill), 'The Way We Were' (starring Robert Redford and for which she sang the US chart-topping title song) and 'Funny Lady'.

Her first venture out of world of MOR and showbiz music was in 1970 when she entered Top 10 with her version of Laura Nyro's **Stoney End**. In late '70s she had hit single with **No More Tears/Enough Is Enough**, a duet with Donna Summer(▶), Barry Gibb produced her in rock/pop vein on **Guilty** LP, which gave her three hit singles.

Now established in every facet of show bizdom—even her record of Lieder and classical art songs earned one million sales. Streisand achieved lifetime ambition when 'Yentl' movie (1983) saw her as producer, director and star. Continued 'oppressed womanhood' theme with starring role in 1987 film 'Nuts' which had 'Oscar' written all over it.

| **Hit Singles:** | US | UK |
|---|---|---|
| People, 1964 | 5 | |
| Second Hand Rose, 1966 | 32 | 14 |
| Stoney End, 1971 | 6 | 27 |
| The Way We Were, 1974 | 1 | 31 |
| Love Theme From A Star Is Born (Evergreen), 1977 | 1 | 3 |
| My Heart Belongs To Me, 1977 | 1 | |
| The Main Event/Fight, 1979 | 3 | |
| Woman In Love, 1980 | 1 | 1 |
| Comin' In And Out Of Your Life, 1981 | 11 | |

**With Neil Diamond:**
You Don't Bring Me Flowers, 1978   1   5

**With Donna Summer:**
No More Tears (Enough Is
  Enough), 1979   1   3

**With Barry Gibb:**
Guilty, 1980   3   34
What Kind Of Fool, 1981   10   —

**Albums (selected):**
My Name Is Barbra (Columbia/Embassy),
  1964
Simply Streisand (Columbia/CBS), 1967
Greatest Hits (Columbia/CBS), 1969 **CD**
Stoney End (Columbia/CBS), 1971
The Way We Were (Columbia/CBS), 1974
Greatest Hits Vol. II (Columbia/CBS),
  1979 **CD**
Guilty (Columbia/CBS), 1980* **CD**
Christmas Album (CBS), 1980 **CD**
Memories (Columbia/CBS), 1981
Yentl (Columbia/CBS), 1983
Emotion (Columbia/CBS), 1984 **CD**
Love Songs (CBS), 1984 **CD**
The Broadway Album (Columbia/CBS),
  1985 **CD**
Funny Girl (CBS), 1985 **CD**
Butterfly (CBS), 1987 **CD**
Colour Me Barbra (CBS), 1987 **CD**
Live Concert At The Forum (CBS), 1987 **CD**
One Voice (CBS), 1987 **CD**
Songbird (CBS), 1987 **CD**
Superman (CBS), 1987 **CD**
Wet (CBS), 1987 **CD**
*With Barry Gibb

# Style Council

UK group formed 1983.

**Original/Current line-up:** Paul Weller,
vocals, guitar, composer; Mick Talbot,
keyboards, composer.

**Career:** When the Jam(▶) disbanded in
December 1982, Paul Weller linked up with
former Merton Parkas, Dexys Midnight
Runners(▶) and Bureau member Talbot to
form Style Council, an outfit heavily influenced
by Weller's long-time interest in soul in general
and Motown in particular.

Highly politically motivated, Style Council
played first gig at May Day concert in Liverpool
for Campaign for Nuclear Disarmament and
Merseyside Unemployment Centre and later
in year captured mood of a rare British summer
with **Long Hot Summer** EP.

**Our Favourite Shop, Style Council.
Courtesy Polydor Records.**

Released in March 1983, debut single
**Speak Like A Child** peaked at four on UK
chart. Further hits carried group through
1984 leading to 'Best Debut Group Of The
Year' award in America's New Music Awards.

Raising money for striking British coal
miners and widow of taxi-cab driver David
Wilkie, killed during miners' dispute, Weller
and Talbot put together Council Collective
with aid from Steve White, Junior Giscombe,

Dizzy Heights, Animal Nightlife's Leonardo
Chignoli, Heaven 17's Martin Ware, Vaughn
Toulouse, American soul singer Jimmy
Ruffin(▶) and Weller's girlfriend D.C. Lee to
cut version of **Soul Deep**.

Weller's poltical stance was reflected in
his election as president for Britain of International Youth Year in 1985 and participation
in the Red Wedge tour in aid of UK Labour
Party in early 1986.

A run of excellent singles, quality in-depth
albums and well received concert dates
around the world all helped establish Style
Council as a pop act with deeper appeal than
transcient chart success.

| Hit Singles: | US | UK |
|---|---|---|
| Speak Like A Child, 1983 | — | 4 |
| Money Go Round, 1983 | — | 11 |
| Long Hot Summer, 1983 | — | 3 |
| Solid Bond In Your Heart, 1983 | — | 11 |
| My Ever Changing Moods, 1984 | 29 | 5 |
| Groovin', 1984 | — | 5 |
| Shout To The Top, 1984 | — | 7 |
| Walls Come Tumbling Down, 1985 | — | 6 |
| The Lodgers, 1985 | — | 13 |
| Have You Ever Had It Blue, 1986 | — | 14 |
| It Didn't Matter, 1987 | — | 9 |
| Wanted, 1987 | — | 20 |

**Albums:**
Café Bleu (Polydor), 1984 **CD**
Our Favourite Shop (Polydor), 1985 **CD**
Home And Abroad (Polydor), 1986 **CD**
Home And Abroad (Live) (Polydor), 1986
Cost Of Loving (Polydor), 1987 **CD**
Introducing The Style Council (Polydor),
  1987 **CD**

# Donna Summer

US vocalist, composer.
Born Boston, Massachusetts, September,
1950.

**Career:** Dropped out of high school to pursue
ambition to become singer. Joined rock group
and played small-time gigs around Boston.

Eventually moved to New York, auditioning
for part in Broadway production of 'Hair'.
Instead was offered part in German version of
show and moved to Germany. Roles in several
European productions followed, and Summer
settled in Mannheim.

In 1975 started recording with Oasis
Records producers Giorgio Moroder and Pete
Belotte. Result was disco-sex epic **Love To
Love You Baby**, a repetitive electronic-
orientated single that united quasi-orgasmic
moans and groans with metronomic disco
beat. Picked up by Casablanca in US, single
became enormous worldwide hit, despite
protests from various moralist groups.

Greatly helped by astute business and
musical sense of Moroder and Belotte,
Summer quickly became acknowledged Queen
of '70s disco, releasing series of singles and
albums that combined memorable melodies,
robotic rhythms and sensual lyrics.

Perhaps surprisingly, in late '70s Summer
began to show she was not simply disco
puppet. Records revealed more maturity, and
1979 duet with Barbra Streisand(▶), **No
More Tears (Enough Is Enough),** matched
her with vocal talents of Streisand.

In 1980 Summer signed with Geffen and
entered new phase: recorded more of her own
material, and became devout Christian, dropping overtly sexual image. Her **State Of
Independence** was widely regarded as best
soul single of 1982, but her creatives forces
have so far best been harnessed in Michael
Omartian-produced **Cats Without Claws**
album.

Avowed intention of becoming 'all-round
entertainer' seems even more likely to bear

fruit. However, as an artist who built her career
on a huge following in the discos, especially in
the gay clubs, she upset many when, as a
born-again Christian, she launched an anti-
homosexuality campaign.

**Love To Love You Baby, Donna Summer.
Courtesy Oasis/Casablanca Records.**

| Hit Singles: | US | UK |
|---|---|---|
| Love To Love You Baby, 1975 | 2 | 4 |
| I Feel Love, 1977 | 6 | 1 |
| Down Deep Inside (Theme from | | |
|   The Deep), 1977 | — | 5 |
| I Remember Yesterday, 1977 | — | 14 |
| Love's Unkind, 1977 | — | 3 |
| I Love You, 1977 | 37 | 10 |
| Rumour Has It, 1978 | 53 | 19 |
| Last Dance, 1978 | 3 | 51 |
| MacArthur Park, 1978 | 1 | 5 |
| Heaven Knows, 1979 | 4 | 34 |
| Hot Stuff, 1979 | 1 | 11 |
| Bad Girls, 1979 | 1 | 14 |
| Dim All The Lights, 1979 | 2 | 29 |
| On The Radio, 1980 | 5 | 32 |
| The Wanderer, 1980 | 3 | 48 |
| Love Is In Control (Finger On | | |
|   The Trigger), 1982 | 10 | 18 |
| State Of Independence, 1982 | 41 | 14 |
| I Feel Love, 1982 | — | 22 |
| She Works Hard For The Money, | | |
|   1983 | 10 | 25 |
| Unconditional Love, 1983 | — | 14 |
| Dinner With Gershwin, 1987 | 48 | 13 |

*With Barbra Streisand:*
No More Tears (Enough Is
  Enough), 1979   1   3

**Albums:**
Love To Love You Baby (Oasis/Casablanca),
  1975
A Trilogy Of Love (Casablanca), 1977
Four Seasons Of Love (Casablanca), 1977
I Remember Yesterday (Casablanca/
  Embassy), 1979

The Deep (Casablanca), 1977
Once Upon A Time (Casablanca), 1977
Shutout (with Paul Jabara) (Casablanca),
  1977
Live And More (Casablanca), 1978
Bad Girls (Casablanca), 1979
On The Radio (Casablanca), 1979
The Wanderer (Geffen), 1980
Walk Away (Casablanca), 1980 **CD**
Greatest Hits Volume 1 (Casablanca), 1980
Greatest Hits Volume 2 (Casablanca), 1980
Donna Summer (Geffen), 1982 **CD**
Cold Love/Grand Illusion (Warner Bros),
  1982 **CD**
She Works Hard For The Money (Mercury),
  1983 **CD**
Cats Without Claws (Warner Bros), 1984 **CD**
The Summer Collection (Mercury), 1985 **CD**
All Systems Go (WEA), 1987 **CD**
I Love To Dance (Perfect), 1987

# Supertramp

UK group formed 1969.

**Original line-up:** Roger Hodgson, vocals,
bass, keyboards; Richard Davies, vocals,
keyboards; Dave Winthrop, reeds; Richard
Palmer, guitar; Bob Miller, drums.

**Career:** Hodgson and Davies formed band
with aid of wealthy benefactor and convinced
A&M to take chance on recording them. A&M
wasn't particularly impressed with first effort
and didn't release it in US. Miller left and was
replaced by Kevin Currie. Frank Farrell joined
on bass to allow Hodgson's move to guitar on
second album. Band broke up after LP failed
to dent charts and Scandinavian tour met
with indifferent audiences.

Hodgson and Davies regrouped with Douglas Thompson on bass and John Anthony
Helliwell on reeds (both ex-members of Alan
Brown set). Bob Benberg (ex-Bees Make
Honey) took over drums. Using production
talents of Ken Scott, band recorded million-
selling **Crime Of The Century**.

In 1977, band moved lock stock and barrel
to US, relocation artistically reflected in mega-
selling album **Breakfast In America**, which
spawned a handful of hit singles. Low-key
persona ensured that cutback to fourpiece
(Davies, Helliwell, Thompson and Benberg) did
not lower band in public estimation. 1985 set
**Brother Where You Bound** was tenth of
career.

**Below: Supertramp model the bearded
millionaire look.**

**Current/Final line-up:** Davies; Douglas Thompson, bass; John Helliwell; Bob Benberg, drums.

**Hit Singles:**

| | US | UK |
|---|---|---|
| Dreamer, 1975 | — | 13 |
| Give A Little Bit, 1977 | 15 | 29 |
| The Logical Song, 1979 | 6 | 7 |
| Goodbye Stranger, 1979 | 15 | — |
| Take The Long Way Home, 1979 | 10 | — |
| Breakfast In America, 1979 | — | 9 |
| Dreamer, 1980 | — | 15 |
| It's Raining Again, 1983 | 11 | 26 |

**Albums:**
Supertramp (A&M), 1970
Indelibly Stamped (A&M), 1971
Crime Of The Century (A&M), 1974 **CD**
Crisis? What Crisis? (A&M), 1975
Even In The Quietest Moments (A&M), 1977
Breakfast In America (A&M), 1979 **CD**
Paris (A&M), 1980
Famous Last Words (A&M), 1982 **CD**
Brother Where You Bound (A&M), 1985
Autobiography Of Supertramp (A&M), 1986 **CD**
Free As A Bird (A&M), 1987 **CD**

# The Supremes

US vocal group formed 1959.

**Original line-up:** Diana Ross; Mary Wilson; Florence Ballard; Barbara Martin.

**Career:** Originally known as Primettes, formed by Mary Wilson, Florence Ballard, Diane (Diana) Ross(▶) and Betty Anderson in Detroit. Anderson quickly replaced by Barbara Martin. Group did local gigs with male group the Primes (later the Temptations(▶)) and recorded for Lupine without great success.

In 1960 they came to attention of emerging local entrepreneur Berry Gordy, who signed them to Tamla Motown. Over the next few years group acted as back-up singers and recorded handful of moderately successful singles. Barbara Martin dropped out in 1962 and group carried on as trio.

Turning-point came when Gordy assigned writing/production team Holland/Dozier/Holland(▶) to group in 1963; **Where Did Our Love Go** became US No. 1 and massive worldwide hit in 1964. Next three years saw trio become most successful female vocal group in pop history, with slew of international chart-toppers.

From 1966 group was billed as Diana Ross and the Supremes, Gordy already singling out Ross as potential solo superstar. Florence Ballard left to pursue unsuccessful solo career (ending in untimely death of heart attack in 1976). Replacement was Cindy Birdsong, formerly of Patti LaBelle and the Bluebelles. Hits continued, although not on such a massive scale, until Diana Ross left group in 1969 to achieve superstardom. Between 1964 and 1969 group had notched up 12 No. 1 hits.

Although Ross' departure (she was replaced by Jean Terrell) was expected to deal mortal blow to group's success, more major hits were forthcoming, starting with **Up The Ladder To The Roof** in 1970. Couplings with Temptations and Four Tops(▶) also helped keep Supremes at forefront during this period.

After 1972 group began to look slightly old-fashioned against new, more militant stance of black music; it also suffered from personnel changes. Mary Wilson continued to tour and record with various line-ups until 1977 when group broke up. Wilson pursued as yet not particularly successful career as solo artist.

Supremes' '60s output with Holland/Dozier/Holland ranks among finest pop music ever. They were also influential in making black music a major international force, combining glamour, real talent and touch of soul hitherto missing from many female vocal line-ups. In retrospect, group may appear simply as launch pad for Diana Ross, but Supremes' records still stand up as classics.

**Final line-up:** Mary Wilson; Cindy Birdsong; Jean Terrell.

**Hit Singles:**

| | US | UK |
|---|---|---|
| Where Did Our Love Go, 1964 | 1 | 3 |
| Baby Love, 1964 | ·1 | 1 |
| Come See About Me, 1964 | 1 | 27 |
| Stop! In The Name Of Love, 1965 | 1 | 7 |
| Back In My Arms Again, 1965 | 1 | 40 |
| Nothing But Heartaches, 1965 | 11 | — |
| I Hear A Symphony, 1965 | 1 | 39 |
| My World Is Empty Without You, 1966 | 5 | — |
| Love Is Like An Itching In My Heart, 1966 | 9 | — |
| You Can't Hurry Love, 1966 | 1 | 3 |
| You Keep Me Hangin' On, 1966 | 1 | 8 |
| Love Is Here And Now You're Gone, 1967 | 1 | 17 |
| The Happening, 1967 | 1 | 6 |
| Reflections, 1967 | 2 | 5 |
| In And Out Of Love, 1967 | 9 | 13 |
| Love Child, 1968 | 1 | 15 |
| I'm Livin' In Shame, 1969 | 10 | 14 |
| Some Day We'll Be Together, 1969 | 1 | 13 |
| Up The Ladder To The Roof, 1970 | 10 | 6 |
| Stoned Love, 1970 | 7 | 3 |
| Nathan Jones, 1971 | 16 | 5 |
| Floy Joy, 1972 | 16 | 9 |
| Automatically Sunshine, 1972 | 37 | 10 |
| Baby Love, 1974 | — | 12 |

*With The Four Tops:*

| | US | UK |
|---|---|---|
| River Deep Mountain High, 1971 | 14 | 4 |

*With The Temptations:*

| | US | UK |
|---|---|---|
| I'm Gonna Make You Love Me, 1969 | 11 | 3 |
| I Second That Emotion, 1969 | — | 18 |

**Albums:**
Live At The Talk Of The Town (Motown), 1968
Greatest Hits (Motown), 1968
Love Child (Motown), 1969
Greatest Hits Volume 2 (Motown), 1970
Baby Love (—/MFP), 1973

Anthology (Motown), 1974
At Their Best (Motown), 1978
Stoned Love (—/MFP), 1979
Greatest Hits (featuring Mary Wilson) (Motown), 1981
Motown Superstars Series Volume 1 (Motown/—), 1982

*With The Temptations:*
TCB (Motown), 1969

*With The Four Tops:*
The Magnificent Seven (Motown), 1971

*Mary Wilson Solo:*
Mary Wilson (Motown), 1979

# Talking Heads

US group formed 1976.

**Original/Current line-up:** David Byrne, vocals, guitar; Chris Frantz, drums; Tina Weymouth, vocals, bass, synthesiser; Jerry Harrison, vocals, guitar, keyboards.

**Career:** Byrne, Frantz and Weymouth met at Rhode Island School of Design in early '70s. Trio began working, living, and then playing music together. In 1976 they decided to expand line-up and asked ex-Modern Lovers Harrison to join. Harrison had grave doubts about any further involvement with music business and had applied for graduate school, but later agreed to join provided he could finish semester.

Band cashed in on Sire Records' search for 'new wave' groups and recorded **Talking Heads: 77**. Upon release it was clear Heads didn't fit into neat category. (Interestingly, Sire's other new wave groups, such as Dead Boys, also failed.)

Next album, **More Songs About Buildings And Food**, may have overloaded on ideas Byrne picked up while studying design (cover was modern mosaic of band made up of polaroid prints), but it also contained music which moved mind and soul. Single **Take Me To The River** earned heavy radio play and opened up audience. Band had become intellectual favourites. **Fear Of Music** LP was instant critical success and won notice in UK.

Band members became involved in variety of private projects. Byrne worked on albums with Brian Eno(▶), Harrison released solo LP. Weymouth/Frantz enjoyed considerable outside success with Tom Tom Club(▶).

This activity alone could have caused a delay before next release, but **Remain In Light** was soon out, and went beyond sparse

sound of previous LPs. **Light** explored African rhythms, added side group of musicians, and generally destroyed any possible preconceptions about band. Supporting tour included expanded line-up so that audiences could hear new efforts. Band emphasised change by including live material going back to early days as well as new material for LP, **The Name Of This Band Is Talking Heads**.

Subsequent albums, particularly 1985 release **Little Creatures**, consolidated Byrne's reputation as a writer/musician. In 1986, Byrne realised career-long ambition with release of **True Stories** movie and album an intensely personal vision which received critical acclaim and success on art-house circuit.

True Stories, Talking Heads.
Courtesy EMI Records.

**Hit Singles:**

| | US | UK |
|---|---|---|
| Once In A Lifetime, 1981 | — | 14 |
| Burning Down The House, 1983 | 9 | — |
| Road To Nowhere, 1985 | — | 6 |
| And She Was, 1986 | — | 17 |
| Wild Wild Life, 1986 | — | 43 |

**Albums:**
Talking Heads: 77 (Sire), 1977 **CD**
More Songs About Buildings And Food (Sire), 1978 **CD**
Fear Of Music (Sire), 1979 **CD**
Remain In Light (Sire), 1980 **CD**
The Name Of This Band Is Talking Heads (Sire), 1982
Speaking With Tongues (Sire), 1983 **CD**
Stop Making Sense (EMI), 1984 **CD**
Little Creatures (EMI), 1985 **CD**
True Stories (EMI), 1986 **CD**
Naked (EMI), 1988 **CD**

*David Byrne Solo:*
Music For The Knee Plays (EMI), 1985

# James Taylor

US vocalist, composer, guitarist.
Born Boston, Massachusetts, March 12, 1948.

**Career:** Taylor's mother passed her interest in music on to her children—thus Taylor's decision to try musical career following high school. In 1967 he recorded some tapes with friend Danny Kortchmar in New York as the Flying Machine. He moved to Notting Hill area of London and passed demos of his work to new Beatles company, Apple Ltd. **James Taylor** was released and ignored, though it included his excellent **Carolina In My Mind**.

With Apple falling into disarray, Taylor returned to US. After bouts of depression, and another round of mental institutions (his first had been while still in high school), with support of producer Peter Asher (Linda Ronstadt(▶)), he finally signed with Warner

**Left: Talking Heads in 1988 with David Byrne (right).**

Bros. Taylor's painful expression, deep intro spection and laid-back delivery began selling well. **You've Got A Friend** single reached No.1 in US and his popularity peaked in 1972 In 1973 he married Carly Simon(▶) (they divorced in late '70s). He branched out and encouraged siblings Livingston and Kate Taylor in their musical careers

**Mud Slide Slim, James Taylor. Courtesy Warner Bros Records.**

Surprisingly, in view of his writing credentials, Taylor chose to finish decade with re-working of Sam Cooke's **Wonderful World** and The Drifters **Up On The Roof**, which nonetheless maintained his chart status. Eighties have seen sporadic album releases, but selective high-profile concert appearances (July 4 Disarmament Festival in the USSR, Prince's Trust gala in UK, both 1987) have done more to keep Taylor in the public eye.

| Hit Singles: | US | UK |
|---|---|---|
| Fire And Rain, 1970 | 3 | 42 |
| You've Got A Friend, 1971 | 1 | 4 |
| Don't Let Me Be Lonely Tonight, 1973 | 14 | — |
| Mockingbird (with Carly Simon), 1974 | 5 | 34 |
| How Sweet It Is, 1975 | 5 | — |
| Handy Man, 1977 | 4 | — |
| Your Smiling Face, 1977 | 20 | — |
| (What A) Wonderful World, 1978 | 17 | — |

*With J.D. Souther:*

| | | |
|---|---|---|
| Her Town Too, 1981 | 11 | — |

**Albums:**
James Taylor (Apple), 1968
Sweet Baby James (Warner Bros), 1970 **CD**
James Taylor & The Original Flying Machine (Springboard/DJM), 1971
Mud Slide Slim* (Warner Bros), 1971
One Man Dog (Warner Bros), 1972
Walking Man (Warner Bros), 1974

**Below: James Taylor, a major '70s star still active in the '80s.**

Rainy Day Man (Trip/DJM), 1975
Gorilla (Warner Bros), 1975
In The Pocket (Warner Bros), 1976
The Best Of James Taylor (Warner Bros), 1976
JT (Columbia/CBS), 1977 **CD**

Greatest Hits (Warner Bros), 1977 **CD**
Flag (Columbia/CBS), 1979
Dad Loves His Work (Columbia/CBS), 1981 **CD**
That's Why I'm Here (Columbia/CBS), 1986 **CD**
Classic Songs (WEA), 1987 **CD**
*Released as double album, UK only, 1975

# Tears For Fears

UK group formed 1980.

**Original/Current line-up:** Roland Orzabel, guitar, vocals; Curt Smith, bass, vocals.

**Career:** Pretentious pop duo who, on reflection, may be no more than the Peter and Gordon of the '80s.

Orzabel and Smith first met in early '70s, and played in variety of nondescript bands before signing with Phonogram as Tears For Fears (name comes from Arthur Yanoff's book 'Prisoners Of Pain'). First single **Suffer The Children** recorded in home town of Bath with David Lord on synthesisers.

Temporary alliance with producer Mike Howlett (A Flock Of Seagulls, China Crisis, Thompson Twins, etc), before Chris Hughes (Adam And The Ants, Wang Chung, etc) took charge. Debut LP **The Hurting** was released in 1983.

However, it was **Songs From The Big Chair** set, which propelled them to international superstardom. Album spawned three major hits, including worldwide number one **Everybody Wants To Rule The World** (later theme as **Run The World**, for hunger relief in Africa). Duo subsequently decided to take indefinite sabbatical, which was broken by re-working of old hits at the beginning of 1988.

| Hit Singles: | US | UK |
|---|---|---|
| Mad World, 1982 | — | 3 |
| Change, 1983 | — | 4 |
| Pale Shelter, 1983 | — | 5 |
| Mother's Talk, 1984 | — | 14 |
| Shout, 1985 | 1 | 4 |
| Everybody Wants To Rule The World, 1985 | 1 | 2 |
| Head Over Heels, 1985 | 3 | 12 |

**Albums:**
The Hurting (Mercury), 1983 **CD**
Songs From The Big Chair (Mercury), 1985 **CD**

# The Temptations

US vocal group formed 1961.

**Original line-up:** Otis Williams; Melvin Franklin; Eldridge Bryant; Eddie Kendricks; Paul Williams.

**Career:** Formed in Detroit in 1961 from amalgam of elements from Otis Williams and the Distants (Otis Williams, Franklin, Bryant) and the Primes (Kendricks, Paul Williams). Temptations were recording for Tamla Motown a year later but it was not until David Ruffin replaced Bryant in 1963 (his brother Jimmy Ruffin had been offered job but declined) that breakthrough came. The contrast between lead vocals of Kendricks — high, sweet and soft — and Ruffin — gritty and emotion-laden — provided formula for success: thanks were also due to promising young songwriter and producer Smokey Robinson(▶).

The Robinson-penned, Kendricks-led **The Way You Do The Things You Do** gave them 1963 hit. Two years later, with Ruffin singing lead, **My Girl** brought them to forefront among black vocal groups, overtaking Curtis

Mayfield's Impressions(▶) in mass popularity.

In 1966 group started working with writer/producer Norman Whitfield who exploited more biting version of Motown sound with ballsy **Ain't Too Proud To Beg, I Know (I'm Losing You)** and others, counter-balanced by some smooth ballad efforts.

After Ruffin split for solo career, Dennis Edwards was brought in from the Contours and Whitfield took opportunity to push Temptations in new musical direction. So-called 'psychedelic soul' style evolved, with dramatic use of recording effects and rock-influenced arrangements which made **Cloud Nine, Runaway Child, Running Wild, Can't Get Next To You, Psychedelic Shack** and **Ball Of Confusion** such totally distinctive hits.

A return to soft balladry saw **Just My Imagination** earn Temptations first platinum single award, and marked last appearance of solo-bound Kendricks; now seriously ill, Paul Williams also left (he died soon after). Their replacements were Damon Harris (the Vandals) and Richard Street (the Monitors).

Further Whitfield-produced progressive soul hits came with **Superstar, Take A Look Around, Papa Was A Rolling Stone** and the monumental **Masterpiece** album.

Following departure of Harris (replaced by Glenn Leonard in 1975) and Edwards (in 1979), group seemed to lose much of its fire. Whitfield having moved on to mastermind Undisputed Truth, then Rose Royce, plus his own label, Temptations' subsequent work lacked sense of direction.

After unsuccessful stint with Atlantic, group returned to home base at Motown with Edwards back in line-up for 1980 **Power** album though he soon left again. A 'Temptations Reunion' brought most of original line-up back together but only on temporary basis and as group started new run of hits (**Treat Her Like A Lady, Up On The Roof** with unlikely lead vocalist Bruce Willis).

Kendrick and Ruffin, who featured on 1982 **Reunion** set, are now working as duo following 1985 success with Hall & Oates.

**Current line-up:** Franklin; Ron Tyson; Otis Williams; Richard Street; Ali-Ollie Woodson.

| Hit Singles: | US | UK |
|---|---|---|
| The Way You Do The Things You Do, 1964 | 11 | — |
| My Girl, 1965 | 1 | 43 |
| It's Growing, 1965 | 18 | 45 |
| Since I Lost My Baby, 1965 | 17 | — |
| My Baby, 1965 | 13 | — |
| Ain't Too Proud To Beg, 1966 | 13 | 21 |
| Beauty Is Only Skin Deep, 1966 | 3 | 18 |
| (I Know) I'm Losing You, 1966 | 8 | 19 |
| All I Need, 1967 | 8 | — |
| You're My Everything, 1967 | 6 | 26 |
| (Loneliness Made Me Realise) It's You That I Need, 1967 | 14 | — |
| I Wish It Would Rain, 1968 | 4 | 45 |
| I Could Never Love Another (After Loving You), 1968 | 13 | 47 |
| Cloud Nine, 1968 | 6 | 15 |
| Run Away Child, Running Wild, 1969 | 6 | — |
| Get Ready, 1969* | 29 | 10 |
| Don't Let The Joneses Get You Down, 1969 | 20 | — |
| I Can't Get Next To You, 1969 | 1 | 13 |
| Psychedelic Shack, 1970 | 7 | 33 |
| Ball Of Confusion (That's The World Is Today), 1970 | 3 | 7 |
| Just My Imagination (Running Away With Me), 1971 | 1 | 8 |
| Superstar (Remember How You Got Where You Are), 1971 | 18 | 32 |
| Take A Look Around, 1972 | 30 | 13 |
| Papa Was A Rollin' Stone, 1972 | 1 | 14 |
| Masterpiece, 1973 | 7 | — |
| *In 1966, US | | |

*With Diana Ross and Supremes:*

| | | |
|---|---|---|
| I'm Gonna Make You Love Me, 1969 | 2 | 3 |
| I Second That Emotion, 1969 | — | 18 |

**Albums:**
Greatest Hits (Gordy/Motown), 1967
Cloud Nine/Puzzle People (Motown), 1969/1970 **CD**
Psychedelic Shack (Gordy/Motown), 1970
Psychedelic Shack/All Directions (Motown), 1970/1972 **CD**
Puzzle People (Gordy/Motown), 1970
Greatest Hits Volume II (Gordy/Motown), 1972
All Directions (Gordy/Motown), 1972
Masterpiece (Gordy/Motown), 1973 **CD**
Anthology Vols 1 & 2 (Motown), 1977 **CD**
Temptations (—/Motown), 1977
Sing Smokey (—/Motown), 1979
Power (Gordy/Motown), 1980
20 Golden Greats (—/Motown), 1980
Reunion (Gordy/—), 1981
All The Million Sellers (Gordy/Motown), 1982
Get Ready (—/Pickwick), 1982
Give Love At Christmas (—/Motown), 1982
Surface Thrills (Motown), 1983
Back To Basics (Motown), 1983
Truly For You (Motown), 1984
Touch Me (Motown), 1985
17 Greatest Hits (Motown), 1985 **CD**
Song For You (Motown), 1986 **CD**
25the Anniversary (Motown), 1986
To Be Continued (Motown), 1986
Live At The Copa/With A Lot O Soul (Motown), 1987 **CD**

*With The Supremes:*
TCB (Tamla Motown), 1969

*David Ruffin & Eddie Kendricks:*
(with Hall & Oates): Live At The Apollo (RCA), 1985

**Sheet Music, 10cc. Courtesy Mercury Records.**

# 10 cc

UK group formed 1972.

**Original line-up:** Eric Stewart, guitar, vocals; Graham Gouldman, bass, vocals; Lol Creme, guitar, vocals; Kevin Godley, drums, vocals.

**Career:** In June 1970, Stewart, Creme and Godley had worldwide hit as Hotlegs with **Neanderthal Man**. Godley and Creme had first met at art school; Stewart had been in the Mindbender (who had 1966 UK Top 5 Hit with **Groovy Kind Of Love**). Graham Gouldman, another Mindbenders, joined Hotlegs for 1970 UK tour supporting Moody Blues(▶); wrote Yardbirds(▶) hit **For Your Love**. Stewart had set up Strawberry Studios in Stockport, Cheshire, and in 1971 Neil Sedaka(▶) recorded his comeback album **Solitaire** there with Stewart, Gouldman, Godley and Creme. Returned following year to cut **The Tra La Days Are Over** (Gouldman had met Sedaka while he was working as a songwriter for the Kasenatz-Katz organisation in New York's

**10cc (debut LP with Rubber Bullets). Courtesy UK Records.**

Brill Building).

Godley and Creme came up with **Donna**, a clever parody (as much of their work is) of US '50s hits, and took song to Jonathan King who released it on his new UK label, King, changing band's name to 10 cc. Record made No. 2. First chart-topper **Rubber Bullets** scored in 1973.

Following debut album **10 cc**, band played first live gigs at Douglas, Isle Of Man, in August 1973, adding Paul Burgess on drums; toured US twice in 1974.

Switching to Phonogram early in 1975 for third album, **The Original Soundtrack,** group continued run of hits; peaked creatively with classic single **I'm Not In Love**.

After guesting with Rolling Stones(▶) at Knebworth in August 1976, band was depleted in October when Godley and Creme decided to leave for subsequently successful career as duo.

With Stewart and Gouldman now firmly in control of creative aspect, Stuart Tosh, Rick Fenn and Tony O'Malley joined 10 cc in April 1977, debuting on May UK tour. Duncan Mackay was added on keyboards 10 months later.

Group's planned Japan/Australia tour was cancelled after motorcycle accident to Gouldman in Japan. He was soon back in action writing and recording score for that year's 'Animalympics' movie and title song for movie 'Sunburn'. Stewart produced Sad Cafe's(▶) second album as well as songs for French movie 'Girls'; recorded own solo album in 1981. Further outside production work came for Gouldman with the Ramones and Gilbert O'Sullivan in 1981.

Godley and Creme went on to become successful artists in own right. Pair also developed parallel career as video makers, becoming much in demand as video became essential part of pop promotion process. Gouldman eventually formed Wax duo with US AOR artist Andrew Gold.

**Current line-up:** Stewart; Gouldman; Stuart Tosh, drums; Rick Fenn, guitar; Tony O'Malley, keyboards; Duncan Mackay, keyboards.

| Hit Singles: | US | UK |
|---|---|---|
| Donna, 1972 | — | 2 |
| Rubber Bullets, 1973 | — | 1 |
| The Dean And I, 1973 | — | 10 |
| Wall Street Shuffle, 1974 | — | 10 |
| Life Is A Minestrone, 1975 | — | 7 |
| I'm Not In Love, 1975 | 1 | 1 |
| Art For Art's Sake, 1975 | — | 5 |
| I'm Mandy Fly Me, 1976 | 60 | 6 |
| Things We Do For Love, 1976 | 5 | 6 |
| Good Morning Judge, 1977 | — | 5 |
| Dreadlock Holiday, 1978 | 44 | 1 |
| Under Your Thumb, 1981 | — | 3 |
| Wedding Bells, 1981 | — | 7 |

*Godley & Creme:*
| | | |
|---|---|---|
| Cry, 1985 | 17 | 19 |

**Albums:**
10 cc (UK), 1973
Sheet Music (UK), 1974
Original Soundtrack (Mercury), 1975
How Dare You (Mercury), 1976
Deceptive Bends (Mercury), 1977
Live And Let Live (Mercury), 1977
Bloody Tourists (Mercury), 1978 **CD**
Greatest Hits (Mercury), 1979 **CD**
Things We Do For Love (Mercury), 1979
Look Hear (Warner Bros/Mercury), 1980
Greatest Hits, 71-78 (Polydor/—), 1981
Ten Out Of Ten (Warner Bros/Mercury), 1981 **CD**
In Concert (—/Contour), 1982
Windows In The Jungle (Mercury), 1983

*Godley & Creme:*
Consequences (Mercury), 1977
'L' (Mercury), 1978
Freeze Frame (Polydor), 1979
Ismism (Polydor), 1981
Birds Of Prey (Polydor), 1983
The History Mix (Polydor), 1986 **CD**

# Ten Years After
UK group formed 1967.

**Original/Final line-up:** Alvin Lee, Gibson ES 335 guitar, vocals; Chick Churchill, keyboards; Leo Lyons, bass; Rick Lee, drums.

**Above: Alvin Lee, leader of Ten Years After in 1967, and of Ten Years Later in 1977, although the latter band did not equal the former's fame.**

**Career:** One of major bands to emerge from mid-'60s blues revival movement in UK. Formed by Lee and Lyons who met in Nottingham and worked together in Hamburg for a time. On returning to Britain; met music scholar Ric Lee while working in West End production and formed the Jaybirds. Adding Chick Churchill, changed name and came to critics' attention via appearances at London's Marquee Club. Group signed to Decca's Deram subsidiary who put out first album without waiting to score any hit singles (an unusual move in those days).

Famed American promoter Bill Graham heard album and booked group for his Fillmore Auditorium venues in US. Subsequent albums and appearance at massive Woodstock rock festival (and in the 'Woodstock' movie in which their 11-minute opus **Goin' Home** scored heavily) established world reputation for fast and furious blend of blues and heavy rock.

Introduced electronic effects for **A Space In Time** and moved into more pensive

**Right: Phil Lynott (left) and Scott Gorham of Thin Lizzy.**

direction; album was US smash. But, by 1973, Lee was disillusioned with group's direction and exhaustive tour schedules (a record 28 US tours before they broke up), describing band as 'a travelling jukebox'.

Members took time off for solo projects and Lee retired to 15th-century country home to build studio and record gospel singer Mylon Lefevre. Churchill's solo album **You And Me** appeared in 1973. **Ten Years After** set that year was live album compiled from concerts in Amsterdam, Rotterdam, Frankfurt and Paris.

A month before band's scheduled spring 1974 UK tour, Lee appeared at London's Rainbow with own hastily assembled nine-piece band. Show was released on disc as **Alvin Lee And Co In Flight**.

Ten Years After's own Rainbow appearance a month later was sell-out. It proved to be their last British stage appearance as Lee set off to tour world as Alvin Lee And Co.

In May 1975, Alvin Lee declared Ten Years After defunct and Ric Lee formed own band. However, just one month later Ten Years After were back on road for US tour to fulfill contractual obligations before final split. Lee formed Ten Years Later in 1977 with Tom Compton drums, and Mick Hawksworth, bass; released two LPs, **Rocket Fuel** 1978) and **Ride On** (1979). Since then, Alvin Lee has recorded further solo efforts; Chick Churchill has become professional manager at Chrysalis Music, and Leo Lyons has worked as producer, notably with UFO.

| Hit Singles: | US | UK |
|---|---|---|
| Love Like A Man, 1970 | — | 10 |

**Albums:**
*Ten Years After:*
Ten Years After (Deram), 1967
Undead (Deram), 1968
Stonehenge (Deram), 1969
Ssssssh (Chrysalis), 1969
Cricklewood Green (Chrysalis), 1970
Watt (Chrysalis), 1970
Alvin Lee & Co (Deram), 1972
A Space In Time (Columbia/Crysalis), 1972
Rock 'n' Roll To The World (Columbia/Chrysalis), 1972
Recorded Live (Columbia/Chrysalis), 1973
Positive Vibrations (Columbia/Chrysalis), 1974
Goin' Home (Deram/Chrysalis), 1975
Classic Performances (Columbia/Chrysalis), 1977
Hear Me Calling (—/Decca), 1981
Goin' Home, Their Greatest Hits (London/—), 1975
Original Recordings Vol. 1 (See For Miles), 1987
Original Recordings Vol. 2 (See For Miles), 1987

*Ten Years Later:*
Rocket Fuel (Polydor), 1978
Ride On (Polydor), 1979

*Alvin Lee Solo:*
Free Fall (—/Avatar), 1980

RX5 (Atlantic/—), 1981

*With Mylon Lefevre:*
Road To Freedom (Columbia/CBS), 1973

# Thin Lizzy
UK group formed 1970

**Original line-up:** Phil Lynott, Fender Precision, Ibanez basses, lead vocals; Eric Bell, lead guitar; Brian Downey, drums.

**Vagabonds Of The Western World, Thin Lizzy. Courtesy London Records.**

**Career:** Hard-rocking group equally at home with blues ballads, Thin Lizzy was accessible and electric on record, skillfully showmanlike in concert.

First hit was **Whiskey In The Jar.** Hard-driving 1972 version of traditional folk song reached No. 6, staying in charts for eight weeks, but next three singles flopped. By then Eric Bell, disturbed by Irish troubles, left group after Belfast concert, to be briefly replaced by Gary Moore, until Scott Gorham and Brian Robertson were added as guitarists.

In summer 1974 band signed with Vertigo label and made Reading Festival debut. More albums followed and UK, European and US tours, but three more singles failed to make charts. Then, five years and five LPs after first release, **Jailbreak** album provided **The Boys Are Back In Town** single, which entered Top 10 in UK and US charts. Title single also made charts and album reached Top 10 on both sides of Atlantic. Melody Maker's readers' poll voted band 'brightest hope'. However, summer 1976 US tour was cancelled when Lynott contracted hepatitis and winter US tour was postponed when Robertson injured hand in brawl.

Next two singles made 1977 charts. Band headlined Reading Festival, topped bill on US tour, and **Bad Reputation,** their eighth album, reached No. 4. Video of Rainbow Theatre concert in March 1978 was shown on television in many countries but not in Britain. Albums and singles continued to reach charts; pick-up band called the Greedy Bastards formed and Robertson left the group going on to Motorhead(▶), to be replaced by

Gary Moore. Moore's single, **Parisienne Walkways** co-written by Lynott, reached No. 8 in 1979. Thin Lizzy's **Black Rose**, released same month, topped album charts.

Tours still beset by troubles; three European dates were cancelled when Lynott got food poisoning and Moore was sacked for missing two US dates. Ex-Pink Floyd(▶) guitarist Snowy White joined group in 1980. The same year Lynott's solo album **Solo In Soho** reached No. 28. Band toured Japan and Australia, and further albums and singles made UK Top 30. In 1981 **The Adventures Of Thin Lizzy,** compilation of 10 years of hits, was successful (helped by £250,000 television advertising campaign). With Darren Warton, keyboards, and John Sykes, guitar, band played farewell gig at Reading Festival, August '83. Lynott and Downey then formed five-piece Grand Slam, which attracted less attention than Lynott's well documented personal problems (marriage, drinks, drugs). Phil Lynott eventually succumbed to indulgent lifestyle, dying in January 1986.

**Final line-up:** Lynott; Downey; Darren Wharton, keyboards; John Sykes, guitar.

| Hit Singles: | US | UK |
|---|---|---|
| Whiskey In The Jar, 1973 | — | 6 |
| The Boys Are Back In Town, 1976 | 12 | 8 |
| Don't Believe A Word, 1977 | — | 12 |
| Dancin' In The Moonlight (It's Caught Me In The Spotlight), 1977 | — | 14 |
| Rosalie—Cowgirl's Song, 1978 | — | 20 |
| Waiting For An Alibi, 1979 | — | 9 |
| Do Anything You Want To, 1979 | — | 14 |
| Killer On The Loose, 1980 | — | 10 |
| Killers Live (EP), 1981 | — | 19 |

*Phil Lynott & Gary Moore:*
| | | |
|---|---|---|
| Out In The Fields, 1985 | — | 5 |

*Gary Moore Solo:*
| | | |
|---|---|---|
| Parisienne Walkways, 1979 | — | 8 |
| Run For Cover (10). 1985 | | |

*Phil Lynott Solo:*
| | | |
|---|---|---|
| Yellow Pearl, 1981 | — | 14 |

**Thin Lizzy (debut album). Courtesy London Records.**

**Albums:**
Thin Lizzy (London/Decca), 1971
Shades Of A Blue Orphanage (—/Decca), 1972
Vagabonds Of The Western World (London/Decca), 1973
Night Life (Mercury/Vertigo), 1974
Fighting (Mercury/Vertigo), 1975
Jailbreak (Mercury/Vertigo), 1976
Johnny The Fox (Mercury/Vertigo), 1976
Remembering (—/Decca), 1976
Bad Reputation (Mercury/Vertigo), 1977
Live And Dangerous (Warner Bros/Vertigo), 1978
Rocker (1971-1974) (London/—), 1978
Black Rose (Warner Bros/Vertigo), 1979
Chinatown (Warner Bros/Vertigo), 1980

Renegade (Warner Bros/Vertigo), 1981
Adventures Of (—/Vertigo), 1981
Thunder And Lightning (Warner Bros/Vertigo), 1983
Collection (Castle Collectors) **CD**
Lizzy Killers (Vertigo) **CD**

*Phil Lynott Solo:*
Solo In Soho (Warner Bros/Vertigo), 1980
The Philip Lynott Album (Warner Bros/Vertigo), 1982
Making Love From Memory (MCA/—), 1982

# .38 Special
US group formed 1979.
**Original line-up:** Donnie van Zant, guitar, vocals; Don Barnes, guitar, vocals; Jeff Carlisi, guitar; Steve Brookins, drums; Ken Lyon, bass.

**Career:** Founded by van Zant, younger brother of late Ronnie, vocalist with Lynyrd Skynyrd(▶). Band follows same route as illustrious predecessors — triple lead guitar breaks, macho bar-room 'proud to be Southern' lyrics — albeit somewhat mellower.

First self-titled album was released in 1977; featured guest spot from Dan Hartman on vocals. For third album **Rockin' Into The Night,** Lyon was replaced by Larry Lundstrom. Titletrack made 43 in US singles chart. Band consolidated position in US pop lists with two further entries in 1981. **Hold On Loosely** made No. 27, **Fantasy Girl**, 52.

.38 Special broke through to first division in '82 when album **Special Forces** made US Top 10. LP cuts **Caught Up In You** and **You Keep Runnin' Away** earned singles placings. Ironically more successful than their splinter, the Rossington-Collins Band, .38 Special are filling void left by Skynyrd.

**Current line-up:** van Zant; Barnes; Carlisi; Brookins; Larry Lundstrom, bass, vocals; Jack Grondin, drums.

| Hit Singles: | US | UK |
|---|---|---|
| Caught Up In You, 1982 | 10 | — |
| If I'd Been The One, 1983 | 19 | — |
| Back Where You Belong, 1984 | 20 | — |

**Albums:**
.38 Special (A&M), 1977
Special Delivery (A&M), 1978
Rockin' Into The Night (A&M), 1979
Wild Eyed Southern Boys (A&M), 1981
Special Forces (A&M), 1982
Tour De Force (A&M), 1984

# Thompson Twins
UK group formed 1977.
**Original line-up:** Tom Bailey, vocals, keyboards; John Roog, guitar; Pete Dodd, guitar; Chris Bell, drums.

**Career:** Named after detective characters from 'Tin Tin' cartoons, The Thompson Twins were conventional four-piece before becoming an unweildy septet; recorded two albums with this format, **A Product Of . . .** and **Set**.

First gained attention with dancer **In The Name Of Love**, before pruning line-up. Remaining trio (Currie, Bailey and Leeway) hired producer Alex Sadkin to record **Quick Step And Sidekick** in idyllic Bahamas. Album reached number two in UK charts, and spawned series of hit singles, including inventive **Love On Your Side**.

Band broke worldwide in 1984 with release

of **Hold Me Now** single, which made both UK/US top tens, and sold over five million copies.

A return to Compass Point studios in the West Indies resulted in **Into The Gap**, with Sadkin this time joined by Tom Bailey in production chair. Album reached triple platinum status in Britain.

With Bailey now in control of production, Twins began new LP. Work halted, however, when Bailey succumbed to exhaustion.

Group re-assembled in June '85 in New York, and finished album with Nile Rodgers co-producing with fully fit Bailey. Titled **Here's To Future Days**, set contained strong anti-heroin song **Don't Mess With Dr. Dream**. Commitment to social issues resulted in strong CND involvement, as well as appearance on 'Live Aid'(▶).

Only cloud on Thompson Twin's bright horizon was cancellation of October '85 UK tour due to liquidation of promoter Paul Loasby's company. Group resumed live work with US marathon in November 1985, but in April 1986 Leeway left, leaving others to continue as duo.

**Current line-up:** Bailey; Alannah Currie, keyboards, saxophone, vocals.

| Hit Singles: | US | UK |
|---|---|---|
| Love On Your Side, 1983 | — | 9 |
| We Are Detective, 1983 | — | 7 |
| Hold Me Now, 1983 | 3 | 4 |
| Doctor Doctor, 1984 | 11 | 3 |
| You Take Me Up, 1984 | — | 2 |
| Sisters Of Mercy, 1984 | — | 13 |
| Don't Mess With Dr. Dream, 1985 | — | 15 |
| Lay Your Hands On Me, 1985 | 6 | — |

**Albums:**
A Product Of (Arista), 1981
Set (Arista), 1982
Quickstep And Sidekick (Arista), 1983 **CD**
Into The Gap (T-Label), 1984 **CD**
Here's To The Future Days (Arista), 1985 **CD**
Close To The Bone (Arista), 1987 **CD**

# George Thorogood And The Destroyers
US group formed 1974.
**Original line-up:** George Thorogood, guitar, harmonica; Jeff Simon, drums; Bill Blough, bass.

**Career:** Thorogood began by playing bars and small clubs in Wilmington, Delaware, then up and down East Coast. Music was rockin' R&B with early Stones(▶) influence. John Forward saw band at Joe's Place (Cambridge, Mass.) in summer 1975 and was

**Above: Delaware slide boy—blues influence reflected in the playing style of George Thorogood.**

struck by 'feel' they had for old standards, achieved by deliberate choice of small amps and by avoiding state of art electronics.

Two years of deals and negotiations by Forward led to contract with small ethnic blue grass label, Rounder Records. Self-titled album startled Rounder by selling strongly in every city where band had recently played. Second album also overloaded Rounder's independent distribution system as sales picked up nationally by word of mouth. Recognising his limits, Thorogood refused to take his 'traditional rock'n'roll' to larger venues; band had to use phoney names so crowds could get into their usual gigs. (MCA released set of early demo tapes made in 1974 (with bassist Michael Lenn) when considering whether to sign band; group has subsequently rejected any connection with effort.)

Third Rounder LP sold well enough for label to turn band over to Capitol Records and go back to folk/bluegrass artists. With **Bad To The Bone**, band had an album likely to be found in most US record shops. Real forte has always been live performances. Nothing on record can capture fire of Thorogood playing slide guitar in small crowded atmosphere. As opening act for Rolling Stones' 1981 US tour, George Thorogood may have won wider exposure, but with same sense of compromise the Glimmer Twins may have felt when leaving behind Crawdaddy Club.

**Current line-up:** Thorogood; Blough; Simon; Hank Carter, saxophone.

**Albums:**
George Thorogood And The Destroyers (Rounder/—), 1978 **CD**
Move It On Over (Rounder/Sonet), 1978
Better Than The Rest (MCA), 1979
More George Thorogood And The Destroyers (Rounder/Sonet), 1980
Bad To The Bone (EMI America/—), 1982

**Move It On Over, George Thorogood & The Destroyers. Courtesy Sonet Records.**

Maverick (EMI), 1985
Live (EMI), 1986
Born To Be Bad (Manhattan), 1988

# Three Dog Night
US group formed 1968.

**Original line-up:** Danny Hutton, vocals; Cory Wells, vocals; Chuck Negron, vocals; Joe Schermie, bass; Floyd Sneed, drums; Jim Greenspoon, keyboards; Mike Allsop, guitar.

**Career:** Original members were all LA-based musicians passing through small local groups and doing session work. Hutton instigated idea of group based on three lead vocalists and recruited Wells and Negron. According to Eskimo lore, the colder the night, the more dogs are brought in to sleep with, coldest being 'three dog night'. Despite name, however, band was far from cold and almost immediately began picking up US gold records.

Although albums sold extremely well, group remained primarily a singles factory. **Joy To The World** was *the* No. 1 US single of 1971. By 1972 when hits stopped, band became disjointed. Jack Ryland replaced Schermie, and second keyboards player, Skip Konte, joined. Then band disappeared.

Nova-like career came at time when singles were disdained by 'serious' rock crowd, so it was easy to dismiss band as having little or no impact. Yet Three Dog Night must be fondly remembered for turning non-original material into joyful celebration all their own. Possibility of re-formation was being discussed when this volume went to press.

**Final line-up:** Hutton; Wells; Negron; Sneed; Greenspoon; Jack Ryland, guitar; Kip Konte, keyboards.

**Hit Singles:**

|  | US | UK |
|---|---|---|
| One, 1969 | 5 | — |
| Easy To Be Hard, 1969 | 4 | — |
| Eli's Coming, 1969 | 10 | — |
| Celebrate, 1970 | 15 | — |
| Mama Told Me (Not To Come), 1970 | 1 | 3 |
| Out In The Country, 1970 | 15 | — |
| One Man Band, 1970 | 19 | — |
| Joy To The World, 1971 | 1 | 24 |
| Liar, 1971 | 7 | — |
| An Old Fashioned Love Song, 1971 | 4 | — |
| Never Been To Spain, 1971 | 5 | — |
| The Family Of Man, 1972 | 12 | — |
| Black And White, 1972 | 1 | — |
| Pieces Of April, 1972 | 19 | — |
| Shambala, 1973 | 3 | — |
| Let Me Serenade, 1973 | 17 | — |

**Albums:**
Joy To The World—Greatest Hits (MCA/Anchor), 1974
Best Of (MCA/—), 1975 **CD**

*Worth Searching Out:*
It Ain't Easy (Dunhill/Stateside), 1970
Harmony (Dunhill/Probe), 1971

# Peter Tosh
Jamaican vocalist, composer, guitarist.
Born Peter McIntosh, Kingston, Jamaica, October 19, 1944; died September 11, 1987.

**Career:** A fervent preacher of Rastafarian ethic, Peter Tosh has established himself as leading figure of Jamaica's alternative culture, first as member of influential Wailers, alongside late Bob Marley(▶) and Bunny (Wailer) Livingstone, then as solo artist allied—in

**Above: "Legalise it and I will advertise it" said Peter Tosh, but they didn't ...unfortunately.**

somewhat unlikely fashion—to Mick Jagger and Keith Richard via Rolling Stones(▶) Records.

An adept musician by early teens, playing steel guitar, acoustic guitar and keyboards, Tosh met fellow Wailers in Kingston ghetto suburb Trenchtown, sharing socially aware songwriting, taking themes from politics, religion, poverty and social repression. Among his songs for Wailers were **Get Up, Stand Up, One Foundation** and **400 Years**.

When trio split up (1974) Tosh's work took on increasingly revolutionary nature which led to beating by Jamaican police in 1975. From this experience came his banned **Mark Of The Beast** and an ever more radical stance as in **Legalise It** (also banned, but big JA hit nonetheless) which called for legalisation of marijuana. 1977 album **Equal Rights** summed up Tosh's crusade against racism and oppression with outspoken demand for recognition by blacks of Africa as the true homeland.

Switching from Virgin to Rolling Stones Records in 1978 brought Tosh support of Jagger and Richard. He teamed with revered reggae sidemen Sly Dunbar(▶) (bass) and Robbie Shakespeare(▶) (drums) to guest on Stones' American tour. His classic **Bush Doctor** album of 1978 included the superb **(You Gotta Walk) Don't Look Back** single which, in limited-release dub version, featured Jagger and Richard on back-up vocals to Smokey Robinson(▶) composition.

Two more Rolling Stones Records, LPs and 1981 appearance at London's Rainbow theatre furthered Tosh's international appeal, while love-song duet with Gwen Guthrie on **Nothing**

**But Love** showed a softening lyrical approach.

More recently, looked to re-form the Wailers with Bunny Livingstone, and the pair had re-recorded classic cuts before Tosh was brutally murdered in an attempted burglary at his home in September, 1987.

**Albums:**
Legalise It (Columbia/Virgin), 1976
Equal Rights (Columbia/Virgin), 1978
Bush Doctor (Rolling Stones), 1978
Mystic Man (Rolling Stones), 1979
Wanted Dread And Alive (EMI/Rolling Stones), 1981
Captured Live (EMI), 1984
No Nuclear War (Parlophone), 1987 **CD**

# Toto
US group formed 1978.

**Original line-up:** Bobby Kimball, vocals; Steve Lukather, guitar; David Paich, keyboards; Steve Porcaro, keyboards; David Hungate, bass; Jeff Porcaro, drums.

**Career:** All original line-up bar Kimball were notable Los Angeles session musicians — credits for various members include Steely Dan, Boz Scaggs, Aretha Franklin, Leo Sayer, Earth, Wind & Fire, Jackson Browne, Barbra Streisand and many more. Group named either after Dorothy's dog in 'Wizard Of Oz' film, or Kimball's real surname (supposedly 'Toteaux'). Successful first LP featured in US LP chart for most of 1979 and spawned three US hit singles, but second and third LPs were rather less notable; due, according to Lukather, to fame arriving too quickly for group to adapt to it.

However, 1982 LP gave group highest placing in album chart in US, plus three US and two UK hit singles. Resulted in domination of 1983 Grammy Award Ceremony, winning seven categories; group also returned to UK charts. This coincided with another Porcaro brother, Mike, replacing David Hungate as bass player.

Toto's involvement with 'Dune' soundtrack album in 1984 saw band as instrumental outfit, Kimball having left for solo career. Replacement was Fergie Frederiksen (ex-Trillion). Regarded as epitome of AOR, Toto have nonetheless had inspired moments.

**Below: A young Pete Townshend (circa 1964) and a Rickenbacker he no doubt smashed to pieces later.**

**Current line-up:** Lukather; Paich; Steve Porcaro; Jeff Porcaro; Mike Porcaro, bass; Fergie Frederiksen, vocals.

**Hit Singles:**

|  | US | UK |
|---|---|---|
| Hold The Line, 1978 | 5 | 14 |
| Rosanna, 1982 | 2 | 12 |
| Africa, 1982 | 1 | 3 |
| I Won't Hold You Back, 1983 | — | ? |
| I'll Be Over You, 1986 | 8 | — |

**Albums:**
Toto (Columbia/CBS), 1978 **CD**
Hydra (Columbia/CBS), 1979
Turn Back (Columbia/CBS), 1981 **CD**
Toto IV (Columbia/CBS), 1982 **CD**
Isolation (Columbia/CBS), 1984
Fahrenheit (CBS), 1986 **CD**

**Toto (debut album). Courtesy CBS Records.**

# Pete Townshend
UK guitarist, composer, vocalist, multi-instrumentalist.
Born London, May 19, 1945.

**Career:** Townshend grew up in Ealing, West London, son of singer Betty Dennis and sax player Cliff Townshend, who played in the Squadronaires. Spent summers at holiday camps where father played in bands. His grandmother bought him his first guitar when he was 12.

Townshend wrote his first song, **It Was You**, at 16 (actually recorded by the very early Who, in 1963, before Keith Moon joined, but never released). In 1965 he began 20-year career writing for the Who(▶).

Townshend's first departure from the band came in 1972 when he released **Who Came First,** an album of songs either about his Indian master Meher Baba, or included because Baba liked them. (Various Baba-orientated LPs done with other Baba-lovers were previously recorded, but these were never intended as official Townshend releases.) **Who Came First** gave the public a very different taste of Townshend. Playing guitar without vengeance known as trademark in Who, Townshend created an atmosphere of relaxation with excellent acoustic sound accompanied by a clear and sincere, if not technically magnificent, voice. Up until this point, Townshend's voice was not often heard at length, as Roger Daltrey(▶) handled Who vocals.

Next official solo release, **Rough Mix**, didn't come until 1977, when Townshend teamed up with ex-Small Faces(▶), Faces(▶) singer/composer/bass player Ronnie Lane. Though LP had a 'Baba flavour', the references were quite subtle, and the sound was more upbeat. Only mildly successful initially, it has remained a steady seller, and has been re-released several times.

In 1980 Townshend truly made his mark as solo artist with **Empty Glass**. The single **Let**

173

**My Love Open The Door,** made it into the US Top 10, (matching most successful Who single in US, **I Can See For Miles**) and several other tracks received massive US airplay. Townshend's voice, under producer Chris Thomas, had improved dramatically. Lyrical content was more intellectual and more personally revealing than Daltrey would have agreed to had the material been offered the Who. Many expected great things from Townshend's future solo work; there was no

**Scoop, Pete Townshend's demos. Courtesy Atco Records.**

doubt about who was the main creative force behind the Who.

Unfortunately, the much-anticipated **All The Best Cowboys Have Chinese Eyes** LP in 1982 didn't quite measure up to **Empty Glass.** A bit too heady and abstract for some, it confused the general public with its experimental song structure, and sometimes bizarre lyrics. The stream-of-consciousness effect was balanced by a couple of energetic, almost Who-style tracks, but overall the LP lacked cohesiveness. When around the time of its release, Townshend gave several confessional interviews attesting to personal confusion and unhappiness, and even alcohol and drug addiction during much of its recording, this was understandable.

Early 1983 brought new LP of old material, a double LP collection of Townshend's personal demos, some done for the Who, some just for himself, entitled **Scoop.** In February '83, Townshend received the Lifetime Achievement Award from the British Record Industry.

Townshend has done some solo live shows, usually for charity (Rock Against Racism and Amnesty International gigs in '79), and performs and records with a wide variety of artists. Anti-drug crusade in 1985 attracted national attention, and he is still busy at his own recording studios.

**Guitars:** 1964-66: Rickenbacker 6 and 12 strings, 1967-68: Fender Stratocaster,

Telecaster, 1969-71: Gibson SG, 1972: Gibson Les Paul Deluxe, 1979: Schecters.

**Hit Singles:**

|  | US | UK |
|---|---|---|
| Let My Love Open The Door, 1980 | 9 | — |

**Albums:**
Who Came First (Decca/Track), 1972
Rough Mix (MCA/Polydor), 1977
Empty Glass (Atco/WEA), 1980 **CD**
All The Best Cowboys Have Chinese Eyes (Atco/WEA), 1982
Pete Townshend Scoop (Atco/Atco), 1983
White City (Atco), 1985

# Toyah

UK vocalist, composer.
Born Toyah Ann Wilcox, Kings Heath, Birmingham, May 18, 1958.

**Career:** Left school in 1976 to take up place at Birmingham Old Rep Drama School; two months later was offered co-starring role in BBC-TV play 'Glitter'. Appearance in this led to place with National Theatre, and Toyah never returned to drama school.

Career as actress burgeoned, and in 1978 Toyah developed musical side of talent by forming eponymous band. Started gigging between acting jobs, one of which was a part in the Who(▶)'s 1979 film 'Quadrophenia'.

In 1979 she signed to Safari Records and released single **Victims Of The Riddle** and 33rpm six-track single **Sheep Farming In Barnet.** Both attracted critical attention and generated sales in alternative outlets.

1980 saw album **The Blue Meaning** make UK Top 40, and later in year **Toyah Toyah Toyah,** a collection of live tracks, confirmed success.

Breakthrough to wider public came in 1981 with release of four-track EP **Four From Toyah,** featuring **It's A Mystery.** It was a major hit, a were next three single releases (**Four More From Toyah** also being an EP). **Anthem** made No. 2 in album charts.

In 1982 Toyah consolidated record success while continuing to be greatly in demand as an actress. Voted top female vocalist in several UK polls, though she has yet to make any impact in US.

Without doubt extremely talented (and a particularly convincing actress), Toyah appeals to wide audience with her very personal brand of sophisto-punk. Her vivid appearance (in particular her amazing hairstyles and brilliant make-up which she does herself) and energetic stage act guarantee strong following for live work, and her versatility indicates continued success. Was

convincing star of Derek Jarman's bizarre movie interpretation of 'The Tempest' in 1984, and made short work of leading role in West End production of 'Trafford Tanzi'.

**Hit Singles:**

|  | US | UK |
|---|---|---|
| Four From Toyah (EP), 1981 | — | 4 |
| I Want To Be Free, 1981 | — | 8 |
| Thunder In The Mountains, 1981 | — | 4 |
| Four More From Toyah (EP), 1981 | — | 14 |

**Albums:**
The Blue Meaning (—/Safari), 1980
Toyah Toyah Toyah (—/Safari), 1980
Anthem (—/Safari), 1981
The Changeling (—/Safari), 1982
Warrior Rock (Toyah On Tour) (—/Safari), 1982
Love Is The Law (Safari), 1983
Minx (Epic), 1985

# Traffic

UK group formed 1967

**Original line-up:** Steve Winwood, guitar, keyboards, vocals; Dave Mason, guitar; Jim Capaldi, drums; Chris Wood, saxophone, flute.

**Career:** Traffic emerged following Winwood's(▶) departure for Spencer Davis Group(▶) in which Winwood played dominant role. Mason(▶) and Capaldi previously played in Birmingham group Deep Feeling. Wood had played sax in ska-influenced Locomotive. In spring 1967, retired to a Berkshire cottage in Aston Tirrold, coining cliché 'getting it together in the country'.

Six months later, debut **Paper Sun,** a powerful and evocative summer single, climbed to No. 5 in UK charts. Follow-up **Hole In My Shoe,** with its dream-like imagery and schoolgirl's voice, was even more commercial and reached No. 2.

First album **Mr Fantasy** revealed individual talents of all members, indicating this was no one-man band. Another Top 10 single, film theme **Here We Go Round The Mulberry Bush,** revealed Mason's ability to pen commercial tunes, in contrast to others' heavy jazz leanings. This apparently caused incompatibility, culminating in Mason's departure in December 1967. Within six months he returned, contributing four songs to **Traffic,** but left again in October 1968 and group folded. Live/studio **Last Exit** was erratic and unsatisfactory finale.

After short stay in ill-fated Blind Faith(▶), Winwood worked on projected solo album **Mad Shadows,** which ended up as Traffic reunion, minus Mason. Re-formed trio released **John Barleycorn Must Die** in April 1970, a superb fusion of jazz, rock, R&B and folk. Unit was bolstered by induction of Rick Grech (ex-Family(▶), Blind Faith), and later Jim Gordon (session drummer) and Reebop Kwaku-Baah (congas). Mason again returned temporarily and this short-lived aggregation played six gigs, captured for posterity on **Welcome To The Canteen,** a surprisingly impressive live album.

During December 1971 US tour, **The Low Spark Of High Heeled Boys** met critical acclaim. However, Grech and Gordon quit and Winwood fell ill with peritonitis amid rumours of Traffic's imminent dissolution. During lull in group activity, Capaldi cut solo **Oh How We Danced** at Muscle Shoals. Formed partnership with rhythm section David Hood and Roger Hawkins, who joined Traffic for Jamaican-recorded **Shoot Out At The Fantasy Factory.** Muscle Shoals sessioneer

**Left: Traffic (from left) Steve Winwood, Chris Wood, Jim Capaldi, Dave Mason — the original quartet.**

Barry Beckett was added on keyboards for 1973 world tour, which included some of their finest live performances as evidenced on German-recorded **On The Road.**

When Shoalsmen returned to States in autumn 1973, Rosko Gee from Gonzalez was brought in as bassist. As quartet (Winwood/Wood/Capaldi/Gee) cut final album **When The Eagle Flies,** which revealed Winwood concentrating heavily on keyboards/synthesiser. Period of indecision ended in December 1974 with Capaldi and Winwood pursuing solo careers.

Traffic were responsible for some of the finest music to emerge from Britain in the late '60s/early '70s. While many contemporaries fell into self-parody or became victims of self-indulgent '70s art rock, Traffic continued to produce music of increasing complexity, originality and quality.

Chris Wood died in July 1983 of liver failure.

**Final line-up:** Winwood; Capaldi; Wood; Rosko Gee, bass.

**Hit Singles:**

|  | US | UK |
|---|---|---|
| Paper Sun, 1967 | — | 5 |
| Hole In My Shoe, 1967 | — | 2 |
| Here We Go Round The Mulberry Bush, 1967 | — | 8 |

*Jim Capaldi Solo:*

|  | US | UK |
|---|---|---|
| Love Hurts, | — | 4 |

(see also Mason and Winwood entries)

**Albums:**
Mr Fantasy (Island), 1967 **CD**
Traffic (Island), 1968 **CD**
Last Exit (Island), 1969
Best Of Traffic (Island), 1969
John Barleycorn Must Die (Island), 1970 **CD**
Welcome To The Canteen (Island), 1971
Low Spark Of High Heeled Boys (Island), 1971 **CD**
Shoot Out At The Fantasy Factory (Island), 1973
On The Road (Island), 1973*
Where The Eagle Flies (Island), 1974
*Issued in single *and* double LP form.

*Jim Capaldi Solo:*
Oh How We Danced (—/Island), 1972
Short Cut Draw Blood (Antilles/Island), 1975
The Contender (—/Polydor), 1978
Electric Nights (Polydor), 1979
Sweet Smell Of Success (—/Carrere), 1980
Let The Thunder Cry (WEA), 1981
Fierce Heart (WEA), 1983
One Man Mission (WEA), 1984

# John Travolta

US vocalist, actor.
Born Englewood, New Jersey, February 18, 1954.

**Career:** Of Italian/Irish parentage; dropped out of high school at 16 to pursue acting career. After gaining experience in summer stock, commercials and off-Broadway shows, made way to Hollywood where he played bit parts in various movies.

Part in touring version of 'Grease' led to role in Broadway version. First important break was leading role in TV show 'Welcome Back Kotter' in 1975. Next two years also saw parts in movies 'Devil's Rain', 'Boy in the Plastic Bubble' and 'Carrie'. During this period signed recording contract with Midsong, gaining three Top 40 entries.

Major turning-point came with main role in massively successful 1977 movie 'Saturday Night Fever'. Although Travolta did not sing in film, it established him as teen idol, and paved

way for impact in 'Grease' in 1978. Travolta and co-star Olivia Newton-John(▶) scored hugely with songs from movie; Travolta's solo efforts also charted internationally.

Follow-up movies 'Moment By Moment', 'Urban Cowboy' and 'Stayin' Alive' were comparatively disastrous, whilst 'Blow Out' at least had a script. Reunion with Olivia Newton-John, 'Two Of A Kind' is best forgotten—and has been.

Although primarily an actor, Travolta possesses pleasant if unspectacular singing voice. Hits with Newton-John were classics of lightweight pop-rock genre.

**Hit Singles:**

| | US | UK |
|---|---|---|
| Let Her In, 1976 | 10 | — |
| Sandy, 1978 | — | 2 |
| Greased Lightnin', 1978 | 47 | 11 |

*With Olivia Newton-John:*

| | | |
|---|---|---|
| You're The One That I Want, 1978 | 1 | 1 |
| Summer Nights, 1978 | 5 | 1 |

**Albums:**
Grease Soundtrack (RSO), 1978

*With Olivia Newton-John:*
Two Of A Kind (EMI), 1983

# Terence Trent D'Arby

US singer, composer.
Born New York, 1962.

**Career:** Son of Pentecostal Minister father and gospel singer mother, raised in Chicago, played drums at church meetings. Took up boxing, then enlisted in US army at 18, posted to Germany, where he bought bass guitar and joined local rock band, The Touch, who split up just as they were about to hit big time.

Secured worldwide deal with CBS on strength of tape of own songs and made sensational live appearances on UK TV pop show 'The Tube' which catapulted him into public attention. Immediately dubbed 'The New Prince Of Pop' by influential UK magazine New Musical Express and undertook several interviews where he proclaimed himself to be 'a genius'.

Finding an audience in UK, debut single, **If You Let Me Stay** was fiery, pleading soul ballad. Follow-up **Wishing Well** was much rockier.

Debut album **Introducing The Hardline According to Terence Trent D'Arby** mixed R'n'B, pop, and soul with a hard-edged modern production from Heaven 17's Martyn Ware, yielding two more hit singles in UK in **Dance Little Sister** and **Sign Your Name**. In early 1988, he finally gained success in America with release of **Wishing Well** single.

Obvious influences include Michael Jackson, Rod Stewart, Stevie Wonder and Rolling

**Terence Trent D'Arby's first album. Courtesy CBS Records.**

Stones (covered two Jagger-Richards songs on B-side of **Sign Your Name** single), but merges them in such a way to create a seamless, effortless style very much his own.

Genius? Of course not, but true star and essential addition to every record collection.

**Hit Singles:**

| | US | UK |
|---|---|---|
| If You Let Me Stay, 1987 | — | 7 |
| Wishing Well, 1987 | — | 4 |
| Dance Little Sister, 1987 | — | 20 |
| Sign Your Name, 1987 | — | 2 |

**Albums:**
Introducing The Hardline According To (CBS), 1987 **CD**

# Triumph

Canadian group formed 1975.

**Original/current line-up:** Rik Emmett, vocals, guitar; Mike Levine, bass, keyboards; Gil Moore, drums, vocals.

**Career:** Formed in Streetsville, Ontario, Triumph was inspired by fellow Canadians Rush(▶) to play thunderous music in small clubs and venues throughout province. Two LPs provided modicum of interest in Canada, but little elsewhere.

Extensive touring in US honed down band's sound and finally sparked audience support. **Progression Of Power** album suggested Triumph might yet produce unique image worthy of heavy-metal success. This was further indicated on excellent **Allied Force** and **Never Surrender** LPs.

In UK, Triumph remains relatively unknown. Early material was released collectively in 1979 but failure to tour in UK provides little opportunity for impact.

Hard work and exciting stage act have improved Triumph to point that band deserves a listen. Further improvement might yet win support needed to move group out of 'just another band' category.

During their 1984 tour they played to over a million fans, and the music was celebrated on a double album **Stages** (1985). The band

returned to the studios to make **The Sport Of Kings** released in 1986. With Rik Emmett a regular guitar poll winner, Triumph grew ever more popular and in late 1987 they released their ninth album **Surveillance**.

Mixing hard rock with more melodic material, the band experimented with a guitar synthesizer and also introduced a classically trained keyboard player, Dave Tkaczuk to several tracks, together with guest guitar virtuoso, Steve Morse, who was featured in a guitar dual with Emmett on **Headed For Nowhere**.

**Current line-up:** Emmett; Levine; Moore; Dave Tkaczuk, keyboards.

**Albums:**
Triumph (RCA/Attic), 1976
Just A Game (RCA), 1979
Rock'n'Roll Machine* (RCA/Attic), 1979
Progression Of Power (RCA), 1980
Allied Forces (RCA), 1980 **CD**
Never Surrender (RCA), 1982
Thunder 7 (MCA), 1985 **CD**
Stages (MCA), 1985 **CD** (Double)
Sport Of Kings (MCA), 1986 **CD**

*Debut LP **Triumph** with one track less

# The Troggs

UK group formed 1966.

**Original line-up:** Reg Presley, vocals; Chris Britton, guitar; Pete Staples, bass; Ronnie Bond, drums.

**Career:** Formed in Andover, Hants, the Troggs were discovered by record producer Larry Page who signed them to management deal and secured recording contract with Fontana.

After debut in BBC Radio's 'Saturday Club' and TV's 'Thank Your Lucky Stars', they recorded American writer Chips Taylor's **Wild Thing**. Featuring Reg Presley's moody vocal and ocarina playing, the record lived up to title, being one of wildest records ever cut in UK. Its originality was rewarded with a million sales and American chart-topping status (where it was, most unusually, available on

*Left: A talent for mixing musical genres with ease, Terence Trent D'Arby.*

two record labels—Fontana and Atco.

Presley himself penned the follow-up **With A Girl Like You**, a UK chart-topper which also went gold, and again available on both Fontana and Atco in US.

The classic **I Can't Control Myself** and **Any Way That You Want Me** gave them four UK Top-10 hits in very first year. Another million-seller came in 1967 with **Love Is All Around** (also a Presley composition).

Peter Staples was replaced by Tony Murray in 1969 and group's recording career went into decline despite mini-hit with novel version of Beach Boys(▶) **Good Vibrations.**

However, stunning stage act created fanatically loyal following in Germany, France, Holland, Britain and, particularly, in America, which sustained them through the '70s despite lack of activity.

With no further line-up changes, group today continues to earn good money on cabaret/club circuits, despite lack of recording success.

**Current line-up:** Presley; Britton; Bond; Tony Murray, bass.

**Hit Singles:**

| | US | UK |
|---|---|---|
| Wild Thing, 1966 | 1 | 2 |
| With A Girl Like You, 1966 | 29 | 1 |
| I Can't Control Myself, 1966 | 43 | 2 |
| Any Way That You Want Me, 1968 | — | 8 |
| Give It To Me, 1967 | — | 12 |
| Night Of The Long Grass, 1967 | — | 17 |
| Love Is All Around, 1967 | 7 | 5 |

**Albums:**
The Troggs Tapes (Private Stock/Penny Farthing), 1975
Live At Max's Kansas City (Max's Kansas City), 1979
Golden Hits (Astan), 1984

*Worth Searching Out:*
Wild Thing (Atco/Fontana), 1966
Best Of (Rhino), 1985

**Wild Thing, Troggs. Courtesy Fontana Records.**

# Robin Trower

UK guitarist, composer.
Born London, March 9, 1945.

**Career:** Trower began in a Southend band, Paramounts. Co-member Gary Brooker went on to form Procol Harum(▶). After recording **Whiter Shade Of Pale**, Brooker asked Trower to join Harum and he stayed from 1967-71. He left because of dissatisfaction with limited guitar sound.

Trower had become a great admirer of Jimi Hendrix(▶), as evidenced by his **Song For A Dreamer**, which he contributed to his final Harum LP, **Broken Barricades**. Instead of going for guitar hero role, Trower tried to form group to be called Jude. This effort failed, but introduced him to ex-Stone The Crow bassist/vocalist Jim Dewar. In mid-1972, he and Dewar formed Robin Trower Band with drummer Reg Isadore. First LP, **Twice Removed From Yesterday**, produced some spacy riffs which some found exhilarating, but others considered a Hendrix rip-off.

**Twice Removed From Yesterday, Robin Trower. Courtesy Chrysalis Records.**

Band was ignored in UK, but did well in the US. Unfortunately, each subsequent release pushed Trower further into axe hero role. Ex-Sly Stone drummer Bill London replaced Reg Isadore on third LP, **For Earth Below**. This line-up recorded next five LPs, by which time recycled Hendrix lines were no longer interesting.

Trower then teamed up with London and Jack Bruce(▶) to form BLT. LP of same name made US Top 40 in 1981. Isadore joined band for **Truce** LP.

Trower's guitar work can be interesting (**Bridge Of Sighs** was chosen as early CD release for Chrysalis), if somewhat derivative. Among peers (Pat Travers, Ted Nugent, Mick Jones, Rich Williams) he clearly ranks as one of best. His big US following should keep him gainfully employed for some time to come.
Guitar: Fender Stratocaster.

**Albums:**
Twice Removed From Yesterday (Chrysalis), 1973
Bridge Of Sighs (Chrysalis), 1974
For Earth Below (Chrysalis), 1975
Robin Trower Live (Chrysalis), 1975
Long Misty Days (Chrysalis), 1976
In City Dreams (Chrysalis), 1977
Caravan To Midnight (Chrysalis), 1978
Victim Of Fury (Chrysalis), 1980
Time Is Short (Chrysalis), 1983
Back It Up (Chrysalis), 1983
Beyond The Mist (Music For Nations), 1985

*Bruce, London, Trower:*
BLT (Chrysalis), 1981

*Bruce/Trower:*
Truce (Chrysalis), 1982

# The Tubes
US group formed 1972.

**Original/current line-up:** Fee Waybill, vocals; Bill Spooner, guitar; Vince Welnick, keyboards; Rich Anderson, bass; Michael Cotten, synthesiser; Roger Steen, guitar; Prairie Prince, percussion.

**Career:** Formed by Bill Spooner with art school friends, group immediately gained devoted following in San Francisco's Bay Area. Combined often heavy rock with outrageous satire and became known for bizarre creations such as Quay Lude (drugged-out superstar) and Dr Strangekiss (a crippled Nazi, sounding not unlike Tom Jones). Semi-clad girls were also well to the fore.

Signed record deal with A&M in 1975, releasing **The Tubes** same year. With Al Kooper as producer, set included Rocky Horror style classics, notably **White Punks On Dope**, later a Top 30 UK hit.

By third album **Now**, Tubes had recruited Minge Lewis to produce more mainstream work. Late '70s also saw them tempering theatrical outrage by limiting appearances of dancing girls, possibly to avoid accusations of blatant sexism. Braved a purely musical, non-theatrical, club tour in 1980, which was only partially successful.

Fourth album **Remote Control**, produced by Todd Rundgren(▶), failed to break any new ground and caused renewed friction with record company. Finally recorded unreleased album for A&M, for which Waybill refused to contribute vocals. Reputedly left their record company following finance dispute.

Signed deal with Capitol, which led to 1981-82 tour, taking in Sweden, Norway, Germany, France, Holland, Portugal, Italy and Britain. **The Completion Backward Principle** (a phrase borrowed from the methodology of salesmanship) saw group assigned to producer David Foster (Boz Scaggs, Hall & Oates) in attempt to record hit album. Although work showed flashes of old humour, it was obvious compromise, and Tubes now seem part of the very system they once parodied so effectively, as con-

**Below: The outrageous Tubes toned down their act to find success.**

**Above: Ike and Tina Turner in happier days before their divorce.**

firmed by their 1983 US AOR hit **She's A Beauty.**

| Hit Singles: | US | UK |
|---|---|---|
| She's A Beauty, 1983 | 10 | — |

**Albums:**
The Tubes (A&M), 1975 **CD**
Young And Rich (A&M), 1976
Now (A&M), 1977
What Do You Want From Live (A&M), 1978
Remote Control (A&M), 1979
The Completion Backward Principle (Capitol), 1981
Outside Inside (Capitol), 1983
Trash (A&M), 1986

# Tina Turner
US vocalist.
Born: Annie Mae Bullock, Brownsville, Tennessee, November 26, 1938.

**Career:** When Ike and Tina Turner's long-term working and marital relationship split amidst much acrimony, it seemed like end of the line for one of soul music's most gifted vocalists. For while Tina had fronted the steady flow of hits, everyone knew that Ike Turner was the key to it all, writing much of the material, heading the band, playing superb guitar and keyboards, choreographing the dazzling stage shows and making all the business deals. Tina seemed destined to end her days singing the old hits at second-rate cabaret venues.

But in 1982 an invitation to join Heaven 17 for joint vocals on **Ball Of Confusion** for the UK group's new album, brought Tina to London. Heaven 17's Greg Walsh and Martin Ware then produced Tina on version of Al Green's **Lets' Stay Together** which went Top Ten and spawned a sell-out European tour. Record hit in US too and sold a million.

With Capitol Records now 100 per cent behind her revived career, Tina scored in 1984 with **Private Dancer** album, crop of hit singles, including Grammy Award winning **What's Love Got To Do With It?**

Now regarded as rock music's number one lady, Tina started her long career very much in the R&B vein. Her sister had been dating member of Ike Turner's Kings Of Rhythm in St. Louis and Tina eventually persuaded Ike to let her sing. Ousting Ike's first wife and pianist Bonnie Turner both in the band and home, Tina sang lead on **A Fool In Love** when another of Ike's vocalists failed to make the session. Result was an R&B number two.

Ike, who had helped earlier careers of B.B. King, Bobby Bland and Howlin' Wolf (among others), masterminded stunning Ike and Tina Turner Revue featuring the Ikettes backing group (of which P.P. Arnold, Merry Clayton and Bonnie Bramlett were all one-time members).

The all-singing, all-dancing revue plus records on wide range of labels, including milestone **River Deep Mountain High**, produced by Phil Spector, took Ike and Tina from R&B 'chittlin' circuit' to highest realms of rock, helped by endorsement of Rolling Stones.

Linking with major Liberty/Minit/United Artists set-up, Ike and Tina veered heavily toward rock while also cutting heavy blues-oriented material, and Tina appeared as the Acid Queen in screen version of The Who's rock opera 'Tommy'.

Ike's bizarre behaviour finally split the relationship, Tina walking out in 1974 with nothing but clothes she stood up in.

Many traumas and a whole decade later she was right back on top while Ike, the man on whom she had seemed totally dependent, lost his fortune and passed into obscurity.

It took almost a decade for Tina to smash back into the public consciousness with **Private Dancer**, but from then on her career snowballed. Slew of her singles brought her to attention of new generation of record buyers, and she made well-received movie debut in **Mad Max (Beyond The Thunderdome)**. Since 1984 Tina has maintained superstar status with sell-out concerts, Live Aid duet with Mick Jagger and platinum album **Break Every Rule**. Has also received extensive exposure via Pepsi-Cola TV commercials.

Almost unique in her metamorphosis from soul star to rock icon, Tina Turner looks set to garner further success and acclaim in late 80s. One of entertainment industry's most luscious fifty-year-olds, Tina has nevertheless indicated that she may want to take like easier in foreseeable future, so barnstorming concert appearances may be reduced. Aficionados can get full lowdown on rock diva's eventful life in best-selling autobiography 'I Tina'.

**Hit Singles:**

| | US | UK |
|---|---|---|
| Let's Stay Together, 1983 | 26 | 6 |
| What's Love Got To Do With It, 1984 | 1 | 3 |
| Better Be Good To Me, 1984 | 5 | — |
| Private Dancer, 1985 | 7 | 26 |
| We Don't Need Another Hero, 1985 | 2 | 3 |
| One Of The Living, 1985 | 15 | — |
| Typical Male, 1986 | 1 | 33 |
| Two People, 1986 | — | 43 |
| What You Get Is What You See, 1987 | 15 | — |

*With Bryan Adams:*

| | US | UK |
|---|---|---|
| It's Only Love, 1985 | 19 | 29 |

**Albums:**
Private Dancer (Capital), 1984 **CD**
Break Every Rule (Capital), 1986 **CD**
So Fine (Entertainers), 1987 **CD**
Too Hot To Handle (Thunderbolt), 1987

Happy Together, The Turtles. Courtesy White Whale Records.

# The Turtles

US group formed 1965.
**Original line-up:** Howard Kaylan, vocals; Mark Volman, vocals; Al Nichol, guitar; Chuck Portz, bass; Jim Tucker, guitar; Don Murray, drums.

**Career:** While still at Westchester High School (LA) in 1962, Kaplan (change to Kaylan came later), Nichol and Portz formed surf band, the Nightriders. Murray, who attended nearby school, joined on drums. In February 1963 band added Volman, and changed name to Crossfires.

With various rhythm guitarists, this line-up recorded some obscure singles, and played at local high-school dances. Jim Tucker eventually took rhythm guitar spot. (Band occasionally billed itself as folk group, Crosswind Singers.) The new, but very small, White Whale label offered a contract on condition that name be changed yet again. Band's manager suggested 'Tyrtles' to cash in on UK-sounding name; band agreed on 'Turtles'.

The Byrds(▶) had just hit with Dylan cover,

**Mr Tambourine Man**, so Turtles' first release, **It Ain't Me, Babe**, sounded like perfect progression in folk-rock fusion. **Let Me Be** and **You Baby**, both written by 'protest' songwriter P. F. Sloan, followed debut into charts. First LP was released in 1965 and, as was typical of time, carried lots of covers and some filler. The surprise is that the jangling sound on **Wanderin' Kind** and **Love Minus Zero** sounds as fresh and novel today as it did then.

Next single was self-penned **Grim Reaper Of Love**; being different in texture and sound from expected Turtles mould, it barely made charts. White Whale regrettably put pressure on Kaylan/Volman to stop releasing original material. Next release, **Outside Chance,** missed completely, but included new drummer John Barbata (later of Jefferson Starship(▶)). Then Portz left; Jim Pons (ex-Leaves) joined.

By early 1967, band had been a year without a hit, a bad sign in the golden age of singles. However, **Happy Together** went to US No. 1, and put band back in spotlight. Turtles' next release, **She'd Rather Be With Me**, made No. 3 in US.

By 1968, band wanted to assume self-production. After two misses, they came up with US No. 6 **Elenore,** but the public seemed to miss ironic mockery of song, so band overloaded potshots on next LP. **The Turtles Present The Battle Of The Bands** was unequalled in its loving snipes at rock styles until Nick Lowe's(▶) **Jesus Of Cool/Pure Pop For Now People** LP.

The Turtles lost Tucker while touring UK, (he wasn't replaced. As sessions were to begin for new LP, Barbata also quit and John Seiter (ex-Spanky And Our Gang) came in. Line-up of Kaylan, Volman, Nichol, Pons and Seiter lasted rest of band's lifetime. New LP was to be straight-ahead rock, and admirer Ray Davies (Kinks(▶)) agreed to produce it. Despite strong material and Davies credentials, album failed to hit at a time when LPs were beginning to determine success and status.

Band continued to tour with greatest hits package, making 'unhip' decision to play White House at Tricia Nixon's request. Failure to produce hit records caused growing problems with White Whale, which led to legal hassles; band quietly disappeared in 1970.

Kaylan and Volman have most interesting Turtles history. Unable to record under their own name because of lawsuits, the duo took names of two Turtles roadies and joined Frank Zappa(▶) as Phlorescent Leech and Eddie. Their appearance in '200 Motels' was promising and promoted comic image. As Flo & Eddie, they released several LPs, backed Marc Bolan(▶), promoted a radio show, and in general maintained zany side of Turtles into '70s and '80s.

Considering their brilliant sound and good sense of humour, it is puzzling that the Turtles haven't exerted greater influence. They remain a highly underrated cult band; though recordings during their heyday have become somewhat collectable.

**Final line-up:** Kaylan; Volman; Nichol; Jim Pons, bass; John Seiter, drums.

**Hit Singles:**

| | US | UK |
|---|---|---|
| It Ain't Me Babe, 1965 | 8 | — |
| You Baby, 1966 | 20 | — |
| Happy Together, 1967 | 1 | 12 |
| She'd Rather Be With Me, 1967 | 3 | 4 |
| You Know What I Mean, 1967 | 12 | — |
| She's My Girl, 1967 | 14 | — |
| Elenore, 1968 | 6 | 7 |
| You Showed Me, 1969 | 6 | — |

**Albums:**
*As The Crossfires:*
Out Of Control (Rhino/—), 1981

*As The Turtles:*
Happy Together Again (—/Philips), 1975
It Ain't Me Babe (Rhino/—), 1982
Great Hits Of The Turtles (Rhino/—), 1982

*Worth Searching Out:*
You Baby (White Whale/—), 1966
Happy Together (White Whale/London), 1967
Golden Hits (White Whale/—), 1967
Battle Of The Bands (White Whale/London), 1968
Turtle Soup (White Whale/—), 1969
Wooden Head (White Whale/—), 1970
20 Greatest Hits (Rhino), 1986 **CD**

Above: Conway Twitty, rock'n'roller turned country music superstar.

# Conway Twitty

US vocalist, guitarist, composer.
Born Harold Lloyd Jenkins, Friars Point, Mississippi, September 1, 1935.

**Career:** Former rock 'n' roll singer, turned country performer, Twitty scored in late '50s with teen anthems **I Need Your Lovin'** and **It's Only Make Believe** (which he co-wrote). Many in business saw him as MGM's answer to Elvis Presley.

Transition to country started in mid-'60s. First C&W chart record was **Guess My Eyes Were Bigger Than My Heart** (1966), and since then he has maintained continuous stream of hit singles and albums.

Twitty was coupled with Loretta Lynn(▶) for series of duets in early '70s, and pair earned Country Music Association Vocal Duo Of The Year awards in '72, '73, '74 and '75.

A baseball protégé (he turned down chance of going pro), Twitty is welcome change from the schmaltz-laden stereotypes rife in Nashville. His powerful baritone is still a major draw at concerts.

**Hit Singles:**

| | US | UK |
|---|---|---|
| It's Only Make Believe, 1958 | 1 | 1 |
| Mona Lisa, 1959 | 29 | 5 |
| Danny Boy, 1959 | 10 | — |
| Lonely Blue Boy, 1960 | 6 | — |

**Albums (selected):**
Looking Back ( – /Polydor), 1975
Georgia Keeps Pulling On My Ring (MCA), 1978
It's Only Make Believe ( – /Pickwick), 1981
Southern Comfort (Elektra/—), 1982
Greatest Hits (MGM/—), 1982
No. 1 Classics Volume 1 (Elektra), 1982
Early Favourites (Accord/—), 1982
Number Ones (MCA/—), 1982
Shake It Up Baby (—/Bulldog), 1982

*With Loretta Lynn (selected):*
Feelins (MCA), 1975
United Talent (MCA), 1976
Very Best Of (MCA/—), 1976

# U2

UK group formed 1979.

**Original/Current line-up:** Bono 'Vox' Hewson, vocals; Dave 'The Edge' Evans guitar, keyboards; Adam Clayton, bass; Larry Mullen, drums.

**Career:** Inspired by London's new, young bands in 1976, Bono and the 'The Edge' decided to form own group in Dublin. Fellow mates Clayton and Mullen joined, and name U2 was taken, with implication that every fan could join in the music as well.

Bono described band as beginning with three chords, but with special enthusiasm. Pub gigs led to local record contract with CBS. Two singles, released in Ireland only, gained

The Joshua Tree, U2.
Courtesy Island Records.

cult status in UK. Island Records became interested and took over band, releasing **11 O'clock Tick Tock** in May 1980.

UK critics began falling over themselves to cite U2 as next big thing. When **Boy** LP was released, U2 were hailed as *the* hope of rock's future. Band ignored press and pushed on, establishing close rapport with audiences. **I Will Follow** was issued as strong single.

Touring in US brought band into contact with producer Sandy Pearlman (Blue Oyster Cult/Dictators/Clash) and for time he was considered for second LP. Some New York sessions were produced but ultimately band returned to Steve Lillywhite.

1981 single **Gloria** received heavy airplay and made UK Top 40. When **October** LP was released, expected revisionism set in and critics carped that U2 was really just another '60s band because of basic guitar, bass, drum sound. Band continued to ignore press and found audiences growing everywhere.

1982 tour introduced music from forthcoming **War** album, which subsequently entered UK listings at No. 1, and established bands credentials in US. First chart single **New Years Day** made UK top ten in January, 1983. Evangelical outlook had not restricted U2's development, although group were still struggling to impress critics still sceptical of 'message' contained in their music. **Red Sky** set (1985) saw journalistic 'about face', and preceded appearance in Live Aid concert which further spread international appeal.

By 1987, U2 were generally considered premier band of the moment, and 18 month world tour promoting **Joshua Tree** album left very little geographically for them to conquer. Obligatory cover of Time magazine confirmed acceptance from mainstream of rock business. U2's biography **Unforgettable Fire** written by former professional soccer player Eamon Dunphy (published Autumn 1987) quickly became surprise best-seller, despite band's subsequent distancing from project.

**Hit Singles:**

| | US | UK |
|---|---|---|
| New Years Day, 1983 | — | 10 |
| Two Hearts Beat As One, 1983 | ← | 18 |
| Pride, 1984 | — | 3 |
| The Unforgettable Fire, 1985 | — | 6 |
| With Or Without You, 1987 | 1 | 4 |
| I Still Haven't Found What I'm Looking For, 1987 | 1 | 6 |
| Where The Streets Have No Name, 1987 | 13 | 4 |

**Albums:**
Boy (Island), 1980 **CD**
October (Island), 1981 **CD**
War (Island), 1983 **CD**
The Unforgettable Fire (Island), 1984 **CD**
Under A Blood Red Sky (Island), 1985 **CD**
Joshua Tree (Island), 1987

# UB40

UK group formed 1977.

**Original line-up:** Ali Campbell, vocals, guitar; Robin Campbell, guitar, vocals; Brian Travers, saxophone; Earl Falconer, bass; Jimmy Lynn, keyboards; Jim Brown, drums; Norman Hassan, percussion; 'Yomi' Babayemi, percussion.

**Career:** Band came together in West Midlands; as most members were unemployed, took name from unemployment benefit form.

Inter-racial outfit, UB40 pioneered specifically British brand of melodic reggae, combining smooth vocals and liquid saxophone fill-ins with relaxed reggae beat. At first amateurish band quickly tightened up sound and by 1979 were undertaking gigs. That same year Lynn left, replaced by Michael Virtue, Babayemi returned to his native Nigeria; Astro joined as resident toaster/ vocalist. That year group also signed to local Graduate label; second single, **King/Food For Thought**, took them into Top 5.

**The Best Of, UB40.
Courtesy Dep Records.**

Debut album **Signing Off** was also major hit, prompting band to form their own **Dep International** label in 1981.

Relatively quiescent couple of years passed until band released **Labour Of Love** in 1983. Album featured slick covers of reggae classics, and struck major chord with public; former Neil Diamond/Tony Tribe hit **Red Red Wine** became UK number one and established band internationally. Further hit singles ensued, reinforcing outfit's position as number one pop-reggae outfit. In 1985 Ali Campbell duetted with Pretenders' vocalist Chrissie Hynde on remake of Sonny and Cher's **I Got You Babe**, again hitting number one spot.

UB40 have continued to maintain popularity, helped by clever choice of material and smooth, relaxed vocal sound. Overall approach dates back to ska/rock steady roots of Jamaican

music, and is more accessible to broad audience than much current roots reggae.

**Current line-up:** Ali Campbell; Robin Campbell; Travers; Falconer; Brown; Hassan; Astro, toaster, vocals; Michael Virtue, keyboards.

**Hit Singles:**

| | US | UK |
|---|---|---|
| King/Food For Thought, 1980 | — | 4 |
| My Way Of Thinking/I Think It's Going To Rain, 1980 | — | 6 |
| The Earth Dies Screaming/ Dream A Lie, 1980 | — | 10 |
| Don't Slow Down/Don't Let It Pass You By, 1981 | — | 16 |
| One In Ten, 1981 | — | 7 |
| Red Red Wine, 1983 | 34 | 1 |
| Please Don't Make Me Cry, 1983 | — | 10 |
| Many Rivers To Cross, 1983 | — | 16 |
| Cherry Oh Baby, 1984 | — | 12 |
| If It Happens Again, 1984 | — | 9 |
| Don't Break My Heart, 1985 | — | 3 |
| I Got You Babe (With Chrissie Hynde), 1985 | 28 | 1 |
| All I Want To Do, 1986 | — | 41 |
| Sing Our Own Song, 1986 | — | 5 |
| Maybe Tomorrow, 1987 | — | 14 |
| Rat In Mi Kitchen, 1987 | — | 12 |

**Albums:**
Signing Off (—/Graduate), 1980
Present Arms (—/Dep International), 1981
Present Arms In Dub (—/Dep International), 1981
The Singles Album (—/Graduate), 1982
UB44 (—/Dep International), 1982
Live (—/Dep International), 1983
Labour Of Love (—/Dep International), 1983 **CD**
Geffery Morgan (—/Dep International), 1984 **CD**
Baggariddim (—/Dep International), 1985 **CD**
The UB40 File (—/Dep International), 1985
Signing Off (Sound), 1980 **CD**
Rat In The Kitchen (DEP), 1986 **CD**
More Music (Sound), 1986 **CD**
Best Of (DEP), 1987

# UFO

UK group formed 1970.

**Original line-up:** Phil Mogg, vocals; Pete Way, bass; Andy Parker, drums; Mick Bolton, guitar.

**Career:** When UFO formed, their style of music was called hard rock. **UFO 1** and **Flying** were totally unnoticed in UK/US but became popular in Germany and Japan. Bolton left and remaining trio became core of UFO through various personnel changes. Michael Schenker(▶) met UFO while with Scorpions, who opened a German tour. He took guitar spot on **Phenomenon** which became underground cult LP in US.

**Force It** and **No Heavy Petting** LPs showed off Schenker's growing heavy-metal guitar abilities; the latter album also saw band expand range by adding Danny Peyronel on keyboards. **Lights Out** album provided stage favourites **Love To Love** and title song. Paul Raymond was now on keyboards and band developed highly competent stage show. In UK they had become major draw without compromising to punk or new wave.

Growing reputation was boosted by

**Left: Ireland's finest export of the '80s, U2, with Bono (right).**

**Obsession**, but live **Stranger In The Night** finally broke band in US. For exciting heavy metal, this LP is excellent introduction. Unfortunately, it marked departure of Schenker who left to form Michael Schenker Group. Paul Chapman, who had guested on LP, took over his spot full time.

In hindsight, this period began demise of band. **No Place To Run** saw Raymond replaced by Neil Carter. LP was too slickly produced by George Martin and missed edge given by Schenker. **The Wild, The Willing And The Innocent** album met fair reviews but did nothing new or exciting. Worse, Mogg's stage performances were becoming erratic because of personal problems and pressures. Way managed to contend with deteriorating situation for one more LP, but mid-1982 brought announcement he was leaving to form Fastway with ex-Motorhead(▶) guitarist, Fast Eddie Clarke.

Band recorded **Making Contact** in 1983 with Carter doubling on keyboards and bass. UFO set off on European tour with Billy Sheehan as guest bassist. Then at February 1983 Athens show Mogg collapsed, and audience nearly rioted. Cutting short tour, group quickly returned to UK so that Mogg could rest up. A month later plans were announced for UK tour, following which UFO would disband. However, Mogg has since kept fragile line-up together.

During 1987 Phil Mogg recorded a series of demos in America with Atomik Tommy M on guitar, Jim Simpson (drums), and Paul Gray

**Strangers In The Night, UFO. Courtesy Chrysalis Records.**

(bass), which they hoped would lead to a major record deal. When this wasn't forthcoming the tracks were released by UK label FM Revolver as a 'musical scrapbook' in April 1988. On December 23, 1987 UFO played for rock magazine Metal Hammer's Christmas Party at London's Astoria, then a few months later Phil Mogg began writing new material with Pete Way hoping to reform UFO with its original line-up.

**Current line-up:** Mogg; Paul Raymond, guitar; Paul Grey, bass.

**Albums:**
UFO 1 (—/Beacon), 1971
Flying (—/Beacon), 1972
Phenomenon (Chrysalis), 1973
Force It (Chrysalis), 1975
No Heavy Petting (Chrysalis), 1976
Lights Out (Chrysalis), 1977
Obsession (Chrysalis), 1978
Strangers In The Night (double, live), (Chrysalis), 1979
No Place To Run (Chrysalis), 1979
The Wild, The Willing And The Innocent (Chrysalis), 1981
Mechanix (Chrysalis), 1982
Making Contact (Chrysalis), 1983
Misdemeanor (Chrysalis), 1985
Anthology (Raw Power), 1987 **CD**

# Ultravox

UK group formed 1975.

**Original line-up:** John Foxx (real name Dennis Leigh), vocals; Billy Currie, violin, keyboards, synthesiser; Chris Cross (aka Chris St John), bass; Stevie Shears, guitar; Warren Cann, drums.

**Career:** Foxx, from Chorley, Lancs, met Cross when latter moved from London to join Preston band Stoned Rose. After recruiting other three (Cann born in Canada, others British), formed band named Tiger Lily, with intention of playing like early Roxy Music(▶). Signed with small Gull label, released version of Fats Waller's **Ain't Misbehavin'**, title music to X-rated film of same name. No success, but single reissued in '80s on even smaller Scottish label, Dead Good Records.

Band also known in early days by such names as the Zips, the Innocents, London Soundtrack and Fire Of London, but by 1976 had settled on name of Ultravox! (exclamation mark later dropped).

Signed with Island in 1976, releasing three LPs and numerous singles, all unsuccessful, despite growing cult following. In 1978, Shears left, replaced until 1979 by Robin Simon. That same year, Foxx departed to embark on partially successful solo career, which continues today. Currie, Cross and Cann decided to stay together, even though group dropped by Island at this time. Recruited

James 'Midge' Ure as singer/guitarist — Ure had played with Currie in Visage, part time band for both, led by Steve Strange. Ure's previous career had included Slik, a Scottish pop band who topped UK charts in 1976 with **Forever And Ever**, Rich Kids, formed by ex-Sex Pistol(▶) bassist Glen Matlock (Ure was also invited at one point to join Sex Pistols, but declined), and temporary work with Thin Lizzy(▶).

When Ure joined Ultravox, group adopted fresh direction with synthesisers, which had

started when Foxx was singer, and signed with Chrysalis. Ever since, they have enjoyed substantial success in UK, and to a lesser extent in other countries, with unbroken run of hit singles, plus several successful LPs.

While they have also worked on outside projects (Currie with Visage until early 1983, Ure also with Visage, as well as solo records and 1983 collaboration with Mick Karn of Japan, Cross making videos with Ure, and Cann writing film music), suspicion exists that group may have become too set in their ways.

**Left: Ultravox, masters of synthesised sound. From left, Cross, Currie, Ure, Cann.**

Ure's continued success and creditable endeavours with Bob Geldof in Band Aid(▶) project have somewhat tempered group's activities.

**Current line-up:** Midge Ure, vocals, guitar, synthesiser; Currie; Cross; Cann.

**Hit Singles:**

| | US | UK |
|---|---|---|
| Vienna, 1981 | — | 2 |
| All Stood Still, 1981 | — | 8 |
| The Thin Wall, 1981 | — | 14 |
| The Voice, 1981 | — | 16 |
| Reap The Wild Wind, 1982 | — | 12 |
| Hymn, 1982 | — | 11 |
| Visions In Blue, 1983 | — | 15 |
| We Came To Dance, 1983 | — | 18 |
| Dancing With Tears In My Eyes, 1984 | — | 3 |
| Love's Great Adventure, 1984 | — | 12 |
| Same Old Story, 1986 | — | 31 |
| All Fall Down, 1986 | — | 30 |

*Midge Ure Solo:*

| | | |
|---|---|---|
| No Regrets, 1982 | — | 9 |
| If I Was, 1985 | — | 1 |
| Call Of The Wild, 1986 | — | 27 |

**Albums:**
Ultravox! (Island), 1977
System Of Romance (Antilles/Island), 1978
Vienna (Chrysalis), 1980 **CD**

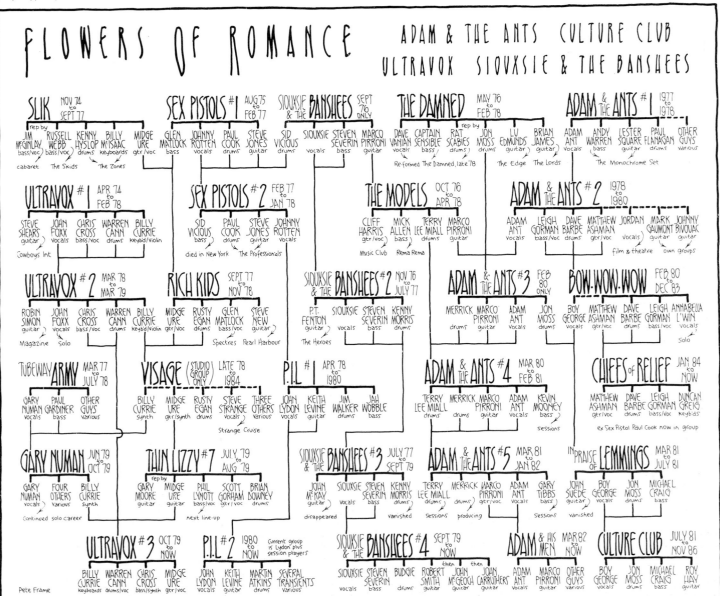

Three Into One (Antiles/Island), 1980*
Rage In Eden (Chrysalis), 1981 **CD**
Quartet (Chrysalis), 1982 **CD**
Monument (Soundtrack) (Chrysalis), 1983
Lament (Chrysalis), 1984 **CD**
Collection (Chrysalis), 1985 **CD**
U-Vox (Chrysalis) **CD**
*compilation

*Midge Ure Solo:*
The Gift (Chrysalis), 1985 **CD**

*Worth Searching Out:*
Ha! Ha! Ha! (Island), 1977

# Undertones

UK group formed 1975.

**Original/Final line-up:** Feargal Sharkey, vocals; John O'Neill, guitar; Damian 'Dee' O'Neil, guitar; Mike Bradley, bass; Billy Doherty, drums.

**Career:** Formed in Derry, Northern Ireland, band went unnoticed until mid-1978 when UK press discovered Irish music scene. **Teenage Kicks** EP was put out on independent label; John Peel played a role in getting band exposure by including EP on his radio show.

Undertones' first LP captured brash, young sound. With a cover deliberately derivative of Who's(▶) **My Generation** LP, Undertones struck pose of an '80s band aware of rock's past. Critics praised band's freshness, and UK concerts won large audiences.

Focus of band was Sharkey's quavering vocals, which always seemed ready to break down but just managed to last to end of each song. This kept concerts interesting, but band stalled on record. **Hypnotised** was termed average by critics but **Positive Touch** was condemned as repetitive.

Undertones retreated to Northern Island in 1982 to rework sound, as evident from **The Sin Of Pride** Set. With band now on crest of a wave, Sharkey's solo aspirations prompted group's demise.

First success for Sharkey was 1983 hit **Never Never**, released under name of Assembly, outfit co-led by former Yazoo and later Erasure maestro Vince Clarke.

But major breakthrough was not to come until 1985, when fervent **A Good Heart Is Hard To Find** touched chord with British public, taking number one spot. Debut album **Feargal Sharkey** went on to sell more than two million copies worldwide.

Latterly artist has become purveyor of contemporary pop with hint of soul, as exemplified by Alison Moyet, Level 42 and others. By all accounts an astute businessman, Sharkey looks set to pursue long and successful career.

**Hit Singles:**

|  | US | UK |
|---|---|---|
| Jimmy, Jimmy, 1979 | — | 16 |
| My Perfect Cousin, 1980 | — | 9 |
| Wednesday Week, 1980 | — | 11 |
| It's Going To Happen, 1981 | — | 18 |
| *Feargal Sharkey Solo:* | | |
| A Good Heart Is Hard To Find, 1985 | — | 1 |
| You Little Thief, 1986 | — | 5 |
| *Feargal Sharkey with Vince Clarke in Assembly:* | | |
| Never Never, 1983 | — | 4 |

**Albums:**
Undertones (Fame), 1979 **CD**
Hypnotised (Sire), 1980
Positive Touch (Harvest/EMI), 1981
The Sin Of Pride (—/Ardeck), 1983
Cher O' Bowlies (Compilation) (EMI) **CD**

*Feargal Sharkey Solo:*
Feargal Sharkey (Virgin), 1985 **CD**

# Uriah Heep

UK group formed 1969

**Original line-up:** Mick Box, guitar; David Byron, vocals; Ken Hensley, keyboards; Alex Napier, drums; Paul Newton, bass, vocals.

**Career:** Box and Byron asked Ken Hensley to leave Toe Fat and formed Uriah Heep. Napier and Newton had been with Box and Byron in their old band Spice; Newton had known Hensley in earlier band, Gods, and introduced him to Heep. While recording first LP, Napier left, to be replaced by Nigel Olsson, who quit after recording sessions for Elton John(▶). Heep auditioned Keith Baker as new drummer.

Following second LP, Baker left. Ian Clarke joined for one year and one album. Hensley finally convinced Toe Fat mate, Lee Kerslake, to take drums. Band also replaced Newton with Mark Clarke who quit after few months. Throughout this flux, band was object of critical attack rivalled only by that directed towards Grand Funk Railroad(▶). Gary Thain joined on bass and band took off as international stars. Based on vague sorcery, **Demons And Wizards** and **The Magician's Birthday** LPs were full of mystic connotations. The same line-up also recorded highly underrated **Uriah Heep Live** LP which predates heavy metal without the boring repetition that sometimes plagues genre.

Thain developed drug problems which led to his firing in early 1975. (He died in December 1975.) John Wetton (later of Asia(▶)) joined for 18 months. **Return To Fantasy** and **High And Mighty** were recorded during this period.

Even though LPs were as strong as ever Heep lost audience and internal dissent began tearing band apart. Wetton and Byron left in August 1976. Box, Hensley and Kerslake signed up John Lawton for vocals and Trevor Bolder (ex-David Bowie(▶)) on bass. This line-up recorded **Firefly, Innocent Victim** and **Fallen Angel** as band continued downward slide. Reshuffle again occurred before recording of excellent **Abominog**, which appeared after most fans assumed band was gone for good.

Despite being dropped by Bronze label, Heep continued to work, and secured deal with CBS at end of 1984.

**Current line-up:** Box; Lee Kerslake, drums; Peter Goalby, vocals; John Sinclair, keyboards; Trevor Bolder, bass.

**Albums (selected):**
Very 'Eavy, Very 'Umble (—/Vertigo), 1970

**Above: Uriah Heep must be termed survivors, despite continual line up changes in the band.**

Uriah Heep (Mercury/—), 1970
Salisbury (Mercury/Vertigo), 1971
Demons And Wizzards (Mercury/Bronze), 1972 **CD**
The Magician's Birthday (Mercury/Bronze), 1972
Sweet Freedom (Warner Bros/Bronze), 1973
Wonderworld (Warner Bros/Bronze), 1974
The Best Of (Mercury/Bronze), 1975
Innocent Victim (Warner Bros/Bronze), 1977
Fallen Angel (Chrysalis/Bronze), 1978
Conquest (—/Bronze), 1980
Dreamer (—/Bronze), 1982
Head First (Mercury/Bronze), 1983
Equator (Portrait), 1985
Abominog (Castle Classics) **CD**
Anthology (Raw Power) **CD**

# Richie Valens

US vocalist, guitarist, composer.
Born Los Angeles, California, May 13, 1941; died February 3, 1959.

**Career:** Took up guitar age nine; became popular entertainer while in high school, appearing at school functions and local dances with own group, the Silhouettes. Spotted by Bob Keene of Del-Fi Records and signed to contract. First single **Come On Let's Go** was moderate success in US with cover version by Tommy Steele reaching UK Top 10.

Mexican background apparent in many recordings, with adaptation of traditional Mexican song **La Bamba** becoming best-known example; released with **Donna**, which became Valens' biggest hit. Made film debut in late 1958 singing **Ooh My Head** in rock 'n' roll teen drama movie 'Go Johnny Go'.

Embarked on first major tour through Mid-West US in January 1959. Halfway through tour, co-star Buddy Holly(▶) chartered plane to fly to next engagement; Valens won seat on aircraft by flipping coin with guitarist Tommy Allsup. Valens died with Holly and Big Bopper when plane crashed into snow-covered cornfield.

Death at age 17 cut short promising career, and Valens left relatively few recordings. However, he established chicano strain of rock, paving way for artists like Chris Montez. Interest in Valens leapt following success of 1987 biopic 'La Bamba', and fellow East LA denizens Los Lobos took Valens' hits into charts all over again.

**Hit Singles:**

|  | US | UK |
|---|---|---|
| Donna/La Bamba, 1958 | 2 | — |

**Albums:**
His Greatest Hits (—/President), 1970
Rock Lil' Darlin (—/Joy), 1971
History Of (Rhino), 1985

# Luther Vandross

US vocalist.
Born New York.

**Career:** Born and raised in New York, Vandross' earliest musical instincts were strongly encouraged by his family including an older singer who sang with the doo-wop group The Crests. Early musical influences included Aretha Franklin, Dionne Warwick and Diana Ross. In 1972 Vandross met Ken Harper, writer of the hit Broadway show The Wiz who included Vandross' song **Rejoice (A Brand New Day)** in the production.

Two years later Vandross arranged and sang backing vocals on David Bowie's Young Americans LP which included his song **Fascination**. He then worked with Bette Midler on her Songs For The New Depression LP and through her producer Arif Mardin starting doing sessions for Carly Simon, Chaka Khan and the Average White Band.

On the strength of session work Vandross formed his own progressive R&B band called Luther which broke up after only a couple of hits. He then signed with Epic Records as a solo artist (1981) and recorded a succession of finely-crafted albums which showcased his wide emotive range and helped him to slowly

Above: Luther Vandross, still getting to know how to make the record-playing public want him.

build up a strong following.

Vandross' fifth album **Give Me The Reason** included a surprisingly jazzy treatment of the Dionne Warwick classic **Anyone Who Had A Heart**; the title track was from the 'Ruthless People' soundtrack.

His 1987 London dates were all sell-outs in spite of the fact that Vandross has yet to score a big hit record in the UK. His style of emotive soul is guaranteed to keep him in the frontline however, and it can only be a matter of time before he achieves big UK success on vinyl.

Give Me The Reason, Luther Vandross. Courtesy Epic Records.

**Hit Singles:**

| | US | UK |
|---|---|---|
| I Really Didn't Mean It, 1987 | 16 | — |
| Stop To Love, 1987 | 12 | — |

**Albums**
Never Too Much (Epic), 1981
Busy Body (Epic), 1984
The Night I Fell In Love (Epic), 1985 **CD**
Forever For Always For Love (Epic), 1987
Give Me The Reason (Epic), 1987 **CD**

Left: Van Halen, with extrovert singer David Lee Roth in scarf.

# Van Halen

US group formed 1974.
**Original line-up:** David Lee Roth, vocals; Edward Van Halen, Gibson Flying V guitar; Mike Anthony, bass; Alex Van Halen, drums.

**Career:** Netherlands-born Van Halen brothers originally trained as concert pianists; family relocated in Pasadena, California. Formed group (originally known as Mammoth) with Roth and Anthony (both born in US Mid-West), and became popular local attraction through combination of loud and energetic heavy metal and Roth's very tight trousers. Due to inability to attract record deal, began promoting own gigs; used every possible attention-grabbing trick — like parachuting into stadium gig in successful attempt to upstage the headlining band.

By 1977, group were attracting audiences of 3,000. Warners Bros' A&R man Ted Templeman saw them playing in Hollywood club and signed them immediately.

Subsequent albums, all produced by Templeman, achieved major US chart success. **1984** LP contained superb **Jump** single.

At end of 1985 Roth left to pursue solo ambitions, scoring considerable success. Van Halen reconstituted with veteran metal merchant Sammy Hagar and went on to record biggest album of career, multiplatinum-selling **5150**. Disc also spawned US hit single **Why Can't This Be Love?**

Van Halen seem likely to continue as major draw, cornerstone of success being pyrotechnic guitar playing of Eddie Van Halen. Regarded by many as hottest fretboard artist in the business, Van Halen guested on Michael Jackson's all-time best selling album **Thriller**.

**Current line-up:** Edward Van Halen; Anthony; Alex Van Halen.

**Hit Singles:**

| | US | UK |
|---|---|---|
| Dance The Night Away, 1979 | 15 | — |
| Pretty Woman, 1982 | 12 | — |
| Jump, 1984 | 1 | 7 |
| I'll Wait, 1984 | 13 | — |
| Panama, 1984 | 13 | — |
| Why Can't This Be Love, 1986 | — | 8 |
| Love Walks In, 1987 | 14 | — |

*David Lee Roth Solo:*

| | | |
|---|---|---|
| California Girls, 1985 | 3 | — |
| Just A Gigolo/I Ain't Got Nobody, 1985 | 12 | — |

**Albums:**
Van Halen (Warner Bros), 1978 **CD**
Van Halen II (Warner Bros), 1979 **CD**
Women And Children First (Warner Bros), 1980
Fair Warning (Warner Bros), 1981
Diver Down (Warner Bros), 1982 **CD**
1984 (Warner Bros), 1984 **CD**
5150 (WEA), 1986 **CD**
*David Lee Roth Solo:*
Crazy From The Heat (Warner Bros), 1985

# Vangelis

Greek composer, keyboard player.
Born Vangelis Papathanassiou.

**Career:** During '60s came to prominence in native land as leader of Aphrodite's Child, who scored notable Euro hit with **Rain And Tears** single (1968) and **666** double LP (1972). Another member of group Demis Roussos later became famous for easy-listening hits.

After group split, Vangelis relocated to Paris to establish reputation as serious composer. Worked on score for film 'L'Apocalypse Des Animaux' with director Frederick Rossiff for notable LP. Moved to London in 1974. Initially regarded as flatulent upstart, Vangelis ignored major commercial failure and continued to work on electronic/synthesiser music through several poor-selling albums.

By 1980, had teamed with ex-Yes(▶) vocalist Jon Anderson—had been tipped to join Yes some years previously—for series of album projects. Crowning achievement is his work for multiple Oscar award winning 'Chariots Of Fire' movie, which won him Oscar for best score. Further film projects have included 'Blade Runner'. 'Bounty' and 'Mask'.

In 1985 Vangelis moved into yet another musical field when he wrote score for Royal Ballet's version of 'Frankenstein'.

**Hit Singles:**

| | US | UK |
|---|---|---|
| Chariots Of Fire (Main Theme), 1981 | — | 12 |

Below: Jon Anderson (left) and Vangelis Papathanassiou joined forces in 1980.

| | US | UK |
|---|---|---|
| Chariots Of Fire — Titles, 1982 | 1 | 41 |

*With Jon Anderson:*

| | | |
|---|---|---|
| I'll Find My Way Home, 1981 | 51 | 6 |

**Albums:**
Heaven And Hell (RCA), 1975
Albedo 0.39 (RCA), 1976
Spiral (RCA), 1977
Beauborg (RCA), 1978
Hypothesis (Affinity), 1978
Best Of (RCA), 1978
China (Polydor), 1979 **CD**
Short Stories (Polydor), 1979
See You Later (Polydor), 1980
Chariots Of Fire (Polydor), 1981 **CD**
Friends Of Mr. Cairo (Polydor), 1981
Private Collection (Polydor), 1983
Magic Moments (RCA), 1984
Spiral (RCA), 1984
Opera Sauvage (Polydor), 1984 **CD**
Soil Festivities (Polydor), 1984 **CD**
Apocalypse Des Animaux (Polydor), 1985 **CD**
Ignacio (Phonogram), 1985 **CD**
Invisible Connections (DGG), 1985 **CD**
Mask (Polydor), 1985 **CD**
Le Fete Sauvage (Phonogram), 1986 **CD**

# Bobby Vee

US vocalist.
Born Robert Velline, Fargo, North Dakota, April 30, 1943.

**Career:** Formed first band the Shadows in 1959. Made first appearance in hometown as direct result of Buddy Holly's(▶) death in plane crash on February 3. Holly and rest of 'Winter Dance Party' had been due to appear in Fargo that evening; Vee's group brought in as replacement. First record on local label, **Suzy Baby**, became local hit and was released nationally on Liberty, who signed Vee to long-term deal. In attempt to take over where Buddy Holly had left off, producer Snuff Garrett had Vee cover Adam Faith's(▶) UK hit **What Do You Want**, which in turn had been inspired by Holly's last recordings with pizzicato strings. Release failed but next single, **Devil Or Angel**, made Top 10, followed by Hollyish **Rubber Ball**, which became first of many UK hits.

During next three years, Vee became established as purveyor of Brill Building pop songs, with best material from Gerry Goffin and Carole King(▶), who wrote biggest hit **Take Good Care Of My Baby**. Although records and image were 'manufactured' to appeal to same market as Frankie Avalon(▶) and Fabian(▶), Vee's records had more lasting appeal due to careful production. Collaboration with Crickets in 1962 resulted in excellent **Bobby Vee Meets Crickets** album and sell-out tour of UK, with guests spots in 'Just For Fun' teen-movie. Appeal faded in mid-'60s despite attempts to score with contemporary material and 'fluke' comeback in 1967 with **Come Back When You Grow Up**.

Attempted further comeback in '70s under real name, but despite interesting album failed to make impression. Became Bobby Vee again in order to capitalise on old hits in nostalgia market.

**Hit Singles:**

| | US | UK |
|---|---|---|
| Devil Or Angel, 1960 | 6 | — |
| Rubber Ball, 1960 | 6 | 4 |
| How Many Tears, 1961 | — | 10 |
| Take Good Care Of My Baby, 1961 | 1 | 3 |
| Run To Him, 1961 | 2 | 6 |
| Please Don't Ask About Barbara, 1962 | 15 | 29 |
| Sharing You, 1962 | 15 | 10 |
| Punish Her, 1962 | 20 | — |
| A Forever Kind Of Love, 1962 | — | 13 |
| The Night Has A Thousand Eyes, 1962 | 3 | 3 |
| Charms, 1963 | 13 | — |
| Come Back When You Grow Up, 1967 | 3 | — |

**Albums (selected):**
Golden Greats (Liberty/—), 1968
Singles Album (—/Fame), 1982

# Suzanne Vega

US composer, vocalist.
Born New York.

**Career:** Encouraged into arts background by Puerto Rican father, she attended New York High School of Performing Arts (as portrayed by "Fame" movie and TV series) studying dance.

Grew up reading Sylvia Plath's introspective poetry and listening to Leonard Cohen and early (acoustic) Bob Dylan. Began performing self-composed songs in NY club scene and

**Solitude Standing, Suzanne Vega. Courtesy A&M Records.**

attracted attention of lawyer Ron Fierstein and studio engineer Steve Addabbo who immediately offered to manage her. Abbaddo also became her record producer when a deal with A&M was signed.

Vega soon gained image as 80s version of Joni Mitchell — cute, fey and lonely, clutching acoustic guitar for support — but insisted on still wearing battered old leather jacket on stage and refused to wear dresses.

Debut LP Suzanne Vega established her as strong songwriter in traditional vein but only reached wider audience in 1986 with **Left Of Centre** featured in "Pretty In Pink" youth movie and became surprise hit single.

Followed by **Marlene On The Wall** hit, sell-out world tour and **Solitude Standing**

album which showed sharper, more modern approach. Finally achieved true star status with hit single **Luka**, which concerned child cruelty, forcing even critics to view Vega with respect and admiration. Only the future will tell whether she adapts and thrives or returns to a musical ghetto of soft/folk-rock.

**Hit Singles:**

| | US | UK |
|---|---|---|
| Marlene On The Wall, 1985 | — | 21 |
| Left Of Centre, 1986 | — | 32 |
| Luka, 1987 | — | 3 |

**Albums:**
Suzanne Vega (A&M), 1985 **CD**
Solitude Standing (A&M), 1987 **CD**

# The Velvet Underground

US group formed 1966.
**Original line-up:** Lou Reed, guitar, vocals; John Cale, guitar, bass, viola; Maureen Tucker, drums, percussion.

**Career:** Ill-assorted group of talented subversives came together in New York's fertile and bustling 'alternative' music scene in 1966 — Cale(▶), a Welsh child prodigy, Reed(▶), a classically trained trumpet player, and Tucker, one of few female drummers to succeed in rock.

Outlook was direct and dramatic opposite of the 'flower power' scene that was burgeoning at that time. Group mercilessly spotlighted drugs, death and the bizarre. Struggled in NYC's underground clubs until discovery by media idol/artist Andy Warhol. He added Nico, one of his protégées, promoted them, and designed cover of first album, **The Velvet Underground And Nico** (1967).

Group's image, outlook and sound were shocking and incomprehensible at times. Literate, half-spoken vocals and dark slashing sound did not suit audience looking for peace and love, and connection with Warhol led some to view them as publicity stunt. Their pervading influence is now obvious in punk, new wave and Euro-pop, however.

Nico left after first album. Group recorded two more albums on Verve/Polydor, **White Light/White Heat** 1968) and **The Velvet Underground** (1969), but they were too controversial to meet with commercial success. In 1970 Cale and Reed left, both to pursue varied and lengthy solo careers. Morrison was joined by Bill and Doug Yule briefly, but the Velvets' natural life had come to an end by 1972.

**Final line-up:** Morrison; Bill Yule, drums; Doug Yule, guitar, bass, keyboards.

**Albums:**
White Light/White Heat (Verve), 1968 **CD**
The Velvet Underground (MGM), 1969 **CD**
Loaded (Cotillion/Atlantic), 1970
Live (with Lou Reed) (Mercury), 1969
Velvet Underground Live (Cotillion/Atlantic), 1970
VU (Polydor), 1985 **CD**
Another View (Polydor, Germany) **CD**

*Worth Searching Out:*
The Velvet Underground And Nico (Verve), 1967 **CD**

Left: Likened to Joni Mitchell, Suzanne Vega gained star status with Luka.

# Gene Vincent

US vocalist, composer.
Born Vincent Eugene Craddock, Norfolk, Virginia, February 11, 1935; died Hollywood, California, October 12, 1971.

**Career:** Took up music seriously following disablement due to leg injuries received in motorcycle accident at Norfolk Naval Base while merchant seaman. By 1956 secured regular spot on country music station WCMS with DJ 'Sheriff' Tex Davis acting as manager. Recorded demo of **Be-Bop-A-Lula** at WCMS studio and won contract with Capitol Records, who regarded Vincent as 'answer' to Elvis Presley. **Lula** rapidly became hit but despite making charts again in 1957 Vincent's popularity declined in US.

During short-lived road career with Blue Caps, Vincent was regarded as wildest rock 'n' roll act on and off stage, leaving wrecked hotels and dressing rooms in wake. Poor management and money problems with group forced him to cease touring in US. Continued to record for Capitol, occasionally producing classic tracks. Generally recording career lacked direction, with producer Ken Nelson veering towards MOR standards in attempt to broaden appeal.

During 1960 found new popularity in Britain with appearances on Jack Good's 'Boy Meets Girl' TV show. Despite setback of further injuries received in April 1960 car crash that killed Eddie Cochran(▶), continued to tour UK regularly and became hero of teddy-boy movement; scored several minor UK hits on Capitol before final decline to smaller labels and smaller club dates.

By 1969 Vincent was shadow of former self, beset by personal problems and alcoholism. Returned to California in 1971, where attempts to once again revive career failed. He died later that year from heart failure undoubtedly related to drink problems.

Cult following established during lifetime

**Below: The charismatic Gene Vincent, in Capitol Studios during the '50s.**

shows no sign of diminishing and echoes of Vincent's stye are still found in many rockabilly revival groups, notably in chart successes of the Stray Cats(▶).

| Hit Singles: | US | UK |
|---|---|---|
| Be-Bop-A-Lula, 1956 | 7 | 16 |
| Bluejean Bop, 1956 | — | 16 |
| Lotta Lovin', 1957 | 13 | — |
| My Heart, 1960 | — | 16 |
| Pistol Packin' Mama, 1960 | — | 15 |

**Albums:**
Gene Vincent's Greatest (Fame), 1977
The Gene Vincent Singles Album (Capitol), 1981
Gene Vincent and Eddie Cochran — Together Again (Capitol), 1980
Gene Vincent and Eddie Cochran — Rock 'n' Roll Heroes (Rockstar), 1981
The Bop They Couldn't Stop (Magnum Force), 1981
Dressed in Black (Magnum Force), 1982
Ain't That Too Much (Everest), 1982
Birdoggin' (Bulldog), 1982
For The Collectors Only (Magnum Force), 1984
I'm Back And I'm Proud (Nightflite) **CD**
Songs Of The James Dean Era (Capitol) **CD**
Born To Be A Rolling Stone (Charly), 1987 **CD**

*Gene Vincent and the Shouts:*
Shakin' Up A Storm (EMI), 1983

# Loudon Wainwright III

US composer, guitarist, vocalist.
Born Chapel Hill, North Carolina, September 5, 1947.

**Career:** Wainwright began appearing in East Coast clubs and bars in the late '60s. He clearly emphasised the folk side of rock by relying on acoustic guitar and funny between-songs patter. In 1971 Atlantic brought out **Album I** which continued folk trend with macabre subject matter. **Album II** emphasised outrage for sake of outrage à la Lenny Bruce.

Switching to Columbia, Wainwright found sense of balance between humour and making a point. **Album III** captured Wainwright at his best; **Red Guitar** tipped hat to Pete Townshend's(▶) stage antics, and **Dead Skunk** got into US Top 20. Wainwright also had realised limits of self-accompaniment and on this LP began using session musicians for recording and as back-up group on stage. He married Kate McGarrigle(▶) in 1973 and she appeared on **Unrequited** LP. (They had separated by 1978.)

Although always minority taste, Wainwright retains faithful following. Fans include British comedian/satirist Jasper Carrott, who featured Wainwright as resident troubadour in recent TV series.

| Hit Singles: | US | UK |
|---|---|---|
| Dead Skunk, 1973 | 16 | — |

**Albums:**
Album I (Atlantic), 1971
Album II (Atlantic), 1972
Album III (Columbia/CBS), 1973
Attempted Moustache (Columbia/CBS), 1974
Unrequited (Columbia/CBS), 1975
T-Shirt (Arista), 1976
Final Exam (Arista), 1978
Live One (—/Radar), 1979
Fame And Wealth (—/Demon), 1983

# Tom Waits

US composer, vocalist, pianist.
Born Pomona, California, December 7, 1949.

**Career:** Waits entertained small audiences on West Coast in early '70s. His rough voice and sparse back-up (usually piano, stand-up bass, drums and sax) evoked atmosphere of '50s Beatniks rather than '60s rock. Waits' tales of survival on other sides of tracks drew attention of Elektra, who signed him in 1973.

Waits' compositions started to get recorded by other artists and he opened for variety of acts from Charlie Rich to Frank Zappa. He has continued working throughout US and Europe but, despite rave critical approval, he remains cult figure on outskirts of rock. Waits' songs about lowlife are perceptive and poignant observations rather than critical judgements and his music seems best suited to dark, smoke-filled basement clubs and Bohemian cafés. This perhaps limits his potential for mass appeal, though he recently contributed to score for Francis Ford Coppola film; 'One From The Heart', and appeared in Coppola's movies 'Rumble Fish' (1983) and 'Cotton Club' (1985).

In recent years, more accessible output and burgeoning cult status threaten to combine to elevate Waits to mainstream success.

**Albums:**
Closing Time (Elektra), 1973
The Heart Of A Saturday Night (Elektra/Asylum), 1974
Nighthawks At The Diner (Asylum), 1975
Small Change (Asylum), 1976
Foreign Affairs (Elektra), 1977
Blue Valentine (Asylum), 1978
Heartattack And Vine (Asylum), 1980
Bounced Checks (Asylum), 1981
Swordfish Trombones (Island), 1983 **CD**
Asylum Years (Asylum), 1984 **CD**

Rain Dogs (Island), 1985 **CD**
Franks Wild Years (Island), 1987 **CD**

**Above: Franks Wild Years, Tom Waits. Courtesy Island Records.**

**Left: Consistently shying away from popular acclaim, cult figure Tom Waits.**

# Rick Wakeman

UK keyboard player, composer.
Born London, May 18, 1949.

**Career:** Born into musical family; father was professional pianist. Studied piano from age four. On leaving school attended Royal College of Music when he started to make mark as session musician. Eventually gave up studies in favour of recording world. Provided keyboards expertise for many top artists, including David Bowie(▶), T. Rex(▶) and Cat Stevens(▶) during late '60s/early '70s.

In 1970 Wakeman was asked to join emergent Strawbs(▶), and stayed with band for 16 months. But after Yes(▶) lost keyboards man Tony Kaye, they persuaded Wakeman to quit Strawbs(▶) and join them, which he did in summer 1971.

While with Yes, Wakeman became keyboard star, adding prodigious technique and classical influence to Yes' sometimes flatulent music. But, having already released one solo album, **Six Wives Of Henry VIII**, Wakeman split to pursue solo career in 1974.

Next album, **Journey To The Centre Of The Earth**, was huge success on both sides of Atlantic, and Wakeman built spectacular stage show around it. With following album, **The Myths And Legends Of King Arthur**, he went step further and produced musical spectacular on ice at London's Empire Pool, complete with 45-piece orchestra and 48-piece choir.

Continuing to make solo records, Wakeman nevertheless rejoined Yes in 1976, staying with group until end of 1979.

Quitting long-time label A&M in 1979, Wakeman did not record for two years until he came up with elaborate visionary work **1984** for Charisma. This became Top 30 UK album, and put Wakeman back on path of success. Following earlier excursions into film music **Lisztomania** (1975) and **White Rock** (1976), he scored horror movie 'The Burning' in 1982, following it with music for World Cup movie **G'Olé** in spring 1983.

Latterly Wakeman has kept relatively low profile, although upsurge of interest in so-called 'New Age' music has brought him back into favour in certain circles. It has also recently been reported that former champion carouser has become reformed character, espousing Christianity.

**Below: Keyboard maestro Rick Wakeman, an electro-pop pioneer.**

**Albums:**
Six Wives Of Henry VIII (A&M), 1973
Journey To The Centre Of The Earth (A&M), 1974
Myths And Legends Of King Arthur (A&M), 1975
Lisztomania (A&M), 1975
No Earthly Connection (A&M), 1976
White Rock (Soundtrack) (A&M), 1976
Criminal Record (A&M), 1977
Best Known Works (A&M), 1978
Rhapsodies (A&M), 1979
1984 (Charisma), 1981
The Burning (Charisma), 1982
G'Olé (Charisma), 1983
Silent Night (TBG), 1985
Country Airs (Coda), 1986 **CD**
The Family Album (President), 1987 **CD**
The Gospels (President), 1987 **CD**
New Age Collection (President), 1987 **CD**
Live At Hammersmith (President) **CD**
Crimes Of Passion (Soundtrack) (President), 1987

# Jerry Jeff Walker

US composer, guitarist, vocalist.
Born Onetona, New York, March 16, 1942.

**Career:** Legend has it that Walker left home as soon as possible to seek fame and fortune as folk singer. Several years of work followed until Beatles(▶) and Dylan(▶) killed off coffee-house scene. Various folk groups began transmuting into the Byrds(▶), Lovin' Spoonful(▶), Mamas And Papas(▶), Buffalo Springfield(▶). In this atmosphere Walker formed Circus Maximus in 1966. he made one good if unoriginal, folk-rock album, then left as rest of band wanted to follow on to next 'in' thing: jazz rock.

Returning to his first love, Walker made country-folk LP for Circus Maximus label, then split to ATCO when Vanguard showed no interest in releasing his style of music. It was while recording three ATCO LPs that Walker wrote **Mr Bojangles**, since covered countless times and US Top 10 hit for Nitty Gritty Dirt Band(▶).

On moving to Austin, Texas, Walker began exploring local talent and developing cowboy music in Willie Nelson(▶)/Waylon Jennings(▶) mould. His low-key approach hardly meshes with rock's high-powered business cycle of record, tour, record. His reluctance to sacrifice private life for life on road has kept following extremely limited. MCA (his label since 1972) seems content with this approach and Walker continues to play game his own way, i.e. to make music for fun and not to worry about size of audience.

**Above: The highly individual Jerry Jeff Walker, pictured in the '70s.**

**Albums:**
Mr Bojangles (Bainbridge/—), 1968
Driftin' My Way Of Life (Vanguard), 1969
Jerry Jeff Walker (MCA), 1972
Viva Terlingua (MCA/—), 1973
Walker's Collectables (MCA), 1974
Ridin' High (MCA), 1975
It's A Good Night For Singing (MCA/—), 1976
A Man Must Carry On (MCA), 1977
Contrary To Ordinary (MCA), 1978
Jerry Jeff (Elektra), 1978
Too Old To Change (Elektra), 1979
Best Of (MCA/—), 1980
Reunion (MCA), 1981
Cowjazz (MCA/—), 1982

# Joe Walsh

US guitarist, vocalist, composer.
Born Wichita, Kansas, November 20, 1947.

**Career:** First gained attention as star of the James Gang(▶), a Cleveland-based band who toured with the Who(▶) gathering critical raves. Walsh was propelling force of group, providing songs and fierce hard-rock guitar. Quit in 1971 and with drummer Joe Vitale and bassist Kenny Passarelli recorded solo LP, **Barnstorm**. After idea of developing Barnstorm into a working band fell apart, he recorded two albums. One, **The Smoker You Drink, The Player You Get,** went gold in 1973; from it came Top 30 single **Rocky Mountain Way**.

Signed with MCA in 1974. Released fairly interesting live LP, **You Can't Argue With A Sick Mind** (1976). Joined the Eagles(▶) same year, becoming part of that group's best line-up, Walsh's guitar adding bite to band's progressive LA harmonies. Continued with his solo projects; contributed theme song for movie 'The Warriors' in 1978, and played on sessions for Randy Newman(▶), Emerson, Lake and Palmer(▶), and Warren Zevon(▶), among others. Had hit single with **Life's Been Good to Me** from **But Seriously Folks** LP.

In 1982 the Eagles announced their break-up. Walsh worked with John Entwistle(▶) on his **Too Late The Hero** album then the following year began major US tour opening for Stevie Nicks. Continues to record solo with limited success.

| Hit Singles: | US | UK |
|---|---|---|
| Life's Been Good To Me, 1978 | 12 | 14 |
| All Night Long, 1980 | 19 | — |

**Albums:**
*Barnstorm:*
Barnstorm (Dunhill/Probe), 1972
(See also James Gang, Eagles)

*Solo:*
The Smoker You Drink, The Player You Get (Dunhill/Probe), 1973 **CD**
So What (Dunhill/Probe), 1974
You Can't Argue With A Sick Mind (ABC-MCA/Anchor), 1976 **CD**
But Seriously Folks... (Asylum), 1978
Best Of (ABC-MCA/—), 1978 **CD**
There Goes The Neighborhood (Asylum), 1981
You Bought It You Name It (Warner Bros), 1983 **CD**
The Confessor (Warner Bros), 1985
Got Any Gum (WEA), 1987 **CD**
Live (MCA), 1986

**So What, Joe Walsh. Courtesy ABC Records.**

# Jennifer Warnes

US singer.
Born Orange County, California.

**Career:** Made her professional debut at seven wrapped in an American flag singing the "Star Spangled Banner" accompanied by 300 accordians. Weaned on the Los Angeles folk circuit, Warnes took the female lead in the West Coast production of "Hair", and also had a weekly stint on the Smothers Brothers Comedy Hour television programme.

She made one album for Warner Brothers produced by John Cale before signing to Arista. Single **Right Time Of The Night** reached the UK charts in 1975 followed by **I Know A Heartache When I See One** from the **Shot Through The Heart** album.

Associated next with a number of major themes, including the Academy award-winning **It Goes Like It Goes** from "Norma Rae" in 1979, in 1981 she performed Randy Newman's **One More Hour** for his ragtime score, and it received an Oscar nomination.

Her biggest hit to date is **Up Where We Belong** from "An Officer And A Gentleman", duetted with Joe Cocker and a number one single in US, Canada, the UK, and Australia, as well as winning an Oscar, a Golden Globe award, a Grammy, and the Grand Prix Award at the Tokyo Music Festival.

**Famous Blue Raincoat** features songs written by Leonard Cohen, including several originals, with Cohen contributing vocals to the track "Joan Of Arc".

Never afraid to take unconventional musical routes, Warnes' solo chart success has been less than that for many contemporaries but she has gained respect for her individual approach to new musical projects.

| Hit Singles: | | US | UK |
|---|---|---|---|
| *(With Joe Cocker)* | | | |
| Up Where We Belong, 1985 | | 1 | 1 |
| *(With Bill Medley)* | | | |
| The Time Of My Life, 1987 | | 1 | — |

**Albums**
Shot Through The Heart (Arista), 1979
Best Of (Arista), 1982
Famous Blue Raincoat (RCA/Cypress), 1987 **CD**

**Famous Blue Raincoat, Jennifer Warnes. Courtesy RCA Records.**

# Dionne Warwick

US vocalist.
Born East Orange, New Jersey, December 12, 1941.

**Career:** Studied music from age six. Sang with family gospel group Drinkard Singers. After further music training at Hart College of Music in Connecticut, Warwick (she has gone back and forth between Warwick and Warwicke spellings) moved to New York and became back-up singer. Often worked with sister Dee Dee, and aunt Cissy Houston.

Songwriters/producers Burt Bacharach and Hal David were impressed by her work on Drifters'(▶) session and arranged contract with Sceptre Records. Warwick's first solo release, written by them, was **Don't Make Me Over**; it became US hit and started huge run of success for Bacharach-David-Warwick partnership. Team created some of classiest romantic pop music ever recorded; Bacharach's distinctive and often subtle melodies, David's above-average lyrics and Warwick's ethereal but soulful voice combined to produce clutch of classics.

Nevertheless, by late '60s formula was wearing thin and Warwick attempted to revive flagging career by switching to Warner Bros and experimenting with various producers. Arrived back in limelight through pairing with Spinners on **Then Came You**, a 1974 No. 1.

Second major phase of career started with signing to Arista. Barry Manilow(▶)-produced 1979 LP **Dionne** was million-seller, and further Arista albums have also scored heavily. Latterly Warwick has enjoyed greater than ever success.

A talented artist with truly distinctive vocal approach, Warwick has managed to avoid

Left: Jennifer Warne's output has been occasional so far, but never lacking in quality.

in 1945. He became company's musical father figure, helping to nurture many careers, including those of his sidemen Otis Spann (his half-brother), Little Walter, Jimmie Rodgers(▶), and emergent R&B/rockers Bo Diddley(▶) and Chuck Berry(▶).

Waters, a true giant of the blues, was indisputably the major figure of Chicago blues scene through the '50s (when he logged 12 American R&B chart hits) and into '60s. Some of his best-known songs, **Rollin' Stone, Got My Mojo Working**, and **Mannish Boy**, became fodder for countless British and American R&B/rock bands, most notably the Rolling Stones(▶) (named after Waters' hit) and Johnny Winter(▶). In recent years he recorded for Winter's Blue Sky label, and still showed enormous musical powers despite ailing health, which culminated in death from heart failure in 1983.

### Albums (selected):
Can't Get No Grinding (Chess), 1973
Back In The Early Days (—/Syndicate), 1977
Hard Again (Blue Sky), 1977
I'm Ready (Blue Sky), 1977
Live (Blue Sky), 1977
Chess Masters (Chess), 1981
King Bee (Blue Sky), 1981
Hoochie Coochie Man (Blue Sky), 1983
Rare And Unissued (Chess), 1985
Collection (De-Ja Vu), 1985 **CD**
On Chess Vol. 1 (1948-1951), 1986 **CD**
On Chess Vol. 2 (1951-1959), 1986 **CD**

*Worth Searching Out:*
Electric Mud (Cadet), 1968

worst excesses of MOR while at same time steering clear of disco route. Her perfectionist approach ensures that she will be able to pursue successful career for years to come.

**Heartbreaker, Dionne Warwick.
Courtesy Arista Records.**

### Hit Singles:
| | US | UK |
|---|---|---|
| Anyone Who Had A Heart, 1964 | 8 | 42 |
| Walk On By, 1964 | 6 | 9 |
| You'll Never Get To Heaven, 1964 | 34 | 20 |
| Reach Out For Me, 1964 | 20 | 23 |
| Message To Michael, 1966 | 8 | — |
| Alfie, 1967 | 15 | — |
| I Say A Little Prayer/Valley of The Dolls, 1967 | 4 | — |
| Valley Of The Dolls/I Say A Little Prayer, 1968 | 2 | 28 |
| Do You Know The Way To San Jose, 1968 | 10 | 8 |
| Promises Promises, 1968 | 19 | — |
| This Girl's In Love With You, 1969 | 7 | — |
| You've Lost That Lovin' Feeling, 1969 | 16 | — |
| I'll Never Fall In Love Again, 1970 | 6 | — |
| I'll Never Love This Way Again, 1979 | 5 | — |
| Deja Vu, 1979 | 15 | — |
| Heartbreaker, 1982 | 10 | 2 |
| All The Love In The World, 1983 | — | 12 |
| That's What Friends Are For, 1985 | 1 | 16 |

*With Detroit Spinners:*
| Then Came You, 1974 | 1 | 9 |

*With Jeffrey Osbourne:*
| Love Power, 1987 | 12 | — |

### Albums:
Greatest Hits Volume 1 (—/Hallmark), 1973
Greatest Hits Volume 2 (—/Hallmark), 1973
Greatest Hits Volume 3 (—/Hallmark), 1974
Greatest Hits Volume 4 (—/Hallmark), 1975
Collection (—/Pickwick), 1976 **CD**
Dionne (Arista), 1979
No Night So Long (Arista), 1980
Golden Collection (—/K-Tel), 1981
Hot Live & Otherwise (Arista), 1981
Friends In Love (Arista), 1982 **CD**
Heartbreaker (Arista), 1982 **CD**
Golden Hits Volume 1 (—/Phoenix), 1982
Golden Hits Volume 2 (—/Phoenix), 1982
So Amazing (Arista), 1983 **CD**
Without Your Love (Arista), 1985 **CD**
Reservations For Two (Arista), 1987 **CD**

Walk On By And Other Favourites (Charly), 1988 **CD**
20 Greatest Hits (Bescol), 1988 **CD**

# Muddy Waters
US vocalist, guitarist, composer.
Born McKinley Morganfield, Rolling Fork, Mississippi, April 4, 1915; died April 30, 1983.

**Career:** Raised on a plantation in Clarksdale, Mississippi, where he was discovered and recorded by folklorist Alan Lomax for the Library of Congress in 1941. Walters joined the great wartime black exodus to the Northern industrial cities, settling in Chicago in 1943 and quickly establishing himself in its vibrantly exciting blues circuit.

Leonard and Phil Chess signed Waters to their Aristocrat label (soon re-named Chess)

**Below: Muddy Waters on stage in the '70s with his trusty Fender Telecaster.**

**Muddy Mississippi Waters Live.
Courtesy Blue Sky Records.**

# Wax
UK/US duo formed 1986.

**Current line-up:** Andrew Gold, vocals/keyboards; Graham Gouldman, guitar/bass/vocals.

**Career:** American Gold (son of Hollywood composer Ernest Gold, former keyboard player with Linda Ronstadt and Jackson Browne, but also successful solo artist himself) and Englishman Gouldman (sixties songwriter and former member of The Mindbenders and Hotlegs) were introduced in 1982; Gold then co-wrote three tracks with Gouldman and fellow 10CC member Eric Stewart for band's **Ten Out Of Ten** album.

When 10CC dissolved in 1984, Gold joined Gouldman in UK to continue writing material with no clear aim as to use. After two months' work together, christened themselves Wax, signed record deal with RCA and released 1986 debut album, **Magnetic Heaven** to critical and commercial indifference. Two singles **Right Between The Eyes** and **Hear**

Above: Wax duo Graham Gouldman (left) late of 10cc, with his partner Andrew Gold.

**No Evil** failed to chart.

1987 saw release of second album, **American English**, spawning deserved UK Top 10 hit single **Bridge To Your Heart** followed by minor hit of title track.

Given their backgrounds in high-quality pop music, it's no surprise Wax's music relies heavily on instant melodies and clever arrangements, blending together attributes of 10CC, Billy Joel and Steely Dan, but without their lyrical bite or musical innovation.

Towards mid-1988, Wax were rehearsing for first-ever concert dates and planning third album. Unlikely to inspire lifetime devotion but always to be relied on for catchy pop songs, Gold and Gouldman — whether together or apart — will be around for many, many years.

**Hit Singles:**     US   UK
Bridge To Your Heart, 1987    —   12

**Albums:**
Magnetic Heaven (RCA), 1986 **CD**
American English (RCA) 1987

Below: Joe Zawinul, founder member of jazz/rockers Weather Report.

# Weather Report

US group formed 1970.

**Original line-up:** Josef Zawinul, keyboards, synthesiser; Wayne Shorter, saxophones; Miroslav Vitous, bass; Alphonse Mouzon, drums; Airto Moreira, percussion.

**Career:** Most durable of all jazz/rock aggregations that sprung to life in late '60s/early '70s. Formed by Austrian (born Vienna) Zawinul and Shorter (born Newark, NJ).

Hold impressive jazz credentials: Zawinul worked with Cannonball Adderley; Miles Davis (recorded **Bitches Brew**); composed standards **Mercy Mercy Mercy** and **In A Silent Way**; earned Grammy in 1967 for best instrumental performance. Shorter (ex-Art Blakey, Miles Davis) was prominent tenor player before switching affection to alto sax. Czech-born Vitous had recorded/performed with Art Farmer, Freddie Hubbard, Brookmeyer-Terry Quintet, Miles Davis, Stan Getz and Herbie Mann. Brazilian Airto worked with Lee Morgan and Miles Davis. South Carolinan Mouzon recorded/performed with Roy Ayers and did sessions for Roberta Flack(▶) and Gene McDaniels.

Moreiro quit shortly after release of debut **Weather Report** (1970). LP earned plaudits from jazz and rock critics alike; set recording pattern of tight percussive music with emphasis on interplay between Zawinul and Shorter. Tracks were totally melodic, opening new avenues for those usually reluctant to listen to normal complexity of jazz

Unit has subsequently undergone various personnel changes: Vitous left in 1974 after release of **Mysterious Traveller**. Replace-

ment Jaco Pastorius remained until 1979 and **Mr Gone** set. Bass duties were taken over by Abe Laboriel. Mouzon moved to McCoy Tyner group in '72, and then Larry Coryell's 11th House. Is now prominent session player and sometime leader of own band. Drum seat was permanently filled by Pete Erskine (ex-Stan Kenton and Maynard Ferguson) in 1978. Percussionists who have graced group's work include Alex Acuna, Ishmael Wilburn, Tony Williams. Steve Gadd and Eric Garratt, group drummer from 1972-76. Weather Report had earned various poll honours throughout world before band split in 1987, also the year that former member Jaco Pastorins was killed. They had been regular recipients of 'Downbeat' magazine's Best Group plaudit. Debut album also won Downbeat award. Unit's popularity had extended worldwide, particularly Japan; they were infrequent but welcome visitors to Europe. Weather Report's authority in jazz/rock market had outlasted all contemporaries. Zawinful and Shorter have gone separate ways.

**Final line-up:** Zawinful, Shorter, were core of constantly changing line-up.

**Albums:**
Weather Report (Columbia/CBS), 1970
I Sing The Body Electric (Columbia/CBS), 1972
Sweetnighter (Columbia/CBS), 1973
Mysterious Traveller (Columbia/CBS), 1974
Tail Spinnin' (Columbia/CBS), 1975
Black Market (Columbia/CBS), 1976 **CD**
Heavy Weather (Columbia/CBS), 1977 **CD**
Mr Gone (Columbia/CBS), 1978
8.30 (Columbia/CBS), 1979
Night Passage (Columbia/CBS), 1980 **CD**
Weather Report (Columbia/CBS), 1981
Procession (Columbia/CBS), 1983
Domino Theory (Columbia/CBS), 1984 **CD**
Sportin' Life (Columbia/CBS), 1985

# Wham!

UK duo formed 1982.
George Michael, vocals; born George Michael Panos, London, June 26, 1963.
Andrew Ridgeley, guitar; born Jan. 1963.

**Make It Big, Wham!
Courtesy Epic Records.**

**Career:** Michael and Ridgeley as teenage North Londoners had been in various no-hope groups before joining forces in summer 1982 and recording as duo, co-writing material. First single **Wham! Rap (Enjoy What You Do)** was well received by pop press and in clubs, but not played on daytime radio due to so-called contentious lyrics concerning problems faced by jobless youth.

Second single **Young Guns (Go For It)** covered lyrical ground, but achieved radio play to become Top 3 hit at end of 1982. Follow-up **Bad Boys**, released March 1983, made No. 2 in UK; first LP **Fantastic** followed. Early part of 1984 was spent writing material

Left: George Michael and Andrew Ridgeley of Wham! before their farewell concert. Now with solo careers of differing levels of success.

*George Michael Solo:*
(See separate entry)

**Albums:**
Fantastic (—/Innervision), 1983
Make It Big (Epic), 1984
The Final (Epic), 1986 **CD**

# Whitesnake

UK group formed 1978.
**Original line-up:** David Coverdale, vocals; Micky Moody, guitar; Bernie Marsden, guitar; Jon Lord, keyboards; Neil Murray, bass; David Dowle, drums.

**Career:** Coverdale joined 1973 Deep Purple(▶) line-up and stayed with band until its demise in 1976. 1977 saw release of solo LP, **Whitesnake**. It disappeared but Coverdale had more success with next solo project, **Northwinds**. Once legal problems were sorted out (allowing him to play live again), Coverdale formed stable line-up. Band released **Trouble** while undertaking extensive UK tour. Sound was basic R&B-influenced rock, pioneered decade before by Deep Purple and others.

**Snakebite** and **Love Hunter** continued in same style with danger of Whitesnake becoming cliché. Dowle was replaced by Purplemate Ian Paice to roughen up edges of band's backbeat.

**Fool For Your Loving** single proved band could reach mass appeal. **Ready An' Willing** sold well enough to encourage recording of double live set, **Live In The Heart Of The City** (title reflected place of origin: Hammersmith Odeon, London). **Come An' Get It** was next release and revealed basic problem: music was loud and energetic, but it sounded as if everyone could play it in their sleep. **Saints An' Sinners** saw revised line-up, and continuing personnel changes have bugged band. Most significant was departure of Lord upon re-formation of Deep Purple(▶) in 1984. Current members now seek to restore fortunes.

Latterly however reconstituted band has gone from strength to strength, conquering US and world with platinum album **Whitesnake** and developing genre that might be called 'designer metal'. Videos feature moody Coverdale with moody girls, all with identical highly-moussed 'glamour' hairstyles.

Band's time has finally come, and outfit looks set to join higher echelons of bankable stadium-rockers.

**Current line-up:** Coverdale, Neil Murray, bass; Cozy Powell, drums; Richard Bailey, keyboards; John Sykes, guitar.

| Hit Singles: | US | UK |
|---|---|---|
| Fool For Your Loving, 1980 | 53 | 13 |
| Don't Break My Heart Again, 1981 | — | 17 |
| Still Of The Night, 1987 | — | 16 |
| Here I Go Again, 1987 | 1 | 9 |
| Is This Love?, 1987 | 2 | 9 |

The most recent album, Whitesnake. Courtsey EMI Records.

**Albums:**
Trouble (United Artists), 1978
Love Hunter (United Artists), 1979
Ready An' Willing (Mirage/United Artists), 1980
Live In The Heart Of The City (Mirage/United Artists), 1980
Come An' Get It (Atlantic/Liberty), 1981
Saints An' Sinners (—/Liberty), 1982
Trouble (Fame), 1982
Lovehunter (Fame), 1984
Slide It In (Liberty), 1985
Whitesnake (EMI), 1987 **CD**

**Below: Former boutique salesman David Coverdale (left) of Whitesnake infamy.**

for **Make It Big** LP, which was recorded in South of France. Set contained Wham!'s first UK number one single **Wake Me Up (Before You Go Go)**.

Group established international following in 1985, touring China and breaking through in States. Wham! claimed Chinese tour had cost them £1m; publicity value was further heightened when member of support band stabbed himself on flight to Canton.

Subject to frivolous gossip-mongering in Britain's tabloid press, duo found it hard to be taken seriously, despite undoubted talent; Michael was recipient of 1985 Ivor Novello 'Songwriter of the Year' award. Pair also featured in Band Aid and Live Aid events, 1985, but in early '86 there were reports of split because of management problems.

Beneath pop image, Wham! undoubtedly have knack for Motown-influenced commercial material. Films may be their future, most certainly for George Michael, while Andrew Ridgeley may be content to crash racing cars.

Meanwhile both members of duo were attracting individual attention, Ridgeley for typical 'pop-star' antics (crashing racing cars, drunken horseplay) and Michael for songwriting talent (1985 Ivor Novello Songwriter Of Year Award.)

Inevitable split came in 1986, with Ridgeley going on to do little other than attract attention of gossip columnists, Michael embarking on hugely successful career as solo artist.

One hit followed another, with Michael increasingly showing himself to be a vocalist of real class (witness creditable performance on duet with soul diva Aretha Franklin.)

At time of writing Michael's **Faith** album is topping US charts, having spun off slew of hit singles, and artist is one of most successful solo acts in world. Interesting character who combines liberal social attitudes with penchant for pop star high life, Michael is all-round talent who can undoubtedly look forward to long shelf-life.

| Hit Singles: | US | UK |
|---|---|---|
| Young Guns (Go For It), 1982 | — | 3 |
| Bad Boys, 1983 | — | 2 |
| Club Tropicana, 1983 | — | 4 |
| Club Fantastic Megamix, 1983 | — | 15 |
| Wake Me Up (Before You Go Go), 1984 | 1 | 1 |
| Freedom, 1984* | 3 | 1 |
| Last Christmas, 1984 | — | 1 |
| Everything She Wants, 1985 | 1 | 2 |
| I'm Your Man, 1985 | 20 | 1 |
| Edge Of Heaven, 1987 | 9 | — |

*1985 in US

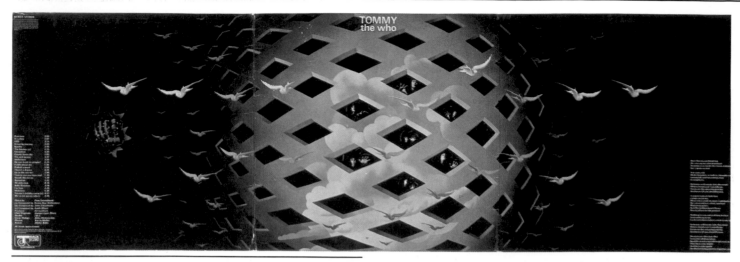

# The Who

UK group formed 1964.

**Original line-up:** Pete Townshend, guitar, keyboards, vocals; Roger Daltrey, vocals; John Entwistle, bass, horns, vocals; Keith Moon, drums.

**Career:** While at Acton County Grammar School, Townshend(▶) and Entwistle(▶) joined Daltrey's(▶) band the Detours in 1962. Townshend's mother got boys audition with Commercial Entertainments Ltd's Bob Druce; they were soon doing gigs on his club circuit, playing mostly R&B and Top 10 covers. Originally a five-piece, Detours went through several singers and guitarists until Daltrey switched from guitar to vocals; they then stayed a four-piece with Townshend on lead, Entwistle on bass, and Dougie Sandom on drums. Became Who when they saw another band named Detours on TV. Were introduced to Helmut Gorden, an enterprising door-knob manufacturer; he became manager, took all earnings and put band on weekly wage.

More influential, however, was Pete Meaden, a fast-talking, pill-popping freelance publicist enamoured with the world of 'mods' — Meaden decided Who were perfect for mod audience; convinced band to change name to High Numbers (a 'number' being a mod). He introduced them to the fashions of Carnaby Street. Wrote and produced a mod single for them, **I'm The Face/Zoot Suit**, on Fontana in July 1964; it flopped, despite widespread publicity, probably because Meaden had simply written new lyrics to Slim Harpo's **Got Love If You Want It**.

Band didn't really arrive at the perfect formula until one night at the Royal Oldfield Hotel. A cocky young kid in the audience announced he could play drums better than their drummer (a substitute — Sandem had left band), and proved it by demolishing the drumkit in the interval; Keith Moon(▶) was in.

Meaden had ideas, but no money, so when Kit Lambert stopped by the Railway Hotel in Harrow to see High Numbers, he persuaded them to let him, and his partner Chris Stamp, take over management. Meaden was dropped, and band became Who again. It was at the Railway that Townshend smashed his first guitar: he accidentally broke the neck of his 12-string Rickenbacker on very low ceiling; mishap getting no reaction from audience, Townshend proceeded to smash it to smithereens. This got such a reaction that Lambert encouraged Townshend (and Moon, who followed suit and kicked over his drumkit) to continue instrument-destroying as a publicity stunt. Became the traditional ending to a Who performance.

Lambert bought Townshend two Vortexian tape recorders; he came up with first demo, **I**

**Can't Explain**, which later sold itself to Kinks(▶) producer Shel Talmy. Talmy became Who producer; got band recording contract with US Decca, then UK Decca. While in residency Tuesday nights at Marquee Club in Soho in early '65, still playing mostly R&B covers, Who recorded **I Can't Explain** at Pye Studios. Helped by first 'Top of the Pops' appearance, single went to No. 8 in UK. From then on Townshend continued to write 90% of Who material (Entwistle contributed remainder).

Four months later, second single, **Anyway, Anyhow, Anywhere**, which featured feedback (then so revolutionary that their record company sent it back, convinced strange noises were a mistake), went to No. 10 in the UK and became signature tune for TV's music show 'Ready, Steady, Go'. Third single that year not only surpassed others in sales, reaching No. 2 in UK, but also in notoriety. **My Generation** was soon adopted as anthem for the young with its controversial angry, stuttered lyric, 'Hope I die before I get old'.

With three hit singles and first LP, **My Generation (The Who Sing My Generation** in US), doing well, bookings were up. Earnings trebled, yet Who remained in debt because of continued instrument smashing. On top of financial worries, there were personality clashes, internal power struggles, constant threats to split up (which continued for 20 years), and management/producer problems. With conflict on all sides, Who ended up in legal battle with Shel Talmy over **Substitute**, their next single. Despite being released on two different labels it reached No. 5 in Britain, and Talmy bowed out for a percentage. Lambert produced single that followed, **I'm A Boy**, which climbed to No. 2 in UK. Later that year, band had first US hit, **Happy Jack**, followed by success with seemingly innocent song about masturbation, **Pictures Of Lily**, and slightly psychedelic Top 10 hit both sides of the Atlantic, **I Can See For Miles**. The Who had moved away from mod, and after brief pop art phase (Union Jack jackets, target T-shirts, slightly longer hair) dabbled briefly in semi-hippie look until late '60s.

First live dates in America were with Murray the K show in New York. Later that year toured extensively in US as support for Herman's Hermits(▶), a tour that made them rather unpopular with hotel managers. It was their appearance at Monterey Pop Festival, aided by first national US TV appearance on the Smothers Brothers Show, that sold them to America. Both shows made use of smoke bombs and self-destrucion.

Until **Tommy**, the Who were basically a singles band. Neither **A Quick One** nor **The Who Sell Out** LPs did particularly well. Though **Sell Out** had brilliant basis for an album — a radio station format with adverts and jingles between tracks—the cover, with Daltrey sitting in bath of baked beans, drew more attention.

Top: The triptych cover of Tommy. The Who. Courtesy Polydor Records. Left: The Who, circa 1965-what youthful innocence!

Above: A feature of early Who shows was an instrument destroying finale, apparently conceived by the group in order to avoid encores.

In 1969 Who released their long-awaited double LP **Tommy**; A 'rock opera' concept album chronicling the adventures of a deaf, dumb and blind boy, with spiritual overtones, it was dedicated to Townshend's Indian master Meher Baba. From now on Who music was more obsessed with problems of adolescent males, as lyrics grew more politically, socially and spiritually thought-provoking. Daltrey became more of a front man; band spent two years performing **Tommy** live in its entirety, taking it eventually to several European opera houses. Received 14-minute standing ovation at NY's Metropolitan Opera House. One of the most familiar Who images of era was Daltrey in long blonde curls and leather fringe twirling his mike, and Townshend in white boiler suit doing scissor leaps, performing **Tommy**, was part of the Woodstock festival; Woodstock absolutely confirmed Who's future success in US.

In 1970 released **Live at Leeds**; many critics regard it as fine example of live Who concert. The Who have long been considered one of the top live acts in rock 'n' roll. Few can match their intensity and versatility and few moments in rock are more universally moving than the **See Me, Feel Me** finale.

After very trying work on another ambitious concept LP, **Lifehouse**, failed, remains were salvaged to make **Who's Next**, first LP produced by Glyn Johns, and first to feature synthesisers, used frequently thereafter.

The next major project, **Quadrophenia**, returned to sound of band's early days, and again used mod culture as vehicle to address adolescence. **Quadrophenia** was vastly underrated (criticised mostly for over-orchestration), only fully appreciated in 1979 when repackaged as movie soundtrack for Who film of same name, which coincided with the UK rebirth of the mod movement.

By 1975, all four Who members had made at least one solo album. Entwistle put together **Odds & Sods**, an LP of old Who rarities to appease fans, but no new Who material was being recorded.

It seemed that nothing could match the success of **Tommy**; in 1975 it was Ken Russell's 'Tommy' film, with Daltrey in leading role, and soundtrack LP, which brought band whole new following, rather than new album, **Who By Numbers**. Poorly received, melancholy **Numbers** addressed problems of ageing; single **Squeeze Box** made US Top 20 and UK Top 10.

Back on the road in 1975-76, the Who were selling out soccer stadiums; May '76 concert at Charlton Athletic Ground earned them a place in the Guinness Book of World Records for loudest concert.

After problems with Lambert and Stamp, Bill Curbishley stepped in as manager. There was a long lull in recording until 1978 when **Who Are You** was completed. The LP and single of the same name were Who's biggest sellers since original **Tommy**.

Untimely death of drummer Keith Moon on September 7, 1978 forced Who to consider

The original Quadrophenia album, The Who. Courtesy Polydor Records.

The Kids Are Alright, soundtrack compilation. Courtesy Polydor Records.

folding, but by early '79 pressed on with ex-Small Faces(▶), Faces(▶) drummer Kenney Jones. Jones made live debut with new Who at London's Rainbow; soon press was hailing 1979 'Year of the Who'. Extensive touring and two successful Who films 'The Kids Are Alright', a film biography of the band, and 'Quadrophenia' with accompanying Who soundtracks put Who back in business. However, year ended in tragedy when 11 Who fans were crushed to death at Cincinnati concert on December 3, 1979. Devastated, Who again considered disbanding, but continued US tour well into 1980.

**Face Dances** in 1981, the first new material in three years, was produced by Bill Szymcyzk. Some thought it innovative, but most considered it wrong for the Who. Single **You Better, You Bet** made US Top 20, but at this point the Who were being largely ignored in UK. Worry over responsibility of the band and the efforts of balancing stardom with family life drove Townshend to drink and drugs. Some felt the Who were finished. But Townshend pulled himself together, going completely straight in early '82. Much relieved, the other members were anxious to contribute to next LP (returning to producer Glyn Johns) **It's Hard**, which erased bad press of **Face Dances**; in conjunction with tours in US, LP proved band was still strong.

In 1982 band decided to call it a day, going out in style with US 'Farewell Tour' which was hottest concert ticket of year, grossing 40 million dollars. Band regrouped for 1985 'Live Aid' show at Wembley, and continue to get together again when occasion calls for it (1988 BPI awards ceremony, for example.) Townshend works as editor for British publishing company Faber while continuing with solo projects like 1986's **White City** album/video. Daltrey continue to record solo (results receiving mixed reception), and while no doubt still hoping to die before he gets old, was recently seen as TV spokesman for American Express.

The Who were undoubtedly one of great bands of 60s/70s, potent mixture of rebel sensibility and explosive creativity. Interesting contributions may still be expected from individual members.

**Current line-up:** Townshend; Daltrey; Entwistle; Kenney·Jones, drums.

**Left: Meaty, Beaty, Big & Bouncy (back cover), The Who. Courtesy Polydor.**

**Below left: Bearded Pete Townshend onstage in 1971.**

**Below: US Tour 1980, with Pete Townshend (right) and Kenney Jones.**

| Hit Singles: | US | UK |
|---|---|---|
| I Can't Explain, 1965 | — | 8 |
| Anyway, Anyhow, Anywhere, 1965 | — | 10 |
| My Generation, 1965 | — | 2 |
| Substitute, 1966 | — | 5 |
| I'm A Boy, 1966 | — | 2 |
| Happy Jack, 1966 | 24 | 3 |
| Pictures Of Lily, 1967 | 51 | 4 |
| I Can See For Miles, 1967 | 9 | 10 |
| Pinball Wizard, 1969 | 19 | 4 |
| The Seeker, 1970 | 44 | 19 |
| See Me Feel Me/Overture From Tommy, 1970 | 12 | — |
| Won't Get Fooled Again, 1971 | 15 | 9 |
| Let's See Action, 1971 | — | 16 |
| Join Together, 1972 | 17 | 9 |
| 5.15, 1973 | 45 | 20 |
| Squeeze Box, 1975 US, 1976 UK | 16 | 10 |
| Substitute (re-issue), 1976 | — | 7 |
| Who Are You, 1978 | 14 | 18 |
| You Better, You Bet, 1981 | 18 | — |

**Albums:**
Tommy (Decca/Track), 1969 **CD**
Live At Leeds (Decca/Track), 1970 **CD**
Who's Next (Decca/Track), 1971 **CD**
Meaty, Beaty, Big & Bouncy (Decca/Track), 1971†
Quadrophenia (MCA/Track), 1973 **CD**
Odds & Sods (MCA/Track), 1974
A Quick One/Sell Out (MCA/Track), 1974*
Magic Bus/My Generation, 1974*
Tommy (soundtrack) (Polydor/Polydor), 1975
The Who By Numbers (MCA/Polydor), 1975
The Story Of The Who (—/Polydor), 1976†
Who Are You (MCA/Polydor), 1978
The Kids Are Alright (soundtrack) (MCA/Polydor), 1979
Quadrophenia (soundtrack) (Polydor/Polydor), 1979
My Generation (re-issue) (—/Virgin), 1979
Live At Leeds/Who Are You (—/Polydor), 1980*
Face Dances (Warner Bros/Polydor), 1981
Hooligans (MCA/—), 1981†
It's Hard (Warner Bros/Polydor), 1982 **CD**
Who's Greatest Hits (MCA/—), 1983†
Rarities (—/Polydor), 1983
One Upon A Time, (Polydor), 1983
The Singles (Polydor), 1984 **CD**
*Double Re-issues
†Compilations

# Kim Wilde

UK vocalist.
Born Kim Smith, London, November 18, 1960.

**Career:** Daughter of seminal UK rock 'n' roller Marty Wilde, Kim embarked on training for non-musical career at Hertfordshire Art College. After singing on demos made by brother Ricky, attracted attention of notable producer/record company owner Mickie Most. He supervised mixing of **Kids In America**, produced by Ricky and written by Marty and Ricky. Single released on Most's RAK label in early 1981 reached No. 2; hit with three further singles in UK Top 20 during 1981 — **Chequered Love, Water On Glass** and **Cambodia** — all created by same family team.

First LP reached Top 3 in UK in 1981; less successful in US when released where in 1982, although **Kids In America** was sizeable US hit 18 months after UK release. 1982 was far less successful—two smaller hit singles and **Select** LP minor chart item— but Kim embarked on first tour which was generally well received.

Artist remained in public eye during mid-eighties, but achieved major US breakthrough in 1987 by time-honoured method of covering classic Motown hit. **You Keep Me Hanging On** hit number one spot at end of May that year. Competent if not outstanding vocalist, Kim Wilde also has looks and presence, and has potential to develop into major international star.

**Hit Singles:**

|  | US | UK |
|---|---|---|
| Kids In America, 1981 | 25 | 2 |
| Chequered Love, 1981 | — | 4 |
| Water On Glass, 1981 | — | 11 |
| Cambodia, 1981 | — | 12 |
| View From A Bridge, 1982 | — | 16 |
| Rage To Love, 1985 | — | 19 |
| You Keep Me Hangin On, 1986 | 1 | 2 |
| Another Step, 1987 | — | 6 |
| Say You Really Want Me, 1987 | — | 29 |
| Rockin Around The Xmas Tree (with Mel Smith), 1987 | — | 1 |

**Albums:**
Kim Wilde (EMI/RAK), 1981
Select (—/RAK), 1982
Catch As Catch Can (—/Rak), 1983
Best Of (—/Rak), 1984 **CD**
Teases And Dares (MCA), 1984 **CD**
Very Best Of (EMI), 1984 **CD**
Another Step (MCA), 1987 **CD**

# Jackie Wilson

US vocalist,
Born Detroit, June 9, 1934; died 1984.

**Career:** Possessor of one of the finest tenor voices in popular music idiom Wilson's hit record career has spanned three decades. During brief spell as boxer in late 1940s, won amateur Golden Gloves welterweight title.

Singing began in church. Performed with Ever Ready Gospel Singers before taking secular path in 1951 for session with Dizzy Gillespie's Dee Gee label. Later that year sang in talent show at Paradise Theatre, Detroit; heard by Billy Ward, whose group the Dominoes were then hot with **Sixty Minute Man**. Ward, impressed, took phone number then called months later when Clyde McPhatter quit Dominoes. Wilson replaced him to sing lead/second tenor; sang with group for four years on King/Federal Records, his soaring

tenor tones distinctive in melismatic delivery of ballads like **Rags To Riches**.

When Dominoes moved to Decca in 1956, Wilson stayed with them for while then left for solo career. Sang in local clubs until spotted by Al Green, manager of Johnny Ray and LaVern Baker. Signed with Brunswick Records under supervision of house bandleader Dick Jacobs; has remained Brunswick artist. Wilson was mainstay of roster for more than a decade with lengthy succession of hits, adapting style to keep up with times. Hits included **Reet Petite** (1957), **Lonely Teardrops** and classy ballad **To Be Loved** (1958).

Maintained stylistic variations and fought with orchestration over the years until 1963, when he injected R&B feeling with **Baby Workout**.

In 1966 Wilson began recording in Chicago (instead of New York); with move came transfusion of new ideas from producers Carl Davis and Sonny Sanders. More mainstream soul output of danceable songs like **Whispers, Higher and Higher** and **I Get The Sweetest Feeling** resulted. Wilson was transformed into soul star.

Formula lost commercial impact by early '70s and Wilson began searching for new ideas and material. Brief liaison with Eugene Records and Chi-Lites was unsuccessful.

On September 29, 1975, Jackie suffered heart-attack while singing at Latin Casino in Camden, New Jersey; lapsed into coma, suffered severe brain damage, and was confined to Cherry Hills Medical Center in New Jersey before death in 1984.

Ironic postscript to career was provided when reissued **Reet Petite** topped UK charts for four weeks in 1987; success almost equalled by reissued **Higher And Higher**. Wilson was also portrayed in hit movie about Richie Valens, 'La Bamba'.

**Hit Singles:**

|  | US | UK |
|---|---|---|
| Reet Petite, 1957 | — | 6 |
| Lonely Teardrops, 1959 | 7 | — |
| That's Why (I Love You So), 1959 | 13 | — |
| I'll Be Satisfied, 1959 | 20 | — |
| Night/Doggin' Around, 1960 | 4 | — |
| Doggin' Around/Night, 1960 | 15 | — |
| (You Were Made For) All My Love/ A Woman, A Lover, A Friend, 1960 | 12 | — |
| A Woman, A Lover, A Friend/ (You Were Made For) All My Love, 1960 | 15 | — |
| Alone At Last, 1960 | 8 | 50 |
| My Empty Arms, 1961 | 9 | — |
| Please Tell Me Why, 1961 | 20 | — |
| I'm Comin' On Back To You, 1961 | 19 | — |
| Baby Workout, 1963 | 5 | — |
| Whispers (Gettin' Louder), 1966 | 11 | — |
| (Your Love Keeps Lifting Me) Higher And Higher, 1967 | 6 | — |
| I Get The Sweetest Feeling, 1972 | 35* | 9 |
| (Your Love Keeps Lifting Me) Higher And Higher, 1969 | — | 11 |
| Higher And Higher, 1987 | — | 15 |

*Charted in US in 1968

**Albums (selected):**
My Golden Favourites (Brunswick/Coral), 1962
My Golden Favourites Volume 2 (Brunswick/Coral), 1962
Higher And Higher (Brunswick), 1967 **CD**
Greatest Hits (Brunswick), 1968
Classic (Skratch), 1984
Reet Petite (Ace) **CD**
Very Best Of (Ace) **CD**

*Worth Searching Out:*
Baby Workout (Brunswick/—), 1964
Higher And Higher (Brunswick/MCA), 1967

# Johnny Winter

US guitarist, vocalist, composer.
Born Leland, Mississippi, January 23, 1944.

**Career:** Fluid guitarist who lived for traditional blues and R&B; spent teens playing with younger brother Edgar(▶) in local Texan bands. Later began working as session player and recorded several LPs for regional release in South. **Austin, Texas, About Blues, Early Times, Before The Storm, First Winter, The Johnny Winter Story** and **The Progressive Blues Experiment** all contain material from this period.

**Johnny Winter And, Johnny Winter. Courtesy CBS Records. The Winter Brothers had their heyday in the '70s.**

One of these albums was mentioned in 'Rolling Stone' article covering local scene in Texas; New York Scene club owner Steve Paul then located Winter and signed him to management contract. He proclaimed Winter next rock 'superstar' and the hype was on.

Columbia offered one of largest recording contract's ever given new talent and promptly packed Winter off on national tour. When Winter's atmospheric blues did not transpose to large concert halls, he overhauled his back-up band. Steve Paul took the Scene's house band and reorganised the McCoys (**Hang On Sloppy**) to back Winter; key figure in line-up was Rick Derringer(▶).

Columbia was faced with competition from Winter's old material, which had been bought up and re-issued by various cash-in outfits. As a result, Winter's new material failed to mark up expected sales. More importantly, music tastes began to change in US as younger kids failed to support blues revival. Despite several excellent LPs (**Johnny Winter And, Johnny Winter And Live**), strain on Winter exceeded his ability to cope and rock's 'next superstar' retired with drug habit.

**Still Alive And Well** didn't appear until 1973 but showed Winter was still talented and capable of recording strong effort. However, its critical success failed to produce significant sales and next two Johnny Winter LPs began to sound as if he was desperately trying to produce a commercial success.

In 1977, Winter began extended collaboration with Muddy Waters(▶). If this signalled end of Winter's hopes for superstardom, it also marked his return to true strength as blues guitarist: simple, clean and traditional music which revitalised interest in Muddy Waters' career.

Like so many other 'next big thing' hypes Winter never came close to matching the stupendous expectations placed on him. Only now can his early Columbia masterpieces be appreciated.

**Albums:**
Johnny Winter (Columbia/CBS), 1969
Second Winter (Columbia/CBS), 1969
Johnny Winter And (Columbia/CBS), 1970

Johnny Winter And . . . Live (Columbia/CBS), 1971
Still Alive And Well (Columbia/CBS), 1973
Saints And Sinners (Columbia/CBS), 1974
Captured Live (Blue Sky), 1976
Nothin' But The Blues (Blue Sky), 1977
White, Hot, And Blue (Blue Sky), 1978
Ready For Winter (Accord/—), 1981
Raised On Rock (Blue Sky), 1981
Early Winter (President), 1984
Serious Business (Sonet), 1985

*With Edgar Winter:*
Together Live (Blue Sky), 1976

*Worth Searching Out:*
The Johnny Winter Story (double) (Blue Sky), 1980

# Stevie Winwood

UK vocalist, composer, multi-instrumentalist.
Born Birmingham, England, May 12, 1948.

**Career:** Generally acclaimed as one of Britain's greatest white R&B vocalists. Career began in 1961, playing with trombonist Rico and later the Muff Woody Jazz Band (featuring his brother Muff Winwood). At 15, Steve and Muff joined Spencer Davis Rhythm 'n' Blues Quartet.

Professional career began following year, by which time Winwood had assimilated many musical influences, including folk, jazz, pop, blues and soul. Newly named Spencer Davis Group(▶) achieved some lowly chart placings before breaking big in 1965/66 with string of hits and two No. 1s, **Keep On Running** and **Somebody Help Me**. In spite of title, it was Winwood who gained critical attention and approval for powerhouse vocals and impressive guitar and piano work; it came as no surprise when he announced his decision to form new unit in 1967.

Traffic(▶) provided Winwood with greater freedom to develop his musical ideas. Two highly acclaimed albums, **Mr Fantasy** and **Traffic**, were boosted by three hit singles: **Paper Sun, Hole In My Shoe** and **Here We Go Round The Mulberry Bush**. By early 1969, Winwood was tempted by a more ambitious plan and formed world's first supergroup — Blind Faith(▶), with Cream's Eric Clapton and Ginger Baker, and Family's Rick Grech. Group were hyped to ludicrous proportions and individual egos suffocated natural talents. After recording one album, and touring America (following much-publicised appearance in Hyde Park), Faith folded.

Winwood began '70s guesting with Ginger Baker's(▶) Air Force, but soon began work on solo album **Mad Shadows**, which finally emerged as Traffic re-formation. Over next

**Above: Steve Winwood, man of many bands and solo star of the '80s.**

**Arc Of A Diver, Steve Winwood.
Courtesy Island Records.**

four years, Traffic recorded four more studio albums, all critically acclaimed.

Winwood's solo career was preceded by two years of silence, punctuated by appearances on albums by Viv Stanshall, Jim Capaldi, Sandy Denny, Toots and the Maytals (▶) and George Harrison(▶). Such eclectic musical activities proved sufficient inspiration for first solo, finally released in 1977. Ever restless, Winwood continued with related projects, including concert with Georgie Fame(▶) and appearances on Stomu Yamashta's **Go Live From Paris** and Marianne Faithful's **Broken English**.

Second solo **Arc Of A Diver**, a Top 5 US hit, revealed imaginative use of electronic keyboard instruments and synthesiser, continuing experiments begun on first effort. Lyrical contributions by Will Jennings, George Fleming and Viv Stanshall seemed erratic in quality, but hit single **While You See A Chance** made US Top 10. 1982 work, **Talking Back To The Night**, consolidated rather than improved solo reputation. Winwood undertook his first tour as solo artist during summer 1983. In spite of illustrious history, the once

precocious teenage talent has yet to produce the work of genius of which many believe him still capable. Nevertheless, high quality of artist shows little sign of atrophying as middle age beckons.

Winwood's somewhat low-key, almost patchy career turned full-circle upon release of **Back In The High Life** LP in 1986, the title track earning this uniquely talented performer two Grammys in 1987 for Record Of The Year and Best Pop Vocal.

**Hit Singles:**

| | US | UK |
|---|---|---|
| *With Traffic:* | | |
| (See separate entry) | | |
| *Solo:* | | |
| While You See A Chance, 1980 | 9 | — |
| Higher Love, 1986 | 1 | 13 |
| Valerie, 1987 | 9 | 19 |
| Freedom Overspill, 1987 | 16 | — |
| The Finer Things, 1987 | 4 | — |
| Back In The High Life Again, 1987 | 10 | — |

**Albums:**
*With Traffic:*
(See separate entry)

*Solo:*
Steve Winwood (Island), 1977 **CD**
Arc Of A Diver (Island), 1980 **CD**
Talking Back To The Night (Island), 1982 **CD**
Back In The Highlife (Island), 1986 **CD**
Chronicles (Island), 1987 **CD**

# Bill Withers

US vocalist, composer, guitarist.
Born Slab Fork, West Virginia, July 4, 1938.

**Career:** Born into rural family, Withers showed no particular aptitude for music as child. Served in US navy for nine years, only started singing and playing guitar afterwards, in 1964.

While working in aircraft factory he began composing songs, and was eventually signed by independent Sussex label in 1971. First album, **Just As I Am**, was produced by Booker T. Jones and featured clutch of sensitive and original songs. Single from album, **Ain't No Sunshine**, eventually went gold and has since become a standard, recorded by everyone from Michael Jackson(▶) to Roland Kirk.

Second album, **Still Bill**, confirmed emergence of major new talent and notched up even greater success. By now Withers was also performing live with superb rhythm section (guitarist Benorce Blackman, bass player Melvin Dunlap and drummer James

**Left: Bill Withers can afford to smile after charting for ten years.**

Gadson), winning over audiences with combination of appealingly unstylised voice, distinctive material and modest, almost diffident manner. Style coalesced best elements of black music and singer/songwriter tradition.

After a superb live double album and one more studio album, Withers split from Sussex to join Columbia roster. Since that time his career has progressed in fits and starts. His albums have generally been little more than pleasant, and sales have not been spectacular. However, in 1978 he scored major international hit with **Lovely Day**.

Most recent success has been as guest artist on two superb singles, **Soul Shadows** by Crusaders(▶) and **Just The Two Of Us** by Grover Washington. Both showed his vocal prowess to be undiminished, and had they been released under his own name would have undoubtedly put him right back at top. Bill Withers continues to be held in high regard, both as songwriter and vocalist, and is likely to be in demand for some time to come.

**Hit Singles:**

| | US | UK |
|---|---|---|
| Ain't No Sunshine, 1971 | 3 | — |
| Lean On Me, 1972 | 1 | 18 |
| Use Me, 1972 | 2 | — |
| Lovely Day, 1978 | 30 | 7 |
| Just The Two Of Us (with Grover Washington Jr.), 1981 | 2 | 34 |

**Albums:**
Best Of (Sussex), 1975
Menagerie (Columbia/CBS), 1978
'Bout Love (Columbia/CBS), 1978
Greatest Hits (Columbia/CBS), 1980
Watching You Watching Me (CBS), 1985

*Worth Searching Out:*
Just As I Am (Sussex), 1971
Still Bill (Sussex), 1972
Live At Carnegie Hall (Sussex), 1973

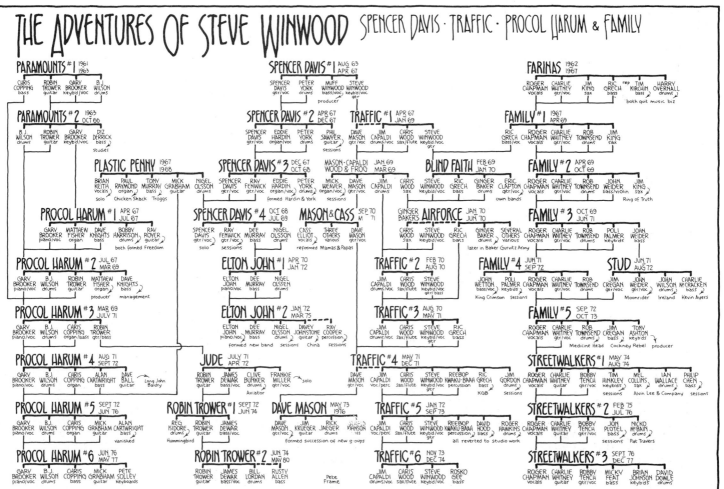

# Stevie Wonder

US vocalist, composer, multi-instrumentalist.
Born Stevland Morris, Saginaw, Michigan, May 3, 1950.

**Career:** One of the most important and consistent of contemporary artists, Stevie Wonder showed early interest in music. Although blind since birth, by age eight was proficient on piano, harmonica, drums and bongos.

Family moved to Detroit when Wonder was child; at age 10 he was introduced to nascent Tamla Motown label by family friend Ronald White, one of the Miracles. Period of grooming followed, during which time several moderately successful singles were released. Wonder gained experience on live work on Motown's touring 'revues', quickly winning reputation as exciting vocal/instrumental act.

First major success came in 1963 with **Fingertips**, recorded live and featuring Stevie's urgent vocalising and harmonica playing against jumping brass background. Record made No. 1, as did album from which it was taken, **Twelve Year Old Genius**. Nevertheless, next few singles were not particularly successful: right format for youthful prodigy had not yet been found.

Wonder solved problem himself with **Uptight**, released in 1966. Self-penned, and featuring vocals without harmonica, it made No. 3 in US and became massive international hit. It heralded string of international successes, most self-written, others taken from wide range of sources, including Bob Dylan(▶) (**Blowin' In The Wind**) and cabaret repertoire (**For Once In My Life**).

By end of '60s Wonder was becoming somewhat restless within confines of Motown 'family', although reluctant to make break completely. He was already producing other artists, and felt capable of taking full control of his career. Crucial point was release of album **Signed, Sealed And Delivered** in 1970. Entirely produced by Wonder, it won award for best soul album of 1970 and gave him confidence to pursue own path.

In 1970 Wonder met and married Syreeta Wright (marriage later broke up). Syreeta contributed to **Where I'm Coming From** album, which heralded new phase of Wonder music in experimental direction.

Following year saw Wonder attain majority, at which time all previous earnings became available to him. Artist then set up Taurus Productions; although gaining independence from Motown, company remained as distributor of all Wonder products.

New freedom prompted important musical leap forward with **Music Of My Mind**, a one-man tour-de-force featuring variety of electronic keyboards. Album alienated some old fans, but brought Wonder to attention of new rock audience, and eventually went gold. It also paved way for album which established commercial viability of new Wonder music, **Talking Book**. Full of songs which have since become standards — **You Are The Sunshine Of My Life, You've Got It Bad, Girl, Superstition, I Believe (When I Fall In Love It Will Be Forever)** — **Talking Book** was first in series of award-winning platinum albums that became synonymous with name Stevie Wonder in '70s.

'70s also saw Wonder sign record-breaking financial agreement with Motown—a guaranteed $13 million between 1975 and 1982. He became one of most often-awarded artists, with 14 Grammies between 1974 and 1977 alone. He gained reputation for keen socio-political awareness (particularly of black issues) and became symbol of spirit of liberation. Double album **Songs In The Key Of Life,** was regarded by many as one of *the* albums of the decade.

Entering '80s as strongly as ever with **Hotter Than July**, Wonder continued to exert huge influence. In 1982 he was given Award of Merit by American Music Awards, a citation which only does scant justice to enormous contribution he has made to popular music. Revered by his peers as much as by public, Wonder is sure to continue to push back boundaries throughout '80s and beyond.

Late 1987 album **Characters** marked return to funky style of earlier career, move welcomed by longtime fans.

Below: **Stevland Morris, aka Stevie Wonder, circa 1966.**

**Hit Singles:**

| | US | UK |
|---|---|---|
| Fingertips Part 2, 1963 | 1 | — |
| Uptight (Everything's Alright), 1966 | 3 | 14 |
| Nothing's Tood Good For My Baby, 1966 | 20 | |
| Blowin' In The Wind, 1966 | 9 | 36 |
| A Place In The Sun, 1966 | 9 | 20 |
| I Was Made To Love Her, 1967 | 2 | 5 |
| I'm Wondering, 1967 | 12 | 22 |
| Shoo-Be-Doo-Be-Doo-Da-Day, 1968 | 9 | 46 |
| For Once In My Life, 1968 | 2 | 3 |
| I Don't Know Why, 1969 | 39 | 14 |
| My Cherie Amour, 1969 | 4 | 4 |
| Yester-Me, Yester-You, Yesterday, 1969 | 7 | 2 |
| Never Had A Dream Come True, 1970 | 26 | 6 |
| Signed, Sealed, Delivered, I'm Yours, 1970 | 3 | 15 |
| Heaven Help Us All, 1970 | 9 | 29 |
| We Can Work It Out, 1971 | 13 | 27 |
| If You Really Love Me, 1971 | 8 | 20 |
| Superstition, 1973 | 1 | 11 |
| You Are The Sunshine Of My Life, 1973 | 1 | 7 |
| Higher Ground, 1973 | 4 | 29 |
| Living For The City, 1974 | 8 | 15 |
| He's Misstra Know It All, 1974 | — | 10 |
| Don't You Worry 'Bout A Thing, 1974 | 16 | — |
| You Haven't Done Nothing, 1974 | 1 | 30 |
| Boogie On Reggae Woman, 1975 | 3 | 12 |
| I Wish, 1976 | 1 | 5 |
| Sir Duke, 1977 | 1 | 2 |
| Send One Your Love, 1979 | 4 | 52 |
| Masterblaster (Jammin'), 1980 | 5 | 2 |
| I Ain't Gonna Stand For It, 1980 | 11 | 10 |
| Lately, 1981 | — | 3 |
| Happy Birthday, 1981 | — | 2 |
| That Girl, 1982 | 4 | 39 |
| Do I Do, 1982 | 13 | 10 |
| I Just Called To Say I Love You, 1984 | 1 | 1 |
| Love Light In Flight, 1985 | 17 | — |
| Part-time Lover, 1985 | 1 | 3 |
| Go Home, 1986 | 22 | — |
| Overjoyed, 1986 | — | 17 |
| Skeletons, 1987 | 19 | — |

*With Paul McCartney:*

| | US | UK |
|---|---|---|
| Ebony And Ivory, 1982 | 1 | 1 |

**Albums:**

Tribute To Uncle Ray (Motown), 1963
Jazz Soul Of Little Stevie (Motown), 1963
Twelve Year Old Genius Recorded Live (Motown), 1963
With A Song In My Heart (Motown), 1964
Uptight (Motown), 1966 **CD**
Down To Earth (Motown), 1966 **CD**
I Was Made To Love Her (Motown), 1967 **CD**
Some Day At Christmas (Motown), 1967
For Once In My Life (Motown), 1969 **CD**
My Cherie Amour (Motown), 1969 **CD**
Live At The Talk Of The Town (Motown), 1970
Where I'm Coming From (Motown), 1971
Greatest Hits (Motown), 1972
Greatest Hits Volume 2 (Motown), 1972
Music Of My Mind (Motown) **CD**
Talking Book (Motown), 1972 **CD**
Innervisions (Motown), 1973 **CD**
Fullfillingness First Finale (Motown), 1974 **CD**
Songs In The Key Of Life (Motown), 1976
The Secret Life Of Plants (Motown), 1979
Hotter Than July (Motown), 1980 **CD**
Signed (Motown), 1981 **CD**
Stevie Wonder's Original Musiquarium 1 (Motown), 1982 **CD**
People Move Music Play (Motown), 1983
Woman In Red (Motown), 1984 **CD**
In Square Circle (Motown), 1985 **CD**
Original Musiquarium Vol 2, 1985 **CD**
Essential Stevie Wonder (Motown), 1987

**Below: Little Stevie Wonder had his first No. 1, Fingertips, at age 13.**

Below: Original Musiquarium 1.
Courtesy Motown Records.

Below: For Once In My Life.
Courtesy Motown Records.

Above: Stevie Wonder bringing together
black and white in the '60s.

Above Inset: A contender in the '80s,
still promoting racial harmony.

Below: Stevie going strong in the '70s.

# Roy Wood

UK vocalist, composer, multi-instrumentalist. Born Ulysses Adrian Wood, Birmingham, November 8, 1946.

**Career:** Learned guitar in early teens and joined/formed numerous groups, including the Falcons, the Lawmen, Gerry Levene and the Avengers, and Mike Sheridan and the Nightriders (who recorded Wood's composition **Make Them Understand**). Following expulsion from Moseley College of Art, Wood became more involved in group work, finally forming the Move(▶) in 1964. Impressive line-up of Bev Bevan (drums), Carl Wayne (vocals), Chris 'Ace' Kefford (bass) and Trevor Burton (guitar) was enlisted from cream of small-time Birmingham groups. Signed to opportunist manager Tony Secunda, they established themselves via residency at London's Marquee Club. Burgeoning interest led to recording contract with Deram. First single, **Night Of Fear,** reached No. 2 in early 1967, and was followed by eight other hits, all composed by Wood, one of the cleverest and most appealing songwriters of the era. Psychedelia, flower power, early rock 'n' roll and classical pastiche were some of the themes explored on successive single releases.

As years passed, Wood's influence over group increased. From **Fire Brigade** onwards he assumed lead vocals as well as songwriting credits.

Following two essentially pop albums, **The Move** and **Shazam,** Wood was anxious to undertake more ambitious work. Acknowledged as a singles group in Britain, Move were gradually accepted as serious musicians in the States (despite limited popularity). Musical direction became increasingly diverse and uncertain towards end of decade; during final stage of career they flirted with heavy metal (**Brontosaurus, When Alice Comes Down To The Farm**) and rock revivalism (**Californian Man**). Wood's desire for music of greater complexity resulted in creation of Electric Light Orchestra(▶), whose aim was to continue the exploratory work begun by the Beatles(▶) on such songs as **Strawberry Fields Forever** and **I Am The Walrus.**

After recording one hit album and single (**10538 Overture**), the ever-restless Wood left ELO in the hands of Jeff Lynne in order to pursue another new project. Soon a new group, Wizzard, emerged, comprising Rick Price (guitar), Bill Hunt (piano/harpsichord/French horn), Hugh McDowell (electric cello), Nick Pentelow (sax), Mike Burney (sax), Keith Smart (drums) and Charlie Grima (drums). Wood took lead role with new image, including multi-coloured hair and warpaint. First single, **Ball Park Incident,** was an intriguing production, echoing Phil Spector's wall-of-sound '60s work.

Subsequent singles were even more impressive and included two celebrated No. 1's, **See My Baby Jive** and **Angel Fingers.** These and the haunting Spector-like festive hit, **I Wish It Could Be Christmas Everyday,** confirmed Wood's ability to write/produce hits that were the equal of his finest '60s work. Nevertheless, inability to produce albums of equivalent interest remained a failing from the early days. A brave attempt at rock revivalism, **Eddy And The Falcons,** proved commercially unsuccessful, causing Wood to lose interest.

In mid-70s he revived the pseudo-heavy metal experimentation of **Brontosaurus** in a revamped Wizzo, but his work was ill-timed. A simultaneous shot at solo fame produced the impressive hit **Forever,** an affectionate tribute to Neil Sedaka(▶) and the Beach

Boys(▶). Solo albums **Boulders** (1970) and **Mustard** (1975) were again erratic, though they demonstrated his total control as producer, engineer and designer (he even painted the cover!).

Late '70s and '80s proved barren for Wood, while his protégé Lynee has reaped a fortune with ELO. Wood's great strength and weakness has always been his peripatetic nature, but his past record remains exemplary—composer of all Move's hits, the mastermind behind the original ELO, and the creator of some of early '70s finest UK singles via Wizzard. A multi-talented producer, arranger, singer, songwriter and manipulator of pop genres, it would be a mistake to write him off despite his inconspicuous profile on the current scene.

| Hit Singles: | US | UK |
|---|---|---|
| (See also Move and ELO) | | |
| *With Move:* | | |
| (See separate entry) | | |
| *With ELO:* | | |
| 10538 Overture, 1972 | — | 9 |
| *With Wizzard:* | | |
| Ball Park Incident, 1972 | — | 6 |
| See My Baby Jive, 1973 | — | 1 |
| Angel Fingers, 1973 | — | 1 |
| I Wish It Could Be Christmas Everyday, 1973 | — | 4 |
| Rock'n'Roll Winter (Looney's Tune), 1974 | — | 6 |
| Are You Ready To Rock, 1974 | — | 8 |
| *Solo:* | | |
| Dear Elaine, 1973 | — | 18 |
| Forever, 1973 | — | 8 |
| Going Down The Road, 1974 | — | 13 |
| Oh What A Shame, 1975 | — | 13 |

**Albums:**
*With Move:*
(See separate entry)
*With ELO:*
The Electric Light Orchestra (Harvest), 1971
*Solo:*
Boulders (Harvest), 1973
Mustard (Jet), 1975
The Roy Wood Story (Harvard), 1976
On The Road Again (Automatic), 1979
The Best Of (70-74) (MfP), 1985
Starting Up (Legasy), 1987
*With Wizzard:*
Wizzard Brew (Harvest), 1973
Eddy And The Falcons (Warner Bros), 1974
See My Baby Jive (Harvest), 1974
*Roy Wood Wizzo Band:*
Super Active Wizzo (Warner Bros), 1977

# XTC

UK group formed 1977.

**Original/Current line-up:** Andy Partridge, guitar, vocals; Colin Moulding, bass, vocals; Barry Andrews, keyboards; Terry Chambers, drums.

**Drums And Wires, XTC. Courtesy Virgin Records.**

**Career:** Partridge organised XTC as punk band in Swindon, near London. **This Is Pop?** single attracted some attention and revealed XTC to be power-pop group in punk clothing. This became more apparent by time solid third album, **Drums And Wires,** appeared in 1979.

Next LP yielded minor hit, **Sergeant Rock,** which earned some US airplay and write-off as lightweight by UK press. In 1982 **Senses Working Overtime** put band back in UK charts, and double LP **English Settlement** (cut to single LP for US market) received critical approval. End of 1982 produced singles compilation (UK only) **Waxworks**. In promotional move, this album was issued for limited time with second LP, **Beeswax,** comprising B-side.

After illness hit leader Partridge, band gave up heavy touring schedule while continuing to record. Subsequent albums were well received by critics (particularly Todd Rundgren-produced 1986 offering **Skylarking**), but major commercial breakthrough continues to elude band.

| Hit Singles: | US | UK |
|---|---|---|
| Making Plans For Nigel, 1979 | — | 17 |
| Sergeant Rock, 1981 | — | 16 |
| Senses Working Overtime, 1982 | — | 10 |

**Below: A mug shot of XTC, with prime mover Andy Partridge (with glasses) looking less than amused.**

**Albums:**
White Music (Virgin-Epic/Virgin), 1978 **CD**
Go 2 (Virgin-Epic/Virgin), 1978
Drums And Wires (Virgin-Epic/Virgin), 1979 **CD**
Black Sea (Virgin), 1980 **CD**
English Settlement (Virgin), 1982 **CD**
Waxworks: Some Singles 1977-1982 (—/Virgin), 1982
Beeswax: Some B-sides 1977-1982 (—/Virgin), 1982
Mummer (Virgin), 1983 **CD**
Go Too (Virgin), 1984 **CD**
Big Express (Virgin), 1984 **CD**
Compact XTC (Virgin), 1986 **CD**
Skylarking (Virgin), 1986 **CD**

# The Yardbirds

UK group formed 1963.

**Original line-up:** Keith Relf, vocals, harmonica; Anthony 'Top' Topham, guitar; Chris Dreja, guitar; Paul Samwell-Smith, bass; Jim McCarty, drums.

**Career:** First version of Yardbirds grew out of Kingston Art School band, the Metropolitan Blues Quartet. Eric Clapton(▶) replaced Topham in late 1963, before band took over residency vacated by Rolling Stones(▶) at Crawdaddy Club in Richmond. Band generated strong cult following on London and Home Counties club circuit, and toured Europe with blues legend Sonny Boy Williamson.

Signed by Columbia, they released **Five Live Yardbirds** in 1964 (only in UK), essential listening for anyone wanting to know what British R&B was all about. Album increased band's following, as did **Sonny Boy Williamson And The Yardbirds,** released same year. 1965 saw shift in direction when band recorded **For Your Love,** written by Graham Gouldman then of Mindbenders, later of 10 cc(▶). An unusual yet thoroughly commercial rock/pop song, far removed from band's R&B orientation, it catapulted the Yardbirds into charts on both sides of Atlantic, making No. 3 in UK and No. 6 in US.

Success was consolidated by release of two more Graham Gouldman singles, **Heart Full Of Soul** and **Evil Hearted You**. Clapton, however, quit after **For Your Love**, unable to reconcile himself to move away from band's roots, and joined John Mayall's(▶) Bluesbreakers. Jimmy Page was asked to replace Clapton, but declined and recommended Jeff Beck(▶), another ex-art college musician, who accepted.

1966 saw further stresses and personnel changes. Now a hot live act, band was continually touring, which didn't suit Paul Samwell-Smith. He pulled out to concentrate on production. Chris Dreja moved to bass, and Jimmy Page, then an in-demand session musician, agreed to second offer, joining Beck on guitar. Relatively minor hit **Happenings Ten Years Time Ago** was only single with this line-up.

By end of year Beck had also left. Following fairly disastrous album produced by Mickey Most, and a couple of unsuccessful American singles, Relf, McCarty, Page and Dreja called it a day in July 1968.

Relf and McCarty formed folk duo Together, then founded Renaissance(▶), but their post-Yardbirds career was not particularly auspicious. Relf died in accident at home in 1976. Dreja became a photographer, while Page formed New Yardbirds which metamorphosised into supergroup Led Zeppelin(▶) (managed by former Yardbirds road manager Peter Grant).

Yardbirds' influence was greater than their actual success and paved the way for guitar-dominated psychedelic/heavy rock bands of late '60s and '70s. Now, virtually all recordings have become collectors' items, and Yardbirds are regarded as one of all-time legendary rock bands.

**Final line-up:** Relf; McCarty; Jimmy Page, guitar; Dreja.

**Hit Singles:**

| | US | UK |
|---|---|---|
| For Your Love, 1965 | 6 | 3 |
| Heart Full Of Soul, 1965 | 9 | 2 |
| Evil Hearted You/Still I'm Sad, 1965 | — | 3 |
| I'm A Man, 1965 | 17 | — |
| Shapes Of Things, 1966 | 11 | 3 |
| Over Under Sideways Down, 1966 | 13 | 10 |

**Albums:**
Yardbirds With Sonny boy Williamson (Mercury/Fontana), 1964
Five Live Yardbirds (—/Charly), 1964
The Yardbirds (—/CBS), 1966
Great Hits (Epic/—), 1967
Remember (—/Starline), 1971
Eric Clapton And The Yardbirds (Springboard/—), 1972
Yardbirds Favourites (Epic), 1972
Yardbirds Featuring Eric Clapton (—/Charly), 1975
Yardbirds Featuring Jeff Beck (—/Charly), 1975
Shapes Of Things (Springboard/Charly), 1977
Single Hits (—/Charly), 1982
Afternoon Tea (Rhino/—), 1982
For Your Love (Accord/—), 1982
Classic Cuts (Topline) **CD**
First Recordings (Bellaphon) **CD**
Roger The Engineer (Edsel) **CD**

**Below: Yes on stage shortly before split up in the early 1980s.**

Greatest Hits (Charly) **CD**

*Worth Searching Out:*
Having A Rave-up With The Yardbirds (Epic/—), 1971
Live Yardbirds Featuring Jimmy Page (Epic), 1971*
*Withdrawn

**Five Live Yardbirds. Courtesy EMI Records.**

# Yes

UK group formed 1968.
**Original line-up:** Jon Anderson, vocals; Chris Squire, bass; Peter Banks, guitar; Tony Kaye, organ; Bill Bruford, drums.

**Career:** After 12 years in nowhere bands Anderson chanced upon Squire in Soho night-club; line-up of Yes was completed by members of their previous bands. Debut LP **Yes** took Beatles(▶)/Byrds(▶) originals and expanded them into almost unrecognisable baroque extravaganzas; sound deliberately emulated classical influence of ELP's(▶) Keith Emerson.

Follow-up **Time And A Word** LP added superfluous strings and did not sound innovative as intended. In 1971 Banks left; he was replaced by Steve Howe (ex-Syndicate, In Crowd, Budast, Tomorrow). This line-up produced **The Yes Album**, which showed that original intention to fuse rock/classical music remained band's driving force Significantly, Banks added synthesiser and Yes recorded completely original music for the LP.

Kaye was replaced by Rick Wakeman(▶) (ex-Strawbs) whose classical training coincided with band's direction. **Fragile** LP took on symphonic sound closely associated with Yes. In 1972 Alan White (ex-Plastic Ono Band) took over drums for what many consider best Yes line-up.

Growing integration of technological advances and classical idioms exploded on **Close To The Edge** (recorded before Bruford had left drum slot to play with King Crimson(▶)). New line-up proved that complex, orchestral compositions translated well on stage with live set, **Yessongs**. This triple set also betrayed problem with Yes music: the line between innovative exploration and overblown pretension.

Next double LP **Topographic Oceans** sank under its own weight and convinced Wakeman to jump ship. (He had released successful solo album **Six Wives Of Henry VIII** in 1973.) Patrick Moraz (keyboards) joined August 1974. His classical training allowed him to assume Wakeman's mantle with little difficulty, as evidenced on **Relayer** LP and in live shows. Wakeman rejoined in 1976 when Moraz quit Yes as fans were flooded with plethora of various solo efforts and spin-offs.

1977's **Going For The One** dredged up same old Yes conventions and music seemed slightly foolish in light of new wave. Wakeman left after **Tormato** and then — a shock to Yes fans — so did Anderson; Anderson went on to solo work and Vangelis(▶). Buggles duo

Trevor Horn (guitars) and Geoff Downes (keyboards) joined in 1980 for US/UK tours and recording of **Drama** LP. Then not with a bang, but with a short press announcement, Yes folded altogether. Howe and Downes reappeared in Asia(▶) with Carl Palmer and John Wetton in 1981.

Although it seemed that the techno rock maestros had packed their last stadium, at the time of writing a new album **Big Generator** was in the pipeline and a world tour was being discussed. In any event, Yes at their best were an exciting band which foreshadowed synth explosion of '80s.

**Final line-up:** Squire; Trevor Horn, guitar, vocals; Steve Howe, Gibson Howe Model guitar (based on Switchmaster); Geoff Downes, keyboards; Alan White, drums.

**Hit Singles:**

| | US | UK |
|---|---|---|
| Roundabout, 1972 | 13 | — |
| Wonderous Stories, 1977 | — | 7 |
| Owner Of A Lonely Heart, 1983 | 1 | — |
| Love Will Find A Way, 1987 | 30 | — |
| Rhythm Of Love, 1988 | 40 | — |

**Albums:**
Yes (Atlantic), 1969
Time And A Word (Atlantic), 1970
The Yes Album (Atlantic), 1971 **CD**
Fragile (Atlantic), 1971 **CD**
Close To The Edge (Atlantic), 1972 **CD**
Yessongs (Atlantic), 1973 **CD**
Tales From Topographic Oceans (Atlantic), 1973
Relayer (Atlantic), 1974
Yesterdays (Atlantic), 1975
Going For The One (Atlantic), 1977
Tormato (Atlantic), 1978
Drama (Atlantic), 1980
Yesshows (Atlantic), 1980
Classic Yes (Atlantic), 1981 **CD**
90125 (Atlantic) **CD**
Big Generator (Atlantic) **CD**

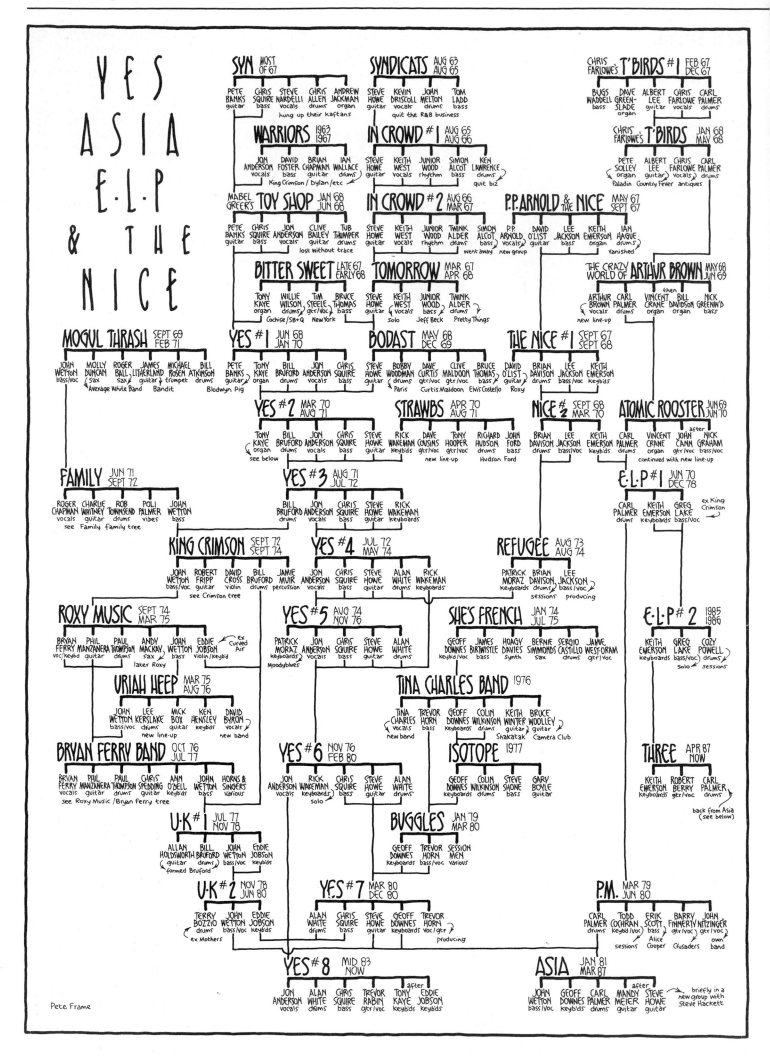

Pete Frame

# Neil Young

Canadian vocalist, composer, guitarist.
Born Toronto, Ontario, November 12, 1945.

**Career:** Son of well-known Toronto sports writer, who gave Neil ukelele for Xmas, 1958. Graduated to banjo, then guitar soon after. Early influence was Hank Marvin of Shadows(▶). After short-lived group the Jades, joined first real band the Squires in 1963. By late 1964 began to arrange and write for them. During this period, met Stephen Stills(▶) and Richie Furay, whom he would later join in Buffalo Springfield(▶). Became coffee-bar folk singer in New York, then met Bruce Palmer, a member of Mynah Birds (led by Rick Matthews, who later found fame as Rick James(▶) in '80s). Mynah Birds, with Young a member, cut several still unreleased tracks for Motown, but arrest of James as deserter from US Navy effectively killed group.

Young moved to Los Angeles with Palmer in early 1966; reunited with Stills and Furay in freeway traffic jam. Quartet decided to form group the Herd, with drummer Dewey Martin (ex-Dillards). Changed group name to Buffalo Springfield after steamroller of same name; began gigging in spring 1966. After meeting Byrds(▶), became embroiled in LA folk/rock and country/rock scenes.

With several line-up changes in rhythm section (Palmer departed and later returned, Young left and rejoined, Jim Messina joined early 1968), Buffalo Springfield lasted until May 1968, leaving three excellent LPs and five hit singles, only one of which, **For What It's Worth**, made US Top 10.

After working as folkie, Young acquired record deal with Reprise. First solo LP released start of 1969. Then formed band Crazy Horse(▶), who provided backing for second classic LP, **Everybody Knows This Is Nowhere**. After recording third LP, Young was invited to join Crosby, Stills & Nash, and briefly group became Crosby, Stills, Nash & Young(▶) for **Déjà Vu** LP, double live album and performance at Woodstock Festival. Personality clashes led Young back to solo career; **After The Goldrush** and **Harvest** were commercially and artistically successful. But Young turned back on success with 1973 release of **Journey Through The Past**, soundtrack to film produced by Young. Subsequent three LPs permeated by melancholy songs and performances, as Young refused to follow easy commercial path.

Late 1975 LP **Zuma** saw return to form of earlier LPs, with attacking guitar solos and instantly recognisable vocals from Young. Briefly worked with Stephen Stills, but union short-lived. Next LP, **American Stars 'n' Bars**, included assistance from Linda Ronstadt(▶) and Emmylou Harris(▶), joining stellar list of guests on previous Young records such as Crosby, Stills, Nash, Jack Nitzsche, Rick Danko and Levon Helm (the Band(▶)), Nils Lofgren(▶) and others. Three-LP set **Decade**, a self-compiled retrospective, released in late 1977, almost whole year before **Comes A Time**, which encountered many delays due to track changes, remixes, cover art alteration, etc. New era arrived with **Rust Never Sleeps** and **Live Rust**, once again with backing from Crazy Horse, to whom Young has returned several times in his career. Concept included major tour, made into film 'Rust Never Sleeps'.

Young then worked at length on film project 'Human Highway'. Directed and acted in movie, along with Dean Stockwell, Russ Tamblyn and Devo(▶). During this period (1980-81) also released two more albums. In 1982, began using synthesisers and electronic instruments; eventually invited many of

Above: Neil Young, dwarfed by his stage equipment, from his strange film, Rust Never Sleeps.

past friends from backing bands to assist him in making **Trans**, including Nils Lofgren, guitar; Ben Keith, pedal steel, keyboards; Bruce Palmer, bass; Joe Lala, percussion; and Ralph Molina, drums. Group toured in support of **Trans**. While new electronic direction admirable in some ways, peculiar sounds tended to alienate long-standing Young fans, who preferred his earlier work. However, following is extremely faithful, and new direction regarded by many as experiment from which their hero will emerge and return to intense electric rock of most influential periods (1969-1973 and 1975-1979).

**Hit Singles:**

|  | US | UK |
|---|---|---|
| *With Buffalo Springfield:* | | |
| (See separate entry) | | |
| *Crosby, Stills, Nash & Young* | | |
| Woodstock, 1970 | 11 | — |
| Teach Your Children, 1970 | 16 | — |
| Ohio, 1970 | 14 | — |
| *Solo:* | | |
| Heart Of Gold, 1972 | 1 | 10 |

**Albums:**
*With Buffalo Springfield:*
(See separate entry)

*Crosby, Stills, Nash & Young:*
Deja Vu (Atlantic), 1970
Four Way Street (Atlantic), 1971
So Far (Atlantic), 1974*
*Compilation

*With Crazy Horse:*
Life (Geffen), 1987 **CD**

*Solo:*
Neil Young (Reprise), 1968
Everybody Knows This Is Nowhere (Reprise), 1969
After The Goldrush (Reprise), 1970 **CD**
Harvest (Reprise), 1971 **CD**
Journey Through The Past (Reprise), 1972
Time Fades Away (Reprise), 1973
On The Beach (Reprise), 1974
Tonight's The Night (Reprise), 1975
Zuma (Reprise), 1975
Long May You Run (Stills/Young Band), 1976
American Stars 'n' Bars (Reprise), 1977
Decade (Reprise), 1977*
Comes A Time (Reprise), 1978
Rust Never Sleeps (Reprise), 1979
Live Rust (Reprise), 1979
Hawks And Doves (Warner Bros), 1980
Re-ac-tor (Warner Bros), 1981
Trans (Warner Bros), 1982
Everybody's Rockin' (Geffen), 1983
Landing On Water (Geffen), 1986 **CD**
Best Of (Warner Bros), 1987 **CD**
*Compilation

# Paul Young

UK vocalist.
Born: November 30, 1955.

**Career:** More than 700 shows up and down Britain from 1979 to 1982, fronting the fondly remembered eight-piece soul review Q-Tips, provided perfect grounding for the talents of Paul Young who has become leading British exponent of 'blue-eyed soul'.

When Q-Tips broke up, Young retained services of keyboard player Ian Kewley, his regular songwriter partner, and began work on **No Parlez** album which built on chart-topping success of **Wherever I Lay My Hat** single—CBS's most successful domestic release in its 18 year history.

A sell-out debut tour of UK and lengthy European tour plus six weeks in USA caused vocal strain and temporary loss of top six notes in his range. Therefore planned major

**Secrets of Association, Paul Young Courtesy CBS Records.**

Wembley concert with Elton John was cancelled, and another US tour was deferred. There was a gap of over 18 months between **No Parlez** and follow-up album **The Secret Of Association** which featured superlative version of Ann Peebles' soul classic **I'm Gonna Tear Your Playhouse Down**.

During hiatus, Young re-vamped his Royal Family backing outfit, Johnny Turnbull replacing Steve Bolton on guitar, Matt Irving joining as second keyboard player, and respected black singers George Chandler, Jimmy Chambers and Tony Jackson replacing the Fabulous Wealthy Tarts (Maz Roberts and Kim Leslie). Drummer Mark Pinder, bass player Pino Palladino and Ian Kewley completed line-up.

1987 album **Between Two Fires** achieved platinum status in UK, but latterly Young's career seems to have stalled slightly. Although still highly successful, artist seems unsure of best direction to take (As witnessed by preparedness to appear second on bill to Genesis at Wembly concerts.)

Excellent singer and appealingly unpretentious personality, Young has potential to scale heights of international stardom, but time may be running out for now-veteran artist.

**Hit Singles:**

|  | US | UK |
|---|---|---|
| Wherever I Lay My Hat (That's My Home), 1983 | — | 1 |
| Come Back And Stay, 1983† | 22 | 4 |
| Love Of The Common People, 1983 | — | 2 |

**Below: Blue-eyed soulster Paul Young, who burst upon UK music scene in 1983 with high-grade R&B material, and has since made number 1 in USA.**

197

| | | |
|---|---|---|
| I'm Gonna Tear Your Playhouse Down, 1984* | 13 | 9 |
| Everything Must Change, 1985 | — | 9 |
| Everytime You Go Away, 1985 | 1 | 4 |
| Tomb Of Memories, 1985 | — | 16 |
| Wonderland, 1986 | — | 24 |

†1984 in US
*1985 in US

**Albums:**
No Parlez (CBS), 1983 **CD**
The Secret Of Association (CBS), 1985 **CD**
Between Two Fires (CBS), 1986 **CD**
Live At Last (CBS), 1986 **CD**

*Paul Young & The Q-Tips:*
Live (Hallmark), 1985

# ZZ Top

US group formed 1970.

**Original/Current line-up:** Billy Gibbons, Gibson Les Paul guitar, vocals; Dusty Hill, Fender Telecaster bass, vocals; Frank Beard, drums.

**Career:** Gibbons was exciting guitarist in local Houston, Texas, band of late '60s, Moving Sidewalks. When that project fell apart, he and manager Bill Ham planned new group. Beard joined and, after failure to find right combination through auditions, recommended Hill. Drawing on traditional country blues and delta music, ZZ Top added hard white rock to come up with own version of high-energy music. Band quickly established reputation as powerful opening act, challenging headliners to match their performances.

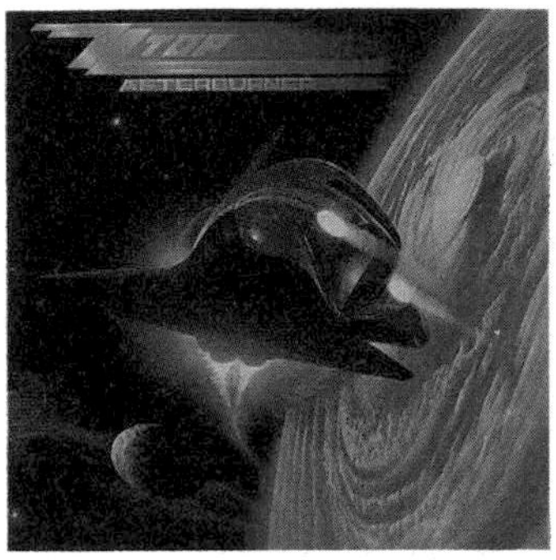


**Afterburner, ZZ Top.**
**Courtesy Warner Bros Records.**

**First Album** received only local interest but **Rio Grande Mud** reflected growing audience by eventually going gold. **Tres Hombres** in 1973 put band into big time and provided US hit single **La Grange**. Forever touring as boogie band, ZZ Top now headlined massive concerts and **Fandango!** quickly followed **Tres Hombres** to platinum. From studio side of LP **Tush,** with its raunchy euphemisms, merited heavy airplay. Following **Téjas** LP and massive World Wide Texas Tour (1976-77), ZZ Top decided to take a vacation which turned into three-year hiatus.

**Dequello** LP returned trio to prominence in 1979 and group subsequently enjoyed international chart success with 1983 set **Eliminator** and 1985 album **Afterburner**. Single **Gimme All Your Lovin'** heralded renewed single chart action. The beat (chug-a-lug) goes on.

| **Hit Singles:** | US | UK |
|---|---|---|
| Tush, 1974 | 20 | — |
| Gimme All Your Lovin', 1984 | 37 | 10 |
| Legs, 1984 | 8 | 16 |
| Sleeping Bag, 1985 | 8 | 27 |
| Rough Boy, 1986 | — | 23 |

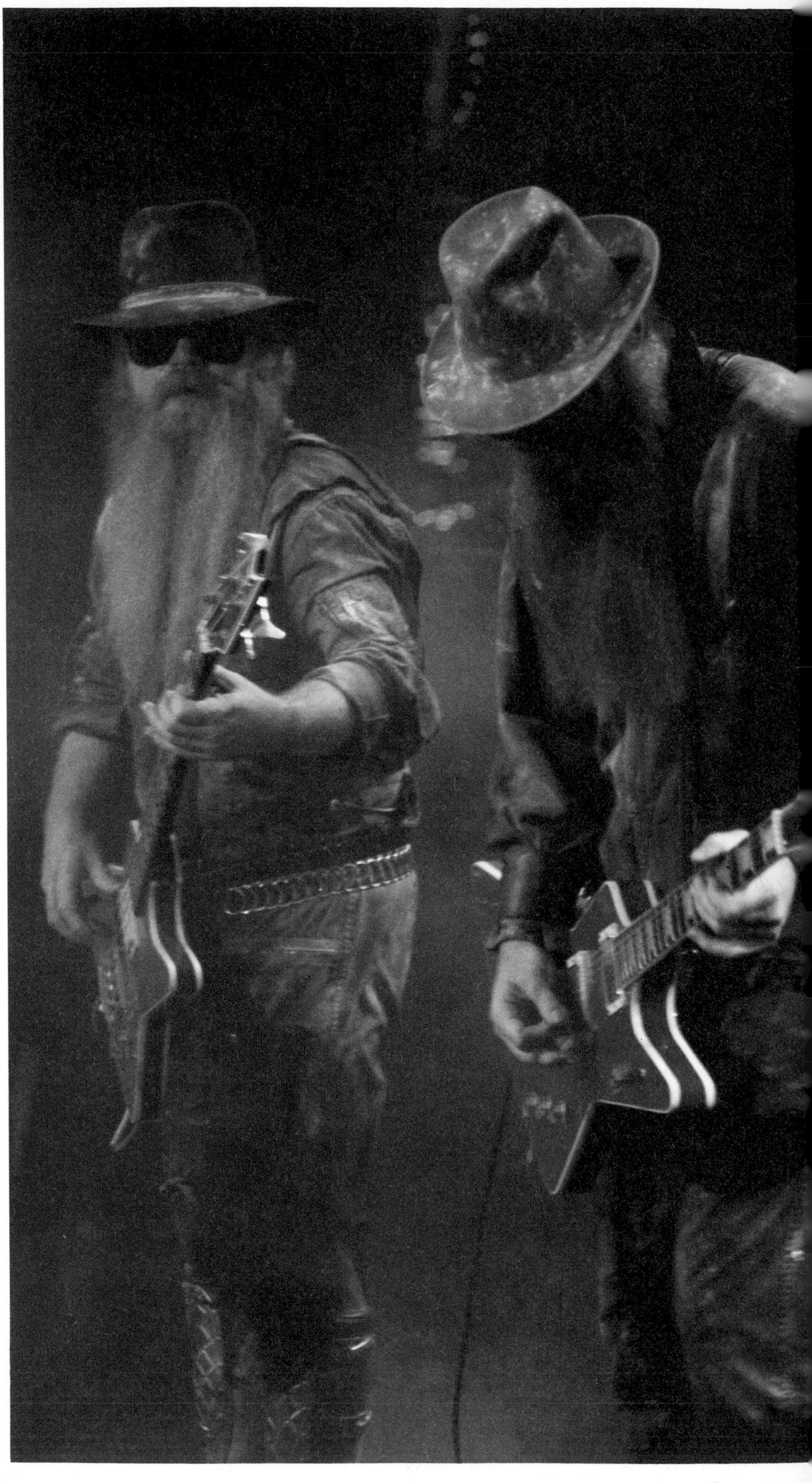

**Albums:**
First Album (Warner Bros), 1971 **CD**
Rio Grande Mud (Warner Bros), 1972 **CD**
Tres Hombres (Warner Bros), 1973 **CD**
Fandango! (Warner Bros), 1974 **CD**
Téjas (Warner Bros), 1976 **CD**
Best Of (Warner Bros), 1977 **CD**
Dequello (Warner Bros), 1979 **CD**
El Loco (Warner Bros), 1981 **CD**
Eliminator (Warner Bros), 1983 **CD**
Afterburner (Warner Bros), 1985 **CD**
Sixpack (Warner Bros) **CD**

# Frank Zappa

US composer, guitarist, vocalist.
Born Francis Vincent Zappa Jr., Baltimore, Maryland, December 21, 1940.

**Career:** Raised on East Coast until age 10, then moved to West Coast with family, which may explain schizoid musical career. Early interests ranged from Edgar Varese to R&B to '50s doo-wop. Practical experience included high-school band Blackouts, recording Don Von Vliet (also ex-Blackout and re-named Captain Beefheart(▶) by Zappa), and producing naughty sex tape for local vice squad (which earned light jail sentence and draft exemption).

Zappa joined group Soul Giants which, according to legend, played first gig on Mothers' Day. MGM couldn't cope with name 'the Mothers' so added 'of Invention'. Original line-up of Ray Collins, Jimmy Carl 'Token Indian' Black, Roy Estrada and Dave Coranda immediately went for record number of personnel changes. Coranda left in horror at Zappa's master plan for world domination.

Tom Wilson (Dylan(▶), Velvet Underground(▶), producer) recorded debut **Freak Out** in early 1966. Double bonanza of over-the-top social commentry, **Freak Out** demanded a little thinking to get behind satire to strange music underlying it. Zappa became touted as rock's sharpest sociologist. The highly intelligent interviews he gave revealed distaste for any trends or fashions. With further personnel changes, Zappa recorded **Absolutely Free** which questioned lack of freedom in modern society. If rock fans felt smug, claiming to be outside that society, they missed point of **We're Only In It For The Money** which lampooned Beatles(▶) **Sgt. Pepper** and rock's under-30 audience in one blow.

Claiming all his work was one extended piece, Zappa overloaded his modern classical influences into free-form solo **Lumpy Gravy** LP. Zappa's band seemed to disappear although he continued to use many of the same musicians. In late 1967 he started work on two simultaneous recording projects. **Cruising With Ruben And The Jets** appeared first and provided return to satire of early albums. In fact, Zappa reproduced '50s feel so faithfully from cover and liner notes to sound itself, it's questionable whether he intended a put-down or tribute; Sha-Na-Na(▶) or Rocky and the Replays never did better. **Uncle Meat**, soundtrack for never made movie, indicated Zappa's fascination for all forms of media.

**Burnt Weeny Sandwich** proved to be Mothers' last album. **Weasels Ripped My Flesh** (1970) was released under Mothers name but was compilation of old and live material. Zappa formally announced Mothers' demise in October 1969 press release, and promptly buried himself in running two new

**Left: Texan boogie band as they appeared early 1988, headed for twentieth anniversary together.**

labels (Bizarre and Straight) while producing groups on outer fringe of rock respectability (early Alice Cooper(▶), GTO's, Beefheart, Wild Man Fischer). Old Mothers Lowell George and Roy Estrada went on to form Little Feat(▶). Jimmy Carl Black and Bunk Gardner formed Geronimo Black, while Art Tripp joined Captain Beefheart.

Zappa kept Ian Underwood (guitar, keyboards) for second solo album **Hot Rats.** When released, it was hard to tell difference between Zappa alone and Zappa with Mothers. This was apparent when next LP, **Chunga's Revenge,** featured many musicians who eventually made up the Mothers used in **200 Motels** movie and soundtrack. These last two projects made particular use of vocalists Howard Kaylan and Mark Volman (ex-Turtles(▶)).

Zappa jammed with John Lennon(▶) and appeared on **Sometime In New York** LP (1972). Then he took Mothers (who, of course had undergone several more personnel changes) on tour and released two live albums: **The Mothers: Fillmore East-June 1971** and **Just Another Band From LA.** End of '71 saw poor European tour (band's equipment lost in Montreux fire) and serious injury to Zappa when pushed from stage at Rainbow Theatre, London. Zappa continued to release (some say grind out) material, either solo **(Waka Jawaka)** or with Mothers **(Grand Wazoo)**. Although assured of certain level of sales, Zappa seemed to want wider approval of his ideas. His writing moved closer to simple rock. Lyrics began to lose bite and became more scatological. If shock tactics didn't get him into Top 10, he'd titillate his way there.

New record deal with Warners emphasised efforts to make hit record. **Overnite Sensation** missed mark but **Apostrophe** finally rose high in US charts. In gratitude Zappa hired marching band to play past Warners' office. Next two LPs, **Roxy And Elsewhere** and **One Size Fits All**, took step back to live recordings as if Zappa was content to resume his role outside mainstream rock. **Bongo Fury** was also primarily live but featured reunion with old friend Captain Beefheart. Beefheart's appearance signalled end of dispute between the two stretching back to Zappa's production of the Captain in late '60s. One year passed before **Zoot Allures** appeared. Then as if possessed, Zappa began releasing albums every few months. **Sheik Yerbouti** (1979), **Joe's Garage Act 1** (1979) and **You Are What You Is** (1981) are all excellent. **Ship Arriving Too Late To Save A Drowning Witch** (1982) contains **Valley Girl** single by Zappa and Moon Unit (his daughter). It was counterculture's answer to Frank/Nancy Sinatra(▶) duet of '60s, comprised of Southern California's teenage jargon, a language of its own. Latterly Zappa has involved himself in struggle against right wing/fundamentalist moves to censor rock lyrics, while Moon Unit has achieved further fame as video jockey. Meanwhile guitarist son Dweezil is proving to be chip off the old block, forging solid reputation as sessioneer and also working as presenter on MTV.

Guitars: D'mini-Les Paul, the Strate.

**Albums:**
Uncle Meat (Bizarre/Reprise), 1969
Hot Rats (Bizare/Reprise), 1969 **CD**
Burnt Weeny Sandwich (Bizarre/Reprise), 1969
Weasels Ripped My Flesh (Bizarre/Reprise), 1970
Chunga's Revenge (Bizarre/Reprise), 1970
The Mothers: Fillmore East, June 1971 (Bizarre/Reprise), 1971

Above: Frank Zappa's wry smile indicates all's well with this enigmatic and consistently adventurous Mother of rock music.

200 Motels (United Artists), 1971
Just Another Band From LA (Bizarre/Reprise), 1972
Waka/Jawaka — Hot Rats (Bizarre/Reprise), 1972
Grand Wazoo (Bizarre/Reprise), 1972
Overnite Sensation (DiscReet), 1973 **CD**
Apostrophe (DiscReet), 1974 **CD**
Roxy And Elsewhere (DiscReet), 1974
One Size Fits All (DiscReet), 1975
Bongo Fury (DiscReet), 1975
Zoot Allures (DiscReet), 1976
Zappa In New York (DiscReet), 1978
Studio Tan (DiscReet), 1978
Sheik Yerbouti (DiscReet), 1979
Sleep Dirt (DiscReet), 1979
Orchestral Favourites (DiscReet), 1979
Joe's Garage Act I (Zappa/CBS), 1979
Joe's Garage Acts II & III (Zappa/CBS), 1979
Tinsel Town Rebellion (Barking Pumpkin/CBS), 1980
You Are What You Is (Zappa/CBS), 1981
Shut Up And Play Yer Guitar (Barking Pumpkin/CBS), 1981

Ship Arrived To Late To Save A Drowning Witch (Barking Pumpkin/CBS), 1982
The Man From Utopia (Barking Pumpkin/CBS), 1983
Rare Meat—Early Productions of Frank Zappa (Del Fi/—), 1983
Them Or Us (EMI), 1984
Thing Fish (Capitol), 1985
Does Humour Belong In Music (EMI), 1986 **CD**

*Worth Searching Out:*
Freak Out (MGM/Verve), 1966
Absolutely Free (MGM/Verve), 1967
We're Only In It For The Money (DiscReet), 1968 **CD**
Lumpy Gravy (MGM/Verve), 1968
Cruising With Ruben And The Jets (MGM/Verve), 1968
Mothermania — The Best Of The Mothers (MGM/Verve), 1968

**The classic cover of Weasels Ripped My Flesh, Mothers Of Invention. Courtesy Bizarre/Reprise Records.**

## A

**ACE** – Short-lived British soul-influenced group. Topped US charts in 1975 with moody **How Long** from **Five-A-Side** album.

**ADAM ANT** – British singer who came to prominence with New Romantic Movement of late seventies/early '80s. Latterly pursuing career as actor.

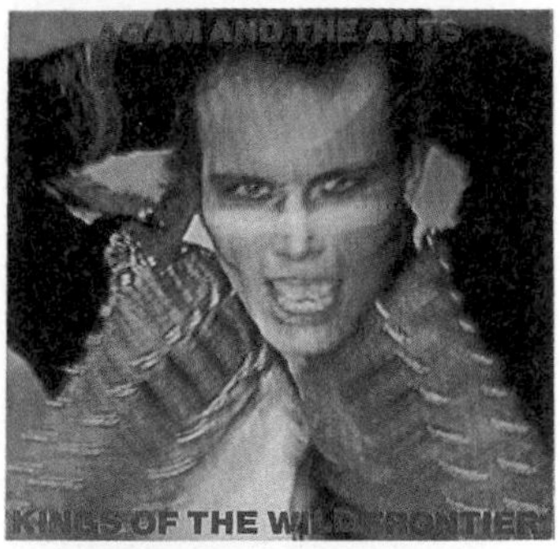

**Kings Of The Wild Frontier, Adam and the Ants. Courtesy CBS Records. Adam has since gone solo.**

**KING SUNNY ADE** – Nigerian performer of good time African music whose 'juju' sounds have attracted large audiences in both the US and UK.

**AIR SUPPLY** – Australian band who scored well in the American singles chart in the early '80s, most notably with **All Out Of Love** and **The One That You Love**, both penned by vocalist, UK-born Graham Russell.

**JAN AKKERMAN** – Former lead guitarist of Dutch band Focus which enjoyed success during '70s. A reticent, introverted character, he has since cut selection of excellent solo albums, of which **Live** (1979) is a standout.

**ALABAMA** – Consistent performers who broke into the US pop charts with **Feels So Right** in 1981 after a decade in the country listings. Now enjoying platinum status with albums.

**HERB ALPERT** – The 'A' in A&M Records, Alpert and his Tijuana Brass were chart regulars in the early '60s. Rejuvenated recording career with low-key disco offerings from late '70s.

**MOSE ALLISON** – Highly individual white blues jazz singer/pianist. Much recorded and a major influence on British stars such as Georgie Fame.

**CARLOS ALOMAR** – US guitarist, highly regarded leader of David Bowie's stage band for many years. Has also worked with John Lennon, Bette Midler, Chuck Berry and R&B greats Wilson Pickett and James Brown. Married to former Chic vocalist Robin Clark.

**ALTERED IMAGES** – UK synth band behind cutesy, squeaky, goo-goo vocals of Clare Grogan (who had part in film 'Gregory's Girl'). Had promising start with 1981 hits **Happy Birthday** and **I Could Be Happy,** but sound now wearing thin.

**AMEN CORNER** – Cardiff-based mod band which topped UK charts with **Half As Nice** (1969) and enjoyed four other Top 20 records. Name changed to Fairweather (after lead singer Andy Fairweather-Low) in 1970 when they had Top 5 hit with **Natural Sinner.**

**AMERICA** – US trio who peaked with lilting **Horse With No Name** in 1972. CSN&Y 'soundalike' formula surprisingly returned outfit to American top ten in 1982 with **You Can Do Magic.**

**THE AMERICAN BREED** – Scored in 1967 with **Bend Me Shape Me.** Originally called Gary and the Nite Lights, they hailed from Chicago.

**LAURIE ANDERSON** – One woman show from America, best known for socially perceptive lyrics and electric sound. Most recent success was single **O Superman,** which reached No.2 in the UK in 1981.

**PAUL ANKA** – Canadian teen idol who topped US/UK charts in 1957 with **Diana.** Subsequently scored 35 further Top 60 entries in America before settling down on nightclub circuit. Wrote English lyrics to **My Way,** which assured already wealthy artist (art collection, property) of royalties in old age.

**ANNETTE** – Annette Funicello was regular face in '60s spate of 'beach party' movies. Launched with Top 10 US single **Tall Paul** on Walt Disney's Vista label; followed through with string of crass but commercially successful singles.

**APRIL WINE** – Canadian HM outfit from Nova Scotia who cracked US LP listings in 1980.

**ARGENT** – Former member of Zombies, Argent is a first division keyboard performer who has settled nicely into film/studio work after a couple of decent hit singles from the early '70s, notably rock anthem **Hold Your Head Up.**

**ARRIVAL** – Liverpool pop band. Scored in 1970 with **Friends** and **I Will Survive,** but folded three years later, three of members becoming nucleus of Kokomo.

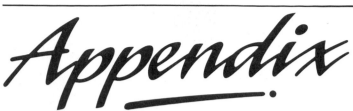

# Appendix

Sheer lack of space prevents us including a full entry on the following acts, but we would like to recognise their contributions to rock music.

**ART OF NOISE** – Electro invention of notable producer Trevor Horn. Success of **Beat Box** and **Close (To The Edit)** achieved by dynamic videos rather than muted group image.

**ASHFORD & SIMPSON** – Premier US songwriters – **Ain't No Mountain High Enough, You're All I Need To Get By, Ain't Nothing Like The Real Thing, Reach Out And Touch,** etc, etc – who found chart success as performers with dynamic **Solid** in 1985.

**ASSOCIATION** – Slick pop group who featured their five-part harmonies on series of major hits throughout late '60s. Topped US charts twice with **Windy** (1967) and **Cherish** (1966). Rumours of band's reunion have been rife since 1975, but still no show.

**CHET ATKINS** – Country guitarist whose influence permeates all kinds of American guitar music. Now head of RCA Records in Nashville.

**ATLANTA RHYTHM SECTION** – Distinguished band of session musicians (featuring guitarist Barry Bailey) who scored five US Top 20 hits in late '70s. Re-make of **Spooky,** originally recorded by Classics IV, (whose line-up included current ARS guitarist J.R. Cobb and group's manager Buddy Buie), was group's last major success.

**BRIAN AUGER** – From jazz pianist to R&B organist, he featured John McLaughlin in his first group. Then formed Brian Auger Trinity which by mid-1965 had become Steampacket with Long John Baldry, Rod Stewart and Julie Driscoll fronting on vocals. After band split, Auger and Driscoll had 1968 hit with **This Wheel's On Fire.**

**FRANKIE AVALON** – US teen idol from late fifties who scored with succession of teen anthems, most notably US No 1 **Venus** (1959).

**AVERAGE WHITE BAND** – Scottish outfit led by Hamish Stuart and Alan Gorrie whose potential was unfulfilled after series of exciting hit singles, of which **Pick Up The Pieces** topped the US charts in 1975.

**HOYT AXTON** – Best known as songwriter with hits for Steppenwolf, Three Dog Night, Ringo Starr, Tiny Tim and Joan Baez. Cut series of fine country rock albums in own right. His mother wrote Elvis Presley's hit **Heartbreak Hotel,** and was partner in formation of Stax label.

**Below: Every mother's favourite son, 'Buster' Bloodvessel (in chair) leads Bad Manners with aggression, wit and not inconsiderable style.**

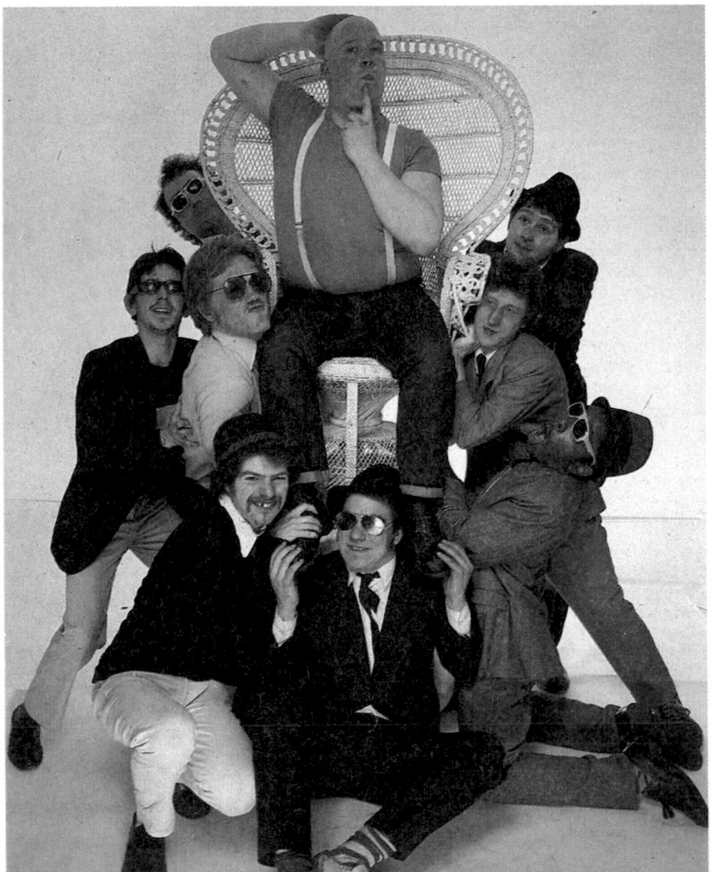

## B

**B-52's** – One of the earliest US new wave bands who sprung to fame with wacky **Rock Lobster** (1979). Continued in similar vein with songs like **Party Gone Out Of Bounds.** Hilarious lyrics, but sound gets repetitive after first LP.

**BURT BACHARACH** – Enormously successful New York-based songwriter, notably in partnership with Hal David. On Staff at Scepter/Wand Records they wrote hits for Chuck Jackson, Tommy Hunt, Maxine Brown and, most notably, Dionne Warwick – including classics **Anyone Who Had A Heart, Walk On By** and **You'll Never Get To Heaven.** Partnership dissolved after 'Promises Promises' musical. From 1963 on, Bacharach recorded own albums for MCA and A&M and starred in countless TV specials. Most recent success was 1986 chart-topping Michael McDonald/Patti Labelle duet **On My Own.** Married to Carole Bayer-Sager.

**THE BACHELORS** – Irish balladeer group (brothers Declan and Con Clusky plus Sean Stokes). Their old-hat 'Tin Pan Alley' format competed successfully with Merseybeat explosion; had 10 Top 20 hits between 1963-1967.

**BACHMAN-TURNER OVERDRIVE** – Formed from the remnants of Guess Who, Canadians Randy Bechman and Fred Turner have earned a place in rock history if for nothing but staying power. Topped US singles chart in 1975 with oft-revised **You Ain't Seen Nothing Yet.**

**BADFINGER** – Beatles' protégés; scored in 1970 with McCartney's **Come And Get It.** Founder and songwriter Peter Ham committed suicide in 1975.

**BAD MANNERS** – Group of North Londoners led by shaven-headed behemoth Doug Trendle (aka Buster Bloodvessel) whose cockney sing-a-longs endured for a couple of years in the '80s.

**JOHN BAEZ** – Peacenik from the early sixties whose magnificent vocal style enhanced folk/rock protest scene. Ironically, the country classic **The Night They Drove Old Dixie Down** provided her with her only top ten success.

**GINGER BAKER** – Best known as drummer for Cream. Upon band's demise, formed short-lived Blind Faith, then Airforce then Baker-Gurvitz Army. More recent ventures have included Ginger Baker's Nutters, and Bakerland. He currently lives in Italy.

**LONG JOHN BALDRY** – Seminal figure on British R&B scene. Served with Cyril Davies R&B All Stars, taking over band and re-naming it the Hoochie Coochie Men on Davies' death in January 1964. Gave Rod Stewart his first break (as second singer) and then joined Steampacket, also with Stewart. From Bluesology (which also included Elton John), moved into pop with 1967 UK chart-topper **Let The Heartaches Begin.** Football anthem **Mexico** marked by big, full voice.

**BANANARAMA** – UK all-girl trio paired with Fun Boy Three for 1982 hit **Really Saying Something.** Also hit with **Shy Boy** on own. A bit weak vocally, lacking energy overall. Probably best-suited to back-up work.

**BARCLAY JAMES HARVEST** – Manchester-based British cult band with critically acclaimed albums for EMI's Harvest label and Polydor.

**H.B. BARNUM** – Major US black arranger, composer. Had hits with Robins, Lou Rawls, Irma Thomas, the Osmonds and many Motown acts. Recorded own piano/vocal albums for RCA in '60s.

**BOBBY BARE** – First hit, **The All-American Boy,** a parody on Elvis Presley, made US No. 2 in 1958 but label credit went to his friend Bill Parsons. Subsequently became major pop/country artist with classic **Detroit City** and **500 Miles Away From Home,** plus brilliant reading of Kris Kristofferson's **Me And Bobby McGee.**

**JOHN BARRY** – John Barry Seven instrumental group backed countless British pop package shows between 1957-1962 before wider fame was won with TV and movie film tunes, most notably work on the 'James Bond' series and 'Out of Africa'.

**Cupid's In Fashion, Average White Band. Courtesy RCA Records.**

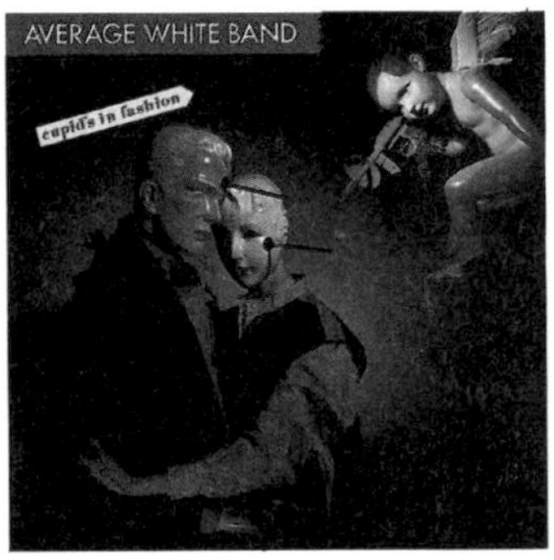


**LEN BARRY** – Had big hit as member of Dovells with **Bristol Stomp** (1961), then became successful blue-eyed soul singer on own with Philadelphia classics **1-2-3** and **Cry Like A Baby.**

**SHIRLEY BASSEY** – Welsh-born daughter of West Indian seaman. Made UK charts with cover of Harry Belafonte's **Banana Boat Song.** After two-year chart hiatus, London Palladium appearances helped establish her as major recording, concert and cabaret star with torch-ballad successes **As Long As He Needs Me, You'll Never Know, What Now My Love** and **I (Who Have Nothing).**

**MIKE BATT** – Producer of psychedelic band Hapshash and the Coloured Coat, moved into lushly-orchestrated own-name albums of rock covers. Had 1975 solo hit with **Summertime City,** then captured weeny-bopper market with his music for 'The Wombles' TV series.

**BAUHAUS** – Post-punk British outfit, pioneers of gothic rock who achieved cult following in early '80s.

**BAY CITY ROLLERS** – 70s manufactured phenomenum, this Scottish band were never out of the UK singles chart for nearly seven years, and even topped US listings with **Saturday Night** in 1975.

**THE BEAT** – Enterprising UK group whose quirky lyrics endeared UK fans. Upon demise, band spawned Fine Young Cannibals and General Public.

**THE BEAU BRUMMELS** – Launched as 'America's answer to the British invasion', their soft-rock approach paved way for the Byrds, Turtles and others with 1965 hits **Laugh Laugh** and **Just A Little.**

**FREDDIE BELL AND THE BELLBOYS** – Pioneer rock 'n' rollers. Appeared with Bill Haley in 1955 'Rock Around The Clock' movie and were first US rockers to visit UK, touring with Tommy Steele in 1956. Scored on British charts with **Giddy Up A Ding Dong.**

**MAGGIE BELL** – Blues and soul-laced Scottish singer. Fronted admirable Stone the Crows which featured Les Harvey on lead guitar. After band split, following Harvey's death from electrocution on-stage at Swansea, she released superb if uncommercial solo albums.

**BELLESTARS** – Seven-piece all-girl group evolved

from Bodysnatchers who make funky, brassy dance music. Early hit singles were covers **Iko Iko** and **The Clapping Song. Sign Of The Times** (1983) indicated some originality, 1986 line-up reduced to trio.

**CLIFF BENNETT** — UK blue-eyed soulster, his brassy Rebel Rousers group scored with covers of the Drifters' **One Way Love** and Beatles' **Got To Get You Into My Life.** Later formed heavier Toe Thumb with little success.

**BROOK BENTON** — Gospel-rooted black rock 'n' roll balladeer. With Belford Hendricks and producer Clyde Otis he co-wrote his first three big hits **It's Just A Matter Of Time, Endlessly** and **Thank You Pretty Baby** in 1959. Consistently in charts (including million-selling duets **Baby (You've Got What It Takes)** and **Rockin' Good Way** with Dinah Washington) until 1963. Bounced back in 1970 with classic rendition of Tony Joe White's **Rainy Night In Georgia.**

**BIG BOPPER** — One-hit wonder J.P. Richardson, alias the Big Bopper, was top Texan radio DJ. Scored worldwide with rock 'n' roll novelty **Chantilly Lace** (1958). Had minor success with follow-up **The Big Bopper's Wedding,** but died February 3, 1959, in air crash (with Buddy Holly and Richie Valens). Also a successful songwriter, he penned Johnny Preston's **Running Bear** hit.

**BIG BROTHER AND THE HOLDING COMPANY** — The San Francisco-based group which springboarded Janis Joplin to superstardom.

**BIG OZZIE BAND** — Australian rockers with concern over ecology in the '80s. Single **Midnight Oil** has placed them in spotlight and many great things are expected of them in the future.

**THE BIG THREE** — Highly respected Liverpool group of early '60s that failed to follow Beatles and others to international success, despite Brian Epstein's management.

**ELVIN BISHOP** — Emerged from Paul Butterfield Blues Band to form own highly respected funky rock band highlighting his delicious guitar style and solid vocals.

**BILL BLACK** — American stand-up bassist featured on Elvis Presley's early Sun recordings. Moving to electric bass, formed Bill Black Combo in 1959 and enjoyed six US top twenty hits. After his death in 1965, the Combo continued with Willie Mitchell replacing Black.

**CILLA BLACK** — Friend and close associate of the Beatles, launched to stardom by Brian Epstein with covers of US soul hits, then veered towards MOR via cabaret and regular TV shows.

**BLACK OAK ARKANSAS** — Raunchy Southern boogie band. Earned gold in 1974 for **High On The Hog** album.

**BLANCMANGE** — UK duo Neil Arthur and Stephen Luscombe make lighthearted pop in style of biggest hit **Living On The Ceiling.** Check out 1982 single **God's Kitchen/I've Seen The World.**

**BOBBY BLAND** — Classic blues vocalist, whose smooth styling has kept him in the public eye over a 30-year career.

**THE BLASTERS** — Los Angeles-based outfit formed by brothers Phil and Dave Alvin who have been on verge of mega-success since early punk-styled albums.

**BLIND FAITH** — Archetypal 'supergroup' formed in 1969 featuring Eric Clapton, Steve Winwood, Ginger Baker and Rick Grech. London Hyde Park concert which attracted 100,000 punters was highlight of this short-lived venture.

**BLOOD SWEAT AND TEARS** — Bombastic but innovative brass-rock aggregation from late '60s who survived a decade on the back of million selling singles **You've Made Me So Very Happy, Spinning Wheel** and **And When I Die.**

**MIKE BLOOMFIELD** — American blues guitarist whose greatest success came from partnership with Al Kooper. Unfulfilled talent who died in 1981.

**DAVID BLUE** — Singer/songwriter, friend of Bob Dylan and stalwart of Greenwich Village folk-rock scene. Classy albums on Warner Bros, Elektra and Asylum.

**BLUE MINK** — Anglo/American pop outfit who benefitted from writing prowess of vocalist Roger Cook. Never cracked US charts despite cosmopolitan sound personified by UK success **Melting Pot.**

**BLUES BROTHERS** — Film venture formed by John Belushi and Dan Ackroyd, which featured former Booker T & MG's sideman Steve Cropper and 'Duck' Dunn. Live concerts were a riot; excesses killed Belushi in 1982.

**BLUES PROJECT** — New York white blues band formed by Danny Kalb and featuring Al Kooper and Steve Katz (who went on to create Blood Sweat and Tears). Influence far exceeded their record sales.

**COLIN BLUNSTONE** — Classy British singer/songwriter remembered as lead singer of the Zombies and for 1971 solo hit **Say You Don't Mind.**

**GRAHAM BOND** — Early days as modern jazz alto-sax player led him into British R&B boom of early '60s. Switching to organ he replaced the deceased Cyril Davies in Blues Incorporated before forming own group, which included Ginger Baker, Jack Bruce and John McLaughlin. After demise of Graham Bond Organization he was involved in several bands, including Ginger Baker's Airforce

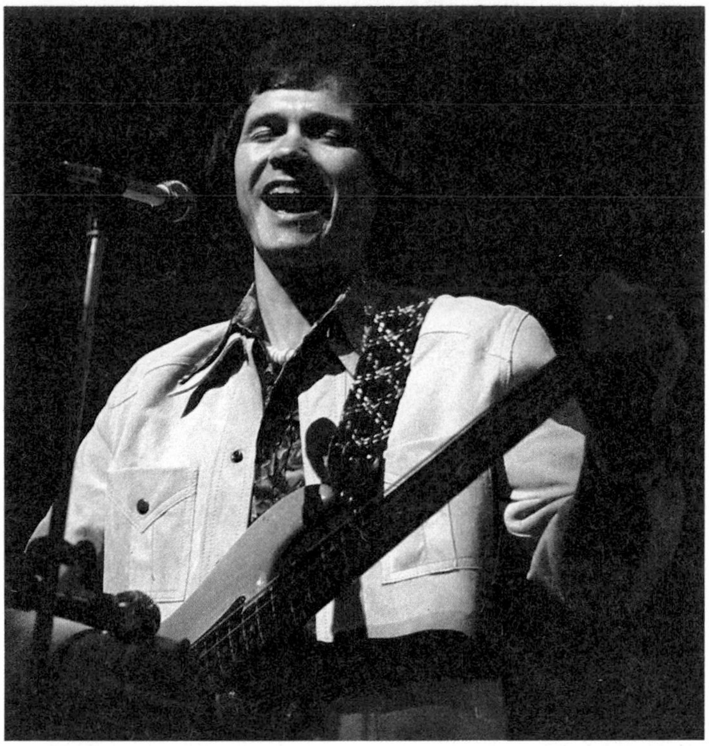

**Above: David Gates, lead singer of Bread, solo artist and prolific songwriter.**

before falling to death under London Underground train in 1974.

**BONEY M** — West Indian vocal/instrumental group with several semi-religious UK pop hits, including **Daddy Cool, Sunny, Ma Baker, Belfast, Rivers Of Babylon/Brown Girl In The Ring** (No. 1), **Rasputin, Mary's Boy Child** (also No. 1) and **Hooray! Hooray! It's A Holi Holiday** in the late '70s.

**BONZO DOG (DOO DAH) BAND** — British rock band with penchant for humorous material, led by Viv Stanshall, Neil Innes and Roger Ruskin Spear. Had outrageously funny stage act and UK Top 5 single with **The Urban Spaceman** in 1968.

**BOOKER T AND THE MG'S** — Influential Memphis-based quartet featuring the best of the Stax session men Booker T. Jones (organ), Steve Cropper (guitar), Duck Dunn (bass) and Al Jackson, Jr (drums). Their classic instrumental **Green Onions** remains a firm dance favourite.

**PAT BOONE** — Next to Elvis, the most successful US solo singer of the rock 'n' roll era (though his music was somewhat right of MOR and relied on clean-cut 'all-American Boy' image). Raised in Nashville and married to daughter of country star Red Foley; came to prominence with bland cover versions of black rock 'n' roll hits by Fats Domino **(Ain't That A Shame)** and Little Richard **(Tutti Frutti, Long Tall Sally).** Then switched to 'moon in June' romantic ballads with **Love Letters In The Sand, April Love** and others. Had 24 Top 20 hits of which novelty item **Speedy Gonzales** was best credential for his inclusion in a rock book. Daughter Debbie had major hit in 1977 with **You Light Up My Life.**

**BOW WOW WOW** — One of Malcolm McLaren's rare failures, this effete quartet led by vocalist Annabelle Lewin nonetheless made UK charts in 1982 with **Go Wild In The Country** and **I Want Candy.**

**THE BOX TOPS** — Super Memphis-based blue-eyed soul band. Topped charts in 1967 with **The Letter.** As much a vehicle for songwriting/arranging/producing talents of Dan Penn, Spooner Oldham and Chips Moman as for Alex Chilton's distinctively husky lead vocals.

**BREAD** — Sugary American pop outfit led by David Gates whose ear for a weepy ballad kept group in charts for most of the '70s.

**BRECKER BROS** — Mike (tenor sax, flute, soprano sax) and Randy (trumpet) Brecker are stalwarts of US session scene. Worked with Stevie Wonder, Janis Joplin, James Taylor, Johnny and Edgar Winter, John Lennon, Carly Simon, David Allen, Patti Austin and countless others. Recorded own selection of jazz-funk albums for Arista.

**BRINSLEY SCHWARZ** — Launched with biggest PR hype of all-time (a complete jet-load of UK journalists being flown out to see them perform at New York's Fillmore East). Backlash worked against them. Despite some fine mixtures of blues-rock and soft-rock harmonies they could not fight way into major league and broke up in 1975.

**DAVID BROMBERG** — American guitarist, also dobro player (though inferior vocalist) who has worked with Bob Dylan, Willie Nelson, Gordon Lightfoot, Rick Derringer, and Sha Na Na among others. Large selection of solo LPs recorded for Columbia and Fantasy (from 1971-1977) feature many live recordings.

**ELKIE BROOKS** — Superior smokey-voiced songstress. Emerged from Da Da and Vinegar Joe to become major solo concert attraction and notch massive-selling albums, notably **Pearl.**

**ARTHUR BROWN** — Zany UK rock personality who scored with powerful **Fire** (1968). The Crazy World Of Arthur Brown was staggering in-concert spectacle but was never properly captured on disc.

**JACK BRUCE** — Former Cream bassist/vocalist whose career began promisingly with **Songs For A Tailor** LP. Later work was less successful although he remains active in music.

**FELICE AND BOUDLEAUX BRYANT** — Nashville-based composers who wrote **Bye Bye Love, Wake Up Little Suzie, Bird Dog** and other hits for Everly Brothers, **Raining In My Heart** for Buddy Holly and **Let's Think About Living** for Bob Luman. Recorded own albums in '60s.

**ROY BUCHANAN** — Served on rock 'n' roll session scene (with Dale Hawkins, Bob Luman, Freddie Cannon, etc.) before re-emerging in '70s as highly acclaimed guitar star on Polydor.

**TIM BUCKLEY** — One of rock's great 'might have beens', this Washington folkie turned rocker scored heavily with 1972 LP **Greetings From LA**. Died from drug overdose in 1975.

**BUCKS FIZZ** — 1981 Eurovision winners with **Making Your Mind Up.** Highly produced pop in Abba mould has done well in the UK since, with such hits as **The Land Of Make Believe** and **My Camera Never Lies** (both No. 1s).

**BUFFALO SPRINGFIELD** — Pioneer San Franciscan band from '60s featuring Stephen Stills, Neil Young, Richie Furay and later Jim Messina. Melodic style enjoyed one US hit **For What It's Worth** (1967).

**DORSEY BURNETTE** — Bass player in brother Johnny's famed rock 'n' roll trio. Had own hits with big ballads **Tall Oak Tree** and **Big Rock Candy Mountain.** Also wrote hits for Jerry Lee Lewis and Ricky Nelson.

**JOHNNY BURNETTE** — US rocker whose **Dreamin'** and **You're Sixteen** have stood the test of time. Died in a boating accident in 1964.

**Songs For A Tailor, Jack Bruce. Courtesy Polydor Records.**

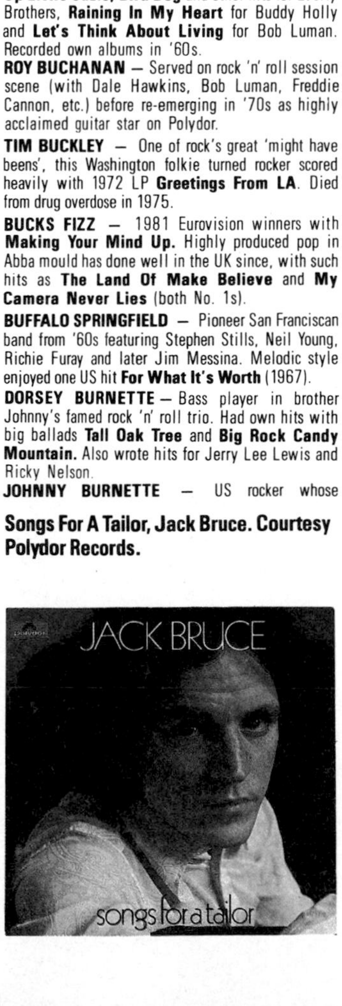


**JAMES BURTON** — Sought after guitar sessioneer who came to public attention as Presley sideman in '70s, and, more recently, as a member of Emmylou Harris's Hot Band. Also worked with Ricky Nelson group in 50s/60s.

**PRINCE BUSTER** — King of bluebeat, who influenced generation of British bands like UB 40 and Specials.

**PAUL BUTTERFIELD** — With his Blues Band, became major concert attraction in '60s and '70s before HM scene overwhelmed him. This talented vocalist/harmonica player surrounded himself with ace musicians like Mike Bloomfield, Elvin Bishop and David Sanbourne. Died of drug-related causes in 1987.

**JERRY BYRNE** — White New Orleans rock 'n' roller. Cut 1958 pounding classic **Lights Out** with black producer Harold Battiste.

## C

**JOHN CALE** — Founder of Velvet Underground, later rock/theatrical experimentalist.

**J.J. CALE** — Enigmatic modern country performer who threatened to turn the world on its ear in early '70s with barrage of tastefully laid back material, of which **After Midnight** is now a classic.

**GLEN CAMPBELL** — Former session guitarist whose smooth vocals enhanced Jim Webb's classic work **By The Time I Get To Phoenix** and **Wichita Lineman**. Now established cabaret favourite and television performer.

**CANNED HEAT** — Pioneering US blues band who scored in US/UK singles charts with **On The Road Again** (1968). Founder members Al Wilson and Bob Hite both died of heart attacks.

**FREDDIE CANNON** — Boston native brought to fame via Philadelphia-based Swan Records and 'American Bandstand' TV show. 18 hits in a row — notably hard-rocking **Tallahassie Lassie** and **Way Down Yonder In New Orleans. Palisades Park** made him major star of tail-end of rock 'n' roll's golden '50s.

**CARAVAN** — Long-established Canterbury-based outfit formed around guitarist Pye Hastings and keyboard-player Dave Sinclair (who quit in 1971, and again in 1975 after short reunion with group). Popular concert act during '70s, who never made impact on charts despite excellent albums, particularly **If I Could Do It All Over Again I'd Do It All Over You.**

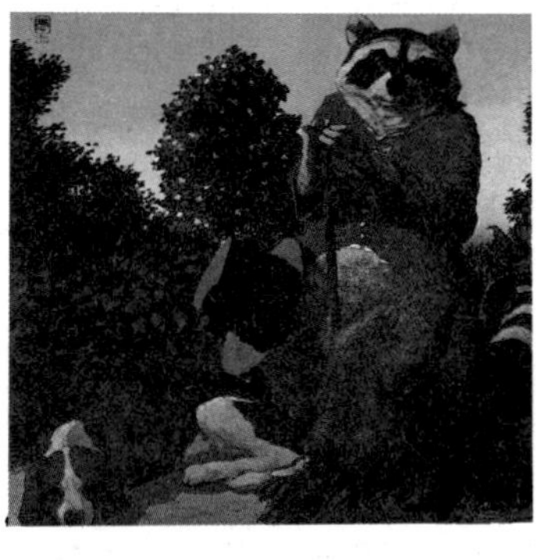

**Naturally, J.J. Cale. Courtesy Shelter Records.**

**LARRY CARLTON** — Premier US session guitarist whose own output has placed him firmly at the pinnacle of the jazz/rock movement. Featured on **Hill Street Blues** theme hit single, and with artists such as The Crusaders, Steely Dan and Art Garfunkel.

**ERIC CARMEN** — Former Raspberry who hit US No 2 with **All By Myself** in 1976.

**CARLENE CARTER** — Talented country rock singer, daughter of country star June Carter. Now married to Nick Lowe. Paul Carrack played keyboards in her excellent backing band.

**JOHNNY CASH** — The 'Man In Black' whose straight-down-the-line approach to country music has endeared him to audiences from the mid-fifties.

**DAVID CASSIDY** — Star of popular 'The Partridge Family' US TV series. Became massive hero of teeny-bopper audiences in early '70s before being ousted by Donny Osmond and Michael Jackson. Continues to act.

**CATE BROS** — Ernie (keyboards) and Earl (guitar) Cate received acclaim in late '70s as powerful live act. Record sales proved sporadic, despite excellent Steve Cropper-produced albums.

**THE CHAMPS** — Highly rated US instrumental combo who topped charts with debut hit **Tequila** (1958). Their raunchy singles are now prized collectors' items. Latter-day members Jimmy Seals and Dash Crofts went on to further success as Seals and Crofts duo.

**BRUCE CHANNEL** — R&B-flavoured rocker. **Hey Baby** made US No. 1 in 1962. Went on to tour UK with Beatles in same year. Fluid harmonica playing set Channel apart from dozens of contemporaries.

**CHAS AND DAVE** — Modern-day Flanagan and Allan, Chas Hodges (ex-Head Hands & Feat) (piano, vocals) and Dave Peacock (bass, vocals), both former session musicians, have achieved record and concert success with clever cockney patois lyrics, which they call 'Rockney', coupled with solid rock base.

**CHEAP TRICK** — Innovative American quartet led by guitarist Nick Nielson who had solitary US chart with **I Want You To Want Me** in 1979. Consistent LP performers.

**CHEECH AND CHONG** — Popular hippy comic duo discovered by Lou Adler (who produced their recent movie). Tommy Chong was once member of Canadian soul outfit Bobby Taylor and the Vancouvers and co-wrote their classic Motown cut **Does Your Mama Know About Me.** Pair (Cheech Marin is Mexican/American, Chong Chinese/American) are now cult film stars through appearances in series of US Government drug abuse movies.

**CHIC** — Archetypal late '70s disco outfit formed by Nile Rodgers and Bernard Edwards whose **Le Freak** and **Good Times** both made US no 1.

**CHILLIWACK** — Your basic US band with better than average harmonies; most recently enjoying US success with '80s hits like **My Girl (Gone, Gone, Gone)** and **Whatcha Gonna Do (With My Heart).**

**THE CHIPMUNKS** — Studio creation (sounding like a 33 rpm record on 45 speed) of David Seville. The perky **Chipmunk Song** sold three and a half million copies proving that either poor taste was alive and well in 1958, or that a lot of children talked parents into buying it.

**JIMMY CLANTON** — White New Orleans kid who scored initially with black-sounding R&B ballad **Just A Dream;** then promoted as all-American boy-next-door with million-selling **Venus In Blue Jeans** (1962).

**STANLEY CLARKE** — Dextrous American bass player who ventured into heavy funk after establishing himself in jazz field. Work best personified by collaboration with keyboard player George Duke as Clarke/Duke project.

**CLASSICS IV** — Backing band on hits for Billy Joe Royal and the Tams, they scored in 1967 with ballady **Spooky.** Guitarist James Cobb and group's arranger/producer Buddy Buie went on to join the Atlanta Rhythm Section.

**JIMMY CLIFF** — Ace Jamaican reggae star who peaked with **The Harder They Come** movie and album in 1972. Maintains high profile in West Indies.

**GEORGE CLINTON** — Mastermind behind the P. Funk organisation which has included Parliament, Funkadelic, Parlet, The Brides Of Funkenstein, etc. Novelty approach has restricted this talented musician's audience.

**BILLY COBHAM** — Prolific jazz-rock drummer who has worked with everyone from Miles Davis to James Brown. Stream of competent albums has kept Cobham in the foreiront of instrumentalists, and his reputation has ensured 'sell-out' notices for his drum clinics.

**COCTEAU TWINS** — Whimsical UK trio led by Elizabeth Frazer and Robin Guthrie, whose tuneful melodies may yet find a broader acceptance beyond that of the 'Indie Chart'.

**LEONARD COHEN** — 'Laughing Len', purveyor of lugubrious bedsit ballads was nonetheless influence on many '70s singer/songwriters. Best remembered for **Suzanne** and **Hey That's No Way To Say Goodbye.**

**JUDY COLLINS** — Highly respected 'folkie' who established huge following in the '60s with melodic albums for Elektra. Best known for version of **Amazing Grace,** a 1970 top twenty hit on both sides of the Atlantic.

**PERRY COMO** — King of the crooners — with '50s hits like **Tina Marie, Magic Moments** and **Catch A Falling Star.** His top-rated TV show provided admirable showcase for many emergent R&B and rock acts as well as influencing teen fashion trends.

**RITA COOLIDGE** — Tennessean lady who was discovered whilst working with Delaney & Bonnie. Laid back vocal style was fashionable in late '70s when she enjoyed her greatest single success. Once married to Kris Kristofferson.

**LARRY CORYELL** — Jazz guitarist who sounded more comfortable in his home surroundings than on myriad of jazz-rock offerings from '70s.

**CRAZY HORSE** — Former Neil Young back-up band, whose heyday was before death of guitarist/vocalist Danny Whitton in 1974. Re-formed units met less success despited quality work.

**THE COWSILLS** — Pop-harmony family group earned gold discs for **The Rain, The Park And Other Things** (1967) and **Hair** (1969).

**FLOYD CRAMER** — Top session pianist at RCA's Nashville Studios. Backed hits by Elvis Presley, Chet Atkins, Jim Reeves and others, and enjoyed million-seller in own right with atmospheric **Last Date** (1960).

**THE CREATION** — UK mod/pop group in Who mould; Shel Talmy produced their minor hits in 1966. Now mostly of interest to '60s collectors of music on the genre.

**MARSHALL CRENSHAW** — Solid American vocalist/guitarist whose contract with Warner Bros has produced decent albums, particularly self titled debut offering from 1982.

**THE CRICKETS** — With guitarist/singer Sonny Curtis and drummer Jerry Allison (the constant core of a changing line-up), the Crickets started out as Buddy Holly's backing group, splitting from him shortly before his death. In 1962 they toured and recorded with Bobby Vee, enjoying two UK hits. After break-up in 1975, Curtis and Allison played on Eric Clapton's 1970 solo albums, following which Crickets were re-formed.

**THE CRITTERS** — Covered John Sebastian's **Younger Girl** from debut Lovin' Spoonful album to score memorable if minor 1966 hit.

**ARTHUR 'BIG BOY' CRUDUP** — Mississippi bluesman whose originals, **That's All Right** and **My Baby Left Me,** provided early hit material for Elvis Presley.

**JIM CROCE** — Croce was killed in an air crash in 1973 at the height of his career, and this laid-back singer/songwriter was surely destined to add to his collection of chart albums and singles, of which **Time In A Bottle** is now a classic.

**CHRISTOPHER CROSS** — Rotund US vocalist/guitarist who exploded onto the rock scene with his sensational self-titled debut album in 1980. Has threatened to re-affirm this success, but the effort may be too much for him.

**RODNEY CROWELL** — One of the brightest of the new breed of country performers, Crowell's songs have been recorded by a host of living legends, including Willie Nelson, Waylon Jennings and Emmylou Harris (he was once a member of her Hot Band). Bob Seger's version of **Shame On The Moon** made US top five in 1983.

**CRUSADERS** — Crack jazz/funk aggregation featuring Wilton Felder and Joe Sample, which has, at various stages of line-up, included Wayne Henderson, Larry Carlton and long-time drummer Stix Hooper. Scored with guest singers on singles **Street Life** (Randy Crawford) and **Soul Shadows** (Bill Withers).

**CURLY LEADS & SWITCHES** — Legendary R&B outfit who produced classic **Plug Me In** album in early '60s. Curly (real name Maximillian De Frost) was grandson of French Ambassador to US who joined with local black musicians after moving to Louisiana. Now noted chef in French quarter of New Orleans, but still playing part-time.

**KING CURTIS** — Wonderful R&B tenor sax player who fronted own band, as well as playing for Buddy Holly, Coasters, Donny Hathaway, and Aretha Franklin. 1971 classic album **Live At The Fillmore West** proved testament to career that was cut tragically short when he was stabbed to death in New York the same year.

**JOHNNY CYMBAL** — Tribute to those mainstays of the '50s black R&B group sound, **Hey Mr Bass Man,** made Top 20 in 1963.

## D

**DALE AND GRADE** — Their 1963 cover of Don and Dewey's R&B hit **I'm Leaving It Up To You** took the Lousiana duo to top of US charts.

**CHARLIE DANIELS BAND** — Hard working country-rock unit led by wily vocalist/violinist/guitarist Daniels. Had major chart success in 1979 with **The Devil Went Down To Georgia.**

**DANNY AND THE JUNIORS** — Group of Italian Americans from Philadelphia whose **At The Hop**

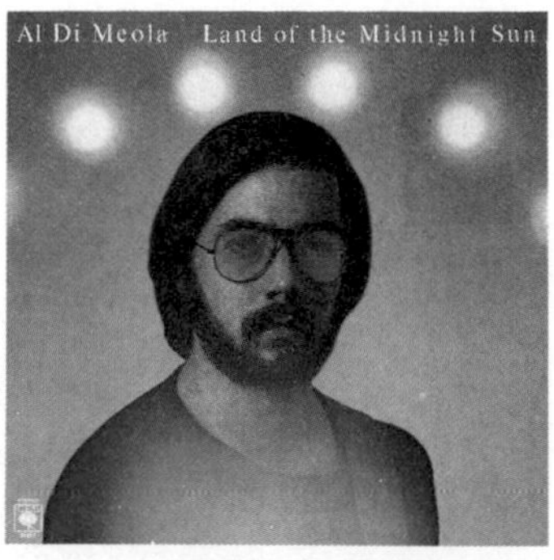


**Land Of The Midnight Sun, Al Di Meola. Courtesy Columbia Records.**

(1957) remains one of the all-time great rock 'n' roll waxings.

**BOBBY DARIN** — Influential '50s rocker cum crooner whose divided loyalties restricted success. Nonetheless left legacy of classic material including **Mack The Knife, Things, Splish Spash** and **Multiplication** following death from heart attack in 1973.

**JAMES DARREN** — Philadelphia contemporary of Frankie Avalon, Steve Alaimo and Fabian. His corny but catchy **Goodbye Cruel World** made him a star in 1961.

**DARTS** — London-based doo-wop revivalists who charted a dozen times in UK between 1977 and 1980, including a trio of No. 2s **Come Back My Love, Boy From New York City** and **It's Raining** in 1978.

**DAVE DEE, DOZY, BEAKY, MICK AND TICH** — British mid-'60s pop band with 10 UK Top 20 entries to credit, including 1968 chart-topper **The Legend Of Xanadu.**

**BILLIE DAVIS** — Teamed with Mike Sarne for novelty item **Will I What?,** then charted as solo in 1963 with **Tell Him** before linking up with ex-Shadows' bass player Jet Harris for long and traumatic relationship. In 1967 cut classic soulful version of **Angel Of The Morning.**

**SPENCER DAVIS GROUP** — Popular Midlands (UK) outfit best remembered as Stevie Winwood's first band. Had single success on both sides of the Atlantic, with **Gimme Some Lovin'** making both US and UK top tens.

**JOEY DEE AND THE STARLIGHTERS** — Resident band at the Peppermint Lounge in New York, their **Peppermint Twist** rode the dance craze wave in 1961. Felix Cavaliere, Eddie Brigati and Gene Cornish were in group in 1963 before moving on to form the Young Rascals.

**KIKI DEE** — Powerful English vocalist who has never attained deserved recognition. Biggest chart record **Don't Go Breaking My Heart** (1976) cut with Elton John, but **Amoreuse** remains her classic track. Once signed to Motown.

**JACKIE DE SHANNON** — Enormously talented — and underrated — Californian singer/songwriter prolifically recorded by Liberty. **Needles And Pins**

**Below: Crusader's reed man (and occasional bass player) Wilton Felder.**

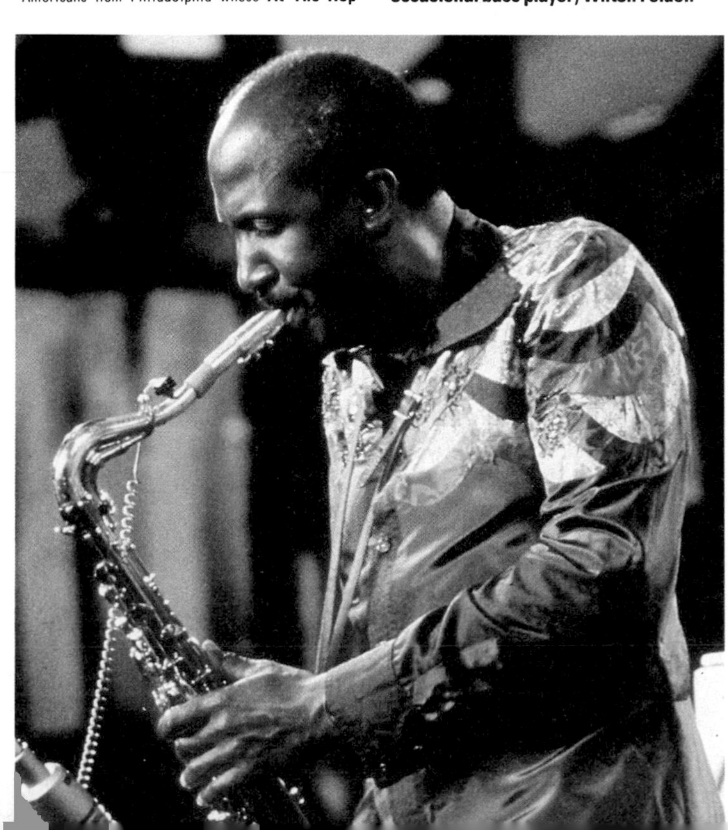

was major hit for British group the Searchers.

**DELANEY & BONNIE** — 'Blue-eyed' soul duo whose superlative bands featuring at various times Eric Clapton, Leon Russell, Rita Coolidge, Duane Allman, Jim Keltner and Bobby Whitlock made waves in early '70s.

**DEODATA** — Brazilian musician who first came to fame with his version of **Also Sprach Zarathustra (2001 Theme)** in 1973. Now an in-demand film/session man.

**AL DI MEOLA** — Outrageously talented guitarist who has flirted with a variety of music. His jazz-rock work is best personified by his association with Paco De Lucia and John McLaughlin.

**WILLIE DIXON** — Long-time producer and composer at Chess Studios where he nurtured major talent. A workmanlike double bass player, has released many quality blues albums. Best known composing credits include **I'm A Man, Hootchie Kootchie Man,** and **Wang Dang Doodle.**

**THOMAS DOLBY** — UK vocalist electro-pop wizard with mad-scientist looks to match. First UK hit was **Windpower.** Actually broke in the US first with **She Blinded Me With Science** (1982) accompanied by fantastic video featuring Magnus Pyke.

**DOLLAR** — UK duo with several hits from 1978-1982, most notably **Love's Got A Hold On Me, Mirror Mirror** and **Give Me Back My Heart.** After 3-year break, reformed in 1986.

**RAL DONNER** — Chicago-born, New York-based Elvis Presley soundalike. 1963's **I Got Burned** was best effort among string of chart entries.

**THE DOVELLS** — Philadelphian blue-eyed soul group with penchant for dance craze discs which earned them eight hits in four years. Lead singer Len Barry went on to solo fame.

**DR. FEELGOOD** — Underrated English rock band who have soldiered on entertaining audiences for nearly 20 years with their brand of homegrown R&B. Made UK top ten in 1979 with **Milk And Alcohol.**

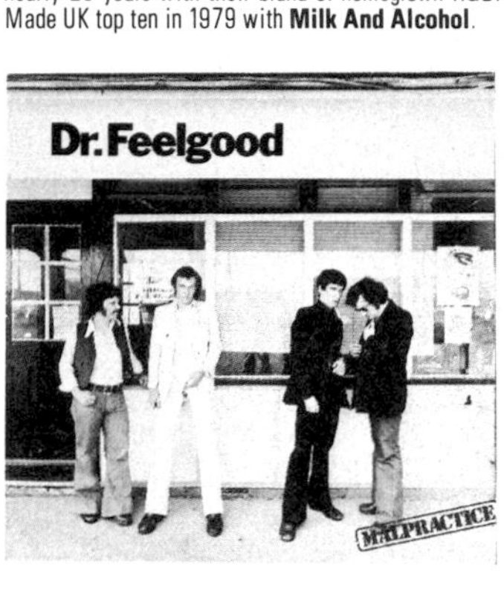


**Malpractice, Dr. Feelgood. Courtesy United Artists Records.**

**JULIE DRISCOLL** — Started as secretary of the Yardbirds' fan club and climbed to stardom as a singer. Fronted Steampacket with Rod Stewart and Long John Baldry, then in partnership with Brian Auger had 1968 hit with cover of Dylan's **This Wheel's On Fire.** Married to jazz/classical composer Keith Tippett.

**LES DUDEK** — Talented US guitarist/producer who has been involved with various projects throughout '70s and '80s. Has cut several solo albums, as well as recording with Allman Bros, Steve Miller. Had own Dudek, Finnegan, Krueger Band before joining Cher for **Black Rose** LP and group of same name.

**SLY DUNBAR & ROBBIE SHAKESPEARE** — Leading Jamaican reggae sidemen (drums and bass respectively) who have featured on a host of hit singles as well as cutting own albums.

**JOHNNY DUNCAN** — Tennessee-born country singer/guitarist. Married British girl and settled in UK on discharge from army. Replaced Lonnie Donegan as resident skiffle singer in Chris Barber's band, then formed own Blue Grass Boys making UK No. 2 with **Last Train To San Fernando** (1957).

**JAMES DUNLAP** — US drummer, former member of Watts 103rd Street Rhythm Band. Joined Bill Withers group in early '70s. Now leading session player and Michael Jackson's regular studio drummer.

## E

**THE EASYBEATS** — Formed in Australia where they had four chart-toppers in quick succession. Went to Britain in 1966 and cut worldwide hit **Friday On My Mind.** After lesser hits, group broke up in 1969.

**ECHO & THE BUNNYMEN** — Liverpool-based pop unit who have hovered on fringes of international stardom since 1982.

**RANDY EDELMAN** — US singer/songwriter, and excellent piano player, particularly popular in UK. Charted in UK during 1976 with re-make of **Concrete And Clay** and **Uptown Uptempo Woman.**

**ELECTRIC FLAG** – Rock/soul supergroup bringing together guitar wizard Mike Bloomfield, Nick 'The Greek' Gravenites and black drummer Buddy Miles, plus brass. Hard-hitting sound wowed audience at 1967 Monterey Pop Festival but albums disappointed.
**RAMBLING JACK ELLIOTT** – Itinerant American folk singer/songwriter. Companion to Woody Guthrie while in teens and major influence over Bob Dylan.
**BRIAN ENO** – Former Roxy Music alumnus who has built reputation as synth innovator and experimental video artist.
**JOE ELY** – Powerful country rock singer whose MCA albums have shown snatches of lyrical genius.
**THE EQUALS** – UK pop-soul band (two blacks, two whites). Topped chart with **Baby Come Back** (1968); had further hits with **Viva Bobby Joe** and **Black Skin Blue Eyed Boys.** Eddy Grant went on to solo stardom in '80s.

## F

**FABIAN** – Glamour boy from the 50s who stuck around in TV movies and revival shows. Real name Fabiano Forte.
**MARIANNE FAITHFULL** – Ex-convent schoolgirl most remembered for notorious liaison with Mick Jagger. The Jagger-Richard song **As Tears Go By** was her best and biggest record.
**GEORGIE FAME** – Sprang to prominence with his band the Blue Flames during UK "blues boom" of the sixties. Later switched to lightweight pop material, which established career longevity. Career highs for this talented vocalist/keyboard player were concert performances with Count Basie and Harry South big bands.
**CHRIS FARLOWE** – UK male vocalist with hits in the mid-'60s, namely No. 1 single **Out Of Time.**
**CHARLIE FEATHERS** – Influential Mississippi rockabilly singer/guitarist. Never a hitmaker but a cult figure during '70s.
**JOSE FELICIANO** – Multi-talented performer whose brilliant re-working of Doors **Light My Fire** should have meant eternal superstardom. However, all-encompassing musical outlook has limited chart success.
**THE FIXX** – UK group who got exposure in the US with melancholy hit **Stand Or Fall** (1982).
**ROBERTA FLACK** – US vocalist/pianist whose career was established by classic ballad **The First Time I Ever Saw Your face**. Also enjoyed chart success with Donnie Hathaway.
**FLAMIN' GROOVIES** – San Franciscan favourites of Continental audiences having built cult following for their purist approach to rock 'n' roll in '50s/Beatles' mould.
**FLASH AND THE PAN** – Australian group formed from remnants of Easybeats. Unusual sound is readily identifiable by nasal vocals that sound as if singer is locked in a box. Recently re-entered US/UK chart scene with **Waiting For A Train** (1983).
**FLASH CADILLAC AND THE CONTINENTAL KIDS** – Rock 'n' roll revivalists from Colorado.
**FOCUS** – First Dutch band to become rock superstars thanks to distinctive blend of rock, modern jazz and the classics. **Sylvia** and **Hocus Pocus** both scored in 1973 Thijs van Leer (keyboards, flute) and Jan Akkerman (guitar) had some solo success.

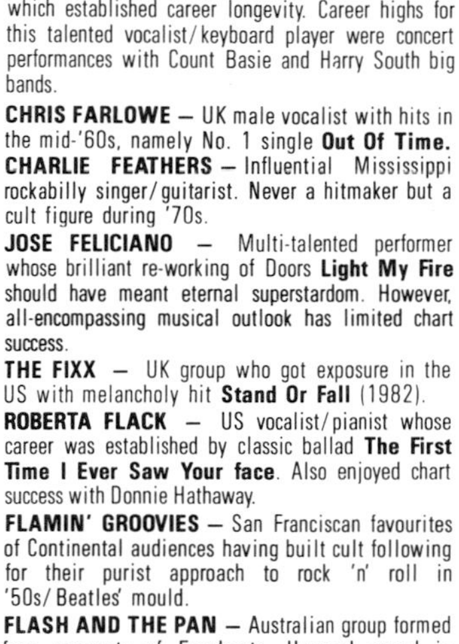

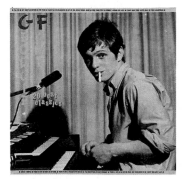

**20 Beat Classics, Georgie Fame. Courtesy RSD Records.**

**FLAT & SCRUGGS** – American guitar/banjo duo who firmly established bluegrass music as a popular music form with **Foggy Morning Breakdown**, theme from the movie Bonnie & Clyde. Also scored title music for the Beverly Hillbillies TV series.
**A FLOCK OF SEAGULLS** – Melodic Liverpool band who flirted with charts in early '80s, and also saw gold album success in USA with **Listen** (1983).
**FLYING BURRITO BROS** – Seminal outfit who introduced country music to the 'drop-out' generation. Members included the late Graham Parsons, Chris Hillman, Sneaky Pete Kleinow, Bernie Leadon and Michael Clark.
**DAN FOGELBURG** – American singer/songwriter on the fringes of the first division who became a US

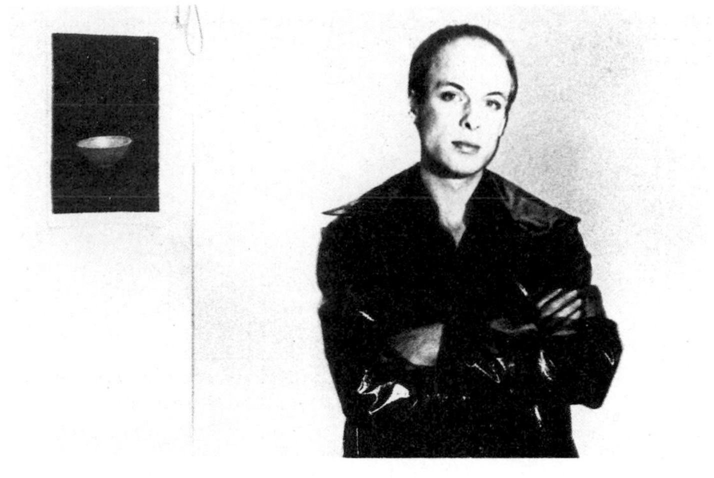

**Above: Brian Eno, who left Roxy Music, went on to work with David Bowie.**

chart regular following **Same Old Lang Syne** in 1981.
**FOGHAT** – US/UK aggregation formed by ex-patriot Brits – Tony Stevens, Dave Peverett and Roger Earl (all ex-Savoy Brown) in 1972. Group enjoyed album/concert success in US during '70s while being totally ignored in Britain.
**WAYNE FONTANA** – Leader of the Mindbenders. Hit UK No. 2 with cover of Major Lance's **Um Um Um Um Um Um'** then went to No. 1 in US, No. 2 in UK, with **Game Of Love** (1965). Had solo charters after group broke up in 1966.
**FRANKIE FORD** – Black New Orleans stalwart Huey 'Piano' Smith cut **Sea Cruise** for Ace Records. Label wiped off his vocals and substituted those of their great white hope Frankie Ford for 1959 Top 20 classic. Same format was adopted for follow-up **Alimony.**
**TENNESSEE ERNIE FORD** – Seminal rockabilly performer, who dominated C&W charts during '50s and '60s, as well as scoring pop success, most notably wiht **Sixteen Tons** in 1955.
**THE FORTUNES** – Birmingham, England, group that cut Coca Cola's familiar theme **It's The Real Thing,** as well as the pirate radio theme **Caroline.** Scored big US/UK hits with **You've Got Your Troubles, Here It Comes Again** and **This Golden Ring,** thanks to their classy harmonies.
**FOURMOST** – Early '60s UK pop/Mersey group, produced by Brian Epstein, who scored with hits **Hello Little Girl** and **A Little Loving**.
**THE FOUR PREPS** – Barber-shop harmonies won them late '50s hits and made them major influence on nascent Beach Boys.
**KIM FOWLEY** – Important figure of Los Angeles 'garage rock' scene. Wrote and produced for Jayhawks, B. Bumble and the Stingers, Hollywood Argyles, Rivingtons, and Paul Revere and the Raiders. Worked in England throughout 1965, producing Rockin' Berries, P.J. Proby, Cat Stevens, Soft Machine and others. Worked Stateside on first Mothers Of Invention album. Cut run of solo albums besides writing hit songs for Byrds, Emerson, Lake and Palmer, Helen Reddy and many more.
**CONNIE FRANCIS** – American pop singer of the late '50s and early '60s who enjoyed five year run of top twenty action in US and UK. In 1960 achieved three double sided million sellers: **Mama/Teddy, Everybody's Somebody's Fool/Jealous Of You** and **My Heart Has A Mind Of It's Own/Many Tears Ago**. Career more or less halted by rape at knife-point in 1974 and subsequent psychological problems.
**STAN FREBERG** – Recorded classic send-ups of Presley's **Heartbreak Hotel,** the Platters' **The Great Pretender** and Harry Belafonte's **Banana Boat Song** in '50s.
**JOHN FRED AND THE PLAYBOY BAND** – White Louisiana band had brief moment of glory with international 1967 hit **Judy In Disguise (With Glasses)** in 1967.
**FREDDIE AND THE DREAMERS** – Lightweight British pop act of '60s. Freddy Garrity's on-stage leapings inspired Chubby Checker record **Do The Freddie,** which group then recorded as their seventh and final hit. Still active on cabaret circuit.
**BOBBY FULLER FOUR** – Recorded 1966 hits **I Fought The Law** and **Love's Made A Fool Of You,** but Fuller was shot dead within months.
**JERRY FULLER** – Managed minor hits of his own but wrote biggies for Ricky Nelson (including **It's A Young World**) and Gary Puckett and the Union Gap **(Young Girl).**
**FUN BOY THREE** – London trio formed by ex-members of The Specials; UK chart regulars from 1981 (also teamed with Bananarama) before splitting in 1983.
**BILLY FURY** – British teen icon who had slew of hit singles in '60s, most notably **Halfway To Paradise** and **Jealousy**. Died of heart attack in 1983.

## G

**STEVE GADD** – Premier New York session drummer. Worked with Joe Cocker, Stanley Clarke, Paul Simon, Ringo Starr (sic), Dr John, Lee Ritenour, Steely Dan, Kate and Anna McGarrigle. Was featured in Simon & Garfunkel Central Park concert in 1981. Member of Stuff.
**ERIC GALE** – Premier US session guitarist who has worked with a myriad of top class talent including King Curtis, Marvin Gaye, Diana Ross, Steely Dan, Aretha Franklin and Paul Simon, with whom he featured in Simon's movie One Trick Pony. Has cut steady stream of jazz-rock albums.
**GALLAGHER & LYLE** – Scottish duo whose A&M output included hit singles **I Want To Stay With You** and **Heart On My Sleeve**. Graham Lyle has subsequently provided material for Tina Turner and Art Garfunkel.
**GANG OF FOUR** – Aggressive English group who have been on the verge of national success for some time. Personnel changes and lack of musical direction have certainly stunted growth despite decent LP product.
**DON GIBSON** – Legendary country performer/writer who penned **I Cant Stop Loving You, Oh Lonesome Me, Sweet Dreams, Legend In My Time**, etc. Made pop charts in US/UK with **Sea Of Heartbreak** in 1961.
**MICKEY GILLEY** – Cousin of Jerry Lee Lewis and regular entrant in lower reaches of country charts; enjoys cult status thanks to '50s rockabilly cuts.
**JIMMY GILMER AND THE FIREBALLS** – Studio musicians at Norman Petty's new Mexico base; they provided him with over-dubs for various Buddy Holly demo tapes before scoring four US hits between 1959 and '61 and three more in 1968-69. **Sugar Shack** (1963) made US No. 1.
**GERRY GOFFIN** – Major '60s songwriter with then wife Carole King. Made several unsuccessful solo albums.

**Below: Champion fiddler Byron Berline on stage with the Flying Burritos.**

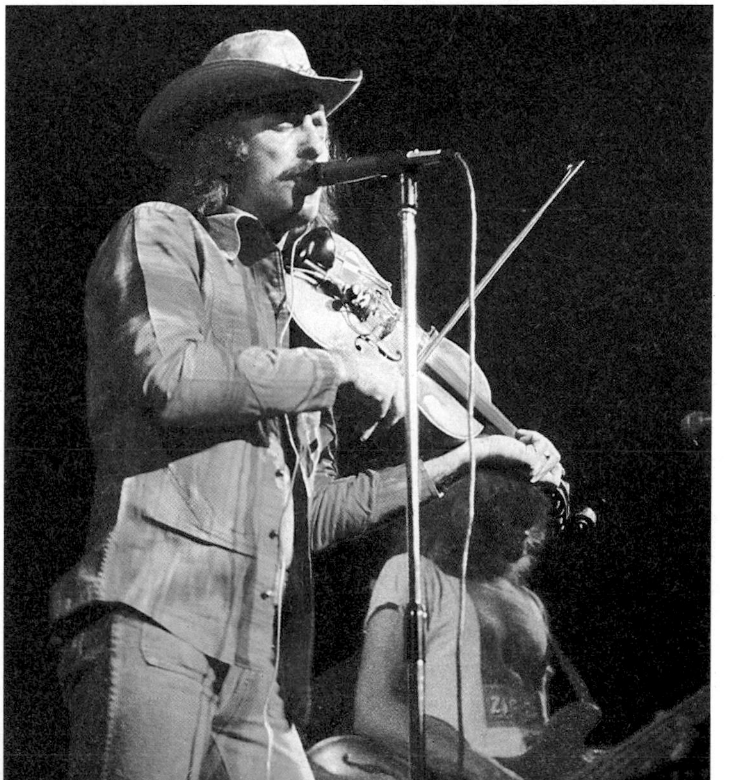

**GOLDEN EARRING** – Dutch band who've been around for a while, mostly in the background except for big transatlantic hit **Radar Love** (1973 and 1977). Had some US success via MTV with **Twilight Zone** (1982).
**GONG** – Adventurous French/Australian/English band that included Bill Bruford (ex-Yes) and guitarists Steve Hillage and Allan Holdsworth among its members. Officially split in 1977, but re-formed temporarily until 1979.
**CHARLIE GRACIE** – Pretender to Presley's throne while the king was on military service. Biggest hit came with **Butterfly** (1957).
**GRANDMASTER FLASH AND THE FURIOUS FIVE** – US vocalist and back-up men. Scored with rapping single **The Message** in the UK in 1982.
**DOBIE GRAY** – Former soul star **(The In Crowd)** who moved to the country-rock field with varying degrees of success. Cut classic **Drift Away** album (title track made US top ten) in 1973.
**RICK GRECH** – French-born bass guitarist; emerged from Family to join short-lived Blind Faith with Eric Clapton. Progressed to Ginger Baker's Airforce Traffic and the Crickets before working with Eric Clapton again in 1973.
**ELLIE GREENWICH** – Major writer from New York's famed Brill Building school, in partnership with Jeff Barry. Came up with hits for such Phil Spector acts as the Crystals, the Ronettes and Bob B. Soxx and the Blue Jeans. Recent Broadway show 'Leader Of The Pack' celebrated some of her greatest hit songs.
**THE GROUNDHOGS** – Earthy British R&B band (taking name from John Lee Hooker song) led by wizard guitarist Tony McPhee. Admirable albums for United Artists.
**JAMES GUERICO** – Chicago catalyst. Produced **Kind Of A Drag** hit for Buckinghams in 1966. Joined Mothers Of Invention on guitar in 1968. Produced second and biggest-selling Blood Sweat and Tears album. Masterminded Chicago Transit Authority (Chicago). Set up Caribou studios in Colorado (where Elton John and others recorded). Produced, directed and scored 'Elektra Glide In Blue movie. Became Beach Boys' manager in 1975 and appeared on stage with them.
**GUESS WHO** – Canadian rockers who spawned Bachman-Turner Overdrive after successful career which included several US hit singles.
**ADRIAN GURVITZ** – Flash guitarist and former member of Gun, Three Man Army, Baker-Gurvitz Army and Moody Blues' drummer Graeme Edge's Band. Made UK Top 10 in 1982 with trite single **Classic.**
**ARLO GUTHRIE** – Son of legendary Woody Guthrie and spokesman for the 'Woodstock' generation of the late '60s. Best known work is **Alice's Restaurant**.
**WOODY GUTHRIE** – Left-wing idealist whose politics restricted career, but who nonetheless left legacy of classic songs such as **This Land Is Your Land**.

## H

**H.P. LOVECRAFT** – Chicago acid-rock outfit formed in 1966. Hauntingly mystic albums.
**MERLE HAGGARD** – Staunch right-wing country artist whose compelling **Okie From Muskogee**

outraged anti-Vietnam war faction in 1970. Has been mainstay of US C&W charts for two decades.

**TOM T. HALL** – Influential country performer/songwriter with string of superb albums. Wrote Jeannie C. Riley hit **Harper Valley PTA.**

**JOHNNY HALLYDAY** – France's answer to Elvis Presley — with a lot of Gene Vincent influence thrown in. Cut countless major American and British hit songs in French and managed to stay at top during two decades, but found little recognition beyond Continent, where he enjoyed superstar status.

**ALBERT HAMMOND** – London-born, Gibralter-raised US West Coast stalwart. Hit big in 1972 with **It Never Rains In Southern California.**

**JOHN HAMMOND JR** – Son of Columbia/CBS's venerated A&R man. Among best — and most esoteric — of white blues singers to emerge in '60s. String of superior albums, including **Triumvirate,** cut in 1973 with Mike Bloomfield and Dr John.

**HERBIE HANCOCK** – Classically-trained jazz pianist who moved from the uncertain confines of the Miles Davis Group to a dazzling new career in jazz-rock. Has returned to his roots, whilst retaining international audience; composed music for impressive movie Round Midnight in 1986.

**PAUL HARDCASTLE** – Re-mix engineer who sprang to prominence with anti-war disco item **19** in 1985.

**ROY HARPER** – Former hippy, he enjoyed some success with series of folk-styled albums in '60s and early '70s. Rock superstars including Jimmy Page, Dave Gilmour, Ronnie Lane, and Keith Moon have guested on LPs and live performances. Output restricted by poor health over last six years.

**HARPERS BIZARRE** – Purveyors of lightweight but classy five-part pop harmonies. Scored with Paul Simon's **59th Street Bridge Song (Feelin' Groovy)** and re-makes of Cole Porter's **Anything Goes** and Glenn Miller's **Chatanooga Choo Choo.** Producer Ted Templeman was outfit's drummer.

**JET HARRIS AND TONY MEEHAN** – Erstwhile members of the Shadows. Guitarist Harris and drummer Meehan had three monster instrumental singles: **Diamonds, Scarlet O'Hara** and **Applejack** in 1963.

**ALEX HARVEY** – Powerful Scottish performer who came close to major international success in the seventies with The Sensational Alex Harvey Band. Died of a heart attack in 1981, a decade after his brother Les was killed onstage with his group Stone The Crows.

**MOLLY HATCHET** – Originally rock trio, formed by guitarist Dave Hlubek, burgeoning line-up coincided with string of successful US albums.

**DONNY HATHAWAY** – Cult soul performer whose inspired work was cut short by suicide in 1979. His classic album remains **Live,** although pop fans will remember his teaming with Roberta Flack on singles such as **Where Is The Love** and **The Closer I Get To You.**

**RICHIE HAVENS** – Black American troubadour who earned considerable reputation in early '70s for frenetic guitar style and heartfelt vocals.

**DALE HAWKINS** – Superior Louisiana rockabilly singer who injected heavy R&B flavour into his 1957 masterpiece **Susie Q.**

**RONNIE HAWKINS** – Candian rocker whose parties would have made Nero blush. Members of his Hawks backing group later became The Band.

**SCREAMING JAY HAWKINS** – Theatrical American pianist/vocalist famous for classic **I Put A Spell On You** and coffin-bound stage apperances.

**ISAAC HAYES** – Shaven-headed soul guru who turned from songwriter to star performer for legendary Memphis-based Stax label. Best remembered for **Shaft** movie soundtrack.

**HEAD EAST** – Obscure US outfit despite some enterprising material and a fine series of albums for A&M since **Flat As A Pancake** (1975).

**ROY HEAD** – White Texan R&B singer remembered for **Treat Her Right** biggie.

**HEATWAVE** – Multi-national soul outfit led by Rod Temperton and Johnny Wilder, who cut seven hit singles from 1977, including **Boogie Nights** and classic R&B ballad **Always And Forever.** Car crash paralysed Wilder in 1979, whilst Temperton went onto success with Michael Jackson and his **Off The Wall** LP.

**HEAVEN 17** – Stylish UK band formed from remains of original Human League (Martyn Ware, Ian Craig Marsh), now based around lead singer Glenn Gregory. Appealing disco-electronic sound and futuristic/socio-ecological lyrics have provided hits **(We Don't Need This) Fascist Groove Thing** and **Temptation.** Debut LP **Penthouse And Pavement** (1981) deserves a listen.

**BOBBY HEBB** – As youngster once played spoons with Bo Diddley! Reputed to be first black artist to appear on Nashville's Grand Ol' Opry show. Had UK No. 2 with soul ballad **Sunny.**

**DICK HECKSTALL-SMITH** – Graduated from jazz and rock 'n' roll into R&B as sax player with Blues Incorporated before progressing through Graham Bond Organization, John Mayall's Bluesbreakers and Colosseum to solo albums and session work.

**THE HERD** – Built by songwriters Ken Howard and Alan Blakeley around teen-appeal good looks of Peter Frampton (billed as 'The Face Of 1968'). After run of hits, Frampton left to form Humble Pie with Steve Marriott, then found subsequent solo success while the Herd fell apart.

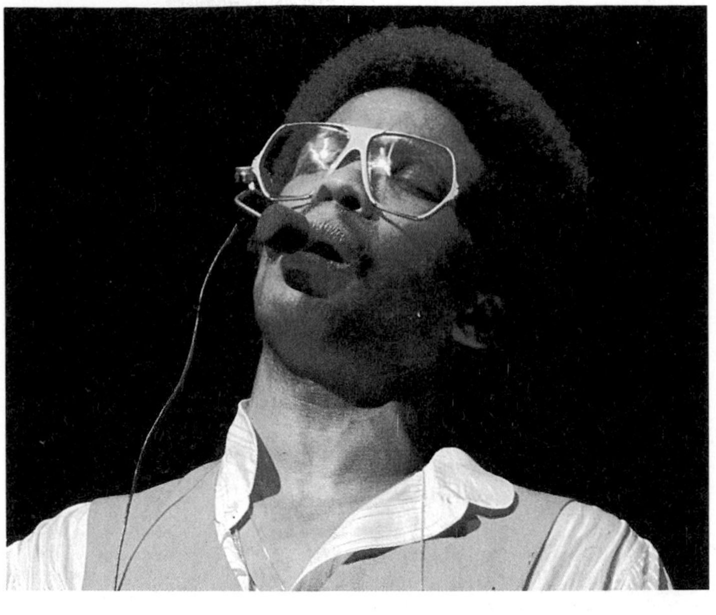

**Above: Herbie Hancock, a jazz superstar, who moved into rock in the 1970s.**

**HOLLAND / DOZIER / HOLLAND** – Legendary Motown songwriters responsible for host of classic material before moving to Hot Wax and later HDH labels.

**HOOKFOOT** – Superior British rock band formed from session men working behind Elton John and others at DJM Records.

**JOHNNY HORTON** – Country-pop singer best remembered for epic **Battle Of New Orleans.** Died in November 1960 car crash.

**HOT CHOCOLATE** – Errol Brown-led band who dominated UK charts in '70s and '80s with pleasing sould-tinged dance material including **So You Win Again, You Sexy Thing** and **It Started With A Kiss.**

**HUMBLE PIE** – Limited high volume rockers formed by former Small Face Steve Marriot, and Peter Frampton. Fizzled out in mid '70s.

**HUSKER DU** – Minneapolis trio that emerged in 1981 with **Land Speed Record,** an exhilarating hardcore collection. By **New Day Rising** (1985), their finest album, the songs had become more melodic, but still sizzled with emotional intensity and huzzsaw guitars. After three more albums, the Huskers disbanded in 1987. Their work stands as a high-water mark of American punk music.

**BRIAN HYLAND** – Scored at 15 with crass **Itsy Bitsy Teeny Weeny Yellow Polka Dot Bikini.** Friend and protégé of Del Shannon, he redeemed himself with **Sealed With A Kiss** (1962) and superb Shannon-produced version of Curtis Mayfield-penned **Gypsy Woman** (1970).

## I

**ICEHOUSE** – Australian band formed by guitarist/vocalist Ira Davies in 1978. Enjoyed UK hit in 1983 with **Hey Little Girl.**

**FRANK IFIELD** – British-born (Coventry), raised in Australia. Returned to UK in 1959 to establish himself with falsetto flavour ballads and outbreaks of yodelling. Hit No. 1 with **I Remember You, I'm Confessin' Lovesick** and **Wayward Wind.**

**IMPRESSIONS** – US soul trio led by Curtis Mayfield, who penned group's classic cuts including **Amen, People Get Ready** and **It's Alright.**

**INCREDIBLE STRING BAND** – Glasgow-based jug band. Flowered into fully fledged folk-rock outfit with well-made hippy-orientated albums.

**INNER CIRCLE** – Jamaican reggae outfit destined for superstardom until death of founder Jacob Miller. Recorded **Everything Is Great** UK chart hit in 1979.

**IRON BUTTERFLY** – American rock quintet whose **In-A-Gadda-Da-Vida** album was elephantine accompaniment to all zonked-out early '70s social occasions.

**IT'S A BEAUTIFUL DAY** – Superior San Francisco post-psychedelia rock band hinged around violin sound of classically trained leader David La Flamme.

**Too Hot To Handle, Heatwave. Courtesy GTO Records.**

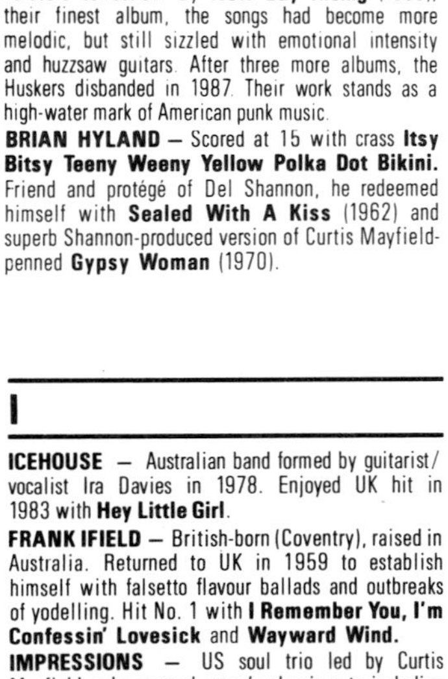


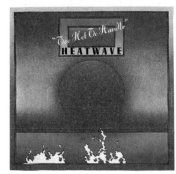

## J

**TERRY JACKS** – Rod McKuen translated **Seasons In The Sun** from the Jaques Brel French original for the Beach Boys. They recorded but never released it. Instead a version by Canadian Terry Jacks crashed the charts. Previously he had sold more than four million records in partnership with his wife Susan Pesklevits as the Poppy Family.

**BOB JAMES** – Jazz-rock keyboard specialist who has scored plays and movies, whilst turning out regular diet of jazz and funk albums. Has also recorded with guitarist Earl Klugh.

**RICK JAMES** – US vocalist originally signed by Motown as writer/producer. Own career has been overshadowed by artists he has collaborated with including Teena Marie and Eddie Murphy.

**THE JAMES GANG** – US group which flourished upon recruitment of guitar superstar Joe Walsh. Split in mid-'70s, having seen career tumble when Walsh departed to join The Eagles.

**TOMMY JAMES AND THE SHONDELLS** – Their cover of Raindrops' **Hanky Panky** on local Michigan label Snap remained obscure for two years; it was then picked up for national distribution by Roulette and rocketed to No. 1. Subsequent hits included **Money Money, Crimson And Clover** and **Crystal Blue Persuasion.**

**JAPAN** – Effete British quartet who were on fringes of mega-success before band's figurehead David Sylvian left for as yet unsuccessful solo career.

**JAY AND THE AMERICANS** – Had 18 US chart entries between 1962 and 1977. Clean-cut all-American image was fostered by ace producer Wes Farrell.

**WAYLON JENNINGS** – Modern country all-rounder happiest when recording and touring with close pals Willie Nelson and Tompall Glaser, collectively known as 'The Outlaws'.

**JOAN JETT & THE BLACKHEARTS** – Well-established American band led by former Runaway Joan Jett, who have established reputation with non-stop gigging and solid studio work.

**JOHNNY AND THE HURRICANES** – Formed at high school in Toledo, Ohio, Johnny and the Hurricanes scored with series of rock 'n' roll instrumentals between 1959/61, of which **Red River Rock** remains a favourite.

**PAUL JONES** – After role as lead singer with Manfred Mann, enjoyed British solo hits and went on to rewarding career as actor. Founder member of Blues Band, which disbanded in 1984.

**TOM JONES** – Started out as Presley-style rock 'n' roller. After years in obscurity, discovered by Gordon Mills who took him to London, changed his name (from Thomas J. Woodward) and took him to No. 1 with Mills-penned **It's Not Unusual** (1965). Seven weeks at No. 1 the following year, **Green Grass Of Home** paved way to Las Vegas, TV spectaculars and superstardom. Though his performances were often over-the-top, at his best Jones could be extremely soulful and commanded wide respect from black American R&B artists.

**GEORGE JONES** – Acknowledged as one of the finest vocalists in American music, Jones overcame severe drink problem (which cost him his marriage to Tammy Wynette) to re-establish career in country charts from late '70s.

**RICKIE LEE JONES** – Jazzy troubadour whose quirky ditties looked set to earn her major stardom in early '80s, but whose promise has yet to be totally fulfilled.

**JUICY LUCY** – Blues-based UK band fronted by vocals of former Zoot Money Big Roll Band bass player Paul Williams. Scored with 1970 version of Bo Diddley's **Who Do You Love?**

**BILL JUSTIS** – Birmingham, Alabama-born Memphis rock 'n' roll session stalwart. Hooting alto-sax playing earned him 1957 million-seller with **Raunchy.**

## K

**KC AND SUNSHINE BAND** – Good-time US disco outfit led by Harry Casey who were dance favourites throughout '70s. Casey secured songwriting reputation with Grammy for Betty Wright's **Where Is The Love?** in 1975. Resurfaced in 1983 with UK No. 1 **Give It Up.**

**KAJAGOOGOO** – '80s version of the Bay City Rollers. Weak, contrived pop from the makers of Duran Duran, nevertheless very popular in the UK (particularly with the pre-teen set).

**THE KALIN TWINS** – A five-week stint at No. 1 in UK with **When** (1958) led to a British tour, but despite success of follow-up **Forget Me Not,** they quickly sank into obscurity.

**EDEN KANE** – Richard Sarstedt took his stage name from title of Orson Wells' movie 'Citizen Kane'. Run of UK hits from 1961 to '62 included No. 1 **Well I Ask You.** Re-emerged in '70s with brothers Clive and Peter as the Sarstedt brothers.

**KANSAS** – US heavy metal outfit whose success was masterminded by Monkees and Archies mentor Don Kirshner. **Point Of Know Return** LP represents their best work.

**JERRY KELLER** – Scored with delightful **Here Comes Summer** in 1959. Also wrote 1965 hit **Almost There** for Andy Williams.

**JOHNNY KIDD AND THE PIRATES** – Image-laden British rockers. Kidd (Frederick Heath) co-penned their 1960 debut hit **Shakin' All Over,** arguably the most authentic rock 'n' roll original ever cut in Britain. Influenced early '60s bands. Johnny Kidd died in 1966, but Pirates continued.

**Sign Of The Times, Bob James. Courtesy Columbia Records.**

**THE KINGSMEN** – Place in rock history assured by superlative 1964 re-make of Richard Berry's R&B number **Louie Louie.**

**THE KINGSTON TRIO** – Folksy pop harmony group. Made No. 1 in 1958 with Civil War movie theme **Tom Dooley.**

**EARL KLUGH** – American virtuoso guitar player, who specialises in smooth jazz-rock on collection of classical guitars.

**KNACK** – Short-lived LA pop band that never lived up to critics' expectations after 1979 hit **My Sharona.**

**BUDDY KNOX** – Texan country singer turned rock 'n' roller. Cut his 1957 **Party Doll** and **Hula Love** hits at Norman Petty's studio in Clovis, New Mexico.

**ALEXIS KORNER** – Father figure of British R&B explosion of '60s. Later sang lead with successful studio band CCS. Fronted excellent R&B/blues prog. on BBC radio 'til death in 1984.

**LEO KOTTKE** – Superb US acoustic guitarist with roots in folk. Giddying release of albums since debut set **Circle Around The Sun** in 1970.

**KRAAFTWERK** – German synthesizer duo who surprisingly made charts on both sides of the Atlantic with **Autobahn** in 1975. They take themselves less seriously than their audience.

**BILLY J. KRAMER AND THE DAKOTAS** – Members of Brian Epstein's Merseybeat stable. Six British Top 20 records in two years, included Lennon/McCartney songs **Do You Want To Know A Secret, Bad To Me, I'll Keep You Satisfied** and **From A Widow.**
**KROKUS** – Swiss HM outfit led by vocalist Marc Scorace and guitarist Fernando Von Arb who have competed successfully in the international head-bangers market.

## L

**FRANKIE LAINE** – Still a major concert draw over forty years since his stage debut, Laine peppered the charts during the '50s with such classics as **Rawhide** and **Sixteen Tons**.
**RONNIE LANE** – Originally half of Small Faces songwriting duo with Steve Marriott. Went on to Faces, then quit to work with own back-up band Slim Chance. Scored in 1974 with **How Come** and **The Poacher.** In 1977 recorded mellow **Rough Mix** LP with Pete Townshend. Despite handicap of multiple sclerosis continues to write and occasionally perform.
**RONNIE LAWS** – Former member of Earth Wind & Fire who is regular in US R&B and pop charts with his classy alto playing and vocalising.
**ALBERT LEE** – Highly respected London guitarist who emerged from Chris Farlowe's Thunderbirds and was later member of Poet and the One Man Band and Head Hands and Feet before stint with the Crickets, and permanent role with Emmylou Harris band.
**GARY LEWIS AND THE PLAYBOYS** – Son of Hollywood comedian Jerry Lewis, Gary and his group had seven breezy US pop hits in just two years in mid-'60s.
**JOHN LEYTON** – UK TV actor who scored in 1961 with Joe Meek-produced No. 1 **Johnny Remember Me.** Went back to acting for roles in major movies including 'The Great Escape' 'Von Ryan's Express', and 'Krakatoa: East of Java'.
**GORDON LIGHTFOOT** – Canadian vocalist/guitarist/pianist/composer whose pleasant interpretation of own material has earned valuable niche in recording industry. International success highlighted by **If You Could Read My Mind** single in 1970, and as part of Bob Dylan's 'Rolling Thunder Review' a year later.
**LITTLE RIVER BAND** – Antipodean sextet whose ear for a melody won hearts of American audiences and permanent place in charts from 1977 thru' '82. **The Night Owls** (1981) may yet become a classic.
**LOGGINS AND MESSINA** – American soft-rock duo who enjoyed major success in early '70s. Since split in 1976, Loggins has gone on to score movies (Caddyshack) as well as notch up several hit singles (**Whenever I Call You Friend, I'm Alright, Footloose**) Loggins also co-wrote Doobies' classic **What A Fool Believes** with Michael McDonald.
**LULU** – Astute management has kept this bouncy Scottish songstress at the top of the showbiz tree for two decades. Re-issued **Shout** was hit again in 1987, although singer has not depended on chart success since recent move into theatrical career.
**LOBO** – Aka Kent Lavoie, had million-seller in 1971 with **Me And You And A Dog Named Boo.**
**JACKIE LOMAX** – Emerged from Liverpool group the Undertakers to record for Apple under aegis of George Harrison.
**TRINI LOPEZ** – A folksy sing-along style with a Latin flavour was the formula which took Trini Lopez to success with **If I Had A Hammer, La Bamba** and **Lemon Tree** in early to mid-'60s.
**LOVERBOY** – Canadian HM quintet with regulation issue perms and tight pants whose music is fodder for the masses.
**FRANKIE LYMON AND THE TEENAGERS** – Young lead singer Frankie Lymon sadly died from heroin overdose after period as child star with '50s group. **Why Do Fools Fall In Love** (1956), **I'm Not A Juvenile Delinquent,** and **Baby Baby** (both 1957) are now classics.
**LORETTA LYNN** – "The Coal Miner's Daughter" who overcame family hardship to establish herself in the hearts of the country faithful. Excellent autobiographical movie featured tour de force performance by Sissy Spacek.

## M

**MAISONETTES** – London group who scored with clever Motown soundalike **Heartache Avenue** in 1982.
**HARVEY MANDEL** – White Detroit blues rock guitarist who has recorded prolifically under own name and as member of Canned Heat and John Mayall's Bluesbreakers. Also did session work with Love, the Ventures, Charlie Musselwhite and others.
**AL MARTINO** – American balladeer. Had '70s UK hit with **Spanish Eyes,** which he originally recorded in 1955.
**JOHN MARTYN** – British singer/songwriter whose soulful left-field approach has kept him at

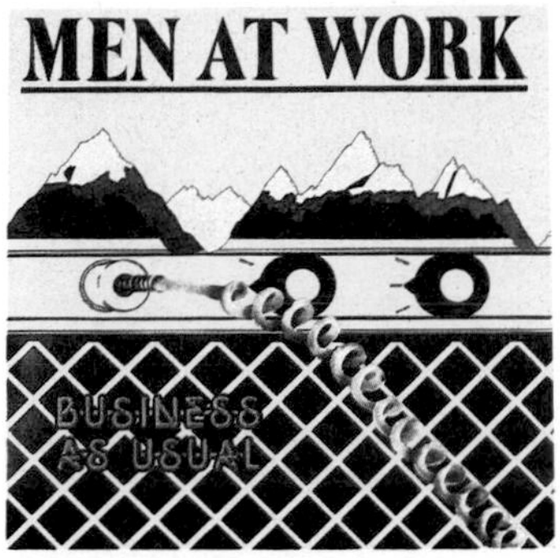


**Business As Usual, Men At Work. Courtesy Epic Records.**

arm's length from major success, despite string of well-crafted albums.
**MC5** – Tough, uncompromising American band formed in late '60s who were forerunners to the punk movement a decade later.
**CHARLIE McCOY** – Superb country-rock harmonica player who has appeared on many of Bob Dylan's records, as well as being member of Nashville sessioneers' group Area Code 615.
**THE McCOYS** – Covered the Vibrations' **My Girl Sloopy** as **Hang On Sloopy** for 1965 gold disc. Later became back-up band for Johnny Winter. Guitarist Rick Derringer went on to work with Edgar Winter and cut solo album **All American Boy.**
**SCOTT McKENZIE** – The man who sang the 1967 hippy flower-power love and peace anthem **San Francisco (Be Sure To Wear Some Flowers In Your Hair).**
**RALPH McTELL** – Long-established UK folk purveyor whose loyalty to that music has prevented consistent national attention. Made UK charts in 1974 with **Streets Of London.**
**MELANIE** – Diminutive but powerful voiced vocalist who enjoyed best moments with magnificent **Lay Down** (with Edwin Hawkins Singers) and **Ruby Tuesday** singles. Ahmet Ertegun produced **Photograph** album in 1975 for Atlantic signalled end of creative period.
**THE MEMBERS** – UK white reggae band formed around lead singer Nick Tesco. Enjoyed some US success with lighthearted single and popular MTV video **Working Girl**, until Tesco left in 1983.
**MEN AT WORK** – Australian soft-rockers who scored two successive US number one singles with **Who Can It Be Now?** and **Down Under** (also a UK number one) in 1982.
**THE MERSEYBEATS** – Liverpool band. Scored with cover of Jackie De Shannon-penned Dionne Warwick hit **Wishin' And Hopin'** and **I Think Of You** in 1964. After brief break-up, re-emerged as Merseys duo to score with **Sorrow.**
**METERS** – Classic New Orleans R&B/funk band who were sought after backing unit for wide variety of artists, including Fats Domino, Lee Dorsey, Irma Thomas, Robert Palmer and Paul McCartney. Founder Art Neville now appears with brother Aaron as the Neville Brothers.
**LEE MICHAELS** – Multi-instrumentalist (mainly guitar, keyboards) who enjoyed long tenure with A&M label. Scored US Top 10 in 1971 with **Do You Know What I Mean.** His band once featured Doobie drummer Keith Knudsen.
**BETTE MIDLER** – Buxom chanteuse whose ribald stage persona has successfully translated into movie medium, with star appearances in The Rose, Ruthless People, Down And Out In Beverley Hills, Outrageous Fortune and others.
**JOHN MILES** – UK guitarist/vocalist from Jarrow who scored with ambitious **Music** in 1975, and disco-oriented **Slowdown** a year later. Has subsequently remained in second division of rock performers despite undoubted talent.
**BUDDY MILES** – Large-framed drummer who earned his reputation as a session-man in the sixties. Worked with Hendrix in Band Of Gypsies, and later formed The Buddy Miles Band. Founder member of cult group The Electric Flag.
**FRANKIE MILLER** – Scottish R&B vocalist whose gravelly recordings eventually wore down his audience. Made UK top ten in 1978 with **Darlin'**.
**ROGER MILLER** – Novelty country-pop hits out of Nashville with **Dang Me** (1969), King Of The Road (1965) and **England Swings** (1965).
**RONNIE MILSAP** – Blind (since birth) American country vocalist/pianist whose soulful performances have earned a host of Grammy awards. A regular in the C&W and pop charts in the US.
**THE MINDBENDERS** – Originally led by Wayne Fontana, they split from him and found success in 1965 with **Groovy Kind Of Love.** Guitarist Eric Stewart later became member of 10cc.
**MISSING PERSONS** – Formed by Bozzio Bros in 1980, this American band should have made major impact, having learnt the ropes with artists such as Frank Zappa, and with producer Ken Scott at the helm.
**GUY MITCHELL** – Tin Pan Alley-styled pop singer who dabbled in rock 'n' roll, notably with **Singing The Blues** (1956), covered in UK by Tommy Steele.
**WILLIE MITCHELL** – Legendary Memphis producer and multi-instrumentalist who has been a cornerstone of the Tennessee R&B sound for over thirty years. Most widely known for work with Al Green.
**MODERN ROMANCE** – Up-tempo '80s combo with brassy-heavy, latin-tinged party music approach, evident on UK hits **Everybody Salsa, Ay Ay Ay Ay Moosey,** and **Best Years Of Our Lives.** Also quite popular in foreign regions, such as South America.
**ZOOT MONEY** – With his powerful Big Roll Band, was a mainstay of British R&B/soul club scene and cut some fine records of which only **Big Time Operator** made chart impact. From his band, Paul Williams went on to front Juicy Lucy while Andy Somers (Summers) ended up in the Police. Money now makes regular appearances as actor in British TV commercials and shorts.

**Below: The Divine Ms. Bette Midler with her prominent features to the fore.**

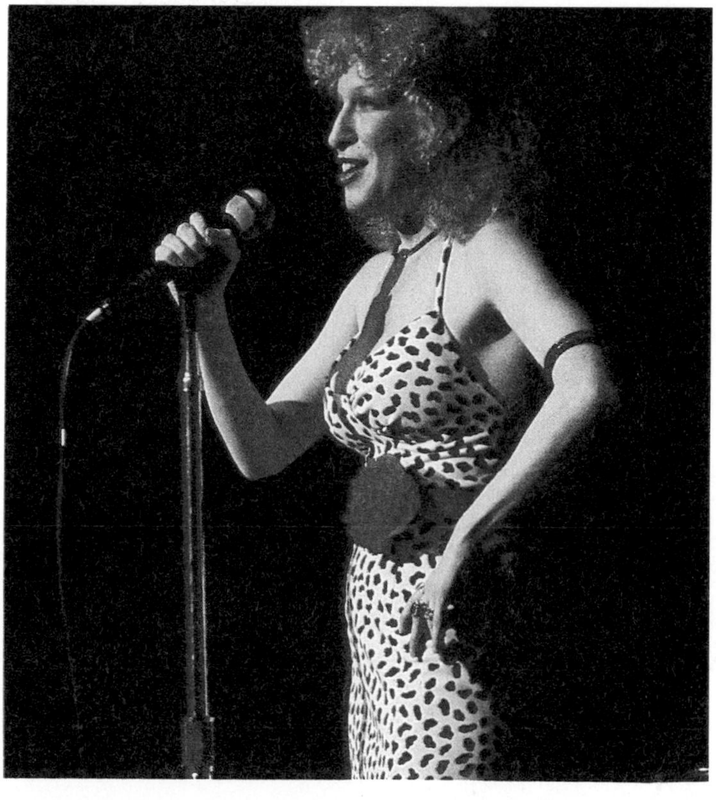

**BILL MONROE** – Founder of bluegrass music, who, with his group the Blue Grass Boys, influenced generations of country and rock performers. Advancing years (born 1911) have not slowed this superlative mandolinist/vocalist.
**MONSOON** – Unique blend of traditional East Indian music and pop, with inspired vocals from young Indian beauty Sheila Chandra. 1982 singles **Ever So Lonely** and **Shakti** definitely worth a listen.
**CHRIS MONTEZ** – Mexicano Californian. Punchy **Let's Dance** was 1962 million-seller as was follow-up **Some Kind Of Fun.**
**SCOTTY MOORE** – Elvis Presley's first manager and his backing guitarist on Sun hits and early tours.
**MOTHER EARTH** – Rock/blues/country showcase for superbly soulful voice of Tracy Nelson. Recorded admirable late '60s albums on Mercury.
**MOTLEY CRUE** – Californian HM quartet who have bludgeoned their way to success in USA, despite mediocre output which is neither as wild nor obnoxious as their image. 1986 UK tour has edged band to international success.
**MOTORS** – UK band formed from remnants of Ducks De Luxe. Charted in UK during 1978 with **Airport** and **Forget About You.** Strong material supplied by bassist Andy McMaster and guitarist Nick Garvey.
**MOUNTAIN** – Archetypal melodic HM outfit led by the gigantic Lesie West on guitar, whose first album **Nantucket Sleighride** is a feast of tasty guitar licks, sharp vocals, and topflight songs.

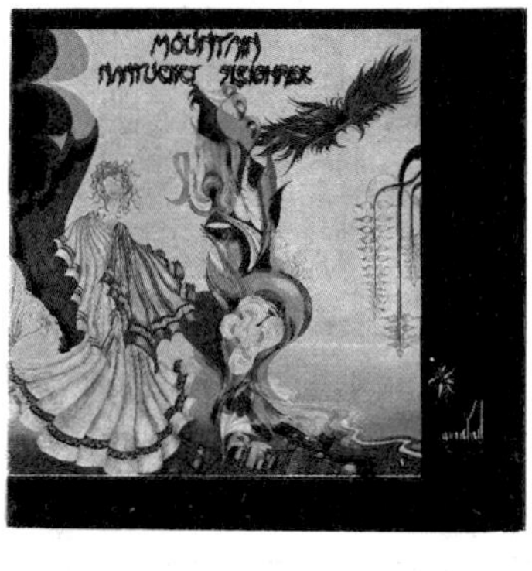

**Nantucket Sleighride, Mountain. Courtesy Windfall Records.**

**MUD** – Basic British beat group used as vehicle for the songs of Nicky Chinn and Mike Chapman, before going into self-production and achieving run of Top 20 singles. Mud's two No. 1 singles in the UK were **Tiger Feet** (1974) and **Oh Boy** (1975).
**MUNGO JERRY** – Up-dated jug band with skiffle flavour made Mungo Jerry rave success of 1970 open-air concerts; led to million-selling smash **In The Summertime.** Further hits established big following on Continent, which band's leader Ray Dorset has exploited skilfully through to '80s.
**ANNE MURRAY** – Nova Scotia-born easy-listening country singer with enormous following. From first big hit **Snowbird** in 1970, material has crossed over into pop charts.

## N

**JOHNNY NASH** – US soul singer whose smooth style earned him several hit singles in the late '60s/early '70s, most notably **Hold Me Tight** and **I Can See Clearly Now**.
**NAZARETH** – Scottish heavy metallers led by rough-house vocalist Dan McCafferty who charted in the early '70s with some regurgitated and predictable rock 'n' roll 45s.
**FRED NEIL** – Influential component of Greenwich Village folk scene. From his debut Elektra album **Bleeker And MacDougal, Candy Man** was later covered by Roy Orbison and **The Other Side Of Life** by the Lovin' Spoonful. Most successful song was **Everybody's Talkin',** recorded by Harry Nilsson for soundtrack of 'Midnight Cowboy'.
**SANDY NELSON** – American session drummer who scored a couple of instrumental hits pre-Beatles, notably the percussion anthem **Let There Be Drums**.
**WILLIE NELSON** – Top-flight American country star, whose bedraggled appearance belies a smooth writing and vocal style personified by the lilting **Always On My Mind**.
**MICHAEL NESMITH** – Left the super-successful Monkees pop outfit to find solo recognition for his polished brand of country rock and his First National Band. Best known solo hits are **Joanne** and **Rio.** Now successful with film/video production.
**NITTY GRITTY DIRT BAND** – Innovative folk/bluegrass band who have maintained a regular album output since 1970. In 1977, became first US band to tour USSR.
**THE NEW YORK DOLLS** – Flashy glam-rock band with strong transvestite overtones and ear-splitting

sound, which won lots of publicity but limited record sales. They broke up in 1975. David Johansen went on to US solo success in '80s.

**THE NEWBEATS** — Perky falsetto sound made **Bread And Butter, Everything's Alright** and **Run Baby Run** (1964-65) into hits for this Nashville-based trio.

**MICKEY NEWBURY** — Superior country writer who adapted **American Trilogy** single covered successfully by Elvis Presley. His own material has been recorded by Andy Williams, Kenny Rogers, Jerry Lee Lewis and Ray Charles among others. His finest work can be found on Elektra LPs.

**THE NICE** — Formed as backing band for P.P. Arnold they made showy rock albums. Caused controversy by burning the Stars and Stripes during their stage renditions of **America.** Keyboard virtuoso Keith Emerson went on to found Emerson Lake and Palmer.

**NIGHT RANGER** — Yet another band caught in '70s time warp. **Don't Tell Me You Love Me** video showcases them as one of the most unbearable bunch of poseurs on MTV. However, someone in America's buying this stuff.

**LAURA NYRO** — New York singer who cut masterpiece **Eli And The Thirteenth Coming,** since when she has recorded only sporadically. Wrote pop classics **Stoned Soul Picnic, Wedding Bell Blues, And When I Die and Stoney End.**

## O

**HAZEL O'CONNOR** — 1980 single **Eighth Day** promised great things for this Gucci punk performer, but she quickly dropped from sight, preferring to concentrate on acting career.

**O'JAYS** — Leading soul vocal group, who have charted regularly since their 1972 classic **Backstabbers**. Lead vocalist Eddie Levert can now proudly watch over his two sons who are featured in modern generation R&B outfit Levert.

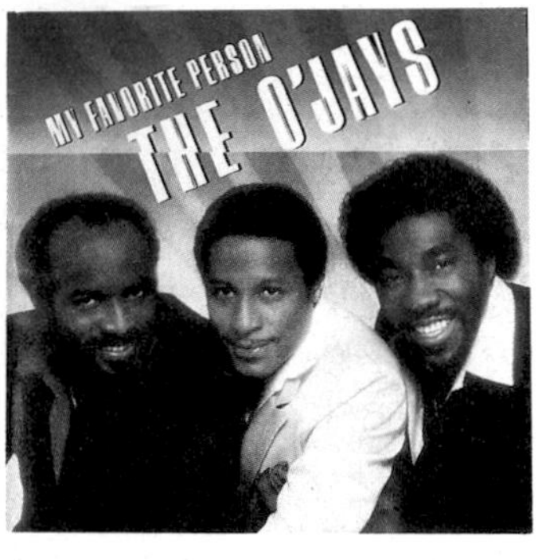


**My Favourite Person, The O'Jays. Courtesy Philly Intl. Records.**

**OAK RIDGE BOYS** — Former gospel stars, this vocal quartet have been permanent fixtures in the country, and, more recently, pop charts in US. Recipients of a host of country music awards as 'Best Vocal Group'.

**PHIL OCHS** — American folk singer with sincere, but heavy-handed lyrical approach, who struggled to survive against quality opposition including Dylan and Baez. Satirical pop/folk mix of album **Greatest Hits** (1970) was his one flirtation with commercial success before suicide in 1976.

**YOKO ONO** — Esoteric talent who took commercial advantage of her marriage to John Lennon in pop field. Better testimony can be found in her avante-garde films and art.

**TONY ORLANDO** — Worked for Don Kirshner cutting demos before being launched as artist in own right in 1961 with **Halfway To Paradise.** Following solo hits in '60s he was re-launched as lead singer of Dawn in '70s for further triumphs. Biggest US/UK Dawn hits were **Knock Three Times** and **Tie A Yellow Ribbon Round The Old Oak Tree.** Also had US weekly TV variety show.

**ORLEANS** — Melodic East Coast band who charted briefly in the USA with outstanding singles **Dance With Me** (1975) and **Still The One** (1976).

**OSIBISA** — Introduced African rock music to British audiences and commanded large following from 1970 to 1976 when **Sunshine Day** gave them their first chart single.

**GILBERT O'SULLIVAN** — Managed to get break with Gordon Mills management outfit by squatting in MAM office reception. Given short-trousers and cloth cap working-class image he scored with thoughtful and melodious songs, hitting pinnacle with transatlantic hit **Alone Again (Naturally)** (1972). Enjoyed total of 12 UK Top 20 records between 1970-1974, including No. 1's **Clair** and **Get Down.**

**OUTLAWS** — Leading exponents of Southern Rock, along with Allman Bros Band and Lynyrd Skynyrd. Voracious appetite for gigs has maintained group's high profile in USA.

**OZARK MOUNTAIN DAREDEVILS** — Country-rock exponents who enjoyed major success in mid-'70s. Charted, however, with pure pop **Jackie Blue** in 1975.

## P

**PABLO CRUISE** — American band led by bassist Bud Cockrell (ex-It's A Beautiful Day) and keyboard/vocalist Cory Lerois (ex-Stoneground) who scored a series of US hit singles from 1977 without really establishing first division credentials.

**GRAHAM PARKER** — Decent British R&B vocalist who led riotous brass-based band Rumour through a succession of exciting but predictable albums from mid-'70s.

**PAUL AND PAULA** — Twee **Hey Paula** hit summit of American charts in 1962, but cloying unisex teenager image saw them quickly fade from prominence.

**PAVLOV'S DOG** — Adventurous US band from New York featuring dual keyboards and falsetto vocalising of David Surkamp. Band split after two eccentric albums recorded in mid-'70s.

**TOM PAXTON** — Self-effacing folk performer who packed concert halls throughout the '70s with his dry humour, and 'spoken' style.

**PEARLS BEFORE SWINE** — US cult band led by Tom Rapp which enjoyed underground success in late '60s/early '70s. After couple of solo albums, Rapp moved to Europe and quit recording scene.

**TEDDY PENDERGRASS** — Former lead vocalist with Harold Melvin and the Bluenotes, Pendergrass quickly established himself as a premier live performer before catastrophic car crash halted career.

**PENTANGLE** — Revered pop/folk unit from the '70s who attracted cult following from British concert audiences.

**PETER AND GORDON** — Peter Asher's actress sister Jane was Paul McCartney's girlfriend, which explains how duo got to record fresh Lennon/McCartney material, bringing them hits with **World Without Love** and **Nobody I Know.** Peter Asher went on to manage James Taylor and Linda Ronstadt.

**BOBBY 'BORIS' PICKETT** — Pickett's imitation of Boris Karloff's spooky voice took **Monster Mash** to the top in 1961.

**PLASMATICS** — Lightweight punk group whose success was based on appearance rather than musical ability, and they will be remembered for nothing more than vocalist Wendy O. Williams erotic stage behaviour.

**POCO** — American country/rock pioneers formed from ashes of Buffalo Springfield (Richie Furay and Jim Messina), who maintained high profile for fifteen years despite countless personnel changes.

**POLECATS** — Modern day rockabilly band from London, who were perhaps too innovative for then punk audience. Split in 1983 after two good albums.

**BILLY PRESTON** — Highly rated keyboard performer who has worked with Little Richard, Sam Cooke and The Stones. Scored notable single success with Syreeta and **With You I'm Born Again** (1979).

**JOHNNY PRESTON** — Recorded solo in 1959, scoring internationally with **Running Bear,** on which vocal chant effects were contributed by the Big Bopper.

**THE PRETTY THINGS** — Anarchic UK R&B/rock band who tried to be even more outrageous than the Rolling Stones. Made some interesting but usually excessively noisy singles, plus competent **S.F. Sorrow** and **Parachute** albums.

**ALAN PRICE** — former Animal and founder of Alan Price Set who has pursued varied solo career. Hit singles included **Simon Smith And His Amazing Dancing Bear** and **The House That Jack Built**. Latterly has concentrated on writing and performing music for television, film and theatre.

**CHARLEY PRIDE** — Black country singer whose style belies background. Quickly overcame prejudice to win respect of redneck audiences. Shelves are overloaded with CMA and Grammy awards.

**Below: Country rockers the Outlaws, popular despite lack of hit singles.**

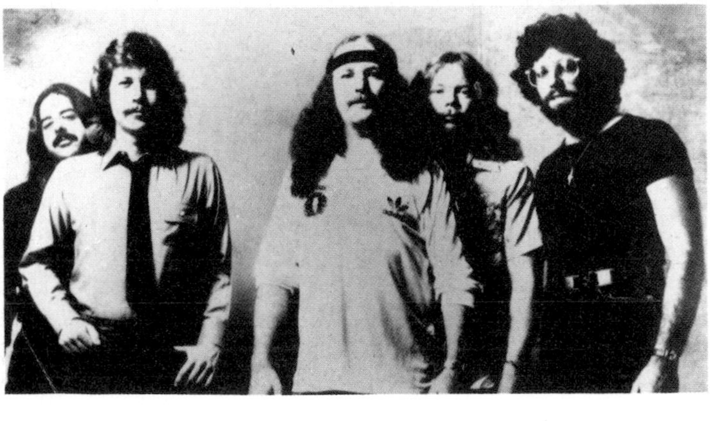

**P.J. PROBY** — US vocalist probably more famous for his then outrageous hairstyles and splitting trousers than his hits **Hold Me, Together, Somewhere** (all 1964) and **Maria** (1965).

**PSYCHEDELIC FURS** — UK new wave band who enjoyed US success courtesy of MTV with single **Love My Way** (1982).

**GARY PUCKETT AND THE UNION GAP** — Civil War-inspired stage uniforms and breezy Jerry Fuller-produced pop songs gave this San Diego group their moments of glory, notably with 1968 chart-topper **Young Girl.**

**PURE PRAIRIE LEAGUE** — Country-rock exponents who cut US top ten single **Let Me Love You Tonight** in 1980.

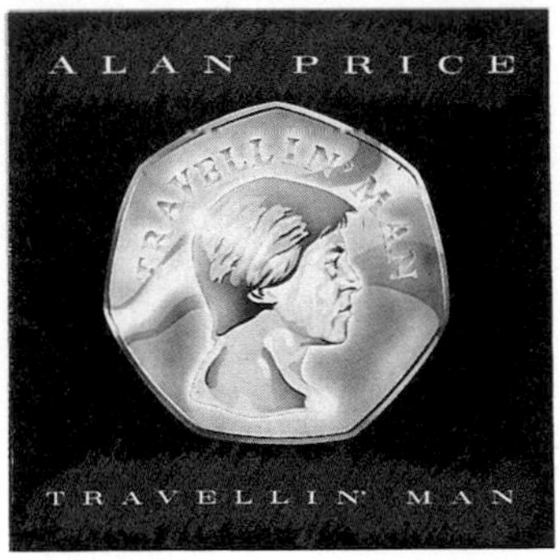


**Travellin' Man, Alan Price. Courtesy Trojan Records.**

## Q

**QUESTION MARK AND THE MYSTERIANS** — Basic garage-rock sounds of **96 Tears** (1966) gave this Flint, Michigan-based Tex-Mex group their lone smash hit.

**QUINTESSENCE** — Eastern-flavoured jazz-rock outfit formed via 'Melody Maker' adverts in 1969. Series of Island albums were aimed at underground hippy audiences.

## R

**EDDIE RABBIT** — Country artist who has made regular inroads into US pop charts. Best known for **Every Which Way But Loose** movie theme, which enjoyed Top 50 status in both US/UK in 1979.

**RARE EARTH** — Bringing heavy rock flavour to essentially soul material, this band launched Motown's Rare Earth label (named after them). Under ace black producer Norman Whitfield, cut classic long versions of such Motown classics as **Get Ready, (I Know) I'm Losing You** and **Ma** in early '70s.

**THE RASCALS** — Pioneer blue-eyed soul band on Atlantic, formed in 1966 as the Young Rascals. Topped charts year later with **Good Lovin'; Groovin'** was 1967 classic. Sheer musicianship made them delightful live attraction. Organist Felix Cavaliere, singer Eddie Brigati and guitarist Gene Cornish had all previously been with Joey Dee and the Starlighters.

**JIM REEVES** — Soft spoken C&W singer who was a pop chart regular until his death in a plane crash in 1964. Subsequently enjoyed posthumous hit records, particularly in UK.

**RENAISSANCE** — Formed by ex-Yardbirds Keith Relf and Jim McCarty, group was major UK concert attraction through '70s, and scored top 10 single **Northern Lights** in 1978. Relf, who left band in 1972, died in 1976.

**THE REPLACEMENTS** — A Minneapolis band renowned for brilliant songwriting and a raucous, sloppy live act. Long independent label favourites of critics and hardcore fans, their fourth album **Let It Be** (1984) won them a contract with Sire Records and brought them a larger following.

**PAUL REVERE AND THE RAIDERS** — US band who thanks to their colourful American Revolutionary War garb (including long hair in ponytails) and strong musicianship made immediate impact when they appeared in 18th-century costumes on Dick Clark's 'Where The Action Is' TV show. Recorded string of pop classics in long career, including American No. 1 **Indian Reservation** in 1971. Band saw many personnel changes, but lead singer Mark Lindsay remained constant factor. Lindsay enjoyed some solo success, including own US TV show in early '70s.

**CHARLIE RICH** — Former rockabilly singer whose country ballads saw plenty of chart action in the early '70s, with **The Most Beautiful Girl** topping US listings (no. 2 in UK) in 1973.

**JEANNIE C. RILEY** — Tom T. Hall's superb lyric of liberated womanhood made **Harper Valley PTA** 1968 the ideal vehicle to take Jeannie soaring up the charts.

**JOHNNY RIVERS** — Personable vocalist/guitarist who became US teen idol in mid-'60s with clever re-makes of R&B hits, including **Memphis, Baby I Need Your Lovin', Maybellene** and **Rockin' Pneumonia-Boogie Woogie Flu.**

**TOM ROBINSON** — Gay activist and radical, who has dented the UK charts on three occasions, most notably with **2-4-6-8-Motorway** in 1977.

**TOMMY ROE** — Buddy Holly soundalike from Atlanta, Georgia, who scored a couple of US No. 1s with his own composition in the '60s, **Sheila** (1962) and **Dizzy** (1969). Now works on US club circuit with own trio.

**KENNY ROGERS** — Country-pop vocalist who has been a chart regular on both sides of the Atlantic since 1968, when his group the First Edition made US no 5 with **Just Dropped In.**

**TIM ROSE** — A member of Big Three folk group with Mama Cass, Rose composed classic **Morning Dew** for his debut/solo album. Also included brilliant **Hey Joe,** which Jimi Hendrix covered successfully. Rose later settled in Britain, setting up band there.

**RUFUS** — Successfully overcame loss of Chaka Khan with **Numbers** set in 1977; band rejoined Chaka for 1981 set **Camouflage.**

**RUN-DMC** — The most popular rap group in the US, Run-DMC combines rap's pounding beat with heavy-metal guitar and a pop sensibility. Originating from Hollis, Queens in New York, Run-DMC were the first group to attract white listeners to rap in large numbers, helping to destroy the segregation of "white" and "black" music that plagued the 1970s. Their 1986 album, **Raisin' Hell** was their most successful to date and contained a funky rap version of Aerosmith's **Walk This Way.**

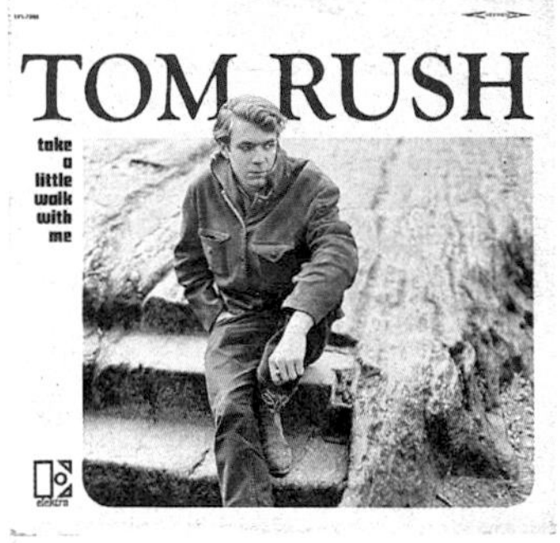


**Take A Little Walk With Me, Tom Rush. Courtesy Elektra Records.**

**TOM RUSH** — Folkie who emerged from burgeoning beatnik generation in the early '60s, but who never shook off cloak of his contemporaries like Dylan and Paxton. Still recording 20 years after debut set **Blues Songs And Ballads.**

**BOBBY RYDELL** — The original Robert Lewis Ridarelli had sensational period in US charts from 1959-64, scoring 22 Top 60 hits, including teen classics **Wild One, Volare** and **The Cha-Cha-Cha.** Still active on supper-club circuit.

## S

**SAD CAFE** — Manchester rock group who looked on horizon of big future after UK top ten single **Every Day Hurts** in 1979, but who virtually disappeared without trace.

**SAGA** — Another formula, heavy-metal band kept in business by the fans of faceless rock in the tradition of Triumph, Rush and the like.

**SAM & DAVE** — US soul duo whose heyday was in '60s, when they belted out a dozen R&B anthems on the Stax label, including **Hold On I'm Coming, Soul Man** (later recorded by Dave Prater (Dave) and Lou Reed) and **I Thank You.**

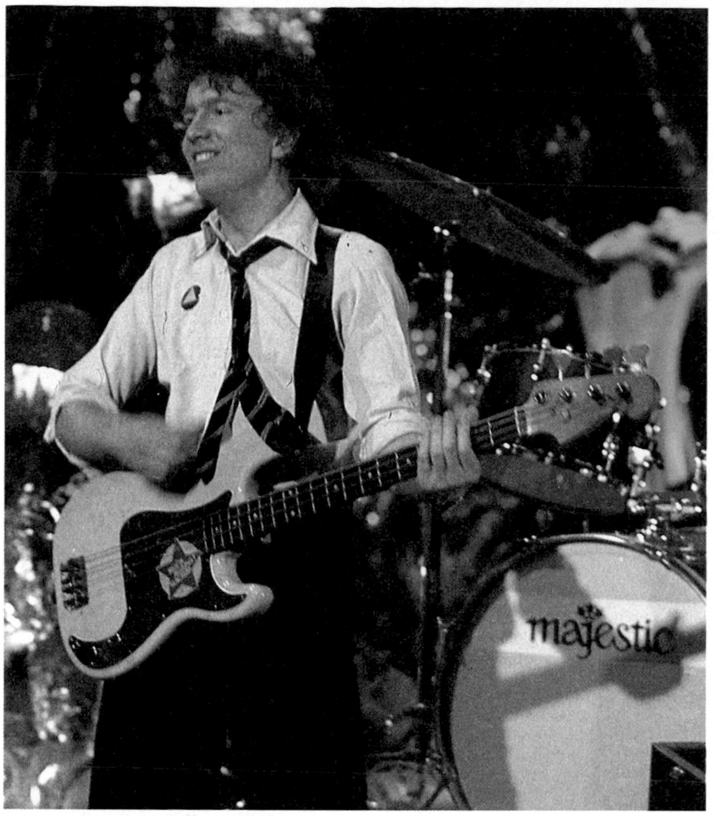


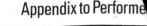

**Above: Tom Robinson, who hit it big in 1977-78, then vanished until 1983.**

**SAVOY BROWN** — English blues band who had approaching two thousand members since formation in 1966, the most notable of which were founder member guitarist Kim Simmonds, and former Chicken Shack axeman Stan Webb.

**SCREAMING LORD SUTCH** — An anachronism throughout his long career and master of the publicity stunt. His **Jack The Ripper** parody kept

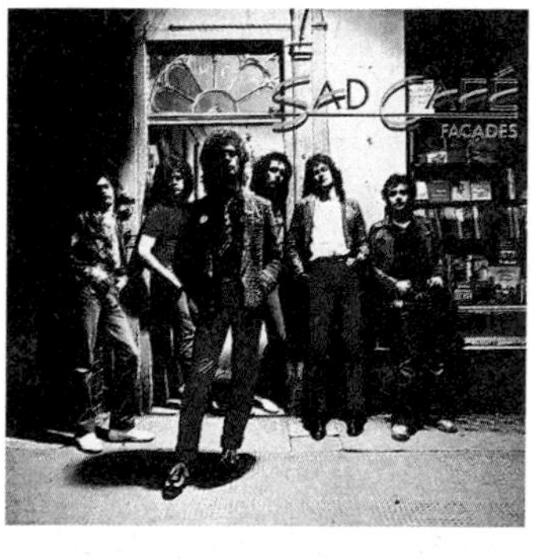


**Facades, Sad Café's 1979 album. Courtesy RCA Records.**

him in work for two decades, although he enjoyed US success with Atlantic album **Lord Sutch And Heavy Friends,** which included his ex-band members Jimmy Page, Nicky Hopkins and Ritchie Blackmore. Now prospective UK parliamentary candidate and founder of Monster Raving Loony Party.

**SEALS & CROFTS** — Lightweight US pop duo who dented US charts in '70s. Jim Seals was former member of The Champs ("Tequila").

**PETE SEEGAR** — The grandaddy of the US folk movement, whose left-wing politics appealed to the college and university set while leaving two generations of middle-class Americans cold.

**SELECTER** — British two-tone reggae band from the Midlands who enjoyed couple of minor hits in UK before disbanding. Vocalist Pauline Black is a promising talent who should re-surface.

**SHA NA NA** — American rock revivalists who starred in Woodstock movie and soundtrack; own recording career was a pale imitation of their live shows.

**SHALAMAR** — Funky US soul trio led by Howard Hewitt who enjoyed single success with collection of inspired electro-disco soul. Founder members Jody Watley and Jeffrey Daniels have since found solo success.

**SHAM 69** — Creation of vocalist Jimmy Pursey whose lyrical content decried social conditions of British working class. Biggest hits were **If The Kids Are United** and **Hurry Up Harry** in 1978. Pursey has subsequently pursued solo career with negligible success.

**HELEN SHAPIRO** — Husky-voiced singer who charted with melodic teen material in early '60s. Topped UK charts with **You Don't Know** and **Walkin' Back To Happiness** in 1961. Still active on cabaret/supper-club circuit.

**PETE SHELLEY** — Formerly lead singer with the Buzzcocks with several hits from 1978-80 such as **Ever Fallen In Love (With Someone That You Shouldn't Have)** and **Promises.** Most notable solo single **Homosapien.**

**BOBBY SHERMAN** — Launched via 'Shindig' TV series, Sherman was archetypal American teen idol and his records were predictably unadventurous though they gave him a 1969-1970 chart run.

**SHOOTING STAR** — Ten year veterans of American rock scene, sextet broke through upon release of 1982 set **Three Wishes.**

**SHOWADDYWADDY** — UK's answer to Sha Na Na, this collection of MOR rockers were mainstays of UK pop listings for five years from 1974, scoring 10 top ten singles.

**PETER SKELLERN** — UK singer/songwriter/pianist from Lancaster with a penchant for wistful '30s-flavoured material. Won UK/US success with debut single **You're A Lady.** Has cut run of highly entertaining albums, often using softly muted brass band to add Northern England feel.

**SKY** — Brainchild of classical guitarist John Williams, group were popular concert attraction, particularly in UK, with uneasy amalgam of rock and classics.

**JIMMY SMITH** — American jazz organist whose sound from the Hammond organ inspired a thousand R&B keyboard players in the '60s.

**PATTI SMITH** — Chicago-born rock 'n' roll poetress, whose self-indulgence left her floundering after chart single **Because The Night** in 1978.

**Below: Styx, monsters in America, but almost unknown in Britain.**

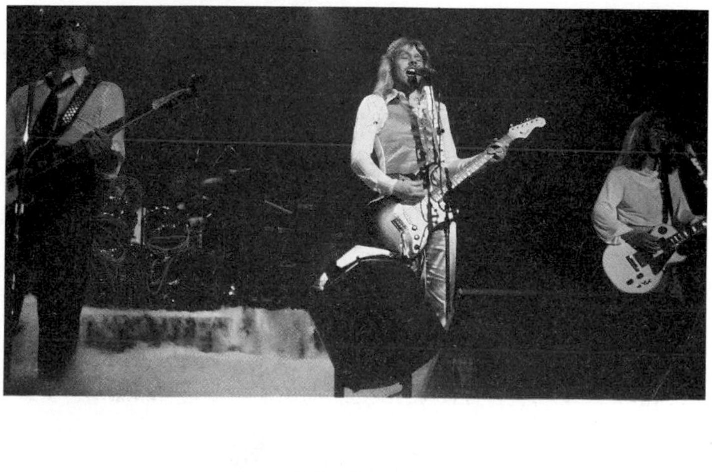

**SOFT MACHINE** — Seminal UK jazz-rock band, whose members have included Robert Wyatt, Kevin Ayers, Mike Ratledge and Hugh Hopper. Broke up in 1979.

**JOE SOUTH** — Influential session guitarist/writer/producer; worked with The Tams, Joe Smith, Simon & Garfunkel, Aretha Franklin, Bob Dylan, etc. etc. Scored own success in 1969 with classic **Games People Play.**

**J.D. SOUTHER** — Guitarist founder of ill-fated Souther (John David), Hillman (Chris), Furay (Richie) band which did not live up to enormous potential during two-album 18-month tenure. Has enjoyed modicum of solo success while recording with Linda Ronstadt (for whom he wrote superb **Heart Like A Wheel),** Warren Zevon, Joe Walsh and Christopher Cross.

**SPARKS** — Novelty American pop group formed by Mael Bros in 1974. Unusual presentation eventually lost support, despite run of UK chart singles from 1974.

**CHRIS SPEDDING** — Anonymous guitar hero of countless recording sessions, had taste of solo glory with **Motorbiking** hit on Mickie Most's Rak label in 1975.

**SPINNERS** — Superb US black vocal group known as the Detroit Spinners in the UK; formed in the '50s and still working in the '80s. Enjoyed most chart success between 1961 and 1978 with US/UK hits like **It's A Shame, Could It Be I'm Falling In Love, Ghetto Child, Rubberband Man** and US No.1 **Then Came You.** Best work featured lead vocalist Phillipe Wynne.

**SPOOKY TOOTH** — Major band on late '60s progressive rock scene in Britain; had only moderate success with albums. Dogged by frequent personnel changes, including loss of American-born founder Gary Wright. Three-year hiatus from 1970-1973 didn't help.

**RICK SPRINGFIELD** — US singer/guitarist who's never quite made the big time, but who's hung in there for over a decade with such hits as **Speak To The Sky** (1972), and more recently **Jessie's Girl** (a No. 1 in 1981), **I've Done Everything For You** (1981), **Don't Talk To Strangers** (No.2 in 1982) and **Affair Of The Heart** (1983). Played Dr. Noah Drake on US soap 'General Hospital'.

**BILLY SQUIER** — Annoying poseur who relies mostly on good looks for appeal. Nevertheless has come up with some good hooks on US hits like **Everybody Wants You** (1982).

**STAPLE SINGERS** — Gospel family who found favour in singles charts in early '70s. Lead singer Mavis later went on to successful solo career.

**ALVIN STARDUST** — A '60s star as Shane Fenton, he burst into charts with new name and black leather image. Chart-topping **Jealous Mind** and further hits were also written by Shelley.

**AL STEWART** — Scottish guitarist/vocalist whose lightweight but intriguing style saw chart action with **Year Of The Cat** (1977) and **Time Passages** (1978).

**STIFF LITTLE FINGERS** — Irish high-energy quartet who saw a promising career disappear when founder member Jake Burns called it a day. Made UK top twenty in 1980 with **At The Edge.**

**STEVE STRANGE** — Poseur extraordinaire who landed recording contract. Charted (as Visage, with Midge Ure of Ultravox) in UK with **Fade To Gray** (1980), **Mind Of A Toy** (1981), **Damned Don't Cry** (1982) and **Night Train** (1982).His main talent lies in attracting similarly precious individuals to various London nightspots.

**STRAWBS** — Formerly The Strawberry Hill Boys, folk trio from London suburbs led by Dave Cousins, group evolved into popular rock quartet (featuring Rick Wakeman) before splitting in late '70s. Cousins now runs radio station in West country.

**STRAY CATS** — New York rockabilly trio who had decent chart run in early '80s (**Rock This Town** made both UK and US top tens) before splitting in 1984.

**STUFF** — Aggregation of superstar sessioneers, including Steve Gadd (drums) Cornell Dupree (guitar), Eric Gale (guitar), Richard Tee (keyboards), Gordon Edwards (bass) and Chris Parker (drums). Their Warner Bros albums have, naturally enough, contained magical moments.

**STYLISTICS** — Excellent US black vocal group who've managed several US/UK pop singles from 1972-76, including **I'm Stone In Love With You, Break Up To Make Up, Rock 'N' Roll Baby, You Make Me Feel Brand New, Let's Put It All Together, Sing Baby Sing, Can't Give You Anything (But My Love),** and more.

**STYX** — US AOR band formed in 1970 with succession of hit singles in US from 1975. 1979 number one single **Babe** is typical of their pleasant but unremarkable style.

**SURVIVOR** — '70s styled American AOR band whose them from Rocky III **Eye Of The Tiger** was major '82 smash. Have maintained success with similarly crafted material, including US Football theme **American Heartbeat.**

**SUTHERLAND BROS AND QUIVER** — Iain and Gavin Sutherland amalgamated their own unit with pub-rock band Quiver in 1972, remaining on fringe of national success for seven years. Brothers are best known for composition **Sailing,** an international hit for Rod Stewart, and their own soulful **Arms Of Mary,** a UK Top 10 entry in 1976.

**BILLY SWAN** — Bill Black Combo and Clyde McPhatter both scored with Swan's composition **Lover Please.** After stint as roadie for country stars, became Monument Records' staff producer, working on Tony Joe White's **Polk Salad Annie** hit. As an artist he adopted soft-rocking style to achieve No. 1 with **I Can Help** (1974).

**SWEET** — Unpretentious pop band who secured regular UK chart placings from 1971 to 1978. Brainchild of Nickey Chinn, Michael Chapman songwriting/production partnership, who wrote **Blockbuster** No. 1 for group in 1973.

**SWINGING BLUE JEANS** — Liverpool band led by vocalist/ guitarist Ray Ennis who had string of UK hits, **Hippy Hippy Shake, You're No Good,** etc. (and couple of minor US chart entries) in mid-'60s.

## T

**TANGERINE DREAM** — German synthesiser outfit popular in Europe since formation in 1967. Current members Edgar Froese, Christoph Frank and Johannes Schmoelling have also been active on solo projects. Recorded soundtrack for James Caan movie 'Thief' ('Violent Streets' in UK) in 1981.

**TEARDROP EXPLODES** — UK outfit formed in 1978 who achieved two UK top ten singles, **Reward** and **Treason,** in 1981. Image maker and guiding light Julian Cope split band in 1982.

**TOMMY TEDASCO** — The 'man of 1000 jingles' (as well as countless TV and music scores) is probably most often-hired guitarist on West Coast, having started out in '60s with Jan & Dean. Has also worked for Beach Boys, Fats Domino, Stephen Bishop, Judy Henske, Maria Muldaur, Michael Nesmith, Dory Previn and Elvis Presley. Contributes regular 'Studio Log' column for US magazine 'Guitar Player' and is author of guitar instruction volume. Has cut a couple of solo guitar albums in a jazz vein.

**NINO TEMPO AND APRIL STEVENS** — Tempo played sax on Bobby Darin records before signing to Atco as duo with his sister and notching No. 1 with Deep Purple. In late '70s, Tempo came back to prominence as an instrumentalist, riding disco boom with his Fifth Avenue Sax band.

**TENPOLE TUDOR** — Tartan punk from Eddie Tenpole and his look-alike band, who specialised in raucous, sing-along pub-style tunes, anachronistic clothes and Scottish nationalism. 1981 hits **Swords Of A Thousand Men** and **Wunderbar** typical of sound. Founder Eddie Tudor-Pole has returned to acting since demise of band, appearing in 'Absolute Beginners' and 'Sid & Nancy'.

**THIRD WORLD** — Jamaican soul/reggae outfit who should have achieved superstardom after magnificent **Now That We've Found Love** single in 1978.

**B.J. THOMAS** — One of pop's anomalies, a soulful singer who has contented himself with lifeless MOR material. His anthem is whimpish **Raindrops Keep Fallin' On My Head,** but also enjoyed seven other US Top 20 entries from 1969-75.

**RICHARD AND LINDA THOMPSON** — Folk duo who enjoyed solo and group success (Richard with Fairport Convention) before teaming up. Rolling Stone magazine nominated their 1982 collection **Shoot Out The Lights** as 'Album Of The Year'. Subsequent break-up of marriage has resulted in separate 1985 albums, but pair later toured together again. Richard Thompson is reckoned one of the best guitarists in rock, but has preferred to maintain low profile.

**THUNDERCLAP NEWMAN** — Andy Newman met The Who's Pete Townshend at art college. Formed Thunderclap Newman with Jimmy McCullough and Speedy Keene. Townshend produced through the Who's Track label; group scored in 1969 with **Something In The Air** but success was not sustained. McCullough went on to play with Stone the Crows, then Wings.

**JOHNNY TILLOTSON** — Melodic **Poetry In Motion** (1958) made star of this former country

**Tom Verlaine. Courtesy Elektra Records.**

singer. Eight-year run found him consistently on the American charts, his other biggie being **It Keeps Right On A-Hurtin'**.

**TINY TIM** — Long-time Greenwich Village weirdo. Appeared in 1968 'You Are What You Eat' movie and 'Laugh-In' TV series before bizarre re-make of **Tiptoe Through The Tulips** single and **God Bless Tiny Tim** album shot him to temporary international prominence.

**KEITH TIPPETT** — Respected jazz and neo-classical composer. Has played keyboards on King Crimson and Soft Machine albums. Married to Julie Driscoll, of **This Wheel's On Fire** fame.

**THE TOKENS** — Originally purely a studio outfit, with such luminaries as Neil Diamond, Neil Sedaka and Carole King playing on records. Eventually working band of Hank Medress, Jay Seigel, Phil Matgo and Mitch Margo was formed. Folksy style gave them American No. 1 with **The Lion Sleeps Tonight**.

**THE TORNADOS** — Put together as London-based session band by producer Joe Meek; became the Tornados when they started to work as Billy Fury's backing outfit. 1962 brought enormous organ-dominated space-flavoured instrumental hit **Telstar**. Guitarist Heinz left for solo career with material based on his fascination with Eddie Cochran, scoring with single **Just Like Eddie** (1963).

**TOWER OF POWER** — San Francisco-based R&B rock outfit at forefront of brass-laced bands of early '70s. Original vocalist Lenny Williams has enjoyed chart status with enterprising soul material.

**THE TREMELOES** — As backing group to Brian Poole they had UK No. 1 with cover of Contours' US soul hit **Do You Love Me?** Poole quit in 1965 for solo stardom but soon sank — returning to job as a butcher — while his erstwhile support went on to run of seven Top 10 hits from 1967-1970, including chart-topping cover of Four Seasons' oldie **Silence Is Golden**.

**BONNIE TYLER** — Gifted Welsh vocalist who saw renewed chart action in the '80s with Jim Steinman penned **Total Eclipse Of The Heart** ('83), and then powerful **Holding Out For A Hero** ('85).

## U

**THE UNITED STATES OF AMERICA** — Lone eponymous album (1968) for Columbia was superbly innovative slice of progressive rock, parodying everything from **Sargeant Pepper** to Jefferson Airplane.

**PHIL UPCHURCH** — Noted US session guitarist (Cat Stevens, Howlin' Wolf, George Benson, Quincy Jones, etc) who charted in 1962 with million-selling dance opus **You Can't Sit Down**. Has released sporadic solo albums.

## V

**VANDENBERG** — **Burning Heart** single/video typifies the deluge of hard rock/hippy clones in the US.

**VANILLA FUDGE** — US (E. coast) band whose claim to fame was turgid version of **You Keep Me Hangin' On**. Drummer Carmine Appice and bassist Tim Bogert went on to bigger things.

**VENTURES** — US instrumental group who inspired generation of 'beat bands' in early '60s. Their **Walk Dont Run** (1960) is now rock classic.

**TOM VERLAINE** — Founder of Television, this talented New Jersey guitarist/vocalist is sure to achieve international success when the rough edges have worn down.

**BOBBY VINTON** — Major US pop artist in early '60s with decidedly MOR ballad material like **Roses Are Red, Blue Velvet, Blue On Blue** and **I Love How You Love Me**. Makes maximum use of Polish heritage in well-worked, but corny, cabaret show.

**Right: Wishbone Ash on stage.**

## W

**WALKER BROS** — American trio who achieved teen success in UK in mid-'60s with succession of powerful pop ballads. Re-formed in 1976 for one-off single **No Regrets**.

**JUNIOR WALKER** — Motown stalwart whose screaming sax and vocals generated a dozen hit singles for the label in the sixties and seventies, most notably **Shotgun** and **Roadrunner**.

**WALL OF VOODOO** — Mexican/American LA band with unique blend of cultures evident in off-the-wall music. Hit single **Mexican Radio** (1982).

**WAR** — Brass-based soul aggregation who enjoyed brightest moments with Eric Burdon as lead vocalist.

**CLIFFORD T. WARD** — Singer/songwriter from English Midlands who went Top 10 with melodious debut single **Gaye** in 1973; scored again in 1975 with **Jigsaw Girl**.

**JIMMY WEBB** — Wrote songs for Johnny Rivers and Fifth Dimension, who recorded for Rivers' Soul City label, to establish self as major LA-based writer. Fifth Dimension's **Up Up And Away**, Glen Campbell's **By The Time I Get To Phoenix** and Richard Harris's **MacArthur Park** were among his formidable triumphs. In 1970 Webb started touring and signed own contract with Reprise the following year leading to albums for variety of labels.

**BERT WEEDON** — Veteran British session guitarist who charted with cover of Virtues' **Guitar Boogie Shuffle** in 1959 to make him one of longest-toothed rock 'n' rollers. Has wielded considerable influence over younger musicians thanks to his highly proficient technique.

**IAN WHITCOMB** — Active on UK R&B scene, Whitcomb went to US West Coast on holiday, recording version of **Sporting Life** to notch minor hit. Jerry Dennon flew to Dublin, where Whitcomb was studying, to record **You Turn Me On**. A US Top

**Above: One of the finest voices of the '80s, so far in a '60s style, Mari Wilson.**

**Tammy Wynette. Courtesy Epic Records.**

10 hit in 1965, it missed in UK. Whitcombe subsequently stayed in US and turned author.

**MARTY WILDE** — Member of the Larry Parnes school of British rock 'n' rollers. Resident on TV's 'Oh Boy!' and 'Boy Meets Girl' shows, he had string of British hits at tail-end of '60s, starting with **Endless Sleep** in 1957. Tried to launch son Ricky as British teeny-bopper idol, without success; did better with daughter Kim Wilde who ranks as major artist of '80s in own right.

**PAUL WILLIAMS** — Diminutive US writer who, wrote hits for Carpenters and Barbra Streisand among others. Is currently carving out successful career as singer/writer/ actor in movies and on television. In demand as soundtrack composer as well.

**DON WILLIAMS** — Low-key C&W performer who sent middle-aged ladies crazy with his old-fashioned, but well-crafted ditties. **I Recall A Gypsy Woman** made UK top twenty in 1973.

**HANK WILLIAMS** — Arguably the king of country music, he penned classic songs **Cold Cold Heart**, **Your Cheating Heart, Hey Good Lookin, Jambalaya** and **Take These Chains From My Heart** before death from heart attack caused by usual rock excesses in 1953.

**MARI WILSON AND THE WILSATIONS** — Mari Wilson started as the Queen of the beehive hairdo — in keeping with '60s image: female vocalist with back-up singers set up. Biggest hit **Just What I Always Wanted** (1982). Changed image in 1986 but with no success as yet.

**PETE WINGFIELD** — Keyboard player with British R&B band Jellybread, diverted into sessions for Freddie King, Van Morrison, Colin Blunstone and others before own 1975 transatlantic hit **Eighteen With A Bullet**. Later a member of the Olympic Runners soul band. Toured with Van Morrison in '70s.

**EDGAR WINTER** — Sax-blowing, keyboard-playing brother of Johnny (and also an albino), the younger Winter's hard-driving brand of R&B placed him in both American and British singles charts with **Frankenstein** in 1972.

**WISHBONE ASH** — Pillars of 'twin lead guitar' syndrome, these UK rockers had fifteen year career before calling it a day in 1982.

**LINK WRAY** — Legendary swamp-rock guitarist of Shawnee Indian extraction. Big hit with **Rumble** instrumental in 1958 followed by long spell in obscurity before re-emergence with hypnotic if at times strangely metered albums.

**GARY WRIGHT** — Former member of Spooky Tooth (keyboards, vocals) who stormed US charts in 1976

with **Dream Weaver** album and single. Currently records in own home studio.

**ROBERT WYATT** — Soft Machine drummer turned British progressive rock guru. Scored in 1974 with surprise Cockney version of **I'm A Believer**. Re-emerged in 1983 with Elvis Costello-penned Falklands War comment **Shipbuilding**.

**TAMMY WYNETTE** — Country legend and champion of the down-trodden housewife, Wynette's working class anthems **D.I.V.O.R.C.E.** and **Stand By Your Man** have been the backbone of a 20 plus year career. Formerly married to George Jones.

## Y

**THE YOUNGBLOODS** — Formed by talented New York singers Jesse Colin Young and Jerry Corbitt, who shared lead vocal role. Expanded group became resident at Café Au Go Go in 1966 with strong jug-band/folk-rock flavour. After cutting Dino Valenti's **Get Together** in 1957 (Top 10 in 1959 on re-release) they moved to West Coast, cutting much acclaimed **Elephant Mountain** and other fine albums before folding in 1969, leaving Young to continue as respected solo artist.

**TIMI YURO** — Diminutive white girl singer with amazingly soulful voice, reminiscent of black star Esther Phillips. At her finest on R&B ballads, she benefited from lush yet totally sympathetic Nashville string arrangements. Scored with **Hurt** (1961) and superb albums, before moving into MOR and disappearing from scene due to marital problems.

## Z

**ZAGER AND EVANS** — Fashionably futuristic lyrics of **In The Year 2525** made this duo from Omaha, Nebraska, 1969's most successful one-hit wonders.

**WARREN ZEVON** — US singer/songwriter best known for 1978 single **Werewolves Of London**. Somewhat of a cult figure.

**ZOMBIES** — Intelligent UK pop group from '60s who charted with **She's Not There** in 1964. Founder Rod Argent (keyboards) and Colin Blunstone (vocals) later enjoyed solo success.

**Odyssey And Oracle, The Zombies. Courtesy CBS Records.**